OXFORD COMMENTARIES ON INTERNATIONAL LAW

General Editors: *Professor Philip Alston*, Professor of International Law at New York University, and *Professor Vaughan Lowe*, Chichele Professor of Public International Law in the University of Oxford and Fellow of All Souls College, Oxford.

The Rights of Minorities in Europe

The Rights of Minorities in Europe

A Commentary on the European Framework Convention for the Protection of National Minorities

Edited by

MARC WELLER

OXFORD
UNIVERSITY PRESS

This book has been printed digitally and produced in a standard specification in order to ensure its continuing availability

OXFORD
UNIVERSITY PRESS

Great Clarendon Street, Oxford OX2 6DP
United Kingdom

Oxford University Press is a department of the University of Oxford. It furthers the University's objective of excellence in research, scholarship, and education by publishing worldwide.

Oxford is a registered trade mark of Oxford University Press in the UK and in certain other countries

Reprinted 2012

British Library Cataloguing in Publication Data
Data available

Library of Congress Cataloging in Publication Data
Data available

ISBN 978-0-19-920762-6

This volume, published under the auspices of the European Centre for Minority Issues and the Centre of International Studies, University of Cambridge, is dedicated to Professor Sir Elihu Lauterpacht; QC, CBE

EUROPEAN CENTRE FOR MINORITY ISSUES

UNIVERSITY OF CAMBRIDGE

Preface

Minority issues have long been a sensitive topic for governments. Given that international law is made by governments, it comes as no surprise that international minority rights have lagged behind the development of other branches of human rights. Up until the 1990s, there were no significant international human rights instruments addressing minorities. The sole exception was a single provision in the International Covenant on Civil and Political Rights clarifying that persons belonging to minorities shall not be denied the right, in community with the other members of their group, to enjoy their own culture, to progress and practise their own religion, or to use their own language.

It took the shock of the interethnic violence that afflicted Eastern Europe with the unfreezing of the Cold War to spark a renewed interest in the field. In 1992, a non-binding Declaration on the Rights of Persons Belonging to National or Ethnic, Religious and Linguistic Minorities was adopted by the UN General Assembly. However, it was within the Council of Europe area that the first human rights treaties focusing specifically on minorities were adopted. Following upon the European Charter for Regional or Minority Languages of 1992, the European Framework Convention for the Protection of National Minorities (FCNM) was adopted in 1994. The Convention—the first comprehensive treaty addressing minority rights anywhere—entered into force in 1998, having attracted the requisite twelve ratifications surprisingly swiftly. In fact, the FCNM now boasts a respectable membership of thirty-five states. While there are some notable absences, even within the EU membership, this is a solid result.

The adoption of the Framework Convention attracted little jubilation, however. When analysing the Convention, many of the leading human rights scholars were profoundly sceptical. They noted the fact that the Convention was not cast in the form of a Protocol to the European Convention for the Protection of Human Rights and Fundamental Freedoms. This meant that the rights established in the Convention would not become subject to the review of the European Court of Human Rights. There was no 'hard' enforcement mechanism attached. Instead, the commitments of the parties were to be assessed by what appeared to be a weak Advisory Committee. The Committee itself, while composed of independent experts, seemed to function under the political control of the Council of Europe Committee of Ministers. Moreover, the substantive provisions of the Convention were at times cast in rather general terms, leading to some doubts as to whether these were in fact really 'hard' legal obligations. This concern was amplified by the fact that the treaty was established as a 'Framework' Convention, leaving it up to the parties to determine how they would implement these general obligations.

Of course, academic scholars can never be wrong—especially legal scholars. Nevertheless, one can observe an ever-growing respect for the achievements of the Council of Europe and of the Framework Convention. Despite its general character, states have generally taken seriously the commitments made when signing the Convention. Of course, over the past five or six years of the operation of the Convention, the situation of minorities has not dramatically improved across all of Europe. However, the Convention has generated a greater sense of accountability on the part of governments where the treatment of minorities is concerned and the states parties have reported substantively and generally at length on implementation to the Advisory Committee. While much remains to be done, there have been important, albeit incremental, advances in the situation of many minorities across Europe.

The purpose of this commentary is not, however, to assess the quality of implementation of the Convention in each of the states concerned. That task is being performed by the Advisory Committee and by NGOs that are contributing to, and commenting upon, the ongoing monitoring process between governments and the Council of Europe. Instead, this project seeks to review the content of the legal obligations that were adopted exactly ten years ago. The aim of this undertaking is to add more precise meaning to the at times general provisions of the Convention, and to record their advancing interpretation in state practice.

International law is driven by the practice of states and of other actors that enjoy legal competence in the international sphere, such as international organizations. The submissions of states to the Council of Europe provide clear evidence of their own interpretation of the legal obligations they have contracted into. Often, this understanding will require a significantly higher level of performance than might be gleaned from the text of the Convention itself. Moreover, the authoritative responses from the Advisory Committee, and the Committee of Ministers itself, add to this advancing and ever more detailed interpretation of the Convention.

Hence, a decade after the adoption of the Convention, and at the point of conclusion of the first monitoring cycle of implementation by the Council of Europe, it appeared appropriate to subject this by now very significant body of practice to scholarly analysis. This analysis draws on an exegesis of the negotiating history of the individual provisions of the Convention and on state practice outside of the framework of the Convention, but it is chiefly informed by the implementation practice of the states parties and the Council of Europe organs.

Through this work, we hope to offer a far more detailed and refined understanding of the individual obligations contained in the Convention. In addition to the increasing specificity of meaning that we have identified, this commentary also exhibits the increasing ambition of these obligations. Expectations of state performance are increasing over time, and it is our task to illuminate this enhanced level of legal provision. This will not only be relevant when seeking to further advance minority issues within Europe. Given that only Europe has thus far generated a binding legal text of this kind, we believe that its analysis and interpretation may also be of relevance to the attempts to enhance minority rights in other regions. Indeed, this project was also informed by a wish to support the efforts of creating a binding legal standard on minority rights at the universal level.

While the Convention itself is fairly short, what has resulted from this project is a rather substantive legal commentary. We have been blessed with an unusually high-powered team of authors, including most of the leading experts in the field, other than those who are members of the Advisory Committee. As we wanted to undertake a review of the Convention 'from the outside', we did not find it appropriate to draw on those who have done so much to advance our understanding of it from within. However, we are very pleased to have been able to persuade Professor Rainer Hofmann, formerly the President of the Advisory Committee, to contribute a substantive introduction. Professor Hofmann also attended a review conference, where the drafts of individual sections of the commentary were discussed amongst the team of authors. Professor Asbjørn Eide, who served for many years as the Chair of the Working Group on Minorities of the UN Sub-Commission for the Promotion and Protection of Human Rights and has now joined the Advisory Committee as its President, adds the broader context from the perspective of the UN in the second introductory chapter.

While this project was conducted outside the Council of Europe, we are pleased to acknowledge the consistent help we have had from the Secretariat of the Framework Convention in Strasbourg and in particular Mark Neville, the Director of that office, and his impressive staff. This co-operation was particularly essential during the phase of data collection, when the Council of Europe supported the creation by ECMI of an electronic databank of materials relating to the FCNM. That databank, which presents the negotiating documents, the state reports, and pronouncements of the Advisory Committee according to the structure of Articles of the FCNM can be found at **www.ecmi.de/doc/CoE_Project/**.

Of course, where such a distinguished group of authors is involved, it is neither desirable nor possible to impose a rigidly common ideology and approach on all of the contributions. For ease of use, we have ensured that all contributions follow a common format. During meetings of the team of authors, we have discussed our respective positions and some modifications have resulted from these exchanges. Ultimately, however, each section of the commentary remains an expression of the views of the author. Throughout the text of the commentary, we have followed an article-by-article approach. However, given the technical nature of the concluding provisions, starting with Article 24, we have abandoned that approach at that point. Instead, we are covering Articles 24–6, addressing the monitoring mechanism, as one single contribution. Similarly, the concluding provisions of the Convention are presented in one final section.

In addition to the team of commentators, we have had a great deal of help in bringing this project to a successful conclusion within a very short period of time. First of all, we very gratefully acknowledge the support of the VW Foundation, who have generously funded this endeavour. In raising the necessary funds for this project, we have had the help of Professor Sir Elihu Lauterpacht, QC, CBE, and Professor James Crawford, QC, of the University of Cambridge, and Professor Christian Tomuschat of the Humboldt University of Berlin.

At the European Centre for Minority Issues, where this project originated and was carried out, Dr H. E. Alexander Morawa and Ms Kyriaki Topidi contributed to the initial organization of the project and organized the commentators' workshops. Further organizational tasks were performed by Ms Colleen French and Ms Marnie Lloydd, who also arranged the sub-editorial process that was carried out with great efficiency and effectiveness by them and by Denika Blacklock, Alcidia Moucheboeuf, Teddy Florrea and Jenny Filkins, under the management of Ms French. In addition, we are very grateful for the last minute corrections completed by Ms Josee Lavoie. We also gratefully acknowledge the support of Oxford University Press, in particular Mr John Louth, who supported this project with immediate enthusiasm, Ms Gwen Booth, and Mr Edwin Pritchard, whose professionalism and speed in adding this work to their list is greatly appreciated.

Marc Weller

Flensburg
31 August 2004

Table of Contents

Selected Abbreviations

AC	Advisory Committee
ACHR	American Convention on Human Rights
AJIL	*American Journal of International Law*
Banjul Charter	African Charter on Human and Peoples' Rights
CAHMIN	Ad Hoc Committee for the Protection of National Minorities
CDCC	Council for Cultural Co-operation
CDDH	Council of Europe Steering Committee for Human Rights
CDMM	Council of Europe Steering Committee on Mass Media
CEDAW	Convention on the Prohibition of All Forms of Discrimination against Women
CERD	International Convention on the Elimination of All Forms of Racial Discrimination
CMLR	*Common Market Law Review*
CoE	Council of Europe
COLPI	Constitutional and Legal Policy Initiative
CoM	Committee of Ministers
Comm.	Communication
Copenhagen Document	1990 Document of the Copenhagen Meeting of the Conference on the Human Dimension of the Conference on Security and Co-operation in Europe
CPT	European Committee for the Prevention of Torture
CRC	Convention on the Rights of the Child
CSCE	Conference on Security and Co-operation in Europe
DH-MIN	Committee of Experts for the Protection of National Minorities
ECDL	European Commission for Democracy through Law (also: Venice Commission)
ECHR	European Convention for the Protection of Human Rights and Fundamental Freedoms
ECJ	European Court of Justice
ECMI	European Centre for Minority Issues

ECOSOC	Economic and Social Council of the United Nations
ECRI	European Commission against Racism and Intolerance
ECtHR	European Court of Human Rights
ECommHR	European Commission of Human Rights
EHRR	European Human Rights Reports
EPIL	*Encyclopedia of Public International Law*
ETS	European Treaty Series
EU	European Union
FCNM	Framework Convention for the Protection of National Minorities
FUEN	Federal Union of European Nationalities
GAOR	United Nations General Assembly Official Record
HCNM	OSCE High Commissioner on National Minorities
HRC	UN Human Rights Committee
ICCPR	International Covenant on Civil and Political Rights
ICESCR	International Covenant on Economic, Social, and Cultural Rights
ICJ	International Court of Justice
ILC	International Law Commission
ILM	International Legal Materials
ILO	International Labour Organization
IMT Charter	London Charter of the International Military Tribunal
JEMIE	*Journal on Ethnopolitics and Minority Issues in Europe*
Lund Recommendations	Lund Recommendations on the Effective Participation of National Minorities in Public Life
MRG	Minority Rights Group International
NGO	non-governmental organization
NYIL	*Netherlands Yearbook of International Law*
ODIHR	OSCE Office for Democratic Institutions and Human Rights
OSCE	Organization for Security and Co-operation in Europe
Oslo Recommendations	The Oslo Recommendations Regarding the Linguistic Rights of National Minorities
PA	Parliamentary Assembly
PCIJ	Permanent Court of International Justice
PHARE	originally: Poland and Hungary Action for the Reconstruction of the Economy

PHARE CBC	PHARE Cross Border Co-operation Programme
RHDI	*Revue héllenique de droit international*
TEC	Treaty Establishing the European Community
TEU	Treaty of the European Union
TRNC	'Turkish Republic of Northern Cyprus'
UDHR	Universal Declaration of Human Rights
UN	United Nations
UN Declaration on Minorities	UN Declaration on the Rights of Persons Belonging to National or Ethnic, Religious and Linguistic Minorities
UNESCO	United Nations Educational, Scientific, and Cultural Organization
UNGA	United Nations General Assembly
UNMIK	United Nations Interim Administration Mission in Kosovo
UNTS	United Nations Treaty Series
VCLT	Vienna Convention on the Law of Treaties
Vienna Document	1989 Concluding Document of the Vienna Follow-up Meeting of the Conference on Security and Co-operation in Europe
YBECHR	*Yearbook of the European Convention on Human Rights*

Notes on Contributors

Gudmundur Alfredsson is Professor of Law at Lund University and Director of the Raoul Wallenberg Institute of Human Rights and Humanitarian Law. He was a member of the OSCE/HCNM Expert Group which drafted the Lund Recommendations on the Effective Participation of National Minorities in Public Life, is a member of the UN Sub-Commission on the Promotion and Protection of Human Rights and its Working Group on Minorities, and is the author of numerous publications on human rights and international law issues.

Matthew Draper served as Junior Legal Officer at the OSCE Office of the High Commissioner on National Minorities from 2002 to 2004. He presently lives in New York City and works for Sullivan & Cromwell LLP, an international law firm.

Asbjørn Eide is Senior Fellow and former Director of the Norwegian Institute of Human Rights and formerly a member of the United Nations Sub-Commission on Promotion and Protection of Human Rights and the chair-person of its Working Group on Minorities. He is the former Secretary-General of the International Peace Research Institute in Oslo, and the author of numerous books and articles on peace and conflict issues and human rights. He has now joined the Council of Europe FCNM Advisory Committee.

Geoff Gilbert is a professor in the Department of Law and the Human Rights Centre at the University of Essex in the United Kingdom. He has published widely in the field and he is the Editor-in-Chief of the *International Journal of Refugee Law*. He was Director of the Human Rights Centre's OSCE Project which received funding from the Foreign and Commonwealth Office. He has been an academic contributor to the UN Working Group on Minorities and prepared reports for it.

Lauri Hannikainen is the former Director of the Northern Institute for Environmental and Minority Law at the University of Lapland and Professor at the School of Law, University of Turku, Finland. He is currently a member of the European Commission against Racism and Intolerance at the Council of Europe.

Hans-Joachim Heintze is a Researcher and Associate at the Institute for International Law of Peace and Armed Conflict at the Ruhr-Universität

Bochum and President of the International Association for the Study of the World Refugee Problem (AWR). He has both taught and lectured on humanitarian, human rights, and international law around the world, and is the author of many specialized contributions on minority rights.

Peter Hilpold is Professor at the Institute of Public Law and Political Science at the University of Innsbruck, Austria, where he specializes in public international law and the law of the European Union. Among his many works on minority rights is a major monograph, *Modernes Minderheitenrecht* (Vienna, 2001).

Rainer Hofmann is Professor of International Law and Director of the Walther-Schücking-Institute for International Law, University of Kiel, Germany, the former President of the Advisory Committee of the Council of Europe Framework Convention for the Protection of National Minorities, a Member of the Board of the European Centre for Minority Issues, Flensburg, and a member of the academic advisory board on international law to the German Foreign Ministry. He has published extensively in the field of human and minority rights.

Sally Holt is Research Fellow at the Centre for International Cooperation and Security, University of Bradford, UK. From 2000 to 2004 she was Legal Officer at the Office of the High Commissioner on National Minorities (HCNM) of the Organization for Security and Co-operation in Europe (OSCE). Prior to that she held positions as a researcher for 'Rights and Humanity', a UK-based non-governmental organization focusing on economic, social, and cultural rights, and as a case officer for a firm of solicitors representing asylum seekers in the UK.

Jennifer Jackson-Preece is a Lecturer at the London School of Economics and the author of a leading analysis of minority protection in Europe, *National Minorities and the European Nation-States System* (Oxford, 1999).

Zdenka Machnyikova is a legal expert specializing in the protection of minorities under international law and the relationship between human rights and conflict prevention. She was until recently Senior Legal Adviser to the OSCE High Commissioner on National Minorities. In her work with the OSCE she has analysed and evaluated legislation and provided advice regarding policy, law, and practice affecting minority rights and interethnic relations in many European countries. Among other OSCE work in this field, she participated in the elaboration of the Oslo Recommendations Regarding the Linguistic Rights of National Minorities (1998), the Lund Recommendations on Effective Participation of National Minorities in Public Life (1999), and the Warsaw

Guidelines to Assist National Minority Participation in the Electoral Process (2001). Along with John Packer and Steven R. Ratner, she is an editor of the forthcoming volume, *Contemporary Issues in the Protection of Minorities in Europe* (2004).

Tove H. Malloy is a Senior Research Associate at the European Centre for Minority Issues, Flensburg, Germany, currently on leave from the Danish Ministry of Foreign Affairs. She holds a doctorate in Government from the University of Essex and an MA in Humanities from Odense University (now Southern Denmark). She has previously taught at the European Master Programme in Human Rights and Democratization in Venice, Italy, and has represented the Danish government in international fora on post-conflict resolution for Rwanda and Bosnia, transition and development in Albania, as well as indigenous affairs issues. She is the Managing Editor of the *European Yearbook for Minority Issues* and author of *National Minority Rights: A Critical View of the Post-1989 European Discourse*. Her main research areas are legal and political theory with current interests in the notion of identity in international law and national minority 'regions' in the enlarged EU.

John Packer was the first Director of the Organization for Security and Co-operation in Europe's (OSCE) High Commissioner on National Minorities in The Hague. A distinguished scholar, Packer has years of experience participating in major international missions relating to human and minority rights violations and conflict prevention in several countries. He has lectured in numerous universities and in 2003–4 was Visiting Assistant Professor of International Law at the Fletcher School of Law and Diplomacy and a Fellow at the Carr Center for Human Rights Policy at Harvard University's John F. Kennedy School of Government. The author of various publications, he is Associate Editor of the *Human Rights Law Journal* and a member of the editorial boards of several scholarly journals including the *International Journal on Minority and Group Rights*.

Patrick Thornberry is Professor of International Law at Keele University in the United Kingdom, and has published widely in the field of public international law and human rights, specializing in the rights of minorities and indigenous peoples, and racial discrimination, including *Indigenous Peoples and Human Rights* (2002) and *Minority Rights in Europe* (2004). He is currently rapporteur of the UN Committee on the Elimination of Racial Discrimination and has chaired the Minority Rights Group and maintains links with a range of NGOs and organizations of indigenous peoples.

Kyriaki Topidi is a doctoral candidate at the School of Politics and International Studies of Queen's University Belfast, where she is studying the legal aspects of EU minority rights.

Fernand de Varennes is a Senior Lecturer at Murdoch University School of Law, Perth, Australia. He has published widely on language rights, indigenous peoples and minority rights, international law, and ethnic conflicts. He is also a former Director at the Asia-Pacific Centre for Human Rights and the Prevention of Ethnic Conflict and the founding Editor-in-Chief of the *Asia-Pacific Journal on Human Rights and the Law*. He is recognized as one of the world's leading legal experts on language rights and is the 2004 LINGUAPAX Award laureate. He is Senior (Non-Resident) Research Associate at the European Centre for Minority Issues in Flensburg, Germany.

Marc Weller is the Director of the European Centre of Minority Issues in Flensburg, Germany, a lecturer in international law at the University of Cambridge, and a Fellow of the Lauterpacht Research Centre for International Law and Hughes Hall. His writings mainly focus on conflict management, issues of international law, and human and minority rights. He has acted as legal adviser to several governments and organizations.

Table of Cases

CERD

ECJ

ECtHR and ECommHR

HRC

IACHR

ICJ

PCIJ

International Instruments, National Legislation, and Implementation Bodies

Council of Europe Official Documents on the Framework Convention

ALBANIA

ARMENIA

AUSTRIA

AZERBAIJAN

BOSNIA AND HERZEGOVINA

BULGARIA

CROATIA

CYPRUS

CZECH REPUBLIC

DENMARK

ESTONIA

FINLAND

GERMANY

HUNGARY

IRELAND

ITALY

LIECHTENSTEIN

LITHUANIA

MALTA

MOLDOVA

NORWAY

POLAND

ROMANIA

RUSSIAN FEDERATION

SAN MARINO

SERBIA AND MONTENEGRO

SLOVAK REPUBLIC

SLOVENIA

SPAIN

SWEDEN

SWITZERLAND

THE FORMER YUGOSLAV REPUBLIC OF MACEDONIA

UKRAINE

UK

THE FRAMEWORK CONVENTION FOR THE PROTECTION OF NATIONAL MINORITIES: AN INTRODUCTION

Rainer Hofmann

I. Background

The goal of this introductory chapter is to give an overview of the major procedural and some of the general substantive issues raised by, and connected with, the Framework Convention for the Protection of National Minorities (FCNM) at the advent of its second monitoring cycle. Prior to engaging in this analysis, however, it seems appropriate to briefly present the drafting history of the FCNM and its main features.

The FCNM is clearly a result of the impressive renaissance of international efforts to safeguard the rights of persons belonging to national minorities. This trend started when, subsequent to the demise of the socialist regimes in Europe, the international community came to understand that unsettled majority–minority relations constituted a serious threat not only to the internal peace and security of the states concerned, but also to peace and security in Europe as a whole. Consequently, both the Conference for Security and Co-operation in Europe (CSCE)/Organization for Security and Co-operation in Europe (OSCE) and the Council of Europe (CoE), as the two most relevant international organizations in the human rights field in Europe have, since the early 1990s, been actively engaged in an attempt to stabilize majority–minority situations that have potential to result in ethnic violence or even civil strife and war.

Whereas the work of the OSCE High Commissioner on National Minorities (HCNM) is particularly aimed at preventing such developments[1] by means of diplomacy and political pressure, the Council of Europe, with its strong tradition of initiating negotiations and providing fora aimed at the drafting of legally binding instruments, chose a different approach. This strategy resulted in the adoption of two treaties: The Council of Europe Draft European Charter for Regional or Minority Languages of 5 November 1992, which entered into force on 1 March 1998[2] and has been ratified by seventeen states as of 15 July 2004;[3] and the Framework Convention. The latter was adopted on 10 November 1994 by the CoE Committee of Ministers and was opened for signature on 1 February 1995. It entered into force on 1 February 1998 and, as of 15 July 2004, has been ratified by thirty-five states.[4] Already, by January 2002 the FCNM had been ratified by thirty-four states, making it, within a short period of time, one of the Council of Europe treaties with the highest number of members.

[1] For recent reviews of the activities of the OSCE High Commissioner on National Minorities, see S. Holt, 'The Activities of the OSCE High Commissioner on National Minorities: January 2001–May 2002', *European Yearbook of Minority Issues*, 1 (2001/02), 565–89; and M. Draper, 'The Activities of the OSCE High Commissioner on National Minorities: June 2002–June 2003', *European Yearbook of Minority Issues*, 2 (2002/3), 475–91.

[2] Council of Europe (CoE), European Charter for Regional or Minority Languages (adopted 5 November 1992, entry into force 1 March 1998), ETS 148, Strasbourg, 1992.

[3] Armenia, Austria, Croatia, Cyprus, Denmark, Finland, Germany, Hungary, Liechtenstein, the Netherlands, Norway, Slovakia, Slovenia, Spain, Sweden, Switzerland, and the United Kingdom. For a recent review of developments under the Charter see A. Bultrini, 'Developments in the Field of the European Charter for Regional or Minority Languages', *European Yearbook of Minority Issues*, 2 (2002/3), 435–43.

[4] Albania, Armenia, Austria, Azerbaijan, Bosnia-Herzegovina, Bulgaria, Croatia, Cyprus, Czech Republic, Denmark, Estonia, Finland, Germany, Hungary, Ireland, Italy, Liechtenstein, Lithuania, Malta, Moldova, Norway, Poland, Portugal, Romania, the Russian Federation, San Marino, Serbia and Montenegro, Slovakia, Slovenia, Spain, Sweden, Switzerland, the former Yugoslav Republic of Macedonia, Ukraine, and the United Kingdom. The FCNM has been signed, but not yet ratified by Belgium, Georgia, Greece, Iceland, Latvia, Luxembourg, and the Netherlands. Three Council of Europe member states have not yet taken any action with a view to being bound by the FCNM: Andorra, France, and Turkey.

Although the FCNM is not the first instrument relevant to the protection of national minorities developed by the Council of Europe, it is the most comprehensive document in the field. Its particular relevance derives from the fact that it is the first legally binding, multilateral treaty to address the protection of national minorities in general. Moreover, in Article 1, it is expressly stated that the protection of national minorities constitutes an 'integral part' of the international protection of human rights; thus, the FCNM is to be considered a member of the European family of human rights treaties with consequences attached to its interpretation. It should also be noted that throughout the entire drafting process, the thirty-two experts constituting the Ad Hoc Committee for the Protection of National Minorities (CAHMIN), specifically established for that task by the Committee of Ministers, took into close consideration the relevant international documents, among which the pertinent provisions of the 1990 Copenhagen and other CSCE/OSCE instruments were of particular importance. This was the result of an agreement reached at the 1993 Vienna Summit of Heads of State and Governments of the Council of Europe member states to transform, to the greatest possible extent, the political commitments of the CSCE/OSCE instruments into legal obligations. Incidentally, the resulting decision to draft a Framework Convention for the Protection of National Minorities discontinued efforts to produce an Additional Protocol to the European Convention for the Protection of Human Rights and Fundamental Freedoms (ECHR), providing for a comprehensive, judicial protection of the rights of persons belonging to national minorities.[5]

The FCNM consists of a Preamble and thirty-two articles that are grouped into five sections. Section I contains general principles, including the above-mentioned Article 1, according to which the protection of national minorities and persons belonging to such minorities constitutes an integral part of the international protection of human rights. Also, Article 3(1) FCNM stresses that every person belonging to a national minority is free to choose to be treated, or not to be treated, as a member of a minority, with no disadvantage arising from such a decision.

Section II is the main operative part of the FCNM and contains those principles which states parties are obliged to implement by means of domestic legislation and policies, and through bi- and multilateral treaties. These elements cover a wide range of issues, such as: the principle of non-discrimination in

[5] See, in particular, Council of Europe Parliamentary Assembly Recommendation 1201/EC of 1 February 1993 on an Additional Protocol on the Rights of Minorities to the European Convention on Human Rights [1993].

Article 4(1); the promotion of effective equality in Article 4(2); and the conditions regarding the preservation and development of the culture, as well as the religion, language, and traditions of national minorities in Article 5(1). Articles 7 and 8 guarantee freedom of assembly, association, expression, thought, conscience, and religion, while Article 9 seeks to facilitate access to and the use of media. Furthermore, Articles 10 and 11 deal with: linguistic rights relating, *inter alia*, to the use of minority languages in private and in public, as well as before administrative authorities; the use of one's own name and the use of minority languages for the display of information of a private nature; and for topographical names. Rights linked with education, such as the right to learn and to be instructed in the minority languages (Articles 12, 13, and 14), and to participation in the cultural, economic, public, and social life (Article 15) also fall under this section. Moreover, Articles 5(2) and 16 prohibit forced assimilation, while Article 16 further protects rights to transfrontier contacts and co-operation.

Section III contains some important principles on the interpretation of the FCNM. In particular, pursuant to Article 21, its provisions may not be construed in such a way as to contain a right to engage in activities that might jeopardize the territorial integrity and political independence of a state. In this context, it must be stressed that this statement precisely reflects the present situation under international law according to which the protection of national minorities is not concerned with the internationally protected right of peoples to self-determination. On the other hand, the FCNM does not exclude the establishment of structures of personal and territorial autonomy for the benefit of national minorities; it simply does not explicitly regulate this issue. That said, such structures might prove the best solutions to preserve and to promote the distinct identity of a national minority, in specific situations and under certain conditions. Finally, Article 22 makes clear that the FCNM may not be construed as limiting higher standards of human rights protection ensured in other international instruments under national legislation.

Section IV sets out the main aspects of the monitoring mechanism, which will be dealt with in greater detail below. Among the final provisions included in Section V, the character of the FCNM as an 'open' treaty, to which non-member states of the Council of Europe may join with an invitation from the Committee of Ministers, deserves particular attention. As a provision contained in Article 25, it was obviously drafted with a view to include OSCE member states, especially Armenia, Azerbaijan, Bosnia-Herzegovina, and the former Federal Republic of Yugoslavia, which all acceded to the FCNM before becoming member states of the Council of Europe.

II. Analysis

This section will begin with a discussion of the specific character of the FCNM as a 'Framework' convention and its consequences, and will continue with an overview of the monitoring system established during the first cycle of monitoring. It will then address some general issues relevant during the first cycle of monitoring and that will continue to be of relevance during the second cycle of monitoring. These subjects include: questions relating to the personal and territorial scope of application of the FCNM; the excessive confidentiality of the monitoring process, which results in a lack of transparency; and other thematic issues such as the situation of Roma.

A. The Specific Character of the FCNM

The specific character of the FCNM as a 'framework convention' is reflected in Section II, its main operative part. It contains those provisions on principles which states parties are obliged to implement by means of domestic legislation and policies, and through bi- and multilateral treaties. In other words, this section mostly consists of programmatic provisions,[6] meaning that member states are under a legally binding obligation to ensure the compatibility of their domestic legislation and its practical application with the principles enshrined in the FCNM. On the other hand, this means that states parties are under no legally binding obligation to ensure the direct applicability of the substantive provisions of the FCNM before their administrative and judicial authorities. They may, however, opt to do so in order to add to their compliance with the obligations flowing from the FCNM.

At times, the specific obligations established in the FCNM are in the form of provisions seemingly drafted as compromise formulations. In some instances, this might be true, especially considering the difficulties within CAHMIN to agree upon acceptable wording. However, there might also have been situations when the drafters deliberately opted for somewhat more vague formulations. In view of the fact that minority situations in Council of Europe member states differ most considerably with regard to their characteristics, and often constitute politically highly sensitive issues, it is essential for the FCNM

[6] The only exception is Art. 3(1) FCNM which guarantees the *right* of every person belonging to a national minority to freely choose to be treated, or not to be treated, as belonging to a national minority and that no disadvantage shall result from this choice or the exercise of the rights connected to that choice. Notwithstanding the wording of Arts. 6, 7, and 11(3) FCNM, these articles can be construed as providing for the legal *rights* of persons belonging to national minorities since they deal with rights guaranteed in the European Convention for the Protection of Human Rights and Fundamental Freedoms (ECHR), which is in force in all states parties to the FCNM.

to allow for flexible interpretation and application of its provisions, taking the complexity of minority situations into account. From a strictly positivist point of view, this aspect of the FCNM can be criticized. From a practitioner's point of view, however, this is the only possible solution. Finally, the specific character of the FCNM determines the structure of its monitoring system. The domestic implementation of obligations flowing from any framework convention cannot be subject to international judicial control. Judicial action results in clear 'either-or' decisions that are not compatible with a more flexible approach. This is the case for the increasingly relevant jurisprudence of the European Court of Human Rights (ECtHR) as concerns alleged violations of rights guaranteed under the ECHR and its Additional Protocols and held by persons belonging to national minorities.[7] Therefore, a monitoring system based upon periodic state reports and geared towards the establishment of a continuous and constructive dialogue between state authorities and representatives of national minorities and civil society, facilitated by the supervisory organs acting as catalysts for such a process, is indeed the most appropriate way to achieve the ultimate goal of the FCNM. This goal remains to address unstable minority–majority relations that have a clear potential to destabilize peace and security in Europe.

B. Overview of the Monitoring System under the FCNM

This overview of the monitoring system established under the FCNM will begin with a survey of its legal basis, and will continue with a presentation of the pertinent practice developed during the first cycle of monitoring of the two supervisory bodies, the Committee of Ministers and the Advisory Committee. Finally, it will conclude with an outlook on decisions taken to improve the efficiency and transparency of the monitoring system for the second cycle of monitoring.

1. The Legal Basis

According to Articles 24 and 26 FCNM, the Committee of Ministers, assisted by the Advisory Committee, is entrusted with evaluating the implementation of the FCNM. In order to achieve this aim, the states parties are required to

[7] On this issue, see G. Pentassuglia, 'Minority Issues as a Challenge in the European Court of Human Rights: A Comparison with the Case Law of the United Nations Human Rights Committee', *German Yearbook of International Law*, 46 (2003), 401–51. For recent reviews, see R. Medda-Windischer, 'The Jurisprudence of the European Court of Human Rights', *European Yearbook of Minority Issues*, 1 (2001/2), 487–534 and R. Medda-Windischer, 'The Jurisprudence of the European Court of Human Rights', *European Yearbook of Minority Issues*, 2 (2002/3), 445–69.

submit a report giving full information on legislative and other measures taken to give effect to the principles of the FCNM, within one year of its entry into force for the respective state party, as stated under Article 25. Further reports are due every five years, and whenever the Committee of Ministers requests them.

Article 26 FCNM mandates the Committee of Ministers to determine the rules concerning the composition of the Advisory Committee and its procedure. To this end, the Committee of Ministers adopted Resolution (97)10, the Rules on the Monitoring Arrangements under Articles 24 to 26 of the Framework Convention for the Protection of National Minorities on 17 September 1997.[8]

The Advisory Committee is composed of eighteen ordinary members. Each state party may nominate candidates who meet the qualifications and capacities required for membership, namely: recognized expertise in the field of protection of national minorities; and with an understanding that they will serve the Committee effectively, independently, and impartially in their individual capacities as ordinary members. The same requirements apply to the so-called 'additional members' who, pending their appointment to the Advisory Committee in accordance with the rotation system established in Resolution (97)10, assist the ordinary members in evaluating state reports from their nominating state party. Complementing the tasks of the Committee of Ministers, the main tasks of the Advisory Committee are to examine the state reports, which are made public by the Council of Europe upon receipt from the state party,[9] and to prepare an opinion on the measures taken by the state party concerned to meet its obligations under the FCNM.[10] According to the legal basis of the Advisory Committee's monitoring activities laid out in Resolution (97)10, it may: request additional information from a state party;[11] receive information from other sources such as individuals and non-governmental organizations, taking this information into account when establishing its opinions;[12] actively seek information from other sources;[13] and hold meetings with government representatives and other persons.[14]

The Advisory Committee transmits its opinions to the Committee of Ministers,[15] which then assesses the adequacy of the measures taken by the state party concerned, resulting in *conclusions*. Where appropriate, it may also

[8] CoE Resolution on the Rules Adopted by the Committee of Ministers on the Monitoring Arrangements under Articles 24 to 26 of the Framework Convention for the Protection of National Minorities, 97(10), 601st meeting (1997). Hereinafter this decision will be referred to as Resolution (97)10. On this document, see M. Weckerling, 'Der Durchführungsmechanismus des Rahmenübereinkommens des Europarates zum Schutz nationaler Minderheiten', *Europäische Grundrechte Zeitschrift*, 24 (1997), 605.

[9] Resolution 97(10), 601st meeting (1997), Rule 20.

[10] Above, n. 9, Rule 23.

[11] Above, n. 9, Rule 29.

[12] Above, n. 9, Rule 30.

[13] Above, n. 9, Rule 31.

[14] Above, n. 9, Rule 32.

[15] Above, n. 9, Rule 23.

adopt *recommendations* on further steps to be taken by the respective states parties.[16] The conclusions and recommendations of the Committee of Ministers are made public upon their adoption,[17] together with any comments the state party may have submitted in respect of the opinion delivered by the Advisory Committee.[18] These opinions shall, as a rule, be made public together with the conclusions of the Committee of Ministers.[19] Moreover, the Advisory Committee's responsibilities also extend to monitoring and following up on the conclusions and recommendations of the Committee of Ministers.[20]

2. *The Practice*

On this legal basis, the Advisory Committee and the Committee of Ministers developed their respective monitoring practices during the first cycle of monitoring. This section describes the evolution of these practices and briefly presents the structure of the *follow-up* procedures.

(a) Practice of the Advisory Committee

Immediately after the Secretariat of the Council of Europe received a state report,[21] it was transmitted to all members of the Advisory Committee.[22] In addition to a copy of the state report, members of the respective working group

16 Resolution 97(10), 601st meeting (1997), Rule 24. 17 Above, n. 16, Rule 25.

18 Above, n. 16, Rule 27. 19 Above, n. 16, Rule 26. 20 Above, n. 16, Rule 36.

21 In this context, it must be stressed that the Advisory Committee has faced the problem of delayed state reports (for an overview see, Advisory Committee on the Framework Convention for the Protection of National Minorities, Introduction to the Framework Convention for the Protection of National Minorities, Appendix 1, *Chart of Signatures and Ratifications and Status of Monitoring Work*, H(1998) 005 Rev. 11 **www.coe.int/T/E/human_rights/minorities** 17 August 2004). In this case, the President of the Advisory Committee informs the Permanent Representative of the respective state at the Council of Europe of this situation. If the state report is delayed by more than one year, the President of the Advisory Committee informs the Chairman of the Committee of Ministers who then decides upon the action to be taken. Pursuant to an initiative by the Advisory Committee, on 19 March 2003 the Committee of Ministers decided that based upon a specific mandate by the Committee of Ministers, the Advisory Committee may commence its monitoring activities in the absence of a state report. The first decision of this kind was taken on 3 September 2003 with respect to Bosnia-Herzegovina; the state report of which had been more than two years overdue.

22 As of 15 July 2004, the Advisory Committee had received all state reports due for the first cycle of monitoring, with the exception of Portugal's. In chronological order, these were: San Marino, Cyprus, Finland, Liechtenstein, Croatia, Czech Republic, Italy, Slovakia, Denmark, Hungary, Romania, the United Kingdom, Malta, Ukraine, and Estonia in 1999; Germany, the Russian Federation, Moldova, Austria, Slovenia, and Spain in 2000; Norway, Switzerland, Sweden, Armenia, Albania, Lithuania, and Ireland in 2001; Azerbaijan, Poland, and Serbia and Montenegro in 2002; Bulgaria and the former Yugoslav Republic of Macedonia in 2003; and Bosnia-Herzegovina in 2004. As to reports due for the second cycle of monitoring, the Advisory Committee had received state reports from Liechtenstein, Croatia, Hungary, Denmark, Moldova, Italy, Czech Republic, and Slovenia by 15 July 2004. All reports are available at **www.coe.int/T/E/human_rights/minorities** 17 August 2004.

received all pertinent information available at the Secretariat,[23] including reports of other monitoring bodies such as the UN Human Rights Committee, the Committee under the Convention on the Elimination of Racial Discrimination (CERD), the European Commission against Racism and Intolerance (ECRI), and of international organizations such as the OSCE. Also of particular relevance were NGO reports by organizations such as Minority Rights Group (MRG), the International Helsinki Federation, and other organizations representing national minorities in a given country.

In its first meeting, the members of the working group identified those issues which they felt were in need of additional factual information in order to adequately assess the implementation of the FCNM in the state concerned. On the basis of this information, a questionnaire was drafted and sent to the competent authorities of that state, subsequent to its adoption by the plenary. In most cases, the questionnaire replies proved to be sources of valuable information.

Probably the most important procedural aspect leading to the drafting of an opinion proved to be the country visits by the respective working groups, on invitation by the government concerned. From the very beginning, the working groups established the practice of meeting not only with representatives of government and other state organs such as members of parliament, ombudspersons, and judges, but also with representatives of national minorities and knowledgeable members of civil society. In addition to these consultations, such country visits regularly included visits to regions where persons belonging to national minorities reside. This was done to obtain a better understanding of concerns *in situ*, and to add to the visibility of the FCNM and its monitoring system.[24] All such country visits proved to be informative and were characterized by the determination of all parties to assist the working group in open, frank, and co-operative discussions to understand the extent to

[23] Early on, the Advisory Committee decided to set up country-specific working groups, which are primarily responsible for establishing the necessary contacts with governments and other actors in a given country. These contacts are meant to facilitate the conduct of country visits, when appropriate, and for drafting the text of the opinion to be submitted to the plenary, which alone is entitled to adopt (with the majority of its ordinary members) an opinion and transmit it to the Committee of Ministers.

[24] During the first cycle of monitoring, visits were conducted in: Finland and Hungary in 1999; Slovakia, Denmark, Romania, Czech Republic, Croatia, Cyprus, and Italy in 2000; Estonia, the United Kingdom, Germany, Moldova, Ukraine, Armenia, and Austria in 2001; Slovenia, the Russian Federation, Norway, Albania, Switzerland, Lithuania, and Sweden in 2002; Ireland, Azerbaijan, Poland, Serbia and Montenegro, the former Yugoslav Republic of Macedonia, and Bulgaria in 2003; while the visit to Bosnia-Herzegovina took place in 2004. Only the government of Spain did not invite a working group to conduct a visit. In view of the specific situation in Liechtenstein, Malta, and San Marino, and the information available, the respective working groups felt that their work on the state reports could be completed without country visits.

which the provisions of the FCNM had been implemented. In addition, these discussions regularly addressed shortcomings in domestic application and the ways and means to reduce them. Following a final meeting, the working group identified the essential aspects of its draft opinion.

This draft opinion was then transmitted to the plenary for a first reading and, with the amendments agreed, put to a vote. The ordinary or additional member elected by the state party concerned was always invited to comment upon the draft opinion, but was not entitled to participate in the vote on the adoption of the opinion. Notably, the vast majority of opinions were adopted with overwhelming majorities, quite often unanimously.[25] The opinions adopted were then transmitted to the governments concerned and to the Committee of Ministers, meaning to the Ministries of Foreign Affairs of all member states of the Council of Europe.

On 30 November 2001, the Advisory Committee decided to introduce changes to the structure of its opinions. In particular, it discontinued the practice of submitting a 'Proposal for conclusions and recommendations by the Committee of Ministers' (Section V of the earlier opinions). In its place, a new Section IV, entitled 'Main findings and comments of the Advisory Committee' was introduced. It also decided to submit 'Concluding Remarks' in Section V instead of Section IV. Made in light of the first country-specific decisions on the implementation of FCNM taken by the Committee of Ministers in October 2001, these changes were effective immediately and applied to all subsequent opinions adopted in the first cycle of monitoring.

Finally, like most other monitoring bodies established under human rights treaties, the Advisory Committee has been faced with the problem of delayed state reports. When this situation arose, the President of the Advisory Committee informed the Permanent Representative of the respective state at the Council of Europe. If the state report was delayed by more than one year, the President informed the Chairman of the Committee of Ministers who then

[25] As of 15 July 2004, the Advisory Committee had adopted the following thirty-four opinions: for Denmark, Finland, Hungary, and Slovakia on 22 September 2000; for Liechtenstein, Malta, and San Marino on 30 November 2000; for Croatia, Cyprus, Czech Republic, and Romania on 6 April 2001; for Estonia and Italy on 14 September 2001; for the United Kingdom on 30 November 2001; for Germany, Moldova, and Ukraine on 1 March 2002; for Armenia and Austria on 16 May 2002; for Albania, Norway, the Russian Federation, and Slovenia on 12 September 2002; for Lithuania, Sweden, and Switzerland on 21 February 2003; for Azerbaijan and Ireland on 23 May 2002; for Poland, Serbia and Montenegro, and Spain on 27 November 2003; and for Bosnia-Herzegovina, Bulgaria, and the former Yugoslav Republic of Macedonia on 28 May 2004. Thus, immediately after the end of the first cycle of monitoring, the Advisory Committee had concluded its work for thirty-four out of thirty-five states parties. Portugal's state report, due on 1 September 2003, had not yet been received as of 15 July 2004.

decided upon action to be taken. Such actions have still not prevented some member states from failing to meet their reporting obligations.[26] In the spring of 2003, therefore, the Advisory Committee approached the Committee of Ministers to obtain authorization to begin monitoring even in the absence of the initial state report in cases of particularly lengthy delays. Its view was that persistent delays might result in some member states escaping without any monitoring under the FCNM, raising serious challenges to the credibility of the entire monitoring mechanism. On 19 March 2003, the Committee of Ministers authorized the Advisory Committee to submit a proposal on the commencement of the monitoring process without the prior receipt of a state report in cases where the report was delayed by more than twenty-four months. Along with the proposal, information received by the state concerning the reason for the delay had to be submitted. If no delegation requested discussion on the matter, the Committee of Ministers would make an immediate decision.[27]

(b) Practice of the Committee of Ministers

Actual discussion on the opinions of the Advisory Committee, as well as of the comments submitted by both the government of the respective state and other governments, took place in the Rapporteur Group on Human Rights (GR-H), a sub-body of the Committee of Ministers. Representatives of the Advisory Committee introduced the opinions and were also invited to present their views. This practice has strengthened the constructive dialogue between the two monitoring bodies under the FCNM and added considerably to their mutual understanding.

This atmosphere of co-operation and constructive dialogue was also well reflected in the comments by the governments concerned.[28] In most instances, they largely consisted of information on developments that had taken place

[26] The following state reports were received with a delay exceeding fifteen months: Armenia (due 1 September 1999, received 11 June 2001), Austria (due 1 July 1999, received 15 November 2000), Azerbaijan (due 1 October 2000, received 4 June 2002), Bosnia-Herzegovina (due 1 June 2001, received 20 February 2004), Bulgaria (due 1 September 2000, received 9 April 2003), Moldova (due 1 February 1999, received 29 June 2000), Slovenia (due 1 July 1999, received 29 November 2000), Spain (due 1 February 1999, received 19 December 2000), Switzerland (due 1 February 2000, received 16 May 2001), and the former Yugoslav Republic of Macedonia (due 1 February 1999, received 23 September 2003).

[27] See Committee of Ministers CM/Del/Dec(2003)832/4.2E, 2003. Based on this decision and pursuant to a proposal by the Advisory Committee, the Committee of Ministers authorized the commencement of monitoring with respect to Bosnia-Herzegovina, on 3 September 2003. Its state report had been due on 1 June 2001. The state report was, in fact, submitted on 20 February 2004, just three days before the working group left for its visit to that country.

[28] These comments are available under **www.coe.int/T/E/human_rights/minorities** 17 August 2004.

after the adoption of the opinion, and could frequently be seen as reactions to concerns raised in the opinion or during the meetings held in the context of the visits to the countries in question. In addition, governments were given an opportunity to express their views if they disagreed with the findings of the Advisory Committee.

Significantly, the conclusions and recommendations of the Committee of Ministers have been guided by the Advisory Committee opinions. This is reflected in the conclusions both commending the good practices established by the state party concerned, and indicating the shortcomings in its implementation of obligations flowing from the FCNM. Furthermore, the Committee of Ministers always recommended that the state party take these conclusions into account together with the various findings of the Advisory Committee. Finally, it has consistently invited the states parties to continue the dialogue in progress with the Advisory Committee, and to keep it regularly informed of measures taken in response to the conclusions and recommendations set out in the resolutions.

Thus, all twenty-six country-specific resolutions adopted by the Committee of Ministers so far[29] clearly reflect the pertinent findings of the Advisory Committee. In fact, all relevant issues which the Advisory Committee has identified in the concluding remarks of its opinions were also addressed in the conclusions of the Committee of Ministers. This, together with the fact that the Committee of Ministers consistently recommended that states continue their dialogue with the Advisory Committee, keeping it regularly informed of new developments and of measures taken to implement the conclusions and recommendations set out in the resolutions, clearly indicate the value that the Committee of Ministers attaches to the Advisory Committee's role in monitoring the implementation of the state obligations flowing from the FCNM. Furthermore, it shows the strong determination of both monitoring bodies to further strengthen the established, continuous, and constructive dialogue between themselves, state governments, and the national minorities concerned, as the best means to monitor and improve the domestic implementation of the provisions of the FCNM.

[29] As of 15 July 2004, the Committee of Ministers had adopted resolutions with respect to the following states parties: Denmark and Finland (on 31 October 2001); Hungary and Slovakia (on 21 November 2001); Liechtenstein, Malta, and San Marino (on 27 November 2001); Croatia and Czech Republic (on 6 February 2002); Cyprus (on 21 February 2001); Romania (on 13 March 2002); Estonia and the United Kingdom (on 13 June 2002); Italy (on 3 July 2002); Armenia, Germany, and Moldova (on 15 January 2003); Ukraine (on 5 February 2003); Norway (on 8 April 2003); the Russian Federation (on 10 July 2003); Lithuania, Sweden, and Switzerland (on 10 December 2003); Austria (on 4 February 2004), Ireland (on 5 May 2004), and Azerbaijan (on 13 July 2004).

(c) *The Follow-Up Procedure*

Concerning the follow-up procedure, it is important to note that the Committee of Ministers has stressed the essential relevance of the follow-up procedure of the monitoring mechanism established under the FCNM, in all adopted resolutions. This procedure is to consist of a continuous dialogue between the governments concerned and the Advisory Committee, serving as a forum to discuss the measures which states parties have taken, or should take, to implement the findings of the Advisory Committee and the conclusions and recommendations of the Committee of Ministers.

In contrast to most existing international human rights treaties monitoring systems, states parties are not only obliged to report periodically, but they also have a legal duty to maintain a continuous dialogue with the Advisory Committee. In addition, the comments of the governments concerned, on the respective opinions of the Advisory Committee, must be seen as an essential part of that dialogue since they largely contain information on recent developments, often directly relating to concerns raised and comments made by the Advisory Committee. Moreover, governments are expected not only to regularly submit information as to the measures taken in response to the specific conclusions of the Committee of Ministers, but also to report on initiatives taken on the Advisory Committee's detailed and specific comments.

Thus, the resolutions of the Committee of Ministers have entrusted the Advisory Committee with a vital role in the follow-up procedure. They reflect its confidence in the capacity of the Advisory Committee to perform its tasks responsibly within the monitoring mechanism, based upon a legally sound interpretation of the provisions of the FCNM.

Another more important element of the follow-up procedure is its capacity to increase public awareness and knowledge of the Advisory Committee's opinions and to stimulate a constructive dialogue on the domestic level. To this end, it is essential that the opinions be made easily accessible to the public and be translated not only in to the official language(s) of the state party concerned, but also into relevant minority languages. Nevertheless, seminars have constituted the most important aspect of the follow-up procedure.[30] Since early 2002, fifteen such seminars have been held in: Finland, Croatia, Estonia, Romania, and Hungary (in 2002); in Armenia, Germany, Slovakia, Ukraine, Moldova, and the Czech Republic (in 2003); and in Cyprus, Italy, the Russian Federation, and Norway (in the first half of 2004). While only some of these were open

[30] The programmes of these follow-up seminars are available at **www.coe.int/T/E/ human_rights/ minorities** 17 August 2004.

to the general public, all were attended by competent government officials, representatives of national minorities, members of civil society, and representatives of the Advisory Committee. They offered ideal opportunities to present the contents of the opinions of the Advisory Committee and pertinent government comments, as well as to engage in fruitful exchanges of views on measures to be taken by the respective governments, with a view to complying with the pertinent resolutions of the Committee of Ministers. Even more important, however, is the possibility they offer to react immediately to ongoing developments, and to engage in discussions with governments concerned before submission of the next state report. In this context, it should be mentioned that one of the major subjects discussed during the follow-up seminar held in Bratislava on 8 July 2003 concerned allegations that, in some hospitals in Eastern Slovakia, young Roma women had been sterilized without their prior and informed consent. This discussion related to the establishment of a group of experts to investigate these allegations. Regrettably, the Slovak authorities did not endorse the proposal of the representative of the Advisory Committee to include non-Slovak experts in the group. It is to be expected that this issue will receive utmost attention during the second cycle of monitoring.

3. Outlook for the Second Cycle of Monitoring

In the initial stages of the first cycle of monitoring, the length of the process was unacceptable. Although the time required has been considerably shortened as the Advisory Committee and Committee of Ministers have developed and refined their practices, long time periods remain a concern. In view of the advent of the second cycle of monitoring, which began in February 2004, when several states parties were due to submit their second state reports, the Advisory Committee decided on two steps to streamline procedures and, in particular, to shorten the period between the submission of the state report and the adoption of the opinion of the Advisory Committee. First, it adopted a general 'Outline for State Reports for the Second Cycle of Monitoring'[31] in which states parties were strongly encouraged to report on all those measures they have taken in response to the conclusions and recommendations of the Committee of Ministers—which implicitly include the findings of the Advisory Committee expressed in its opinions—and on any other steps made to further improve the implementation of the state obligations flowing from the FCNM. Furthermore, the Advisory Committee decided to

[31] Advisory Committee on the Framework Convention for the Protection of National Minorities, Outline for State Reports to be Submitted under the Second Monitoring Circle, in Conformity with Article 25 Paragraph 1 of the Framework Convention for the Protection of National Minorities, ACFC/INF (2003) 001, 2003. This general outline was approved by the Committee of Ministers on 15 January 2003.

send specific questionnaires to each state well in advance of the submission date for the second state report. These country-specific questionnaires are based upon the contents of the first opinion of the Advisory Committee, pertinent comments of the respective government, and results of the follow-up procedure, including follow-up seminars and information that the Secretariat of the FCNM might have received from various sources.

These questionnaires are expected to facilitate the drafting of state reports considerably. In particular, if state reports are drafted with the active participation of organizations representing national minorities and civil society, they should offer an excellent basis for discussions to be held during the Advisory Committee country visits. This would allow for country visits to be conducted within a few months after the receipt of the state report. In turn, this would enable the Advisory Committee to adopt its opinions within less than twelve months after the receipt of the second state reports. To this end, the 8 April 2003 decision of the Committee of Ministers to renew all authorizations granted to the Advisory Committee for the first cycle of monitoring to the second one, is to be welcomed. This was generally seen as a strong expression of respect for, and appreciation of, the Advisory Committee's work so far.

If, in the second cycle of monitoring, even more states make the opinions of the Advisory Committee accessible to the public soon after their adoption, a truly continuous dialogue between all parties involved might develop. Such continuous dialogue would complement the follow-up procedures and, if sufficient funding is found, could consist of more than only one follow-up seminar per country to better account for current developments.

Unfortunately, the late submission of state reports has considerably hampered the commencement of the second cycle of monitoring. As of mid-July 2004, the Secretary-General of the Council of Europe had only received nine of the twenty-two state reports due by that time.[32] Hopefully, these violations of unambiguous treaty obligations are only a sign of states' 'reporting fatigue' and will not diminish the momentum created by both states parties and monitoring bodies in the second stage of the first cycle of monitoring.

[32] The following state reports were received: Liechtenstein (received 25 March 2004, due 1 March 2004), Croatia (received 13 April 2004, due 1 February 2004), Hungary (received 7 May 2004, due 1 February 2004), Moldova (received 7 May 2004, due 1 February 2004), Denmark (received 14 May 2004, due 1 February 2004), Italy (received 14 May 2004, due 1 March 2004), Czech Republic (received 2 July 2004, due 1 April 2004), Slovenia (received 6 July 2004, due 1 July 2004), and Estonia (received 16 July 2004, due 1 February 2004). This means that the following state reports remained outstanding: Cyprus, Finland, Germany, Romania, San Marino, Slovakia, Spain, and the former Yugoslav Republic of Macedonia (all due 1 February 2004); Ukraine and the United Kingdom (both due 1 May 2004); Bosnia-Herzegovina and Malta (both due 1 June 2004); and Austria (due 1 July 2004).

C. The Personal Scope of Application of the FCNM

The drafters of the FCNM have never agreed on a definition of the term 'national minority' and, thus, have failed to provide the monitoring bodies with a clear indication as to the FCNM's scope of application. This has prompted several states to add declarations to their instruments of ratification,[33] usually limiting the breadth of their FCNM obligations to groups commonly referred to as 'old' or 'traditional' minorities, that is, those having long-lasting ties with the territory on which they reside and being nationals of the state of which that territory is a part. These states wish to exclude 'new' minorities from the personal scope of application of the FCNM. Some states took a similar approach indicating in their state reports that the FCNM covered only 'old' minorities, whereas other states opted for broader and more inclusive approaches, making the FCNM applicable also to 'new' minorities.

In view of the intricate legal problems raised by such declarations,[34] and after considerable internal deliberations, the Advisory Committee decided to make use of the flexibility inherent in the wording of the FCNM and adopted a pragmatic and flexible approach, at least with respect for the first cycle of monitoring. It began by underlining that, in the absence of a definition of 'national minority' in the FCNM, the states parties had to examine the personal scope of application to be granted to the FCNM within their respective countries. The position of each government was, therefore, deemed to be the outcome of this examination. The Advisory Committee continued by noting that, on the one hand, states parties have a margin of appreciation in this respect in order to take into due account the specific circumstances prevailing in their countries and that, on the other hand, this margin of appreciation must be exercised in accordance with general principles of international law and the fundamental principles set out in Article 3 FCNM. The Advisory Committee stressed, in particular, that the implementation of the FCNM should not be a source of arbitrary or unjustified distinctions. For this reason, the Advisory Committee considered that examining the scope of application given to the implementation of the FCNM by each state party was part of its duty, in order

[33] For the text of these declarations, see **www.coe.int/T/E/human_rights/minorities** 17 August 2004.

[34] These issues concern questions of legal quality (they might constitute declarations, interpretative declarations, or even disguised reservations), as well as ones of legal effects (are they considered to be binding upon the Advisory Committee and the Committee of Ministers?). For a thorough discussion of these complex issues, see R. Bank and J. A. Frowein, 'The Effect of Member States' Declarations Defining "National Minorities" upon Signature or Ratification of the Council of Europe Framework Convention for the Protection of National Minorities', *Zeitschrift für ausländisches öffentliches Recht und Völkerrecht*, 59 (1999), 649–75.

to verify that no such arbitrary or unjustified distinctions were being made by the states parties. Furthermore, it considered that it had to verify the proper application of the fundamental principles set out in Article 3 FCNM.[35] The Advisory Committee approach on this matter reflects its general tendency to avoid unnecessary confrontation with governments. Instead, it seeks to engage in constructive dialogue with a view to settling any disagreements over the interpretation of the FCNM. Finally, it should be mentioned that the Advisory Committee expressly stated that it agreed with, and welcomed, the approach by the Austrian and the German authorities to consider that members of a national minority living outside the minority's traditional settlement area, in principle, are also entitled to protection under the FCNM.[36]

As regards the issue of the potential applicability of the FCNM to persons belonging to 'new' minorities, the Advisory Committee maintained that some of its provisions, such as Article 11(3), with its explicit reference to areas traditionally inhabited by persons belonging to a national minority, would only be applicable to 'old' minorities. In contrast, it is clear that Article 6(1) FCNM applies to 'all persons living on the territory' of a given state party, including persons belonging to 'new' minorities.[37] Furthermore, it seems possible to argue that other provisions, such as Articles 3, 5, 7, and 8 FCNM could also be applicable to persons belonging to 'new' minorities, at least in certain circumstances. Based upon this analysis, the Advisory Committee opted again for a

[35] See, for example, Advisory Committee on the Framework Convention for the Protection of National Minorities, Opinion on Albania, ACFC/INF/OP/I (2003) 004, 2002, paras. 17–22, where the Advisory Committee held that the a priori exclusion of the Egyptians, as a group having resided for centuries in Albania, from the personal scope of application of the FCNM was incompatible with Art. 3 FCNM. Advisory Committee Opinion on Denmark, ACFC/INF/OP/I (2001) 005, 2000, paras. 13–25 reached the same conclusion with respect to, *inter alia*, the Roma, a finding which was confirmed in the pertinent conclusions of the Committee of Ministers. In other, less clear situations, the Advisory Committee opted for a more pragmatic approach and called upon the governments concerned to discuss the issue with the representatives of the groups concerned; see, for example, Advisory Committee Opinion on Austria, ACFC/INF/OP/I (2002) 009, 2002, paras. 12–20 concerning inhabitants of Vienna of Polish origin; Advisory Committee Opinion on Romania, ACFC/INF/OP/I (2002) 001, 2001, paras. 14–18 concerning the Csangos; Advisory Committee Opinion on Sweden, ACFC/INF/OP/I (2003) 006, 2003, paras. 13–19 concerning the inhabitants of Scania and Gotland; Advisory Committee Opinion on Ukraine, ACFC/INF/OP/I (2002) 010, 2002, paras. 13–16 concerning the Rusyns; and Advisory Committee Opinion on the United Kingdom, ACFC/INF/OP/I (2002) 006, 2001, paras. 11–16 concerning the Cornish.

[36] Advisory Committee Opinion on Austria, ACFC/INF/OP/I (2002) 009, 2002, para. 16 and Advisory Committee Opinion on Germany, ACFC/INF/OP/I (2002) 008, 2002, para. 16.

[37] See, for example, Advisory Committee Opinion on Austria, ACFC/INF/OP/I (2002) 009, 2002, para. 35; Advisory Committee Opinion on Germany, ACFC/INF/OP/I (2002) 008, 2002, paras. 37–40; Advisory Committee Opinion on Italy, ACFC/INF/OP/I (2002) 007, 2001, para. 40; Advisory Committee Opinion on Norway, ACFC/INF/OP/I (2003) 003, 2002, para. 36; and Advisory Committee Opinion on Sweden, ACFC/INF/OP/I (2003) 006, 2003, para. 37

flexible approach, making it possible to consider the inclusion of persons belonging to such groups in the application of the FCNM on an article-by-article basis. As a result, the Advisory Committee expressed its opinion that competent state authorities should consider the issue in consultation with those concerned.[38] It must be stressed, however, that the Advisory Committee clearly favours an inclusive approach, as is demonstrated by statements either welcoming such an approach by a government[39] or supporting developments towards the de facto implementation of such an approach.[40]

In the international discussion on the term 'national minority', there is no consensus as to whether persons differing from the majority population with respect to religion only might be considered a national minority, thus falling under the personal scope of application of international instruments aimed at the protection and promotion of the distinct identity of national minorities. As regards the FCNM, this issue has been resolved through Advisory Committee practice. In its opinion on Cyprus, it dealt extensively with the situation of the Maronites and, to a lesser extent, with other religious groups such as the Latin and Armenian communities.[41] This position was later shared by the Committee of Ministers.

Another highly controversial issue is the question as to whether persons belonging to an indigenous people can be considered a national minority in a legal sense. In this context, the Advisory Committee held the opinion that recognizing a group of persons as an indigenous people does not exclude persons belonging to that group from the protection afforded by the FCNM, since the fact that a group of persons may be entitled to a different form of protection cannot by itself justify their exclusion from other forms of protection.[42]

[38] See, for example, Advisory Committee Opinion on Austria, ACFC/INF/OP/I (2002) 009, 2002, para. 20; Advisory Committee Opinion on Germany, ACFC/INF/OP/I (2002) 008, 2002, para. 18; Advisory Committee Opinion on Hungary, ACFC/INF/OP/I (2001) 004, 2000, para. 14; Advisory Committee Opinion on Italy, ACFC/INF/OP/I (2002) 007, 2001, para. 17 and Advisory Committee Opinion on Switzerland, ACFC/INF/OP/I (2003) 007, 2003, para. 24

[39] See, for example, Advisory Committee Opinion on the United Kingdom, ACFC/INF/OP/I (2002) 006, 2001, para. 14.

[40] See, for example, Advisory Committee Opinion on Croatia, ACFC/INF/OP/I (2002) 003, 2001, para. 17; Advisory Committee Opinion on Estonia, ACFC/INF/OP/I (2002) 005, 2001, para. 17; Advisory Committee Opinion on Sweden, ACFC/INF/OP/I (2003) 006, 2003, para. 16.

[41] Advisory Committee Opinion on Cyprus, ACFC/INF/OP/I (2002) 004, 2001, paras. 18–21, 41, 42; see also Advisory Committee Opinion on Armenia, ACFC/INF/OP/I (2003) 001, 2002, para. 19 with respect to the Yezidis.

[42] See the Advisory Committee Opinion on Finland, ACFC/INF/OP/I (2001) 002, 2000, paras. 21–9 concerning Sami; Advisory Committee Opinion on Norway, ACFC/INF/OP/I (2003) 003, 2002, para. 9, 19 concerning Sami; Advisory Committee Opinion on Russia, ACFC/INF/OP/I (2003) 005, 2002, para. 26 regarding the numerically small nations of the North; and Advisory Committee Opinion on Sweden, ACFC/INF/OP/I (2003) 006, 2003, para. 18 concerning Sami.

D. The Territorial Scope of Application of the FCNM

Some states parties to the FCNM are faced with complex issues as a result of the fact that their respective governments cannot exercise effective control over all parts of the state territory concerned. This applies to Cyprus, with respect to the part of the country presently under Turkish occupation; Moldova with respect to the part of the country frequently referred to as Transnistria; and Serbia and Montenegro with respect to the UN-administered province of Kosovo. Notwithstanding the fundamental historic, factual, and legal differences between these situations, the approach chosen by the Advisory Committee in its opinion on Cyprus is particularly interesting.[43]

In its opinion on Cyprus, the Advisory Committee pointed out that in examining the measures taken to give effect to the provisions of the FCNM, it had only taken account of the territory under government control. Thus, the situation in areas beyond the control of the government of Cyprus fell outside the scope of its opinion. This approach seemed to constitute the only viable position since it respected both the territorial integrity of Cyprus, and the factual limitations faced by the Cypriot government as concerns effective control over all Cypriot territory.

In this context, particular attention should be paid to recent developments concerning the possibility of monitoring the implementation of the provisions of the FCNM in Kosovo. While it is clear that the FCNM applies in Kosovo, in principle, as a result of the accession to that treaty by the former Federal Republic of Yugoslavia, it is equally apparent that the government in Belgrade is prevented from exercising effective control over that area by virtue of the pertinent United Nations Security Council Resolution 1244 (1999) establishing the international administration in Kosovo. Therefore, the 30 June 2004 Committee of Ministers authorization for the Secretary-General of the Council of Europe to conclude an agreement with the United Nations Interim Administration Mission in Kosovo (UNMIK), in order to monitor compliance with the standards of the FCNM and facilitating the monitoring arrangements in accordance with the FCNM in Kosovo,[44] is noteworthy. Following the conclusion of this agreement on 23 August 2004 in Priština, the Committee of Ministers, assisted by the Advisory

[43] Advisory Committee Opinion on Cyprus, ACFC/INF/OP/I (2002) 004, 2001, para. 7. The same approach was followed in the Advisory Committee Opinion on Moldova, ACFC/INF/OP/I (2003) 002, 2002, para. 10 with respect to Transnistria; and in the Advisory Committee Opinion on Serbia and Montenegro, ACFC/INF/OP/I (2004) 002, 2003, para. 9 with respect to Kosovo.

[44] CoE Decision of the Committee of Ministers on the Agreement between the United Nations Interim Administration Mission in Kosovo (UNMIK) and the Council of Europe on Technical Arrangements Related to the Framework Convention for the Protection of National Minorities, CM/Del/Dec(2004)890/2.1b, 890th meeting, 2004 and the Monitoring Agreement are available at **https://wcm.coe.int/ViewDoc.jsp?id=102391&Lang=en** 17 August 2004.

Committee, will be entitled to monitor the implementation of the FCNM in Kosovo. To that end, and within six months following the entry into force of that agreement, UNMIK should submit full information on legislative and other measures taken to give effect to the principles set out in the FCNM. This submission shall be made public, as will the opinion of the Advisory Committee and the pertinent conclusions and recommendations of the Committee of Ministers. In effect, UNMIK will have accepted the same obligations regarding the implementation of the FCNM in Kosovo and its monitoring as any state party to the FCNM. This is particularly relevant, even outside the context of the FCNM, since it will be the first time that a United Nations body exercising interim administration over a territory will have accepted being under the scrutiny of an international monitoring system as mandated by a human rights treaty.

E. The FCNM as a 'Living Instrument'

As with any international human rights instrument, the question arises as to whether the provisions of the FCNM ought to be interpreted in a dynamic manner, whether it constitutes a 'living instrument', or whether the implementation of its provisions should be monitored in view of the contents given to them by the respective states parties at a given moment in time. In examining the compatibility of the system of individual declarations of linguistic affiliation, applicable in the Italian province of Bolzano (Bozen), for example, the Advisory Committee concluded that any measures taken must be flexible enough to allow for developments over time.[45] This statement must be interpreted as a clear indication that the Advisory Committee, when interpreting the provisions of the FCNM, fully adheres to the approach chosen by the European Court of Human Rights when interpreting provisions of the ECHR, namely to consider Council of Europe human rights instruments as living instruments, subject to dynamic interpretations. This means that all measures taken by states parties in favour of a particular national minority should be constantly monitored to determine their continued need to achieve their original goal: should they be maintained, or if they are no longer relevant, should they be adapted to a changed context in order to prevent stagnation?

F. Lack of Transparency

A widely, and rightly, criticized shortcoming of the monitoring system under the FCNM is the duration of the confidential stage of the monitoring cycle.

[45] Advisory Committee Opinion on Italy, ACFC/INF/OP/I (2002) 007, 2001, para. 18.

Pursuant to Rule 25 of Resolution (97)10, the conclusions and recommendations of the Committee of Ministers should be made public upon adoption, while according to Rule 26, the opinions of the Advisory Committee should be made public at the same time, 'unless in a specific case the Committee of Ministers decides otherwise'. Finally, under Rule 27, comments by states parties to be submitted to the Committee of Ministers within four months of the receipt of the pertinent opinion, pursuant to a decision taken by the Committee of Ministers on 7 February 2001, should also be made public together with the conclusions and recommendations of the Committee of Ministers and the opinions of the Advisory Committee. In view of the considerable periods of time often needed by the Committee of Ministers to adopt its resolutions,[46] strict observance of these rules has resulted in situations in which the entire monitoring cycle exceeds two years.

In view of the widely held conviction that opinions of the Advisory Committee, constituting the major substantive elements of the monitoring activities under the FCNM, should be introduced into the public domain as early as possible to stimulate public dialogue between all parties concerned, many quarters welcomed the 7 February 2001 decision of the Committee of Ministers to allow the government concerned to make the pertinent opinion public, together with its comments, even before the adoption of conclusions and recommendations by the Committee of Ministers.

The Finnish government was the first to make use of this possibility on 6 July 2001, and became an example followed by the governments of Slovakia, Liechtenstein, and Hungary in 2001; of Romania, the Czech Republic, Estonia, the United Kingdom, Germany, and Austria in 2002; Norway, Albania, Switzerland, Sweden, and Lithuania in 2003; and Azerbaijan and Serbia and Montenegro in 2004. Particularly commendable was the decision of the government of Serbia and Montenegro which, so far, has been the first and only government to publicize the opinion of the Advisory Committee even before it had submitted its response to the Committee of Ministers, adding considerable transparency to the monitoring process. Another positive example was set by the German government, which annexed pertinent comments by organizations representing national minorities residing in Germany

46 Examples where the pertinent resolution, as of 15 July 2004, had not yet been adopted include: Albania (opinion adopted 12 September 2002) and Slovenia (opinion adopted 12 September 2002). Another case in point is Austria, with respect to which the resolution was adopted on 4 February 2004, whereas the pertinent opinion had been adopted on 16 May 2002. It should be added, however, that the reason for the enormous delay in these three cases—normally the Committee of Ministers needs less than one year to adopt its resolution—is action taken by third states within the Committee of Ministers.

to its own comments. This step constitutes a welcome initiative to continue the dialogue between the government and those organizations established in the process of drafting the German state report. Both of these approaches should, in the opinion of the Advisory Committee, be emulated by other governments.

In contrast, the governments of Armenia, Croatia, Cyprus, Denmark, Ireland, Italy, Malta, Moldova, the Russian Federation, and San Marino were not prepared to adhere to this practice. With regard to practices in these states, the opinions of the Advisory Committee were only made public upon adoption of the conclusions and recommendations of the Committee of Ministers. This means that, as of 15 July 2004, the opinions of the Advisory Committee on the state reports of Poland, Slovenia, and Spain were not yet in the public domain. In addition, the opinions adopted on 27 May 2004 on Bosnia-Herzegovina, Bulgaria, and the former Yugoslav Republic of Macedonia had not yet been made publicly available; it should be noted, however, that as of 15 July 2004, the four-month period within which governments are invited to submit their comments on the opinions of the Advisory Committee had not elapsed. Notwithstanding the beneficial reduction in length of the confidential stage of the monitoring cycle, it is hoped that even more states will adhere to the practice of early publication of the opinions of the Advisory Committee. Ideally, these should be made accessible to the public upon their adoption by the Advisory Committee.

G. The Availability of Statistical Data and the Conduct of Censuses

An apparent lack of adequate statistical data has the ability to hamper the monitoring process of the implementation of the FCNM in many ways. Throughout the first cycle of monitoring, therefore, the Advisory Committee has stressed the necessity to collect and process data by way of censuses or other means to define the numerical size and geographical distribution of national minorities, *inter alia* as a *conditio sine qua non* for any pertinent government policy to be successfully implementable, and to allow persons belonging to national minorities to express their identity freely. On the other hand, the Advisory Committee recognized that, in some countries, persons belonging to national minorities themselves might be reluctant to identify themselves in view of specific historical experiences.[47] In such situations, the Advisory

[47] In particular, this is the position of German Sinti and Roma who feel that the availability of such data facilitated the Holocaust. See the Advisory Committee Opinion on Germany, ACFC/INF/OP/I (2002) 008, 2002, para. 23.

Committee called for the use of other methods, with the co-operation of the national minorities concerned, such as estimates based on ad hoc studies.[48] In any case, the principle of confidentiality, as set out, *inter alia*, in the Committee of Ministers' Recommendation (97)18 Concerning the Protection of Personal Data Collected and Processed for Statistical Purposes, must be strictly respected, and consultations with representatives of national minorities should be sought to ensure that census categories are appropriately defined.

Another important aspect to be respected in the conduct of censuses, is the voluntary nature of any statement regarding a person's belonging to a certain group, as reliance on FCNM protection is optional, as clearly expressed in Article 3 FCNM. This means that the FCNM only applies if it is chosen by the persons concerned and to the extent that they wish. Therefore, the Advisory Committee has consistently stressed that, in a census, answers to any question regarding a person's ethnic affiliation must not be made mandatory.[49] On the other hand, it is equally important that there be a possibility to express one's belonging to a certain national minority confidentially.

H. The Situation of Roma and Travellers

A review of the thirty-four Advisory Committee opinions adopted so far clearly shows the vulnerability of Roma and Travellers, particularly women. Considering the reports of many of the states parties, the Advisory Committee had to conclude that such persons continue to face widespread discrimination and disadvantages in socio-economic and other societal settings, including in the field of education. It is therefore essential that activities aimed at improving the specific situations of Roma and Travellers continue, and that they be substantially increased, at national and international levels, if need be. The Advisory

[48] See, for example, Advisory Committee Opinion on Armenia, ACFC/INF/OP/I (2003) 001, 2002, para. 31; Advisory Committee Opinion on Austria, ACFC/INF/OP/I (2002), 009, 2001, para. 22; Advisory Committee Opinion on Azerbaijan, ACFC/INF/OP/I (2004) 001, 2003, para. 27; Advisory Committee Opinion on the Czech Republic, ACFC/INF/OP/I (2002) 002, 2001 para. 28; Advisory Committee Opinion on Germany, ACFC/INF/OP/I (2002) 008, 2002, para. 24; Advisory Committee Opinion on Hungary, ACFC/INF/OP/I (2001) 004, 2000, para. 17; Advisory Committee Opinion on Moldova, ACFC/INF/OP/I (2003) 002, 2002, para. 36; Advisory Committee Opinion on Norway, ACFC/INF/OP/I (2003), 003, 2002, para. 27; Advisory Committee Opinion on Romania, ACFC/INF/OP/I (2002) 001, 2001, para. 26; Advisory Committee Opinion on Serbia and Montenegro, ACFC/INF/OP/I (2004) 002, 2003, para. 45; and Advisory Committee Opinion on Slovakia, ACFC/INF/OP/I (2001) 001, 2000, para. 21.

[49] See, for example, Advisory Committee Opinion on Estonia, ACFC/INF/OP/I (2002) 005, 2001, para. 19; Advisory Committee Opinion on Russia, ACFC/INF/OP/I (2003) 005, 2002, para. 30; Advisory Committee Opinion on Ukraine ACFC/INF/OP/I (2002) 010, 2002, para. 22.

Committee shared this assessment, and strongly welcomed and fully supported pertinent initiatives by various governments and numerous NGOs, both in and outside the Council of Europe.

III. Conclusion and Outlook

At the end of the first cycle of monitoring, there can be no doubt that the FCNM has become the major legal instrument for the protection of national minorities in Europe.[50] The competent monitoring bodies have established and consolidated their practices to include a range of novelties for the activities of bodies working in a system based on periodic state reports: regular country visits, for example, are conducted to gain information *in situ* on the adequacy of the measures taken by the respective state to implement its obligations flowing from the FCNM. It is also important to note the establishment of a continuous and constructive dialogue within which the follow-up seminars, another innovation, play an extremely important role.

Concerning the substance of the provisions of the FCNM, it would not be realistic to expect considerable precision of the vaguely formulated FCNM provisions after only five years of monitoring. This commentary is part of an effort to move towards greater precision. Indeed there are a number of clarifications and advances to be found in the soft jurisprudence of the Advisory Committee. This soft jurisprudence from the Advisory Committee, continuous and constructive dialogue between the Advisory Committee and representatives of governments and national minorities, and dialogue between the Advisory Committee and the academic world on the strength of this commentary, could form the basis for future precision of FCNM provisions.

[50] For well-balanced stock taking and a critique of the results achieved so far, see the papers presented at the Conference to mark the Fifth Anniversary of the Entry into Force of the Framework Convention for the Protection of National Minorities, Strasbourg, 30–1 October 2003, currently only available at **www.coe.int/T/E/human_rights/minorities** 17 August 2004.

THE FRAMEWORK CONVENTION IN HISTORICAL AND GLOBAL PERSPECTIVE

Asbjørn Eide

I. Introduction: International Co-operation and the Minority Issue

According to Article 1 of the Framework Convention for the Protection of National Minorities (FCNM), '[t]he protection of national minorities and of the rights and freedoms of persons belonging to those minorities forms an integral part of the international protection of human rights, and as such falls within the scope of international co-operation.' By adopting the Convention in 1994, the Committee of Ministers, representing the vast majority of European states including many that had formerly fought wars against each other where ethnic conflicts had been part of the problem, formally recognized and proclaimed that minority protection was 'within the scope of international co-operation'. All European states ratifying the Convention have committed themselves to submit to the procedures established for the implementation of that Convention.

Behind this achievement was a long and tumultuous European and world history. This chapter takes the commitment expressed in Article 1 as a starting point for a historical exploration of its antecedents and its global acceptance. The journey starts with the origin and contextual relevance of the words 'falls within the scope of international co-operation'. The term 'international', as well as the composite terms 'international law' and 'international co-operation', are post-Westphalian concepts that could not have materialized before the emergence in Europe of the so-called 'nation-states' as the building blocks in the international political architecture. That process spread to the rest of the world by the nineteenth and twentieth centuries, but often with features different from those of European developments.

'International co-operation' took an even longer time to emerge as a concept, and the purposes of state co-operation were not always aimed at protecting nationalities or minorities. At times quite the opposite was intended. 'International protection of human rights' appeared only when commitments to international co-operation had reached an advanced stage; indeed, this notion did not become part of international law until the establishment of the United Nations, and even then it remained rudimentary until the main human rights conventions had been adopted, and the machinery had been established for their monitoring or implementation.[1]

When that stage was initiated by the adoption of the Universal Declaration of Human Rights (UDHR), 'minority protection' was not considered to be an aspect of human rights at the UN or the Council of Europe. It was thought that the respect and protection of individual rights, including prevention of discrimination, would make the special protection of minorities unnecessary and possibly harmful. It took another two decades before the UN started to address issues of minority protection cautiously, and another two decades before the issue was seriously addressed, both by the UN and the Council of Europe.

[1] In this respect, the Council of Europe was way ahead of both the UN and the regional organizations, as it had established the European Commission on Human Rights and the European Court of Human Rights during the 1950s.

The formulation 'protection of international minorities and of the rights and freedoms of persons belonging to those minorities' in Article 1 reflects a dilemma and a duality that has never been resolved, and is unlikely to be in the near future: the individual versus the collective approach to minority protection. This dichotomy reflects the fact that while the rights of persons belonging to minorities are issues of human rights, the protection of minorities has a wider set of justifications to take into account: the maintenance of group identity; the prevention of conflict; and the search for state stability.

In our time, international co-operation is organized both at the regional and the global level. It is, therefore, important to look outward, to examine the approaches to minorities by the United Nations as the global organization, and to compare the European model with those in other regional systems. This chapter explores some of the issues involved in placing the Framework Convention in its historical and its wider international contexts.

II. Developments up to the Second World War

A. The Emergence in Europe of an International System of States

The term 'international' appears to have been used, for the first time, by Jeremy Bentham. It first appeared in his *Introduction to the Principles of Morals and Legislation* (written in 1780 and published in 1789), concerning the codification of laws. As an introductory issue, he pointed out the need to distinguish between what should be regulated by internal law, including disputes between private persons of different states (what we now call international private law), on the one hand and on the other, 'transactions between sovereigns as such, for the subject of that branch which may be properly and exclusively termed international'.[2] The distinction between the internal and the international had not been self-evident prior to this point in time. It was a product of the gradual development of the modern state system, which by convenience is generally claimed to have started with the Peace of Westphalia in 1648 ending the Thirty Years War on the European continent.

[2] Jeremy Bentham's *Introduction to the Principles of Morals and Legislation* contains his most famous presentation of the utility principle but discusses also the limits and purpose of legislation. It has appeared in several editions, including one edited by J. H. Burns and H. L. A. Hart (The Athlone Press, London, 1970), and reprinted in paperback with new introduction by F. Rosen (Clarendon Press, Oxford, 1996). The quote in the text above is taken from J. Bowring, *The Works of Jeremy Bentham*, i (Edinburgh 1838, reprint New York, 1962), 149 (publisher unknown) and is quoted here from O. Brunner, W. Conze, and R. Koselleck (eds.), *Geschichtliche Grundbegriffe* (Ernst Klett, Stuttgart, 1982), 369.

Transactions 'between sovereigns as such' were included under Bentham's term 'international'. 'Nations' were those territories and peoples under the control of a sovereign, either a person (emperor, king) or a collective government. 'Nations' were not, in his terminology, or in subsequent international law, understood in an ethnic sense. He referred to 'state-nations', whose territory and subjected peoples might vary and change over time, though his own country, Britain, was already territorially quite fixed. Bentham did not mention the term 'international co-operation', which at that point in time would have been a utopian idea. In the eighteenth century, the major powers were in almost constant conflict over colonial possessions and over territories and influence on the European continent.

A brief reminder of earlier history may be useful here. During the High Medieval period in Europe, the papacy and the Holy Roman Empire formed a framework quite different from the later state system. With feudalism at its base, the sense of a '*respublica Christiana*' had developed: a united Christendom, with the papacy claiming a kind of universal jurisdiction. It pretended that local rulers and kings, and even the Holy Roman Emperor, were subject to higher authority, ultimately based on the Christian religion as interpreted by the Pope. Within this belief, there could be no clear distinction between 'internal', 'international', and 'law' in the public sphere, as distinct from customs and regulations relating to private transactions. Instead, it was loosely associated with 'natural law', which in turn was interpreted as 'divine' law.

Two sets of challenges in the sixteenth and seventeenth centuries brought fundamental changes to these notions. The first matter was the rise and consolidation of new territorial states, in particular France and England, whose increasingly absolutist rulers refused to be subject to any external authority, be it the Emperor of the Holy Roman Empire or the Pope. This marked the emergence of state-nations and of the conception of 'sovereign' and 'sovereignty' in the modern sense. The second challenge was the Protestant revolt against religious authority and the doctrine of the papacy. Implicit in this challenge, which started as a purely religious dissent, was the fundamental question of legitimate rule by kings and princes. At a time when religion had strong influence on the minds of people, kings and emperors sought their legitimacy in divine authority ('by the Grace of God'). As long as Central and Western Europe[3] were unified by one religion interpreted by one religious leader, the

[3] The Great Schism occurred much earlier, in a process ending around 1050. This movement refers to the break between the Western and Eastern Part of Christianity which led to the establishment of the Orthodox Church, that was headquartered in Constantinople in collaboration with the Emperor of Byzantium. Most of the territory of the Byzantine Empire was later overrun by the Ottomans, who

Pope, he could wield considerable influence over the population, especially over whether they accepted their rulers.

The Protestant revolt allowed the opportunity for independent-minded rulers to challenge the authority of the papacy and still maintain religious legitimacy, provided their subjects adhered to the religion preferred by the ruler. This was first addressed in the Peace of Augsburg (1555), which confirmed the Augsburg Confession, whereby each prince could determine whether Lutheranism or Roman Catholicism was to prevail in his lands. *Cuius regio, eius religio*, a Latin phrase meaning 'Whose the region is, his religion' was the guiding principle. Conflicts between the Catholic and the various Protestant or Reformed churches continued and were a major factor in the Thirty Years War, which ended in 1648 with the Peace of Westphalia. The peace treaties adopted at this time constituted the final confirmation of the death of the *respublica Christiana*. The system of independent states was consolidated and continued to expand, though states were not yet territorially fixed, with the exception of those in Western Europe. The rest of the continent remained a *mélange* of feudal entities and empires, and its transformation into territorial states did not fully take place until the nineteenth and twentieth centuries.

B. Protection of Religious Minorities

The history of minority protection started in the seventeenth and eighteenth centuries with efforts to provide protection to religious minorities in the aftermath of the religious conflicts in Europe.[4] Religion remained important for the princes and sovereigns as sources of their legitimacy, but religion was also important for the private person. The sovereign imposition of a particular religion to be adhered to in the territory he or she controlled was bound to cause tension and repression. Since territories often changed hands, persons sometimes found themselves being ruled by a new sovereign with a different religion. It was this predicament that led to the first peace treaty provisions for the protection of religious minorities in territories that changed

were ethnically Turkic and followers of Islam. The Russian Tsar was the main Orthodox ruler left to confront the Ottoman Turks. The struggle during the nineteenth century of the peoples of the Balkans for independence from the Ottoman Empire, on religious and national grounds, and the conflicting approaches of European states towards those struggles, was a key element in the emergence of the so-called 'nationalist principle' in international relations.

[4] There are numerous studies on minorities in international relations and international law and it would go far beyond this study to list them here. One of the most recent is G. Pentassuglia, *Minorities in International Law* (European Centre for Minority Issues and Council of Europe Publishing, Strasbourg, 2002), which contains an extensive list of publications in each chapter.

hands.[5] However, the recognition of different religious branches also generated wider debate about freedom of religion for the individual. This notion was to become one of the earliest assertions of human rights, and it also serves to illustrate the movement from collective to individual rights.

The French revolution brought human rights to the foreground, but a number of contrasting effects on the further development of Europe: nationalist sentiments; quest for democratic development; but also strong authoritarian reaction followed the Napoleonic wars and occupations.

C. International Co-operation in 'the Century of Nationalism'—1815 to the First World War

The settlement at the 1814–15 Congress of Vienna gave rise to a form of international co-operation: the Holy Alliance between the Protestant Emperor of Prussia, the Catholic Emperor of Austria, and the Orthodox Tsar of Russia. It was an effort to set back the clock and to recapture the essence of the *respublica Christiania*, only this time to be managed by a three-headed leadership—emperors representing three different versions of Christianity. It was established to restore and preserve the old order, taking action to repress democratic and national movements.

England was not a part of this troika because of the Holy Alliance's excessive reactionary and anti-democratic policies. It was, however, in alliance with the three in the 'Quadruple Alliance', which had been formed to oppose Napoleon and which determined the outcome of the Congress of Vienna. This group was later extended to become the 'Quintuple Alliance' when France joined in 1818. The resulting alliance engaged in international co-operation to repress Italian nationalist uprisings in 1820 and Spanish nationalist movements, but broke up over the Greek wars of independence from the Ottoman Empire, due to conflicting attitudes towards intervention by the great powers. By 1830, the Holy Alliance was basically dead, replaced by the Concert of Europe. This new coalition was an unorganized and vague consensus among the European monarchies favouring the preservation of the territorial and political status quo. The term assumed the responsibility and right of the great powers to intervene and impose their collective will on states threatened by internal

[5] Pentassuglia, above, n. 4, p. 181, mentions the 1731 Treaty of Utrecht in which France gave the Hudson Bay and Acadia to England, guaranteeing the right of the people to exercise the Catholic religion 'insofar as the laws of England permit'. The 1678 Treaty of Nijmegen between France and Holland guaranteed Catholics in Holland freedom of religion and possession of their property.

rebellion, but it was soon shaken by conflicting interests and the 1853–6 Crimean war, which was a direct armed conflict between major parties to the Concert of Europe: Great Britain, France, and Sardinia in support of Turkey on one side, against Russia on the other. From then on, the Concert of Europe was no more than a balance of power, where the states watched each other rather than co-operated.

At the 1856 Peace of Paris which ended the Crimean War, the Ottoman Empire became a member of the European concern, guaranteeing its integrity. In turn, the Sultan made a commitment to improve the status of his Christian subjects who were under European protection. There was no formal follow-up to monitor this international undertaking, however.

The Ottoman Empire continued to decline and the 1856 guarantee of its integrity was not taken seriously. New political entities became independent or autonomous in the Balkans. European powers played diverse roles in these events, co-operating to some extent in the peace settlements, including requirements for the protection of minorities as conditions for international recognition. One of the main examples was the 1878 Congress of Berlin, where Great Britain, Austria-Hungary, France, Germany, Italy, Russia, and Turkey entered into a treaty for 'the Settlement of Affairs in the East' which, among the conditions to recognize the independence of Montenegro, Serbia, and Romania, and the establishment of Bulgaria as a principality under the sovereignty of the Sublime Porte, also set requirements for the respect of civil and political liberties, religious freedom, and prohibition of discrimination in public affairs, from which minorities would benefit.[6]

International co-operation in these matters did not extend beyond the drafting of treaty requirements. There was no follow-up co-operation, no common secretariat, and no monitoring or complaint-handling body.

D. A Note on Time Zones on Nation-State Formation in Europe

The nineteenth century has been characterized as the age of ethnic or cultural nationalism, the effort to form state territories on the basis of the cultural or ethnic habitat, which has been described as 'the marriage between state and culture'. Gellner has convincingly argued that there are four time zones in Europe in this respect.[7] The first was at the Atlantic rim (England and France

[6] Above, n. 5, p. 182.

[7] E. Gellner, *Conditions of Liberty: Civil Society and its Revivals* (Hamish Hamilton, London, 1994), ch. 15.

in particular), where strong dynasties had already established control over territories roughly correlating to cultural areas in the late medieval period; they were therefore among the first territorial states. The second time zone was the area that had been under the nominal control of the Holy Roman Empire, which had lost all of its significance well before the Napoleonic wars. By the beginning of the nineteenth century, the area was deeply fragmented into different political units, but the fragments essentially belonged to two major cultures: the German and the Italian. Consequently, the century of nationalism in that zone manifested itself in the unification of two major units, Germany and Italy.

From the nationalist perspective, the third zone was much more difficult to reconcile according to the 'one culture, one state model'. According to Gellner, 'there was an appallingly complex patchwork of different cultures, intermixed both geographically and in the social structure, with political, cultural and religious boundaries devoid of any coherence or mutual support. Here both cultures and polities had to be created.' Expanding on his description, these areas had been subjected to separate, externally dominated and culturally different empires: the Ottoman; the Austrian and the German; and the Byzantine Empire, which had left its legacy, *inter alia*, through the Orthodox Church. It was this third zone that caused the greatest difficulty in solving the nationality-minority puzzle at the end of the nineteenth century. This was even more the case during the period of the League of Nations, when the territories had become independent states and the three empires had been dissolved. The application of the nationalist principle continued to be a source of conflict and manipulation in the 1930s and during the Second World War. These conflicts were frozen during the Cold War, but re-emerged with serious consequences after its end, particularly in former Yugoslavia.

The fourth time zone, in Gellner's opinion, corresponds to the general area of the Tsarist Empire. It had many of the same characteristics as the third time zone until the end of the First World War, but its subsequent history diverged from that of the Balkans or Central Europe. With the exception of Finland and the Baltic countries, which became independent after the Russian revolution, the rest of the Tsarist Empire was maintained 'under new management' by the Soviet Union.[8] With the weakening and final collapse of the Soviet Union, the nationalist and ethnic conflicts came out in full force after 1988 in Nagorno Karabakh in Azerbaijan, South Ossetia and Abkhazia in Georgia, and in Chechnya in the Russian Federation among others.

[8] Gellner, above, n. 7, ch. 15, p. 116.

E. Sovereignty and Positivism: The Relation to Nationalism and Minority Issues

The nineteenth century is considered the golden age of 'classical' international law. It represented an effort to break completely with the natural law of the past and to reject the notion that there were higher principles or laws binding states. Therefore, the assertion of full state sovereignty was closely associated with positivism: the only valid law was a positively stated or recognized law. The positivist doctrine allowed for any kind of legislation and practice, including repressive and inhumane legislation, such as that of Germany under Hitler. Under the positivist doctrine, international law was only binding to the extent that states consented to it by their free, sovereign will. Included in their free, sovereign will was also the right to use force against other states when so chosen. Nationalism had an ambiguous place in this process. Once the nation-state had been established, nationalism reinforced the sense of absolute sovereignty and rejected any right of others to interfere with its treatment of its minorities. Nonetheless, empires that controlled and repressed nationalities had the same sovereign right as nation-states to repress nationalist movements inside their borders. Other European states were faced with the dilemma of whether they could or should intervene to protect minorities or nationalities within empires or multi-ethnic states, thereby challenging state sovereignty. The Ottoman Empire, represented by Turkey, was never quite seen as European and, consequently, was subject to more interventions than others, but uncertainties and doubts persisted throughout the century as to the justifications for intervention.

F. International Co-operation for the Protection of Minorities: The League of Nations

Convened in 1919 following the Second World War, the Paris Peace Conference served in part to settle past disputes through a number of peace treaties with the defeated states of Germany, Austria, Hungary, Bulgaria, and Turkey, and to adopt a blueprint for the future through the establishment of the League of Nations, the brainchild of US President Woodrow Wilson.

The League of Nations was established 'to promote international cooperation and to achieve international peace and security'. It was the first effort to develop international co-operation on issues of political importance, and to move from the pattern of international conferences and congresses of the past to an organized co-operation with a secretariat and regular meetings. As such, it was the beginning of a new stage in international law, the initiation of a law of co-operation, distinct from a law of coexistence. The main purpose of this co-operation was to constrain states from using force against each other; instead they were to resort to a cumbersome, internationally regulated process of peaceful resolution of conflict, before acts of war could be undertaken. Co-operation with the aim of reducing numbers of armaments also ties in to this thinking. Other important areas were also covered: the members of the League committed themselves to co-operate for the promotion of fair labour conditions (which led to the establishment of the International Labour Organization (ILO)); for the prevention of trafficking in women and children; and to secure just treatment of the native inhabitants of the territories under their control. Another important part of the co-operation was the international monitoring of the implementation of the mandate obligations by states that were entrusted with the mandates of territories formerly belonging to the states defeated during the war.

The Covenant of the League of Nations included no provision for international co-operation for the protection of minorities, nor was there any proposal to set up a general system to this end. President Wilson drafted a provision requiring new states, as a precondition to their recognition as independent states, to bind themselves to give the same equal treatment in law and in fact to 'all racial or national minorities' as that accorded to the racial or national majority of the people. The proposal was finally dropped, however, since it would be undesirable to impose special obligations on a special group of states in the Covenant, which was built on the implicit assumption of state equality.

Minority protection under the League was, therefore, not based on the Covenant, but on special minority treaties signed at the Paris Peace Conference or contained in special chapters regarding minorities in peace treaties. This legal basis could also be found in unilateral declarations made before the League's existence and noted through resolutions by the League upon the admission of certain newly independent states. Some bilateral treaties were placed 'under the guarantee' of the League.[9]

Minority protection under the League only extended to independent countries or those that had had their borders extended due to the peace settlement or due to the upheavals in Russia, such as the independence of the three Baltic states. Special concern with minority protection in these countries must be seen as an effort to mitigate the consequences of the imperfect implementation of the principle of national self-determination, promoted by President Wilson in his 14 points.

[9] A comprehensive listing can be found in A. Spiliopoulou Åkermark, *Justifications of Minority Protection in International Law* (Justus Förlag, Uppsala, 1997), 104–5.

The implementation of the principle of national self-determination in Central Europe, where a mosaic of different ethnic groups lived interspersed with one another, required a strengthened system of minority protection. The guarantees implicit in the treaties and undertakings listed above were twofold: in the first place, the affected states undertook an obligation to implement the protective system in their internal order. In the second instance, alleged violations could be brought to the attention of the League by its members, other states, or through petitions from affected minorities. The Permanent Court of International Justice, created in connection with the establishment of the League, was given the competence to exercise jurisdiction over disputes concerning the interpretation of the treaties when requested by the Council. Upon request, it could also give advisory opinions and did so in a number of cases. The minorities could not, however, address the Court, as they had no *locus standi*.

The minority protection system met with some success during the first decade of the League, but gradually failed for multiple reasons. Some of the states that were obliged to protect their minorities through treaties or other undertakings refused to apply them after some time, as they became the subjects of increasing popular resentment. Part of the problem was the selectiveness of these obligations. Only some states, all of them from Eastern Europe, were subjected to the League's control system. There was some debate about the desirability of replacing the sketchy minority protection system with a general system for the protection of human rights, applicable to all member states. This informed the system which was later established after the Second World War by the United Nations, but no action was taken in that direction during this period.

There has been wide discussion as to whether the minority protection of the League was a failure. Undoubtedly, it would have been more legitimate if it had been applied generally. On the other hand, the most prevalent needs appeared to be in those new or redrawn states in 'the third time zone' (Gellner) rather than in states that had already been consolidated. It was not foreseen that nationalism in settled states could go to the extremes that occurred in Hitler's Germany, for example.

Many of the problems arose from the actual peace treaties themselves adopted at the Paris Peace Conference in 1919. To a large extent, the settlements were based on a vindictiveness that was harmful for the future of Europe. At the insistence of France and Britain, the Versailles treaty with Germany exacted enormous reparations from the new, democratic German government under the Weimar Republic, to compensate for damages incurred by the defeated German Kaiser and his government, including a fifteen-year French occupation of the Rhineland. Both measures were devastating barriers to the reconstruction and development of German economy and society. Together with the impact of the Great Depression, starting in 1929, these measures served to undermine the democratic government and contributed to the emergence of the extreme nationalists led by Hitler.

The main problem, however, was that the European states were not yet sufficiently ready for the kind of international co-operation required for effective protection. The continued assertion of unlimited state sovereignty, combined with increasingly intolerant nationalism aggravated by turbulence resulting from the economic depression, undermined the minority protection system, and even the League itself.

The system of unbridled state sovereignty led to an accumulation of tensions that had built up since Westphalia. The first major outburst resulted in the Napoleonic wars, the second major crisis led to the First World War, and, in spite of the efforts of the League, a third explosion occurred in 1939–40. It took another and even more devastating world war to demonstrate that the system was untenable and that more extensive co-operation was necessary, even if it modified the notion of state sovereignty.

Nevertheless, the post-First World War treaties were the forerunner of a more general minority system for two reasons. In the first place, most of the treaties and declarations were modelled on the original Polish-German treaty with some general principles emanating from particular commitments. Secondly, since the League of Nations was entrusted with the task of receiving petitions and ruling on claims of violated minority rights under the treaties, case law emerged with significance for post-Second World War developments.

III. Minorities in the Age of the United Nations

A. The United Nations and International Co-operation

The Charter of the United Nations reflects a vision of a far more comprehensive and intensive international co-operation than the Covenant of the League had envisaged. The Charter proposed a world order built on the threefold purpose set out in Article 1: the maintenance of international peace, including the protection of the territorial integrity of states against external aggression and intervention; the development of friendly relations among nations, taking into account the principles of sovereign equality and self-determination of peoples; and the achievement of international co-operation to resolve problems of economic, social, cultural, or humanitarian character, including the promotion and encouragement of respect for human rights and fundamental freedoms without distinction as to race, sex, language, or religion. In this sense, 'sovereignty' is qualified by the 'equality' and 'self-determination' of peoples, and requires the respect of strong states for the territorial and political integrity of weaker ones. It also necessitates all states to abstain from using armed force except in self-defence, and to participate in international co-operation in broad fields, including the promotion of and respect for human rights.

The United Nations organization was established 'to employ international machinery for the promotion of the economic and social advancement of all peoples', as set out in the Preamble of the Charter. Thus, a substantial international secretariat was created, indicating the wide scope of intended co-operation as compared to any earlier efforts.

B. Human Rights the New Foundation

The most revolutionary aspect of the UN Charter is its introduction of human rights as a core purpose for international co-operation. The Preamble of the Universal Declaration of Human Rights states that 'recognition of the inherent dignity and of the equal and unalterable rights of all members of the human family is the foundation of freedom, justice and peace in the world' and Article 1 proclaims that 'all human beings are born free and equal in dignity and rights'. The Declaration, given its intended worldwide application, was a historically unprecedented event.[10] It espouses interrelated and interdependent civil, political, economic, social, and cultural rights adopted as a package, the premiss being that the different rights were interdependent and therefore indivisible.

A major feature of the human rights system established under the United Nations was its strong emphasis on equality and non-discrimination in the treatment of each individual. The principle was set out in the UN Charter itself and made the core pillar of the Universal Declaration. Traditional ethno-nationalism had not treated members of minorities as equals, and the intention was to change this outlook. Nevertheless, while there was strong support for the principle of equality and non-discrimination during the drafting of the Declaration by the Commission on Human Rights in 1947–8, there was not much support for the inclusion of rights of minorities or their members.

[10] A detailed presentation of the background to, and the drafting and content of, the Universal Declaration of Human Rights, is found in G. Alfredsson and A. Eide (eds.), *The Universal Declaration of Human Rights: A Common Standard of Achievement* (Nijhoff, The Hague, 1999).

Several proposals for articles on the rights of minorities or their members were presented by the Secretariat and by the delegations of Denmark, Yugoslavia, and the USSR, but did not find majority support. The Chair of the Commission, Eleanor Roosevelt (USA), argued against the inclusion of any such provision. She referred to a regional conference held in Lima in 1938, where it had been affirmed that a system for the protection of ethnic, linguistic, or racial groups could not be applied in the Americas, 'where minorities as such did not exist', a position repeated at the Inter-American Conference on Problems of War and Peace, held at Chapultepec in February 1945. The Chapultepec Conference had affirmed that closed and homogeneous groups that demanded the status of minorities were not desired in the Americas.[11] The lines were, thus, drawn between the 'new states' of the Americas and those of Western Europe on the one hand, and the countries of Central and Eastern Europe on the other, with Belgium taking an intermediate position.

Some argued that the universal, individual human rights contained in the Declaration would, in themselves, provide the necessary protection of minorities as a consequence of the principle that everyone, without discrimination, was entitled to every right contained in the Declaration. The representative of the United Kingdom argued that the rights of all minorities were in effect, fully protected in the proposed Declaration, making specific rights for minorities superfluous; '. . . thus, article 16 guaranteed to them freedom of religion, article 17 freedom of the press and opinion, article 18 freedom of assembly, article 23 the choice of education, article 25 the right to participate in the cultural life of the community, and article 2 expressly protected minorities'.[12] While subsequent developments have shown that the individual rights contained in the Declaration are not sufficient to protect minorities, those rights are nevertheless essential as part of the platform for their protection. Everyone is entitled to enjoy universal human rights without distinction on the grounds of race, language, or ethnic, religious, or national origin. Members of minorities, as well as majorities, are entitled to all ordinary human rights, both in relation to the state and in relation to the organizations set up by the minorities themselves. Everyone is entitled to freedom of expression and information, in whatever language he or she prefers, which clearly also includes his or her own

[11] Inter-American Conference on Problems of War and Peace, Act of Chapultepec—Declarations on Reciprocal Assistance and American Solidarity (adopted 6 March 1945, entry into force 8 March 1945), Resolution XL, 1945, E/CN.4/AC2/SR 9.

[12] United Nations, *Yearbook of the United Nations 1948–49* (United Nations, New York, 1949), 544. Please note that the final numbering of the Declaration changed after his statement: freedom of religion and belief became Art. 18; freedom of opinion and expression became Art. 19; the right to education became Art. 26 and the provision of cultural rights became Art. 27. Art. 2 remained the same.

minority language. Similarly, everyone is entitled to hold and to practise any religion and belief of his or her own choice, within limits set for the purpose of protecting public order or public morals.

The right of members of minorities to full freedom of association, as well as to freedom of expression and information, is of particular importance in assuring that minorities effectively participate in the social, economic, cultural, and political life of larger societies. These are rights to which all human beings are entitled, including members of minorities. Finally, freedom of movement within a state as well as the right to leave any state and return to one's own is also important for the establishment and maintenance of free association. A proposal by the representative of the United Kingdom to omit any reference to minority protection from the draft Declaration was accepted with the backing of the United States, and with China and India as co-sponsors.[13]

The resistance in adopting specific minority rights was led by a coalition of the 'new' states of the Americas and those 'old' states in Europe which had a long history of nation building. Principally, support for minority rights came from Central and Eastern Europe, including the USSR. Among the few Asian and African states members of the UN in 1948, only India appears to have taken an active part in the discussion on minority rights. Initially the Indian representative expressed some support for minority protection, possibly seeing it as a tool to end the discrimination to which Asian migrants were confronted in the West and in South Africa. Later the Chinese and Indian representatives joined the United Kingdom and other Western states in opposing any provision on minority protection in the Declaration, due to the prominence of the principle of non-discrimination within it.

C. Minority Protection Efforts by the Sub-Commission

The General Assembly, in its Resolution 217 C(III), which was adopted together with the resolution adopting the Universal Declaration, justified its decision not to include any provision on minority protection by observing that the minority problem was complex and delicate with particular characteristics in each state. Since it was difficult to find a common solution to these complex issues, and taking into account the universal character of the Declaration on Human Rights, the Assembly decided not to include any provision on minorities in the Declaration. Instead, it transferred the matter to the Sub-Commission on Prevention of Discrimination and Protection of Minorities,

[13] Discussions during the drafting of the Universal Declaration of Human Rights, 1948, UN Doc. E/CN.4/99 and 104, UN Doc. E/CN.4/SR 73 and 74.

which would undertake 'a thorough study of the problem of minorities' for the United Nations, to take effective measures for the protection of racial, national, religious, or linguistic minorities.

As a contribution to the work of the Sub-Commission, the UN Secretariat issued a memorandum,[14] elaborating the relationship between the prevention of discrimination and the protection of minorities. This memorandum emphasized the fundamental differences between the two objectives, and concluded that the two had to be handled separately. The term 'discrimination', on the one hand, implied any act or conduct that denied equality of treatment to certain individuals because they belonged to particular groups. In order to prevent discrimination, some method to suppress or eliminate any conduct that denied or restricted a person's right to equality had to be found. The protection of minorities, in contrast, upheld distinctions that were voluntarily maintained by the group concerned. This, to a large extent, required positive action. The memorandum referred to the rendering of services, such as the establishment of schools in which teaching would be in the child's mother tongue. According to the memorandum, this was required to achieve real equality. If the child was not taught in his or her own language, he or she would be discriminated against when compared to the majority who were taught in their mother tongue.

The Sub-Commission energetically sought to fulfil its dual mandate to develop standards for the prevention of discrimination and for the protection of minorities. It was relatively successful in its standard-setting activities concerning non-discrimination, among them the drafting of what became the International Convention on the Elimination of All Forms of Racial Discrimination (CERD). With regard to minority rights and protection, the Sub-Commission met strong resistance in its political bodies. In 1950, ECOSOC cancelled the Sub-Commission altogether. It was reinstated at the insistence of the General Assembly in 1951, but it was careful to avoid minority issues for many years.

During this period one modest achievement had been made: the Sub-Commission proposed a special provision to be inserted in the draft of the International Covenant on Civil and Political Rights (ICCPR).[15] The debate in the Sub-Commission on the proposed provision revealed the existence of two broad schools of thought. According to the first school, the minority group

[14] Memorandum Submitted by the Secretary-General, Definition and Classification of Minorities, Compilation of Definitional Proposals over a Forty-Year Period (1950), UN Doc. E/CN.4/1987/WG.5/WP.1.

[15] Sub-Commission on Prevention of Discrimination and Protection of Minorities, Report of the Sub-Commission (1950), UN Doc. E/CN.4/358 (1950) paras. 39–41.

itself was the beneficiary of the protection to be afforded, while for the second, the beneficiary was the individual member of the group. The second group won the debate. The draft finally proposed by the Sub-Commission, and subsequently adopted by the General Assembly as Article 27 ICCPR, reads, '[p]ersons belonging to ethnic, religious or linguistic minorities shall not be denied the right, in community with other members of their group, to enjoy their own culture, to profess and practice their own religion or to use their own language.'[16] This provision was substantially weaker than that which the Sub-Commission had originally intended. First of all, the right was vested in individuals rather than groups, and secondly, it imposed passive obligations on states.

The Sub-Commission did not resume its work on minority issues until several years after the adoption of the ICCPR (1966). In 1971, it appointed Francesco Capotorti as Special Rapporteur to undertake a study of the implications of Article 27 of the Covenant.[17] The resulting study, completed in 1977, remains the most thorough UN report on the subject. In the study's preface, the Rapporteur notes some of the obstacles to genuine acceptance by states of the idea of special protection for minorities: any international system may be viewed as a pretext for interference in a state's internal affairs; the usefulness of a uniform approach in such profoundly different contexts is questionable; preservation of the identity of minorities is seen as a threat to state unity and stability; and the need for special protection could be used to justify reverse discrimination. 'In short', Capotorti concluded, 'governments would prefer to have a free hand in their treatment of minorities.'[18] His principal suggestions for future action focused on the formulation of standards to supplement Article 27, the development of new international methods for implementation, and the adoption of bilateral or regional arrangements.[19] As a follow-up, the Commission established a working group to draft a declaration on the rights of minorities in 1978.[20] For many years, however, opinions were too divided to make any progress.

16 Above, n. 15, para. 42.

17 F. Capotorti, *Study of the Rights of Persons Belonging to Ethnic, Religious and Linguistic Minorities* (1977), UN Doc. E/CN.4/Sub.2/384 and Add. 1–6, republished in the UN Centre for Human Rights, New York, 1991.

18 Above, n. 17, p. iv.

19 ibid.

20 At its 34th session, in 1978, the Commission established an open-ended working group, pursuant to resolution 5(XXX) adopted by the Sub-Commission, recommending the drafting of a declaration on the rights of members of minorities, within the framework of the principles set out in the International Covenant on Civil and Political Rights (ICCPR) (adopted 16 December 1966, entered into force 23 March 1976) 999 UNTS 171, Art. 27; a draft declaration proposed by Yugoslavia (E/CN.4/L.1367/Rev.1) was submitted to the working group to serve as a basis for discussion.

D. Renewed Efforts in the 1990s

In 1990, as a reaction to the emergence of numerous conflicts in Central and Eastern Europe, the Commission accelerated its work and completed its draft of a declaration on the rights of minorities in 1991. In 1992 the Declaration on the Rights of Persons Belonging to National or Ethnic, Linguistic, and Religious Minorities was adopted by the General Assembly.[21]

Also in 1990, the Sub-Commission initiated a study on peaceful and constructive approaches to situations involving minorities, entrusted to the present author. The final report was presented to the Sub-Commission in 1993.[22] The study called for a comprehensive strategy by states to address minority issues. The strategy was to include: assured equal treatment in the common domain; allowances for pluralism in unity through policies in the fields of languages, education, and culture; and allowances for territorial decentralization, facilitating effective participation for regionally concentrated minorities, but based on democratic, not ethnocratic principles. It also called for increased attention to minority issues by specialized agencies and other UN bodies. The study further recommended the establishment of a United Nations Working Group to promote the implementation of the 1992 Declaration. A subsequent Working Group was set up by the Sub-Commission in 1995 and has since met annually. It has significantly contributed to growing attention by the UN and its members to minority issues. The Working Group has a mandate to: review the promotion and practical realization of the 1992 Declaration; seek solutions to problems involving minorities, including the promotion of mutual understanding between and among minorities and governments; and recommend further measures appropriate for the promotion and protection of the rights of persons belonging to national or ethnic, religious, and linguistic minorities.

Four categories of observers participate in the activities of the Working Group on Minorities. The first comprises government officials who provide information on steps taken to promote the principles of the Declaration. The second consists of representatives from United Nations agencies and regional bodies, who contribute information on their field activities as they relate to national minorities. The third group is composed of representatives from non-governmental organizations that deal with minority issues as part of their

[21] UN Commission on Human Rights, Declaration on the Rights of Persons Belonging to National or Ethnic, Religious and Linguistic Minorities, Final Report of the Commission's Working Group, UNGA Res. 47/135 (1992), UN Doc. E/CN.4/1992/48.

[22] Sub-Commission on Prevention of Discrimination and Protection of Minorities, Res. 1993/34 on the Protection of Minorities, United Nations High Commissioner for Human Rights, UN Doc. E/CN.4/Sub.2/1993/34 and Add. 1–4. Addition 4 contains the recommendations of the study.

mandate. Finally, scholars and professional researchers involved in the field of minorities and group accommodation, who provide the Working Group with empirical material, analysis, and ideas for improved approaches to the minority issues, make up the fourth group.

The Working Group seeks to act as a forum for dialogue and the exchange of ideas, information, and experiences which can lead to proposals for constructive group accommodation and further measures to promote and protect the rights of minorities. To date, it has examined steps taken at national, bilateral, regional, and global levels; the causes of problems affecting minorities; forcible displacements of populations and the return of persons who have been displaced; the facilitation of dialogue between and among minorities and governments; prevention and early warning mechanisms; patterns of media presentation and the role of the media in promoting mutual tolerance and understanding; issues of effective participation by minorities; and integration versus autonomy as policy options in addressing minority problems. In addition, emphasis has been placed on the need for appropriate multicultural and intercultural education not only for minorities, but also for majorities.

IV. Indigenous Peoples: A Separate Track

During the 1970s, the Sub-Commission identified indigenous peoples as a category in need of particular protection. While no formal definition has been adopted, indigenous peoples are generally understood to be descendants of the populations that inhabited the country, or a geographical region to which the country belongs, at the time of conquest or colonization, or the establishment of present state boundaries. Furthermore and irrespective of their legal status, indigenous peoples retain some or all of their own social, economic, cultural, and political institutions.[23] Among indigenous peoples are the Amerindians or native Americans on both the North and South American continents; the Inuit, Sami, and other groups who have settled in Arctic regions from Alaska and Canada, through Northern Scandinavia and Northern Russia including Siberia; the Australian Aborigines; and the Maoris of New Zealand. Many

[23] International Labour Organization (ILO), Convention No. 169 concerning Indigenous and Tribal Peoples in Independent Countries (adopted 27 June 1989, entry into force 5 September 1991), Art. 1(*b*) concerning indigenous and tribal peoples in independent countries. This is not a binding definition for the United Nations, but generally captures what is intended to be included in the category. Normally, it would be added that they must be non-dominant in the national society as a whole.

indigenous peoples exist both in Africa and in Asia, but there is controversy over the scope of the definition as it applies to them.

In many parts of the world, indigenous peoples have been dispossessed of their original lands and resettled in places with different environmental conditions. This has meant that they have been deprived of access to basic resources, such as water and food sources, as well as their sacred lands and sites. Such forced removal has not only disrupted the lives of indigenous peoples, but has also destroyed their social and legal orders in the process, and led to hunger, disease, despair, and death. As a result, indigenous peoples have been marginalized in the states where they live and frequently subjected to severe discrimination.

During the 1970s the Sub-Commission prepared a study on 'the Problem of Discrimination against Indigenous Populations' and the Secretariat of the United Nations carried out extensive research in support of the study.[24] The process of collecting information for the study lasted more than ten years, making it the most comprehensive source of information available on the situation of indigenous peoples.[25] During the same period, international indigenous organizations rapidly increased their activities.

In 1982, a Working Group on Indigenous Populations[26] was established to develop new standards on the rights of indigenous peoples. It was the first international forum allowing for the continuous participation of representatives of indigenous peoples. The unique feature of the standard-setting process within the Working Group was that it was carried out with the full participation of the intended beneficiaries, the indigenous peoples, rather than being performed solely by governments and experts. Nothing comparable has been attempted in other standard-setting exercises. In 1993, the Group finished a draft declaration on indigenous rights,[27] which was adopted by the Sub-Commission in 1994 and subsequently transferred to the Commission.

[24] Massive research was co-ordinated by Augusto Willemsen Diaz, a staff member of the UN Human Rights Division, of Guatemalan nationality.

[25] This was due in large part to the efforts of Secretariat member Augusto Willemsen Diaz, who made the protection of indigenous populations his lifelong commitment.

[26] Working Group on Indigenous Populations, The Draft Declaration on the Rights of the Indigenous Peoples, ESC Res. 1982/34, UN ESCOR, UN Doc. E/1982/82. Note that in the resolution, and also otherwise in the UN official language, the concept used is 'indigenous populations', while in the present chapter 'indigenous peoples' is used. This is deliberate.

[27] The draft text can be found as annex to Sub-Commission Resolution 1994/45, UN Sub-Commission on Prevention of Discrimination and Protection of Minorities, Report of the Sub-Commission on Prevention of Discrimination and Protection of Minorities, 46th session, (1994), UN Doc. E/CN.4/Sub.2/1994/56, pp. 105–15.

Debate on the draft declaration on indigenous rights is currently taking place in the Commission, which has set up its own working group to examine it. Observers representing indigenous peoples have access to the negotiations, which have become much more drawn out and difficult than expected. In 2000, ECOSOC established the Permanent Forum on Indigenous Affairs, which meets every year as an advisory body to discuss indigenous issues related to economic and social development, culture, the environment, education, health, and human rights. In general, indigenous peoples place great emphasis on collective land rights, local autonomy, and self-determination, but proposals regarding land rights and self-determination have encountered opposition from some governments, while the content of the right to self-determination remains unclear. Some negotiating parties understand it as a unilateral right to secession, something many governments are not ready to accept; however, many indigenous peoples would be satisfied with a degree of territorial autonomy in regions which have remained their traditional areas of residence and where they form a majority.

The ILO has also been concerned with the prevention of discrimination against members of tribal and indigenous populations. In 1957 it adopted its first Convention (No. 107) on Tribal and Indigenous Population, but its assimilationist approach made it unpalatable to those whom it was intended to benefit. Subsequently, and in parallel to the efforts of the Sub-Commission, the ILO thoroughly revised it to become Convention No. 169 on Indigenous and Tribal Peoples in Independent States, adopted in 1989. This Convention uses the term 'peoples', one that many indigenous representatives preferred to the term 'population', which was used in the 1957 Convention (No. 107). Government fears that the term 'people' would be used to assert the right of peoples to self-determination was addressed in Article 1(3)'s disclaimer, where the term people was defined so that its use would 'not be construed as having any implications as regards the rights which may attach to the term under international law'.

Indigenous persons in most cases also qualify as belonging to minority groups and can avail themselves of the international protection of minorities, where available. In countries that have ratified ILO Convention No. 169, their rights regarding land and autonomy are stronger than under international minority provisions, and in such cases they prefer to make use of the ILO Convention rather than those on minority protection.[28]

[28] This is the position of the Sami, the indigenous people in Norway, for example.

V. The Global and the Regional

International law and co-operation began in Europe, as did the issue of minority protection. The League of Nations broadened the scope of international co-operation to involve countries, such as Australia, Canada, Japan, China, India, the countries of Latin America, and a small number of Asian and African countries as well. Nevertheless, the focus of minority issues has remained predominantly centred on Central and Eastern Europe.

The United Nations has immensely broadened the number of participants in international co-operation. The organization is presently composed of more than 190 members, the vast majority non-European. Nevertheless, it could be argued that the approach to minority protection remains essentially European, whereas the protection of indigenous peoples focuses mainly on the countries 'beyond the blue line', those that were settled by European colonizers who marginalized the original inhabitants.

Efforts are being made to create more awareness of the minority issues in Africa and Asia. The UN Working Group on Minorities and the one on indigenous populations have held seminars in Latin America, in Africa, and in South-East Asia, exploring the specifics of the minority issues in these regions. In the Americas, the main issue, aside from those of indigenous peoples, is the situation of the Afro-Americans. Resolving this situation is partly a question of eliminating the open or structural discrimination to which these people have been subjected, but also partly to recognize their growing assertion of a separate identity.

The African Charter on Human and Peoples' Rights (Banjul Charter) includes not only the usual civil, political, economic, social, and cultural rights, but also the rights of peoples, which has been interpreted by the African Commission to cover minority rights to some extent. Reporting guidelines to the article on equality (Article 19) request that states provide information on the 'constitutional and statutory framework which seeks to protect the different sections of the national communities', and warns against the domination of certain groups over others. Members of the African Commission also raise issues of minority rights in their examination of state reports.

The African Commission has also established a Working Group on Indigenous Populations/Communities as a subsidiary body. Following the adoption of a working paper on the 'Concept of Indigenous Peoples in Africa', the Commission charged the Working Group with gathering information on the situation of indigenous peoples, undertaking country visits, and formulating recommendations. The terms minorities and indigenous peoples are often used interchangeably in Africa, and the enabling resolution of the Working Group expressly refers to minorities. Promoting minority rights is still quite sensitive in Africa, however, and the African Commission has to proceed with caution in its effort to build up minority protection measures.

There is no corresponding regional organization in Asia and there are great difficulties in building up regional international co-operation in this region, where the majority of the world's population live. For the time being the only mechanisms available to minorities seeking protection are those of the United Nations, but it must be recognized that the UN Working Group on Minorities, and that on Indigenous Populations, still have very limited influence on the developments in the Asian region.

In Europe, the Conference on Security and Co-operation in Europe (CSCE), now the Organization for Security and Co-operation in Europe (OSCE), was instrumental in broadening regional co-operation when the Council of Europe was still a predominantly West European organization. Since the 1990 Human Dimension Conference in Copenhagen however, the role of the High Commissioner on National Minorities has played an enormously important part in promoting respect for minorities in his conflict prevention efforts.

Nonetheless, it is clear that of any body advocating national minority rights, the Council of Europe has the most elaborated minority rights standards, after having adopted the European Charter on Regional and Minority Languages in 1992, and the European Framework Convention for the Protection of National Minorities in 1994, which is the subject of the present book.

THE TITLE AND THE PREAMBLE[1]

Tove H. Malloy

Title

The Framework Convention for the Protection of National Minorities

The title and the preamble of an international agreement are not decisive in assessing the substance of its provisions but may be relied upon for interpretation purposes. In this instance, it is clear that the FCNM is a binding agreement under international law, subject to the customary international law reflected in the Vienna Convention on the Law of Treaties. For interpretation purposes, the title of the FCNM adds four important points to the character and the interpretation of the treaty.

First, the title refers to a framework agreement between states. A framework agreement means that the instrument can include a number of programme-type provisions which create no directly enforceable rights for individuals and whose implementation will be left to the states concerned in terms of their internal legislation. Programme-type provisions merely set certain objectives

[1] I would like to thank the members of the FCNM Commentary project for valuable comments received during the second meeting of the group in Cambridge, March 2004. In particular I would like to thank Marc Weller for his enthusiastic support in getting this chapter through its various stages. Any mistake and views expressed are my own.

for states regarding the protection of national minorities. The reference to a framework allows states a wider measure of discretion enabling them to take their own particular circumstances into account.[2] Nevertheless, it may also encourage the creation of subjective rights for persons belonging to national minorities, as well as established models for bilateral agreements concerning the protection of national minorities.

Secondly, the title establishes the beneficiaries of the FCNM: national minorities. This designation raises a number of issues, all of which will be pursued further in the analysis of the Preamble and in the substantive parts of this commentary. First, there is the fact that the title speaks of national minorities, rather than 'persons belonging to national minorities'. The latter version would be more consistent with the substantive provisions throughout the FCNM. This usage was chosen to communicate an emphasis on individual rights enjoyed in community with others, as opposed to collective rights enjoyed by groups. In that way, the FCNM follows the pattern of the 1992 UN Declaration on the Rights of Persons Belonging to National or Ethnic, Religious, and Linguistic Minorities (UN Declaration on Minorities) and Article 27 of the International Covenant on Civil and Political Rights (ICCPR), both of which refer to persons belonging to minorities. Given the repeated invocation of this formula throughout the substantive provisions of the text, it would be misleading to interpret the somewhat shorter form of the title as a direct endorsement of group rights.

Thirdly, the title refers to *national* minorities. This wording is not necessarily in accordance with usage at the universal level, where reference is often made not only to national, but also to ethnic, religious, and linguistic minorities, as evidenced in the UN Declaration. Instead, the FCNM follows the European regional practice confirmed by the Concluding Document of the 1990 CSCE Meeting on the Human Dimension in Copenhagen (the Copenhagen Document). As the FCNM does not include a definition of a national minority, the practice of referring to national minorities rather than ethnic and other types of minorities in the title could be seen as somewhat problematic. National minorities are usually seen as the historic minorities which resulted from the redrawing of European borders after the major

[2] Steering Committee for Human Rights (CDDH), Final Activity Report of the CDDH for the Attention of the Committee of Ministers, CDDH (93) 22, 1993. See also the Preparatory Work of the Ad Hoc Committee for the Protection of National Minorities (CAHMIN), Explanatory Report to the Framework Convention for the Protection of National Minorities, CAHMIN H(1995) 010, 1995, section D.

conflicts of the twentieth century. A particularly restrictive view would hold that national minorities are only those groups that were divorced by the drawing or redrawing of boundaries from their kin state. Hence, a national minority without an external kin state would not qualify. Moreover, whereas national minorities are usually citizens of European states, members of other ethnic groups may not be citizens. This has led one commentator to argue that the European system is less generous to minorities.[3] Furthermore, a number of states have deposited declarations nominating only certain groups as 'national minorities', purporting to leave out others.[4] The controversial issue of a definition of a national minority is addressed elsewhere in this volume in detail, but it suffices to note at this stage that in practice this issue is being addressed in a less restrictive way.

Finally, the title of the FCNM leads us to consider the concept of protection. Again, this concept will be addressed at greater length below in the chapter on Article 1. For now, we might note that protection has connotations that are both positive and negative. On the positive side, the invocation of 'protection', even in the title, somewhat negates the designation of the instrument as a 'framework' agreement. While it is left to states to determine how they achieve the results required by the agreement, it is clear that they are indeed internationally responsible for achieving them. Protection implies a proactive stance, guaranteeing the existence, safety, and development of the identity of national minorities. On the negative side, one might note that international discourse on majority–minority relations has advanced considerably on the concept of protection. Protection implies a helpless position of the individual members of national minorities vis-à-vis the all-powerful state—a state that has to be restrained from harming the national minority through national minority protection. In fact, this is how the term arose during the League of Nations era when individuals found themselves as national minorities under the authority of an alien, and perhaps hostile, state due to territorial change. Of course, it is now clear that national minority issues need to be considered in a much broader perspective, which translates protection into proactive obligations fostering the development of national minority identities and extending to the full and effective equality of national minorities within the state.

[3] A. Eide, Commentary to the Declaration on the Rights of Persons Belonging to National or Ethnic, Religious and Linguistic Minorities, 2001, UN Doc. E/CN.4/Sub.2/AC.5/2001/2.

[4] The classic case is the one of Germany declaring that only citizens are considered national minorities, leaving the large Turkish community without protection.

Preamble

The member States of the Council of Europe and the other States, signatories to the present framework Convention,

Considering that the aim of the Council of Europe is to achieve greater unity between its members for the purpose of safeguarding and realising the ideals and principles which are their common heritage;

Considering that one of the methods by which that aim is to be pursued is the maintenance and further realisation of human rights and fundamental freedoms;

Wishing to follow-up the Declaration of the Heads of State and Government of the member States of the Council of Europe adopted in Vienna on 9 October 1993;

Being resolved to protect within their respective territories the existence of national minorities;

Considering that the upheavals of European history have shown that the protection of national minorities is essential to stability, democratic security and peace in this continent;

Considering that a pluralist and genuinely democratic society should not only respect the ethnic, cultural, linguistic and religious identity of each person belonging to a national minority, but also create appropriate conditions enabling them to express, preserve and develop this identity;

Considering that the creation of a climate of tolerance and dialogue is necessary to enable cultural diversity to be a source and a factor, not of division, but of enrichment for each society;

Considering that the realisation of a tolerant and prosperous Europe does not depend solely on co-operation between States but also requires transfrontier co-operation between local and regional authorities without prejudice to the constitution and territorial integrity of each State;

Having regard to the Convention for the Protection of Human Rights and Fundamental Freedoms and the Protocols thereto;

Having regard to the commitments concerning the protection of national minorities in United Nations conventions and declarations and in the documents of the Conference on Security and Co-operation in Europe, particularly the Copenhagen Document of 29 June 1990;

Being resolved to define the principles to be respected and the obligations which flow from them, in order to ensure, in the member States and such other States as may become Parties to the present instrument, the effective protection of national minorities and of the rights and freedoms of persons belonging to those minorities, within the rule of law, respecting the territorial integrity and national sovereignty of states;

Being determined to implement the principles set out in this framework Convention through national legislation and appropriate governmental policies. Having agreed as follows:

I. Background to the Preamble

The Preamble provides a narrative version of the political sentiments and intentions agreed upon in Vienna in 1993 by the heads of states and governments of the Council of Europe during their first ever summit meeting. The resulting Vienna Declaration of the Summit of Heads of State and Governments (the Vienna Declaration) called for the incorporation of the normative decisions taken during the summit into international law. These held that respect for national minorities is essential for stability and peace in Europe, that a climate of tolerance and dialogue promotes participation, and that members of national minorities should be able to develop their culture through language rights. The issues raised in the Preamble are clearly stated in the Vienna Declaration, and they indicate the thoughts of the various heads of states and governments setting out the terms of reference for the drafting of the FCNM. The general view was that territorial ambitions, aggressive nationalism, intolerance, and totalitarian ideologies are aberrations that have no home in Europe. Hatred and war threaten all regions, not only regions in conflict. The guiding principle was that conflicts destroy rather than construct and consolidate Europe. The European continent must unite to consolidate peace and stability, commit to pluralism and parliamentary democracy, uphold the indivisibility and universality of human rights, promote the rule of law, and a common cultural heritage enriched by diversity. In short, Europe must become a vast area of democratic security. In stating these sentiments, the heads of states and governments expressed their awareness that the protection of national minorities is an essential element of stability and democratic security.

Similar sentiments to those offered in the Vienna Document and the Preamble to the FCNM had been voiced in the opening recitals of the Copenhagen Document. The Copenhagen Document opened with references to pluralistic democracy, the rule of law, human rights and fundamental freedoms, ideals of democracy, political pluralism, and free elections while also calling for further steps to be taken in the direction of implementing these ideals. Most importantly, though, it recognized that these are prerequisites for progress in setting up the lasting order of peace, security, justice and co-operation in Europe. Similarly, the preamble to the 1992 UN Declaration on Minorities highlighted political and social stability of states and linked stability directly to the promotion and protection of the rights of persons belonging to national or ethnic, religious, and linguistic minorities. In contrast, the Preamble to the Council of Europe's 1992 European Charter on Regional and Minority Languages (hereafter Language Charter) speaks of not security and stability but principles of democracy and cultural diversity in relation to the promotion and protection of minority languages.

A. Issues

The Preamble sets out the reasons for drawing up the FCNM and explains certain basic concerns of its drafters. The structure of the Preamble to the FCNM is a classic one. It enumerates and establishes the who, what, how, and why of the treaty, the parties to the treaty, the aim of the treaty, the methods by which the treaty is to be realized, and the reasons why the treaty was drafted. I find it convenient to group the paragraphs of the Preamble in the following analytical categories: technical provisions (paragraphs 1, 12, and 13), programme provisions (paragraphs 2, 5, 6, 7, 8, and 9) and foundational provisions (paragraphs 3, 4, 10, and 11). Before turning to an interpretation of each of these, it might be helpful to introduce the overall background to their drafting history and that of the FCNM in general.

B. History

The history of the Preamble itself pre-dates the drafting of the FCNM. At the request of the Hungarian, Italian, and Yugoslavian authorities, the European Commission for Democracy through Law (the Venice Commission) had drafted a proposal for a convention for the protection of national minorities and submitted a draft to the Committee of Ministers (CM) in 1991.[5] This proposal was not adopted, however. Nevertheless, together with the Vienna Declaration and the Copenhagen Document, this earlier document became the guiding text for the drafters when writing the Preamble to the FCNM.

In 1992 the CM commissioned the Steering Committee for Human Rights (CDDH) to study the possibility of formulating specific legal standards relating to the protection of national minorities in the spirit of the ECHR as well as

[5] European Commission for Democracy through Law (ECDL), Proposal for a European Convention for the Protection of Minorities and Explanatory Report, CDL-MIN (93) 6 and 7, 1993.

work carried out within the UN and the CSCE. In its terms of reference, it asked the CDDH to carry out the work in the light of the draft European Convention for the protection of minorities, drawn up by the Venice Commission, as well as an Austrian proposal for an additional protocol to the ECHR and other proposals for legal solutions.[6] During a meeting in May 1992, the CDDH set up a working group, the Committee of Experts for the Protection of National Minorities (DH-MIN) to which it passed on the terms of reference assigned by the CM.[7] The original terms of reference were replaced by the CM in 1993 with a request to the CDDH to propose specific legal standards relating to the protection of national minorities. In addition to the texts listed in the first terms of reference, the CM this time added the Draft Additional Protocol to the European Convention on Human Rights proposed in the Parliamentary Assembly's 1993 Recommendation 1201.[8] The work on the second terms of reference resulted in a report recommending a number of proposals for possible action. The report was submitted to the CM in September of 1993.[9] In addition to the proposals for action, the report included a discussion of general aspects, of the definition of the term 'national minority', of collective rights and freedoms, and of the choice of instrument.

In November 1993, the CM established an Ad Hoc Committee for the Protection of National Minorities (CAHMIN). Its terms of reference reflected the decisions taken in Vienna. The CAHMIN, made up of experts from the Council of Europe's member states, started work in late January 1994, with the participation of representatives of the CDDH, the Council for Cultural Co-operation (CDCC), the Steering Committee on the Mass Media (CDMM), and the Venice Commission. The High Commissioner on National Minorities of the CSCE and the Commission of the European Communities also took part, as observers.

The CAHMIN began its work on the Preamble at its first meeting in February 1994 and retained it on the agenda until its last meeting in October of the same year. A preliminary draft Preamble was prepared by the Council of Europe's Secretariat and presented to the drafters during the first CAHMIN meeting, but the final product resulted from discussions among experts. The drafting of the Preamble gave rise to some discussion in the CAHMIN. In addition to the substantive issues of a definition of a national minority and

6 Committee of Ministers Decision No. CM/535/210592 of May 1992, [1992], 476th meeting.

7 CDDH 32nd meeting, 18–22 May 1992.

8 Committee of Ministers Decision No. CM/554/090393 of 9 March 1992, [1992], 476th meeting.

9 Steering Committee for Human Rights (CDDH), Final Activity Report of the CDDH for the Attention of the Committee of Ministers, CDDH (93) 22, 1993.

references to 'solidarity' and 'ethnic cleansing', the CAHMIN's discussions on the Preamble focused on linguistic issues and on inserting references to existing international standards relating to national minority protection.

C. Context

The legal context of the Preamble is of course the provisions enshrined in the articles of the FCNM. Thus, as each paragraph of the Preamble previews at least one if not more provisions in the FCNM, I will refer to these as they become relevant in the analysis of each paragraph below.

II. Analysis

Preambles do not stipulate rights or obligations, rather they are narratives that seek to establish legitimacy with regard to the origins and purposes of a piece of legislation, to outline the processes that led to the enactment of the legislation, and to better communicate these rationales to the document's multiple audiences.[10] Preambles may point to established legal standards and obligations, but they do not establish these. However, according to Article 31(2) of the Vienna Convention on the Law of Treaties, a preamble is part of the context of an international treaty and may be drawn upon to establish the meaning of its provisions and to clarify their purport. This means that preambular provisions may fill lacunae in treaties either positively, by supplementing what has been expressly stipulated, or negatively, by limiting the scope of certain provisions.[11] Indeed, the International Court of Justice (ICJ) has affirmed this by including preambles in its interpretation of treaties either to elucidate the meaning of clauses, or to indicate the juridical climate in which the operative clauses should be read.[12] Moreover, the ICJ has affirmed that a preamble may even have binding character.[13] If we take a preamble as integral to treaty interpretation, one might also argue that a preamble can be as binding as any other part of a treaty. Of course, if there were a conflict of understanding between a preamble and an operative clause, the latter would prevail. As noted above, it is

[10] K. Roach, 'The Uses of Audiences of Preambles in Legislation', *McGill Law Journal*, 47 (2001), 129–59.

[11] H. D. Treviranus, 'Preamble', *Encyclopaedia of International Public Law* (1984), 1097–8.

[12] *Asylum Case (Colombia* v. *Peru)*, 1950 ICJ 266, 282; *Case Concerning Rights of Nationals of the United States of America in Morocco (France/United States of America)*, 1952 ICJ 176, 196; G. Fitzmaurice, 'The Law and Procedure of the International Court of Justice, 1951–4', *British Yearbook*, 33 (1957), 203–38 at 227–9.

[13] Above, n. 12.

convenient first to consider the technical provisions of the Preamble, setting out the character of the instrument, its parties, and its legal nature. There will then follow a consideration of the more programmatic elements of the Preamble, offering insights into the aims and intentions of the drafters. Finally, reference will be made to the foundational paragraphs of the Preamble which embed the FCNM in the field of human rights and link it to other instruments.

A. Technical Provisions

The technical provisions are contained in the first paragraph, enumerating the states parties, as well as the twelfth and thirteenth paragraphs, addressing the implementation of the FCNM.

> The member States of the Council of Europe and the other States, signatories to the present framework Convention,

The first paragraph has three main components. First, it indicates that the FCNM may be signed and ratified by member states of the Council of Europe thus drawing the link to the twelfth paragraph which invites member states to become parties to the agreement. Secondly, it invites non-members to sign the instrument. Non-member states wishing to sign and ratify the instrument must be invited by the CM. It is understood that the non-member states which may be invited to sign are those states which participate in the OSCE co-operation.

Thirdly, it specifies that the FCNM will be open for signatures. This links it directly to Article 27 and Article 29 where the conditions for signing the instrument stipulate that signing the FCNM is subject to ratification, acceptance or approval, and deposit with the Secretary-General of the Council of Europe. Ratification refers to the process of approval within each member state's democratic bodies which may vary from state to state. Ratification is only fully accomplished when a signatory state has deposited its ratification document with the Secretary-General of the Council of Europe. According to Article 29, the FCNM would come into force on the first day of the month following the expiration of a period of three months after the date on which twelve member states have deposited their ratification documents. This happened on 1 February 1998. Once in force, the CM may after consultation with the other contracting states invite non-member states having signed the FCNM to accede as well as invite other non-member states which have not yet signed to sign the instrument.

> Being resolved to define the principles to be respected and the obligations which flow from them, in order to ensure, in the member States and such other States as may become Parties to the present instrument, the effective

> protection of national minorities and of the rights and freedoms of persons belonging to those minorities, within the rule of law, respecting the territorial integrity and national sovereignty of states;

The penultimate paragraph presents a clear proposal that stipulates the objectives of the FCNM and reminds the parties to the instrument that the principles laid out in the FCNM must be respected and effectively implemented. Aside from the reference to national minorities as opposed to persons belonging to national minorities addressed above in the section on the Title, five elements of this paragraph merit discussion.

First, the Secretariat of the Council of Europe had initially proposed a reference to the 'creation' of legal obligations. This was however countered by a proposal suggested by the Swiss delegation that the parties should be 'resolved to define the principles'.[14] The Slovak delegation had also tabled a proposal.[15] This pertained mainly to a different linguistic constellation. Eventually, the wording of the Swiss proposal was adopted.

Secondly, the reference to the rights and freedoms of persons belonging to minorities was made for two reasons. One, the drafters wished to make it clear that no collective rights of national minorities were envisaged, but that the rights and freedoms flowing from the FCNM may be exercised individually or in community with others. It thus recognized the possibility of joint exercise of those rights and freedoms, which is distinct from the notion of collective rights. Two, the states recognize that protection of a national minority can be achieved through protection of the liberal ideals of rights and freedoms of individuals belonging to national minorities.

Thirdly, the reference to the rule of law is to ensure that the states implement the provisions through law adhering to the principle that all public acts must be subject to law. Moreover, it allows for the monitoring body of the FCNM to test that the acts which implement the provisions comply with constitutional, human rights and other legislation through effective and credible judicial procedures. This also includes all private acts which must be consistent with the law. Finally, it ensures that all individuals have access to remedies to vindicate their rights.

Fourthly, effective protection of national minorities refers to the fact that the protection of national minorities which forms an integral part of the protection of human rights does not fall within the reserved domain of the states but that the principles of the FCNM must be implemented through state legislation

[14] Ad Hoc Committee for the Protection of National Minorities (CAHMIN), Proposals Concerning the Preliminary Draft Framework Convention for the Protection of National Minorities, CAHMIN (94) 14 Rev., 1994, p. 22.

[15] Above, n. 14, p. 20.

and appropriate policies. Thus, effective protection clearly refers to the legally binding nature of the FCNM. This links the paragraph to Article 19, which outlines the conditions of possibility for any limitations, restrictions, or derogations. When the undertakings included in the FCNM have an equivalent in other international legal instruments, in particular the ECHR, only the limitations, restrictions, or derogations provided for in those instruments are allowed. When the undertakings set forth in the FCNM have no equivalent in other international legal instruments, the only limitations, restrictions, or derogations allowed are those which are relevant and provided for by other legal instruments. The issues of restrictions and derogations will be addressed in detail in the chapter on Article 19 in this commentary. But it should be noted here that the paragraph requests the states 'ensure' that the provision is effectively implemented. This is relatively significant as in earlier versions of the draft the word 'assure' had been used. In the final stages of drafting, the Directorate of Legal Affairs suggested substituting 'ensure' for 'assure'. Given the binding connotation of the former term, the Directorate was able to strengthen the reach of the FCNM by the stroke of a pen.

Finally, the reference to territorial integrity (and national sovereignty) indicates that the drafters of the FCNM wished to assure signatory states that the instrument adhered to the foundational ideals of international law. By referring to the principle of territorial integrity incorporated into international law since the Treaty of Westphalia and laid out in the UN Charter, Article 2, the drafters called upon the old revered principle in international law whereby states agree not to interfere in each other's internal affairs, and when they have disputes to settle these by peaceful means in such manner that international peace and security, and justice, are not endangered. This means that states which are members of the UN must refrain from using the threat of force against the territorial integrity and political independence of any state. The drafters thus assured the signatory states that there would be no risks to state sovereignty involved in signing and ratifying the FCNM. Moreover, by juxtaposing the reference to territorial integrity with that of national sovereignty, the drafters underscored this idea and made it absolutely clear that the state-centrist approach of international law would prevail.[16] State sovereignty,

[16] It should be noted that the use of the adjective 'national' here is problematic. Wishing to qualify the notion of sovereignty as a prerogative of the state, the drafters' reference to national sovereignty rather than state sovereignty results in the well-known ambiguity in international law between the nation and the state. Incidentally, the word 'national' was used several times during CAHMIN discussions in reference to both territory and state sovereignty; a curious circumstance given the known fact that nation does not usually coincide with state.

considered the key constitutional safeguard of the structure of international order, is the focus of Article 21 discussed elsewhere in this volume.

> Being determined to implement the principles set out in this framework Convention through national legislation and appropriate governmental policies

The thirteenth paragraph sets the goal of the FCNM and requires ratifying states to implement the principles of the FCNM in domestic legislation and government policies. Thus, it refers back to the reference to the rule of law in the previous paragraph. However, the purpose of this paragraph is also to indicate that the provisions of the FCNM are not directly applicable. Thus, it is not concerned with the law and practice of the parties in regard to the reception of international treaties in the internal order. In spite of its technical nature, there should be no doubt that the FCNM is a legally binding instrument, requiring its provisions to be translated into municipal law. This means that although the provisions leave the signatory states a measure of discretion in their implementation of the objectives, providing them a margin of appreciation, they are obliged to implement these provisions legally.

B. Programmatic Provisions

The programmatic provisions address the issues which the political leaders of Europe proposed for a contractual relationship with the people of Europe. These were highly ambitious. Thus, the programmatic provisions speak of unity, ideals and principles of common heritage, stability, democratic security and peace, pluralist democracy, identity, tolerance and dialogue, and transfrontier co-operation. The programmatic provisions also refer to issues which were highly sensitive in the early 1990s. The right to existence is perhaps the most profound issue to be established as a basic human right by the international community since the Second World War. Other themes such as identity, tolerance, dialogue, and transfrontier co-operation weighed heavily on the minds of the heads of states when they instructed the Secretariat of the Council of Europe to draw up an instrument for the protection of national minorities.

> Considering that the aim of the Council of Europe is to achieve greater unity between its members for the purpose of safeguarding and realising the ideals and principles which are their common heritage;

The second paragraph has a number of important components. First, it refers to the Council of Europe's mission of aiming toward European unity.

This presents a clear link to Article 1 of the statute of the Council of Europe and the declaration in the Vienna Declaration that the 'end of the division of Europe offers an historic opportunity to consolidate peace and stability'. Similar narrative is also found in the first preambular paragraph of the Venice Commission draft. The aim of unity became increasingly attainable after the events of 1989 and the unification of Germany, but was dampened by the conflicts in the Balkans.

Secondly, it speaks of safeguarding and realizing ideals and principles. To safeguard something in legal terms refers to the protection of something through legal enactment. Thus, the ideals and principles set out in the FCNM must be legally safeguarded. The reference to realizing is of course a call for the signatory states to enter into an active mode and seek to obtain the ideals in question.

Thirdly, it defines the ideals and principles as those which are part of the common heritage of the member states of the Council of Europe. Common heritage is not easily defined for a large region such as that of the Council of Europe. It has recently been up for debate in connection with the drafting of the European Union's Constitution and resulted in some controversy in terms of what constitutes European heritage. In earlier versions of the second paragraph, the draft referred to a common 'European' heritage, but as this phrase was taken out of the final version, the drafters of the FCNM may have had unusual foresight.

> Being resolved to protect within their respective territories the existence of national minorities;

The fifth paragraph refers to three issues in international law, the principle of the responsibility to protect discussed above, the question of respective territories, and the right to existence. With regard to the reference to the signatory states' respective territories, the drafters wished specifically to obligate the states to offer protection within the entire territory belonging to each sovereign state. This draws on Article 29 of the Vienna Convention on the Law of Treaties which stipulates that unless a different intention appears from the treaty or is otherwise established, a treaty is binding upon each party in respect to its entire territory. The conditions on territorial reach applicable for the FCNM are set out in Article 30 which provides for signatory states to specify the territory or territories for whose international relations it is responsible to which the FCNM will apply. This provision could be applicable for signatory states with overseas territories or autonomous national minority regions. Denmark, Finland, Portugal, and Spain did not make use of this provision even though all have autonomous overseas regions for whose international relations they are responsible. Such specification is of course not necessary for the agreement to be applicable to the entire territory of a state if the populations of the autonomous territories are not ethnically different from the majority of the population. However, it may result in ambivalence if a declaration is made as to which national minorities are protected under the agreement and these do not reside in an autonomous region while other national minorities living in autonomous regions are not mentioned.[17] The issue of territorial reach is also significant in Europe where a number of national minorities are kin-state minorities, and the fear of irredentism has not as yet been eradicated. It is of course prescient that the drafters managed to insert this principle just a few years before a member state of the Council of Europe proposed to employ extraterritorial reach to protect its kin minorities.[18]

With regard to the concern of the member states of the Council of Europe regarding the risk to the existence of national minorities, this should be seen in light of the crises in the Balkans. The right to existence in international law is essentially the right to life as enshrined in Article 2 of the ECHR and Article 3 of the UDHR. Discussions in the CAHMIN on ethnic cleansing influenced the drafting of this paragraph, as the ethnic cleansing perpetrated during the Bosnian conflict was arguably one of the darkest moments in recent European history. The fact that the international community could not prevent another European catastrophe emanating from ethnic cleansing after the efforts following the Second World War questioned the effectiveness of existing international relations and international law. Thus, a large majority of the CAHMIN was in favour of condemning ethnic cleansing in the Preamble.

Referring to ethnic cleansing in a human rights instrument is a complex undertaking, and referring to the right to existence does not easily translate into a condemnation of ethnic cleansing. The Concluding Document to the 1992 CSCE Helsinki follow-up meeting included such a condemnation. In the seventeenth paragraph of that document, ethnic cleansing through the use of force and resettlement is explicitly condemned. The CAHMIN settled on a more

[17] This was the model followed by Denmark. By declaring that there is only one national minority in Denmark, the Germans living in Southern Jutland, but not declaring that the territorial reach excludes the overseas autonomous regions of Greenland and the Faeroes, the Danish government made the interpretation of the application of the FCNM ambiguous.

[18] The case of the so-called 'Status Law' adopted by the Hungarian Parliament in June 2001 reaches beyond the territorial state of Hungary. See also R. Hofmann, 'Preferential Treatment of Kin Minorities and Monitoring of the Implementation of the Framework Convention for National Minorities', European Commission for Democracy through Law (ed.), *The Protection of National Minorities by their Kin-state, Science and Technique of Democracy*, 32 (Council of Europe (CoE), Collection Science and Technique for Democracy (ECDL), Strasbourg, 2002), 235–60.

cautious approach. The fifth paragraph of the Preamble was inspired by Article 1(1) of the 1992 UN Declaration on minorities which holds that states shall protect the existence and the national or ethnic, cultural, religious, and linguistic identities of minorities and shall encourage conditions for the promotion of these identities. A number of suggestions were tabled condemning violations of international law and human rights, including: ethnic cleansing; forced expulsion; deportation; and threatening the existence of national minorities. These suggestions drew inspiration from the 14 February 1994 CM declaration on Bosnia and Herzegovina as well as its 11 September 1992 declaration on the conflict in the former Yugoslavia. It was however agreed that given the sensitive nature of this issue any such text should be carefully drafted in order to avoid conveying a wrong message. Time constraints and concerns about the sensitive nature of this issue eventually prevented the CAHMIN from adopting a text on ethnic cleansing. The principle to protect having evolved into sanctioning humanitarian intervention on the grounds of large-scale ethnic cleansing, a reference to ethnic cleansing would certainly have been in place in the Preamble. The lack of a condemnation may have weakened the impact of the Preamble.

> Considering that the upheavals of European history have shown that the protection of national minorities is essential to stability, democratic security and peace in this continent;

The sixth paragraph of the Preamble of the FCNM addresses the call in the Vienna Declaration to consolidate peace and stability. It does so by referencing three fundamental principles in European international relations. First, it puts the protection of national minorities in connection with stability. The function of creating stability is of course entrusted to the OSCE but the concerns of the heads of states and governments of the Council of Europe over territorial ambitions, aggressive nationalism, intolerance, and totalitarian ideologies expressed in the Vienna Document were significant enough for the drafters to wish to include a reference to stability. Secondly, the paragraph refers to democratic security. This ideal is similarly threatened by the totalitarian ambitions listed above, and the drafters wished to draw attention to the fact that the promotion of national minority rights would contribute to guarding against these.

Thirdly, the paragraph refers to the ideal of peace. As bilateral and interstate agreements are seen as important sources of stability and peacemaking efforts, the sixth paragraph of the Preamble previews Article 2 of the FCNM which calls for applying good faith and a spirit of understanding and tolerance in conformity with the principles of good neighbourliness, friendly relations, and co-operation between states. Article 2 has given rise to comments made by both the Parliamentary Assembly (PA) and the Advisory Committee (AC) to the FCNM. In its Recommendation 1492 (2000), the PA recommended that the CM call upon member states to improve and further develop international co-operation in minority rights protection, both bilaterally and multilaterally.[19] In its 14 September 2001 opinion, the AC rejoined that with regard to bilateral relations, Article 2 FCNM outlines the principles of good neighbourliness, friendly relations, and co-operation between states, while Article 18 urges states to conclude bilateral and multilateral agreements and encourage trans-frontier co-operation.[20] Thus, the relevance of Article 2 as well as 18 is important when reading the sixth paragraph of the Preamble.

For reasons not explained in the *travaux préparatoires*, the reference to the upheavals of European history was taken out during drafting, but was reintroduced in the final stages.[21] One might speculate that this was a stylistic concern. Otherwise, there would seem little reason not to retain the reference.

> Considering that a pluralist and genuinely democratic society should not only respect the ethnic, cultural, linguistic and religious identity of each person belonging to a national minority, but also create appropriate conditions enabling them to express, preserve and develop this identity;

In referring to the ability to develop one's identity in the seventh paragraph, the drafters highlighted a number of conditions relevant to creating an environment in which one may be able to develop one's identity. First, it referred to a pluralist and genuinely democratic society. While it is not possible to assess what the drafters had in mind when referring to a genuinely democratic society, a pluralist democratic society is usually seen as a society where divergent values and identities are able to coexist in a peaceful manner. Thus value pluralism may be seen as conducive to an environment where respect and tolerance as well as dialogue help shape the social and political agendas. Value pluralism is of course the guiding principle behind this reference, and while there is no consensus in political theory as to how this may be achieved, there is little argument that pluralism is a democratic ideal necessary to render societal organization ethical.[22] Secondly, the paragraph stipulates that respect

[19] Parliamentary Assembly of the Council of Europe, Recommendation 1492/2000, The Rights of National Minorities, 2001.

[20] CoE, Opinion on Parliamentary Assembly Recommendation 1492/2000, 2001. See also Advisory Committee on the Framework Convention for the Protection of National Minorities, ACFC/MR/INF (2001) 004, 11th Meeting, Meeting Report, 2001.

[21] CAHMIN, 7th Meeting, CAHMIN (94) 32, 1994, p. 19.

[22] Value pluralism was first defended by Isaiah Berlin in his influential essay 'The Pursuit of the Ideal'. See I. Berlin, 'The Pursuit of the Ideal', in *The Proper Study of Mankind* (Farrar, Straus and

for the various identities of persons belonging to a national minority is essential. I will discuss respect below in connection with the call for tolerance inasmuch as respect and tolerance are closely related.

Thirdly, the seventh paragraph calls for creating appropriate conditions for members of national minorities to develop their identity. Thus, it seeks to impose duties on the signatory states to both respect the identities of national minorities and create the best conditions for these identities to flourish. Personal identity is a controversial concept which enjoys divergent views in political philosophy as to how it is formed. While some see personal identity as an acquired set of characteristics,[23] others view it as a question of ascribed characteristics.[24] In either case, personal identity is formed through a process of mirroring oneself against the Other.[25] Moreover, personal identity is seldom static, but rather multifaceted and multi-layered.[26] Individuals usually identify at several levels with several groups or communities, through interaction with others. At times, self-identification results in exclusionary actions, but mostly it provides for a rich fabric of human capital.[27] Identity in international law is further discussed in the chapter on Article 5 below. Here, it suffices to observe that in international law, identity is not a right, rather international law uses language such as preservation, development, and enjoyment of identity.

Finally, the paragraph stipulates that the conditions must be of such character that they enable members of national minorities not only to express their identities but also to preserve and develop these. The paragraph may thus be seen as strongly action-guiding, calling for conditions which allow for the preservation and development of national minority identity. Again, it was the Vienna Declaration, specifically Appendix II, which was the inspiration here. Appendix II stipulated that states should create the conditions necessary for persons belonging to national minorities to develop their culture, while preserving their religion, traditions, and customs. This paragraph is thus at the heart of the

Giroux, New York, 1997). See also J. Raz, *The Morality of Freedom* (Clarendon Press, Oxford, 1988) and W. A. Galston, *Liberal Pluralism: The Implication of Value Pluralism for Political Theory and Practice* (Cambridge University Press, Cambridge, 2002).

[23] S. Macedo, *Liberal Virtues: Citizenship, Virtue, and Community in Liberal Constitutionalism* (Clarendon Press, Oxford, 1990).

[24] C. Taylor, *Sources of the Self: The Making of the Modern Identity* (Harvard University Press, Cambridge, Mass., 1989).

[25] W. E. Connolly, 'Taylor, Foucault and Otherness', *Political Theory*, 13/3 (1985), 365–76.

[26] J. Tully, *Strange Multiplicity: Constitutionalism in an Age of Diversity* (Cambridge University Press, Cambridge, 1995).

[27] W. E. Connolly, *Identity/Difference: Democratic Negotiations of Political Paradox*, expanded edn. (University of Minnesota Press, Minneapolis, 2002).

compassion that found its way into the FCNM and signifies the vital importance of personal identity when addressing the rights of national minorities.

The seventh paragraph should be read in the context of Article 5 FCNM, which in addition to calling for the promotion of conditions necessary to preserve identity, spells out that states should refrain from using assimilation policies and practices. Given that this paragraph calls for states to create conditions under which members of national minorities may express and develop their identities, it actually employs stronger language than Article 5 proper. The seventh paragraph may also be read in the context of Article 15 which requires states to create the conditions necessary for the effective participation of members of national minorities in cultural, social, and economic life and in public affairs inasmuch as an important element in expressing and developing one's identity is participation. In an early version of the Preamble, the seventh paragraph referred to the cultural identity of all persons, but this was later replaced by the list of specific identities of members of national minorities.[28]

> Considering that the creation of a climate of tolerance and dialogue is necessary to enable cultural diversity to be a source and a factor, not of division, but of enrichment for each society;

The language of the eighth paragraph is empathetic and sets the stage for the provision to promote tolerance and prevent intolerance laid out in Article 6. It thus concerns the perpetuation of spheres of influence, intolerance, and totalitarian ideologies described in the Vienna Declaration. This paragraph addresses the aspect of tolerance as a tool by which we may enhance democracy by drawing on a number of issues. First, the drafters referred to cultural diversity as an enrichment of society, thus indicating that they wished to purvey a more progressive and positive view of diversity than heretofore seen in European international relations. Secondly, they called for states to create conditions under which tolerance and dialogue can be fostered. This again is a strong attempt to impose positive obligations on states; certainly stronger than the language employed in Article 6, which calls for encouraging a spirit of tolerance. Moreover, the eighth paragraph refers to a climate of tolerance and dialogue, meaning a comfortable, positive environment. While perhaps insignificant, the choice of climate rather than environment could imply an inclusive approach. Thirdly, the drafters referred to cultural diversity as a source of enrichment which can thrive in a climate of tolerance and dialogue. Here it is important to note that it refers to cultural diversity not national

[28] See also the discussion on the eighth paragraph.

diversity, even though the instrument relates to the protection of national minorities. This most likely should be pinned down to the fact that the drafters worked on the assumption that national identity is a cultural attribute ascribing identity rather than a national attribute meaning a political and social notion. The difficulty of defining cultural apart from national is of course behind this general usage.

Fourthly, the reference to tolerance is a concept in the minority rights debate that most agree is important, but of which few understand the meaning. Although it is discussed in greater depth in the chapter on Article 6 in this volume, it might be useful to note that tolerance and toleration are used interchangeably. It is however possible to distinguish between the two notions. Toleration refers to a mental and rational notion, whereas tolerance refers to a physical, and often non-rational notion.[29] Toleration comes in different shades, but two meanings have emerged as general knowledge. One interpretation refers to a narrow scope toleration, an act of moral disapproval, or rather a 'non-act' in terms of leaving someone alone.[30] The second, more positive notion refers to a form of acceptance of the other's right to existence that builds on a sentiment of respect.[31] While narrow-scope toleration makes social interaction difficult, positive toleration can promote the virtue of showing respect and perhaps even promote human interaction. Respect is important to one's self-esteem. It is not entirely clear, however, that the positive notion would help individuals foster self-esteem and self-respect inasmuch as it does not require human interaction. Neither definition of toleration extends far enough to promote a climate of tolerance and dialogue as well as mutual respect. This is why the drafters of the FCNM called for both tolerance *and* dialogue in the Preamble. Choosing the word dialogue rather than intercultural dialogue is perhaps interesting since the drafters had wished to encourage cultural diversity in this paragraph. Moreover, dialogue can be exclusionary as it refers in its strict sense to only two interlocutors. Nevertheless, in Article 6, the drafters refer to intercultural dialogue. The problem with dialogue is of course that it is often used as a generic term for multilogue.[32]

[29] I am indebted to my colleague Sally Holt of the HCNM for making me clarify this argument.

[30] S. Mendus, *Toleration and the Limits of Liberalism* (Macmillan, Basingstoke, 1989), 5.

[31] K. O. Apel, 'Plurality of the Good? The Problem of Affirmative Tolerance in a Multicultural Society from an Ethical Point of View', *Ratio Juris*, 10/2 (1997), 199–212; S. Leader, 'Three Faces of Toleration in a Democracy', *Journal of Political Philosophy*, 4/1 (1996), 45–67 as well as 'Toleration without Liberal Foundations', *Ratio Juris*, 10/2 (1997), 139–64; M. Walzer, *On Toleration* (Yale University Press, New Haven, 1997). See also S. Mendus (ed.), *The Politics of Toleration* (Edinburgh University Press, Edinburgh, 1999).

[32] See J. Tully, *Strange Multiplicity: Constitutionalism in the Age of Diversity* (Cambridge University Press, Cambridge, 1995).

Aside from changes to clarify the language, the drafting of the eighth paragraph gave rise to only one substantive suggestion. The Turkish delegation proposed adding a reference to solidarity.[33] This proposal did not make it into the final document, however. Solidarity is a notion which usually does not form part of the vocabulary of international law. It is a social and political concept with strong republican overtones, requiring some action on the part of the agent,[34] thus making it difficult to provision in terms of legal obligations.

> Considering that the realisation of a tolerant and prosperous Europe does not depend solely on co-operation between States but also requires transfrontier co-operation between local and regional authorities without prejudice to the constitution and territorial integrity of each State;

The ninth and last paragraph in the section on programmatic provisions contributes to the Preamble as well as the FCNM in an innovative way in international law. This paragraph clearly extends beyond the normal international treaty parameters of setting standards for states and interstate co-operation. It takes into consideration the realization that national minorities in Europe often span across a number of sovereign territories and state borders, as a result of border changes following major bellicose conflicts. Thus, it acknowledges that even in cases where national minorities enjoy a degree of self-administration, either through decentralization or devolution or, in some cases, through autonomy arrangements, transfrontier co-operation may be seen as a means to consolidate peace and stability. This may seem obvious, given that European borders are far less closed than before the process of European integration began. Local and regional authorities are now able to profit from their natural proximity, to engage in cross-border economic and cultural, if not social and political exchanges. However, on a second reading, the great intentions of the drafters may be re-evaluated.

The components of interest in this paragraph are thus first and foremost, co-operation between states versus transfrontier co-operation between local and regional authorities and the issue of prejudice. In addition, a word on a tolerant and prosperous Europe may also be interesting to observers of European relations.

First, by arguing that co-operation betweens states alone does not secure a tolerant and prosperous Europe the drafters show that they are aware that national minorities have been created as a result of the redrawing of Europe's borders after major conflicts and the issue can therefore not be limited to

[33] Above, n. 14, p. 6.

[34] J. Habermas, *The Inclusion of the Other: Studies in Political Theory*, ed. C. Cronin and P. de Greiff (MIT Press, Cambridge, Mass., 1998).

promoting tolerance within state boundaries. Secondly, by suggesting that peace and stability in Europe is dependent on transfrontier co-operation the drafters seem to have taken quite a liberal step. This is because transfrontier co-operation continues to raise fears of secession, and questions of irredentism and separation arise especially on matters regarding kin-state minorities. This furthermore raises questions of nationalism. Do kin-state minorities engage in cross-border relations to preserve their national identity, or do they have a different agenda in mind? If yes, does this question the traditional definition of transnationalism as a view of identity that transcends national boundaries? Certainly, it may have different connotations for kin-state minorities than for academic and political players in international relations.[35] However, fully aware of these diverse interpretations, the drafters inserted a number of qualifiers. First of all, they made sure that the co-operation across borders is restricted to local and regional authorities. This may not seem significant because except for a few regions in Europe where national minorities are regionally defined, or constitute a sub-state nation, national minorities seldom hold power over local and regional authorities. Thus, the transfrontier co-operation to which the drafters refer is essentially co-operation between states. This is why the drafters made sure that there was also a reference prohibiting any prejudice in this co-operation with regard to the constitution and territorial integrity of states.

Nevertheless, the reference to transfrontier co-operation is interesting if held together with the adjective 'prosperous' in the early part of the paragraph. This is because on the neo-liberal view of political economy it has become received knowledge that Europe would not only prosper but also become more tolerant if more people had a better living standard and greater economic opportunities. Economic interaction across borders would promote both of these objectives. While it is questionable whether economic co-operation would promote social and cultural toleration in addition to economic prosperity, the reference to transfrontier co-operation is innovative not so much due to its feeble intent of allowing cross-border contacts to national minorities who have control over local and regional authorities but because it refers to a non-legal ideal of economic neo-liberalism as a tool to create tolerance.

Hence, the ninth paragraph must be read in conjunction with Article 17 FCNM, which while making the necessary provisions for encouraging transfrontier co-operation, imposes conditions on states not to interfere with the right to free and peaceful contacts across frontiers. Given that Article 17 is emphatically worded, and the CAHMIN sought to make a reference to the

[35] The case of the Hungarian 'Status Law' might indicate an alternative interpretation of transnationalism. See above, n. 18.

development of international co-operation early in the drafting process and maintained it throughout, one must accord the drafters the benefit of the doubt that the ninth paragraph is a preambular innovation. Thus, neither the opening recitals of the Copenhagen Document, nor the Preamble to the UN Declaration on Minorities, makes any reference to transfrontier co-operation.

C. Foundational Provisions

The foundational provisions contain the quintessence of all considerations in respect to the FCNM in terms of contextual and referential recitals stating the motives and standards on the basis of which the instrument was concluded. References point to relevant legal standards in order to prevent conflict between treaties. Thus, the foundational provisions refer to the high international standards by which the political leaders wished to abide.

> Considering that one of the methods by which that aim is to be pursued is the maintenance and further realisation of human rights and fundamental freedoms;

The third paragraph reminds its readers that human rights ideals are the objectives by which the aim of unity may be attained. This paragraph draws on the Statute of the Council of Europe, Article 1(*b*), as well as the third preambular paragraph to the ECHR. The proposed text for the paragraph was not changed during the drafting; the original version was adopted in the final text. Nevertheless, two issues merit attention here. First, the reference to human rights standards establishes a link to the provision in Article 1 FCNM that the protection of national minorities and of the rights and freedoms of persons belonging to those minorities form an integral part of the international protection of human rights and international co-operation. Clearly, the drafters wished to combine the aim of peaceful and stable unity with the high standards of the indivisibility and universality of human rights establishing these as the cornerstones of common heritage and as the foundational principles of the Preamble. Secondly, the paragraph calls for not only maintenance of these ideals but also further realization of them. This may be an indication that the drafters wished to draw attention to the fact that they would like to see action in terms of implementation of legal standards.

> Wishing to follow-up the Declaration of the Heads of State and Government of the member States of the Council of Europe adopted in Vienna on 9 October 1993;

The fourth paragraph refers specifically to the international summit meeting of heads of state and governments in Vienna in October 1993 and the

Vienna Declaration. A reference to the 1993 Vienna meeting was deemed essential inasmuch as the decisive step to draw up an instrument on national minority protection was taken during this meeting. The heads of states and governments had agreed that the protection of and respect for national minorities, established as a result of upheavals in European history, should be seen as a contribution to peace and stability. More importantly, they decided to enter into legal commitments regarding the protection of national minorities to this end. Hence, the decisions made during the meeting picked up the momentum of the Copenhagen Document and called for action regarding the protection of national minorities with minimum delay.

The wording of the fourth paragraph was the focus of some discussions in the CAHMIN. The Hungarian delegation[36] suggested a shorter version acknowledging the Vienna Declaration, whereas the Swiss delegation[37] was in favour of the wording 'wishing to implement' the Vienna Declaration. The original phrasing was retained, however, and except for a few changes of linguistic character, the final text was more or less identical with the preliminary text proposed by the Secretariat.

> Having regard to the Convention for the Protection of Human Rights and Fundamental Freedoms and the Protocols thereto;

The tenth paragraph refers to the ECHR and its protocols. While the ECHR does not contain national minority rights as such, except for the prohibition of discrimination on the grounds of membership of a national minority included in Article 14, the fundamental rights enshrined in the ECHR are of course rights which pertain to members of national minorities as well. Thus, the fundamental rights and freedoms of the right to liberty and security, to private and family life, to freedom of expression, to freedom of assembly and association and non-discrimination, just to mention a few, are certainly rights and freedoms from which members of national minorities should benefit. The inclusion of a reference to the protocols is noteworthy as the Council of Europe has subsequently adopted Protocol 12 to the ECHR which seeks to expand the scope of Article 14 of the ECHR and the principle of equality.[38] On its orthodox interpretation the principle of equality does not necessarily provide the conditions of possibility to equality, meaning that equal rights for all may

[36] Ad Hoc Committee for the Protection of National Minorities (CAHMIN), Proposals Concerning the Preliminary Draft Framework Convention for the Protection of National Minorities, CAHMIN (94) 14 Rev., 1994, p. 6.

[37] Above, n. 36, p. 20.

[38] See G. Pentassuglia, *Minorities in International Law* (Council of Europe, ECMI, Strasbourg, 2002), 126–7, P. Thornberry and M. A. Martin Estebanez, *Minority Rights in Europe* (Council of Europe, Strasbourg, 2004), 50–1.

in fact disadvantage some groups who for various reasons may need special rights and entitlements to compete equally in the market place. Protocol 12 therefore stipulates that difference in treatment does not amount to discrimination when it has an objective and reasonable justification. Thus, once Protocol 12 comes into effect, the AC will also be able to monitor the accommodation of national minorities in these terms.

As the ECHR is an essential pillar in the consolidation of peace and stability in Europe, the reference to the instrument here is of course not surprising. The paragraph should be read in the context of Article 23 FCNM, which grants the ECHR a higher position in the hierarchy of European international treaties. The Hungarian delegation to the CAHMIN tabled a different, wordier version of the tenth paragraph, which included reference to the right to use one's own language in private and in public life as an inalienable right in accordance with the principles of the ICCPR.[39] While this proposal was not adopted for this paragraph, it was however followed to some extent in the eleventh paragraph discussed below. The tenth paragraph only underwent a few minor linguistic changes, as well as the elimination of the reference to the ECHR as a 'European' Convention and the deletion of a reference to the Council of Europe.[40] While the deletion of 'European' seems curious indeed, the reference to the Council of Europe may be seen as purely stylistic.

> Having regard to the commitments concerning the protection of national minorities in United Nations conventions and declarations and in the documents of the Conference on Security and Co-operation in Europe, particularly the Copenhagen Document of 29 June 1990;

The eleventh paragraph refers to the ideals on national minority protection adhered to in the UN and the CSCE systems, including the Copenhagen Document. The important aspect here is that the drafters refer to these ideals as commitments. Given that the instruments adopted by the UN and the CSCE (as well as the OSCE) are not legally binding, the drafters perhaps wished to point out that these ideals are nonetheless commitments made by the parties to the instruments. They were thus appealing to the moral conscience of the governments of the signatory states. Modelled on the Vienna Declaration, Appendix II, the reference to the UN system was inserted following a Swiss government proposal.[41] Therefore, the paragraph should be read in conjunction

[39] Above, n. 36, p. 6.

[40] CAHMIN, Summary of the Main Points Raised by the Opinion of the Directorate of Legal Affairs on the Draft Framework Convention, CAHMIN (94) 25, 1994, p. 2. This de-Europeanization is again interesting in light of the otherwise strong efforts to achieve unity in Europe as per the statutes of the Council of Europe.

[41] Above, n. 36, p. 20.

with Article 22 which stipulates that nothing in the FCNM can be construed to limit or derogate from any of the human rights and freedoms which may be ensured under international agreements signed by the ratifying governments.

III. Conclusions and Outlook

Although the final version of the Preamble to the FCNM did not reflect some of the CAHMIN's discussion on controversial issues, it placed the FCNM prominently as a historical and normative instrument in international law and carved a rather innovative position for itself. Its narrative reflects the sentiments characterizing European national minority politics of the early 1990s, and it proposes a contract on national minority accommodation to the member states of the Council of Europe as well as to other states. In a compassionate narrative it conveys the concerns of European policy makers with regard to national minority issues and sets the stage for the propositions, albeit of a programmatic character, made to member states' governments. Although the Preamble includes neither a definition of a minority, nor reference to solidarity or ethnic cleansing, it leaves no doubt that state–minority relations in Europe are a tender issue, deserving much government attention to secure unity, stability, and peace in Europe. Moreover, being cast at times in even more positive language than the operative articles, the Preamble may be seen as supporting a positive reading of the FCNM if included for interpretative purposes. Certainly, the Preamble uses more proactive language than the operative part of the FCNM. While the Preamble maintains the conventional state-centrist approach of international law in stressing territorial integrity, it calls for states to assume positive obligations to protect national minorities and for toleration as a tool to foster social unity. Perhaps, the Preamble to the FCNM is both a piece of art and a tool for action.[42] Furthermore, the fact that the drafters were keenly aware of the kin-state dilemma, while also seeing the economic value of transfrontier co-operation could elevate the Preamble to a prominent position as an innovative narrative to which policy makers can turn, if not for normative standards, perhaps for ethical guidance.

[42] See the debate between Gudmundur Alfredsson and Frank Steketee. G. Alfredsson, 'A Frame for an Incomplete Painting: Comparison of the Framework Convention for the Protection of National Minorities with International Standards and Monitoring Procedures', *International Journal of Minority and Group Rights* (2000), 291–304 and F. Steketee, 'The Framework Convention: A Piece of Art or a Tool for Action?', *International Journal of Minority and Group Rights*, 8 (2001), 1–15.

SECTION I

ARTICLE 1

Hans-Joachim Heintze

The protection of national minorities and of the rights and freedoms of persons belonging to those minorities forms an integral part of the international protection of human rights, and as such falls within the scope of international co-operation.

I. Background

A. Issues

The underlying tension in the concept of minority protection lies in the classical view that states may oppose entitlements that might call into question their sovereignty or territorial integrity. Minority rights, as part of human rights, challenge this assumption. On the one hand, there is a need to reassure governments that the granting of rights to minorities does not undermine these principles. On the other hand, it is equally necessary to ensure that persons belonging to minorities are able to maintain their identity and enjoy their rights as a member of a minority group. This balancing act is performed through the doctrine of minority rights as part of human rights.

I am indebted to Noëlle Quénivet for her invaluable advice and assistance in writing this piece.

Accordingly, Article 1 unambiguously stresses that the protection of national minorities, and of persons belonging to national minorities, forms an integral part of the protection of human rights. This finding, in itself, represents a major step forward in the development of minority rights. As was noted in the introductory section to this book, the idea of protecting minorities by international instruments is as old as religious tolerance, guaranteed, for instance, in the Agreement of Augsburg (1555) and the Peace Treaties of Westphalia (1648). Yet, the real breakthrough in the protection of minorities via international conventions came after the First World War, when the Treaty of Versailles imposed the creation of new states and considerably changed the geography of Europe. There is no doubt that these border shifts had dramatic effects on the populations of some countries. For example, the Hungarians were split among Slovakia, Romania, Ukraine, and Serbia. Inevitably, this division of peoples led to instabilities in the post-war order. The victorious powers, quickly acknowledging the existence of such instabilities, deemed it necessary to offer these newly created minorities adequate protection from acts of revenge carried out by the newly created majorities. The need to prevent the emergence of secessionist demands led the victors to establish a number of protection mechanisms for minority groups under the umbrella of the League of Nations. This international system failed due to the lack of universal acceptance of its rules, a fact particularly visible concerning the protection of minorities since only the states bound by the post-First World War peace treaties were obliged to respect minority regulations, while the great powers of that time were not bound by these norms. The Polish proposal for a global convention on the protection of minorities in 1934 was rejected by France, the United Kingdom, Italy, and Belgium, for example. Moreover, the whole system lost credibility after Nazi Germany misused the idea of minority protection for its expansion.

Since the topic of minority protection had been systematically exploited for hostile purposes, the post-Second World War community of states was very reluctant to grant rights to minorities through their express inclusion in the emerging catalogue of human rights. Instead, while adopting the UN Charter, the states focused on the protection of individual human rights, arguing that this would also protect persons belonging to minorities. The same approach was pursued during the codification of the International Covenant on Civil and Political Rights (ICCPR), adopted in 1966 by the UN General Assembly. It must be stressed that Article 27 ICCPR contains the only universal legally binding norm on minority protection, introducing minority protection firmly into the body of human rights.

Since the end of the Cold War, Europe has witnessed unexpected and bloody explosions of nationalism in its former Communist countries. Several parts of eastern and south-eastern Europe have been devastated by ethnic and religious conflicts, during which hundreds of thousands of persons belonging to minorities were killed, severely injured, or became victims of 'ethnic cleansing'. The European population, shocked by these events, demanded that international organizations develop new mechanisms of minority protection and improve already existing ones.

The first international body to react to this appeal was the Conference for Security and Co-operation in Europe (CSCE), later renamed the Organization for Security and Co-operation in Europe (OSCE). By 1990, all former socialist countries had become CSCE members, having accepted the Copenhagen Document, the first politically binding document to contain a detailed set of commitments towards minorities. It must be added that this document clearly combines minority protection with obligations concerning the rule of law and democratic constitutions. Hence, the CSCE/OSCE broke new ground in the field of minority rights. Recognizing this, other European actors in the field, including the Commission for Democracy through Law (ECDL), proposed that the CSCE promulgate a convention on this topic at the beginning of the 1990s.[1]

B. History

The first attempts to draft a convention were introduced by the ECDL in 1990. Article 1 of that draft reads: 'The States Party to this Convention acknowledge that the international protection of the rights of minorities is a fundamental element of the international protection of human rights, and as such it falls within the scope of inter-State co-operation.' Although the wording of this draft Article 1 is very similar to the final version of the FCNM, there is a fundamental difference. Article 1 was initially supposed to be read in conjunction with Article 4 of the draft that defined the concept of minority.[2]

During discussions, the question arose whether the article should specify that the protection of minorities did not fall within the *domaine réservé* of states

[1] G. Gilbert, 'Minority Rights under the Council of Europe', in P. Cumper and S. Wheatley (eds.), *Minority Rights in a "New" Europe* (Nijhoff, The Hague, 1999), 62.

[2] European Commission for Democracy through Law (ECDL), Preliminary Draft Convention on the Protection of Minorities DAJ.SC.DEMOCRACYCONV.MIN, 1990, Art. 4: 'For the purposes of this Convention, "minority" shall mean a group which is smaller in number than the rest of the population of a State, is not in a dominating position, and whose members have ethnical, religious or linguistic features different from those of the rest of the population, feel solidarity with each other, are guided by the will to safeguard their culture, traditions, religion or languages and aim at equality in facts and in law with the majority.'

(Article 2(7), of the United Nations Charter). Some participants expressed the view that this principle did not reflect the present state of positive law: while this might be so for the protection of the rights of individuals belonging to the minority in the sense of individual rights, it was not so regarding the rights of minorities in the sense of collective entitlements. Other participants considered that the draft legal instrument should go beyond mere consolidation of existing law and be aimed at progressive development. The majority preferred to define the term 'minority'. According to the draft definition, only persons possessing the nationality of the state in whose territory they were residing were covered.

That draft of the ECDL greatly influenced the Parliamentary Assembly, because it opted for the same approach as in its Recommendation 1201, which was meant to be adopted as a Protocol to the European Convention.[3] In fact, the Preamble of the protocol refers to the general obligation to protect the rights of national minorities and Article 1 of the same protocol provides a rather ambiguous definition of the concept of minority in as much as 'the expression national minority' refers to a group of persons in a state who: (*a*) reside on the territory of that state and are citizens thereof; (*b*) maintain long-standing, firm, and lasting ties with that state; (*c*) display distinctive ethnic, cultural, religious, or linguistic characteristics; (*d*) are sufficiently representative, although smaller in number than the rest of the population of that state or of a region of that state; and (*e*) are motivated by a concern to preserve together that which constitutes their common identity, including their culture, their traditions, their religion, or their language. However, Recommendation 1201 with the proposed protocol was rejected in 1993 at the Vienna Summit of the Council of Europe (CoE). It appeared that the codification of minority rights in the European context still faced tremendous resistance, mostly because the concept and nature of minority protection remained vague. Still, at the Vienna Summit Meeting of the CoE on 7 October 1993, the delegates decided to work out a new instrument on the protection of national minorities, resulting in the Framework Convention for the Protection of National Minorities (FCNM) that was opened for signature in 1995.

On 4 November 1993 the Committee of Ministers established an Ad Hoc Committee for the Protection of National Minorities (CAHMIN), composed of experts in the field of minority rights. The terms of reference of CAHMIN reflected the Vienna Decisions of the Summit of the CoE states, which meant

[3] Council Recommendation 1201/93/EC of 1 February 1993 on an Additional Protocol on the Rights of National Minorities to the European Convention on Human Rights, (1993), Parliamentary Assembly of the Council of Europe, 22nd Sitting, Doc. 6742, Art. 5.

that the instrument under consideration was not connected to the European human rights protection mechanisms. CAHMIN started its work in late January 1994. The first product, the preliminary draft opening provisions, contained certain principles of the Framework Convention. The working paper prepared by the Secretariat[4] was based on the ECDL Draft. Article 1 reads: 'The international protection of the rights of national minorities, as well as the rights of persons belonging to those minorities, as guaranteed by the present Convention, is a fundamental component of the international protection of Human Rights, and as such falls within the scope of international co-operation.' This approach of CAHMIN differs from the traditional one, because it refers to the 'rights of the minority', that is to say, the collective rights. All previous documents deal with the protection of the rights of individuals belonging to a minority group. The difference is striking when compared with the revised Federal Union of European Nationalities (FUEN) Draft for an Additional Protocol to the ECHR of 1994, which advocates individual rights only.[5]

It is surprising that there was no further discussion on the question of collective rights for minorities. Instead CAHMIN debates focused on the relationship between minority rights and human rights. The Italian expert argued that confirming that 'the protection of national minorities . . . forms an integral part of the international protection of human rights' did not correctly reflect the Vienna Declaration, which envisioned a document devoted to the protection of minorities, independent and distinct from the international instruments on the legal protection of human rights. However, the intervention of the Italian expert was unsuccessful and finally the CAHMIN stressed that the 'main purpose of Article 1' was to specify that the protection of national minorities is integral to the protection of human rights. The importance of this formulation lies in the fact that minority protection does not fall within the *domaine réservé* of states. Concerning the collective aspect of this article, which contradicts the individualistic human rights approach, CAHMIN underlined without providing any explanation, that the wording made it clear that no collective rights of national minorities were envisaged. This approach cannot be considered satisfactory from the point of legal theory, however, it is common, as has been shown by other CoE documents. The same approach of mixing collective and individual rights has also been taken by the Parliamentary Assembly of the CoE in its Recommendation 1492 (2000), stressing 'the importance of effectively

[4] Ad Hoc Committee for the Protection of the National Minorities (CAHMIN), 1st Meeting, CAHMIN/GR (94) misc. 1, Meeting Report, 1994.

[5] FUEN, Fundamental Rights of Persons belonging to Ethnic Groups in Europe, Draft for an Additional Protocol to the ECHR (Revised FUEN Draft), 1994.

protecting the rights of minorities in Europe. It considers that adequate protection for *persons belonging to national minorities and their communities* is an integral part of the protection of human rights'.[6]

C. Context

It must be noted that there is an overlap between Article 1 and Article 3, and also a close connection between Article 1 and Section III of the FCNM, which deals with general aspects of the relationship between human rights protection and other obligations under international law. In the analysis that follows, there is first a brief introduction to the question of the definition of minorities—a more detailed presentation on this issue can be found under Article 3(1). The question of collective versus individual rights is then dealt with. Thirdly, the key pronouncements of this Article are addressed, establishing minority rights as an integral part of human rights. Finally, the concept of 'protection' of minorities is examined.

II. Analysis

A. Definition of 'National Minorities'

The FCNM contains no definition of the notion of 'national minority', because it was impossible to agree upon one. Former definition attempts, such as Recommendation 1201, have been rejected by states parties, leading to the 1993 ECDL conclusion[7] that the definition of minorities '[was] a delicate problem and one solution might be not to include a specific definition in the text but to rely on the usual meaning of the word'. The CAHMIN followed that recommendation; paragraph 12 of the explanatory report to the FCNM called for 'a pragmatic approach'. The term 'national minorities' consists of two explanatory elements: the noun 'minorities' and the adjective 'national'. The circumstances of groups considered 'minorities' differ greatly from one state to another and it is, therefore, difficult to create a definition that encompasses all categories of minorities. The most controversial points are the minimum size of the minority group and the need for a subjective feeling of solidarity. The situation becomes even more complicated as some states, like France and Turkey, have denied the existence of minorities in the name of national unity. Such

[6] Emphasis added.

[7] ECDL, Explanatory Report to the Proposal for a European Convention for the Protection of National Minorities, CDL-MIN (93) 7, 1993.

states fear that the existence of a commonly agreed definition of a minority supports the regional claims and secessionist movements against which they constantly have to fight.[8] It is symptomatic that both countries made reservations to Article 27 ICCPR to the effect that this article was not applicable. The fear of secessionist movements largely explains the reluctance of many states to reach a consensus on the general definition of the term 'minority'.

Due to the lack of a general definition, international instruments have confined their scope of applicability to certain types of minorities, for example, ethnic, linguistic or religious minorities. An excellent illustration of this approach is provided by Article 27 ICCPR, which enumerates several categories of minorities. These categories can be easily identified, at least in those countries that do not deny the existence of minorities, or that recognize minority groups on their territory. The UN Declaration on the Rights of Persons Belonging to National or Ethnic, Religious, and Linguistic Minorities[9] adds 'national minorities' to the beneficiaries (ethnic, religious, or linguistic minorities) mentioned in Article 27 ICCPR. According to the Commentary of the Working Group on Minorities, this does not mean that the overall scope of application is extended beyond the groups already listed in Article 27. The Commentary states 'there is hardly any national minority, however defined, that is not also an ethnic or linguistic minority'.[10] Therefore an overlap is unavoidable. The Working Group on Minorities clearly rejects the idea that because minorities can be categorized into four groups, their rights have a somewhat different content and strength.

The FCNM confines its realm of applicability to 'national' minorities. This apparently narrows the class of beneficiaries of the rights granted in comparison with the ICCPR. However, the expression 'national minority' is less widely used because it is rather ambiguous in the European context. On the one hand, in France it refers to citizenship, where all citizens of the state belong to the French nation. This understanding is consistent with the 1997 European Convention on Nationality, which defines 'nationality' as 'the legal bond between a person and a State and does not indicate the person's ethnic origin'.[11] On the other hand, the German concept of a national minority follows the idea of a linguistic and cultural community, and is not necessarily related to

[8] F. Benoit-Rohmer, *The Minority Question in Europe, Texts and Commentary* (Council of Europe, Strasbourg, 1996), 12.

[9] UN Declaration on the Rights of Persons Belonging to National or Ethnic, Religious, and Linguistic Minorities, UNGA Res. A/47/135, 1992.

[10] A. Eide, Final Text of the Commentary to the Declaration on the Rights of Persons Belonging to National or Ethnic, Religious, and Linguistic Minorities, UN Doc. E/CN.4/Sub.2/AC.5/2001/2, 1998.

[11] Council of Europe (CoE), European Convention on Nationality, ETS 166, 1997, Art. 1.

citizenship. According to this approach, a national minority must be connected to a larger nation already represented by a state, forming a so-called kin state. This second conceptual framework forms the basis of the mandate of the OSCE High Commissioner on National Minorities (HCNM). Indeed, the HCNM only has a mandate to investigate minority rights issues having an interstate dimension. The OSCE has affirmed that kin states have a legitimate interest in the situation of minorities sharing the same ethnic origin outside their borders.[12] This means that the HCNM is precluded from dealing with minorities living within a single state. Despite this formal distinction, the HCNM has declared on several occasions: 'I know a minority when I see one.' This highlights two distinctions: (1) a minority is a group with linguistic, ethnic, or cultural characteristics distinct from the majority; and (2) it is a group which not only seeks to maintain its identity, but also tries to give stronger expression to that identity.[13] The HCNM's observation reflects the overlap between the protection of ethnic, cultural, linguistic, and religious minorities on the one hand, and national minorities on the other. The same also holds true for the FCNM. In practice, international minority rights aim to protect all those 'who would be in a position of disadvantage and vulnerability vis-à-vis the exercise of democratic power which, in each specific situation, is a function of the constitutional order'.[14] Therefore, the terms used by states, such as 'national minorities', 'nationalities', or 'communities', are without adverse effect, as the right to protection for all groups should be guaranteed regardless of definition. Minority rights law applies to any person belonging to a national, ethnic, linguistic, or religious group in a non-dominant position in the state in which they live.

Despite the absence of a clear general definition of a national minority, it is possible to find some elements of a definition in other provisions of the FCNM. The Preamble states that a pluralist and genuinely democratic society should not only respect the ethnic, cultural, linguistic, and religious identity of each person belonging to a national minority, but it should also create appropriate conditions enabling them to express, preserve, and develop this identity. Moreover, Article 6 FCNM refers to ethnic, cultural, linguistic, and religious identities. It is clear that these are the central criteria that need to be taken into

[12] L. A. Thio, 'Developing a "Peace and Security" Approach towards Minorities' Problems', *International and Comparative Law Quarterly*, 52/1 (2003), 117.

[13] M. van der Stoel, *Peace and Stability through Human and Minority Rights*, (Nomos Verlagsgesellschaft, Baden-Baden, 1999), 45.

[14] Office of the OSCE High Commissioner on National Minorities, Note on the Possible Use of Terminology in the Process of Incorporating into Domestic Law International Standards for the Protection of Minorities, 2003, p. 3.

account to define a minority. Consequently, one can safely conclude 'that we are not too far away from the definition' contained in Recommendation 1201.[15] Alfredsson argues that the necessary elements of the definition are known and largely accepted;[16] many states parties explicitly share this view.[17] Though this definition is not part of the FCNM, it has been raised to the status of a legal obligation by its inclusion in friendship and good neighbourliness treaties drawn up between various member states of the CoE.[18] These treaty obligations might eventually acquire the status of regional customary law,[19] a perspective shared by the Advisory Committee.[20] How the definition issue has been dealt with in practice will be further discussed in the commentary to Article 3.

B. Collective versus Individual Rights

Paragraph 31 of the FCNM Explanatory Report highlights that Article 1 refers to the protection of national minorities and of the rights and freedoms of persons belonging to these minorities. This distinction and the difference in wording make it clear that it does not envisage the collective rights of national minorities. Legal literature has criticized the FCNM for relying exclusively on individual rights to the detriment of group rights. Because of this bias, discriminatory patterns are likely to persist;[21] however, the apparent reason for rejecting the idea of collective rights is that many states fear secessionist demands. In order to overcome these fears, the FCNM acknowledged that the protection of a national minority group could be achieved through the protection of the rights of individuals belonging to that group. The authors of the

[15] H. Klebes, 'The Council of Europe's Framework Convention for the Protection of National Minorities', *Human Rights Journal*, 16 (1995), 93.

[16] G. Alfredsson, 'A Frame with an Incomplete Painting: Comparison of the Framework Convention for the Protection of National Minorities with International Standards and Monitoring Procedures', *International Journal of Minority and Group Rights*, 7 (2000), 291–304 at 296. He mentions: objective characteristics, self-identification, and long association (one or two generations) with the country or territory concerned.

[17] The statement in the Swiss report is typical: 'Since the Framework Convention itself does not define the concept of national minority, Switzerland made a declaration when it ratified the instrument, setting out its interpretation of the concept of national minority. In substance, that declaration is based on proposals made by working groups at international level' (ACFC/SR/2001/002, para. 98).

[18] H.-J. Heintze, 'Bilateral Agreements and their Role in Settling Ethnic Conflicts', in U. Schneckner and S. Wolff (eds.), *Managing and Settling Ethnic Conflicts* (C. Hurst, London, 2004), 189–205 at 197.

[19] Council Recommendation, Rec. 1492/2000/EC of 13 June 2002 on the Rights of National Minorities, 799th meeting, 2002, para. 8.

[20] Advisory Committee on the Framework Convention for the Protection of National Minorities, Opinion Rec. 1492, 2001, para. 4.

[21] Above, n. 16, p. 295.

FCNM chose to concentrate on this point as they had already underscored, in the Explanatory Report to the Convention, that the implementation of the principles set out in the FCNM would be done through national legislation. However, this 'does not imply the recognition of collective rights'.[22] Another reason for this approach may be that persons belonging to national minorities held on to liberal fears that collective rights would endanger the primacy of individual rights.[23] Consequently, the FCNM follows the universally recognized individualistic human rights approach typical of all instruments dealing with minority issues. It signals that the individual *per se*, and not the minority group, is considered to be the rights holder.

This departure point, however, does not solve problems emerging from the consistent group character of minorities. Many persons belonging to national minorities advocate the protection of their group identity, the most important element of their identity being the right to organize themselves as a group. In this vein, they demand the right to use their language, to practise their culture, to influence the content of the education of their children, and to be able to participate in political decisions that affect them.[24] The FCNM tries to resolve the contradiction latent in Article 3(2) by allowing persons belonging to national minorities to exercise their minority rights 'in community with others'. Thus, it recognizes that persons belonging to national minorities cannot avail themselves of the rights listed in the FCNM without the participation of others belonging to the same group. As such, there is undoubtedly a collective dimension encapsulated in Article 1.

C. Protection of National Minorities as an Integral Part of Human Rights

1. *Background to the Human Rights Approach*

The rights of persons belonging to minorities are an aspect of human rights. Embedding minority rights in the human rights environment spells the difference between the League of Nations and the 'modern' minority rights approaches. Minority rights overlap with human rights and, hence, are applicable to persons belonging to minorities. The basic human rights principles of non-discrimination, equality, and participation in the process of self-determination

[22] Preparatory Work of the Ad Hoc Committee for the Protection of National Minorities (CAHMIN), Explanatory Report to the Framework Convention for the Protection of National Minorities, CAHMIN H(1995) 010, 1995, para. 13.

[23] W. Kymlicka, *Multicultural Citizenship* (Oxford University Press, Oxford, 1995), 4–9.

[24] A. Eide, Minorities in a Decentralized Environment, Background Paper, Yalta, 1998.

are particularly relevant to minorities. However, one notes that the inclusion of minority rights in the human rights system generates problems, notably concerning the relationship between non-discrimination and affirmative action. In order to reconcile both approaches, the norm of non-discrimination needs to be interpreted in a more sensitive way, especially when issues of culture and identity are at stake. This is especially true in considering the relationship between individual and collective rights, where the traditional human rights approach—that collective rights should not undermine individual rights—may not apply to situations of minority rights. To better support the integration of minority rights into the body of human rights one should speak of human rights as including the rights of persons belonging to minorities.[25]

The authors of the FCNM appear less interested in the theoretical aspect of integrating minority rights into the human rights system, choosing instead to focus on the fate of national minorities as an international concern. Bearing this in mind, one could argue that leaving states parties to determine who benefits from such a human rights convention runs contrary to this understanding. Therefore, states parties do not enjoy full interpretative licence over the term 'national minority'. Accordingly, a majority of states parties did not declare any beneficiaries of this clause upon ratification. In the absence of a definition of 'national minority', in principle, the protection offered by the FCNM also applies to non-kin-state minorities. This approach is consistent with the application of Article 27 ICCPR.[26] In reality, however, this is a secondary issue since minorities must display a certain stability in their existence. That said, the contribution of individual human rights to minority protection is more important against the background of the prohibition of special discriminatory measures designed to protect and promote the identity of a minority. Nevertheless, the question arises whether citizenship is one of the criteria to identify beneficiaries. In the European context, this criterion has been referred to several times in both the European Charter for Regional or Minority Languages and in Recommendation 1201 of the Parliamentary Assembly, for instance. One must also take into consideration the considerable number of declarations by state parties linking the term 'national minority' to citizenship. Similarly, the criterion of firm and long-standing ties to the state in which a minority group lives sustains the connection between the minority and citizenship.

[25] A. Rönquist, 'The Council of Europe and National Minorities', *Helsinki Monitor*, 1 (1995), 40.

[26] UN Human Rights Committee, General Comment 15/27 (22 July 1986), UN Doc. CCPR/C/21/Rev. 1, para. 7.

2. Implementation of the Human Rights Approach

With an understanding of minority rights as an integral part of human rights, the Advisory Committee requested information on the states parties' participation in, and co-operation with, international organizations, including the identification of relevant international human rights instruments to which they were parties.[27] All state reports provided lists of state participation and co-operation, which resulted in the Advisory Committee noting that the states had ratified a wide range of relevant international instruments. It therefore concluded that, '[o]n the basis of the information currently at its disposal, the Advisory Committee considers that implementation of this article does not give rise to any further observations'. None of the states parties to the FCNM has offered any further information regarding the implementation of relevant international human rights instruments concerning minorities. This may be a consequence of the FCNM's contradictory approach. Although minority rights form 'an integral part of the international protection of human rights', the rights mentioned in the FCNM are not justiciable. This shortcoming pinpoints one of the main criticisms of the FCNM: that modern human rights instruments include national legal remedies and international complaint procedures as a general standard.[28] In light of this weakness, the role of the implementing bodies established by the ECHR has to be taken into consideration. However, these organs have reiterated that the ECHR does not provide an explicit guarantee of minority rights and that 'the protection of individual members of such a minority is limited to the right not to be discriminated in the enjoyment of the Convention rights on the grounds of their belonging to the minority (Article 14 of the Convention)'.[29] This means that the Strasbourg bodies protect minority groups under Article 14 of the ECHR, in combination with the other substantial rights enshrined in the articles of the ECHR.[30] In reality, states enjoy a wide margin of appreciation under the ECHR, which is not conducive to the idea of minority protection. Furthermore, the group dimension of an individual complaint is not taken into consideration. In *Beard* v. *UK*, the European Court of Human Rights (ECtHR) observed 'that there may be said to be an emerging international consensus amongst the Contracting States of the Council of Europe recognising the special needs of minorities and an obligation to protect their

[27] Committee of Ministers, Outline for Reports to be Submitted Pursuant to Article 25 Paragraph (1) of the Framework Convention for the Protection of National Minorities, ACFC/INF(98), 1998.

[28] Above, n. 16, p. 292.

[29] *X* v. *Austria* (8142/78), (1979) EHRR, DR 18 88, 1980: 88, pp. 92–3.

[30] G. Gilbert, 'The Legal Protection Accorded to Minority Groups in Europe', *Netherlands Yearbook of International Law*, 23 (1992), 81–93.

security, identity and lifestyle (. . . in particular the Framework Convention for the Protection of Minorities), not only for the purpose of safeguarding the interests of the minorities themselves but to preserve a cultural diversity of value to the whole community'.[31] Yet, the Court regretted having to come to the conclusion that the consensus was not sufficiently concrete and that it was not possible to derive any guidance from any particular situation.[32]

D. '*Domaine réservé*' and Minority Protection

1. *Background to the Issue of* 'Domaine réservé'

Minority rights, as an integral part of human rights, are now a subject of international co-operation. Although this concept is not uncontroversial, most experts agree that intervention into a sovereign state's internal affairs is possible when the government is committing serious human rights abuses against its population, including against minorities.[33] The exact boundary, however, between a state's right to non-interference in its domestic affairs and the international community's permissible intervention remains uncertain.

The FCNM underlines with the wording of Article 1 that the protection of minorities is the subject of legitimate international interest. Such an approach would have been unthinkable in the context of the CoE a few years earlier.[34] This approach clearly removes any claims formulated by states that the protection of minorities is a matter solely within the competence and sovereignty of the state and, hence, states have exclusive domestic jurisdiction over minority issues. This principle is also reflected in Article 17(1) FCNM, which stresses the importance of maintaining cross-border links with persons belonging to the same group. In this regard, and especially in the light of Article 2 FCNM, states must practise good neighbourliness and friendly relations. The Hungarian Status Law clearly illustrates how minorities can give rise to irredentism. It is hence clear that minority rights as guaranteed by one state can be a legitimate reason for concern in another state.[35] In those cases, a triangulated relationship

[31] *Beard* v. *United Kingdom* (24882/94) (2001), EHRR 422.

[32] Similar arguments to the ECtHR include: *Chapman* v. *United Kingdom* (27238/95) (2001), EHRR 43, *Jane Smith* v. *UK* (25154/94) (2001), EHRR 45, *Coster* v. *United Kingdom* (24876/94) (2001), EHRR 44, *Lee* v. *United Kingdom* (25289/94) (2001), EHRR 46.

[33] R. Uerpmann, 'La Primarité des droits de la personne: licéité ou illicéité de l'intervention humanitaire?', in C. Tomuschat (ed.), *Kosovo and the International Community* (Kluwer Law International, The Hague, 2002), 65–86.

[34] F. Steketee, 'The Framework Convention: A Piece of Art or a Tool for Action?', *International Journal of Minority and Group Rights*, 8/1 (2001), 5.

[35] G. Gilbert, 'The Council of Europe and Minority Rights', *Human Rights Quarterly*, 18/2 (1996), 175.

arises: between national minorities who are citizens or residents of the host country, but have an ethno-cultural affinity with an external 'homeland' or kin state. The settlement of tensions resulting from such a triangle is only possible on the basis of international co-operation.

2. *Implementation of International Co-operation*

In their reports to the Advisory Committee, many states parties outline the need for international co-operation in the field of minority issues. Moldova, for example, declared its 'wish to fulfil its obligations towards the Council of Europe, particularly those arising from the Framework Convention, as part of its policy for international co-operation'. Sweden was interested in promoting international co-operation to protect its inhabitants from all forms of discrimination and also to promote diversity and tolerance. Switzerland considered the protection of national minorities an integral part of the protection of the rights of persons, one which constituted an area of international co-operation: 'Switzerland therefore reaffirmed its conviction that respect for minorities constitutes an integral part of the protection of the rights of persons and consequently is not a matter solely of States' domestic affairs.' The British government also expressed a strong commitment to international co-operation and to protecting ethnic minorities through programmes tackling discrimination and promoting diversity.

E. The Concept of Protection

1. *Background to the Concept*

The CSCE first mentioned the minority issue in the Helsinki Final Act of 1975. This document stipulated that 'the participating States on whose territory national minorities exist will respect the right of persons belonging to such minorities to equality before the law, will afford them the full opportunity for the actual enjoyment of human rights and fundamental freedoms and will, in this manner, protect their legitimate interests in this sphere'.[36] With the Copenhagen Document of 1990, the CSCE demanded from states not only that they respected the rights of persons belonging to national minorities, but also that they undertook more concrete activities in the field of minority rights, combining this issue with democratic statehood.[37] Protection is, therefore, an issue kept to the margins of debate.

[36] Conference for Security and Co-operation in Europe, Helsinki Final Act, 1975, Principle VII.

[37] Second Conference on the Human Dimension of the CSCE, Document of the Copenhagen Meeting of the Conference on the Human Dimension of the CSCE, Copenhagen, 1990, para. 30.

In comparison, the CoE approach is stronger in this regard as it centres on the protection of persons belonging to national minorities. The inclusion of the concept of protection can be traced to the first draft of the ECDL of 1990, which contained a set of protection-based principles. The *travaux préparatoires* show that the term 'protection' of minorities was used to indicate that it did not fall within the *domaine réservé* of states.[38] During negotiations, a second purpose for the inclusion of the term protection arose: international law gradually accepted that not only individuals belonging to minorities, but also minorities as groups had a right to be protected.[39] Furthermore, the opinions of the experts continued to differ as to whether protection should be provided for in legal instruments relating to the protection of national minorities. Some argued that only migrant workers or refugees, not persons of national minorities, would require protection of this nature.[40]

2. *The Concept of Protection in the Context of Minority Rights*

The concept of protection is well established in national law, where it means that states have positive duties towards individuals. For example, the obligation to protect the right to life includes the effective enforcement of the law. Accordingly, the state is obliged to take reasonable steps to provide police and security forces, in order to prevent the loss of life.[41] However, there are limits to a state's positive obligation since the state cannot realistically prevent all forms of violence against individuals on its territory.[42]

From a historical point of view, it was complicated to transform this concept of protection into international law. In traditional international law, reference to the concept of protection can be found only in the notion of 'diplomatic protection', a protection solely exercised by a state vis-à-vis another state.[43] Since modern international law contains obligations *erga omnes*, i.e. the basic rights of the human person owed by states towards the international community as a whole, some corresponding rights and duties of protection 'have entered into the body of general international law'.[44] This means that the

[38] ECDL, Set of Principles on National Minorities Drawn up by the European Commission for Democracy through Law Draft Report of the Fourth Meeting, CD-PV (90) 4 prov., 1990.

[39] ECDL, Explanatory Report to the Proposal for a European Convention for the Protection of National Minorities, CDL-MIN (93) 7, 1993.

[40] Steering Committee for Human Rights (CDDH), Final Activity Report of the CDDH for the Attention of the Committee of Ministers, CDDH (93) 22, 1993.

[41] D. J. Harris et al., *Law of the European Convention on Human Rights* (Butterworths, London, 1993), 39.

[42] *W* v. *UK* (9348/81) (1983), 32 DR 190 at 200.

[43] *Nottebohm Case* (1955), ICJ Rep. 4, p. 4.

[44] *Barcelona Traction Light and Power Co. Case* (1970), ICJ Rep. 3, p. 1.

general understanding of the term 'protection' in international law has become much broader. This is especially true for the whole body of human rights.

In the field of human rights, the general duty to protect can be interpreted in three different manners. First, protection can be understood in the context of vulnerable groups in times of armed conflict, for example, civilians, children, women, and persons *hors de combat* in international humanitarian law.[45] The second meaning deals with situations of mass and gross violations of human rights in which governments are not able or willing to fulfil their obligation to protect those under their jurisdiction. In this case, the need for international protection is obvious. The third meaning concerns groups in need of protection: families; refugees; migrant workers; as well as the general obligation of states to take positive measures to protect their rights.[46] The necessity to protect minorities for the sake of peace was articulated by the Parliamentary Assembly of the CoE in its Recommendation 1492 (2000): 'adequate protection for persons belonging to national minorities and their communities . . . is the only way in which states can reduce ethnic tensions that might give rise to more widespread conflicts'. In order to achieve respect for minority rights, it is vital that states reduce tension and conflict. The pre-emptive protection of minorities, an approach commonly reflected in relevant international instruments, is the means to accomplish this.

In adopting Article 1, states parties to the FCNM followed this approach, demonstrating that they considered national minorities to be in need of international protection. Like the Committee on the Elimination of Racial Discrimination (CERD), the FCNM does not consider minority rights protection as solely 'the right of equality before the law and equal protection of the law', that is to say, a ratification of the status quo. Instead, it encourages states parties to initiate adequate measures promoting full and effective equality between minority and majority populations.[47] This more comprehensive and new approach is particularly striking if one compares the FCNM to the more traditional ICCPR. Article 27 ICCPR is negatively formulated since it states that individuals 'shall *not* be denied the right'[48] ensured therein. On a legal basis this formulation met with severe theoretical criticism because, it was argued, the mere passive stance of the state would not ensure the survival of minorities.[49]

[45] E. Kussbach, 'Protected Persons', in R. Bernhard (ed.), *Encyclopedia of Public International Law*, vol. iii (North-Holland, Amsterdam, 1997), 11–44.

[46] International Covenant on Civil and Political Rights, GA Res. 2200A (XXI) (16 December 1966), 21 UN GAOR Supp. 16, at 52, UN Doc. A/6316, 999 UNTS, Art. 17.

[47] Art. 4(1) FCNM. [48] Emphasis added.

[49] P. Thornberry, *International Law and the Rights of Minorities* (Clarendon Press, Oxford, 1991), 178.

The classical liberal theory of essential equality is not matched by an equality of birth. Therefore, positive measures are necessary to bring those who are vulnerable to the same position as others who are not. As groups with distinct linguistic, cultural, social, and even economic disadvantages, minorities who seek to maintain and develop an identity distinct from the numerical majority are in need of protection. As an example, democratic decision-making processes fail to account for the interests and concerns of minorities.[50] Under these circumstances, protection leads to the recognition of the substantial rights of minorities.

This principle reached general international acceptance in the 1993 UN Declaration on the Rights of Persons Belonging to National, Religious, and Linguistic Minorities which declares in Article 1 that 'States shall *protect* the existence and the national or ethnic, cultural, religious and linguistic identity of minorities within their respective territories and shall encourage conditions for the promotion of that identity.'[51] This wording transcends the tentative approach of Article 27 ICCPR and reflects a greater readiness to accept the collective rights of minorities. This is even more important as existence and identity are aspects of the protection of group rights claimed by minorities.[52] A third requirement of the UN Declaration, which goes beyond mere protection, is to encourage the promotion of the identity of minorities.[53] Consequently, more recent commentaries on the UN Declaration declare that minority protection is based on four tenets: 'protection of existence, non-exclusion, non-discrimination and non-assimilation of the groups concerned'.[54]

In comparison to that of the UN Declaration, the wording of the FCNM is not as clear. Consequently, it may be argued that the understanding of the protection of identity in the FCNM is more restrictive than the one offered in the UN Declaration. Only the Preamble of the FCNM determines that the states are 'to protect' the 'existence' of national minorities within their respective territories. In the light of that preambular paragraph, and according to

[50] J. Packer, 'Problems in Defining Minorities', in D. Fottrell and B. Bowring (eds.), *Minority and Group Rights in the New Millennium* (Martinus Nijhoff, The Hague, 1999), 249.

[51] Emphasis added.

[52] P. Thornberry, 'The UN-Declaration on the Rights of Persons Belonging to National, Religious and Linguistic Minorities: Background, Analysis, Observations, and an Update', in A. Phillips and A. Rosas (eds.), *Universal Minority Rights* (Åbo Akademi University Institute for Human Rights/ Minority Rights Group, Turku, 1995), 39.

[53] A. Eide, Commentary to the Declaration on the Rights of Persons Belonging to National or Ethnic, Religious, and Linguistic Minorities, Working Paper, 1998, UN Doc. E/CN.4/Sub.2/AC.5/1998/WP.1.

[54] A. Eide, Final Text of the Commentary to the UN Declaration on the Rights of Persons Belonging to National, or Ethnic, Religious, and Linguistic Minorities, 2001, UN Doc. E/CN.4/ Sub.2/AC.5/2001/2, para. 23.

the interpretation of the term 'protection', one has to conclude that state obligations under Article 1 FCNM include upholding the right to existence and of identity for national minorities. The exact content of the right to identity is further clarified in connection with Articles 5(1), 6(1), 6(2), and 17(1).

3. Implementation of the Protection of Minority Rights

The implementation mechanism of the FCNM allows for a deeper understanding of the term 'protection' among states parties and implementation bodies. States parties commit themselves to ensuring adequate protection of minorities on their territory. They are, thus, responsible for guaranteeing the competence of the various domestic institutions or bodies in fields that are pertinent to the obligations set forth in the FCNM. In fact, the term 'protection' is often used not only in relation to the individual belonging to the minority, but also vis-à-vis the minority group. This represents the more recent understanding of 'protection',[55] which reflects a progressive development of international law on the legal status of minorities.

Nowadays, this is a commonly accepted understanding. In its 'Opinion on Possible Groups of Persons to Which the FCNM Could be Applied in Belgium',[56] the Venice Commission stressed that only those groups of persons that are actually at risk of domination by the majority deserve protection. Thus, numerical inferiority, though a necessary characteristic, may not be sufficient for a group of persons to qualify as a 'minority' within the meaning of the FCNM. This means that groups in positions of co-dominance cannot benefit from the protection offered by the FCNM. In fact, by virtue of the effective operation of democratic institutions, the FCNM is designed to avoid situations where groups of persons in numerical inferiority to the rest of the population are obliged to yield to the pressure of the majority and to surrender their religious, linguistic, cultural, and historical distinctions.

The meaning of protection according to the FCNM becomes clearer when considered in light of the Committee of Ministers 1998 Outline for the format of state reports.[57] This outline provides some tools for assessing whether or not adequate protection is offered to persons belonging to national minorities. In

[55] B. G. Ramcharan, 'The Concept of Protection in the International Law of Human Rights', in Y. Dinstein (ed.), *International Law at a Time of Perplexity* (Nijhoff, Dordrecht, 1989), 593.

[56] Venice Commission, Opinion on Possible Groups to which the Framework Convention for the Protection of National Minorities could be Applied in Belgium, CDL-A (2002), 50th plenary meeting, 2002.

[57] Outline for Reports to be Submitted Pursuant to Article 25 Paragraph (1) of the Framework Convention for the Protection of National Minorities (Adopted by the Committee of Ministers on 30 September 1998 at the 642nd meeting of the Ministers' Deputies), ACFC/INF (1998) 001.

its first line, it mentions access to justice on issues of protection of persons belonging to national minorities. As a result, states mainly report on developments in the legislative sphere.[58] On the other hand, the government of Estonia, besides reporting on legal issues, provided substantial information on the various steps adopted by the authorities to promote awareness among different minorities about their rights and opportunities. Most promotion was carried out during round tables and seminars. In its evaluation of the Estonian practice, however, the Council of Ministers found that 'the protection of national minorities is not always addressed in an adequate manner in the legislative process and administrative practice'.[59] An analysis of other Advisory Committee comments gives the impression that it considers proper legislation and administration to be sufficient to fulfil the state's obligation to protect national minorities. Yet, comments on other cases suggested that fields of protection, such as language and culture, are equally important and should also be taken into consideration. For example, the Advisory Committee declared, 'Finland has over a period of time made particularly commendable efforts concerning the protection of the Swedish-speaking Finns *and* their status in such areas as media and education.'[60] In the field of cultural protection, the government of Norway informed the Advisory Committee of measures taken to protect the culture and identity of the Sami.[61]

Furthermore, in some states that are party to the FCNM, there remain minority groups without protection under its mandate. Sweden, for instance, reported that it is currently a country characterized by ethnic and cultural diversity, where every fourth inhabitant was born in another country or has parents who were born abroad. The ethnic groups who in recent times have immigrated to Sweden, however, are not regarded as national minorities as they do not satisfy the criteria established by the government.[62]

[58] The German report is a typical example, stating that the protection of minorities is guaranteed as part of the general protection of human rights by the fundamental rights enshrined in the Basic Law: 'This also applies to the justiciability of issues concerning the protection of members of national minorities. Under Article 19, paragraph 4, 1st sentence of the Basic Law, any person whose rights might have been violated by public authority has recourse to the courts. "Public authority" within the meaning of paragraph 4 refers to the entire executive branch, irrespective of whether the latter is qualified as "government" or "administration". Consequently, recourse to the courts is also guaranteed to any member of a national minority.' Germany State Report, ACFC/SR (2000) 1, 2000, para. 2.

[59] Resolution ResCMN (2002) 8 on the Implementation of the Framework Convention for the Protection of National Minorities, para. 1.

[60] Advisory Committee Opinion on Finland, ACFC/INF/OP/I (2001) 002, 2000, para. 55 (emphasis added).

[61] Norway State Report, ACFC/SR (2001) 001, 2001.

[62] Sweden State Report, ACFC/SR (2001) 003, 2001.

III. Conclusion and Outlook

Article 1 reflects the main problems connected with the modern concept of minority protection. The first problem relates to the issue of the dimensions, individual or collective, of this protection. On the one hand, Article 1 speaks about the protection of national minorities, thereby referring to the collective or group dimension of this right. On the other hand, it deals with persons belonging to those minorities, thus clearly adopting an individual approach. This tends to show that minority protection falls in a certain legal grey area between individual and group rights. However, the authors of the FCNM reject such an impression and explicitly underline in the explanatory report that the emphasis is placed upon the protection of persons belonging to national minorities. Therefore one may state that the minority protection forms an integral part of the international protection of human rights. The wording of the second part of Article 1 has the additional advantage of rejecting any objection arguing that the minority protection would be part of the *domaine réservé* of the state. Furthermore, the text underlines that minority protection falls within the scope of international co-operation. In fact, the practice of the states parties proves that the implementation of Article 1 does not create problems concerning the individual/collective dimension of minority protection and its human rights aspect.

Even more difficult to interpret is the wording of Article 1, as it does not provide for a definition of the term 'national minority'. In light of the failure of several definitional attempts, and continuous disagreement among the CoE member states, this lack of definition in the FCNM is not surprising. Nevertheless, in practice, it may create problems. Therefore, the decisions of the Advisory Committee concerning the supervision of the implementation of the FCNM are of utmost importance, and one can hope that this practice will bring some clarification. Furthermore, practice has demonstrated that because the scope of Article 1 and Article 3 overlaps, it is not possible to analyse Article 1 separately from Article 3. However, there is no doubt that Article 1 will, in the future, play an important role as it describes the scope, albeit in vague terms, of the entire Framework Convention.

ARTICLE 2

Peter Hilpold

The provisions of this framework Convention shall be applied in good faith, in a spirit of understanding and tolerance and in conformity with the principles of good neighbourliness, friendly relations and co-operation between States.

I. Background

A. Issues

Article 2 expresses the overall spirit in which the Framework Convention for the Protection of National Minorities (FCNM) should be construed and applied. It has, therefore, been correctly located in the introductory section of the document. The wording of this provision does not necessarily imply a precise relationship between the different principles mentioned, but such a system can be found in viewing the principle of good faith, which stands at the heart of the Convention. First, this principle requires an internal spirit of understanding and tolerance. Its outward expression, in relation to other states parties, translates into the principles of good neighbourliness, friendly relations, and co-operation between states.

B. History

The main inspiration for this provision seems to be the Friendly Relations Declaration of 1970[1] which contains both a principle according to which, '[e]very State has the duty to fulfil in good faith its obligations under the generally recognized principles and rules of international law' and a 'duty of States to co-operate with one another in accordance with the Charter'. This second duty was supplemented by the obligation for states to 'co-operate in the promotion of universal respect for, and observance of, human rights and fundamental freedoms for all, and in the elimination of all forms of racial discrimination and all forms of religious intolerance'. A similar provision can be found in the preliminary draft and the proposal for a European Convention for the Protection of National Minorities elaborated by the European Commission for Democracy through Law.[2] The Ad Hoc Committee for the Protection of National Minorities (CAHMIN) added the wording 'friendly relations and co-operation' to its final draft for Article 2 of the Framework Convention, thereby introducing a more or less explicit reference to the Friendly Relations Declaration,[3] and giving this provision a somewhat different connotation. In this way, the protection of minorities has become an element of stability and cohesion in international relations. In the meantime, minority protection can be seen both as a consequence of greater international co-operation, integration, and stability, as well as a means to achieve these aims in a precise manner.[4]

C. Context

Perhaps more directly than any other provision of the Convention, Article 2 reflects the general philosophy expressed in the Preamble: that tolerance and

[1] Declaration on Principles of International Law concerning Friendly Relations and Co-operation among States in accordance with the Charter of the United Nations UNGA Res. 2625 (XXV), 1970. According to the Ad Hoc Committee for the Protection of National Minorities (CAHMIN) Explanatory Report, the Friendly Relations Declaration is one of several sources of inspiration. As the other sources are not expressly mentioned, it can be assumed that it is the most important one.

[2] European Commission for Democracy through Law (ECDL), Preliminary Draft Convention on the Protection of Minorities [DAJ.SC.DEMOCRACY]CONV.MIN, 1990; ECDL, Proposal for a European Convention for the Protection of National Minorities, CDL-MIN (93) 6, 1993; ECDL, Explanatory Report to the Proposal for a European Convention for the Protection of National Minorities CDL-MIN (93) 7, 22 February 1993.

[3] Above, n. 1.

[4] Advisory Committee on the Framework Convention for the Protection of National Minorities, ACFC-MR-INF (2001) 004, 11th meeting, 2001, Meeting Report on Parliamentary Assembly Recommendation 1492, 2001:'4. The Advisory Committee points out that the protection of national minorities is an integral component of the international protection of human rights and, as such, falls within the ambit of international co-operation. In addition, the Preamble of the Framework Convention recognises that the protection of national minorities is essential to the stability, democratic security and peace of our continent . . .'

co-operation are of pivotal importance for an effective minority protection system. With regard to the normative provisions of the Convention in a narrower sense, Article 2 of the Framework Convention is closely related to all other provisions of the Convention. However, in comparison to some of its other provisions, the expression of this relationship in Article 2 is more immediate and explicit. Its provisions can be seen as giving specific execution, greater elucidation, or at least confirmation, to the general principles and aims that it sets out. In this context Article 6(1) stating that '[t]he Parties shall encourage a spirit of tolerance and intercultural dialogue' is the first provision that bears mentioning.

Questions of good faith are also prominent in Article 16, where parties are asked to 'refrain from measures which alter the proportions of the population in areas inhabited by persons belonging to national minorities and are aimed at restricting the rights and freedoms flowing from the principles enshrined in the present framework Convention',[5] as well as in Article 19, where care is taken to ensure that the restrictions to the principles enshrined in the Convention do not endanger its aim and effect. With regard to the necessity for states parties to engage in more intensive co-operation, Article 18 gives an important further specification, when it requires parties to 'endeavour to conclude, where necessary, bilateral and multilateral agreements with other States, in particular neighbouring States, in order to ensure the protection of persons belonging to the national minorities concerned'.[6]

II. Analysis

A. Structure of the Article

As stated above, the central principle contained in this article is one of 'good faith', requiring the internal adoption of a spirit of understanding and

[5] Gerrymandering has been up to the present time a policy frequently carried out by governments with a view to restricting the territorial scope of minority protection provisions as well as the participatory rights of members of minorities. Such a policy constitutes a clear violation of Art. 2 of the Framework Convention for the Protection of National Minorities (FCNM). In the Advisory Committee on the Framework Convention for the Protection of National Minorities, Opinion on Moldova, ACFC/INF/OP/I (2003) 002, 2002, it has been noted that the Moldovan authorities undertook in December 2001 a revision of the country's administrative-territorial system which also included the functioning of the public local administration. In this context, the Advisory Committee stated the following: 'The Advisory Committee wishes to draw the Moldovan authorities' attention to the need to consult with those concerned by the administrative-territorial changes adopted, in order to ensure that these measures do not infringe the rights and freedoms enshrined in the Framework Convention, including with respect to participation in the decision-making process.' The need to consult stated above can be seen as a derivative of the principle of good faith.

[6] Art. 18(2) FCNM refers to the possibility of transfrontier co-operation.

tolerance and the outward expression of a policy of good neighbourliness, friendly relations, and co-operation.

B. Good Faith

Good faith is a general principle of international law, and perhaps the most important principle of this nature. In this regard, the International Court of Justice (ICJ), in the *Nuclear Test* case, stated:[7] '[o]ne of the basic principles governing the creation and performance of legal obligations, whatever their source, is the principle of good faith. Trust and confidence are inherent in international co-operation, in particular in an age when this co-operation in many fields is becoming increasingly essential.' The content of the principle of good faith has been greatly analysed in international jurisprudence[8] and literature,[9] and its dominant role in treaty interpretation can no longer be contested. In this regard, however, it has to be observed that for those treaties to which the Vienna Convention on the Law of Treaties (VCLT) applies,[10] the principle of good faith is more immediately based in treaty law (Articles 26 and 31(1) VCLT) than the general principles of international law which govern both the observance and interpretation of treaty obligations. At first glance, therefore, it seems rather surprising that the principle of good faith has been given such a prominent role in the Framework Convention, or that it has even been incorporated at all. In fact, the parties to the Framework Convention would have had to account for this principle as parties to the VCLT in any case. Therefore, the inclusion of the obligation to act in good faith adds no material obligation for the parties to the Convention.

This is not a redundant formulation, however. In the first place, and as already mentioned, this criterion provides structure to the whole provision. Secondly, the unique nature of this Convention, as the first modern multilateral treaty for the protection of minorities, has to be kept in mind. It is

[7] *Nuclear Test Cases (Australia* v. *France, N.Z.* v. *France)* [1974] ICJ Rep. 253, p. 268, para. 46.

[8] In addition to the case previously mentioned see, for example, *Border and Transborder Armed Actions, Nicaragua* v. *Honduras*, Judgment, ICJ Rep. 1988, p. 105.

[9] See, for example, A. Verdross, 'Die bona fides als Grundlage des Völkerrechts', in *Festschrift für R. Laun* (Girardet, Hamburg, 1953), 29; B. Cheng, *General Principles of Law—As Applied by International Courts and Tribunals* (Stevens, London, 1953), 105; J. P. Cot, 'La Bonne Foi en droit international public', Cours de l'Institut de Hautes Études Internationales, Paris, 1968/1969; A. d'Amato, 'Good Faith', in R. Bernhardt (ed.), *EPIL* 2 (1995), 599–601; J. P. Müller and L. Wildhaber, *Praxis des Völkerrechts* (Stämpfli, Bern, 2001), 40 ff.

[10] The Vienna Convention on the Law of Treaties (VCLT) applies to treaties between states, which have been ratified since 1980, the year the Convention entered into force. See Vienna Convention on the Law of Treaties (adopted on 23 May 1969, entered into force 27 January 1980), 1155 UNTS 331; 8 ILM 679.

commonly acknowledged that the observance of human rights obligations cannot be guaranteed through the principle of reciprocity, a concept that is paramount in the implementation of bilateral treaties.[11] Primarily, human rights obligations are directed and fulfilled internally, towards a country's own people, rather than towards other states. In internal state matters, therefore, threats of negative reciprocity are meaningless. More and more, however, a noticeable trend has been established whereby human rights protection is a perceived common goal, and this has stimulated competition for the best achievements in this field. As one of many competing claims under the umbrella of human rights protection, the issue of minorities has long been sidelined both because of current international political priorities[12] and because many states continue to perceive minorities as potential competitors for sovereignty in parts or on the whole of their territory. The explicit reference to 'good faith' in the Convention, though technically superfluous, can be seen as a constant reminder to the parties that they have to strive for utmost treaty fidelity, even if other instruments to guarantee implementation are lacking, or if the concept of minority protection is not a particularly popular one at a certain moment in time. As such, this reference can be viewed as a political amplification of an existing obligation. Thirdly, the reference to 'good faith' allows for the inclusion of evolutionary elements where formalized respect for treaty obligations may, in cases of far-reaching societal changes, provide little of the effective protection that this instrument was meant to grant. The leeway offered should be used in good faith, within the limits of the provisions' 'ordinary meaning . . . in their context', and in light of the 'object and purpose' of the treaty.[13] It seems also that the parties to the Framework Convention, in their reports presented pursuant to Article 25(1), have interpreted the obligation to proceed in good faith as an overarching principle. Leaving aside the numerous cases where no specific reference can be found in the reports, respect for this principle is demonstrated either through the general importance that the respective party attributes to the principle of *pacta sunt servanda*, or by a general declaration of commitment to international obligations.

[11] B. Simma, *Das Reziprozitätselement im Zustandekommen völkerrechtlicher Verträge* (Duncker & Humblot, Berlin, 1972), 153; P. Hilpold, 'Das Vorbehaltsregime der Wiener Vertragskonvention', *Archiv des Völkerrechts*, 34/4 (1996), 376–425 at 415 ff).

[12] This was the core of Professor Joseph Kunz's famous statement according to which there are 'fashions in international law just as in neckties. At the end of the first World War, "international protection of minorities" was the great fashion: treaties in abundance, conferences, League of Nations activities, an enormous literature. Recently this fashion has become nearly obsolete. Today the well-dressed international lawyer wears "human rights".' See J. L. Kunz, 'The Present Status of International Law for the Protection of Minorities', *American Journal of International Law*, 48 (1954), 282–7 at 282.

[13] Vienna Convention on the Law of Treaties (VCLT), Art. 31(1).

C. The Spirit of Understanding and Tolerance

The need to apply the Convention in a spirit of understanding and tolerance stems from considerations on the principle of good faith. Tolerance is a necessary prerequisite of any form of minority protection based on a human rights philosophy. It can be argued that tolerance implies a commitment to a multicultural society,[14] but this statement also produces a series of questions. Tolerance can be interpreted as an 'absence of negative discrimination', or as a sort of 'benign neglect'. The minority protection system created after the First World War under the aegis of the League of Nations is widely considered conservationist, without a concept of how different cultural identities in a nation-building process can be reconciled based on mutual respect. In contrast, the Framework Convention ensures that the obligation to act in a spirit of tolerance does not stand alone, but is further qualified by the requirement to demonstrate a spirit of understanding. Tolerance and understanding, therefore, represent a unitary concept. Tolerance based on understanding nurtures an attitude towards minorities characterized by respect and mutual consideration. This also implies the need to grant minorities sufficient social space to enable them to develop according to their own priorities. Ultimately, it could be argued that taking this obligation seriously requires parties to take positive measures. An overall positive attitude towards multiculturalism implies that the different groups also possess the means to develop their identity. Of course, the degree to which parties are required to adopt positive measures will have to be further determined through state practice and will continue to vary according to the situation and the means available to the respective parties.

D. Good Neighbourliness, Friendly Relations, and Co-operation between States

As mentioned, these elements are listed within the Friendly Relations Declaration. The exact relationship between them and the issue of minority protection needs, however, to be further specified. At first sight, it could be argued that, together, these elements caution parties to be prudent not to endanger their favourable relations with other countries when pursuing minority protection goals. This interpretation does not, however, give due regard to the way these elements have been interpreted in the Friendly Relations Declaration and in other international instruments. The Friendly Relations Declaration, itself, explicitly refers to a duty to co-operate in human rights

[14] On the issue of the 'new minorities' see P. Hilpold, 'Neue Minderheiten im Völkerrecht und im Europarecht', *Archiv des Völkerrechts*, 42 (2004), 80–110.

matters. At the Conference for Security and Co-operation in Europe (CSCE) meeting of Experts on National Minorities, which took place 1–19 July 1991 in Geneva, it was confirmed that '[i]ssues concerning national minorities, as well as compliance with international obligations and commitments concerning the rights of persons belonging to them, are matters of legitimate international concern and consequently do not constitute exclusively an internal affair of the respective State'. Therefore, the obligation to apply the provisions of the Convention in good faith encompasses the obligation to co-operate in questions of minority rights. It seems, then, more logical to take the opposite stance with regard to the one presented previously. The principles of good neighbourliness, friendly relations, and co-operation between states do not pose restrictions on this international instrument for the protection of minorities. Instead, attempts to achieve good international relations with neighbouring countries, and the aim of establishing an effective international protection system for minorities, are mutually supportive. This conclusion also corresponds to the traditional position in both legal literature and practice where the protection of minority rights fulfils, *inter alia*, an important role in international security politics.[15]

With regard to state practice on this specific provision of the Framework Convention, it should be noted that several parties have tried to demonstrate their adherence to this obligation, referring to bilateral and multilateral treaties they have concluded to assure further protective measures to minorities.[16] A few words should also be said with regard to a national legislative measure that has given rise to an international dispute: the so-called Hungarian Status Law.[17] This law, which entered into force in 2002, granted particular benefits to people in neighbouring countries deemed to be of Hungarian ethnicity. These benefits were fairly broad and were partly directed at fostering the Hungarian language and culture. At the core of the law was the assumption that the Hungarian nation comprised fifteen million people of which only ten million were living within the boundaries of the Republic of Hungary. Special measures of affirmative action exercised on a transborder level were meant to keep the bonds between the members of this nation alive. The way this aim was pursued, however, stirred up emotional reactions in the neighbouring

[15] A. S. Åkermark, *Justifications of Minority Protection in International Law* (Kluwer Law International, London, 1997), 69.

[16] See, for example, Albania State Report, ACFC/SR (2001) 5, 2001 and the Ireland State Report, ACFC/SR (2001) 6, 2001.

[17] 'Act LXII of 2001on Hungarians Living in Neighbouring Countries' ('Status Law'), Hungarian Parliament, 2001 'on Hungarians living in neighbouring States'.

countries, as it was perceived to be a violation of their national sovereignty. In particular, the actions of Hungarian community organizations that sought to confirm the Hungarian ethnicity of membership applicants seemed to verge on the exercise of sovereign powers on foreign territory. This was also the view of the Council of Europe Commission for 'Democracy through Law' (Venice Commission), from which the Romanian and Hungarian governments had requested an opinion on this issue. The European Commission raised other matters in their monitoring activities during the accession process, primarily regarding discrimination on the basis of ethnicity. This was considered in view of the principle of non-discrimination under EC law and doubts were raised about the proportionality of these measures. Finally, as international pressure mounted in June 2003 the Status Law was significantly modified in order to address criticism. As the modifications to both the extraterritorial and the discriminatory elements largely eliminated the problem, the matter seemed to have been solved, even though the neighbouring countries and the European Commission remained wary with regard to the announced implementation of the legislation. On the whole, the Hungarian Status Law provides an illustrative example of the difficulties a kin state can face when it tries to act in favour of its related minorities in neighbouring countries. It could be argued that the principles set out in Article 2 of the Framework Convention provide fundamental criteria for the reconciliation of the many diverse interests that come into play.[18]

E. Clawback Clauses

The issue of good faith in a broader sense is of particular relevance to the so-called clawback clauses that are dispersed over the entire text of the Framework Convention. These clauses, worded as, or beginning with, 'where necessary'; 'without prejudice to'; 'within the framework of the national legal system'; 'if those persons [that is to say, persons belonging to national

[18] In a press statement of 24 June 2003, the office of the High Commissioner on National Minorities of the OSCE, declared:

'I note that the Act on Hungarians Living in Neighbouring Countries has tended to strain otherwise good relations between Hungary and some of its neighbours. In the spirit of friendly relations, earlier and fuller consultations and better use of existing bilateral instruments and mechanisms might have reduced misunderstandings about the intentions behind the Act.

One can conclude that the deliberations in relation to the Act have demonstrated the importance of the principle that protection of human rights and fundamental freedoms, including for persons belonging to national minorities, is the responsibility of the State having jurisdiction with regard to the persons concerned.'

This statement seems to correspond perfectly to the philosophy behind Art. 2 FCNM.

minorities] so request and where such request corresponds to a real need'; 'as far as possible'; 'where appropriate'; and 'when there is sufficient demand', seem to limit the rights previously granted by the parties. It would be wrong, however, to interpret the Framework Convention as a system of unilateral, spontaneous concessions in regard to which a sufficient number of safeguards have to be introduced to protect the interests of the states parties. Rather, it is the provisions of the Framework Convention which form a legal system with a certain autonomy characteristic of any treaty-based system. Therefore, the limitations included in this treaty have to be interpreted on the basis of this treaty's overall aims, and in the immediate interests of the states parties. The application of the principle of good faith interprets any limitation included in the Framework Convention from the viewpoint of all parties involved, as well as from the perspective of the members of minorities. Interpreted in this way, the clawback clauses further demonstrate that the protection of minorities, as it is understood by the Framework Convention, has also been introduced in the interest of the adhering states parties.

III. Conclusion and Outlook

In conclusion, the provision in Article 2 of the Framework Convention is of enormous importance in elucidating the aim and effect of an otherwise sober and prudent text and acts as a potential source for dynamic, evolutive interpretations of the Convention. With regard to law-making in a stricter sense, Article 2 can be interpreted as an invitation to the single parties to conclude specific, further-reaching agreements on particular minority issues.

ARTICLE 3

Hans-Joachim Heintze

1. Every person belonging to a national minority shall have the right freely to choose to be treated or not to be treated as such and no disadvantage shall result from this choice or from the exercise of the rights which are connected to that choice.
2. Persons belonging to national minorities may exercise the rights and enjoy the freedoms flowing from the principles enshrined in the present framework Convention individually as well as in community with others.

Article 3(1)

I. Background

A. Issues

The Ad Hoc Committee for the Protection of National Minorities (CAHMIN) discussed the right to choose freely to belong to a national minority relatively late in the drafting process of the Framework Convention for the Protection of National Minorities (FCNM).[1] Some experts preferred a provision that linked the 'free choice element' to the exercise of the rights and freedoms of persons belonging to national minorities. Others favoured a provision guaranteeing the free choice between belonging or not belonging to a national minority. Nonetheless, most experts identified certain objective elements that could be used in determining whether or not a person belongs to a national minority in relation to some of the groups in question. At the same time, it was felt that no attempt should be made to define those objective elements. Furthermore, there was consensus on the need to state that no disadvantage should arise from the 'free choice' guaranteed under this provision.

B. History

The first preliminary draft of the European Commission for Democracy through Law (ECDL) of a Convention on the Protection of Minorities considered minority rights to be collective rights.[2] The switch from a collective formulation to an individual one had taken place during the elaboration of the 'Draft Protocol to the European Convention on Human Rights guaranteeing the protection of ethnic groups' in the Steering Committee for Human Rights (CDDH).[3] Put forward by the Austrian Delegation, this Draft Protocol proposal contained provisions that were similar to Article 3 FCNM and consisted

[1] Ad Hoc Committee for the Protection of National Minorities (CAHMIN), 3rd meeting, CAHMIN (94), Meeting Report, 1994.

[2] European Commission for Democracy through Law (ECDL), Preliminary Draft Convention on the Protection of Minorities, DAJ.SC.DEMOCRACYCON.MIN, 1990, Art. 4: 'For the purposes of this Convention, "minority" shall mean a group which is smaller in number than the rest of the population of a State, is not in a dominating position, and whose members have ethnical, religious or linguistic features different from those of the rest of the population, feel solidarity with each other, are guided by the will to safeguard their culture, traditions, religion or languages and aim at equality in facts and in law with the majority.'

[3] Steering Committee for Human Rights (CDDH), Draft Protocol to the European Convention on Human Rights Guaranteeing the Protection of Ethnic Groups Prepared by the Austrian Delegation, CDDH (91) 46, 1991.

of two paragraphs: '(1) To belong to an ethnic group is a matter of a person's individual choice; (2) No disadvantage may arise from the exercise of such choice.' This formulation, focusing on the rights of the individual, was later adopted by the Parliamentarian Assembly of the Council of Europe (CoE) in its Recommendation 1201 and by the ECDL in its proposal for a European Convention for the protection of national minorities.[4] Support for such a statement can be found in the Copenhagen Declaration of the Conference for Security and Co-operation in Europe (CSCE), which declared that to belong to a national minority was a matter of individual choice and no disadvantage should arise from the exercise of that choice.

Although not specifically stated, the text of the aforementioned proposals implies that this principle also applies to the right to choose not to belong to a minority.[5] The Final Activity Report of the CDDH for the attention of the Committee of Ministers[6] also adopted the individually based approach to minority protection, offering different options to formulate the wording to this end.[7] The 1994 Revised Fundamental Rights of Persons belonging to Ethnic Groups in Europe (FUEN) Draft for an Additional Protocol to the ECHR (Revised FUEN Draft) 1994, had the same starting point. It was, nevertheless, surprising that draft Article 3 pleaded for a stronger involvement of the state: '[t]o belong to an ethnic group shall be a matter of individual choice and no disadvantage may arise from the exercise of such choice. The *State Parties undertake* to create the legal, political, cultural and social conditions for such free choice.'[8]

C. Context

Other international instruments contain provisions similar to those contained in Article 3(1) FCNM. The CSCE Copenhagen Document, for example,

[4] ECDL, Proposal for a European Convention for the Protection of National Minorities, CDL-MIN (93) 6, 1993, Art. 2: 'To belong to a national minority shall be a matter of individual choice and no disadvantage may arise from the exercise of such choice.'

[5] CAHMIN, Explanatory Report on the Framework Convention for the Protection of National Minorities, CAHMIN H(1995) 010, 1995, CDL-MIN (93) 7, 1993.

[6] (CDDH), Final Activity Report of the CDDH for the Attention of the Committee of Ministers, CDDH (93) 22, 1993.

[7] Option A: 'An individual shall have the right to choose to be treated as a member of a national minority (to which he belongs) or not, and no disadvantage shall arise from the exercise of that choice.' Option B: 'To belong to a national minority, or to refuse to belong to such a minority, shall be a matter of individual choice freely made and no disadvantage may/shall result from such choice or the renunciation of such choice.'

[8] Fundamental Rights of Persons belonging to Ethnic Groups in Europe (FUEN), Draft for an Additional Protocol to the ECHR (Revised FUEN Draft), 1994. Emphasis added.

determines that 'belonging to a national minority' is a matter of individual choice and that no disadvantage may arise from the exercise of such choice. It adds that no disadvantage may arise for a person belonging to a national minority on account of the exercise or non-exercise of these rights.[9] Concerning the different ways in which individuals are identified as members of a particular racial or ethnic group, the Committee on the Elimination of Racial Discrimination (CERD) stated that such identification should, if no justification existed to the contrary, be based upon self-identification by the individual concerned.[10]

The UN Declaration on the Rights of Persons Belonging to National or Ethnic, Religious, or Linguistic Minorities demands that no disadvantage should result for any person belonging to a minority as a consequence of the exercise or non-exercise of the rights it sets forth. The interpretation of this obligation by the Working Group on Minorities of the Sub-Commission on the Promotion and Protection of Human Rights found that this provision was directed towards both the state and the bodies representing the minority group.[11] The state could not impose a particular ethnic identity on a person through the use of negative sanctions against those who do not wish to be part of that group; nor could persons belonging to minorities be subject to any disadvantage. Some persons, on objective criteria and through the interpretation of others, may be included as part of a group, but may not wish to be identified as such. Under conventional law, responsibility for human rights compliance usually rests with the state; however, the UN Declaration implies duties—at least morally—for persons representing minorities in this respect. Furthermore, states are obliged to prohibit minorities from taking measures imposing their particular rules on persons who do not wish to be part of the minority concerned and, therefore, do not wish to exercise their rights.

In contrast to minority protection, instruments relating to the protection of indigenous peoples not only require persons to identify themselves as indigenous or tribal, but also demand that those persons meet other criteria, such as: descent from the population which inhabited the country or a part of it at the time of the conquest, colonization, or establishment of present state boundaries;

[9] Second Conference on the Human Dimension of the CSCE, Document of the Copenhagen Meeting of the Conference on the Human Dimension of the CSCE, Copenhagen, 1990 **www.osce.org/docs/english/1990-1999/hd/cope90e.htm** 21 July 2004.

[10] Committee On the Elimination of Racial Discrimination (CERD), General Recommendation 8, 38th session, 1990, UN Doc. A/45/18 at 79 (1991), Art. 1, paras. 1 and 4.

[11] P. Thornberry, 'The UN Declaration on the Rights of Persons Belonging to National or Ethnic, Religious or Linguistic Minorities: Background, Analysis, Observations, and an Update', in A. Phillips and, A. Rosas (eds.), *Universal Minority Rights* (Åbo, Åbo Akademi University Institute, 1995), 13–76 at 46.

and, irrespective of legal status, that they retain some or all of their own social, economic, cultural, and political institutions.[12]

Within the FCNM there is an obvious overlap between Article 1 and Articles 3(1) and 3(2), especially as concerns the definition (or absence thereof) of the term minority.

The following elements will be analysed here: (i) the definition issue in the practice of the Advisory Committee; (ii) the freedom of every person to elect or to decline to belong to a national minority; and (iii) the collection of demographic data by government agencies.

II. Analysis

A. The Definition Issue and the Implementation of the FCNM

The rulings of international treaty bodies demonstrate the irrelevance of detailed definitions. Concerning the implementation of Article 27 of the International Covenant on Civil and Political Rights (ICCPR), in case law the Human Rights Committee has held that it applies not only to persons belonging to ethnic, religious, or linguistic minorities but also to indigenous peoples in Canada, Scandinavia, and New Zealand. Persons belonging to indigenous peoples may be understood as belonging to an ethnic, religious, or linguistic minority for the purposes of enjoying the rights mentioned in Article 27.

The Advisory Committee has followed the same approach as the Human Rights Committee. It has underlined that the parties must determine the scope of application in the absence of a definition in the FCNM itself. This means that in the opinion of the Advisory Committee on the one hand, parties are granted a certain margin of appreciation accounting for the specific circumstances prevailing in their country. On the other hand, this must be exercised in accordance with the general principles of international law and fundamental principles as set out in Article 3. In particular, the Advisory Committee stresses that the implementation of the FCNM should not be a source of arbitrary or unjustified distinctions. This understanding of the states parties' obligations follows the line of some scholars: 'States should . . . not be able, by way of unilateral declarations or reservations which seem to go against the very

[12] S. Marquardt, 'International Law and Indigenous Peoples', *International Journal on Group Rights*, 3 (1995), 47–76 at 66.

object and purpose of the exercise, to withhold protection by denying the existence of a minority.'[13]

For this reason, the Advisory Committee examines whether the personal scope adopted by the states parties regarding the implementation of the FCNM does not lead to arbitrary or unjustified distinctions as part of its duty. Furthermore, it considers that it must verify the proper application of the fundamental principles set out in Article 3. In their instruments of ratification, many states explicitly declared that the FCNM contained no definition of the notion of national minorities. As a consequence, they argued that it was up to the individual contracting parties to determine after ratification to which groups it applies.[14] This means it is up to national legislation to define who belongs to a national minority and who is protected by the FCNM, thereby giving individual states the authority to define the scope of application. This provides obvious opportunities for the states parties to include groups that do not fall within the 'traditional' understanding of the term 'national minorities'. In Switzerland, for example, the FCNM has been applied not only to national linguistic minorities, but also to other minority groups of the Swiss population, such as members of the Jewish community and travellers. This demonstrates the irrelevance of labels for the protection of persons belonging to minority groups in need of protection. Some bodies have welcomed the enlarged scope of the definition. The Advisory Committee appreciated 'the inclusive approach' of the United Kingdom in its interpretation of the term 'national minority'. In the UK the scope of the FCNM is based on the broad 'conventional' definition of 'racial group' as set out in the Race Relations Act (1976). Under this Act, 'racial group' is defined as 'a group of persons defined by colour, race, nationality (including citizenship) or ethnic or national origin', including ethnic minority communities. The courts have furthermore interpreted the term and found it to include the Scots, Irish, and Welsh by virtue of their national origin. On a case-by-case basis the courts have also included Roma/Gypsies as well as Irish Travellers (also defined as a racial group for the purposes of the Race Relations (Northern Ireland) Order (1997)), Sikhs, and Jews. The UK's inclusive approach may raise issues of inequalities between groups, however. Jews and Sikhs are mentioned in the decision, while Muslims and other religious groups are not. Even in the UK,

[13] G. Alfredsson, 'A Framework with an Incomplete Picture: Comparison of the Framework Convention for the Protection of National Minorities with International Standards and Monitoring Procedures', *International Journal of Minority and Group Rights*, 7 (2000), 291–304 at 296.

[14] Such declarations were presented by Austria, Belgium, Denmark, Estonia, Germany, Luxembourg, Poland, Slovenia, Switzerland, and Macedonia.

it seems that the lack of definition leaves room for the arbitrary exclusion of certain minorities from the FCNM's scope of application.

The validity of such declarations, therefore, needs to be raised in the light of international treaty law. Without a doubt, general state practice is confusing, with reactions and objections against reservations (or declarations) submitted in unco-ordinated ways and lacking any consistent follow up.[15] Ambiguity also persists over the authority allowed to determine the validity of a reservation. Faced with this uncertainty, scholars argued that with human rights treaties, the rule is that respective treaty bodies have the power to decide on the validity of reservations. This means that, in this case, the Advisory Committee rules on the validity of reservations.[16] Practice shows that the Advisory Committee has not automatically rubber-stamped the declarations and reservations made by the states parties. The Committee examined the declarations and reservations '*inter alia* in order to ensure that they are in line with the general principles of international law and that they are not discriminatory'.[17] In cases where the Advisory Committee has found that another approach could be beneficial, it has not rushed into declaring that a particular community be considered a national minority. Instead, it has urged the state party concerned to discuss this question with the groups involved. As of the end of 2003, ten states parties to the FCNM had added declarations concerning the scope of the Convention to their instruments of ratification. These declarations may be divided into three groups.[18]

The first type defines a national minority using abstract criteria found in national law. For instance, Austria has interpreted the term according to national legislation. Estonia, Luxembourg, and Switzerland have used specific, but abstract criteria to identify national minorities. Non-exhaustively, these include: (i) numerical inferiority to the rest of the population (Switzerland); (ii) requirements for members to be residents of the country (Estonia, Luxembourg, Austria, Poland); (iii) requirements for members to have long-standing, firm, and lasting ties with the state (Estonia, Luxembourg, Austria); (iv) citizenship requirements (Estonia, Luxembourg, Poland); (v) distinct ethnic, cultural, religious, or linguistic identity (Estonia, Luxembourg, Austria); and (vi) motivation to maintain the common culture that currently exists (Estonia).

[15] B. Simma, 'Reservations to Human Rights Treaties—Some Recent Developments', in G. Haffner et al. (eds.), *Liber Amicorum Ignaz Seidl-Hohnveldern* (Carl Heymanns, Cologne, 1998), 664.

[16] J. A. Frowein and R. Bank, 'The Effect of Member States' Declarations Defining "National Minorities" upon Signature or Ratification of the Council of Europe's Framework Convention', *ZaöRV Heidelberg Journal of International Law*, 59/3 (1999), 649.

[17] R. Hofmann, The Framework Convention at the end of the first cycle of monitoring, Filling the Frame, 5th anniversary of the entering into force of the Framework Convention for the Protection of National Minorities, Opening plenary, Strasbourg, 2003, p. 4.

[18] Above, n. 16, p. 673.

The second type clearly identifies national minorities that fall within the scope of the FCNM. States having adopted this approach are: Denmark, Germany, FYR Macedonia, Slovenia, and Sweden. Some states parties offer detailed criteria for the identification of those minorities that are protected. Sweden, for example, has highlighted: (i) *self-identification*—the individual and also the group should have the desire and ambition to retain their identity. Groups with this aim should also occupy a numerically inferior position in society, in relation to the remainder of the population. The determination of the group cannot only be made according to the number of persons within the group, but the strength of the structure and cohesion/unity of the group must also be taken into account; (ii) *religious, linguistic, traditional, and/or cultural belonging*—only one of the listed characteristic features needs to exist, but those that the group demonstrates must distinguish it from the majority in some essential respect; (iii) *historical or long-standing bonds with Sweden*—the government does not consider it possible to determine a limit measured in years. Minority groups whose culture existed in Sweden prior to the twentieth century are generally seen to satisfy this requirement. Some state party declarations of this type include certain groups which, in their opinion, do not constitute national minorities. Germany, for instance, applies this principle with regard to Frisians, as well as to Sinti and Roma, while Slovenia invokes it with regard to Roma. Sweden applies the convention to Sami, Swedish Finns, Tornedalers, Roma, and Jews. Finland made no declaration upon ratification, but in its report it informed the Advisory Committee that the Government Bill for the acceptance of the provisions of the FCNM[19] minorities would read: '. . . at least the Sami, the Roma, the Jews, the Tatars and the so-called Old Russians and *de facto* also the Swedish-speaking Finns will be recognised as minorities for the purposes of the FCNM and therefore enjoy the protection offered by this Convention.' According to the Finnish report, there are other minority groups, including various immigrant groups, that do not fall within the scope of the FCNM. The largest of these are: Russians, Estonians, and Somalis.

States adopting the third type of declaration simply state that there are no national minorities within their territory (Liechtenstein,[20] Malta,[21] and San Marino[22]). Liechtenstein's defence for its membership in the FCNM is an interesting case. It considers its ratification of the FCNM an act of solidarity highlighting its sympathies with the objectives of the Convention.

19 Finland State Report, ACFC/SR (99) 3, 1999.
20 Liechtenstein State Report, ACFC/SR (99) 4, 1999.
21 Malta State Report, ACFC/SR (99) 12, 1999.
22 San Marino State Report, ACFC/SR (99) 1, 1999.

The Advisory Committee, however, expects some consideration of other groups that the government has not considered, at this stage, to be covered by the Convention. Neither Malta nor San Marino submitted any comprehensive information at all. In the absence of this information, and given the limited information obtained from other sources, the Advisory Committee has not been in a position to assess the statement of the Maltese and San Marinian authorities. Other states parties, including Ireland,[23] argue that there is no need for any minority legislation due to their relatively homogeneous population. However, there are many cases in which the Advisory Committee has advised that it would be possible to consider the inclusion of persons belonging to groups which are not recognized as minorities as such, including non-citizens, as appropriate in their application of the FCNM on an article-by-article basis, and has recommended that the authorities consider this issue in consultation with those concerned at some appropriate time in the future.

The decision to define the scope of beneficiaries by formal declarations was accepted by all states parties, with one exception. The Russian Federation explicitly rejected the right of states parties to define national minorities:

> The Russian Federation considers that none is entitled to include unilaterally in reservations or declarations, made while signing or ratifying the Framework Convention for the Protection of National Minorities, a definition of the term 'national minority', which is not contained in the Framework Convention. In the opinion of the Russian Federation, attempts to exclude from the scope of the Framework Convention the persons who permanently reside in the territory of States Parties to the Framework Convention and previously had a citizenship but have been arbitrarily deprived of it, contradict the purpose of the Framework Convention for the Protection of National Minorities.[24]

Without expressly saying so, it was obvious that the Russian declaration was aimed at the situation of the Russian minority in Estonia. The Advisory Committee did not react directly to the Russian statement; however, one may say that there was an indirect reaction by the Advisory Committee. In its general remarks on Estonia, the Committee argued that further efforts were needed to make naturalization more accessible, bearing in mind the high number of stateless persons and the fact that the lack of citizenship often had a detrimental impact on the enjoyment of full and effective equality.[25]

[23] There is no definition of the notion of 'national minority' under Irish law nor is there an enumeration in law of groups which are recognized as national minorities. Cf. Ireland State Report, ACFC/SR (2001) 6, 2001.

[24] Russian Federation State Report, ACFC/SR (99) 15, 2000.

[25] Advisory Committee on the Framework Convention for the Protection of National Minorities, Opinion on Estonia, ACFC/INF/OP/I (2002) 005, 2001, para. 69.

Even when accounting for the Russian declaration and the subsequent practice of the Advisory Committee, the legal status of the declarations remains questionable. It seems clear that according to general international treaty law, the states parties are allowed to interpret their obligations under the FCNM. This right cannot be denied. Therefore, the Russian declaration, which unilaterally rejects the right of states parties to define the term national minority, cannot be imposed on other states parties. Still, the exclusion of certain minority groups from the scope of application of the FCNM through declarations has to be considered a reservation contrary to the purpose of the Convention.[26]

The question of the definition of national minorities also played an important role in connection with the state reports, particularly in the case of Denmark. It declared that the FCNM applied only to the German minority in South Jutland, restricting the Convention's application. Consequently, the Advisory Committee argued that 'the personal scope of application of the Framework Convention in Denmark, limited to the German minority in Southern Jutland has not been satisfactorily addressed'. It noted, in particular, that persons belonging to other groups with long-standing historic ties to Denmark such as Faeroese and Greenlanders seem to have been excluded a priori from protection under the Framework Convention. The same applies to Roma, despite their historic presence in Denmark. The Committee considered this approach to be incompatible with the FCNM and argued that a limited territorial application, leading to the a priori exclusion of certain groups, was not consistent with the Framework Convention. The Advisory Committee, therefore, advised that Denmark should consult with concerned parties and re-examine the scope of application of the Framework Convention.[27]

This Advisory Committee response was rejected by the Danish government, which argued that Denmark's ratification of the Convention was based on the view that neither the FCNM, nor any other international instruments in the field of minorities, contained a definition of the notion of national minority, thus leaving it to the participating states to determine the content of the notion through actual practice. Denmark further contended that in order to define the term 'national minority' one needed to apply general rules of treaty interpretation. Both the history and the aim of the FCNM needed to be taken into account in this case. According to the Preamble of the Convention, the Convention is essential because the upheavals of European history have shown that the protection of national minorities is crucial to maintain political

[26] Above, n. 16, p. 668.

[27] Advisory Committee Opinion on Denmark, ACFC/INF/OP/I (2001) 005, 1999, para. 39.

stability in Europe. Moreover, several parts of the Convention assert that the implementation of the principles of the Convention applies to transfrontier co-operation between local and regional authorities, meaning that the Convention contains certain territorial limitations.[28] In the final section of its comments, the Committee of Ministers drew the conclusion that the personal scope of application of the FCNM merited further consideration by the government of Denmark in consultation with those concerned. Legal scholars often argue that this kind of geographical limitation plainly violates the object and purpose of the FCNM since the goal of protecting the identity of a person belonging to a national minority cannot be limited solely to those persons living in their traditional area.[29]

Another conceptual question is whether indigenous peoples fall into the scope of the FCNM. The Advisory Committee dealt with this issue in connection with the Norwegian report. Norway offers the Sami protection without using the term national minority, arguing that this approach reflects the applicability of the FCNM to indigenous peoples. Furthermore, the Norwegian argument is consistent with views expressed by the Sami Parliament regarding the applicability of the Norwegian policy for national minorities to the persons belonging to this indigenous people.[30] From a legal theoretical perspective, one has to argue that indigenous peoples can, at times, constitute minorities and, therefore, fall within the scope of the FCNM. However, they remain a distinct category due to their relative economic and social underdevelopment and their right to follow their own customs and traditions to a certain extent. There is, furthermore, an obligation to respect their sustained historical continuity with the land that pre-dates the arrival of the dominant population of the state party to the FCNM.[31]

Undoubtedly, the rights of indigenous peoples are not properly addressed in the FCNM. The main instrument at the global level relating to indigenous peoples is the International Labour Organization (ILO) Convention No. 169 concerning Indigenous and Tribal Peoples in Independent Countries. It should, therefore, be welcome that the Norwegian report speaks about 'national minorities and indigenous populations'. This approach reflects the will of indigenous peoples who consider themselves more than minorities. Norway

[28] Comments of the Government of Denmark on the Opinion of the Advisory Committee on the Implementation of the Framework Convention for the Protection of National Minorities in Denmark, GVT/COM/INF/OP/I (2001) 005, 2001.

[29] Above, n. 16, p. 669.

[30] Advisory Committee Opinion on Norway, ACFC/INFO/OP/I (2003) 003, 2002, para. 9.

[31] M. N. Shaw, 'The Definition of Minorities in International Law', *Israel Yearbook on Human Rights*, 20 (1991), 28.

chose not to make a declaration of the personal scope of the FCNM partly because such a declaration could be regarded as a limitation of the scope of the Convention. Another reason was that it might give rise to unintended reactions among persons belonging to the groups in question. During preparations for the ratification of the FCNM, the Norwegian Sami Parliament clearly stated that the Sami did not wish to be included in the declaration, since they preferred to maintain their status as an indigenous people and to protect the strengthened legal status that has been achieved for indigenous peoples through the ILO Convention No. 169. Nevertheless, the Advisory Committee argued that the protection of the FCNM remains available to the Sami. This ensures that persons belonging to this indigenous people can still choose to rely on the protection that the FCNM provides if they wish and further guarantees that the treaties designed for indigenous peoples are not construed as mutually exclusive regimes. Similar problems arose concerning the Crimean Tatars in the Ukraine, whose representatives preferred to use the term 'indigenous people'. The Advisory Committee shared the view held by the government, and a number of representatives of the Crimean Tatars, that the recognition of a group as an indigenous people did not exclude persons belonging to that group from the benefits of protection offered by the FCNM.

This ICCPR practice demonstrates that the issue of indigenous peoples pushed the boundaries of minority rights forward. Most of the cases under the Optional Protocol to Article 27 ICCPR concern indigenous peoples, for example.[32] Denmark's viewpoint differs, however. It holds the view that the citizens of Greenland and the Faeroe Islands are covered by Article 1 ICCPR and cannot be characterized simultaneously as minorities under Article 27. This means that the recognition of a group of persons as *an indigenous people* or *a people* excludes the possibility of their benefiting from protection as a 'national minority' at the same time. The Advisory Committee does not share this view, however. The fact that a group of persons may be entitled to a different form of protection cannot, by itself, justify their exclusion from other forms of protection.

B. The Freedom to Choose to be Treated or not as a Person Belonging to a National Minority

The principle of self-identification of persons belonging to minorities is part of the more general freedom of individuals to self-ascription. This choice is necessary to ensure respect for individual autonomy and liberty. An individual

[32] *Sandra Lovelace* v. *Canada*, Comm. No. 24/1977, 1981, UN Doc. CCPR/C/OP/1, 83, 1984.

may possess several identities that coexist in the private and public spheres. In modern societies, where persons are changing places to a greater extent, many persons have multiple identities that coincide, coexist, or form layers, reflecting their various associations. However, identities are not based solely on ethnicity, nor are they uniform within the same community. Identity can be held by different members to varying degrees and can be more or less salient. This means that the same person might identify herself or himself in different ways for different purposes, depending upon the relevance of identification and arrangement for her or him in a particular situation or context. In the literature on this subject one can find some pertinent examples: a person may choose a certain language for submitting tax forms, yet identify herself or himself differently in a local community for other purposes.[33] This example reflects the freedom of choice—a principle that is fundamental in the field of minority protection.

The freedom of the individual members of a national minority to decide for themselves whether they wish to be associated with a certain national minority, and, therefore, choose to be treated as belonging to that particular national minority, is a fundamental element of the protection of national minorities based on democratic principles. Nobody may be forced against his or her will, either directly or indirectly, to identify him or herself as a member of a national minority. Thus, every person belonging to a national minority can decide for him- or herself whether he or she wishes to be included in the category of persons for whose protection and promotion states need to take measures in compliance with the FCNM. Most legal decisions respect this principle.

The practice of most FCNM states parties corresponds to the principle of self-identification. In Germany, for example, it is each individual's own decision whether he or she chooses to be considered a member of any of the groups protected under the FCNM,[34] and this is neither registered, reviewed, nor contested by the German authorities. In the Czech Republic, '[a]ny form of influencing this choice is prohibited, just as any form or pressure aimed at suppressing one's national identity'.[35] The only exception to general acceptance is Article 2 of the Cypriot Constitution. It lays down the obligation of religious groups and their members to adhere either to the Greek Cypriot or the Turkish Cypriot community. Furthermore, it is impossible for Turkish

[33] Foundation on Interethnic Relations, the Lund Recommendations on the Effective Participation of National Minorities in Public Life and Explanatory Note, The Hague, 1999, I, 4.

[34] Germany State Report, ACFC/SR (2000) 1, 2000, para. 2.

[35] Czech National Council, Charter of Fundamental Rights and Freedoms, 2/1993, Art. 3, para. 2, quoted in Czech Republic State Report ACFC/SR (99) 006, 2001, para. 1.

Cypriots to vote or to celebrate civil marriages with Greek Cypriots. Such obligations and restrictions are not compatible with Article 3 FCNM according to the Advisory Committee.[36] Thus, the Committee of Ministers found the legal obligation of persons belonging to religious groups to elect their representatives to be incompatible with Article 3 and, consequently, recommended that the Cyprus government address the issue.[37]

Most states parties to the FCNM have passed national legislation offering protection to groups that meet some criteria and, therefore, can be regarded as a national, or other, minority. In general, there are three categories of problems with the national legislation in the field of minority rights that can be identified:

1. *The nomination of minorities by governments is at variance with the feelings of persons belonging to minorities*

In some cases, one can identify differences between the opinions of governments nominating minorities and the feelings of persons belonging to these minorities. In order to counterbalance the tensions that this difference of opinion can sometimes create, statements by persons belonging to minority groups are taken very seriously by the Advisory Committee, and constitute an inherent part in the evaluations. According to its mandate, the Advisory Committee has the right to carry out fact-finding activities; in other words it may hold consultations with different groups or communities living within the jurisdiction of the states parties. During such consultations the Advisory Committee has learnt that members of certain communities are not satisfied with their qualification under domestic law. The problems are partly connected to the assumption that communities do not have a kin state. Thus, the Albanian authorities recognize Greeks as a national minority group, while their Macedonian and Montenegrin counterparts identify the Roma and Aromanians/Vlachs as linguistic minorities. The Roma and Aromanians/Vlachs, however, consider the term 'linguistic minority' insufficient in its reflection of the essential elements of their identity, one that they see extending beyond a purely linguistic connotation.[38] Therefore, the Advisory Committee has encouraged the government, in consultation with those concerned, to re-examine the question of

[36] Advisory Committee Opinion on Cyprus, ACFC/INF/OP/I(2002) 002, 2001, para. 21.

[37] Committee of Ministers, ResCMN (2002) 3 on the Implementation of the Framework Convention for the Protection of National Minorities by Cyprus, Council of Europe (CoE), 784th meeting, 2002.

[38] Advisory Committee Opinion on Albania, ACFC/INF/OP/I (2003) 004, para. 20.

the designation 'linguistic minority'. It held the same view concerning the Maronites and Latins in Cyprus,[39] where many persons belonging to these communities were not satisfied with the term 'religious group' as they also shared a specific ethnic origin.

Concerning the UK, the Advisory Committee noted the contradiction between the government's position not to consider the people of Cornwall a national minority and that of numerous persons living in Cornwall who consider themselves a national minority within the scope of the FCNM. These people referred to their Celtic identity, specific history, distinct language, and culture, all of which are criteria set out in the FCNM.[40] In connection with the new census in Britain, the Advisory Committee noted that some persons concerned in this census regretted that they did not have the possibility to declare their affiliation with a particular group (including the Welsh, Cornish, Ulster-Scots, and Roma/Gypsies), even though 'Other' was a choice of affiliation that was listed to mitigate the problem. For its part, the Advisory Committee considered that there should be greater clarity on possible affiliations that are available.[41] As an example to follow in this area, a Welsh publicity campaign was organized to increase public awareness of this option and to further explain affiliation options.

The Advisory Committee has often expressed doubts regarding government assertions that certain groups are well integrated into the majority of the population. Contradicting these viewpoints, persons belonging to minority communities generally make it clear to the Advisory Committee that they prefer to be recognized as a national minority. In this respect, the Advisory Committee notes that persons belonging to these communities define themselves according to their ethnic background, their stated historical roots, their traditions, and their cultural heritage. The Advisory Committee considers that an a priori exclusion of minority group opinions is not compatible with the FCNM and encourages governments, in consultation with those concerned, to re-examine the question of possible designations as a national minority.[42]

The Advisory Committee is especially assertive regarding the a priori exclusion of persons belonging to minority groups by governments and its incompatibility with the FCNM. Denmark's a priori exclusion of Greenlanders

[39] Cyprus State Report, ACFC/SR (99) 2 Ref., 1999, para. 17.

[40] United Kingdom State Report, ACFC/SR (99) 13, 1999, para. 18.

[41] Above, n. 40.

[42] See the Albanian State Report, ACFC/SR (2001) 5, 2001, para. 21 with regards to the Egyptian community in Albania, or the Romanian State Report, ACFC/SR (99) 11 Prov, 1999, para. 18 with respect to the Csango community in Romania.

and Faeroese from the scope of the FCNM is a salient case. Here, the Advisory Committee recommended that the authorities examine the application of the FCNM to these persons, notwithstanding and in addition to any home rule arrangements. During its visit to Denmark, the Committee delegation noted a considerable interest in this matter among the communities concerned.[43] Similarly, persons belonging to the German minority, but living outside the area of Southern Jutland, cannot be excluded a priori from the personal scope of protection of the FCNM.[44] The Advisory Committee made a similar declaration when it took the historic presence of Roma in Denmark into account. Persons belonging to this community cannot be excluded a priori from the scope of application either.[45]

Nonetheless, it is sometimes complicated to identify the collective will of groups that may be considered as minorities. One such group is the Polish community in Austria. Some representatives of this group expressed interest in the possibility of protection under the Austrian Law on Ethnic Groups. After investigating the circumstances that led to the constitution and continuing presence of a Polish community in Austria, however, the federal authorities considered such protection to be inappropriate. They subsequently communicated this decision to the persons concerned, but the latter did not respond to the ruling within the time frame allowed.[46] Similar problems arose in Finland. Representatives of the Swedish Assembly in Finland informed the Advisory Committee that they considered the Swedish-speaking Finns did not constitute a national minority within the scope of the FCNM. Concurrently, a number of persons belonging to this same minority group informed the Advisory Committee that they wished to rely on the protection provided by the FCNM. In its report, the government acknowledged that the Swedish-speaking Finns were de facto covered by the FCNM, leading the Advisory Committee to conclude that Swedish-speaking Finns may indeed rely on the protection of the FCNM.[47]

This de facto approach is common in state practice worldwide. It supports the conclusion that the use of the term minority is not required for the incorporation of international standards of minority protection into domestic law. Some states 'have found it useful to avoid or do away with the term "minority" since, due to locally prevailing understandings or historical reasons, it carries negative connotations in their societies such that its use would be

[43] Advisory Committee Opinion on Denmark, ACFC/INF/OP/I (2001) 005, 2000, para. 20.
[44] Above, n. 43, para. 21. [45] ibid., para. 22.
[46] Austria State Report, ACFC/SR (2000) 3, 2000, para. 19.
[47] Advisory Committee Opinion on Finland, ACFC/INF/OP/I (2001) 002, 2001, para. 16.

confusing, counter-productive or ineffective, and thus, undesirable'.[48] It seems that the Advisory Committee is not ready to adopt such an approach, however, as it has only once been reluctant to use the term national minority with regard to any case it has considered. In the light of special circumstances concerning the Russian minority in the Ukraine, the Advisory Committee recommended that authorities account for the negative connotations of a national minority designation when implementing the FCNM and reflect these considerations in the terminology used.[49]

2. *Territorial Application*

In several cases, the Advisory Committee has criticized the territorial limitations to the scope of the FCNM set out by states. Concerning Albania, the Advisory Committee concluded that the application of 'minority zones', which existed both during and before the former Communist regime and covered areas where national minorities lived traditionally, was still relevant. The teaching of minority languages was a particular talking point here. It was determined, however, that further steps were needed to ensure that no undue limitations were placed on the rights of persons belonging to national minorities living outside these formerly identified 'minority zones', and that it was necessary to clarify this matter with those concerned in both governmental and non-governmental circles.[50] Concerning other states in which national minorities live in their autochthonous settlement areas, the question arose as to whether persons belonging to those minorities, while living outside of their territories, could enjoy the same rights as those who were living within that area. This issue played an important role during discussions on the Denmark home rule for Greenland and the Faeroes debate. Denmark argued that Danish Acts introduced home rule regulations for these communities on a territorially and geographically defined basis, implying that they were not based on ethnic or linguistic criteria. In this context, attention was drawn to the fact that the Faeroes were discussing their full independence with the Danish government, while Greenland was discussing an extension of its autonomy.[51] The Advisory Committee, however, argued that this population could not be excluded a priori from the FCNM because it was applicable to persons of an ethnic Danish origin, living in the home rule areas. Limitations in the territorial application of the FCNM also play a role in Denmark, as only those belonging to the German minority and living inside the area of Southern Jutland fall under the Framework Convention's

[48] OSCE High Commissioner on National Minorities, Note of 31 January 2003, p. 5 (unpublished).
[49] Advisory Committee Opinion on Ukraine, ACFC/INF/OP/I (2002) 010, 2002, para. 20.
[50] Above, n. 39, para. 24.
[51] Denmark State Report, ACFC/SR (99) 9, 1999, para. 16.

scope of protection on an individual basis. The German authorities, however, recognize members of a national minority living outside the minority's traditional settlement area as entitled to protection under the FCNM in principle, a position supported by the Advisory Committee.[52]

Existing national regulations on autonomy also play a role concerning the Finnish-speaking population living in the province of Åland, who can be considered a 'minority-in-a-minority'. Accounting for the extent of autonomy enjoyed by the Province of Åland, the Advisory Committee is of the opinion that protection provided by the FCNM could be extended to the Finnish-speaking population in these territories on issues concerning the competence of the Province of Åland.[53]

The territorial extension of the FCNM's scope for other territories that rely on states for their international relations is an issue in the United Kingdom. Here the Advisory Committee noted that the Bailiwick of Jersey requested that the UK's ratification of the FCNM be extended to include them, mentioning that this would be put forward once draft legislation had been adopted by the Island Legislature.[54]

3. The Criteria of Citizenship

The issue of citizenship plays an overwhelming role in the field of minority protection. Bearing in mind the prevailing situation of minorities in Estonia, the citizenship requirement is not well suited to this case, as a substantial proportion of persons belonging to minorities arrived in Estonia prior to the re-establishment of independence in 1991, and still do not possess Estonian citizenship. The Advisory Committee favours a more inclusive approach to the protection of national minorities than the one currently practised there.[55] Estonia is not the only example of this type of development, however. The German authorities reported the existence of other groups of about 7.49 million persons that they do not consider to be covered by the FCNM at this stage, as they are non-citizens.[56] As of now, the Advisory Committee has not received petitions to be considered a national minority from any of these groups, including both citizens and non-citizens. Yet, the Advisory Committee was of the opinion that it would be possible to consider the inclusion of persons belonging to other groups as appropriate, in the application of the FCNM on

[52] Advisory Committee Opinion on Germany, ACFC/INF/OP/I (2002) 008, 2002, para. 12.

[53] Above, n. 49, para. 18.

[54] Advisory Committee Opinion on the United Kingdom, ACFC/INF/OP/I (2002) 006, 2001, para. 19.

[55] Advisory Committee Opinion on Estonia, ACFC/INF/OP/I (99) 16, 2001, para. 17.

[56] Germany State Report, ACFC/SR (2000) 1, 2000, para. 15.

an 'article-by-article basis'. This viewpoint of the Advisory Committee was sharply rejected by Germany arguing that it set out an abstract definition of the term 'national minorities' for legal applications in the absence of objections raised by contracting states responsible for designating the groups to whom this definition applies. Germany has gone as far as to argue that there is no need for the Advisory Committee to comment on ethnic groups failing to meet one or more of the listed criteria as the Advisory Committee has already expressed its appreciation and acknowledgment of clear definitions regarding the scope of application defined by states parties.

Consequently, Germany has rejected the Committee's thoughts regarding the application of the FCNM to additional groups on an article-by-article basis, as these measures are unlikely to be valuable in the overall context of the state's relationship with these groups. Germany has argued, furthermore, that as it has already expressed in its title, the objective of the FCNM is to protect national minorities; it is not a general human rights instrument for all groups of the population differing from the majority population in one or several respects (ancestry, race, language, culture, homeland, origin, nationality, creed, religious or political beliefs, sexual preferences, for example). Members of these groups are protected by universal human rights and, insofar as they are nationals, guaranteed civil rights. The article-by-article approach would, according to the German government, not only dilute the Convention's objective of protecting national minorities, but it would also assume the risk of creating first- and second-class national minorities. That is to say that some minority groups would benefit from the protection of all rights, while others would only be granted selective rights.[57]

In Norway, citizenship requirements include no strict guidelines for 'national minorities'. The term is understood to apply to minorities with a long-term link to the country. Minority groups must be in the numerical minority and must hold a non-dominant position in society. Furthermore, they must have distinctive ethnic, linguistic, cultural, and/or religious characteristics, making them substantially different from the rest of the population of Norway. The persons concerned must also have a common will to maintain and develop their own identity. The term 'long-term connection' has not been defined, but the Norwegian authorities operate using the international norm that groups must be able to claim a minimum of one hundred years of connection with the state in question.[58] Thus, more recent immigrant groups are not deemed to be national minorities in Norway. The situation is more nuanced, however, in

[57] Germany State Report, ACFC/SR (2000) 1, 2000, para. 15.
[58] Norway State Report, ACFC/SR (2001) 1, 2001, para. 3.1.

the case of Norwegian immigrants with backgrounds from the same groups that have already been granted the status of national minorities in Norway. These immigrants are eligible for measures designed for the national minority, such as language training, even if the individual does not have a long-term connection with Norway. In order for a minority group to be deemed a national minority in Norway, it is usually also required that all or most of the members of the minority group are Norwegian nationals. However, the requirement regarding nationality does not preclude a national minority from comprising individuals who have been granted residency in Norway, but who are not yet Norwegian nationals.

C. Collection of Demographic Data by Government Agencies

Since it is the choice of every individual to declare him- or herself a member of a minority, some states parties neither register nor officially record who is and who is not a member of a national minority. Consequently, there are no official statistics based on ethnic or linguistic features in Germany,[59] Denmark,[60] or Norway.[61] In Finland no statistical data has been collected on national minorities in the country, nor is any data available on ethnic minorities residing in the country, such as the Roma.[62]

This is doubtless in accordance with the obligations under the FCNM. However, the refusal to have such records on ethnic affiliation can sometimes lead to contradictions. For example, only estimated figures are available regarding the members of the various national minorities and other ethnic groups traditionally resident in those states. Usually, under these circumstances the figures are provided by the groups themselves, having been calculated using membership numbers in minority organizations, votes cast for minority party tickets, the number of pupils enrolled in minority schools, and the number of participants in activities or organized events, as has been done in Germany.[63] Finnish personal data protection legislation does not allow registration of any data indicating race or ethnic origin. Therefore, the number of Roma can only be estimated.[64] The situation in Spain is similar, as data collection on ethnic origin is prohibited. As a result, the information on Roma is based on sociological research and surveys carried out at local and regional level by

59 Above, n. 54, para. 4.
60 Advisory Committee Opinion on Denmark, ACFC/INF/OP/I (2001) 005, 2000.
61 Advisory Committee Opinion on Norway ACFC/INF/OP/I (2003) 003, para. 32.
62 Advisory Committee Opinion on Finland, ACFC/INF/OP/I (2001) 002, 2001.
63 Germany State Report, ACFC/SR (2000) 1, 2000, para. 4.
64 Finland State Report, ACFC/SR (99) 3, 1999.

different authors, using different methods, and with different content. These cannot be used for official purposes, although they do give vital information on the situation of the Spanish Roma community.[65] The absence of accurate statistics and records makes it more difficult for organizations providing various humanitarian services to measure the needs of minority groups in a given area. In Hungary, this has been proven to be the case.[66]

Nevertheless, prohibitions of data collection are not absolute. In Finland, for example, the collection of such data for the population register on conditions provided by act of parliament or decree is permitted. There are also separate provisions on the publication of confidential information.[67] In Croatia, declaring one's national affiliation is optional and, when registering, citizens are familiarized with this option. Declaration or non-declaration of one's national affiliation does not have any legal effects.[68] In Poland, the Personal Data Protection Law prohibits the processing of data disclosing racial or ethnic origin. It is only allowed in cases stipulated in the Act itself.[69] In Slovenia, meanwhile, data on nationality can only be collected with the consent of the person to whom the data relates.[70] By the same token, in Ireland no statistical data exists concerning ethnicity, but in the 2002 Census there was a question on membership of the Traveller community.[71] Those completing the census form had the choice of answering yes or no to the question: 'are you a member of the Traveller community?' This enabled members of the Traveller community to indicate their choice as to whether or not they wished to be treated as a member of this group for statistical purposes.

A significant number of examples of recent practice support the conclusion that states respect the free choice of every person belonging to a national minority to be treated or not to be treated as such. There are also problematic cases, however. One case in point is the Italian practice concerning the Ladin- and German-speaking communities in Bolzano province.[72] Unlike Italy's other national minorities, these minority groups are included in the nationwide population census. The aim is to ensure the equitable distribution of political mandates and public sector posts between these three communities.[73] When

[65] Spain State Report, ACFC/SR (2000) 5, 2000.

[66] Hungary State Report, ACFC/SR (99) 10, 1999.

[67] Above, n. 66.

[68] Croatia State Report, ACFC/SR (99) 5, 1999.

[69] Poland State Report, ACFC/SR (2002) 2, 2002.

[70] Slovenia State Report, ACFC/SR (2000) 4, 2000.

[71] Ireland State Report, ACFC/SR (2001) 6, 2001.

[72] Italy State Report, ACFC/SR (1999) 007, 1999.

[73] M. Magliana, 'The Autonomous Province of South Tyrol: A Model of Self-Governance', *Quaderno/Arbeitsheft*, 20 (European Academy, Bozen, Bolzano, 2000), 45.

completing the general census forms, residents of Bolzano province must also fill in an individual declaration of linguistic affiliation. This declaration, which cannot be made anonymously, is retained by the district courts until the following census. The Advisory Committee has pointed out that individual declarations of linguistic affiliation are compulsory and that there is no sufficient guarantee of confidentiality. As census responses remain valid for ten years, each individual's choice stands firm and unchangeable for the same period. Failure to declare one's linguistic affiliation has clear disadvantages since, in the province of Bolzano, all public service posts—at national, regional, provincial, and municipal levels—are allocated among the three linguistic communities in proportion to size. Accordingly, only those having made their declaration of linguistic affiliation can occupy a public service post reserved for their linguistic group. Refusal to declare one's linguistic affiliation also means that the person concerned is unable to exercise certain political rights, including the right to stand as a candidate in municipal, provincial, and regional elections, since a candidate's linguistic affiliation is checked in order to guarantee the strict allocation of political offices among the three communities. In addition, this system poses problems because of the limited freedom of choice it offers. Admittedly, the declaration has a category labelled 'other' in addition to the Ladin, German-speaking, and Italian-speaking groups. But, any person choosing 'other' must also be affiliated to one of the three aforementioned groups to enjoy certain privileges. The Advisory Committee is of the opinion that the current system of individually declaring linguistic affiliation in the province of Bolzano is contrary to the principle of free affiliation and protection of ethnolinguistic data. The inherent tension of this situation was demonstrated when the Advisory Committee criticized the Estonian questionnaire used in the 2000 census as it contained a compulsory question on individual ethnic origin. While appreciating the need for quality data in this field, the Advisory Committee considered that the right not to be treated as a person belonging to a national minority also extends to census situations and that mandatory questions on one's ethnicity are not compatible with this principle. It also considered it essential to protect the resulting census data on ethnicity in an appropriate and discreet manner during processing, in accordance with principles on the protection of personal data collected and processed for statistical purposes.[74]

One acute problem is the disclosure of ethnicity during criminal investigations. In parts of Germany, the authorities have recently decided to replace the personal description form they have used until now. The new personal data form that the police use to register suspects requests data as to whether the

[74] Advisory Committee Opinion on Estonia, ACFC/NF/OP/I (99) 16, 2001, para. 19.

person is East Prussian, West Prussian, or black. This description form also lists physical descriptions such as 'full breasted'. Another heading reads 'Sinti/Rom'. Furthermore, the police were trained to fill in these details based solely on the suspect's physical appearance.[75] The suspect neither had a say in that matter, nor was his or her consent requested. The Advisory Committee was deeply concerned over the use of personal description forms in parts of Germany which permitted any suspect questioned by the police to be classified as belonging to an ethnic group without the person's consent and without him or her even being informed. This practice clearly violates a person's freedom of choice. The Advisory Committee noted that several representatives of Roma/Sinti in Germany strongly opposed this police practice in Bavaria and considered the practice incompatible with Article 3 FCNM. As it seems focused primarily on Roma/Sinti persons, this practice raised questions related to discrimination. A revision of the form succeeded, among other things, in removing the designation 'Sinti/Roma type'. The new structure focuses exclusively on overall terms designating origin (such as 'Mediterranean type'), allowing allocation to certain types on the basis of visually structured instructions for completion of the forms.

Similar problems related to gathering information exist in Slovakia.[76] There is conflicting information emerging from different authorities as to whether governmental bodies continue to collect personal data on the ethnicity of suspects as a general rule, and, in particular, those offenders considered to be of Roma origin. The Advisory Committee has acknowledged that collection of ethnic data may, under certain circumstances, contribute to programmes aimed at ensuring full and effective equality. However, it also found the reports suggesting that such discriminatory data collection continues in Slovakia disconcerting, especially since this practice appears to have no clear legal basis. Another disturbing factor is that this collection has reportedly been carried out, in some cases, at the discretion of the officials concerned and on what they consider to be 'visible characteristics' of a person belonging to a national minority group. Moreover, this determination has been made without the voluntary consent of the accused. The field of law enforcement is not the Advisory Committee's only area of concern in Slovakia, however. It has also documented reports suggesting that non-voluntary collection of ethnicity data is being carried out in a number of other areas, including governmental employment offices and the military forces, again without clear legal basis. The Advisory

[75] Advisory Committee Opinion on Germany, ACFC/INF/OP/I (2002) 008, 2002, para. 19.

[76] Advisory Committee Opinion on Slovakia, ACFC/INF/OP/I (2001), 001, para. 14.

Committee is of the opinion that the collection of personal data on an individual's affiliation with a particular national minority without his or her consent and without adequate legal safeguards does not comply with Article 3 FCNM, as this provision also upholds the right *not* to be treated as a person belonging to a national minority.

III. Conclusion and Outlook

The most complicated and controversial issue of the FCNM is that of personal scope of protection, meaning the definition of the term national minority. Due to the lack of a definition in the FCNM, the Advisory Committee had to opt for a certain approach on this matter. This means in practice that the Advisory Committee takes into consideration the position of the reporting state party, which, in general expresses its policy through declarations or reservations mentioning the recognized minorities. The Advisory Committee examines these declarations/reservations in order to ensure that they are in line with the FCNM and with general principles of international law and that they are not discriminatory. If the Advisory Committee finds that a change in the position of the reporting state party could be beneficial it urges the state to discuss the issue with those groups concerned. Using this procedure the Advisory Committee intends to ensure that states parties do not make arbitrary or unjustified distinctions between the minorities under their jurisdiction. Treaty bodies, like the Advisory Committee, have the power to decide on the validity of such declarations/reservations according to legal literature. These Advisory Committee rulings can be considered as binding on the states parties. Experience shows that in several cases intense discussion has taken place between states parties and the Advisory Committee on these issues. This can be considered the most important contribution of the FCNM to the development of the international minority protection system. Another advantage of the implementation mechanism of the FCNM with regard to Article 3(1) is the fact-finding function of the Advisory Committee which offers persons belonging to minorities the opportunity to articulate their opinion on their status in the society of the states parties. It is unlikely that the Advisory Committee will be able to continue these intensive consultations with governments and minority representatives in the future due to the increasing number of states parties to the FCNM. The experience of the first cycle of monitoring of state reports provides examples of good practice to new states parties and other states looking for practical and useful solutions regarding minority issues, however.

Article 3(2)

I. Background

A. Issues

Although it is very common to use the expression 'rights of minorities', it is not the minority as a whole but the person belonging to a minority who is the holder of the rights. This individualistic approach can be found in all codifications of minority rights. Capotorti mentions three foundations for this approach: (i) historical reasons, because the minority protection system of the League of Nations was originally structured in the form of individual rights; (ii) legal reasons, because there is a need for a coherent formulation of the various human rights. The International Covenant on Civil and Political Rights (ICCPR) lays down only individual rights with the exception of the right to self-determination; and (iii) political reasons, because there is a fear that collective minority rights would increase separatist tendencies as granting rights to minorities might create tension between them and the state. The political leadership of a minority group as an entity would be invested with the authority to represent the interests of that minority vis-à-vis the state.[77] For these reasons, all UN activities in this field deal with persons belonging to minorities from an individualistic perspective. The same is also true for the activities of the Conference on Security and Co-operation in Europe (CSCE)/Organization for Security and Co-operation in Europe (OSCE), and the Council of Europe.

This individualistic approach, whereby rights have been conferred on persons and not on minorities as entities, is on sound grounds and should not be underestimated. However, it is up to the persons belonging to a minority to exercise their rights individually, as well as in community with others, as the rights provided are based on the interests of a collectivity. Thus the holder of the right mentioned in Article 3(2) is not just any individual, but the person as a member of a minority group. This is the most important difference in the concept of the right to self-determination of peoples and minority rights under international law.[78]

B. History

Due to the groundbreaking work of the ICCPR, the codification of Article 3(2) did not encounter much criticism. The precedent-setting 'Draft Protocol to the European Convention on Human Rights guaranteeing the protection of ethnic

[77] F. Capotorti, Study on the Rights of Persons Belonging to Ethnic, Religious, and Linguistic Minorities (1978), UN Doc. E/CN.4/Sub.2/384/Rev.1, paras. 207–9.

[78] A. Cassese, *Self-Determination of Peoples* (Cambridge University Press, Cambridge, 1995), 141–54.

groups' prepared by the Austrian Delegation[79] contains a similar formulation: '[m]embers of ethnic groups may practice and enjoy their rights individually or in community with the other members of their group.' Recommendation 1201 follows the same idea with only marginal differences in phrasing.[80] However, during the work of the Ad Hoc Committee for the Protection of National Minorities (CAHMIN), the Norwegian delegation proposed a wording that was more in accordance with the CSCE Copenhagen Document.[81] Only Romania criticized the wording in question for contrasting with the programmatic character of the rest of the provisions.[82] Despite this criticism, Romania's intervention in CAHMIN was unsuccessful, for it was agreed to keep Article 3 in the proposed version. As a compromise it was decided to raise this point at the level of the Committee of Ministers, but this did not happen.

During the codification process it was underlined that the article does not contain any obligation for states to recognize collective rights. It puts forth that rights flowing from the concept of minority protection can be exercised by a person belonging to a national minority together with other persons, including those belonging to: his or her own national minority; any other national minority; or the majority. It thus recognizes the possibility of joint exercise of those rights and freedoms, which is distinct from the notion of collective rights. Accordingly, the term 'others' should be understood in the widest possible sense and should include persons belonging to the same national minority, to another national minority, or to the majority.[83]

C. Context

During the elaboration of the ICCPR two issues were discussed especially intensely. The first one was whether protection should be accorded to the person belonging to the minority or to the minority group as such. It was underlined that 'any assimilation which might take place must be clearly voluntary'[84]

79 Steering Committee for Human Rights (CDDH), Draft Protocol to the European Convention on Human Rights Guaranteeing the Protection of Ethnic Groups Prepared by the Austrian Delegation, CDDH (91) 46, 1991.

80 Every person belonging to a national minority may exercise his or her rights and enjoy them individually or in association with others in Council Recommendation 1201/1993 of 1 February 1993 on an Additional Protocol on the Rights of National Minorities to the European Convention on Human Rights [1993].

81 'Persons belonging to national minorities may exercise and enjoy [their] [the] rights and freedoms [flowing from this Convention] individually as well as in community with other members of their group', in: Preparatory Work of the Ad Hoc Committee for the Protection of National Minorities (CAHMIN), Proposals Concerning the Preliminary Draft Convention or the Protection of National Minorities, CAHMIN (94) 14 Rev., 1994, p. 10.

82 Above, n. 81, p. 17.

83 CAHMIN, 7th meeting, CAHMIN (94) 32, meeting report, 1994.

84 UN General Assembly, 16th Session (1961) in: UN Doc. A/C.3/SR.1103, para. 39.

and that 'members of the minority groups should not be deprived of the rights enjoyed by other citizens of the same state, so as to enable them to integrate should they so desire'.[85] The second issue regarded the unwillingness of the states to recognize a minority as a collective entity with prospects of acquiring an international legal personality.[86] Article 27 ICCPR, the first post-Second World War codification of minority rights, served as model for the other minority instruments. During the codification of Article 27 the individualistic formulation of the holders of certain rights, meaning 'persons belonging to minorities', was amended by the passage 'in community with the other members of their group'. This adoption reveals a collective element. From the formulation of Article 27, legal literature inferred that the existence of minorities as such is protected because the right of the individual as a minority could otherwise easily become devoid of any substance. Therefore, the difference between an individual and a truly collective right would be rather slight in practice.[87] In illustration, the practice of the Human Rights Committee with respect to Article 27 has been interpreted in an individualist, as well as in a collective manner.[88]

II. Analysis of the Main Issues

A. 'In Community'

The most important aspect of the wording of Article 3(2) is the exercise of the rights 'in community', meaning collectively, whether through associations, cultural manifestations, or educational institutions, or in any other way. According to the Explanatory Report the term 'others' should be understood in the widest possible sense, that is it should include not only persons belonging to one's own minority group, but also persons belonging to other minorities or to the majority.[89] The exercise of rights in community with other members of the group applies not only to minority rights contained in the FCNM, but also to any human right, including the right that persons belonging to minorities should not be subject to any discrimination as a consequence of exercising their rights. This principle is of the utmost importance because governments, administrations, or persons belonging to majorities are often tolerant of persons of other national or ethnic origins until the latter assert their own

[85] UN General Assembly, 16th Session (1961) in: UN Doc. A/C.3/SR.1103, para. 30.

[86] Z. Skurbaty, *As if Peoples Mattered* (Nijhoff, The Hague, 2000), 293.

[87] M. Nowak, *CCPR Commentary* (Engel, Kehl, 1993), 497.

[88] F. Ermacora, 'The Protection of Minorities before the United Nations', *Recueil des cours*, 182 (1985), 308.

[89] Above, n. 5, para. 37.

identity, language, and traditions. Often when they start asserting their rights as persons belonging to a group, discrimination or persecution starts.

In a very tentative manner, Article 3(2) introduces the collective aspect of minority rights, by authorizing the exercise of these rights 'individually as well as in community with others'. Phrased in this way, this individualistic approach inevitably protects the minority as such as a group as well, since without the protection of the group the individual cannot enjoy the freedoms together with other persons belonging to the same group. In fact, Article 3(2) implies the existence of a larger group. Without this implication, the right of a person belonging to the group would be meaningless.[90] Article 3(2) avoids mentioning group or collective rights, however. These terms are the subjects of an ongoing discussion in legal literature.[91] Group rights are granted to the group as such, which means that the group is the holder of these rights.[92] Collective rights are rights given to individuals who belong to a certain group,[93] a description applicable to the FCNM.

When considering the implementation practice, it seems that states parties do not consider the traditional individualistic approach or the collective dimension of minority rights to be problematic. Until now, few state reports have contained information on Article 3(2) and its implementation. Sometimes it is not possible to identify the exact relationship between the information of the reporting state on Article 3(2) and the wording of the text of the FCNM. To a certain extent, this may be considered as proof that states interpret their obligations under Articles 1 and 3 together, as a single one. States parties' reports on Article 3(2) provide only very general information, and reflect their views that minority rights are the rights of the persons belonging to minorities and that the persons concerned enjoy their rights together with others. It appears that the reporting states do not have any problem with the collective dimension involved. Nonetheless, the degree of this collective dimension differs from state to state, according to the needs required by the concrete situation in the state in question. In general, the information provided by the states parties deals with two different aspects: (i) the collective dimension of the rights of persons belonging to minorities; and (ii) the right to form minority organizations.

[90] J. Donnelly, 'Third Generation Rights', in C. Brölmann et al. (eds.), *Peoples and Minorities in International Law* (Nijhoff, Dordrecht, 1993), 134.

[91] V. Segesvary, 'Group Rights: The Definition of Group Rights in Contemporary Legal Debate Based On Socio-cultural Analysis', *International Journal of Group Rights*, 3 (1995), 89–107.

[92] N. Lerner, 'The Evolution of Minority Rights in International Law', in Brölmann et al. (eds.), above, n. 90, 100.

[93] K. Henrard, *Devising an Adequate System of Minority Protection* (Nijhoff, The Hague, 2000), 153.

B. Rights of Persons Belonging to Minorities

Some state reports to the Advisory Committee point to the issue of individual and collective or group rights. Usually they do not provide a clear division between individualistic- and group-oriented approaches. Often states combine individualistic human rights, such as non-discrimination, and group rights, such as the protection of a minority. There are some characteristic examples of state reports dealing with this relationship. Concerning the implementation of Article 3(2), in its report Bulgaria not only considered the minority rights of Roma to be collective rights, but it also conceded that there are some shortcomings in its anti-discrimination legislation and that the mechanisms for its application are not sufficiently effective. In particular, there are no concrete mechanisms and instruments for the implementation of the basic principles of the 'Framework Programme for Equitable Integration of Roma into Bulgarian Society'.[94] The main goals of the Programme, to assist Roma to ensure employment, a satisfactory level of health standards, the urban planning of Roma neighbourhoods, the desegregation of Roma schools, and the study of Romani as a mother tongue, have not been achieved. Correspondingly, the National Council on Ethnic and Demographic Questions, which is empowered to solve these problems, does not possess sufficient powers and administrative capacity. Further, no concrete measures had been taken for the efficient implementation of the FCNM. Thus the government's Programme outlines 'the establishment of an adequate institutional mechanism covering all levels of government with clearly defined responsibilities and powers' as a priority. In this context, the Bulgarian government has envisaged the establishment of a State Agency on Minorities for the prevention of discrimination on ethnic grounds whose activity will be public, that will be charged with the implementation of the state's policy towards minorities, and will include structures conforming to the country's administrative division. One strategic goal of this body, and one of the motives for its creation, is to eliminate any unequal treatment or discrimination against the Roma in Bulgarian society, one of the key priorities of the Bulgarian state.

Hungary considers the right to national and ethnic identity to be a universal human right and the special individual and collective rights of the national and ethnic minorities as fundamental freedoms that the Hungarian parliament respects and enforces in its territory.[95] The report states that the right to national and ethnic identity is a fundamental human right for both individuals and communities, where all minorities are entitled to exist and survive as national and ethnic communities.

[94] Bulgaria State Report, ACFC/SR (2003) 001, 2003.

[95] Above, n. 66.

In contrast, the Constitution of Serbia and Montenegro defines the holders of most minority rights as persons belonging to national minorities.[96] Article 11 of the Constitution deviates from this concept to a certain extent however, by stipulating that Serbia and Montenegro recognizes and guarantees the rights of national minorities (viewing minorities as collectivities) to the maintenance, development, and expression of their ethnic, cultural, linguistic, and other characteristics as well as the use of national symbols, in conformity with international law. On the basis of the above arrangement, it may be concluded that under the Constitution itself, the holders of certain rights are minorities as collectivities. Therefore, the Law on the Protection of Freedoms and Rights of National Minorities recognizes collective rights of minorities. Although it uses the term 'persons belonging to national minorities' in a number of places, there is no doubt that the Law on the Protection of Freedoms and Rights of National Minorities also recognizes the collective rights of minorities. The provision of Article 1(1) of the Law on the Protection of Freedoms and Rights of National Minorities explicitly specifies that it 'shall regulate the manner of exercising individual and collective rights, which are guaranteed to persons belonging to national minorities by the Constitution of Serbia and Montenegro or international treaties'. The said law specifies collective rights, by determining that its provisions govern the protection of national minorities against any form of discrimination in the exercise of freedoms and rights, and provides instruments for safeguarding and protecting the special rights of national minorities to autonomy in the fields of education, the use of language, information, and culture, and to establish institutions for facilitating the participation of minorities in power and the administration of affairs.

C. The Right to Form Organizations

If minorities have a right to form organizations, a strong element of collective rights is inevitably involved. In this connection, some states parties underline this right in their reports concerning Article 3(2).

Albania reports that persons belonging to national minorities living in Albania have the right to exercise all the rights and freedoms guaranteed by law to Albanian citizens, individually or jointly with others, in full equality before the law, and with no discrimination. This means that minorities enjoy the right to unite in organizations and associations and to be elected or to elect their representatives in the elected central or local government structures. They are allowed to propose laws, if the group consists of as many as 20,000 electors;

[96] Serbia and Montenegro State Report, ACFC/SR (2002) 003, 2002.

to practise their religious rituals freely; to study and be taught in school in their mother tongue; as well as to enjoy the specific rights stemming from the principles of the FCNM.[97]

In contrast, Austria argues that there are only a few collective rights under the Austrian minority law, including the right of the National Minority Advisory Councils to deal with pertinent issues, and the right of representative minority organizations to make proposals for the appointment of the members of these councils, including the possibility of certain representative organizations to challenge the composition of the respective Advisory Council by filing a complaint with the Administrative Court. However, some minority organizations in Austria have called for a strengthening of collective rights, primarily the right of associations to take legal action.[98] Germany reports that in addition to individual rights and freedoms, legal provisions have been laid down explicitly for the benefit of political parties of national minorities under federal law and under *Land* legislation, or for bodies representing the interests of a national minority.[99]

III. Conclusion and Outlook

After the first cycle of monitoring of state reports by the Advisory Committee, it seems that Article 3(2) does not create difficulties either for the states or for minority organizations. One also gets the impression that the states parties do not consider Article 3(2) to be an independent norm, but a part of the obligations under Articles 1 and 3(1). Hence, the qualification of minority rights as individual or collective ones can be considered a primarily academic issue. It is not likely that this situation will change in the future, because the stabilization and development of democratic orders in the Council of Europe member states will also increase the opportunities for persons belonging to minorities to exercise their rights and freedoms flowing from the principles enshrined in the FCNM, individually as well as in community with others.

[97] Albania State Report, ACFC/SR (2001) 005, 2001.

[98] Austria State Report, ACFC/SR (2000) 003, 2000.

[99] Germany State Report, ACFC/SR (2000) 001, 2000.

SECTION II

ARTICLE 4

Gudmundur Alfredsson

1. The Parties undertake to guarantee to persons belonging to national minorities the right of equality before the law and of equal protection of the law. In this respect, any discrimination based on belonging to a national minority shall be prohibited.
2. The Parties undertake to adopt, where necessary, adequate measures in order to promote, in all areas of economic, social, political and cultural life, full and effective equality between persons belonging to a national minority and those belonging to the majority. In this respect, they shall take due account of the specific conditions of the persons belonging to national minorities.
3. The measures adopted in accordance with paragraph 2 shall not be considered to be an act of discrimination.

I. Background

A. Issues

Article 4 contains three essential elements of minority rights: (1) the rights of equality before the law and of equal protection by the law; (2) the prohibition of discrimination against a person for reasons of belonging to a minority; and

(3) the introduction of adequate measures for the promotion of full and effective equal rights for majority and minority persons.

Equality before the law and equal protection of the law are frequently denied to minority persons. Usually coupled with discrimination, such denials occur frequently in European countries, notwithstanding general respect for the rule of law and democratic systems of government. There will be variations on the theme from country to country, even different treatments of, and opportunities for, groups within the same country. Evidence of discrimination against minority persons and minority groups is well documented in studies and reports of international[1] and regional[2] organizations and non-governmental organizations.[3]

Democracy and majority rule are not necessarily friendly to, or understanding of, minority desires and needs. Furthermore, the very idea of 'nation-states', a common approach in Europe, may in itself be in contradiction to the rules of equal rights and non-discrimination if or when it brings about the ability and willingness of a national majority, by law or in fact, to impose its identity and culture on others, with the result that within that state there is a second-class status for the minorities. In other words, the minority protection available under the FCNM and other international and regional human rights instruments is much needed.

Discrimination against minorities extends to all sectors of society and across the various rights categories. The identities, cultures, languages, and religions of minority groups are frequently reduced to being second class when compared to those of the majority. Minority persons are less likely to receive full and decent schooling, especially higher education. They are more likely to be unemployed, and when employed, they are likely to earn less and have a harder time getting promotion in the workplace. They often live in poor housing with

[1] Prominent amongst the documentation are the reports by two Special Rapporteurs of the UN Sub-Commission for the Promotion and Protection of Human Rights: F. Capotorti, Study on the Rights of Persons Belonging to Ethnic, Religious and Linguistic Minorities (1977), UN Doc. E/CN.4/Sub.2/384/Rev. 1 and A. Eide, Constructive National Arrangements for Minorities (1993), UN Doc. E/CN.4/Sub.2/1993/34 and Add. 1–4.

[2] See the Secretariat of the Framework Convention for the Protection of National Minorities, Collection of Opinions of the Advisory Committee on the Framework Convention for the Protection of National Minorities, Article by Article, ACFC/I/Secr (2003) 001 Rev. 2, I, II, including evidence reviewed and opinions expressed in connection with the examination of State Reports on Art. 4 as well as a number of other articles. It is striking how frequently discriminatory practices are being confronted by the Advisory Committee. The European Commission against Racism and Intolerance (ECRI) has also on multiple occasions documented discriminatory practices affecting minorities.

[3] Country reports and/or annual reports of Amnesty International, Human Rights Watch, the International Helsinki Federation, and Minority Rights Group International are filled with evidence of equal rights denied and of discrimination against minorities.

a below-average standard of living and social services. In the administration of criminal justice, minority persons face majority justice and are often over-represented in detention centres and prisons. Political representation of minorities at national and municipal levels and in key sectors of public services tends to be marginalized. Autonomous control over internal minority affairs is frequently absent, restricted, and/or tightly regulated by central authorities.[4]

With persisting discriminatory practices negatively affecting educational and employment opportunities as well as political representation, it should not come as a surprise that minority groups often feel that their dignity, their identities, their cultures, and even their existence are threatened. The frequency of violent ethnic and religious conflicts in Europe is undoubtedly related to the second-class status and discriminatory experiences to which minorities are often subjected. With new standards and monitoring institutions put in place by the Council of Europe, the Organization for Security and Co-operation in Europe (OSCE), and the United Nations, improved respect for minority rights is increasingly seen as a useful tool for the prevention of such conflicts or for their resolution and the restoration of peace. The Advisory Committee under the FCNM has clearly paid particular attention to situations where violent conflicts have arisen.[5] Minority rights, with a point of departure in equal rights for everyone, equal treatment, and equal opportunities, are indeed intended to keep the groups content within state borders.

B. History

When the General Assembly adopted the Universal Declaration of Human Rights (UDHR) in 1948, it was decided that the United Nations could not remain indifferent to the 'fate of minorities'.[6] Since then, the formulation of minority rights has proceeded at a slow, but steady, pace in a number of international and regional organizations. The adoption of the FCNM and the establishment of the Advisory Committee are steps in the process.

The growing number of human rights instruments aim to achieve equal rights and non-discrimination for the benefit of minorities. Equal rights and

[4] In terms of adequate special measures concerning participation in national politics and for self-governance, the FCNM does not even come close to the standards suggested by the OSCE High Commissioner on National Minorities, the Lund Recommendations on the Effective Participation of National Minorities in Public Life, The Hague, 1999.

[5] Advisory Committee Opinion on Serbia and Montenegro, ACFC/INF/OP/I (2004) 002, 2003, para. 33, 44.

[6] This was the title of Part C of the UNGA Res. 217 (III) of 10 December 1948. The UDHR was adopted by the same resolution, in Part A. See Universal Declaration of Human Rights (UDHR), UNGA Res. 217 (III), 10 December 1948.

non-discrimination rules are specifically set forth in the context of minorities in several international human rights instruments.[7] These include: the International Covenant on Civil and Political Rights (ICCPR), the International Convention on the Elimination of All Forms of Racial Discrimination (CERD), the Convention on the Rights of the Child (CRC), the Declaration on the Elimination of All Forms of Intolerance and of Discrimination in Education, the ILO Convention No. 169 concerning Indigenous and Tribal Peoples in Independent Countries, and a series of OSCE political documents. The Advisory Committee under the FCNM has also referred to Directives issued by the European Union.[8]

The combination of the desire to eliminate discrimination as a serious human rights problem and to maintain internal and international peace and security, together with the increase in relevant standards, has also seen a new focus of human rights monitoring bodies on minority rights issues. This is true for the Human Rights Committee under the ICCPR, the Committee on Elimination of Racial Discrimination under CERD, the ILO Committee of Experts mainly with reference to Convention No. 169, several special procedures under the UN Commission on Human Rights, such as the Special Rapporteurs on racism and racial discrimination, and on religious intolerance, and the European Commission against Racism and Intolerance (ECRI). The European Court of Human Rights, drawing mainly on Article 14 of the European Convention on Human Rights, has also delivered noteworthy judgments.

Furthermore, and importantly, a number of new minority-specific monitoring or dialogue bodies have been established in the last ten to fifteen years, such as the Advisory Committee under the FCNM, the treaty body under the European Charter for Regional or Minority Languages, the OSCE High Commissioner on National Minorities, the UN Working Group on Minorities, the UN Permanent Forum on Indigenous Issues, and a UN Special Rapporteur on Indigenous Peoples' Rights.[9] All the institutions involved suffer

[7] For compilations of instruments with minority-specific standards, see G. Alfredsson and G. Melander, *A Compilation of Minority Rights Standards: A Selection of Texts from International and Regional Human Rights Instruments and Other Documents* (Raoul Wallenberg Institute, Lund, 1997), Report No. 24; H. Hannum, *Documents on Autonomy and Minority Rights* (Martinus Nijhoff Publishers, Dordrecht, 1993); and P. Thornberry, 'Basic Documents on Minorities and Indigenous Peoples', in *World Directory of Minorities* (Minority Rights Group, London, 1997), 706–801.

[8] See, for example, Advisory Committee Opinion on Ireland, ACFC/INF/OP/I (2004) 003, 2003, para. 29.

[9] At least five European states have acknowledged the presence of indigenous peoples within their borders: Finland, Latvia, Norway, the Russian Federation, and Sweden. As indigenous peoples are generally entitled to minority rights, they are undoubtedly covered by the FCNM.

from serious underfunding, but the decisions and reports from all these bodies are steadily leading to an expansion of the available substantive law.

C. Context

Article 4 is appropriately placed at the outset of Section II of the FCNM, which sets forth a catalogue of guiding principles for the FCNM as a whole. The Article is obviously relevant to, and useful for, the interpretation and the application of practically all the other substantive, programmatic provisions of the Convention. In opinions of the Advisory Committee under the FCNM, clear links between Article 4 and other provisions have often been made, for example: to Article 6 concerning tolerance and dialogue; to Article 12 concerning education; and to Article 15 concerning effective minority participation in cultural, social, and economic life in public affairs.

II. Analysis

A. Structure of the Article

The Article is in three paragraphs. Paragraph 1 spells out the right of equality before the law and of equal protection of the law, and it prohibits any discrimination which would be based on minority membership and characteristics. Paragraph 2 calls for adequate measures in order to promote full and effective equal rights between minority and majority. Finally, paragraph 3 provides that such measures shall not be considered to be an act of discrimination.

As spelled out above, the three guiding principles are properly linked as they belong to a logical whole. Equal rights for everyone is the basic rule. The prohibition of discrimination is supposed to achieve the equal enjoyment and exercise of rights and, when that is insufficient, special or adequate measures are expected to accomplish the same. This three-pronged approach is also contained in other international human rights instruments, although the wording and emphasis may differ in terms of both the strength of the standards and the monitoring institutions.[10]

[10] For a critical examination of the FCNM, see G. Alfredsson, 'A Frame with an Incomplete Painting: Comparison of the Framework Convention for the Protection of National Minorities with International Standards and Monitoring Procedures', *International Journal on Minority and Group Rights*, 7/4 (2000), 291–304.

B. Equal Rights[11]

International human rights instruments repeatedly assert the equal enjoyment of human rights in terms of equality before the law, equal protection of the law, equality before the courts and tribunals, and equal access to public service. Article 1(1) UDHR expresses this eloquently: 'All human beings are born free and equal in dignity and rights.'

In addition to equal treatment in law and by the public authorities, equal rights is usually also meant to cover equal opportunities in the enjoyment and exercise of all human rights. The Explanatory Report accompanying the FCNM says that no separate provision dealing specifically with the principle of equal opportunities has been included: 'Such an inclusion was considered unnecessary as the principle is already applied in paragraph 2 of the article.'[12] Paragraph 2 is about adequate measures which are often meant to include more than merely equal opportunities, but at least equal opportunity is covered.

The requirement of equal treatment and equal opportunities extends across the board to all human rights, that is, civil, cultural, economic, political, and social rights.

C. Non-Discrimination

In respect of the rights of equality before the law and of equal protection of the law, Article 4(1) FCNM spells out that 'any discrimination based on belonging to a national minority shall be prohibited'. Questions about discrimination in law and in fact, drawing on Article 4 in relation to many other articles, are very common when the Advisory Committee considers state reports under the Convention. In order to establish the facts, the Committee has repeatedly called on states to improve national statistics as one important means of establishing whether the provisions of Article 4 are being respected.[13] The minorities which most often are the subject of questions and recommendations are the Roma and the Travellers.[14] The Advisory Committee has also

[11] Although the Explanatory Report accompanying the FCNM refers to the principle of equality, it must be assumed that the intention is to promote and protect the rule of equal rights in line with other international standards. Framework Convention for the Protection of National Minorities and Explanatory Report, CoE Press, Strasbourg, 1995, paras. 38–41, pp. 26–7.

[12] Above, n. 11, para. 40, p. 27.

[13] See, for example, Advisory Committee Opinion on Azerbaijan, ACFC/INF/OP/I (2004) 001, 2003, para. 27, 30, above, n. 5, paras. 44–5, and Advisory Committee Opinion on Lithuania, ACFC/INF/OP/I (2003) 008, 2003, para. 35.

[14] Advisory Committee Opinion on Ireland, ACFC/INF/OP/I (2004) 003, 2003, paras. 34–43, above, n. 5, paras. 34, 39–44; Advisory Committee Opinion on Switzerland, ACFC/INF/OP/I (2003) 007, 2003, para. 28, and Advisory Committee Opinion on Lithuania, ACFC/INF/OP/I (2003) 008, 2003, paras. 32–4.

quoted statements of the ECRI, as the Council of Europe organ with a relevant and explicit non-discrimination mandate.[15]

As described above, unequal treatment and unequal opportunities facing persons belonging to minorities continue to be widely practised or tolerated in the cultural, economic, or educational, political, and social life of most European states and beyond. If in doubt, readers of this book are encouraged to look close to home, to put themselves in the place of minority persons, and to identify instances of such discrimination in their own countries by comparing the actual situations of minority persons with those of the majority.

All the major international human rights instruments, such as the UDHR, the ICCPR, the International Covenant on Economic, Social, and Cultural Rights (ICESCR), CERD, CRC, and regional human rights conventions, prohibit discrimination on grounds which include minority characteristics and/or minority membership. Even the UN Charter, in its Article 1, lists the promotion and encouragement of respect for human rights for all without distinction as to race, language, or religion among the very purposes of the Organization.

The prohibition of discrimination reinforces the rule on the equal enjoyment and exercise of all human rights. The listing of grounds on which discrimination is prohibited may differ from one international instrument to another, but repeated references to national or ethnic origins, race, culture, language, or religion clearly cover traditional minority situations. It is evident from the questioning and opinions of the Advisory Committee that they, for good reasons, look at the same distinguishing features of minorities and rely on the same non-discrimination grounds as are employed in international human rights law, even if the FCNM only refers to 'national' minorities.

In Article 1 CERD and in a 1989 general comment of the Human Rights Committee, the term 'discrimination' is used to cover any distinction, exclusion, restriction, or preference based on any ground associated with minority membership or characteristics and which has the purpose or effect of nullifying or impairing the recognition, enjoyment, or exercise by all persons, on an equal footing, of all rights and freedoms. Furthermore, the Human Rights Committee stated that equal rights do not necessarily mean identical treatment in every instance, and that not every differentiation in treatment will constitute discrimination if the aim is to achieve a purpose legitimate under the Covenant and if the criteria used are reasonable and objective.[16]

[15] See, for example, Advisory Committee Opinion on Azerbaijan, ACFC/INF/OP/I (2004) 001, 2003, para. 24.

[16] UN Human Rights Committee 'General Comment No. 18' on Non-Discrimination (1989), UN Doc. CCPR/C/21/Rev.1/Add.1.

As to the application of the rules on equal rights, non-discrimination, and special measures to specific rights, one can quote Articles 1, 2, and 5 CERD. Here, the ratifying states undertake to guarantee the rights of everyone effectively, without distinction as to race, colour, or national or ethnic origins, and, if necessary, with special measures for equal rights in the enjoyment and exercise of, *inter alia*, the freedoms of thought, conscience, opinion, and expression, and the rights to property, education, training, and participation in cultural activities. The language of the International Convention is more forceful, especially on special measures, but the relationship of Article 4 FCNM with its subsequent programmatic provisions follows a parallel pattern.

The unfortunate selective application by some of the ratifying states, when specifying in declarations or otherwise that the FCNM will only apply to certain minorities, may lead to discrimination between groups within a country and, as a result, to new situations of violent conflict. Similar discriminatory results may arise from bilateral or multilateral agreements between many of the same states.[17]

D. Adequate Measures

Questions concerning special measures arise when the basic rules of the equal enjoyment and the equal exercise of human rights and of non-discrimination are insufficient for minority protection. Article 4 FCNM calls on states 'to adopt, where necessary, adequate measures in order to promote, in all areas of economic, social, political and cultural life, full and effective equality between persons belonging to a national minority and those belonging to the majority'.

According to the Explanatory Report accompanying the FCNM, the promotion of full and effective equality may require the adoption of 'special measures that take into account the specific conditions of the persons concerned. Such measures need to be "adequate", that is in conformity with the proportionality principle, in order to avoid violation of the rights of others as well as discrimination against others.'[18]

Article 4(3) states that 'measures adopted in accordance with paragraph 2 shall not be considered to be an act of discrimination'. In the same Explanatory Report, it further says that 'the purpose of paragraph 3 is to make clear that the measures referred to in Paragraph 3 are not to be regarded as contravening the principles of equality and non-discrimination. Its aim is to ensure persons belonging to national minorities effective equality along with persons belonging to the majority.'[19]

[17] G. Alfredsson, 'Identifying Possible Disadvantages of Bilateral Agreements and Advancing the "Most-Favoured-Minority-Clause" ', in A. Bloed and P. van Dijk (eds.), *Protection of Minority Rights through Bilateral Treaties* (Kluwer Law International, The Hague, 1999), 165–75.

[18] Above, n. 11, para. 9, p. 27.

[19] ibid., para. 41, p. 27.

Demands for adequate measures are present in several international human rights instruments for the purpose of achieving equal rights in fact, but they are more commonly known in these texts as special or concrete measures. Alternatively, they have been referred to as differential or preferential treatment, positive or reverse discrimination, or affirmative action. The label does not matter much, as long as the intentions and results are the introduction of meaningful measures for speeding up the process of eliminating discrimination and achieving equal rights.

In strong language, Article 2(2) CERD provides that states shall take 'special and concrete measures to ensure the adequate development and protection of certain racial groups or individuals belonging to them' in order to guarantee the full and equal enjoyment of all human rights. The Convention also states that such measures are not to be considered discriminatory. Similarly, notwithstanding its negative formulation, the Human Rights Committee has interpreted Article 27 ICCPR to imply the obligation of states to provide special measures of protection.[20]

In the international instruments, special measures for the benefit of minorities are spelled out most clearly in the fields of education, language, and culture, but the measures have also been extended to political, economic, civil and social affairs, religion, and transboundary contacts. In the exercise of political rights, the measures are meant to ensure minority participation in politics and civil service at the national level and an effective contribution to the conduct of local matters. For the purposes of local government, many countries have introduced autonomy or self-government for minorities.

In the Explanatory Report accompanying the FCNM, it is spelled out that the measures 'do not extend, in time or in scope, beyond what is necessary in order to achieve the aim of full and effective equality'.[21] The temporal qualification coincides with international standards. The special measures are temporary and supposed to serve until discriminatory patterns have been eliminated, although in nation-states the measures may have to be in place for extended periods in order to achieve equal treatment and equal opportunities vis-à-vis a dominant majority population.

Special measures for the benefit of minorities should not be seen as constituting privileges within a country. The Advisory Committee under the FCNM has furthermore said that 'such measures must not be considered to be an act of discrimination'.[22] Instead, the measures should be seen as tools intended to elevate persons belonging to minorities and the groups themselves to a position

[20] See UN Human Rights Committee, General Comment No. 23 on the Rights of Minorities (1994), UN Doc. HRI/GEN/1/Rev. 6 (2003), paras. 6(1), 6(2), 7, 9.

[21] Above, n. 11, para. 39, p. 27.

[22] Above, n. 15, para. 28.

of contentment in the equal enjoyment and exercise of all human rights. As such, the special measures are firmly rooted in the rule of equal rights as is non-discrimination.

When commenting on state reports, the Advisory Committee under the FCNM has welcomed and/or recommended a series of measures. Amongst them are the adoption of anti-discrimination legislation in public law, criminal law, and civil law with effective means of implementation;[23] active roles for the courts, tribunals, and independent national institutions in combating discrimination;[24] the incorporation of the European Convention on Human Rights into domestic law;[25] and the dissemination of information, education, and other efforts 'to ensure that individuals are informed of their rights in this sphere and that they have confidence in the relevant authorities to seek remedy when they consider that these rights have been violated'.[26] In other words, the measures are there, but they can still be better described with the adjective 'adequate' and not with 'special'; but one would expect that with increased practice and acceptance, the measures will grow stronger and more specific.

E. Individual and Group Rights

Article 4 FCNM is squarely addressed to minority persons, whereas the parallel provision in Article 2(2) CERD refers to both individuals and groups. ILO Convention No. 169, the UNESCO Declaration on Race and Racial Prejudice, and a few other international human rights instruments have also extended non-discrimination and special measures to minority and indigenous groups. Additionally, in a number of settings, minorities as groups have gained formal or semi-formal access to monitoring and dialogue forums set up by international and regional organizations.

There are good reasons for extending minority rights to group rights.[27] It is natural that minority individuals seek solidarity and strength within a group

[23] See, for example, Advisory Committee Opinion on Azerbaijan, ACFC/INF/OP/I (2004) 001, 2003, paras. 24–5; above, n. 5, paras. 31–2; Advisory Committee Opinion on Sweden, ACFC/INF/OP/I (2003) 006, 2003, paras. 21–3, and Advisory Committee Opinion on Lithuania, ACFC/INF/OP/I (2003) 008, 2003, paras. 28, 30.

[24] Advisory Committee Opinion on Ireland, ACFC/INF/OP/I (2004) 003, 2003, paras. 27–32, 44; above, n. 5, paras. 35–6; Advisory Committee Opinion on Sweden, ACFC/INF/OP/I (2003) 006, 2003, para. 25, and Advisory Committee Opinion on Lithuania, ACFC/INF/OP/I (2003) 008, 2003, para. 29.

[25] Advisory Committee Opinion on Ireland, ACFC/INF/OP/I (2004) 003, 2003, para. 33.

[26] Advisory Committee Opinion on Azerbaijan, ACFC/INF/OP/I (2004) 001, 2003, para. 26. See also Advisory Committee Opinion on Lithuania, ACFC/INF/OP/I (2003) 008, 2003, para. 31.

[27] The use here of the term 'group rights' is intentional. The use of the term 'collective rights' would be misleading in as much as that term encompasses peoples' rights, including the right of self-determination.

and that the group is able to accomplish things that individuals cannot, such as running minority schools or local autonomies. To satisfy minorities from a peace and security perspective, the groups as well as their members must be placed in a position comparable with the majority population.

F. Human Rights Education

Of all measures one can think of for overcoming discrimination, education, in general, and human rights education, in particular, are likely to be the most significant. As to human rights education, this has been recognized again and again, most notably in the proclamation of the UN Human Rights Education Decade (1995–2004), but it has also been stipulated in a long series of human rights instruments.[28]

At a 1990 seminar convened under the auspices of the Programme of Action for the Second Decade to Combat Racism and Racial Discrimination, it was repeatedly affirmed that education was certainly one of the keys to a world free of racism. Education with sensitivity training and community action programmes were said to be essential elements for the creation of a climate of mutual tolerance and understanding between different communities.[29] In reports to the Commission on Human Rights, the Special Rapporteur on contemporary forms of racism, racial discrimination, xenophobia, and related intolerance has stated that he is 'convinced of the importance of education and its far-reaching consequences and suggests that measures should be studied to prevent actions and behaviour giving rise to discrimination—prevention being better than cure'.[30]

III. Conclusion and Outlook

Certain rights and freedoms are particularly important for minorities and for the realization of their rights. In addition to life and physical security, as reflected in the prohibition of genocide and ethnic cleansing, these rights relate to equal treatment, equal opportunities, and non-discrimination, and

[28] G. Alfredsson, 'The Right to Human Rights Education', in A. Eide, C. Krause, and A. Rosas (eds.), *Economic, Social and Cultural Rights: A Textbook*, 2nd rev. edn. (Martinus Nijhoff Publishers, Dordrecht, 2001), 273–88.

[29] UN Secretary-General, *Report of the Seminar on the Political, Historical, Economic, Social and Cultural Factors Contributing to Racism* (Racial Discrimination and Apartheid, UN Centre for Human Rights, HR/PUB/91/3, Geneva, 1990), para. 104.

[30] UN Commission on Human Rights, Report by M. Glélé-Ahanhanzo on Racism in the United States of America (1994), UN Doc. E/CN.4/1994/66, para. 51.

the active employment of these with effective measures, when necessary, for the respect of the rights to dignity, identity, culture, language, education, religion, and other human rights. The contents of Article 4 FCNM stand as a cornerstone for all these necessities if equal rights are to be realized.

The fundamental rules of international human rights law concerning the equal enjoyment of all human rights, as well as non-discrimination in that enjoyment, must apply as a matter of course to persons belonging to minorities; group rights would be beneficial too. The rights must be implementable, and they must be implemented to the highest degree possible and in a reasonable and proportional manner. To that end, special measures are a particularly important and efficient tool for effectively combating long-standing patterns of discrimination and for contributing to more harmonious, peaceful, and prosperous societies.

For the time being, the FCNM is a key element in the work of the Council of Europe towards equal rights for minority persons. The Convention is an improvement on the relative silence in the human rights instruments of the Council that previously existed, and the intentions behind the FCNM adoption are undoubtedly good. Nevertheless, the language of this Convention is weak when compared with existing standards in international human rights instruments. Furthermore, direct minority access to justice within the Council of Europe continues to be limited. Against these weaknesses, the Advisory Committee has repeatedly shown admirable wisdom and courage in its questions on national practices as described in state reports, and the Committee has by now delivered a long series of opinions which definitely point in the right direction.

It can be argued that the FCNM and the Advisory Committee still constitute only a step in an ongoing European legislative and monitoring process. Like other human rights, minority rights should be governed by the rule of law, and disputes about the interpretation and application of the standards should be determined by the courts. When minority individuals and the groups are not satisfied by national courts, they should on special measures have access to the European Court of Human Rights, as they now do to some of the human rights treaty bodies in the UN human rights programme. In addition to Article 14 of the European Convention on Human Rights and eventually Protocol 12 to that Convention, there should be an additional protocol or protocols on minority rights, whereby the door would be opened for the European Court to deal not only with the rules of equal rights and non-discrimination, but also with specific, special measures for the effective realization of minority rights.

ARTICLE 5

Geoff Gilbert

1. The Parties undertake to promote the conditions necessary for persons belonging to national minorities to maintain and develop their culture, and to preserve the essential elements of their identity, namely their religion, language, traditions and cultural heritage.
2. Without prejudice to measures taken in pursuance of their general integration policy, the Parties shall refrain from policies or practices aimed at assimilation of persons belonging to national minorities against their will and shall protect these persons from any action aimed at such assimilation.

Article 5(1)

I. Background

Articles 5 and 6, at least Article 6(1), need to be read together. They are among the least specific provisions of the Framework Convention for the Protection of National Minorities (FCNM) when it comes to imposing obligations on states parties. To be sure, specific measures from domestic law can be seen to fall within the ambit of Articles 5 and 6, but, at least at first glance, there seems little concrete substance that an individual could demand from the state except with regard to Article 6(2). In certain respects, Articles 5 and 6(1) speak to the obligation of the state to ensure conditions for the national minority that allow the individual who belongs to that national minority to enjoy and develop his or her own culture, language, or religion. In that sense, they build on Article 1[1] and complement the provisions that accord rights to individual persons who belong to national minorities.

In one sense, Article 5(1) is a laissez-faire provision: the state promotes conditions for persons belonging to national minorities to maintain and develop their culture, preserving the essential elements of their identity.[2] It is worth noting at the outset that the use of the word 'essential' does not allow the state to adopt a minimalist approach to its obligations under Article 5(1). If anything, 'essential' emphasizes the important role that the state has to play. These characteristics—religion; language; traditions; and cultural heritage—are the very essence of what makes a group a national minority.

[1] See the Drafting History that originally referred to the 'national minority', not the persons who belong thereto. See the Set of Principles on National Minorities drawn up by the European Commission for Democracy through Law (ECDL), draft report, CD-PV (90) 4 Prov., 4th meeting, 1990, and Parliamentary Assembly of the Council of Europe, Council Recommendation 1990/1134/EC, 42nd ordinary session, 14th sitting, 1990, on the rights of minorities.

[2] Conference for Security and Co-operation in Europe (CSCE) Follow-up Meeting, Concluding Document, Vienna, 1989, para. 59: 'They will ensure that persons belonging to national minorities or regional cultures on their territories can maintain and develop their own culture in all its aspects, including language, literature and religion; and that they can preserve their cultural and historical monuments and objects.' See also, the Second Conference on the Human Dimension of the CSCE, Document of the Copenhagen Meeting of the Conference on the Human Dimension of the CSCE, Copenhagen, 1990, para. 33: 'The participating States will protect the ethnic, cultural, linguistic and religious identity of national minorities on their territory and create conditions for the promotion of that identity. They will take the necessary measures to that effect after due consultations, including contacts with organizations or associations of such minorities, in accordance with the decision-making procedures of each State.'

Article 5(1) was formed from two articles in the Venice Commission's Draft Convention on the Protection of Minorities.[3] The original draft gave rights to persons belonging to national minorities rather than imposing an obligation on the state to promote the conditions necessary for these persons to develop and preserve the central characteristics of their national minority group. Parliamentary Assembly of the Council of Europe Recommendation 1134 (1990) on the Rights of Minorities went so far as to accord the rights to the national minority group itself. The Venice Commission's 1993 proposal for a convention for the protection of national minorities accorded some rights to the national minority, and others to persons belonging to the national minority.[4] Once the Ad Hoc Committee for the Protection of National Minorities (CAHMIN) took over the drafting of the Framework Convention, Article 5 began to assume its present form.[5]

Not every one of these differences creates a national minority.[6] Nevertheless, if the state's obligation is to promote the necessary conditions for persons belonging to national minorities to maintain and develop their distinctive characteristics, it must take positive action in a variety of spheres.[7] As the Human Rights Committee has put it in the context of Article 27 of the International Covenant on Civil and Political Rights (ICCPR): '7.2 . . . article 27 of the Covenant requires States parties to accord protection to ethnic and linguistic minorities and the Committee must give due weight to this obligation.'[8] The United Nations 1992 Declaration on the Rights of Persons

[3] ECDL, Preliminary Draft Convention on the Protection of Minorities DAJ.SC. DEMOCRACYCONV.MIN, 1990, Arts. 5, 9.

[4] ECDL, Proposal for a European Convention for the Protection of National Minorities, CDL-MIN (93) 6, 1993. 'Article 3 . . . (2) They shall have the right to the respect, safeguard and development of their ethnical, religious, or linguistic identity . . . Article 6 . . . (1) Persons belonging to a minority shall have the right to freely preserve, express and develop their cultural identity in all its aspects, free of any attempts at assimilation against their will.'

[5] Ad Hoc Committee for the Protection of National Minorities (CAHMIN), Report of the 1st meeting of the CAHMIN Drafting Group, CAHMIN/GR (94) 2 rev., 1994. See also the review of 'culture' carried out by the Council for Cultural Co-operation, Provisions Concerning Culture, CDCC-BU (94) 7 Rev., 1994, pp. 5–7.

[6] CAHMIN, Explanatory Report to the Framework Convention, H (1995) 010, Strasbourg, 1995, para. 43, building on the CSCE, the Geneva CSCE Experts Meeting on National Minorities, Geneva, 1991, III, para. 4. 'They reconfirm that persons belonging to national minorities have the right freely to express, preserve and develop their ethnic, cultural, linguistic or religious identity and to maintain and develop their culture in all its aspects, free of any attempts at assimilation against their will.'

[7] The Explanatory Report makes clear in para. 44, that the national minority's traditions cannot contravene domestic laws and international standards and 'remain subject to limitations arising from the requirements of public order'.

[8] *Sandra Lovelace* v. *Canada*, Comm. No. 24/1977, [1981], UN Doc. CCPR/C/OP/1, 83.

Belonging to National or Ethnic, Religious or Linguistic Minorities,[9] provides a fuller, if equally general, explanation of the function of the state towards the preservation of the national minority:

> Article 4
>
> . . .
>
> (2) States shall take measures to create favourable conditions to enable persons belonging to minorities to express their characteristics and to develop their culture, language, religion, traditions and customs, except where specific practices are in violation of national law and contrary to international standards.
>
> . . .
>
> (4) States should, where appropriate, take measures in the field of education, in order to encourage knowledge of the history, traditions, language and culture of the minorities existing within their territory. Persons belonging to minorities should have adequate opportunities to gain knowledge of the society as a whole.

As Article 4 of the 1992 Declaration makes clear, Article 5(1) overlaps with Article 12 of the Framework Convention. In promoting the conditions necessary for persons belonging to national minorities to maintain and develop their culture, states need to educate the population as a whole about the traditions and cultures of those minorities.

The other major overlap is with Article 4 FCNM as it addresses non-discrimination. To the extent that Article 4 is simply a guarantee of equal treatment for everyone in the state, it has no special relevance to persons belonging to national minorities. All persons within the jurisdiction can benefit from the non-discrimination clause. Article 5 focuses on creating an environment for persons belonging to national minorities to maintain and develop their culture and to preserve their identity as a minority group. Nevertheless, a non-discrimination clause can have particular pertinence to members of a national minority insofar as it is applied to achieve true equality, that is to say, if the state is established in a way that protects the dominant majority, there is no level playing field. The European Court of Human Rights (ECtHR) has recognized that treating two different groups in the same way can discriminate against one of those groups[10] and that a general practice applied to everyone might adversely affect one specific group within the state.[11] Therefore, equal treatment should take precedence over simple non-discrimination.

[9] Adopted by UNGA Res. 47/135, 92nd plenary meeting (18 December 1992).

[10] *Thlimmenos* v. *Greece* (34369/97) (2000) EHRR 161.

[11] *Shanaghan* v. *United Kingdom* (37715/97) (2000) EHRR 326 (3rd Section). See also *Jordan* v. *United Kingdom* (24746/94) (2001) EHRR 323, *McKerr* v. *United Kingdom* (28883/95) (2001)

This chapter will start by considering what is required to 'promote the necessary conditions', including consultation and finance. It will then move on to look at the various characteristics of national minorities, and what states need to do to guarantee that persons belonging to national minorities can maintain and develop their culture, and preserve the essential elements of their identity. Finally, special measures for specific minority groups will be addressed, along with the dilemma that history can never fully be rectified. With respect to Article 5(2), this chapter will examine assimilation and how it completes the 'picture' set out in Article 5(1).

II. Analysis

A. Promoting the Necessary Conditions

Although the language of Article 5 is programmatic and does not lay down the conditions necessary for the maintenance and development of culture, it is not appropriate for this vagueness to be directly translated into implemented domestic legislation, satisfying a state's international obligations under the Framework Convention. In its comment on Ukraine's report under the Framework Convention, the Advisory Committee criticizes the government for its lack of precision: 'Article 6 of the [1992] Law on National Minorities guarantees cultural autonomy for national minorities. This is however formulated only in an extremely general fashion, and the Advisory Committee considers that the content and the reach of this concept would merit being defined and developed in more detail.'[12] It is not enough for the state to leave the minority to sink or swim. There is an obligation to provide an environment in which the minority can flourish if the members so wish. Moreover, the minority must be allowed to flourish as far as possible; there can be no glass ceilings put in the way of developing the minority culture. Article 5(1) requires the state party to *promote* the conditions that are necessary; there must be a positive engagement by the state with the persons belonging to the national minority so as to allow them the opportunity to *develop* their culture. Article 5(1) does not merely

EHRR III, heard at the same time, and *Kelly and Others* v. *United Kingdom* (30054/96) (2000) EHRR (3rd Section). As the Court held in *Shanaghan*: '129. Where a general policy or measure has disproportionately prejudicial effects on a particular group, it is not excluded that this may be considered as discriminatory notwithstanding that it is not specifically aimed or directed at that group. Despite the legitimate concerns about collusion and the specific examples that have been highlighted, the Court does not consider that this can be regarded as establishing a practice or pattern which could be classified as discriminatory within the meaning of Article 14.'

[12] Ukraine State Report, ACFC/SR (99) 14, para. 32.

permit the state to preserve a status quo that effectively leaves the minority group in a cultural ghetto. A pluralistic democracy has to permit the coexistence of a variety of cultures and viewpoints, even those that challenge the state itself.[13] Eide has expressed this most clearly in his commentary on the United Nations 1992 Declaration:

28. Minority group identity requires not only tolerance, but also a positive attitude towards cultural pluralism on the part of the State and the larger society. Not only acceptance, but also respect for the distinctive characteristics and contribution of minorities to the life of the national society as a whole, is required. Protection of their identity means not only that the State should abstain from policies which have the purpose or effect of assimilating minorities into the dominant culture, but also that it should protect them against activities by third parties which have an assimilatory effect. . . .

29. Promotion of the identity of minorities requires special measures to facilitate the maintenance, reproduction and further development of their culture. Cultures are not static; minorities should be given the opportunity to develop their own culture in the context of an ongoing process. That process should be an interaction between the persons belonging to the minority themselves, between the minority and the State, and between the minority and the wider national society.[14]

Thus, there is a positive obligation to involve minority groups in the process of determining what the state has to do to promote the necessary conditions for those groups to flourish and an ultimate obligation to provide finance for such initiatives, as will be considered below.

Before turning to a discussion on consultation and finance, however, it should be acknowledged that it is easier for a state to fulfil its obligations where minority groups are concentrated in one particular region. The fact that the minority is dispersed across several regions is not an excuse for insufficient action. Moreover, it ought to be incumbent upon the state to ensure that the treatment of the minority is equal across its administrative internal boundaries. Acknowledging that additional rights can be afforded where a minority group

[13] *Socialist Party and Others* v. *Turkey* (21237/93) (1998) EHRR 45, para. 47: 'The Court notes that, read together, the statements put forward a political programme with the essential aim being the establishment, in accordance with democratic rules, of a federal system in which Turks and Kurds would be represented on an equal footing and on a voluntary basis. . . . In the Court's view, the fact that such a political programme is considered incompatible with the current principles and structures of the Turkish State does not make it incompatible with the rules of democracy. It is of the essence of democracy to allow diverse political programmes to be proposed and debated, even those that call into question the way a State is currently organised, provided that they do not harm democracy itself.'

[14] A. Eide, Final Text of the Commentary to the Declaration on the Rights of Persons Belonging to National or Ethnic, Religious, and Linguistic Minorities, E/CN.4/Sub.2/AC.5/2001/2.

is found in great concentration in certain areas of the state[15] does not release the state from its obligation to 'promote the conditions necessary for persons belonging to national minorities to maintain and develop their culture, and to preserve the essential elements of their identity' where members of the minority group are found in smaller numbers outside the main areas of settlement.[16]

B. Consultation

Article 15 of the Framework Convention provides for effective participation of the minority, particularly in matters affecting them, and this has a bearing on how the state meets its obligation and promotes the necessary conditions to do so. The national minority has to be involved in the decision-making process, at least in a consultative capacity, for instance. The Advisory Committee has noted in several of its responses to government reports, under Article 25, that consultation is essential with respect to decisions regarding preservation of identity and development of culture, including the allocation of finance.[17] This consultation is especially important vis-à-vis smaller minorities. The Finnish government was commended for leaving decisions on budgetary allocations to the Sami Parliament.[18] In responding to Estonia's report, the Advisory Committee especially emphasized the need to include smaller minorities in the consultation process.[19] While the state might view minorities as one agglomerated whole, especially when fixing

[15] See Art. 10, para. 2, Art. 11, para. 3, Art. 14, para. 2 FCNM.

[16] Advisory Committee Opinion on Italy, ACFC/INF/OP/I (2002) 007, paras. 28, 31 et seq.: '32 . . . The situation of Ladins, distributed in five Alpine valleys and three provinces, is revealing here: whereas the Ladins resident in Bolzano province have long enjoyed very adequate protection, the status of the Ladins in Trento province has improved only of late due to the enactment of Constitutional Law No. 2 of 31 January 2001, which the authorities should ensure is applied appropriately. Outside these two provinces making up the autonomous region of Trentino-Alto Adige, the situation is different. Thus the Ladins living in Belluno province, which lies in an ordinary-statute region, find themselves in a distinctly less favourable position, particularly as regards education and access to the electronic media. Now, the geographical distribution of Ladins and the exclusion of a large proportion of them from certain protection measures tend to make the maintenance of their identity far more problematic. The Advisory Committee notes that efforts have been made to enhance the codification of the Ladin language, which can contribute to its preservation.'

[17] Advisory Committee Opinion on Italy, ACFC/INF/OP/I (2002), 007, 2001, para. 34: 'these measures cannot have the desired effect unless framed and implemented in consultation and collaboration with the Roma community.' See also Advisory Committee Opinion on Romania, ACFC/INF/OP/I (2002), 001, 2001, para. 31; Advisory Committee Opinion on Slovakia, ACFC/INF/OP/I (2001) 001, 2000, para. 24.

[18] Finland State Report, ACFC/SR (99) 3, 1999, para. 23; Croatia State Report, ACFC/SR (99) 5, 1999, at para. 30.

[19] Advisory Committee Opinion on Estonia, ACFC/INF/OP/I (2002) 005: '28. As regards the allocation of this support, the Advisory Committee considers it important that representatives of national minorities are involved in the decision-making process and that the needs of all minorities, including the numerically small ones, are comprehensively addressed.'

budgets and drafting laws, the smaller groups can be in as much danger of assimilation into larger minority groups as from assimilation into the majority:

40. Consulting all minorities directly and actively involving them in the identification and practical implementation of such policies will help them, particularly the numerically smaller minorities, to strengthen their identity while ensuring their integration in Moldovan society. This would also help avoid the risk, reported to the Advisory Committee by certain sources, of these minorities being merged into a population sharing one common factor—the Russian language—with little room to develop their individual identities.[20]

Finally with respect to consultation, although Article 17 promotes links with kin states by national minority groups,[21] support offered through these means cannot act as a substitute for state support.[22] The Framework Convention favours integration without the assimilation of minority groups, requiring subsequent state support in consultation with the national minority.[23]

C. Finance

Possibly the most contentious issue in minority rights is the allocation of finance to minority groups by the state. Article 13(2) of the Framework Convention expressly stipulates that where persons belonging to a national minority establish their own educational establishments, the 'exercise of this right shall not entail any financial obligation for the Parties'. However, during the drafting of Article 5 it was recognized that this wording might impose a financial obligation in certain circumstances.[24] In several reports, the Advisory

[20] Advisory Committee Opinion on Moldova, ACFC/INF/OP/I SR (2000) 2, 2000.

[21] See also European Commission for Democracy through Law (ECDL), *The Protection of National Minorities by their Kin-State* (Council of Europe Publishing, Strasbourg, 2002).

[22] See also the warning note sounded by the High Commissioner on National Minorities (HCNM) regarding the involvement of kin states: 'Protection of minority rights is the obligation of the State where the minority resides. History shows that when States take unilateral steps on the basis of national kinship to protect national minorities living outside of the jurisdiction of the State, this sometimes leads to tensions and frictions, even violent conflict.' Sovereignty, responsibility, and national minorities: Statement by R. Ekeus, OSCE High Commissioner on National Minorities, The Hague, 26 October 2001.

[23] Advisory Committee Opinion on Albania, ACFC/INF/OP/I (2003) 004, 2002: '34 . . . The Advisory Committee considers that further direct initiatives, including funding of such initiatives, should be taken by the authorities in consultation with representatives of the different national minorities, and that there should not be an over-reliance, either on civil society initiatives or on kin-state support from abroad.'

[24] CAHMIN, Report of the 1st meeting of the CAHMIN Drafting Group, CAHMIN (94), 2 Rev, 1994, p. 2. See also A. Eide, 'Commentary to the UN Declaration on the Rights of Persons Belonging to National or Ethnic, Religious and Linguistic Minorities', *UN Guide for Minorities*, part 1, Art. 4(2), para. 56: 'These measures may require economic resources from the State. In the same way as the State

Committee has commended the state for the financial support that it has given to national minorities.[25] However, the Advisory Committee indicated that the over-reliance of Albania, the second poorest state in Europe, on support from kin states for kin minorities was inappropriate.[26] With respect to Armenia, the Advisory Committee's main comments included an instruction to provide greater financial support, following criticisms from leaders of national minority groups.[27] Implicit in this comment is the idea that the state has a duty to provide financial support to national minorities: '94 . . . The Advisory Committee considers that, notwithstanding the country's economic difficulties, the authorities should make additional effort in this field, including supporting the establishment of a cultural centre for national minorities.' Interestingly, the government's response was to explain that in 2002 additional finance would be given, acknowledging that Article 5 does impose both a positive obligation and a financial burden on the state.

Where the state provides financial support, the allocation process has to be inclusive and transparent, with minority groups involved in deciding how resources should be allocated.[28] In this regard, the Czech Republic was implicitly criticized for underfunding 'numerically small national minorities which are those not represented on the Government's Council for National Minorities'.[29] In addition, the state must have a transparent process as to how funds are allocated: '[t]he Advisory Committee therefore encourages the Austrian authorities to elaborate criteria for a more transparent distribution of financial support for national minority cultural activities, and recommends that they make sure that all requests for financial support made by the different organisations representing persons belonging to national minorities are given careful consideration.'[30]

Moreover, devolving decisions to local authorities within the state can leave minorities divided across several regional boundaries with the state caught up in unnecessary bureaucracy.[31] A simplified process recognizing that the object

provides funding for the development of the culture and language of the majority, it shall provide resources for similar activities of the minority.'

25 See, for example, Finland State Report, ACFC/SR (99) 3, 1999, para. 23.

26 Advisory Committee Opinion on Albania, ACFC/SR (2001) 5, 2001, para. 34.

27 Armenia State Report, ACFC/SR (2001) 004, 2001.

28 See the commendation of Finland for devolving allocation to the Sami Parliament—Advisory Committee Opinion on Finland, ACFC/INF/OP/I (2001) 002, 2000, para. 23. See also, Norway State Report ACFC/SR (2001) 1, 2001, para. 29.

29 Advisory Committee Opinion on the Czech Republic, ACFC/INF/OP/I (2002) 002, 2001, para. 32. See also the Italy State Report, ACFC/SR (99) 007, 1999, para. 30.

30 Advisory Committee Opinion on Austria, ACFC/SR (2000) 3, 2000, para. 25.

31 Advisory Committee Opinion on Germany, ACFC/SR (2000) 1, 2000, para. 27.

is to promote conditions for persons belonging to national minorities in order for them to maintain and develop their culture would respond to those cases where the minority group is spread out across the state:

26 ... [The Advisory Committee] notes that the financial support granted to the Sorbs is paid through the Sorbian People's Foundation, whose budget is provided jointly by the Federal authorities, the Land of Brandenburg and the Free State of Saxony. The role of the Foundation is to support measures or projects to foster the Sorbian language and culture. The Advisory Committee considers that this institution . . . is an interesting solution insofar as it clearly exemplifies co-operation in this field between the Federal authorities and the Länder, while at the same time providing a principal partner to whom Sorbian associations seeking to finance their projects can turn.[32]

Wherever possible, the state should devolve decision making on the use of the budget to the minority groups themselves, as Finland has done vis-à-vis the Sami Parliament.[33]

D. Religion

There is less noted about religious minorities in states' Article 25 Reports and the Advisory Committee's opinions when dealing with Article 5 than about linguistic issues. This is not to suggest that religious issues have been fully met by states.[34] Rather this implicit prioritization flows from the day-to-day immediacy of promoting the conditions necessary for maintaining linguistic culture. Indeed, the number of cases involving religious minorities before the ECtHR suggests that the Advisory Committee needs to monitor Article 8 of the Framework Convention carefully. While the rights of religious minorities are a topic for analysis in relation to Article 8 of the Framework Convention, there is at least one aspect of the Strasbourg jurisprudence on Article 9 of the European Convention for the Protection of Human Rights and Fundamental Freedoms (ECHR) that is directly pertinent to Article 5. In the same way that democratic pluralism requires a freedom of expression that may offend, shock, or disturb; the state has to allow for various religious minorities to self-regulate:

The Court recalls that freedom of thought, conscience and religion is one of the foundations of a 'democratic society' within the meaning of the Convention. The pluralism

[32] This might explain the Advisory Committee's criticism of Germany's confusing system for other minority groups. See German State Report, ACFC/SR (2000) 1, 2000, para. 27.

[33] Finland State Report, ACFC/SR (99) 3, 1999, para. 23.

[34] Nor should one overlook the fact that while religion might be the way of identifying a group, it is not the exercise of its faith that is central to its needs. It is debatable how far the state needs to put in place conditions for the group in general so that it can maintain and develop its culture and preserve its religious identity. See Advisory Committee Opinion on Cyprus, ACFC/INF/OP/I (2002) 004, 2002, para. 29 dealing with the Maronites' need for housing and schools to preserve the community.

indissociable from a democratic society, which has been dearly won over the centuries, depends on it. . . . [The] Court does not consider that, in democratic societies, the State needs to take measures to ensure that religious communities remain or are brought under a unified leadership. . . . Although the Court recognises that it is possible that tension is created in situations where a religious or any other community becomes divided, it considers that this is one of the unavoidable consequences of pluralism.[35] The role of the authorities in such circumstances is not to remove the cause of tension by eliminating pluralism, but to ensure that the competing groups tolerate each other (see, *mutatis mutandis, Plattform 'Ärtze für das Leben' v Austria* Series A, vol.139, § 32).[36]

Article 5 of the Framework Convention is designed to allow persons belonging to the national minority to run their own affairs, to enjoy cultural autonomy. The state has a dual role, to avoid unjustified interference and to facilitate steps by the minority group to maintain and develop their own culture. Article 5 is the explicit acknowledgement that the guarantee of freedom of religion for individuals requires necessary conditions to be put in place by the state.

E. Language

There are specific provisions of the Framework Convention dealing with language rights and it is not part of a review of Article 5 to duplicate that analysis. This section will consider the scope of the state's obligation towards the persons belonging to the national minorities, so as to allow them to preserve their linguistic identity and maintain and develop their culture. This particular aspect of Article 5 ties in with obligations the state might already have with respect to the European Charter for Regional or Minority Languages.[37] As paragraph 11 of the Explanatory Report to the Charter clearly states:

The charter sets out to protect and promote regional or minority languages, not linguistic minorities. For this reason emphasis is placed on the cultural dimension and the use of a regional or minority language in all the aspects of the life of its speakers. The charter does not establish any individual or collective rights for the speakers of regional or minority languages. Nevertheless, the obligations of the parties with regard to the status of these languages, and the domestic legislation which will have to be introduced in compliance with the charter, will have an obvious effect on the situation of the communities concerned and their individual members.

[35] Author's footnote: '*cf. Tsarknias* v. *Greece* (45629/99) (1999), EHRR, Second Section, where it was held that the application was inadmissible given that the applicant had tried to disrupt church services.'

[36] *Serif* v. *Greece* (38178/97) (1999), EHRR-IX, Second Section, paras. 49–53.

[37] Council of Europe, European Charter for Regional or Minority Languages, ETS No. 148 (adopted 5 November 1992, entered into force 1 March 1998).

The Charter has a complicated structure[38] and, while it can add substance to the state's obligation towards a linguistic minority under the Framework Convention, it does not provide a direct avenue to improve the rights of persons belonging to that minority. At best, if the expert committee set up under Part IV of the Charter to monitor implementation were to hold that the state's domestic implementation had been deficient, this example could be used by the Advisory Committee when giving its opinion on an Article 25 Report under the Framework Convention.[39]

States parties also need to have regard for the politically binding obligations laid out in the documents of the Organization for Security and Co-operation in Europe (OSCE).[40] As noted above, Article 33 of the Copenhagen Document speaks of protecting and promoting the identity of national minorities, including an obligation to consult with them. In addition, while the OSCE High Commissioner on National Minorities (HCNM) is a tool of conflict prevention rather than an international ombudsperson for minority groups, the Office has consistently used minority rights standards to provide parameters for the proper relationship between the state and national minorities. The Office has been instrumental in providing guidelines as to how certain rights can be implemented at the national level, linguistic minorities being

[38] The Charter has a core set of principles and then a specialized series that is meant to allow states to tailor their obligations to their particular circumstances:

'Article 2—Undertakings

1. Each Party undertakes to apply the provisions of Part II to all the regional or minority languages spoken within its territory and which comply with the definition in Article 1.

2. In respect of each language specified at the time of ratification, acceptance or approval, in accordance with Article 3, each Party undertakes to apply a minimum of thirty-five paragraphs or sub-paragraphs chosen from among the provisions of Part III of the Charter, including at least three chosen from each of the Articles 8 and 12 and one from each of the Articles 9, 10, 11 and 13.

Article 3—Practical arrangements

1. Each Contracting State shall specify in its instrument of ratification, acceptance or approval, each regional or minority language, or official language which is less widely used on the whole or part of its territory, to which the paragraphs chosen in accordance with Article 2, paragraph 2, shall apply.'

[39] Advisory Committee on the Framework Convention for the Protection of National Minorities, Rules of Procedure, 1998, rule 39.

[40] As for the distinction between politically and legally binding rights, see A. Bloed, L. Leicht, M. Nowak, and A. Rosas, 'Monitoring the CSCE Human Dimension: In Search of its Effectiveness', in *Monitoring Human Rights in Europe* (Martinus Nijhoff, Dordrecht, 1993), 51–2. Bloed cites P. van Dijk, 'The Final Act of Helsinki: Basis for a Pan-European System?', *Netherlands Yearbook of International Law*, 110/11 (1980), 97–124: 'The difference should not be exaggerated, as the binding force of [OSCE] commitments is not seriously doubted. . . . "A commitment does not have to be legally binding in order to have binding force" the distinction between legal and non-legal binding force resides in the legal consequences attached to the binding force', not in the binding force as such. Violation of politically, but not legally binding agreements is as unacceptable as any violation of the norms of international law. In this respect there is no difference between politically and legally binding rules.'

a major part of the High Commissioner's work.[41] With respect to language rights, the 1998 Oslo Recommendations Regarding the Linguistic Rights of National Minorities 'provide a useful reference for the development of State policies and laws which will contribute to an effective implementation of the language rights of persons belonging to national minorities, especially in the public sphere'.[42] The implementation of language rights for persons belonging to national minorities properly falls under a consideration of Articles 9 to 14 of the Framework Convention, but the Oslo Recommendations make it clear how a state might fulfil its Article 5 obligations.

At the very least, if a state seeks to 'promote the conditions necessary for persons belonging to national minorities to maintain and develop their culture, and to preserve the essential elements of their identity, namely their . . . language', it should not unnecessarily interfere with the publications, in whatever form, of the minority group. As the ECtHR has held on numerous occasions:

> The Court reiterates the fundamental principles underlying its judgments relating to Article 10 . . . Freedom of expression constitutes one of the essential foundations of a democratic society and one of the basic conditions for its progress and for each individual's self-fulfilment. Subject to paragraph 2 of Article 10, it is applicable not only to 'information' or 'ideas' that are favourably received or regarded as inoffensive or as a matter of indifference, but also to those that offend, shock or disturb. Such are the demands of that pluralism, tolerance and broadmindedness without which there is no 'democratic society'. As set forth in Article 10, this freedom is subject to exceptions, which must, however, be construed strictly, and the need for any restrictions must be established convincingly.[43]

In conclusion, protecting and promoting the identity and culture of linguistic minorities goes to the very root of a pluralistic democracy. Moreover, it is one

[41] Namely, Russians in the Baltics, Greeks in Albania, and Hungarians throughout Central and Eastern Europe and the Balkans.

[42] OSCE, Foundation on Interethnic Relations, The Oslo Recommendations Regarding the Linguistic Rights of National Minorities, Annual Report, The Hague, February 1998.

[43] Taken from *Arslan* v. *Turkey* (23462/94) (1999) EHRR 42, Grand Chamber, para. 44. See also *Baskaya and Okçuoglu* v. *Turkey* (23536/94 and 24408/94) (1999) EHRR 43; *Ceylan* v. *Turkey* (23556/94) (1999) EHRR 44; *Erdogdu and Ince* v. *Turkey* (25067/94 and 25068/94) (1999) EHRR 45; *Gerger* v. *Turkey* (24919/94) (1999) EHRR 46; *Karatas* v. *Turkey* (23168/94) (1999) EHRR 47; *Okçuoglu* v. *Turkey* (24246/94) (1999) EHRR 48; *Polat* v. *Turkey* (23500/94) (1999) EHRR 49; *Sürek and Özdemir* v. *Turkey* (23927/94 and 24277/94) (1999) EHRR 50; *Sürek* v. *Turkey (No. 1)* (26682/95) (1999), EHRR 51; *Sürek* v. *Turkey (No. 2)* (24122/94) (1999) EHRR 52; *Sürek* v. *Turkey (No. 3)* (24735/94) (1999) EHRR 53; and *Sürek* v. *Turkey (No. 4)* (24762/94) (1999) EHRR 54. In addition, see *Marsali* v. *Turkey* (40077/98) (2000), (EHRR), 2nd Section, admissibility; *Zana* v. *Turkey* (26982/95) (2000) EHRR 132, 1st Section, admissibility; *Sener* v. *Turkey* (26680/95) (2000) EHRR 376, 3rd Section.

area where there is a plethora of guidance in various areas allowing the state to facilitate that protection and promotion by persons belonging to national minorities.

F. Culture and Traditions

In one sense, culture is simply an all-encompassing term to describe that which constitutes the identity of the national minority. It is in this sense that it is used in Article 5 when it speaks of maintaining and developing culture, and it therefore applies to all national minorities. However, identity can also consist of 'traditions and cultural heritage'; an aspect of culture not necessarily based on language or religion, but possibly both. Culture in this sense comes to the fore with respect to indigenous peoples and the Roma. Such minority groups might have linguistic and religious differences from the majority, but it is their overall culture that is their defining feature and characteristic:

> The applicant urged the Court to take into account recent international developments, in particular the Framework Convention for the Protection of Minorities, in reducing the margin of appreciation accorded to States in light of the recognition of the problems of vulnerable groups, such as [Roma]. The Court observes that there may be said to be an emerging international consensus amongst the Contracting States of the Council of Europe recognising the special needs of minorities and an obligation to protect their security, identity and lifestyle (see paragraphs 55–59 above, in particular the Framework Convention for the Protection of Minorities), not only for the purpose of safeguarding the interests of the minorities themselves but to preserve a cultural diversity of value to the whole community.[44]

Indigenous peoples are recognized as having distinct rights in addition to those available to minorities,[45] yet they can also assert minority rights.[46] The Roma's status as a national minority is not in question, but like indigenous peoples, it is their traditions and cultural heritage as a whole that define them. The

[44] *Chapman* v. *United Kingdom* (27238/95) (2001) EHRR, Grand Chamber, para. 93.

[45] United Nations Draft Declaration on the Rights of Indigenous Peoples, E/CN.4/SUB.2/1994/2/Add. 1, 1994.

[46] See the series of cases before the Human Rights Committee under Article 27: *Sandra Lovelace* v. *Canada*, Comm. No. 24/1977, UN Doc. CCPR/C/OP/1, 1977, Office of the High Commissioner for Human Rights, para. 83; *Kitok* v. *Sweden*, Comm. No. 197/1985, CCPR/C/33/D/197/1985, 1988; *Bernard Ominayak, Chief of the Lake Lubicon Band* v. *Canada*, Comm. No. 167/1984, UNGAOR, 45th Session, UN Doc. Supp. No. 40, A/45/40, 11 HRLJ 305, 1990; *A.B.* v. *Italy, South Tirol Case*, Comm. No. 413/1990, Decision on Admissibility, 12 HRLJ 25, 1991; *Ilmari Länsman* v. *Finland*, CCPR/C52/D/511/1992, 1994; *J. G. A. Diergaardt (late Captain of the Rehoboth Baster Community) et al.* v. *Namibia*, Comm. No. 760/1997, CCPR/C/69/D/760/1997, 2000; *Apirana Mahuika* v. *New Zealand*, Comm. No. 547/1993, UN Doc. CCPR/C/70/D/547/1993, 2000.

state's obligation under Article 5 of the Framework Convention to promote the conditions necessary remains, but those conditions are more extensive with respect to indigenous peoples and the Roma. In this regard, it is worth noting that the cases dealing with 'way of life' claims before the Strasbourg organs of the ECHR have involved the Sami and the Roma.[47]

The Advisory Committee has gone further than the European Court and Commission of Human Rights. In its opinion responding to Germany's Article 25 Report,[48] it dealt with the case of *Noack* v. *Germany*.[49] *Noack* concerned the relocation of a Sorb[50] village in Germany so as to permit mining for lignite. The applicants were thirteen villagers, the evangelical community, and Domowina, an organization defending Sorb interests. Domowina was held to have no standing to bring a complaint 'contre une mesure qui frappe ses membres',[51] as groups and organizations can bring claims under the ECHR, but they must be victims in their own right.[52] Although the complaint was declared inadmissible and it was found that the cultural association, Domowina, was not a victim and thus had no standing, *Noack* does recognize that the interests of a minority group to preserve its way of life are relevant within ECHR jurisprudence. Part of the Court's reasoning in declaring the application inadmissible was that the Sorb identity would not be destroyed even though the villagers would be displaced by the mining venture:

> A further decisive factor for the Court is that the inhabitants of Horno will be transferred together to a town approximately twenty kilometres from their village of origin and within the area where the Sorbs originally settled. A majority of the inhabitants opted for that town after being consulted on their choice of destination. Even though the transfer means a move and reorganising life in the resettlement area, the inhabitants will continue to live in the same region and the same cultural environment, where the

[47] *G and E* v. *Norway* (9278 and 9415/81) (1983), 35 DR 30, paras. 35–6; *Buckley* v. *United Kingdom* (20348/92) (1995), Commission, 19 EHRR CD 20. Buckley's complaints were, however, rejected by the Court: (23/1995/529/615) (1996), Reports 1996-IV, No. 16; *Chapman* v. *United Kingdom*, above, n. 44; *Jane Smith* v. *United Kingdom* (25154/94) (2001) EHRR 45; *Lee* v. *United Kingdom* (25289/94) (2001) EHRR 46; *Beard* v. *United Kingdom* (24882/94) (2001) EHRR 42; *Coster* v. *United Kingdom* (24876/94) (2001) EHRR 44, Grand Chamber. See also the extensive jurisprudence under the American Convention on Human Rights dealing with indigenous peoples—for example, *Mayagna (Sumo) Awas Tingni Community* v. *Nicaragua (Judgment)*, Inter-American Court of Human Rights, Series C No. 79, 31 August 2001.

[48] Advisory Committee Opinion on Germany, ACFC/INF/OP/I (2002) 008, 2002.

[49] *Noack and Others* v. *Germany* (46346/99) (2000) EHRR, 4th Section.

[50] Sorbs are ethnic Slavs.

[51] See also *Association des amis de Saint-Raphaël et de Fréjus* v. *France* (45053/98) (2000) EHRR, 3rd Section.

[52] See also *Grande Oriente D'Italia di Palazzo Giustiniani* v. *Italy* (35972/97) (1999) (2001) EHRR 496, 4th Section, *Ekin Association* v. *France* (39288/98) (2000) (2001) EHRR 469, 3rd Section.

protection of the rights of the Sorbs is guaranteed by Article 25 of the Constitution of the *Land* of Brandenburg (see Relevant Domestic Law above), where their language is taught in the schools and used by the administrative authorities, and where they will be able to carry on their customs and in particular to attend religious services in the Sorbian language.

Noack is a good example of how minority rights ought to be realized within the state under the ECHR. A balancing exercise needs to take place, on condition that the minority group has a voice in the decision-making process. That having been said, however, the Advisory Committee obviously felt that Germany had not fulfilled its obligations despite the ruling of the European ECtHR in relation to Article 5 of the Framework Convention:

32. The Advisory Committee recalls that Article 5 of the Framework Convention requires the Parties to promote the conditions necessary for persons belonging to national minorities to maintain and develop their culture, and to preserve the essential elements of their identity. As the forced dissolution of municipalities in which members of national minorities traditionally reside is undeniably likely to make the preservation of their identity more difficult, it is essential, for such an action to be compatible with Article 5 of the Framework Convention, that it is taken only as a last resort, when there is no alternative. In the case of the municipality of Horno, where all the legal channels—national and international—have been exhausted, the Advisory Committee considers it to be indispensable that the German authorities make sure that the Sorbian inhabitants concerned can continue to enjoy the rights and facilities they have enjoyed thus far in the cultural and linguistic field. It is also essential that the Sorbian character and culture is clearly visible in the municipality of Forst where the majority of the inhabitants will be resettled. In order to avoid such situations in the future, the Advisory Committee expects that the German authorities will pay due heed to Article 5 of the Framework Convention when weighing any public interest against the legitimate aspirations of the Sorbian people to maintain their culture and preserve their identity.[53]

[53] See also, the opinion of the Advisory Committee Opinion on Finland, ACFC/INF/OP/I (2001) 002, 2000, Art. 5, para. 22: 'Given the importance of reindeer herding, fishing and hunting to the Sami as an indigenous people, the issue of land rights in the Sami Homeland is of central relevance to the protection of Sami culture and their identity. Therefore, the Advisory Committee expresses the wish that the existing dispute over land rights in this area be resolved as expeditiously as possible in a manner that will contribute to the protection of the culture of the Sami without interfering with the rights of the non-Sami population. The Advisory Committee is of the opinion that the central role of the Sami Parliament should be maintained in this process and adequate resources should be secured for the Sami Parliament to carry out its tasks in this sphere. The Advisory Committee further emphasises that, while the issue of land rights is being reviewed, the existing practices relating to the use of the land at issue should be carried out in a manner that does not threaten the maintenance or development of Sami culture or the preservation of their identity. This concerns, *inter alia*, logging operations administered by the National Board of Forestry.'

While the Advisory Committee does not have the same authority to encourage compliance with reference to the Framework Convention as the European Court of Human Rights has with the ECHR, it does address those areas where there is overlap. Given that there is no minority rights provision in the ECHR, it is not fanciful to say that issues concerning the group qua group will be more directly addressed by the reasoning of the Advisory Committee involving Article 5 of the Framework Convention.

G. Effective Participation

While not a specific element of identity among persons belonging to national minorities like 'religion, language, traditions and cultural heritage', effective participation is an essential factor to consider if the state is to promote the conditions necessary to maintain and develop the culture and to preserve the essential elements of that identity.[54] Consultation with the minority group as part of Article 5 has already been discussed as a general matter, while effective participation is required for all under Article 15. It is worth noting that Articles 5 and 15 both speak of promoting or creating the conditions necessary for persons belonging to national minorities to enjoy their rights.

As shown below, a minority group has a right to form its own organizations for self-governance and promotion:[55] 'The inhabitants of a region in a country are entitled to form associations in order to promote the region's special characteristics. The fact that an association asserts a minority consciousness cannot in itself justify an interference with its rights under Article 11 of the [ECHR].'[56] Not only should the state refrain from interfering,[57] it may also

[54] A. Cassese, *Self-Determination of Peoples: A Legal Reappraisal* (Cambridge University Press, Cambridge, 1995); P. Alston (ed.), *People's Rights* (Oxford University Press, Oxford, 2001).

[55] OSCE, Foundation on Interethnic Relations, the Lund Recommendations on the Effective Participation of National Minorities in Public Life, The Hague, 1999, § III promulgated at the request of the OSCE High Commissioner on National Minorities; see also K. Myntti, *A Commentary to the Lund Recommendations on the Effective Participation of National Minorities in Public Life* (Institute for Human Rights, Åbo Akademi University, Turku, 2001), and OSCE Office for Democratic Institutions and Human Rights (ODIHR), Guidelines to Assist National Minority Participation in the Electoral Process, Warsaw, 2001.

[56] *Stankov and United Macedonian Organisation ILINDEN* v. *Bulgaria* (29221/95 and 29225/95) (1998) (2001) EHRR 563, 1st Section, para. 89.

[57] *Sidiropoulos and Others* v. *Greece* (26695/95) (1998) EHRR 55, 57/1997/841/1047, paras. 43–7, where the ECHR held in 1998 that the refusal by the Greek courts to register an organization calling itself 'Home of Macedonian Civilization' violated Art. 11 ECHR (freedom of association). Banning the organization was disproportionate since its proposed aims were purely cultural as depicted from its draft memorandum of association. Despite asserting the existence of a 'Macedonian' minority in Greece, the Greek authorities should have respected the organization's fundamental liberties as derived from the international human rights framework. See also *Stankov* above, n. 56, para. 97, where the

have positive obligations to assist the minority and support it in the formation of such organizations.[58] The Advisory Committee has commended Finland and Norway for their Sami parliaments and the degree of devolution granted to them. It is taken as given that states parties to the Framework Convention will consult with the minority with respect to Article 5 matters in all the responses of the Advisory Committee to Article 25 reports. Therefore, the conditions necessary to allow persons belonging to national minorities to maintain and develop their culture include organizational structures that allow for effective participation in the decision-making process of the state as it pertains to the position of the national minority.

H. Specific Groups

Within any state, the position of some minorities will always require special measures. Often, very substantial minorities will be able to obtain these measures simply through their strength of numbers that cannot be ignored by the government. In other cases, ethnic minorities will have their position enhanced because of their association with another state in the region.[59] However, some minorities still require special measures because their group is small or it has suffered years of prejudice. Equality of treatment is relevant vis-à-vis the majority, but also with respect to other minority groups. Moreover, discriminating between minority groups can be justified if there is a reasonable and objective justification.[60]

When signing or ratifying, several states have entered declarations and reservations, often in order to specify those groups that are to be recognized as national minorities for the purposes of the Framework Convention. As such, other minority groups in the state are disfavoured. However, only the Russian Federation has so far protested this as contrary to the purposes of the Convention.[61] Nevertheless, the Advisory Committee has on several

Court held that democratic principles require states to allow the existence even of political parties with secessionist aims. It is important to note that despite the Court not recognizing the express right to secession, secession should not be excluded as a topic suitable for democratic debate. NB. Incitement to violence, rejection of democratic principles, and seeking the expulsion of others from the territory would all allow for restrictions to the provisions of Art. 11, paras. 97 and 100.

[58] European Centre for Minority Issues (ECMI), Towards Effective Participation of Minorities Principles, E/CN.4/Sub.2/AC.5/1999/WP, Expert Seminar, Flensburg, 1999. For specific limitations, see *Refah Partisi (The Welfare Party) and Others* v. *Turkey* (41340/98, 41342/98, 41343/98, and 41344/98) (2001) EHRR 408, 3rd Section, Grand Chamber. *Gorzelik and Others* v. *Poland* (44158/98), (2001) (2004) EHRR, 4th Section, admissibility, merits, Grand Chamber.

[59] Danes in Germany and Germans in Denmark, or ethnic Hungarians in Romania, are some examples.

[60] Regarding Art. 4, para. 3 FCNM, see *Lindsay and Others* v. *United Kingdom* (8364/78) 1979 3 CMLR 166 paras. 170–1 and *The Liberal Party and Others* v. *United Kingdom* (1982) 4 EHRR 106.

[61] Declaration contained in the instrument of ratification deposited on 21 August 1998.

occasions indicated that certain groups who fall within the remit of the Framework Convention require special measures. Sometimes this is due to the small size of the national minority, particularly if it risks disappearing altogether if the state does not promote special conditions for it.[62] In this manner of thinking, the Advisory Committee advised the Czech Republic that numerically small minorities needed greater support in terms of 'annual state subsidies to assist with the preservation and promotion of the cultural activities, identities, traditions and languages of national minorities'.[63]

Due to the entrenched discrimination that they have faced throughout most of Europe, the other main focus of these special measures has been the Roma. In order to rectify their comparatively worse position in contrast with most other minorities in Europe, the Advisory Committee has recommended several states take particular steps to protect them from discrimination. The argument that history cannot be rectified is defeatist,[64] it has been argued. It might take some time, but states need to address the institutionalized racism that the Roma have experienced.

III. Conclusion and Outlook

Article 5(1) could be used by the Advisory Committee to ensure that states parties to the Framework Convention carry out the most fundamental step in creating a truly pluralistic society: effective dialogue between the state and sub-state entities. Article 5(1), alongside Article 1, acknowledges the role of the state in ensuring that national minorities are neither allowed to be 'frozen in time', nor to 'wither on the branch'. The danger of assimilation is more directly

62 Advisory Committee Opinion on Austria, ACFC/INF/OP/I/ (2002) 009 3, 2002, Art. 5, para. 26 with respect to Czech and Slovak minorities; Advisory Committee Opinion on Cyprus, ACFC/INF/OP/I (2002) 004, 2001, 2 Rev. Art. 5, para. 29, *re* Maronites; Advisory Committee Opinion on Norway, ACFC/INF/OP/I (2003) 003, 2002, Art. 5, para. 34 on the Skogfinns.

63 Advisory Committee Opinion on the Czech Republic, ACFC/INF/OP/I (2002) 002, 2001, Art. 5, para. 32.

64 Namely Comment of the Government of Albania on the Opinion of the Advisory Committee on the Report on the Implementation of the Framework Convention for the Protection of National Minorities in Albania, GVT/COM/INF/OP/I (2003) 004, 2003, para. 35: 'With regard to the Advisory Committee concern for the assimilation of Vlachs/Aromanians in Albania, experts should have in mind that this process of integration is not an event of today, but a result of a long historical process and the passed situation cannot be returned artificially [*sic*]. This does not signify that the particularities of the Vlach community need not to be taken into consideration especially since they have preserved up to the present time their linguistic and cultural features among others. The Albanian state undoubtedly should take measures and encourage the preservation of these features. It is not easy for the Albanian Government to acknowledge the return of the historical assimilating processes taken place [*sic*] in the past centuries, but nevertheless it should support the remaining elements of the above mentioned linguistic identity'.

addressed in Article 5(2), but it is Article 5(1) that reflects the broader, more positive idea of the state providing an environment where persons belonging to national minorities can determine how best to maintain their culture and preserve the essential elements of their identity. In the development of their culture, states are not trapped in a historical time warp, and nor should minorities be.

Article 5(2)

I. Background

Once again, this provision originated in the Venice Commission's Draft Convention on the Protection of Minorities,[65] and needs to be read with Article 16 of the Framework Convention that prevents indirect assimilation through population movements or boundary changes: '[t]he Parties shall refrain from measures which alter the proportions of the population in areas inhabited by persons belonging to national minorities and are aimed at restricting the rights and freedoms flowing from the principles enshrined in the present framework Convention.' The final form of Article 5(2) took some time to resolve in CAHMIN, reflecting the balance between integration and assimilation perspectives. As might be expected, constraints on integration rather than the rejection of assimilation gave rise to the debate.[66] In the end, the references to 'social cohesion' were relegated to the Explanatory Report. It is notable that while CAHMIN called for some examples of what is meant by 'general integration policy' to be included in the Explanatory Report, it is devoid of any such guidance.[67]

II. Analysis

This provision has been formulated both negatively and positively: the state should refrain from assimilating persons belonging to national minorities and should protect them from such processes. Nevertheless, it prohibits neither

[65] ECDL, Preliminary Draft Convention on the Protection of Minorities DAJ.SC. DEMOCRACYCONV.MIN, 1990, Art. 5, 13.

[66] See the proposals of the Austrian and Romanian delegations as set out in CAHMIN, Proposals Concerning the Preliminary Draft Framework Convention for the Protection of National Minorities, CAHMIN (94) 12, 14 Rev., 1994.

[67] CAHMIN, 2nd meeting, CAHMIN (94) 9, Meeting Report, 1994.

a general integrationist policy,[68] such as teaching everyone the national language as provided for by Article 12(1), nor voluntary assimilation by any person belonging to a national minority. The dividing line between integration and assimilation remains very thin,[69] but integration makes the national minority and its culture part of the state, helping to define it, whereas assimilation makes members of the national minority part of the state to the exclusion of their national minority status. In certain ways, Article 5(2) can be seen as the obverse of the obligation under Article 5(1) to promote the conditions necessary so that persons belonging to a national minority can maintain and develop their culture and preserve their identity—voluntary assimilation of individual persons belonging to national minorities is contemplated in Article 5(1).[70] On the other hand, if all the members of a particular national minority decided to assimilate voluntarily, it would call into question the state's commitment to fulfil its Article 5(1) obligations. As such, several issues stemming from Article 5(2) issues have been dealt with above.

The ultimate form of assimilation is enshrined in Article II(e) of the 1948 Genocide Convention,[71] where the crime is deemed to include 'forcibly transferring children of the group to another group'. To fall within the Convention's bounds, the group that it is intended to destroy in whole or in part has to be defined in terms of its national, ethnic, racial, or religious origin. It is clear that in extreme cases assimilation might amount to genocide, but this would be rare, and issues pertaining to the Framework Convention would hardly be paramount in such circumstances. Ethnocide, on the other hand, is not

[68] Above, n. 58, para. 3(1) which indicated that effective participation of the minorities served towards integration of 'all groups as an essential component of peaceful, democratic and pluralist societies'.

[69] J. McGarry and B. O'Leary, 'Introduction: The Macro-political Regulation of Ethnic Conflict', in J. McGarry and B. O'Leary, *The Politics of Ethnic Conflict Regulation* (Routledge, London, 1993), 3, particularly paras. 7, 11. See also W. Kymlicka, *The Rights of Minority Cultures* (Oxford University Press, Oxford, 1995), 28 with respect to the United States: 'a deliberate decision was made not to accept any territory as a state [within the US] unless these national groups were outnumbered'. See also T. Roosevelt, 'Every immigrant who comes here should be required within five years to learn English or leave the country', 1918, cited in B. Bryson, *Made in America* (Morrow, New York, 1994), 143. While there were concentrations of various ethnic groups in different parts of the United States, their desire to integrate meant that English became their first language within a generation—see H. L. Mencken, *The American Language (Abridged)*, cited in Bryson, *Made in America*, 142.

[70] Conference on Security and Co-operation in Europe (CSCE), Meeting of Experts on National Minorities, Geneva, 1991, III, para. 4, which incorporates both ideas into one paragraph: 'They reconfirm that persons belonging to national minorities have the right freely to express, preserve and develop their ethnic, cultural, linguistic or religious identity and to maintain and develop their culture in all its aspects, free of any attempts at assimilation against their will.'

[71] Convention on the Prevention and Punishment of the Crime of Genocide, UNGA Res. 260 (III), 9 December 1948, 78 UNTS No. 1021, 78 (1951).

criminalized if the destruction of culture is all that is encompassed.[72] Nevertheless, such a development would amount to a violation of the human rights of the persons belonging to a national minority, including their rights under the Framework Convention.

More pertinent to the present study is assimilation that falls short of group destruction. As Eide has so clearly noted in relation to Article 1 of the 1992 UN Declaration:[73]

21. The relationship between the State and its minorities has in the past taken five different forms: elimination, assimilation, toleration, protection and promotion. Under present international law, elimination is clearly illegal. The Declaration is based on the consideration that forced assimilation is unacceptable. While a degree of integration is required in every national society in order to make it possible for the State to respect and ensure human rights to every person within its territory without discrimination, the protection of minorities is intended to ensure that integration does not become unwanted assimilation or undermine the group identity of persons living on the territory of the State.

This resonates with the calls for tolerance within a pluralistic society from the ECtHR discussed under Article 5(1).

In practice, the Advisory Committee has found few examples of assimilation in the Article 25 Reports, although indifference to the specific needs of numerically small minorities could ultimately lead to their disappearance. Since Article 5(2) is drafted so that it only covers policies or practices aimed at assimilation, such indifference may not be contrary to Article 5(2), even though it fails to live up to the standards of Article 5(1). With respect to Estonia,[74] the Advisory Committee has, however, noted the thin line between assimilation and integration:

27 . . . The Advisory Committee is of the view that efforts aimed at supporting the culture and identity of persons belonging to national minorities are essential for an integrated society. It follows that such measures should receive increasing attention also in the implementation of the national integration programme, which has, so far, to a large extent focused on the promotion of the state language. In this connection, the Advisory Committee welcomes the Government's commitment to ensure that the programme results in integration and not assimilation of persons belonging to national minorities.

[72] Commission on Human Rights, Technical Review of the United Nations Draft Declaration on the Rights of Indigenous Peoples, UN Economic and Social Council, E/CN.4/Sub.2/1994/2/Add. 1, 46th session, para. 34 et seq.

[73] Above, n. 14.

[74] Advisory Committee Opinion on Estonia, ACFC/INF/OP/I (2002) 005.

III. Conclusion and Outlook

Overall, in the context of the Framework Convention, which operates through the domestic implementation of standards and reports submitted by governments to the Committee of Ministers—with only the Advisory Committee to provide independent scrutiny—it is unlikely that direct assimilation will take place. Rather the focus of discussion will be on whether the state has done enough to promote the necessary conditions under Article 5(1) for persons belonging to national minorities to develop and maintain their culture and preserve their identity.

ARTICLE 6

Geoff Gilbert

1. The Parties shall encourage a spirit of tolerance and intercultural dialogue and take effective measures to promote mutual respect and understanding and co-operation among all persons living on their territory, irrespective of those persons' ethnic, cultural, linguistic or religious identity, in particular in the fields of education, culture and the media.
2. The Parties undertake to take appropriate measures to protect persons who may be subject to threats or acts of discrimination, hostility or violence as a result of their ethnic, cultural, linguistic or religious identity.

Article 6(1)

I. Background

Article 6(1) of the Framework Convention for the Protection of National Minorities (FCNM) stems from the Ad Hoc Committee for the Protection of National Minorities' (CAHMIN) examination of the right to be taught in the minority language and it provides an overview of the integration of the minority group as part of society.[1] In balancing the need for the persons belonging to the national minority to preserve their own culture, and yet be fully integrated into the state, the need for tolerance and intercultural dialogue with respect to everyone else in the state was seen as essential. One can also see its roots in paragraph 36 of the Conference for Security and Co-operation in Europe (CSCE)'s Copenhagen Document:[2] '[e]very participating State will promote a climate of mutual respect, understanding, co-operation and solidarity among all persons living on its territory, without distinction as to ethnic or national origin or religion, and will encourage the solution of problems through dialogue based on the principles of the rule of law.' If Article 12 of the Framework Convention deals with intercultural interaction in the educational sector, then Article 6(1) is intended to extend this principle more generally to society as a whole.[3]

Article 6(1) is a programmatic measure that could hardly give rise to a justiciable claim before any court or other decision-making body. Encouraging 'a spirit of tolerance and intercultural dialogue' and promoting 'mutual respect and understanding and co-operation' are objectives for states to work towards, but it is unlikely that they will ever be fully realized. Nevertheless, Article 6(1) cannot be ignored by states because of its programmatic nature. It is phrased in compelling terms such that states *shall* 'encourage' and 'take effective measures'. Furthermore, its ideals translate into several more substantive provisions in the Framework Convention, such as Articles 4, 11, and 12. Reading the Advisory Committee's opinions, there is also a suspicion that they treat Article 6(1) as a catchall provision.[4] It is important to note from the start, therefore, that the Advisory Committee has used and will, in all likelihood, continue to use

[1] Ad Hoc Committee for the Protection of National Minorities (CAHMIN), 3rd meeting, CAHMIN (94) 13, meeting report, 1994.

[2] Second Conference on the Human Dimension of the CSCE, Document of the Copenhagen Meeting of the Conference on the Human Dimension of the CSCE, Copenhagen, 1990.

[3] See the Norwegian proposal, CAHMIN, Proposals concerning the Preliminary Draft Framework Convention for the Protection of National Minorities, CAHMIN (94) 14 Rev., 1994; CAHMIN, Preliminary Draft Framework Convention for the Protection of National Minorities, CAHMIN (94) 12, 1994.

[4] How one finds that child trafficking, even if it is children belonging to national minorities, falls within Art. 6(1) is less than obvious—see Advisory Committee on the Framework Convention for the Protection of National Minorities, Opinion on Albania, ACFC/INF/OP/I (2003) 004, 2002, para. 41. See also Advisory Committee Opinion on Germany, ACFC/INF/OP/I (2002) 008, 2002, para. 36, concerning the over-representation of Roma and Sinti children in lower secondary schools and special schools for under-achievers; and Advisory Committee Opinion on the Czech Republic, ACFC/INF/OP/I (2002) 002, 1999, para. 49: 'In addition, the State Report indicates that the legal obligation on religious organisations to enlist 10,000 members who are permanently resident in the Czech Republic in order to be registered as legal entities and have access to state subsidies is creating

Article 6(1) to engage with the state to meet its obligations to create a pluralistic society in which the minority group does not just exist, but is a full part of the identity of the state. If Article 5(1) was about states creating the conditions in which the persons belonging to the minority group can develop their culture, Article 6(1) focuses on how a minority group can relate to other state mechanisms and form part of the overall culture of the majority society.

One other issue stands out as needing to be highlighted in this introduction: the scope of the Article. Article 6(1) expressly refers to 'all persons living on the territory', not just persons belonging to national minorities. As such, there is debate about the breadth of its possible application where states have limited the remit of the Framework Convention through reservations or declarations, excluding some national minorities that would otherwise enjoy its benefits and protection.

II. Analysis

A. Linkages with Other Articles of the Framework Convention

The concepts of tolerance, dialogue, and mutual respect are all predicated on equality and non-discrimination.[5] Therefore, Article 4 is directly relevant to Article 6(1). With respect to Austria, the Advisory Committee referred to Article 6(1) when commenting on discrimination faced in employment

practical problems for these organisations. The Advisory Committee appreciates the fact that the Government envisages legislative changes in order to overcome the existing problems.'

It is not that these issues are not important and pertinent to persons belonging to national minorities; it is only that it is difficult to see how they fall within Art. 6.

[5] Favouring one minority over others can give rise to discrimination, leading to greater intolerance towards other minorities. This might arise where there is one more substantial minority group within the state. Problems created by Moldova's quite natural emphasis on Russian language speakers over other Slavic speaking minorities, are a prime example of this development. For further detail, see the Advisory Committee Opinion on Moldova, ACFC/INF/OP/I SR (2000) 2, 2000, para. 45: 'The Advisory Committee is concerned, however, with the existing language gap between two population groups: the majority, on the one hand, who speak the state language, and the Russian-speaking population on the other hand, which includes not only mother tongue Russians but also other Slavic minorities whose languages do not have the same level of protection as Russian. The Advisory Committee considers that the authorities should make sure that developments in the language policy intended to give Russian a higher status do not widen the above mentioned gap. As such a gap is likely to give rise to linguistic intolerance both on the part of the majority and on the part of the national minorities the Advisory Committee considers that the Moldovan authorities should pay special attention to this question when implementing the recently adopted National Minorities Act. Care should be taken that any measures in this respect—be they legislative or otherwise—help to safeguard social cohesion and intercultural dialogue.'

See also *Case Relating to Certain Aspects of the Laws on the Use of Languages in Education in Belgium* v. *Belgium (Merits)* (1474/62) (1968) ECHR 3, pp. 61–71.

matters by Austrian citizens of immigrant background.[6] As regards Cyprus, the Advisory Committee dealt with the manner in which incidences of discrimination are recorded.[7] While the Committee's responses obviously fall within Article 4 in both of these cases, their relationship to Article 6 is a little more tenuous. The overlap with Article 4 is pertinent to Article 6 for those cases where discrimination undermines mutual respect: '[t]he Advisory Committee also refers to its comments in respect of Article 4, to the effect that the practice of placing Roma in camps is not apt to enhance their integration. Placement of Roma in camps of this kind can indeed only aggravate the risks of discrimination against them and is thus not compatible with Article 6 of the Framework Convention.'[8]

The connection between Article 6 and Article 11(3) is clearer. The use of dual language signs in areas where minorities are densely concentrated obviously speaks to the issue of tolerance and mutual respect. In erecting the signs, the state is meeting, in part, its Article 6(1) obligations, as well as those of Article 11(3).[9] Furthermore, Article 12(1) has direct relevance where it states that 'the Parties shall, where appropriate, take measures in the fields of education and research to foster knowledge of the culture, history, language and religion of their national minorities and of the majority'. Moreover, to the extent that fostering knowledge of minority groups falls within Article 6, there is no self-contained limitation to restrict its use to cases only where it is appropriate. Nevertheless, as previously stated, Article 6 is a programmatic duty of the state that does not engender justiciable rights for persons belonging to national minorities.[10] The related provisions are the ones under which the

[6] Advisory Committee Opinion on Austria, ACFC/INF/OP/I (2002) 009, 2002, para. 34.

[7] Advisory Committee Opinion on Cyprus, ACFC/INF/OP/I (2002) 004, 2001. In respect of cases of discrimination, the Advisory Committee notes that no governmental agency appears to be collecting or registering data on such cases. The Advisory Committee is of the opinion that the government should review this state of affairs (see also comments under Art. 4).

[8] Advisory Committee Opinion on Italy, ACFC/INF/OP/I (2002) 007, 2001, para. 39.

[9] Advisory Committee Opinion on Austria, ACFC/INF/OP/I (2002) 009, 2002, para. 29: 'The Advisory Committee acknowledges that an atmosphere of increasing tolerance has gradually developed in Carinthia since the 1972 dispute over place names on signposts, and notes with satisfaction that the results of several studies reveal that coexistence between persons belonging to the majority and persons belonging to the Slovene minority has grown more harmonious.'

[10] Which seems preferable to the messy provision that the CSCE's Geneva Meeting of Experts on National Minorities produced that contains programmatic and normative elements, even within the same sentence. CSCE, Meeting of Experts on National Minorities, Geneva, 1991, IV, para. 3: 'The participating States are convinced that the preservation of the values and of the cultural heritage of national minorities requires the involvement of persons belonging to such minorities and that tolerance and respect for different cultures are of paramount importance in this regard. Accordingly, they confirm the importance of refraining from hindering the production of cultural materials concerning national minorities, including by persons belonging to them.'

content of the right should be examined because it is therethrough that the individual is empowered.

B. Scope of Article 6(1)

Article 6(1) applies to 'all persons living on their territory'. Moreover, Article 6(2) protects 'persons', not just 'persons belonging to' national minorities. At first glance, therefore, Article 6(1) is not limited to persons belonging to national minorities resident on the territory,[11] and the Advisory Committee's opinions on the Article 25 reports of several states illustrate this perspective. For instance, the Committee has applied Article 6(1) to asylum seekers,[12] immigrants, and non-citizens,[13] contrary to the usual understanding of the term 'persons belonging to a national minority' in the European system. Moreover, upon signature or ratification, several states entered declarations or reservations defining the groups that counted as national minorities. Of those states that have been challenged within the scope of Article 6(1), Austria, Denmark, Liechtenstein, and Malta have entered such limiting clauses. In response, they have indicated their disagreement with the alleged remit of Article 6(1) of the Framework Convention as put forward in the opinions of the Advisory Committee.[14] To the extent that the reservations and declarations only define national minority for the purposes of the Convention, they ought to have no substantial bearing on Article 6(1). The wording of Article 6 cannot differ from that found in all the other rights-granting articles by mere chance. Insofar as Article 6(1) is a programmatic obligation for the state that does not establish justiciable rights, it makes sense that its reach be wider than the other provisions. On the other hand, Article 6(1) forms an integral part of the Framework Convention, and arguably all provisions, not just those containing

[11] Human Rights Committee General Comment No. 23 in 'The Rights of Minorities' 15th Session (1994) (50), UN Doc. CCPR/C/21/Rev.1/Add.5, Art. 27, para. 5.1.

[12] Advisory Committee Opinion on Austria, ACFC/INF/OP/I (2002) 009, 2002, para. 32; Advisory Committee Opinion on Czech Republic, ACFC/INF/OP/I (2002) 002, 2001, para. 45; Advisory Committee Opinion on Liechtenstein, ACFC/INF/OP/I (2001) 003, 2000, para. 15; Advisory Committee Opinion on Malta, ACFC/INF/OP/I (2001) 006, 2000, para. 16; Advisory Committee Opinion on Norway, ACFC/INF/OP/I (2003) 003, 2002, para. 36.

[13] Advisory Committee Opinion on Denmark, ACFC/INF/OP/I (2001) 005, 2001, para. 27; Advisory Committee Opinion on San Marino, ACFC/INF/OP/I (2001) 007, 2000, para. 16.

[14] Comments by Liechtenstein on the Opinion of the Advisory Committee on the Framework of National Minorities, GVT/COM/INF/OP/I (2001) 003, 2001: 'With regard to the asylum requests mentioned in paragraph 15 of the report, the Government of Liechtenstein shares the view of the Advisory Committee according to which the promotion by the authorities of a spirit of tolerance and mutual respect between all persons living on the territory of Liechtenstein is important. The issue mentioned in paragraph 15, however, goes beyond the scope of the Framework Convention since it concerns in the case of Liechtenstein foreigners and asylum seekers.'

the phrase 'persons belonging to national minorities', are subject to reservations and declarations. On balance, the distinctive wording of Article 6, together with the fact that the reservations and declarations refer specifically to national minorities, suggest that the wider interpretation should hold sway and definitely does so for any state that has not entered such limitations on the remit of the Framework Convention.

C. Intolerance and Prejudice

Like many other provisions in the Framework Convention, analyses of Article 6(1) have benefited from state visits undertaken on behalf of the Advisory Committee.[15] State visits by the AC, as mandated in Articles 24 to 26 of the Framework Convention, are important when dealing with intolerance and prejudice and there have been direct references to this effect in the reports of those visits.

Aside from the reports on state visits, several opinions of the Advisory Committee have highlighted instances of intolerance and prejudice shown to national minorities. This prejudice comes in several forms, revealing the scope of state duties to protect national minorities from intolerance and prejudice in society as a whole. Most directly, states have a duty to ensure that regional governments implement the international obligations accepted by central governments,[16] and that the police do not show prejudice or intolerance and follow up on complaints.[17] Secondly, there is a need to ensure that the media do not persist in stereotyping minorities.[18] Finally, there is an obligation to counteract prejudiced behaviour in the general population, such as damage

[15] See the examples from visits to Austria, Italy, and Germany.

[16] See the discrimination faced by Slovenes in Carinthia at the hands of the Landeshauptmann in the Advisory Committee's opinion, ACFC/SR (2000) 3, received 15 November 2000, para. 29.

[17] Advisory Committee Opinion on Armenia, ACFC/INF/OP/I (2003) 001, 2002, para. 41 concerning the Yezidis; Advisory Committee Opinion on Czech Republic ACFC/INF/OP/I (2002) 002, para. 39 et seq. concerning the Roma; Advisory Committee Opinion on Italy, ACFC/INF/OP/I (2002) 007, 2001, para. 38, concerning the Roma; Advisory Committee Opinion on Ukraine, ACFC/INF/OP/I (2002) 010, 2002, para. 37 et seq.; Advisory Committee Opinion on the United Kingdom, ACFC/INF/OP/I (2002) 006, 2001, para. 45 et seq.

[18] Advisory Committee Opinion on Albania, ACFC/INF/OP/I (2003) 002, 2002, para. 37 concerning Roma, Egyptians, and Greeks; Advisory Committee Opinion on Finland, ACFC/INF/OP/I (2001) 002, 2000, para. 27 concerning Roma and Russians; Advisory Committee Opinion on Italy, ACFC/INF/OP/I (2002) 007, 2001, para. 37 concerning Roma; Advisory Committee Opinion on Romania, ACFC/INF/OP/I (2002) 001, 2001, para. 34 concerning Roma; Advisory Committee Opinion on Ukraine, ACFC/INF/OP/I (2002) 010, 2002, para. 39, concerning Roma and Jews. See also, International Covenant on Civil and Political Rights (ICCPR) (entered into force 23 March 1976), UNGA Res. 2200A (XXI), 1966, UN Doc. A/6316, Art. 20; *Jersild* v. *Denmark*, (15890/89) (1994) EHRR 33, Grand Chamber.

to bilingual signs,[19] or addressing religious intolerance, particularly towards non-traditional churches and the Jewish community.[20]

While the police definitely form part of the state,[21] state duties vis-à-vis third parties indicate the horizontal responsibilities that the Framework Convention imposes, and which states have to enforce.[22] In turn, this is a logical corollary of the preambular obligation 'to implement the principles set out in this framework Convention through national legislation and appropriate governmental policies'. Thus, the Advisory Committee opinion on the Article 25 Report of Croatia referred to the stance of the various churches, '[i]n addition to governmental authorities, a constructive stance by other relevant actors, such as the Churches operating in Croatia, is essential to solidify a spirit of tolerance and intercultural dialogue.'[23] It is difficult to see how a judicial model of minority rights could try to regulate church behaviour, unless the action was so egregious that it left the state liable for any oversight in protecting individuals from rights violations.[24] To that extent, the programmatic nature

[19] NB Art. 11(3) FCNM. See also, Advisory Committee Opinion on Albania, ACFC/INF/OP/I (2003) 004, 2002, para. 39, concerning Greeks; Advisory Committee Opinion on Norway, ACFC/INF/OP/I (2003) 002, 2002, para. 35, concerning Sami.

[20] Advisory Committee Opinion on Armenia, ACFC/INF/OP/I (2003) 001, 2002, para. 41, concerning non-traditional churches; Advisory Committee Opinion on Austria, ACFC/INF/OP/I (2002) 009, 2002, para. 33 concerning Jews; Advisory Committee Opinion on Ukraine, ACFC/INF/OP/I(2002), 010, 2002, para. 38, concerning religious groups.

[21] On whether one can restrict the freedom of expression of police officers writing in their private capacity—see Comments of the Government of Finland on the Opinion of the Advisory Committee on the Report on the Implementation of the Framework Convention for the Protection of National Minorities in Finland, GVT/COM/INF/OP/I (2001) 002, 2001. See also, ICCPR, above, n. 18.

[22] Or indirectly change behaviour through education and training—see Comments of the Government of Albania on the Opinion of the Advisory Committee on the Report on the Implementation of the Framework Convention for the Protection of National Minorities in Albania, GVT/COM/INF/OP/I (2003) 004, 2003, referring to media training; see Comments of the Government of the Czech Republic on the Opinion of the Advisory Committee on the Report on the Implementation of the Framework Convention for the Protection of National Minorities in the Czech Republic, GVT/COM/INF/OP (2002) 002, 2002, referring to police training.

[23] Advisory Committee Opinion on Croatia, ACFC/INF/OP/I (2002) 003, 2001.

[24] *Agga* v. *Greece (No.2)* (50776/99, 52912/99) (2002) EHRR 671, 1st Section: '60. It is true that the Government argued that, in the particular circumstances of the case, the authorities had to intervene in order to avoid the creation of tension among the Muslims in Xanthi and between the Muslims and the Christians of the area as well as Greece and Turkey. Although the Court recognises that it is possible that tension is created in situations where a religious or any other community becomes divided, it considers that this is one of the unavoidable consequences of pluralism. The role of the authorities in such circumstances is not to remove the cause of tension by eliminating pluralism, but to ensure that the competing groups tolerate each other (see, *mutatis mutandis*, the *Plattform "Ärzte für das Leben"* v. *Austria Judgment* (A/139) (1988), ECHR 139). In this connection, the Court notes that, apart from a general reference to the creation of tension, the Government did not make any allusion to disturbances among the Muslims in Xanthi that had actually been or could have been caused by the existence of two religious leaders. Moreover, the Court considers that nothing was adduced that could

of Article 6(1) of the Framework Convention is a useful complement to the human rights protection regime.

D. Intercultural Dialogue

While a state can try to prevent intolerance and prejudice, promoting intercultural dialogue is a much more ephemeral obligation.[25] Nevertheless, any Article 25 Report has to provide evidence that the state has taken appropriate measures to this end. The opinion relating to Estonia is instructive in this regard:[26]

> With respect to the media, the Advisory Committee notes that the media environment is to a large extent divided between the media consumed by the majority population and that followed by the minority population. As this is a factor that may serve to strengthen existing negative stereotypes and to complicate inter-ethnic dialogue, the Advisory Committee considers that further initiatives to counter this excessive division are needed and welcomes the relevant projects that are already included in the national integration programme.

Moreover, while the concept may be ephemeral, there are a variety of practical steps that can be taken to promote intercultural dialogue. For example, Hungary was advised that de facto separation of schools into Roma and non-Roma was a serious impediment to the promotion of tolerance and intercultural dialogue.[27] In addition, the Norwegian response to a reported lack of awareness amongst the police of minority issues was to establish central and local fora for dialogue with representatives drawn from the police and the various minority groups.[28] Furthermore, it is implicit in the opinion on the Slovak Article 25 report that greater efforts will be needed to promote cultural interaction where the minority is numerically small.[29] Finally, the need for

warrant qualifying the risk of tension between the Muslims and Christians or between Greece and Turkey as anything more than a very remote possibility.'

[25] Although the two are inextricably intertwined, as can be seen by the Advisory Committee Opinion on the Czech Republic, ACFC/INF/OP/I (2002) 002, 2001, para. 38: 'Nevertheless, the Advisory Committee notes that there is still insufficient inter-cultural dialogue in the Czech Republic. Attitudes of intolerance and hostility towards national minorities, especially Roma, are still widespread.' See also, Advisory Committee Opinion on Romania, ACFC/INF/OP/I (2002) 001, 2001, para. 33, concerning Roma.

[26] Advisory Committee Opinion on Estonia, ACFC/INF/OP/I (2002) 005, 2001, para. 31.

[27] Advisory Committee Opinion on Hungary, ACFC/INF/OP/I (2001) 004, 2001.

[28] Comments of the Government of Norway on the Opinion of the Advisory Committee on the Report on the Implementation of the Framework Convention for the Protection of National Minorities in Norway, GVT/COM/INF/OP/I (2003) 003, 2003.

[29] On the positive side, see Advisory Committee Opinion on Hungary, ACFC/INF/OP/I (2001) 004, 2000, para. 25. In this connection, the Advisory Committee also notes that studies suggest that the attitudes of the majority towards the Hungarian minority are most positive in the regions where

close co-operation with the press and other media cannot be underestimated in the practical implementation of intercultural dialogue.[30]

E. Integration

Again, it is difficult to enforce integration,[31] but states are in a better position to encourage it than the more ephemeral idea of intercultural dialogue. One way to accomplish this in a manner directly relevant to minorities throughout the region, is through the relaxation of citizenship laws:[32]

> In the context of enhancing integration measures, the Advisory Committee welcomes the improvements offered by the new Act amending citizenship law, which entered into force on 1 January 2001. This new act provides for children born in Germany of foreign parents to acquire German nationality and substantially shortens the minimum length of residence required before non-citizens can be naturalised. These more flexible provisions can but facilitate the integration into German society and therefore to contribute to the aims of Article 6 of the Framework Convention.

Integration efforts have been made particularly difficult given the redrawing of European borders since 1989, and the consequent difficulties. As such, it is entirely proper that the Advisory Committee has used Article 6 to challenge state practices in this regard: '[f]urthermore, as the lack of citizenship can be a real obstacle to the integration of non-citizens and their participation in political life, the Advisory Committee considers that the Austrian authorities should make sure that the legislation on citizenship is applied fairly and in a non-discriminatory manner to all applicants . . .'[33]

Hungarians constitute a relatively high proportion of the population and where there is constant interaction between the majority and the said minority.

30 Advisory Committee Opinion on Italy, ACFC/INF/OP/I (2002) 007, 2001, para. 35: 'In view of the various submissions made during its visit to Italy and in the light of information made available to it, the Advisory Committee is of the opinion that in general, with the exception of the Roma minority, the linguistic minorities protected by Law No. 482 of 15 December 1999 live on good terms with the rest of the population, and that their relations are marked by great tolerance. It nonetheless considers that Italy could do more to foster intercultural understanding, to which the media for their part could contribute constructively. Consequently, with due respect for the independence of the media, the government could seek to associate them more closely with its action in this matter . . .'

31 Forced integration often tends towards assimilation.

32 Advisory Committee Opinion on Germany, ACFC/INF/OP/I (2002) 008, 2002, para. 40.

33 Advisory Committee Opinion on Austria, ACFC/INF/OP/I (2002) 009, 2002, para. 35; see also, Advisory Committee Opinion on Moldova, ACFC/INF/OP/I (2003) 002, 2002, para. 48: 'The Advisory Committee also notes the existence in Moldova of approximately 4,000–5,000 people of Afro-Asian origin (about 0.1% of the population), including Syrians, Lebanese, Turks, Sudanese and Chinese, some of whom have lived there for more than 10 years without having been able to acquire Moldovan citizenship, because of certain legal and bureaucratic difficulties. The Advisory Committee understands that the Moldovan authorities are looking into the matter and encourages them to find an appropriate solution.'

Education, particularly in relation to the national language, can also assist processes of integration.[34] Equally, in certain circumstances the institution of quotas can be helpful. Correspondingly, part of the Romanian response to the opinion of the Advisory Committee was to indicate that places have been reserved for Roma candidates in the entrance exam for the Police Academy.[35] Given the distrust between the Roma and the police, such a measure should have a direct and tangible impact.

III. Conclusion and Outlook

Given that the Advisory Committee has been prepared to use Article 6(1) as a catchall for a wide variety of issues that have been raised, it would be rash to predict its outlook with any attempt at precision. Nevertheless, Article 6(1) clearly has a specific function in relation to intercultural dialogue and integration. Although its language is programmatic, the mandatory obligation it imposes on states parties means that the Advisory Committee will continue to use it in matters regarding media stereotyping, policing failures, and citizenship laws. Moreover, there is sufficient Advisory Committee practice for it to be clear that Article 6(1) applies to everyone within the state, including refugees and new minorities, not just persons belonging to national minorities. As such, the reservations and declarations made by some states have no bearing on its remit.

Article 6(2)

I. Background

In contrast to the programmatic nature of Article 6(1), Article 6(2) is more normative, requiring states to put measures in place to prohibit hatred towards a minority group because of its identity. Once again, there is considerable overlap with Article 4, which guarantees to persons belonging to national minorities equality before the law and equal protection of the law. Individual guarantees are properly analysed under Article 4, however state obligations also fall within the remit of Article 6(2), and will be examined here.

[34] Advisory Committee Opinion on Germany, ACFC/INF/OP/I (2002) 008, 2002, para. 39.

[35] Comments of the Government of Romania on the Opinion of the Advisory Committee on the Report on the Implementation of the Framework Convention for the Protection of National Minorities in Romania, GVT/COM/OP/INF/I (2002) 001, 2002.

Article 6(2) is drawn from Article 40(2) of the Conference for Security and Co-operation in Europe (CSCE)'s Copenhagen Document, where:

> The participating States clearly and unequivocally condemn totalitarianism, racial and ethnic hatred, anti-semitism, xenophobia and discrimination against anyone as well as persecution on religious and ideological grounds. In this context, they also recognize the particular problems of Roma (gypsies).
>
> They declare their firm intention to intensify the efforts to combat these phenomena in all their forms and therefore will: . . .
>
> —commit themselves to take appropriate and proportionate measures to protect persons or groups who may be subject to threats or acts of discrimination, hostility or violence as a result of their racial, ethnic, cultural, linguistic or religious identity, and to protect their property . . .

The only reason that 'racial' was dropped from the phrasing of this provision was to ensure consistency with the rest of the Framework Convention.[36] It should also be noted in this context, that the European Court of Human Rights (ECtHR) has held that discrimination can amount to inhuman and degrading treatment under Article 3 of the European Convention for the Protection of Human Rights and Fundamental Freedoms (ECHR).[37]

II. Analysis

What clearly emerges from the Article 25 reports is that states must have criminal law in place to address race hate crimes and anti-discrimination laws.[38] The principal areas to be addressed under Article 6(2) seem to concern

[36] CAHMIN, 4th meeting, CAHMIN (94), meeting report, 1994. See also, the International Convention on the Elimination of all Forms of Racial Discrimination (adopted 21 December 1965, entered into force 4 January 1969), UNGA Res. 2106 (XX), 1965, Art. 4.

[37] *East African Asians* v. *the United Kingdom* (4403/70) (1970) ECHR 928; and *Cyprus* v. *Turkey* (25781/94) (2001) ECHR 327, Grand Chamber, para. 310, 311, 499: 'For the Court it is an inescapable conclusion that the interferences at issue were directed at the Karpas Greek-Cypriot community for the very reason that they belonged to this class of persons. The treatment to which they were subjected during the period under consideration can only be explained in terms of the features which distinguish them from the Turkish-Cypriot population, namely their ethnic origin, race and religion. The Court would further note that it is the policy of the respondent State to pursue discussions within the framework of the inter-communal talks on the basis of bi-zonal and bi-communal principles . . . The respondent State's attachment to these principles must be considered to be reflected in the situation in which the Karpas Greek Cypriots live and are compelled to live: isolated, restricted in their movements, controlled and with no prospect of renewing or developing their community. The conditions under which that population is condemned to live are debasing and violate the very notion of respect for the human dignity of its members.'

[38] Advisory Committee Opinion on Romania, ACFC/INF/OP/I (2002) 001, 2001, para. 38, welcoming the new Romanian anti-discrimination law.

the press, the police, and discrimination by both public and private actors.[39] Regarding discrimination, the Advisory Committee criticized Finland for its failure to respond to discriminatory treatment of the Roma. Discrimination is a criminal offence under the Finnish penal code, but there was a demonstrated failure to investigate and prosecute incidents when Roma were denied entry to restaurants.[40] In reports on Romania, the Roma were shown to have suffered direct discrimination in terms of job advertisements and entry to places of entertainment contrary to the demands of Article 6(2).[41]

As for the press, the criticism of Romania noted above also included reference to the fact that editors had gone unpunished despite publishing discriminatory adverts. Nevertheless, Romania has reported that it has obtained a conviction against a journalist for an anti-Semitic article under 'Article 317 of the Criminal Code concerning national and chauvinistic propaganda and incitement to racial or national hatred'.[42] The classic problem remains that certain sections of the press stereotype persons belonging to national minorities, even where legislation exists to prohibit such behaviour:

> The Advisory Committee also notes that certain media continue to present news in a manner likely to kindle ethnic intolerance in the public, or to include negative stereotypes of certain minority groups. The Advisory Committee . . . notes in this context that Article 4.1.a of the Press Act of 26 October 1994 prohibits incitement to national, racial or religious hatred and discrimination. The Advisory Committee therefore considers the Moldovan media themselves should be watching out constantly for this type of problem through their own watchdog bodies.[43]

In addition, the Advisory Committee criticized the United Kingdom because its Press Complaints Commission can only take up a complaint from

[39] Advisory Committee Opinion on Malta, ACFC/INF/OP/I (2001) 006, 2000, para. 17, dealing with discrimination 'in the renting of accommodation and in the access to certain places of entertainment'. NB Malta entered a Declaration on ratification (10 February 2004) that there were no national minorities in Malta, but in the practice of the Advisory Committee, Art. 6 is not limited to national minorities.

[40] Advisory Committee Opinion on Finland, ACFC/INF/OP/I (2001) 002, 2000, para. 25. See also, the prosecution by the Slovak authorities of a restaurant manager who refused to serve Roma in *Miroslav Lacko* v. *Slovakia*, Comm. 11/1998, 2001, CERD/C/59/D/11/1998.

[41] Above, n. 38.

[42] Comments of the Government of Romania on the Opinion of the Advisory Committee on the Report on the Implementation of the Framework Convention for the Protection of National Minorities in Romania, GVT/COM/INF/OP/I (2002) 001, 2002. See also Comments of the Government of Austria on the Opinion of the Advisory Committee on the Report on the Implementation of the Framework Convention for the Protection of National Minorities in Austria, GVT/COM/INF/OP/I (2002) 009, 2002 in response to the opinion of the Advisory Committee regarding the Penal Code that criminalizes inflammatory articles and holds that such material is not protected by freedom of the press.

[43] Advisory Committee Opinion on Moldova, ACFC/INF/OP/I (2003) 002, 2002, para. 47.

an identified individual who has been the victim of pejorative reporting. 'This therefore means that there is a vacuum in which press reports that may contain generally pejorative or prejudicial statements, and may be inaccurate, racist and personally harmful to individuals or the group concerned, cannot be objected to, as they are not directed at a particular person.'[44] There is nothing inherently wrong with self-regulation, but measures must be put in place to ensure that it is effective and comprehensive.

Finally, and with respect to the media, avoiding direct discrimination against national minorities is the basic minimum. Indirect discrimination, such as failure to report events important to the lives of persons belonging to national minorities, must equally be addressed.[45]

The concept of equality before the law requires that the police treat everyone within a territory equally, respecting everyone and providing proper investigation for all complaints.[46] The institutionalized racism that was found to pervade the British police in the Stephen Lawrence Inquiry has to be addressed to meet the United Kingdom's obligations under Article 6(2) of the Framework Convention, for example. Moreover, while incitement to racial hatred was listed as a crime under the UK's Public Order Act 1986, the fact that all prosecutions needed the approval of the Attorney-General meant the law was

[44] Advisory Committee Opinion on the United Kingdom, ACFC/INF/OP/I (2002) 006, 2001, para. 53.

[45] See the praise meted out to Armenia for its apparent success in this field. Advisory Committee Opinion on Armenia, ACFC/INF/OP/I (2003) 001, 2002, para. 39. See also Art. 9 FCNM.

[46] See also *Anguelova* v. *Bulgaria* (38361/97) (2000) EHRR 484, 4th Section; *Moldovan, Rostas et al.* v. *Romania* (41138/98, 64320/01) (2001) EHRR, 1st Section, admissibility partial (3 March 2001) and 2nd Section admissibility final (3 June 2003); *Kalin* v. *Turkey* (31236/96) (2001) EHRR, 3rd Section—where the Court held there was a case to answer with respect to Art. 14 taken together with Arts. 6 and 10—the applicant alleged there was an administrative practice of discrimination based on ethnic origin. In *Nachova and Others* v. *Bulgaria* (43577/98 and 43579/98) (2004) EHRR 89, 1st Section, it was held that failure to carry out a proper investigation by the police could allow the Court to draw negative inferences or shift the burden of proof from the applicant:

'169. In light of the above, the Court considers that in cases where the authorities have not pursued lines of inquiry that were clearly warranted in their investigation into acts of violence by State agents and have disregarded evidence of possible discrimination, it may, when examining complaints under Article 14 of the Convention, draw negative inferences or shift the burden of proof to the respondent Government, as it has previously done in situations involving evidential difficulties. . . .

171. In these circumstances, the Court considers that the burden of proof shifts to the respondent Government, which must satisfy the Court, on the basis of additional evidence or a convincing explanation of the facts, that the events complained of were not shaped by any prohibited discriminatory attitude on the part of State agents. . . .

175. In sum, having regard to the inferences of possible discrimination . . . the failure of the authorities to pursue lines of inquiry—in particular into possible racist motives—that were clearly warranted in their investigation, the general context and the fact that this is not the first case against Bulgaria in which Roma have been alleged to be the victims of racial violence at the hands of State

deemed ineffective in practice.[47] A failure to prosecute has also been noted in relation to Cyprus, including ill-treatment emanating from the police. As with the United Kingdom, the response in Cyprus has been to improve the investigatory process.[48] The Slovak Republic was also reported to have a police culture of failing to investigate Roma and other minorities' complaints. Moreover, the Advisory Committee was concerned that the police were 'over-hesitant to qualify alleged crime as racially motivated'.[49] The Advisory Committee even went so far as to contend that Romania had failed to meet its obligations under Article 6(2) because of the failure of the police to investigate claims by, in particular, the Roma, and because the police engaged in brutality against them.[50] For all states, the failure by the police to treat all persons belonging to national minorities equally before the law must be seen as the most critical dereliction of the state's international obligations.

III. Conclusion and Outlook

Article 6, in general, is distinctive within the Framework Convention because it applies to everyone within the state, not just persons belonging to national minorities. This is particularly relevant with respect to threats and discrimination

agents, and noting that no satisfactory explanation for the events has been provided by the respondent Government, the Court finds that there has been a violation of Article 14, taken together with Article 2, of the Convention.'

Such an approach by the Court would greatly assist persons belonging to national minorities to bring Art. 14 claims where the police do not treat them equally.

47 Advisory Committee Opinion on the United Kingdom, ACFC/INF/OP/I (2002) 006, 2001, para. 52. See also, *LK* v. *The Netherlands*, Comm. No. 4/1991, 1993, UN Doc. CERD/C/42/D/4/1991: '6.4 The Committee cannot accept any claim that the enactment of law making racial discrimination a criminal act in itself represents full compliance with the obligations of States parties under the Convention.'

48 Advisory Committee Opinion on Cyprus, ACFC/INF/OP/I (2002) 004, 2001, para. 32 of the Advisory Committee's opinion; Comments of the Government of Cyprus on the Opinion of the Advisory Committee on the Report on the Implementation of the Framework Convention for the Protection of National Minorities in Cyprus, GVT/COM/INF/OP/I (2002) 004 2001. The Advisory Committee provided the following views where Roma in Hungary did not have their complaints investigated and were subject to police brutality: 'The Advisory Committee considers that there is sufficient reason for the Hungarian authorities to carry out, separately or in the context of the review recommended under Article 4, a full review (1) of the way in which complaints about racially motivated crimes and police brutality are treated, investigated and prosecuted; (2) of the existence of anti-Roma prejudice within the police and prosecuting authorities and (3) the ways in which shortcomings in the current situation can be improved.' Advisory Committee Opinion on Hungary, ACFC/INF/OP/I (2001) 004, 2000, para. 25, 26. Cf. *CP* v. *Denmark* Comm. No. 5/1994, 1994, UN Doc. CERD/C/46/D/5/1994.

49 Advisory Committee Opinion on Slovakia, ACFC/INF/OP/I (2001) 001, 2000, para. 28 et seq.

50 Advisory Committee Opinion on Romania, ACFC/INF/OP/I (2002) 001, 2001, paras. 40–2.

based on ethnicity, language, or religion under Article 6(2). Furthermore, it is necessary for the state to implement criminal laws against hate speech, as well as anti-discrimination laws. If proper respect for other cultures were shown in line with Article 6(1), Article 6(2) would address issues that ought not to arise. Moreover, while there is an obvious link between the two paragraphs of Article 6, Article 6(2) provides the negative reinforcement to complement several other provisions within the Framework Convention, particularly those that address freedom of expression.

ARTICLE 7

Zdenka Machnyikova

The Parties shall ensure respect for the right of every person belonging to a national minority to freedom of peaceful assembly, freedom of association, freedom of expression and freedom of thought, conscience and religion.

I. Background

A. Issues

Article 1 of the Framework Convention for the Protection of National Minorities (FCNM) confirms that the protection of national minorities and of the rights and freedoms of persons belonging to those minorities forms an integral part of the international protection of human rights. In this respect, the inclusion of Article 7 underlines the fact the Framework Convention does not create a new category of rights; rather, minority rights are naturally embedded in the human rights protection system.[1] More specifically, the point of departure

[1] The 1990 Document of the Copenhagen Meeting on Human Dimension of the Conference on Security and Co-operation in Europe, which provided guidance for drafting the FCNM, clearly articulated in para. 30 that 'respect for rights of persons belonging to national minorities as part of universally recognized human rights is an essential factor for peace, justice, stability and democracy in the participating states'. Second Conference on the Human Dimension of the CSCE, Document of the Copenhagen Meeting of the Conference on the Human Dimension of the CSCE, Copenhagen, 1990.

for the protection of national minorities is that the fundamental value of human dignity is equally inherent in all human beings and is accompanied by equal and inalienable rights.[2] In fact, in the European context, it was for a long time believed that proper respect for universal human rights and the principle of non-discrimination would provide sufficient protection for persons belonging to minorities.[3] It is true that a great deal could be accomplished on this basis. As a general rule, if human rights are fully respected then all individuals, whether from a minority or the majority group, will enjoy both the right and the opportunity to pursue their legitimate interests. However, to apply this principle to its full effect sometimes requires that persons belonging to minorities receive strengthened protection and additional rights.

In short, minority standards are supplementary to general human rights. They have been adopted partly to remove any doubt that members of minorities, jointly as well as individually, are fully entitled to all human rights,[4] and partly to ensure that conditions exist by which they can preserve and develop their own identity.[5] The core aspects of this protection of identity are: the rights for persons belonging to national minorities to organize themselves as a group; to use their own language; to be able to preserve, reproduce, and develop their own culture; and to participate in public life. From this perspective, enjoyment of some human rights and fundamental freedoms is of special relevance to the preservation of the identity of a minority group. In particular, these rights and freedoms include: the right to freedom of association and assembly; the right to freedom of expression; and the right to freedom of religion and belief, all of which are preconditions necessary for the preservation of the common spiritual consciousness of a minority and for expression of its common interests and aspirations. This is the main reason why these particular rights are found among the guarantees of the FCNM.

Furthermore, it should be noted that the right to freedom of expression, and the right to association and assembly, are fundamental political rights, and as such are

[2] UNGA, Universal Declaration of Human Rights (UDHR) (adopted on 10 December 1948), UNGA Res. 217 (III) (1948), UN Doc. A/810, Art. 1 affirms that 'All human beings are born free and equal in dignity and rights.'

[3] For instance, within the Council of Europe it was concluded by the Committee of Experts, in considering inclusion of a special provision guaranteeing rights of national minorities in a second additional protocol to the European Convention for the Protection of Human Rights and Fundamental Freedoms (ECHR) in 1973, that from a legal point of view there was no special need to make the rights of minorities the subject of a further protocol to the ECHR. See the Preparatory Work of the Ad Hoc Committee for the Protection of National Minorities (CAHMIN), Explanatory Report to the Framework Convention for the Protection of National Minorities, CAHMIN H(1995) 010, 1995, paras. 1–2.

[4] See the principles expressed in Art. 4 FCNM.

[5] See the principles expressed in Art. 5 FCNM.

important elements of the state's recognition of the plurality of communities and interests within society. The democratic function of these rights is of clear importance for national minorities, as these rights are a prerequisite for the participation of persons belonging to national minorities in public life. History, as well as recent experience, shows that suppression of these rights can lead to the alienation of minorities, to violence, and to their seeking solutions outside the existing framework of the state. In this respect the 1990 Document of the Copenhagen Meeting on the Human Dimension of the Conference on Security and Co-operation in Europe (Copenhagen Document of the CSCE), upon which the legal obligations of the FCNM were built, stressed in the preambular paragraph to the commitments concerning minority guarantees that:

> The participating States recognize that the questions relating to national minorities can only be satisfactorily resolved in a democratic political framework based on the rule of law, with a functioning independent judiciary. This framework guarantees full respect for human rights and fundamental freedoms, equal rights and status for all citizens, the free expression of all their legitimate interests and aspirations, political pluralism, social tolerance and the implementation of legal rules that place effective restraints on the abuse of governmental power.[6]

The importance of ensuring the enjoyment of these fundamental freedoms by national minorities had already been reflected in the development of minority-specific standards. Article 27 of the International Covenant on Civil and Political Rights (ICCPR)[7] set the global minimum standard in specific terms. Rather than simply referring to the general freedoms it requires that the state not deny the right of persons belonging to ethnic, religious, and linguistic minorities to enjoy their own culture, to profess and practise their own religion, or to use their own language. The UN Declaration on the Rights of Persons Belonging to National or Ethnic, Religious, and Linguistic Minorities elaborated on Article 27 in more positive wording in Article 2(1). Paragraph 4 of this same Article specifically underlined the importance of the right of persons belonging to minorities to establish and maintain their own associations. The general principle of enjoying fundamental freedoms without any discrimination and in full equality was also stressed in Article 4(1) of the Declaration. In paragraph 31, the Copenhagen Document likewise underlined the importance of the enjoyment of fundamental rights and freedoms. More significantly, however, paragraph 32 also advanced more specific guarantees regarding the

[6] Above, n. 1, para. 30.

[7] International Covenant on Civil and Political Rights (ICCPR) (adopted 16 December 1966, entered into force 23 March 1976) 999 UNTS 171.

aspects protected by these general freedoms. The relatively modest wording of Article 7 FCNM was the result of efforts by the drafters of the Convention to adopt a more systematic approach to guarantees of minority rights. Their goal was to ensure comprehensive protection through securing, in Article 7, the enjoyment of fundamental freedoms, while at the same time providing protection for particular aspects of these freedoms by incorporating more detailed provisions throughout the Convention.

B. History and Context

The inclusion of Article 7 among the provisions of the FCNM has to be viewed in the wider context of the development of a legally binding instrument concerned with minority protection within the Council of Europe. In 1992 the Council of Europe embarked on examining the possibility of formulating specific legal standards relating to national minorities. A Committee of Experts for the Protection of National Minorities (DH-MIN), which was established under the Steering Committee for Human Rights (CDDH), started to consider an inventory of rights that could be used to formulate specific legal standards for the protection of national minorities. Four categories of rights were identified in this exercise: individual rights and freedoms of persons belonging to national minorities; individual rights and freedoms which could also be exercised jointly; collective rights and freedoms which could be exercised by national minorities; and positive measures to be taken by states. In this context, two specific options were considered for a standard-setting instrument. One was an Additional Protocol to the European Convention for the Protection of Human Rights and Fundamental Freedoms (ECHR),[8] and the other was a separate convention. In the discussion of the rights to be embodied in these instruments, it was asserted that if the option of developing an additional protocol to the ECHR were pursued, it would not be necessary to reaffirm the rights and freedoms already included in the text of the ECHR. However, if a separate convention were created, it would be important to reiterate rights and freedoms already included in the ECHR. In this respect, the argument was advanced that the Convention would be open for signature to other states which were neither members of the Council of Europe nor parties to the ECHR.[9]

[8] European Convention for the Protection of Human Rights and Fundamental Freedoms (ECHR), ETS 5, 1950.

[9] Committee of Experts for the Protection of National Minorities (DH-MIN), 1st meeting, DH-MIN (92) 7, meeting report, 1992, paras. 21–4, p. 5.

In the initial stages, both the proposals for a Special Convention and for a Framework Convention contained three separate articles with detailed guarantees for freedom of association and assembly, freedom of expression, and freedom of religion, replicating to a large extent the language of the ECHR.[10] One expert later suggested that the separate articles be replaced by a summary reference to the ECHR provisions. This proposal was rejected, since it would have put in question the 'didactic' aspect of the provisions of the Framework Convention. Further, it was argued in this context that not all protocols to the ECHR were ratified by all states parties. Finally, objections were raised that existing reservations and declarations regarding provisions of the ECHR could have a negative effect on the implementation of the provisions of the Framework Convention. Ultimately, and although the summary reference to the ECHR was rejected, the idea of grouping the rights in one provision was retained.[11]

To begin with, two different wordings for such provisions were suggested. The first was based on the negative wording of Article 27 ICCPR and the second formula, which was eventually accepted, was phrased as a positive obligation.[12] This option was preferred in particular because it was more in line with the language of the ECHR. Also, as was pointed out by some experts, given the case law of the European Court of Human Rights (ECtHR), such an undertaking is capable of carrying certain positive obligations to protect these freedoms against violations by third parties, that is, to provide horizontal protection.[13]

II. Analysis

A. General Issues

The following analysis provides a basic overview of the nature and scope of the minimum standards pertaining to the cluster of freedoms referred to in Article 7. The analysis does not provide detailed interpretation of these general

[10] Steering Committee for Human Rights (CDDH), Final Activity Report of the CDDH for the Attention of the Committee of Ministers, CDDH (93) 22, 1993, Art. 9, 10, 11.

[11] CAHMIN, 1st meeting, CAHMIN (94) 5, meeting report, 1994, paras. 29–30, pp. 6–7.

[12] Variant II stipulated: 'State Parties shall ensure, without discrimination, the respect of the right of persons belonging to a national minority to freedom of peaceful assembly and to freedom of association, their right to freedom of expression, and their right to freedom of thought, conscience and religion', CAHMIN, 1st meeting, CAHMIN (94) 5, meeting report, 1994, para. 30, p. 7.

[13] CAHMIN, 2nd meeting, CAHMIN (94) 9, meeting report, 1994, para. 34, pp. 6–7.

freedoms in light of other international instruments, as this would go beyond the scope of this chapter. Instead, it focuses mainly on the application of these freedoms under the ECHR and other instruments, as well as in the practice of the states parties, which is of particular relevance to the protection of persons belonging to national minorities. Further, given that separate articles of the FCNM deal specifically with the right to freedom of religion and the right to freedom of expression, and are therefore the focus of discussion in other chapters of this Commentary,[14] this section will address only the basic aspects of protection guaranteed by these rights.

In many respects Article 7 is an unusual provision, as it only provides references to fundamental freedoms without any elaboration of their content. However, as the Framework Convention is constructed as a set of principles and objectives rather than a set of specific rights guaranteed to persons belonging to national minorities, the relative lack of precision does not stand out in the overall context of the Convention. To understand the meaning of the undertakings in Article 7 it is necessary to consider the historical and systematic context of this provision. As mentioned with regard to the *travaux préparatoires*, Article 7 is based on corresponding provisions of the ECHR. In this context, the reference to Article 23 FCNM is of particular relevance as it identifies the relationship between the Framework Convention and the system of protection under the ECHR. It explicitly stipulates that the rights and freedoms flowing from the principles enshrined in the FCNM, insofar as they are the subject of corresponding provisions of the ECHR, shall be understood so as to conform to the latter provisions.[15] While it can be argued that the wording of the rights in Article 7 does not strictly follow the language of the provisions of the ECHR,[16] it is clear from the *travaux préparatoires* of Article 7, and from the inclusion of Article 23 into the FCNM,[17] that the drafters intended these rights to be the same as the equivalent ECHR provisions. At the same time, it is important to bear in mind that the provisions of the ECHR were not designed to respond to the special needs of national minorities. The ECHR's supervisory bodies have been constrained when dealing with different aspects of minority protection[18] by the

[14] See *inter alia* the chapters on Arts. 8, 9, 10, and 11 in this commentary.

[15] For more detailed discussion on the relationship between the FCNM and the ECHR, see the chapter on Art. 23 in this commentary.

[16] See the right to freedom of peaceful assembly and to freedom of association in Art. 11 ECHR; the right to freedom of expression in Art. 10 ECHR; and the right to freedom of thought, conscience, and religion in Art. 9 ECHR.

[17] CAHMIN, 1st meeting, CAHMIN (94) 5, meeting report, 1994, paras. 29–30, p. 7; CAHMIN, Preliminary Draft Framework Convention for the Protection of National Minorities, CAHMIN (94) 12, 1994, Art. D, p. 7.

[18] *Chapman* v. *UK* (27238/95) (2001) ECHR, Grand Chamber, paras. 93–8.

Convention's lack of specific minority provisions, and its relatively limited approach to prohibition of discrimination.[19] Given these limitations, the standards provided by the ECHR have to be seen as a minimum standard in interpreting the scope of obligations under Article 7.[20] In practice, the actual understanding by the parties of their obligations under Article 7 goes beyond the minimum standards offered by the ECHR. The emphasis is on progressive implementation of the provisions of the FCNM: the Convention sets out objectives, which the parties undertake to pursue through their national legislation and relevant governmental policies.[21] The undertaking in Article 7 compels parties to ensure respect for the rights laid down in this provision, specifically for persons belonging to national minorities. As a result, states must take steps to ensure the fulfilment of these undertakings, while taking into account the particular circumstances of national minorities.

In terms of the substance of the provision, the focus of the rights guaranteed in Article 7 is on 'freedom', which provides negative protection against interference by the state or private parties. However, Article 7 does not merely oblige the parties to respect the rights and freedoms embodied in it. Its implementation also requires that parties facilitate the exercise of these rights, in particular by providing a legislative and institutional framework for effective enjoyment of these rights within the state system. Recognition of the need for states to provide legislative guarantees of these freedoms in their domestic legislation is evident from the numerous references in state reports to constitutional provisions ensuring the right to freedom of peaceful assembly, freedom of association, freedom of expression, and freedom of thought, conscience, and religion. As many states have explicitly pointed out, these guarantees are provided for all persons under the jurisdiction of the state, whether belonging to national minorities or not. Only a couple of states have indicated that they have provisions in their constitutions or constitutional laws

[19] Until the recent adoption of Protocol No. 12 to the ECHR, the Convention provided only for the accessory prohibition of discrimination under Art. 14 with regard to the rights guaranteed in the Convention. For a critical evaluation of the European Court of Human Rights approach, see S. Spiliopoulou Åkermark, 'The Limits of Pluralism—Recent Jurisprudence of the European Court of Human Rights with Regard to Minorities: Does the Prohibition of Discrimination Add Anything?', *Journal on Ethnopolitics and Minority Issues in Europe*, 3 (2002).

[20] Above, n. 17, para. 30, p. 7 emphasized 'that in no case the interpretation of the provisions of the Framework Convention should depart from the interpretation given to the corresponding provisions of the ECHR by the European Court of Human Rights'.

[21] CAHMIN, Explanatory Report on the Framework Convention for the Protection of National Minorities, CAHMIN H(1995) 010, 1995, para. 11, 'the approaches and fundamental concepts of the Framework Convention'.

which secure these rights specifically for persons belonging to national minorities.[22]

Concerning detailed measures for the effective enjoyment of the mentioned freedoms, most reporting states refer to generic legislation regulating media, assemblies, associations, religious institutions, and churches, which also apply to national minorities. For instance, in their reports the parties provide specific information on provisions allowing persons belonging to national minorities to acquire legal personality for their minority associations and religious institutions, or to obtain a broadcasting licence. As regards minority-specific legal safeguards, states frequently guarantee persons belonging to national minorities the right to establish minority associations or organizations for the specific purpose of preserving and developing their ethnic and cultural identity.[23] As illustrated below, such associations are often provided with state financial support or are eligible for certain minority entitlements. The conditions and formalities for the establishment and functioning of such associations are entrenched either in generic laws on association[24] or in specific minority acts.[25]

Giving domestic effect to the rights detailed in Article 7 requires measures beyond the simple entrenchment of these rights in national legislation. The specific protection of an individual against violations of these rights must also be a primary concern of the state. As a result, the parties must ensure that persons belonging to national minorities have access to effective judicial and other appropriate remedies in case of a violation of the rights set out in Article 7. State reports confirm that these rights can be vindicated through the courts.[26] Hungary underlined that victims of violations of the rights guaranteed in Article 7 have the right to file a personal complaint to the Constitutional

[22] See, for example, the Slovak Constitution, Art. 34(1) which stipulates: 'The comprehensive development of citizens representing national minorities or ethnic groups in the Slovak Republic is guaranteed, particularly the right to develop their own culture, together with other members of the minority or ethnic group, disseminate and receive information in their mother tongues, associate in minority associations, and the right to create and maintain educational and cultural institutions. Details shall be laid down by law.' In Slovakia State Report, ACFC/SR (99) 8, 1999, para. 17; see also the Constitution of the Republic of Croatia, Art. 15 in Croatia State Report, ACFC/SR (99) 5, 1999, para. 89.

[23] For instance, the Ukrainian Declaration on the Rights of Ukraine's Nationalities, Art. 6 guarantees all nationalities 'the right to establish their cultural centres, societies, friendly associations, and unions. These organizations may carry out any activity directed to development of national culture, take mass measures in the order established by Law, promote setting up of national newspapers, magazines, publishing houses, museums, art groups, theatres, and cinema studios' in Ukraine State Report, ACFC/SR (99) 14, 1999, para. 20.

[24] Moldova State Report, ACFC/SR (2000) 2, 2000, para. 16; Russian Federation State Report, ACFC/SR (99) 15, 2000, para. 23.

[25] Hungary State Report, ACFC/SR (99) 10, 1999, para. 74.

[26] Ireland State Report, ACFC/SR (2001) 6, 2001, para. 64.

Court. It also observed that they have the right to personal complaint, based on the ECHR and the ICCPR, since the rights ensured in Article 7 are established in practically identical form in these conventions.[27]

Further, ensuring these freedoms may involve specific positive obligations to secure their effective exercise by preventing and remedying any infringement of these rights by private actors. This is of critical importance to national minorities since they are often the targets of intolerance, prejudice, media stereotyping, or negative attitudes on the part of local authorities. The *travaux préparatoires* and the Explanatory Report to the FCNM clearly state that Article 7 may imply positive obligations for the parties to protect the freedoms mentioned against violations which do not emanate from the state, that is, to ensure horizontal protection.[28] This means that the parties not only have to abstain from acts infringing the enjoyment of these freedoms, but they also have an obligation to impede third parties from engaging in such acts. In brief, states parties should provide evidence of their best efforts to ensure that private parties acting within their jurisdiction do not prevent persons belonging to national minorities from freely enjoying these rights. The specific scope of these obligations is discussed in greater detail as part of the consideration of particular rights.

Some of the rights guaranteed in Article 7 go beyond the domain of private freedom as their exercise is directed to the outside world, and as such they can be subject to legitimate limitations. Although Article 7 does not expressly provide for any limitations, Article 19 FCNM allows the parties to make limitations which are provided for in equivalent provisions of other international instruments, and in particular in the ECHR.[29] As already noted, the meaning and scope of obligations with respect to the rights in Article 7 correspond to those emanating from the ECHR. As a result, the limitation clauses of the relevant articles of the ECHR are applicable to implementation of the rights guaranteed in Article 7 FCNM.[30] More importantly, any restrictions specified in

[27] Above, n. 25. [28] Above, n. 13, para. 34, pp. 6–7; above, n. 21, para. 52.

[29] Above, n. 21, para. 88; for more detailed discussion on the applicability of the limitation clauses of the ECHR to the FCNM see the chapter on Art. 19 in this commentary.

[30] Art. 9(2) ECHR allows for the following limitations on manifestations of religion and belief: 'Freedom to manifest one's religion or belief shall be subject only to such limitations as are prescribed by law and are necessary in democratic society in the interests of public safety, for the protection of public order, health or morals, or for the protection of rights and freedoms of others' Art. 10(2) ECHR with regard to freedom of expression stipulates that 'The exercise of these freedoms, since it carries with it duties and responsibilities, may be subject to such formalities, conditions, restrictions or penalties as are prescribed by law and are necessary in a democratic society, in the interests of national security, territorial integrity or public safety, for the prevention of disorder or crime, for the protection of health or morals, for the protection of the reputation or rights of others, for preventing the disclosure

the context of implementation of the FCNM cannot go beyond those permitted under the ECHR. In this respect, any conditions, formalities, or restraints imposed by the states parties must be prescribed by law, pursue the legitimate public interest, and be necessary in a democratic society. The ECtHR has interpreted these requirements in great detail and the jurisprudence of the Court provides valuable guidance.[31] As regards state practice, the restrictions established in national laws most frequently cited in the state reports fall within the scope of limitation clauses to international human rights instruments.[32] Notably, from the perspective of national minorities, the parties stress that restrictions cannot be based on language, religion, colour, race, national, or ethnic origin of individuals.[33] More specific limitations affect particular activities. For instance, laws on associations, religious organizations, assemblies, or penal codes frequently prohibit the establishment and functioning of organizations or assemblies whose aim is to incite or propagate racial, ethnic, or religious inequality, or hatred.[34] Another type of limitation mentioned in some state reports concerns categories of persons. The Advisory Committee to the FCNM has drawn attention to the need to eliminate formulations in legislation in which only citizens are explicitly guaranteed enjoyment of the rights spelled out in Article 7, noting that these could affect the enjoyment of the rights by persons belonging to national minorities.[35] In this respect, it should

of information received in confidence, or for maintaining the authority and impartiality of the judiciary.' Art. 11(2) ECHR with regard to permissible limitations on freedom of association and assembly holds that 'No restrictions shall be placed on the exercise of these rights other than such as are prescribed by law and are necessary in a democratic society in the interests of national security or public safety, for the prevention of disorder or crime, for the protection of health or morals or for the protection of the rights and freedoms of others. This article shall not prevent the imposition of lawful restrictions on the exercise of these rights by members of the armed forces, of the police or of the administration of the State.'

[31] The European Court of Human Rights has exercised strict control regarding the limitations imposed on Arts. 9, 10, 11 ECHR as these freedoms protect the core areas which are essential to the proper functioning of pluralist democracies and which lie at the heart of the object and purpose of the Convention. Thus, restrictions which affect fundamental aspects of press freedom and political expression, which entail dissolution of a political party or limit the right to take part in association or lawful and peaceful demonstrations, as well as restrictions on religious pluralism should be subjected to the closest scrutiny; *Manoussakis* v. *Greece* (18748/91) (1996) ECHR 41, para. 44; *Stankov and the United Macedonian Organisation Ilinden* v. *Bulgaria* (29221/95, 29225/95) (2001) ECHR 563, para. 87.

[32] Ireland State Report, ACFC/SR (2001) 6, 2001, para. 61; Sweden State Report, ACFC/SR (2001) 003, 2001, para. 22; Switzerland State Report, ACFC/SR (2001) 2, 2001, paras. 180, 190.

[33] Ireland State Report, ACFC/SR (2001) 6, 2001, paras. 63–4; Sweden State Report, ACFC/SR (2001) 003, 2001, para. 22.

[34] Albania State Report, ACFC/SR (2001) 5, 2001, para. 35; Bulgaria State Report, ACFC/SR (2003) 001, 2003, para. 66; Lithuania State Report, ACFC/SR (2001) 7, 2001, para. 42.

[35] Advisory Committee on the Framework Convention for the Protection of National Minorities, Opinion on Ukraine, ACFC/INF/OP/I (2002) 010, 2002, paras. 40 and 95.

be noted that in human rights treaties, including the ECHR, these rights are granted to everyone under the jurisdiction of the state, including aliens or stateless persons. This principle has also been explicitly highlighted in a number of state reports.[36]

Finally, although the freedoms embodied in Article 7 FCNM apply universally to all, specific attention should, as was stressed in the Explanatory Report,[37] be paid by the parties to their effective enjoyment by persons belonging to national minorities, since they are often subject to direct or indirect discrimination given their distinctive features. Any differential treatment based on grounds such as language, religion, nationality, or national or ethnic origin would be considered discriminatory, unless it is based on objective and reasonable justification and pursues a legitimate aim, and there is a reasonable relationship of proportionality between the means employed and the aim sought to be realized. Moreover, neutral criteria or disguised restrictions may exist that are not specifically designed to exclude representatives of national minorities or particular minority groups, but are applied this way in practice. Reviewing national legislation and procedures, as well as the practice of local authorities, on the basis of the principle of non-discrimination constitutes a vital aspect of a state's implementation of this article. In fact, this is the only area that has to date been addressed by the Advisory Committee in its very sparse comments on Article 7. In reviewing the formalities or limitations in national legislation the Committee warned of conditions that might have a negative effect on persons belonging to national minorities. These conditions will be discussed in greater detail below with respect to particular rights. In this context the implementation of Article 7 is also inextricably linked to the requirement to ensure full and effective equality for persons belonging to national minorities. Accordingly, parties are required to pay specific attention to the particularities of national minorities and, where necessary, provide specific measures to ensure full and effective equality in enjoyment of these rights between persons belonging to national minorities and those belonging to the majority, in keeping with the provisions of Article 4(2) FCNM. There is relatively little focus in the state reports on this aspect of Article 7's implementation. However, in some instances the states mentioned favourable treatment for minority associations with respect to financial subsidies, or the allocation of public buildings and premises for use by national minority groups.[38]

[36] Italy State Report, ACFC/SR (1999) 007, 1999, para. 47; Slovenia State Report, ACFC/SR (2000) 4, 2001, para. 38.

[37] Above, n. 21, para. 51.

[38] Hungary State Report, ACFC/SR (99) 10, 1999, para. 75; Russian Federation State Report, ACFC/SR (99) 15, 2000, para. 23.

B. The Right to Freedom of Association

The right to freedom of assembly and association is one of the central rights, whose free enjoyment is essential for the preservation of the identity of persons belonging to national minorities, since it is geared towards persons uniting and associating to express and protect their common characteristics and interests. In fact, the right to associate with others is a precondition for the existence of a group. More specifically, this right is of great consequence to enjoyment of the rights flowing from the principles enshrined in the FCNM. Article 3(2) FCNM affirms that persons belonging to national minorities may exercise these rights individually, as well as in community with others.[39] Here, the key aspect is the exercise of rights in community, be it through minority associations and organizations, or through assemblies of persons belonging to national minorities such as rallies, demonstrations, or meetings. The collective element of the enjoyment of these rights cannot be put into effect without these pre-existing freedoms of assembly and association. As mentioned above, these rights are primarily defensive in nature, as they allow persons belonging to a national minority to fend off impermissible interference from the state. Persons belonging to national minorities are, therefore, entitled to act together, to assemble in connection with their common interests, and to pursue their aspirations without being subject to formal recognition or approval by the state. If it were otherwise, minorities would be at serious risk of being prevented from asserting their identity and of being subjected to discrimination.

Based on the scope of protection in international human rights treaties, including the ECHR, the right to freedom of association encompasses two main aspects: the right to join (or not to join) an association; and the right to form an association.[40] With respect to the former, the scope of protection of the right to freedom of association affects many issues relating to the establishment and functioning of organizations, such as the right of minority associations to raise funds freely, to affiliate with other national and international

[39] For a more detailed discussion on the collective element of minority rights see the chapter on Art. 3 in this commentary.

[40] These main aspects of the protection have been expressly confirmed in domestic legislation. Finland, for instance, in addition to the right to form and join an association, has also recalled the right to participate in the activities of associations, Finland State Report, ACFC/SR (99) 3, 1999, Art. 7. Germany State Report, ACFC/SR (2000) 1, 2000, para. 74; Hungary State Report, ACFC/SR (99) 10, 1999, para. 54; Switzerland State Report, ACFC/SR (2001) 2, 2001, para. 185.

organizations, and to operate freely without unreasonable governmental interference.[41] The following analysis does not address all the elements of protection provided by this right, but focuses instead on the particular issues that are of critical significance to the enjoyment of this freedom by persons belonging to national minorities.

The right to form an association constitutes the core of the protection provided by this freedom. Although minority associations do not, as a matter of principle, require formal recognition by the state (that is, it must be possible for organizations to be established without prior authorization),[42] their effective functioning in society is often dependent on acquiring legal status. For instance, in its state report, Estonia noted that 'although the right of association does not require formal registration by public authority, in the majority of cases it is in the interest of the founders to found a legal association as a legal persons (in order to own collective property and to be liable for their actions collectively)'.[43] It is also necessary to stress that this general aspect of protection provided by the right to freedom of association is also important for a host of specific provisions in the FCNM, which refers to the establishment of minority organizations and institutions such as Articles 8, 9(2), 13(1), and 15.[44]

As already noted, Article 11 ECHR provides guidance with regard to the content of the right to freedom of association in Article 7, as well as setting the minimum standard for the obligations of the parties. In this respect, the ECtHR confirmed in its landmark judgment *Sidiropoulos & Others* v. *Greece* 'that citizens should be able to form a legal entity in order to act collectively in a field of mutual interest is one of the most important aspects of the right to freedom of association, without which that right would be deprived of any meaning'.[45] Thus, it can be concluded that states have an obligation to create a framework within which associations are able to acquire and enjoy legal personality. This is also the understanding of the parties to the Framework

[41] Art. 17 FCNM, guarantees persons belonging to national minorities the right to establish free and peaceful contacts across frontiers and the right to participate in the activities of national and international non-governmental organizations. For interpretation of the scope of the protection guaranteed by this provision see the chapter on Art. 17 in this commentary.

[42] The principle that no permission from the state authority is necessary for the exercise of this right is explicitly stipulated in the legislation of several countries. See, for example, Czech Republic State Report, ACFC/SR (99) 6, 1999, para. 27(18) (19); Italy State Report, ACFC/SR (1999) 007, 1999, para. 47; Ireland State Report, ACFC/SR (2001) 6, 2001, para. 64; Serbia and Montenegro State Report, ACFC/SR (2002) 003, 2002, para. 59, para. 2.

[43] Estonia State Report, ACFC/SR (99) 16, 1999, para. 33.

[44] For a more detailed discussion see chapters on Art. 8, 9, 13, 15 in this commentary.

[45] *Sidiropoulos & Others* v. *Greece* (26695/95) (1998) ECHR 55, para. 40.

Convention. In their reports, a great number refer to specific legislation allowing persons belonging to national minorities to establish a legal entity, such as acts concerning non-profit associations, co-operatives, unions, political parties, churches and congregations, or civil and commercial codes.[46] Further, it has been confirmed by the ECtHR that the freedom extends not only to formation of an association, but also to its functioning and activities.[47]

Article 11 ECHR does not expressly indicate what types of associations it covers,[48] but the protective scope of the right when it comes to the purposes of associations is generally considered to be broad.[49] The parties to the FCNM refer to diverse forms of associations, such as: non-profit organizations; non-governmental organizations, associations, and foundations; religious denominations; political parties; trade unions; corporations; and other associations functioning for profit, which can be established under domestic legislation.[50] The purposes and aims mentioned in state reports frequently include participation in political, scientific, social, religious, and cultural life, or simply realization of legitimate common interests.[51] In some instances, states restrict the particular nature of non-governmental organizations to non-commercial activities.[52] In this respect, Switzerland has argued that associations that set out to make a profit fall within guarantees of economic freedom.[53] In addressing the exercise of this right by persons belonging to national minorities, many state reports provide extensive lists of minority associations that have been established on the basis of a national minority or ethnic principle. While a large

[46] Estonia State Report, ACFC/SR (99) 16, 1999, para. 33; Armenia State Report, ACFC/SR (2001) 004, 2001, para. 67; Lithuania State Report, ACFC/SR (2001) 7, 2001, para. 42; Moldova State Report, ACFC/SR (2000) 2, 2000, para. 15; Slovakia State Report, ACFC/SR (99) 8, 1999, para. 16; Ukraine State Report, ACFC/SR (99) 14, 1999, para. 20.

[47] *The United Communist Party of Turkey and others* v. *Turkey* (19392/92) (1998) ECHR 1, para. 33.

[48] In contrast with the indicative list of the American Convention on Human Rights (ACHR), OAS Treaty Series No. 36, 1978, 1144 UNTS 123, Art. 16.

[49] For a summary of relevant case law see P. van Dijk and G. J. H. van Hoof, *Theory and Practice of the European Convention on Human Rights*, 3rd edition (Kluwer Law International, The Hague, 1998), 591–3. Regarding the limits of the protection, it is notable that legal persons established under public law, such as public institutions, corporations, or chambers do not fall within the ambit of the protection of this right. See *Le Compte, Van Leuven and De Meyere* v. *Belgium* (6878/75, 7238/76) (1981) ECHR 1, paras. 63–5.

[50] See, for example, Azerbaijan State Report, ACFC/SR (2002) 1, 2002, para. 34; Bulgaria State Report, ACFC/SR (2003) 001, 2003, para. 65; Cyprus State Report, ACFC/SR (99) 2, 1999, para. 43; Estonia State Report, ACFC/SR (99) 16, 1999, para. 33.

[51] See, for example, Lithuania State Report, ACFC/SR (2001) 7, 2001, para. 42; Romania State Report, ACFC/SR (99) 11, 1999, para. 24.

[52] See, for example, Hungary State Report, ACFC/SR (99) 10, 1999, para. 74; Romania State Report, ACFC/SR (99) 11, 1999, para. 24.

[53] Switzerland State Report, ACFC/SR (2001) 2, 2001, para. 187.

number of these organizations have acquired legal status under general acts on association, an approach practised in the majority of states,[54] some countries provide a special status for national minority associations whose activities are aimed at preserving and developing national and cultural identity.[55] However, as will be discussed later in this article, with regard to the legitimacy of imposing conditions, formalities, or limitations on the formation and activities of associations, the right to form an association according to the national minority principle has not been accepted in the practice of some states.

The prescriptions or proscriptions of any state regarding the formation and functioning of associations must strictly follow the requirements established by Article 11(2) ECHR. In the view of the ECtHR, when a state confers legal status it has a right to satisfy itself that an association's aim and activities are in conformity with the rules laid down in legislation, but it must do so in a manner compatible with its obligations under the ECHR.[56] It is difficult to assess to what extent the legislation and practice of states conform to the principles foreseen by the ECHR, as only a handful of states have provided a thorough account of the conditions and limitations they impose on the formation and activities of associations.[57] This is unfortunate and makes it challenging for the Advisory Committee to review whether state practice conforms with Article 7. Nevertheless, limitations have been identified by the Advisory Committee with respect to the imposition of conditions that make it difficult for national minorities to establish their own associations.

The critical issue with regard to enjoyment of this right by persons belonging to national minorities is having the opportunity to form an association that represents national minority interests. As mentioned above, the freedoms of association and assembly enable communities to express and pursue their political interests. National minorities attach a very high importance to the

[54] See, for example, Czech Republic State Report, ACFC/SR (99) 6, 1999, para. 26; Poland State Report, ACFC/SR (2002) 2, 2002, para. 24.

[55] See, for example, Hungary State Report, ACFC/SR (99) 10, 1999, para. 75; Moldova State Report, ACFC/SR (2000) 2, 2000, para. 15; Russian Federation State Report, ACFC/SR (99) 15, 2000, para. 23; Ukraine State Report, ACFC/SR (99) 14, 1999, para. 20.

[56] States have a very narrow margin of appreciation in applying limitations on freedom of association. See above, n. 45, para. 40 where the Court held that 'exemptions . . . are to be construed strictly; only convincing and compelling reasons can justify restrictions on freedom of association. In determining whether a necessity within the meaning of Article 11 § 2 exists, the States have only a limited margin of appreciation, which goes hand in hand with rigorous European supervision embracing both the law and the decisions applying it, including those given by independent courts.'

[57] See, for example, Romania State Report, ACFC/SR (99) 11, 1999, para. 25; Malta State Report, ACFC/SR (99) 12, 1999, para. 6; Switzerland State Report, ACFC/SR (2001) 2, 2001, para. 190; Sweden State Report, ACFC/SR (2001) 003, 2001, para. 22.

maintenance of their identity, and they often vigorously pursue their interests in this regard. European history, as well as recent experience, show that failure to accommodate a minority's special needs and interests often leads to aspirations for self-determination and calls for secession. This can lead states to fear that recognition of minorities would pose a threat to their sovereignty and territorial integrity. Thus, the issue of minority recognition and the registration of their institutions often intersects with political considerations. Some states, in an attempt to keep these tendencies at bay, refuse to accord recognition to ethnic associations because they perceive that seeking recognition of national minority status, and pursuing minority rights, represents a threat to the constitutional order and to the territorial integrity of the state. However, the prohibition of an association or a political party purely on the grounds that it seeks to assert minority identity is considered to be incompatible with freedom of association. In this respect, the conclusions of the ECtHR in *Sidiropoulos & Others* v. *Greece* are of great significance. The Greek authorities had refused to register as an association, a group of persons living in Florina in Northern Greece who considered themselves a Macedonian national minority. The government maintained that registering such an association would be a threat to national security, public order, and Greece's cultural traditions, history, and symbols. The ECtHR held that:

> Territorial integrity, national security, and public order were not threatened by the activities of an association whose aim was to promote a region's culture, even supposing that it also aimed partly to promote the culture of a minority; the existence of minorities and different cultures in a country was a historical fact that a 'democratic society' had to tolerate and even protect and support according to the principles of international law.[58]

In other words, the Court explicitly confirmed that the existence of minorities does not depend on recognition by the state, and that the promotion of the culture of a national minority is a legitimate aim for an association.

States tend to impose stricter conditions on the formation of political parties, as these are a conduit to participation and representation in political life.[59] However, prohibition of ethnic political parties would be incompatible with

[58] *Sidiropoulos & Others* v. *Greece* (26695/95) (1998) ECHR 55, para. 41.

[59] A number of states restrict the right to form or join a political party to citizens, for instance. Although the international standards on freedom of association do not provide for such an exemption, it is unclear, particularly in the light of ECHR, Art. 16, which allows the states parties to impose restrictions on the political activity of aliens, whether such limitations are justified within state margins of appreciation. For examples of differing state practice see Lithuania State Report, ACFC/SR (2001) 7, 2001, para. 42; Romania State Report, ACFC/SR (99) 11, 1999, para. 26; Italy State Report, ACFC/SR (1999) 007, 1999, para. 27; Slovenia State Report, ACFC/SR (2000) 4, 2001, para. 37, n. 42.

the freedom of association.[60] The Advisory Committee affirmed this view when it welcomed Albania's annulment of the law that had restricted national minorities from establishing their own political parties.[61] In this context, the argument that persons belonging to national minorities are able to seek representation through other principal parties does not suffice.[62] Many states have expressly confirmed that the freedom to form political parties on an ethnic basis is ensured in their constitutional system, and have provided numerous examples of the existence of such political parties.[63] However, the formation of political parties on an ethnic basis remains controversial in the practice of some states. For instance, the Advisory Committee has criticized the legislation of the Russian Federation, which prohibits the establishment of political parties formed on 'the grounds of professional, racial, national or religious belonging'. Specifically, the Advisory Committee stated that this phrase (which includes goals aimed at protecting professional, racial, national, or religious interests in charters or programmes, as well as reflecting these goals in the designation of a political party) is open to an interpretation that could limit the legitimate activities of political parties that aim to protect national minorities.[64] A similar prohibition exists in Bulgaria, where political parties based on ethnic, racial, or religious lines are banned. The state uses the argument that such parties express the political will of only one particular circle, and bar access by persons from different backgrounds.[65] In general, it could be asserted that legitimate limits on democratic pluralism do not cover or support such a prohibition. The Opinion of the Advisory Committee reviewing Bulgaria's practice has not yet been released. Another limitation considered unacceptable by the Advisory Committee is the ban on the pursuit of political activities by minority associations. Bearing in mind that activities aimed at protecting minorities may also have a political dimension, the Advisory

[60] OSCE, Lund Recommendations on the Effective Participation of National Minorities in Public Life, The Hague, 1999, Recommendation No. 8.

[61] Advisory Committee Opinion on Albania, ACFC/INF/OP/I (2003) 004, 2002, para. 47.

[62] The Explanatory Report of the Lund Recommendations on the Effective Participation of National Minorities in Public Life with regard to Recommendation No. 8 points out that organization along ethnic lines could be quite problematic. Ideally, the report recommends that parties should be open and should cut across narrow ethnic issues; thus, mainstream parties should seek to include minorities to reduce the need or desire for ethnic parties. However, in some situations communal parties could be the only hope for a national minority to advance their specific interest.

[63] See, for example, Czech Republic State Report, ACFC/SR (99) 6, 1999, para. 26; Hungary State Report, ACFC/SR (99) 10, 1999, para. 74; Romania State Report, ACFC/SR (99) 11, 1999, para. 25; Slovakia State Report, ACFC/SR (99) 8, 1999, para. 18; Serbia and Montenegro State Report, ACFC/SR (2002) 003, 2002, paras. 60–2.

[64] Advisory Committee Opinion on Russian Federation, ACFC/INF/OP/I (2003) 005, 2003, para. 69.

[65] Bulgaria State Report, ACFC/SR (2003) 001, 2003, paras. 66, 68.

Committee underlined that political exclusion should not be interpreted in a manner that hinders the legitimate activities by organizations of persons belonging to national minorities.[66]

The European Court of Human Rights provides further guidance as to where the limits of democratic pluralism fall when it comes to the pursuit of a national minority's interests through associations and political parties. In principle, unless the association promotes the use of violence or acts undemocratically in order to achieve its objectives, restrictions on minority associations or political parties are unlikely to be justified on the grounds of national security, an argument often advanced by states in these cases. In particular, states cannot hinder associations from seeking peaceful and democratic solutions to minority problems, even if their aims call into question the way in which a state is currently organized.[67] However, states can justifiably prohibit the creation of armed organizations.[68] In addition, and as required by international standards,[69] states parties must declare illegal and prohibit organizations which promote and incite racial discrimination and ethnic hatred, and criminalize activities aimed at incitement of racial, religious, or ethnic hatred.[70]

Another important issue from the perspective of implementation of Article 7 FCNM is that recognition of minority associations must be non-discriminatory.[71] This also applies to the treatment of minority associations in general. In order to provide financial support for minority culture, as well as for the enjoyment of some specific minority entitlements, states often require some sort of organizational structure. Refusal to register the associations of some minorities, while providing legal status to others without objective and reasonable justification, would therefore constitute discrimination against such minorities. This question is complicated by the fact that the FCNM does not define a national minority; however, the subjects of protection can be

[66] Advisory Committee Opinion on Russian Federation, ACFC/INF/OP/I (2003) 005, 2003, para. 68.

[67] *The United Communist Party of Turkey and others* v. *Turkey* (19392/92) (1998) ECHR 1, para. 57; see also *The Socialist Party and others* v. *Turkey* (21237/93) (1998) ECHR 45, paras. 46–7; *Refah Partisi (The Welfare Party) and Others* v. *Turkey* (41340/98, 41342/98, 41343/98, 41344/98) (2003) ECHR 87, paras. 97–8.

[68] Hungary State Report, ACFC/SR (99) 10, 1999, para. 74; Bulgaria State Report, ACFC/SR (2003) 001, 2003, para. 65; Romania State Report, ACFC/SR (99) 11, 1999, para. 27.

[69] See Art. 6, para. 2 FCNM; Art. 20 ICCPR; International Convention on the Elimination of all Forms of Racial Discrimination (CERD) (adopted on 21 December 1965, entered into force 4 January 1969), UNGA Res. 2106 (XX), 1965, Art. 4.

[70] Albania State Report, ACFC/SR (2001) 5, 2001, para. 35; Bulgaria State Report, ACFC/SR (2003) 001, 2003, para. 65; Lithuania State Report, ACFC/SR (2001) 7, 2001, para. 42; Romania State Report, ACFC/SR (99) 11, 1999, paras. 25, 26.

[71] Ireland State Report, ACFC/SR (2001) 6, 2001, para. 63.

determined in light of the object and purpose of the Convention.[72] In a number of cases the Advisory Committee has asserted that the protection of the FCNM extends to persons belonging to communities living within the state, which the parties did not consider to fall within the ambit of the Convention.[73] Thus, states cannot a priori exclude certain groups from enjoyment of minority rights under the FCNM. In principle, this would suggest that refusing to register an association of persons who claim to be a national or ethnic minority, and who seek to enjoy specific minority entitlements through such an association, would be contrary to obligations under the FCNM, *inter alia* Article 7 and Article 4. The jurisprudence of the ECtHR is less forthcoming on this point, but this is not surprising, as the ECHR is not geared towards addressing specific minority rights.[74] From the perspective of prohibiting discrimination, it is equally important that any conditions or requirements for registration, even if applied neutrally to all, should not negatively affect national minorities or preclude some of them from registering. In this respect, with regard to Moldovan legislation the Advisory Committee asserted that requiring political parties to have a minimum number of members in at least half the districts of a country is likely to limit the ability of persons belonging to national minorities who do not satisfy this condition to organize political parties.[75]

As required by Article 4(2) FCNM, states parties should also take into account the specific conditions of persons belonging to national minorities and

[72] See European Commission for Democracy through Law (ECDL), Opinion on Possible Groups of Persons to which the Framework Convention for the Protection of National Minorities could be Applied in Belgium, CDL-AD (2002)1, 50th Plenary Meeting, 2002, paras. 5–19.

[73] Advisory Committee Opinion on Finland, ACFC/INF/OP/I (2001) 002, 2000, paras. 16, 17; Advisory Committee Opinion on Denmark, ACFC/INF/OP/I (2001) 005, 2001, paras. 21, 24, 28; Advisory Committee Opinion on the United Kingdom, ACFC/INF/OP/I (2002) 006, 2002, para. 17; Advisory Committee Opinion on San Marino, ACFC/INF/OP/I (2001) 007, 2001, para. 14.

[74] See *Gorzelik & Others* v. *Poland* (44158/98) (2001) (2004) ECHR 869 and 72, paras. 64–6 of judgment of 20 December 2001 and para. 103 of judgment of 17 February 2004 for a rather controversial decision of the Court, in which it did not find that the refusal by Polish authorities to register an association under the name of 'Union of People of Silesian Nationality' was disproportionate interference amounting to a violation of Art. 11 ECHR. The government argued that national minority status confers privileges under domestic law and that no group should have the right to declare itself a nation. It further argued that the community was only an ethnic group, and not a national minority, and that by registering as a national minority association its aim was to circumvent the provisions of the electoral law. The Court held that the group should have been prepared to compromise on, *inter alia*, its name and that Poland was accorded a wide margin of appreciation with respect to the practice of democracy within the state. The Court did not examine whether the refusal to recognize a minority association may entail discrimination directed against this group in comparison to other recognized groups with respect to electoral privileges. For a critical evaluation of the case, see Åkermark, n. 19 above pp. 14–16.

[75] Advisory Committee Opinion on Moldova, ACFC/INF/OP/I (2003) 002, 2002, para. 49.

ensure that they enjoy full and effective equality. In this respect, some parties refer to positive measures to support minority associations in implementing Article 7. For instance, Hungary has explicitly stated that the government's policy not only permits the establishment of minority associations, but also encourages and provides funding for non-profit organizations dealing with the protection of minority rights and the cultivation of minority culture.[76] The provision of governmental facilities and services, such as the use of public buildings, has also been cited in several state reports.[77] This may indeed be a necessary step to ensure that persons belonging to national minorities are able to maintain and develop their culture and preserve the essential elements of their identity.

The right to join or not to join an association implies that membership in an association must be voluntary.[78] As a result, each individual can join associations of his or her choice without having to suffer disadvantage or sanctions because of his or her membership.[79] In this context, persons belonging to national minorities are free to declare or not declare their membership in a minority association.[80] This is an important aspect of the protection provided by the freedom of association, since it allows persons belonging to national minorities to pursue their legitimate interests freely without fear of discrimination or persecution.[81]

C. The Right to Freedom of Assembly

Freedom of assembly, like freedom of association, plays a pivotal role in maintaining and promoting a minority's identity. Freedom of assembly includes the right to call a meeting or a demonstration, organize it, take part in it, or stand aside from it. In this respect, this freedom provides an essential tool for persons belonging to national minorities to participate in public life.

The scope of protection in international standards, *inter alia* Article 11 ECHR and Article 21 ICCPR, is limited to 'peaceful' assemblies. States, therefore, have the right to review whether such assemblies would disturb public order or

[76] Hungary State Report, ACFC/SR (99) 10, 999, para. 75.

[77] Norway State Report, ACFC/SR (2001) 1, 2001, para. 31; Romania State Report, ACFC/SR (99) 11, 1999; Hungary State Report, ACFC/SR (99) 10, 1999, para. 75; Russian Federation State Report, ACFC/SR (99) 15, 2000, para. 23.

[78] See, for example, Switzerland State Report, ACFC/SR (2001) 2, 2001, para. 188.

[79] It should be noted that this freedom is not unlimited, as restrictions on membership in an association may be legitimately imposed on the armed forces, police, or administration of the state. See Art. 11(2) ECHR and Art. 22(2) ICCPR.

[80] See, for example, Sweden State Report, ACFC/SR (2001) 003, 2001, para. 23.

[81] From this perspective, the protection provided in Art. 3 FCNM is highly relevant. For more detailed discussion see the chapter on Art. 3 in this commentary.

pose a threat to, *inter alia*, national security, public safety, and the rights of others. In this connection, they may establish a system of notification for publicly held assemblies. This practice has been cited by certain states, notably for outdoor meetings and rallies.[82] Such measures are fully legitimate, as states are responsible for the maintenance of public order, in particular with regard to street traffic. Moreover, information about and access to such assemblies are necessary for the state to be able to fulfil its duty of protection. In this respect, states may require any proposed assembly to provide information on the object of the gathering; or they may assess the actions of the associations organizing the assembly to ascertain whether they reject democratic principles, and in particular whether they incite violence or hatred against an individual or a population within the state.[83] It is notable, however, that when a minority association that had been declared unconstitutional wanted to hold a peaceful assembly, in *Stankov and the United Macedonian Organisation Ilinden* v. *Bulgaria* the ECtHR found it unacceptable to impose a systematic ban on the holding of peaceful assemblies by such an organization.[84]

In conclusion, parties who are considering preventing an assembly from being held must be able to demonstrate particular grounds to justify their interference, and that the interference is proportionate to the aim pursued. This principle is also explicitly acknowledged in the legislation of some states. Italy, for instance, requires that any prohibition of public assembly must be based on very specific and objective circumstances, and the reason for prohibition must be stated in a separate decision adopted in each case.[85] For example, an assembly would have to pose a direct and imminent danger for public order—mere considerations of expediency would not constitute sufficient grounds for banning a meeting.[86]

There is a close link between the freedoms of assembly and expression, because exercise of the right to freedom of assembly, as well as to freedom of association, inevitably involves holding and propagating specific opinions. Indeed, the essential aim of persons belonging to national minorities, in assembling, is to express and protect their common characteristics and to pursue their collective interests.

[82] Italy State Report, ACFC/SR (1999) 007, 1999, para. 47.

[83] See *Freedom and Democratic Party (ÖZDEP)* v. *Turkey* (23885/94) (1999) ECHR 103, para. 40, as well as *Stankov and the United Macedonian Organisation Ilinden* v. *Bulgaria* (29221/95, 29225/95) (2001) ECHR 563, para. 90.

[84] *Stankov and the United Macedonian Organisation Ilinden* v. *Bulgaria*, above, n. 83, para. 92.

[85] Italy State Report, ACFC/SR (1999) 007, 1999, para. 47; Estonia State Report, ACFC/SR (99) 16, 1999, para. 33; Romania State Report, ACFC/SR (99) 11, 1999, para. 25;

[86] Switzerland State Report, ACFC/SR (2001) 2, 2001, para. 182.

In this context, the European Court of Human Rights has explicitly held that the protection of opinions, and the freedom to express them, are objectives of the freedoms of assembly and association.[87] Such a link is especially relevant for national minority associations and assemblies, especially when public authorities intervene to prevent assembly or association in reaction to statements made by persons belonging to national minorities.[88] In this respect, Sweden explicitly confirmed that no restriction could go as far as to constitute a threat to the free formation of opinions, and that restrictions may not be made on the basis of political, religious, cultural, or other such ideas.[89] The case law of the ECtHR is of particular relevance in considering the implementation of the guarantee in Article 7 FCNM. As was mentioned with regard to legitimate restrictions on associations, unless the assembly in question calls for violence or pursues ideas contrary to the democratic foundations of society, the fact 'that a group of persons calls for autonomy or even requests secession of the country—thus demanding fundamental and territorial changes—cannot automatically justify a prohibition of its assemblies'.[90]

Seen from the perspective of FCNM obligations, providing protection to a minority's assemblies against outside interference, in particular against hindrance of their assemblies by private parties, is another important aspect of the protection warranted by Article 7. This is particularly relevant given that minorities are often the subject of racial discrimination or expressions of ethnic hatred, and the obligation is clearly confirmed by ECtHR case law. In *Plattform 'Ärzte für das Leben'* v. *Austria*, the Court held that the right to freedom of assembly sometimes required positive measures to be taken, even in relations between private parties. Individuals should be able to hold demonstrations without a fear of physical violence from their opponents, for example. In this respect the Court asserted that 'such a fear would be liable to deter associations or other groups supporting common ideas or interests from openly expressing their opinions on highly controversial issues affecting the community. In democracy the right to counter-demonstrate cannot extend to inhibiting the exercise of the right to demonstrate.'[91] In this respect, the *travaux préparatoires* confirm that the drafters intended Article 7 to encompass horizontal protection.[92] This is also the actual understanding of some of the parties to the FCNM.[93]

[87] *Freedom and Democratic Party (ÖZDEP)* v. *Turkey* (23885/94) (1999) ECHR 103, para. 37.

[88] *Stankov and the United Macedonian Organisation Ilinden* v. *Bulgaria* (29221/95, 29225/95) (2001), ECHR, 563, para. 85.

[89] Sweden State Report, ACFC/SR (2001) 003, 2001, para. 22.

[90] Above, n. 88, para. 97.

[91] *Plattform 'Ärzte für das Leben'* v. *Austria* (10126/82) (1988), ECHR, para. 32.

[92] Above, n. 13, pp. 6–7.

[93] Finland State Report, ACFC/SR (99) 3, 1999, Art. 7; Romania State Report, ACFC/SR (99) 11, 1999, para. 25.

Moreover, the parties have a specific obligation under Article 6(2) to protect persons who may be subject to threats or acts of discrimination, hostility, or violence as a result of their ethnic, cultural, linguistic, or religious identity. In this respect, a number of states have reported that their legislation imposes a ban on public assemblies aimed at the incitement of racial, ethnic, or religious hatred, violence, or discrimination.[94]

D. The Right to Freedom of Expression

The specific scope of protection of freedom of expression and freedom of religion, in the context of the present Convention, is the focus of separate chapters of this commentary.[95] To avoid duplicating their analyses, this text will concentrate only on the general aspects of the protection offered by these freedoms as they are of particular relevance to persons belonging to national minorities.

Freedom of expression is indispensable if persons belonging to a national minority are to be able to assert their identity. As with the other freedoms mentioned, this right is fundamentally defensive in nature, providing protection against state interference. The right to freedom of expression includes the right to hold opinions and to receive and impart information.[96] The scope of protection extends not only to the content expressed, but also to the means of imparting such expression through various forms of communication. Protection of both of these aspects is critical to persons belonging to national minorities.

As noted above, some states try to limit expression of a minority's aspirations by prohibiting their meetings, prosecuting their leaders, or banning the distribution of specific materials related to the interests of the national minority. Indeed, a considerable number of applications before the ECtHR have alleged such violations, indicating that Article 7 needs to be carefully monitored by the Advisory Committee. In a great number of cases concerning the Kurdish population in Turkey, the ECtHR has placed particular emphasis on the freedom of expression, which is seen as vital to the preservation of a minority's identity. In this regard, the Court held that:

> Freedom of expression constitutes one of the essential foundations of a democratic society and one of the basic conditions for its progress and for each individual's self-fulfillment. Subject to paragraph 2 of Article 10, it is applicable not only to 'information'

[94] Estonia State Report, ACFC/SR (99) 16, 1999, para. 33.

[95] See chapters on Arts. 8, 9, 10 in this commentary.

[96] See Art. 19 UDHR; Art. 19 ICCPR; Art. 10 ECHR; and the Charter of Fundamental Rights of the European Union, Official Journal of the European Communities, 2000, C 364/1, Art. 11.

or 'ideas' that are favourably received or regarded as inoffensive or a matter of indifference, but also to those that offend, shock or disturb. Such are the demands of pluralism, tolerance and broadmindedness without which there is no democratic society.[97]

Freedom of expression is also essential to the maintenance of a minority's cultural and linguistic identity, as its protection extends to all forms of communication. In this regard, it is of particular importance that language as a vehicle of communication is protected by freedom of expression;[98] correspondingly, Article 7 FCNM guarantees the protection of linguistic freedom. While Article 9(2) FCNM specifically requires that states parties recognize that the right to freedom of expression of every person belonging to a national minority includes the freedom to hold opinions and receive and impart information and ideas in the minority language,[99] the freedom of expression under Article 7 guarantees the right to use any language. The principle that persons belonging to national minorities have the right to use their mother tongue in private and in public without undue state interference has been explicitly confirmed in a number of state reports.[100]

Any restrictions on linguistic expression must strictly follow requirements established by the ECtHR with regard to permissible limitations under Article 10(2) FCNM. In this respect, Denmark asserted that the fact that the issues are raised by a national minority, or that communications are made in a minority language, cannot in itself form a basis for intervention under Danish law.[101] In its Opinion on Estonia, the Advisory Committee expressed concern over provisions of the Estonian State Language Law regarding the signs of private actors, as interpretation of these provisions could be problematic from the point of view of freedom of expression.[102] In reviewing the implementation of the FCNM by Slovakia, the Advisory Committee also concluded that the

[97] See *Arslan* v. *Turkey* (23462/94) (1999) ECHR 42, para. 44, also see above, n. 87, para. 43. For further commentary on this question see G. Gilbert, 'The Burgeoning Minority Rights Jurisprudence of the European Court of Human Rights', *Human Rights Quarterly*, 24 (2002), 755–6.

[98] See, for example, *Ballantyne, Davidson and McIntyre* v. *Canada*, UN Human Rights Committee, 359/1989 and 385/1989 (1993), UN Doc. CCPR/C/47/D/359/1989 and 385/1989/Rev. 1, para. 11(3). The UN Human Rights Committee has indicated in its decision in *Ballantyne, Davidson and McIntyre* v. *Canada*, that the guarantee of freedom of expression in Art. 19 ICCPR also protects the linguistic form of expression.

[99] See also Art. 10, para. 1 FCNM, as well as above, n. 1, para. 32(5).

[100] See, for example, Hungary State Report, ACFC/SR (99) 10, 1999, Art. 9; Italy State Report, ACFC/SR (1999) 007, 1999, Art. 9.

[101] Denmark State Report, ACFC/SR (99) 9, 1999, Art. 9.

[102] Advisory Committee Opinion on Estonia, ACFC/INF/OP/I (2002) 005, 2001, para. 33. For a more detailed discussion of this issue see the chapter on Art. 11 in this commentary.

wording of certain provisions of the State Language Law could, if applied to minority languages, threaten the freedom of expression and assembly of persons belonging to national minorities.[103]

National minorities frequently share their ethnic, cultural, and linguistic identities with the majority population of another country. It is therefore of particular importance to them that the right to freedom of expression is guaranteed regardless of frontiers. States parties are required not to interfere, without legitimate justifications, with the reception of broadcasts from other states, or with the receiving and imparting of ideas and information across their borders by persons belonging to national minorities, through the press and films, for example.[104]

Although persons belonging to national minorities are free to use their mother tongue in the private sphere, the right to freedom of expression alone does not imply that the state has a duty to use or provide for the use of an individual's language of choice in public institutions and in the public administration.[105] However, as shown by the relevant provisions of the FCNM, *inter alia* Article 10(2), the full and effective equality of persons belonging to national minorities may require that state authorities provide for the use of minority languages in public administration.[106]

Finally, the obligation under Article 7 FCNM to respect the right to freedom of expression also entails a duty to provide horizontal protection for expressions of opinion by persons belonging to national minorities. In this respect, the ECtHR expressly held that states have a positive obligation to ensure that the views and opinions of individuals can be imparted in safety.[107] Furthermore, international standards[108] require states to prohibit expressions of advocacy and incitement of national, racial or religious hatred, discrimination, or violence by law.[109]

E. The Right to Freedom of Religion

The protection provided by freedom of thought, conscience, and religion entails a broad range of rights that are of central importance to personal as well

[103] Advisory Committee Opinion on Slovakia, ACFC/INF/OP/I (2001) 001, 2000, para. 30, and Art. 3, para. 1, FCNM.

[104] More detailed discussion on these issues can be found in the chapters on Arts. 9 and 17 in this commentary.

[105] See *Fryske Nasjonale Partij and Others* v. *The Netherlands* (11100/84) (1985) ECHR.

[106] More detailed discussion regarding this issue can be found in the chapter on Art. 10 in this commentary.

[107] *Özgür Gündem* v. *Turkey* (23144/93) (2000), ECHR, paras. 44–6.

[108] See Art. 20 ICCPR; International Convention on the Elimination of all Forms of Racial Discrimination (CERD) (adopted on 21 December 1965, entered into force 4 January 1969), UNGA Res. 2106 (XX), 1965, Art. 4; as well as Art. 6 FCNM.

[109] Romania State Report, ACFC/SR (99) 11, 1999, para. 26.

as group identity. The freedoms of thought and conscience provide individuals with rights to exercise these faculties free from outside influence. Religion and particular beliefs are often the unique features distinguishing members of national minorities from the majority. Therefore, the principle of religious pluralism, embodied in the right to freedom of religion, is a touchstone for the protection of persons belonging to national minorities, and for enabling them to maintain and develop their identities.

International legal instruments do not define the term 'religion' or 'belief' as they try to avoid philosophical as well as ideological controversy. However, the jurisprudence of the ECtHR, in addition to the authoritative interpretation in other instruments, suggests that the term has a very broad meaning. In essence, it includes theistic and atheistic views of the universe, as well as agnostic views. The scope of protection covers traditional religions as well as non-traditional and non-religious beliefs.[110] Although the European Court of Human Rights has confirmed that all kinds of minority views can constitute religious or philosophical convictions,[111] not all views or opinions fall within the remit of Article 9 ECHR. In the case of *Campbell and Cosans* v. *UK*, the Court held that only 'views that attain a certain level of cogency, seriousness, cohesion and importance' are protected.[112] Therefore, religions unable to specify the content of their convictions clearly were not considered protected within the scope of Article 9 ECHR.[113] What is significant for implementation of Article 7 FCNM is that the notion of religion and belief is widely conceived in these instruments, and that states should deal with the different convictions of persons belonging to national minorities in a tolerant and broad-minded manner. This being the case, the protection clearly extends to small or lesser-known, non-traditional religions.

In considering the personal scope of the protection of Article 7, the question arises as to whether the provision applies vis-à-vis religious minorities, or whether it targets protection of the religious beliefs of 'national' minorities

[110] Perhaps the most comprehensive approach has been presented by the UN Human Rights Committee 'General Comment No. 22' on Freedom of Religion, 48th session (1993), UN Doc. HRI/GEN/1 Rev. 1 at 35, which indicates the extent of protection guaranteed by Art. 18: '[the article] protects theistic, non-theistic and atheistic beliefs, as well as the right not to profess any religion or belief. The terms belief and religion are to be broadly construed. Article 18 is not limited in its application to traditional religions or to religions and beliefs with institutional characteristics or practices analogous to those of traditional religions. The Committee therefore views with concern any tendency to discriminate against any religion or belief for any reason, including the fact that they are newly established, or represent religious minorities that may be the subject of hostility by a predominant religious community.'

[111] Pacifist beliefs are one example of this, see *Arrowsmith* v. *UK* (11567/85, 11568/85) (1978) ECHR, p. 49.

[112] *Campbell and Cosans* v. *UK* (7511/76, 7743/76) (1982) ECHR 3, para. 36.

[113] See *X* v. *the United Kingdom* (7291/75) (1978) ECHR, p. 9.

exclusively. As the FCNM does not contain a definition of national minorities, it is left to the states parties, to a large extent, to determine the beneficiaries of the protection of the FCNM within their territories.[114] State practice differs considerably, but a good number of states identify the subjects of protection according to the FCNM Preamble, which calls for protection of ethnic, cultural, linguistic, and religious identities. Frequently only one of the listed features need exist, so for example in some cases religious belief might be the only characteristic that distinguishes the national minority from the majority.[115] However, some states limit the scope of application to specific minorities,[116] or have stipulated that it only recognizes citizens with ethnic characteristics as minorities, and that national minorities in their domestic legal order are not defined according to religious criteria.[117] In this respect, it is important to note that other international instruments extend the protection offered in Article 7 to ethnic, national, linguistic, and religious minorities inclusively.[118] It is also notable that during the drafting of the Convention, the initial proposals accorded this right to 'religious minorities'.[119] The personal scope of the protection of the FCNM is a complex topic discussed in more detail in the chapter on Article 1 in this commentary. However, given the aim of the protection of the FCNM,[120] and taking into account the established practice of the Advisory Committee regarding this question,[121] it would appear that states parties cannot a priori exclude application of this provision

[114] For a detailed discussion on the definition of national minorities and the personal scope of the protection of the FCNM see the chapter on Art. 1 in this commentary.

[115] See, for example, Serbia and Montenegro State Report, ACFC/SR (2002) 003, 2002, para. 65(3.1), which explicitly stated that '[the law] in defining minorities underscores that religion may be one of the features which differentiates a group of citizens of the FR Yugoslavia, constituting a national minority, from majority population'.

[116] Comments of the Government of Denmark on the Opinion of the Advisory Committee on the Report on the Implementation of the Framework Convention for the Protection of National Minorities in Denmark, GVT/COM/INF/OP/I (2001) 005, 2001, Art. 9.

[117] Czech Republic State Report, ACFC/SR (99) 6, 1999, para. 27. However, it seems that the Czech statement contradicts its own argument in expressing that 'the Convention does not define national minorities on the basis of religion, although connection between religious and national identity is apparent in the Preamble of the Convention'.

[118] See Art. 27 ICCPR and the UN Declaration on the Rights of Persons Belonging to National or Ethnic, Religious, or Linguistic Minorities, UNGA Res. 47/135 (18 December 1992), annex 47 UN GAOR 49, 210 (1992), UN Doc. A/47/49.

[119] ECDL, Preliminary Draft Convention on the Protection of Minorities [DAJ.SC. DEMOCRACY]CONV. MIN, 1990, Art. 11; also ECDL, Proposal for A Convention for the Protection of National Minorities, CDL-MIN (93) 6, 1993, Art. 10.

[120] See para. 7, Preamble FCNM and Art. 5(1) FCNM.

[121] Advisory Committee Opinion on Denmark, ACFC/INF/OP/I (2001) 005, 2001, paras. 28, and 29.

to persons belonging to minorities whose sole distinctive feature is their religious belief.

As indicated above, and as confirmed explicitly by some states in their reports,[122] the meaning and scope of the right to freedom of religion in Article 7 is the same as in Article 9 ECHR. The right to freedom of religion in the ECHR,[123] as well as in other instruments,[124] provides an extensive catalogue of rights to be enjoyed by persons belonging to national minorities. It guarantees the right to freedom of thought, conscience, and religion, generally described as *forum internum*.[125] This is a broad category, which includes the right to profess religion or to not profess religion, that is to believe or to have non-theistic views, as well as the right to change religious beliefs. The freedom to have no religious beliefs, or to abstain from the practice or profession of any religion, has also been confirmed in a number of state reports.[126] It is an individual's free choice to belong or not to belong to a religious community. Further, some states have confirmed that their domestic legislation guarantees the right to freely choose religion and to change religion.[127] In this respect, the Committee of Ministers found it unacceptable that Cyprus required persons acquiring Cypriot citizenship to choose to adhere either to the Greek Cypriot or to the Turkish Cypriot community, regardless of whether the individual in question professed a different faith, and called upon state authorities to address this problematic issue.[128]

International standards on freedom of religion also address conversion and religious proselytizing. The right to teach and disseminate one's religion and to

[122] See, for example, Austria State Report, ACFC/SR (2000) 3, 2000, para. 44.

[123] Art. 9(1) ECHR stipulates: 'Everyone has the right to freedom of thought, conscience and religion; this right includes freedom to change his religion or belief and freedom, either alone or in community with others in public or private, to manifest his religion or belief in worship, teaching, practice and observance.'

[124] See, for example, Art. 18 UDHR; Art. 18 ICCPR; Declaration on the Elimination of All Forms of Intolerance and of Discrimination Based on Religion or Belief, UNGA Res. 36/55, 36 UN GAOR, Supp. (No. 51) at 171 (1981), UN Doc. A/36/684, Art. 6; and Conference for Security and Co-operation in Europe (CSCE), Concluding Document Follow-up Meeting, Vienna, 1986–9, para. 16.

[125] P. van Dijk and G. J. H. van Hoof, *Theory and Practice of the European Convention on Human Rights*, 3rd edition, (Kluwer Law International, The Hague, 1998), 541–2.

[126] See, for example, Finland State Report, ACFC/SR (99) 3, 1999, Art. 8; Ireland State Report, ACFC/SR (2001) 6, 2001, para. 66; Norway State Report, ACFC/SR (2001) 1, 2001, para. 32.

[127] See, for example, Estonia State Report, ACFC/SR (99) 16, 1999, para. 33; Poland State Report, ACFC/SR (2002) 2, 2002, para. 24.

[128] Committee of Ministers, Resolution ResCMN (2002) 3 on the Implementation of the Framework Convention for the Protection of National Minorities by Cyprus, 784th meeting, 2002. For state practice, see Comments of the Government of Cyprus on the Opinion of the Advisory Committee on the Report on the Implementation of the Framework Convention for the Protection of National Minorities in Cyprus, GCT/COM/INF/OP/I (2002) 004, 2002.

proselytize can be rather controversial as they may sometimes clash with the right to privacy, and from the perspective of the protection of persons belonging to national minorities, they may interfere with the integrity of some aspects of group identities. In this respect, Article 18(2) ICCPR specifically guarantees freedom from coercion, which would impair a person's freedom to have or to adopt a religion or belief of his choice. This is of great significance to national minorities as the state is precluded from exercising any coercion against persons belonging to national minorities to belong or not belong to a certain religion or belief.[129] This aspect of protection of the freedom of religion is extremely important, as religious minorities have been and, in some cases, still are, the subject of persecution and prejudice. A number of states have noted that their legislation guarantees the right to declare or not to declare religious belief.[130]

The duty to ensure that national minorities are free from coercion under Article 7 FCNM is also supported in the context of other provisions of the FCNM. Article 5(2), in particular, requires parties to refrain from practices designed to bring about the assimilation of persons belonging to national minorities against their will, and protects persons belonging to national minorities from any actions aimed at such assimilation. The prohibition of coercion applies not only to direct forms of physical coercion, but also to indirect forms such as enticement. This is particularly important from the perspective of national minorities if the state guarantees specific privileges, in taxation or access to public offices, on account of adherence to a certain religion. This may negatively impact members of national minorities in choosing whether to belong to a certain religion. The state should, therefore, ensure that national minorities are not discriminated against on the basis of their religious beliefs, and should ensure their full equality in the exercise of their right to freedom of religion. Freedom from state coercion is specifically emphasized in the expressed right of parents to have their children educated in conformity with their religious beliefs and their convictions. Finally, the scope of protection of freedom of religion also addresses the manifestation of religion and belief. Unlike the freedoms of thought and conscience, which cannot be limited, the external expression of faith, meaning every manifestation of religious belief or non-religious conviction extending beyond the purely private sphere, is susceptible to limitations.

[129] See, for example, Ireland State Report, ACFC/SR (2001) 6, 2001, para. 65; Lithuania State Report, ACFC/SR (2001) 7, 2001, para. 44.

[130] See, for example, Estonia State Report, ACFC/SR (99) 16, 1999, para. 35; Serbia and Montenegro State Report, ACFC/SR (2002) 003, 2002, para. 62(1.2); Sweden State Report, ACFC/SR (2001) 003, 2001, para. 23.

The specific obligations of the parties to ensure persons belonging to national minorities enjoy this right are discussed in this volume's chapter on Article 8, which contains more detailed rules with regard to the protection of the manifestation of religion. Given the overlap between Articles 7 and 8 and the more general nature of Article 7, nearly all states parties choose to report information on implementation of the right to freedom of religion under Article 8. The fact remains, however, that Article 7 is much broader in scope. As a result, it is important that the Advisory Committee, in reviewing implementation of Article 7, pays particular attention to those aspects of this right not explicitly covered by Article 8.

III. Conclusion and Outlook

Given that Article 7 contains a number of fundamental freedoms, its scope is extremely broad. This has resulted in states merely providing general information on its implementation, and in the Advisory Committee providing equally limited comments. Of course, the article itself is phrased in very general terms, lacking the detailed rules laid down in other substantive provisions of the Framework Convention. Nevertheless, the connection between the detailed standards of the ECHR and the freedoms specified in Article 7 provides a coherent basis for its interpretation. In this respect, the content of the rights guaranteed by the ECHR should serve as the focal point for states parties when identifying their legal obligations on the enjoyment of these freedoms by persons belonging to national minorities. In this context, although the system of the FCNM does not guarantee self-executing rights, full implementation of Article 7 would require states parties to ensure justiciable rights in their domestic legal order with respect to the fundamental freedoms mentioned in this article.

Article 7 could hardly be said to break new ground when it comes to the development of legal obligations in the field of human rights standards. Nevertheless, it must be stressed that, in contrast with the provisions of the ECHR, the Framework Convention explicitly accords these rights to persons belonging to national minorities. In particular, the FCNM ties the non-discrimination principle with respect to persons belonging to national minorities, and their distinctive characteristics, directly to the implementation of these rights. Arguably, such protection is already guaranteed by the ECHR. However, frequently the European Court of Human Rights does not examine Article 14 violations if it has already established that another substantive provision has been violated. As a result, the contribution of the ECtHR in addressing the needs of minorities through the prohibition of discrimination has been rather limited. Seen in this light, the implementation of the state's obligations under Article 7 takes on enhanced importance. Effective Advisory Committee monitoring could contribute to identifying state practices that result in both direct and, perhaps more importantly, the less easily detectable indirect discrimination against persons belonging to national minorities in the enjoyment of these freedoms.

Regrettably, to date only a few states have treated Article 7 as a substantive provision requiring a detailed review of national legislation and state administrative practice with respect to all aspects of the protection these individual freedoms provide to persons belonging to national minorities. This may be part of the reason why the Advisory Committee has not yet, with the exception of its Opinion on the Russian Federation, found a strong voice in providing comprehensive comments on the implementation of Article 7. Nevertheless, a consistent feature in Advisory Committee monitoring has been to review the permissibility of limitations. Here, however, a more structured review by the Advisory Committee of restrictions in legislative acts, administrative procedures, and the practice of local authorities is to be encouraged. In particular, further clarification of a state's margin of appreciation in imposing limitations or formalities, *inter alia* with respect to the balancing of public interests, such as the promotion of integration or tolerance, and the rights of persons belonging to national minorities, would result in this FCNM provision making a more substantive contribution to the understanding of the scope of protection provided by existing international standards.

With regard to the implementation of particular freedoms, state reports generally say very little about the right to freedom of expression and the right to freedom of religion under Article 7. To a large extent, this is because the vast majority of states provide a detailed examination of their obligations with respect to these freedoms under Articles 8 and 9 FCNM, which are more specific. Therefore, states parties have mainly focused their reporting under Article 7 on the rights to freedom of assembly and to freedom of association. This approach is understandable, as the scope of the obligations established by these articles overlaps. Such state practice serves to underline the interdependence and interconnectedness of the rights guaranteed in the provisions of the Convention. However, the provisions of Article 8 and Article 9 are more specialized, as they provide detailed rules for the implementation of these general freedoms. In this context, it is essential that the Advisory Committee systematically review all aspects of the protection secured by these two freedoms, and encourage states parties to provide a comprehensive account of the implementation of these provisions in their Article 25 reporting obligations, including aspects not covered by the *lex specialis* articles.

Lastly, the implementation of Article 7 has served to highlight that when considering the enjoyment of the freedoms set out in this provision, the obligations of states extend beyond simply combating discrimination. Undeniably, this is the innovative added value of this provision. The FCNM is designed to facilitate minority protection in a positive sense. States parties should, therefore, not only avoid unjustified interference, they should facilitate steps by national minorities to exercise these freedoms. States parties should, therefore, take necessary measures to create an environment in which minorities can maintain and further develop their distinct identities, as foreseen in Article 5 FCNM. In this respect, the practices mentioned in state reports offer a useful point of reference, providing concrete examples of positive measures and of support from public authorities to ensure the functioning of minority associations and assemblies, and religious organizations and institutions.

Given that Article 7 is not novel in substance, its real importance lies in its interconnectedness with the other principles of the FCNM. To maximize the benefit of the protection this article offers persons belonging to national minorities, states parties should examine Article 7 in light of the following principles in determining the extent of their obligations: prohibition of discrimination against persons belonging to national minorities, as foreseen in Article 4; the more specific duty of horizontal protection, concentrating on the principles laid out in Article 5(2) and Article 6(2); and the requirement to promote the conditions necessary for persons belonging to national minorities to maintain and develop their culture and to preserve the essential elements of their identity, as set out in Article 5(1). This comprehensive approach would demonstrate the nuanced role that Article 7 can and should play in the context of the protection provided by this Convention and by the existing body of international human rights standards.

ARTICLE 8

Zdenka Machnyikova

The Parties undertake to recognise that every person belonging to a national minority has the right to manifest his or her religion or belief and to establish religious institutions, organisations and associations.

I. Background

A. Issues

1. Protection of Minorities and Freedom of Religion in International Law

Our beliefs and our conscience are among the most important means for understanding our spiritual and moral existence, and our sense of identity as individuals and members of a larger community. Indeed, the diverse religions and faiths stand as an unrelenting witness to the cultural and intellectual struggle of humankind to come to terms both with the divine and with the material realities of human life. Historically, religion and national identity have been closely intertwined; religion has also had considerable influence over the governance of states.[1] It has shaped and sometimes aggravated the relationship between majorities and minorities or among diverse religious groups, and at

[1] See, for example, Bulgaria State Report, ACFC/SR (2003) 001, 2003, para. 37.

times has resulted in armed conflict and persecution of religious minorities. Even in the modern world, one of the key themes of current international affairs is that extreme doctrines and politicized religion often fuel escalation of internal and external conflicts rather than contributing to the building of peaceful societies.

Ever since the Peace of Augsburg in 1555 set out the principle *cuis regio eius religio*, the relationship between church and state has played a critical role in international relations in Europe, as well as in the treatment of minorities. The 1648 Treaty of Westphalia between the Holy Roman Emperor and the King of France created the foundation of the modern international political system, a construct based on the concept of sovereign states, with each legally entitled to govern its own territory and its own population free of external influence. This treaty extended the Peace of Augsburg's provisions for religious toleration to the Reformed Calvinist Church, which meant all three of the great religious communities of the Empire, Roman Catholic, Lutheran, and Calvinist, were now recognized. To these groups, the member states of the Empire were bound to allow at least private worship and liberty of conscience, in addition to the right of emigration for all religious minorities and dissidents within their domains. Later negotiations in 1767 and 1775, between Poland and Russia, resulted in guarantees of religious rights to dissidents in Poland, while the Congress of Vienna, which resulted in the 1815 Treaty of Vienna, not only provided religious minorities with the freedom to practise their faith, but also granted certain civil rights to Jews. These guarantees were precursors of protections which states later negotiated for ethnic minorities living outside their territory and with whom the state identified. Furthermore, they foreshadowed the creation of the League of Nations treaty systems.[2]

The modern era of international protection of minorities and their religious identity is, however, based on a very different premiss. It is rooted in the concept of universal individual human rights rather than in the protection of exclusive groups based on the proprietary interest of foreign, nation-forming states. The idea that all human beings are entitled to religious freedom has arisen as a by-product of democracy and belief in the dignity of individuals. The 1948 Universal Declaration of Human Rights (UDHR) embodied the principle of religious liberty in Article 18, by which governments declare their neutrality on religious questions, leaving each individual to adopt his or her own

[2] On the League of Nations system, see G. Pentassuglia, *Minorities in International Law: An Introductory Study*, Handbook (Council of Europe, Strasbourg, 2002), i. 26–9.

religious belief without fear of government reprisal.[3] As Nowak has noted, in some respects it is quite surprising that the world community of states was able to adopt international norms guaranteeing religious pluralism, given that attitudes towards religion range from strictly secular states to states that have an established state church.[4]

2. *International Standards on the Right to Manifest One's Religion or Belief*

The right articulated in Article 18 UDHR, to manifest one's religion or belief, was further developed in Article 18 of the legally binding International Covenant on Civil and Political Rights (ICCPR),[5] and in regional contexts in Article 9 of the European Convention for the Protection of Human Rights and Fundamental Freedoms (ECHR),[6] and Article 10 of the Charter of Fundamental Rights of the European Union.[7] Each of these instruments addresses the full scope of the rights to freedom of religion or belief. At the outset, it is worth noting that, from the perspective of protection of minority religious identity, they clearly recognize and protect the communal dimension of religious life. While religion can be an intensely private matter, worshipping together with other adherents of the same faith is often central to the existence of a religion. Thus, the instruments stress that the right involves freedom 'either alone or in community with others' to manifest one's religion, specifically through worship, observance, practice, and teaching. The substantive protection offered by the freedom of religion is reinforced in these instruments by non-discrimination clauses and by provisions guaranteeing equality before the law and equal protection of the law, which prohibit any discrimination on the grounds of 'religion'.[8] The United Nations' 1981 Declaration on the

[3] UNGA, Universal Declaration of Human Rights (UDHR) (adopted on 10 December 1948), UNGA Res. 217 (III) (1948), UN Doc. A/810, Art. 18 stipulates: 'Everyone has the right to freedom of thought, conscience and religion; this right includes freedom to change his religion or belief, and freedom, either alone or in community with others and in public or private, to manifest his religion or belief in teaching, practice, worship and observance.'

[4] On the controversial nature of freedom of religion and the historical background of development of the right to freedom of religion see M. Nowak, *U.N. Covenant on Civil and Political Rights: CCPR Commentary* (N. P. Engel, Strasbourg, 1993), paras. 2–5, pp. 310–12.

[5] International Covenant on Civil and Political Rights (ICCPR) (adopted 16 December 1966, entered into force 23 March 1976) 999 UNTS 171.

[6] European Convention for the Protection of Human Rights and Fundamental Freedoms (ECHR), ETS 5, 1950.

[7] Charter of Fundamental Rights of the European Union, Official Journal of the European Communities, 2000, C 364/1.

[8] See Art. 2(1), (26) ICCPR; Art. 14 ECHR; and Protocol No. 12 to the European Convention for the Protection of Human Rights and Fundamental Freedoms, ETS 177, 2000, Art. 2.

Elimination of All Forms of Intolerance and of Discrimination Based on Religion or Belief (the UN Declaration on the Elimination of All Forms of Intolerance),[9] though not formally binding, distils many of the principles articulated in the ICCPR, and in Articles 2, 3, and 4 it connects the anti-discrimination norms to the protection of religion and belief. The most extensive protection of religious freedoms is that found in the politically binding regional instrument of the Organization for Security and Co-operation in Europe (OSCE). The 1989 Concluding Document of the Vienna Follow-up Meeting of the Conference on Security and Co-operation in Europe (the Vienna Document)[10] details a list of commitments securing the freedom to profess and practise religion but, more importantly from the perspective of minority protection, in paragraph 16 it also secures the rights connected with communal manifestation of religion and sets out the rights to be enjoyed by 'religious communities'. In sum, although the international standards pertaining to the freedom of religion are primarily focused on the equal dignity of individuals they also, by according protection to the communal dimension of the manifestation of religion or belief, provide protections important to the existence and preservation of a minority as a collective.

Common spiritual beliefs, religious tradition, and practice are often the essence of a minority's distinct identity. Allowing members of the group to maintain common consciousness through the exercise of their faith is fundamental for reproduction of a group's identity and for its existence. Thus, protection of the right to profess and practise their religion is of critical importance for members of a religious minority. This is also confirmed in Article 27 ICCPR which affirms that, '[i]n those States in which ethic, religious or linguistic minorities exist, persons belonging to such minorities shall not be denied the right, in community with other members of their group, . . . to profess and practice their own religion . . .'. Whereas Article 27 set the basic universal standard in the field of minority rights, Article 3(1) of the UN Declaration on the Rights of Persons Belonging to National or Ethnic, Religious, and Linguistic Minorities (the UN Declaration on Minorities)[11] provided a more specific standard, implying positive action with the use of the

[9] Declaration on the Elimination of All Forms of Intolerance and of Discrimination Based on Religion or Belief, UNGA Res. 36/55, 36 UN GAOR, Supp. (No. 51) at 171 (1981), UN Doc. A/36/684.

[10] Conference for Security and Co-operation in Europe (CSCE), Concluding Document, Follow-up Meeting, Vienna, 1986–9.

[11] UN Declaration on the Rights of Persons Belonging to National or Ethnic, Religious, or Linguistic Minorities, UNGA Res. 47/135 (18 December 1992), annex 47 UN GAOR 49, 210 (1992), UN Doc. A/47/49.

more positive expression 'to have the right' to profess and practise their own religion freely without interference or any form of discrimination. In addition, as Asbjørn Eide stated in the Commentary to the UN Declaration on Minorities, '[t]he words freely and without interference or any form of discrimination, . . . show that it is not enough for the State to abstain from interference or discrimination. It must also ensure that individuals and organizations of the larger society do not interfere or discriminate.'[12] From the perspective of obligations set out in Article 8 of the Framework Convention for the Protection of National Minorities (FCNM), provisions of the 1990 Document of the Copenhagen Meeting on the Human Dimension of the Conference on Security and Co-operation in Europe (the Copenhagen Document)[13] are of the utmost relevance as they served as a template in the development of the provisions of the Framework Convention. As the Explanatory Report on the interpretation of the FCNM (Explanatory Report)[14] explains, Article 8 combines several elements from paragraphs 32(2), 32(3) and 32(6) of the Copenhagen Document. Paragraph 32(6) provides a general entitlement for persons belonging to national minorities to establish associations and to participate in international non-governmental organizations, while paragraphs 32(2) and 32(3) guarantee more specifically their right to establish and maintain their own religious institutions and to profess and practise their religion.

B. History

As mentioned above, religious tradition is often the essence of a minority's distinct identity, and safeguarding its practice in community with other members of a national minority is a vital means for preserving the minority's common consciousness. This fact is reflected in the inclusion of a specific provision within the FCNM, guaranteeing manifestation of religion and belief specifically to persons belonging to national minorities.[15] The process of defining the protection

[12] A. Eide, Commentary to the UN Declaration on the Rights of Persons Belonging to National or Ethnic, Religious, and Linguistic Minorities, (2001), UN Doc. E/CN.4/Sub.2/AC.5/2001/2.

[13] Second Conference on the Human Dimension of the CSCE, Document of the Copenhagen Meeting of the Conference on the Human Dimension of the CSCE, Copenhagen, 1990.

[14] Preparatory Work of the Ad Hoc Committee for the Protection of National Minorities (CAHMIN), Explanatory Report to the Framework Convention for the Protection of National Minorities, CAHMIN H(1995) 010, 1995, para. 54.

[15] The Preamble of the FCNM emphasized that 'a pluralist and genuinely democratic society should not only respect the ethnic, cultural, linguistic and religious identity of each person belonging to a national minority, but also create appropriate conditions enabling them to express, preserve and develop this identity'.

of religious rights of national minorities in the FCNM went through a number of stages, and the different options considered were to a large extent tied to the efforts of experts to systematize general and specific guarantees in the FCNM.[16] At the stage when a legally binding treaty on the protection of minorities in Europe was still being considered, the initial proposals of the European Commission for Democracy through Law foresaw a specific right to manifestation, which would be guaranteed explicitly to religious minorities.[17] However, when the preliminary drafts of the Framework Convention were discussed in the Steering Committee for Human Rights (CDDH), the scope of this protection was extended and the general right to freedom of thought, conscience, and religion was introduced, following the wording of Article 9 ECHR.[18] The Ad Hoc Committee for the Protection of National Minorities (CAHMIN), charged with drafting the FCNM, decided to group the separate articles on freedom of assembly, freedom of association, freedom of expression, and freedom of thought, conscience, and religion into a single summary provision.[19]

The level of detail to be provided with respect to guarantees of religious rights was the subject of extensive discussion and controversy within CAHMIN. The experts were divided on whether to insert a specific provision focused on the right to establish religious institutions and places of worship, in addition to the general provision on the freedom of religion. At this point, the drafters decided that given the systematic approach adopted for the structure of the Convention further explicit elaboration of the freedom of religion, in what was then Article 2 of Chapter II, would give the impression that this freedom had a privileged position in comparison with other fundamental freedoms mentioned in the draft of Article 2. Two main factors were taken into account, the first being that the right to establish religious institutions was already covered by the general freedom of religion, which is to be read in the light of Strasbourg case law on Article 9 ECHR. The second concerned the already mentioned systematic approach. Some experts were of the view that the specific right connected to freedom of religion should not be mentioned explicitly, unless a similar elaboration was to be provided for the other freedoms included in the article. This option was rejected, however, as it would

16 CAHMIN, 3rd meeting, CAHMIN (94) 13, meeting report, 1994, para. 36, pp. 9–10.

17 European Commission for Democracy Through Law (ECDL), Preliminary Draft Convention on the Protection of Minorities [DAJ.SC.DEMOCRACY]CONV. MIN, 1990, Art. 11; also ECDL, Proposal for a Convention for the Protection of National Minorities, CDL-MIN (93) 6, 1993, Art. 10.

18 Steering Committee for Human Rights (CDDH), Final Activity Report of the CDDH for the Attention of the Committee of Ministers, CDDH (93) 22, 1993, Art. 11.

19 CAHMIN, 1st meeting, CAHMIN (94) 5, meeting report, 1994, paras. 29–30, pp. 6–7.

involve subdividing the existing article into a number of separate provisions within the FCNM. Given the very nature of the Framework Convention, it was considered inappropriate to go into much detail in specifying the freedoms.[20] In the final stages of the drafting process however, the desire to adhere strictly to the systematic approach was outweighed by the benefits of securing specific protection for manifestation of religion and belief for persons belonging to national minorities. In the end, it was decided to further elaborate the general freedom of religion contained in Article 7 by adopting a separate article addressing the right to manifest one's religion or beliefs, including the communal dimension of this right.[21] The final text was based on a Swedish proposal inspired by paragraphs 32(3) and 32(6) of the Copenhagen Document, which guarantee persons belonging to national minorities the right to profess their own religion and also provide a more general standard linked to the establishment and maintenance of minority organizations or associations.[22] Following the example of Article 9 ECHR, the formula 'to profess or practice his or her own religion' was replaced in the final version with the right 'to manifest his or her religion or belief'.[23]

C. Context

The right of persons belonging to national minorities to manifest their religious beliefs is closely connected with freedom of expression, which includes the right to hold opinions and to receive and impart information. With regard to protection of the substance of ideas and opinions, religious expression falls within the broad scope of protection offered by the freedom of expression. This protection is equally important for free manifestation of religion as it also extends to forms and means of communication.[24] Similarly, the freedoms of peaceful assembly and association provide basic preconditions for the enjoyment of public manifestation of religion or beliefs by persons belonging to national minorities.[25] In this respect, the effective implementation of Articles 7, 9, and 10 FCNM is essential to create the environment necessary for the effective enjoyment of the rights guaranteed in Article 8 FCNM. A number of other provisions of the FCNM are also pertinent to the full implementation of

[20] CAHMIN, 3rd meeting, CAHMIN (94) 13, meeting report, 1994, para. 36, pp. 9–10.

[21] CAHMIN, 5th meeting, CAHMIN (94) 19, meeting report, 1994, Art. 8, pp. 4, 26.

[22] CAHMIN, Proposals concerning the Preliminary Draft Framework Convention for the Protection of National Minorities, CAHMIN (94) 14 Rev., 1994, pp. 12, 21; and also CAHMIN, 5th meeting, CAHMIN (94) 19 1994, meeting report, Art. 8, p. 4.

[23] CAHMIN, 6th meeting, CAHMIN (94) 28, meeting report, 1994, Art. 8, para. 36, p. 8.

[24] Bulgaria State Report, ACFC/SR (2003) 001, 2003, para. 70.

[25] Above, n. 24.

the right to manifest one's religion or beliefs. These include Article 4 FCNM, which guarantees full and effective equality of persons belonging to a national minority without any discrimination, as well as Article 5 FCNM, which requires the parties to adopt special measures necessary for maintenance and promotion of the distinct religious identity of national minorities. Horizontal protection and the need to promote religious tolerance, enshrined in Article 6, are also key to the protection of religious communities. Finally, specific rights in some of the other provisions of the Convention assist in supporting the exercise of religious beliefs by national minorities. These include: Article 17, which guarantees contact across frontiers and the right to participate in the activities of non-governmental organizations, both at the national and international levels; Article 12, which requires measures in the field of education to foster knowledge of the culture, history, language, and religion of national minorities and of the majority; and Article 13 which recognizes the right to set up private education and training establishments. The specific implications that implementation of these rights has for Article 8 will be discussed in greater detail below. Finally, Article 23 is of great importance in applying the minimum standards guaranteed by Article 8 because it stipulates that insofar as rights contained in the FCNM are subject to corresponding provisions of the ECHR, they are understood to conform to the provisions of the latter.

II. Analysis

A. Structure of the Article

Article 8 serves as a *lex specialis* provision to the general freedom of thought, conscience, and religion set out in Article 7, as it contains more detailed rules with respect to specific aspects of the right to freedom of religion.[26] In particular, Article 8 requires states to recognize the right to manifest religion or belief. Its protection could be explained as a response to the importance of public exercise and collective practice of religion in preserving the identity of a group. Besides the specific features associated with the expression of religious beliefs, the history of state suppression, to which many religious minorities have been subjected, and still are in some states, provides a particular context for why this right deserves stronger protection. Implicit in the right to manifest one's religion is that one should be able to engage in religious life in community with

[26] Preparatory Work of the Ad Hoc Committee for the Protection of National Minorities (CAHMIN), Explanatory Report to the Framework Convention for the Protection of National Minorities, CAHMIN H(1995) 010, 1995, para. 54.

others of like beliefs, and that this type of communal experience should be determined in accordance with religious beliefs, rather than dictated, monitored, or otherwise impaired by the coercive requirements of the state or private parties.

The wording of Article 8 includes two substantive elements. It requires the states parties to recognize the right to manifest one's religion or belief, the scope of which encompasses a more specific aspect that is emphasized in the second part of the article—the right to establish religious institutions, organizations, and associations. The following analysis will first examine the scope of the protection provided by this provision and then underline the general aspects relevant to implementation of the provision as a whole. A detailed analysis of the two substantive elements mentioned will be carried out in separate sections of this chapter.

B. General Issues

1. Scope of Protection

The right to manifest one's religion encompasses a large catalogue of guarantees that are necessary to ensure free and peaceful enjoyment of this right. For a clearer understanding of the undertakings in Article 8, an examination of the historical and systematic context of this provision is particularly relevant. The Explanatory Report asserts that the content of the provision was inspired by paragraphs 32(2), 32(3), and 32(6) of the Copenhagen Document. Under these provisions, the scope of the obligations of the states parties would include ensuring the rights of persons belonging to national minorities: to profess and practise their religion, including the acquisition, possession, and use of religions materials; to conduct religious education activities in their mother tongue; and to establish and maintain their own religious institutions, organizations, and associations. In this last case, persons belonging to minorities can seek voluntary financial and other contributions as well as public assistance, in conformity with national legislation, as well as participate in international non-governmental organizations.

This context provides somewhat more detail regarding the aims and the content of a state's duties under Article 8. However, the right to manifest one's religion covers a whole host of other essential elements which fall within the scope of protection of this right, and which are not specified in the Copenhagen Document. A detailed reading of the *travaux préparatoires*, as well as a systematic interpretation of Article 7 in the light of Article 23, suggest that the scope of the protection provided in Article 8 is also rooted in Article 9

ECHR.[27] This understanding has been explicitly confirmed by a significant number of states in their reports.[28] The European Court of Human Rights (ECtHR) has produced a respectable amount of case law, which clarifies the scope of the protection provided by the right to manifestation of religion, and which could serve as guidance to states parties in implementing their Article 8 commitments.

2. *Individually or in Community with Others*

Although Article 8 refers to the right of each individual, it also offers protection to a national minority which it needs, as a collective, to manifest its religion. The decision of the drafters to assure the active freedom 'to manifest' one's religion and belief in a separate article clearly shows the important role that the profession of faith plays in preserving a minority group's identity and existence. For similar reasons, the associational dimension of manifestation is stressed through the inclusion of the right to establish religious institutions, organizations, and associations.[29] Evidently, protecting the collective exercise of faith is fundamental to the reproduction of a group's identity and to its existence. Correspondingly, the final text proposed by the Swedish expert included an explicit reference to manifestation of religion 'alone or in community with others'.[30] This phrase, however, was deleted in the final version as a result of the application of the systematic approach, as Article 3(2) FCNM established this

[27] See CAHMIN, 3rd meeting, CAHMIN (94) 13, meeting report, 1994, para. 36, pp. 9–10; and also CAHMIN, 6th meeting CAHMIN (94) 28, meeting report, 1994, Art. 8, para. 36, p. 8.

[28] See, for example, Finland State Report, ACFC/SR (99) 3, 1999, Arts. 7–9; Sweden State Report, ACFC/SR (2001) 003, 2001, para. 23.

[29] During the final stages of the drafting process, despite initial divergent opinions among the delegations on whether to insert a specific provision guaranteeing the right of persons belonging to national minorities to establish their own religious institutions and places of worship, the CAHMIN decided to add a new Art. 8, in addition to the general freedom of religion guaranteed in Art. 7. See CAHMIN, 3rd meeting, CAHMIN (94) meeting report, 1994, para. 36, pp. 9–10; the Swedish proposal, which was adopted in the end, was based on paras. 32(3) and 32(6) of the Copenhagen Document, which guarantee persons belonging to national minorities the right to establish their own religious institutions, organizations, and associations and the general right to establish and maintain organizations or associations. Again, this puts emphasis on securing the collective manifestation of religion or belief by the group. See CAHMIN, Proposals concerning the Preliminary Draft Framework Convention for the Protection of National Minorities, CAHMIN (94) 14 Rev., 1994, p. 12, 21, and also CAHMIN, 5th meeting, CAHMIN (94) 19 1994, meeting report, Art. 8, p. 4.

[30] See CAHMIN, Proposals Concerning the Preliminary Draft Framework Convention for the Protection of National Minorities, CAHMIN (94) 14 Rev., 1994, p. 12, 21; and also CAHMIN, 5th meeting, CAHMIN (94) 19, 1994, meeting report, Art. 8, p. 4; a number of the state reports also confirmed that their legislation explicitly guarantees the enjoyment of this right alone or in community with others. See Denmark State Report ACFC/SR (99) 9, 1999, para. 30; Italy State Report, ACFC/SR (1999) 007, 1999, para. 48.

overarching guarantee for all provisions of the Convention.[31] Notably, the Explanatory Report asserts that the guarantees in the FCNM do not imply the recognition of collective rights.[32] In this respect, the rights of individual members of a national minority, as embodied in Article 8 FCNM, should be understood as a conduit for the protection of a group. Here it is of significance that Article 25 ECHR allows groups and associations to seek redress under Article 9 of the Convention, which is phrased as an individual right. The jurisprudence of the ECtHR has confirmed that groups and associations enjoy the protection of Article 9 in this respect.[33]

3. *Duty of Forbearance*

As regards the obligations of the parties under Article 8, the primary duty of states is to respect the freedom of persons belonging to national minorities to pursue their religious beliefs. The stress here is on the freedom in this right, which is essentially of a defensive character, allowing national minorities to fend off intrusion in this free private domain by the state or third parties. In this respect, the state has a responsibility not to interfere in the religious life of national minorities, and at the same time it has a duty to protect this free space. When it comes to the manifestation of religion, however, this free domain is not absolute and may be limited by the state.[34]

Regarding state practice in implementing the FCNM, the states parties generally refer to their constitutional and legislative provisions securing the right to freedom of religion, including the right to manifest one's religion or belief. This right is normally extended to everybody including persons belonging to national minorities, as a number of states have pointed out. Some states have gone even further and declared that they have specific legislative provisions expressly guaranteeing this right to persons belonging to national minorities.[35] Within their constitutional frameworks, most of the states parties ensure respect for the autonomous existence of religious communities. Indeed, a large number of states have declared that there is neither an official state

[31] For more detailed discussions on the individual and collective elements of the FCNM see chapters on Art. 1 and Art. 3 in this commentary.

[32] Above, n. 14, para. 13.

[33] See, for example, *Metropolitan Church of Bessarabia and Others* v. *Moldova* (45701/99) (2001) ECHR 851, para. 1.

[34] It should be noted that the private exercise of religion and belief, given its nature, cannot be restricted. However, as Nowak above, n. 4, para. 20, p. 319 observed, 'such practice may be termed private only so long as it does not leave that sphere of individual existence and autonomy that does not touch upon the freedom and sphere of privacy of others'.

[35] Lithuania State Report, ACFC/SR (2001) 7, 2001, para. 44; Ukraine State Report, ACFC/SR (99) 14, 1999, para. 22.

religion nor institutional linkage between state and church in their countries, and particularly no state jurisdiction over church affairs as they are governed by the internal rules of the church and by canon law.[36] An express guarantee for religious communities to conduct their internal affairs independently is frequently quoted.[37] This is, of course, an extremely important principle, and an area which merits careful attention by the Advisory Committee. This issue is particularly topical, as a number of states parties have recently emerged from totalitarian regimes, which had both strongly suppressed the freedom of religion and had legislation that allowed a high level of interference in internal church affairs. The remnants of such practices and legislation still exist. As Bulgaria has pointed out in its report, the fall of that country's totalitarian regime was followed by a wave of religious strife within various churches, and this resulted in intrusive attempts by the state to interfere in the internal affairs of religious communities.[38] This is not to say that the state cannot play a constructive role in resolving disputes within religious communities;[39] however, as will be discussed in greater detail with regard to the registration of the churches, it must not substantively assess the beliefs and practices involved.

4. *Positive Obligations*

With respect to Article 8, the question is whether it also entails besides its negative obligation, a positive duty. At a minimum, the parties have a horizontal duty to ensure that national minorities can function peacefully in the pursuit of their religious beliefs, free from interference by a third party.[40] This is particularly important in situations when hostile religious groups confront each other, or when religious customs are made to serve political interests, and religion becomes a divisive factor between minority and majority. In *Metropolitan Church of Bessarabia and Others* v. *Moldova*, the ECtHR considered it unacceptable

[36] See, for example, Albania State Report, ACFC/SR (2001) 5, 2001, para. 39; Germany State Report, ACFC/SR (2000) 1, 2000, para. 58; Lithuania State Report, ACFC/SR (2001) 7, 2001, paras. 44–5.

[37] See, for example, Lithuania State Report, ACFC/SR (2001) 7, 2001, para. 44; Ireland State Report, ACFC/SR (2001) 6, 2001, para. 66.

[38] Bulgaria State Report, ACFC/SR(2003)001, 2003, para. 70; See also *Hasan and Chaush* v. *Bulgaria* (30985/96) (2000) ECHR 509.

[39] See Comments of the Government of Estonia on the Opinion of the Advisory Committee on the Implementation of the Framework Convention for the Protection of National Minorities in Estonia, GVT/COM/INF/OP/I (2002) 005, 2002.

[40] It was pointed out in the *travaux préparatoires* on Art. 7, guaranteeing the general right to the freedom of religion, which was further elaborated in a separate provision of Art. 8, that such provision seems indeed capable of having horizontal effect. See CAHMIN, 2nd meeting, CAHMIN (94) 9, meeting report, 1994, para. 34.

to refuse protection against acts of intimidation to the members of a church which was not officially recognized by the state, on the grounds that only legally recognized activities are entitled to legal protection.[41] The Court confirmed that the obligation of the state to secure peaceful enjoyment of the right to freedom of religion entails an obligation to provide horizontal protection. Besides the implicit obligation under Article 8, horizontal protection is explicitly set out in Article 6(2) FCNM which requires parties 'to take appropriate measures to protect persons who may be subject to threats or acts of discrimination, hostility or violence as a result of their . . . religious identity'. With reference to Article 8, many states parties cite their legislative and institutional guarantees focused on ensuring protection against discrimination based on religion.[42] Some states also mention laws on blasphemy.[43] In their reports, several states parties further highlight their criminal code provisions which penalize acts by individuals that interfere with religious ceremonies, obstruct the activities of religious organizations, ruin or damage religious objects,[44] or incite religious hatred.[45] In considering the United Kingdom's practice, the Advisory Committee on the FCNM held that the lack of comprehensive legislation protecting individuals from religious discrimination and from incitement to religious hatred has an adverse effect on persons belonging to ethnic minorities and called on the government to adopt the necessary legal measures to address this situation.[46] This strongly worded view that the legal obligations of the state under Article 8 require the adoption of comprehensive legislation providing protection against religious discrimination was also supported by the Committee of Ministers.[47] The horizontal protection provided by Article 8 is consistent with obligations imposed by more explicit standards found in other international treaties. Given the history of religious wars and the fact that religious intolerance persists in modern societies, these treaties expressly call for the

[41] Above, n. 33, para. 129.

[42] Bulgaria State Report, ACFC/SR (2003) 001, 2003, para. 71.

[43] Poland State Report, ACFC/SR (2002) 2, 2002, para. 25; and also Advisory Committee on the Framework Convention for the Protection of National Minorities, Opinion on the United Kingdom, ACFC/INF/OP/I (2002) 006, 2002, para. 60.

[44] Albania State Report, ACFC/SR (2001) 5, 2001, para. 39.

[45] See, for example, Moldova State Report, ACFC/SR (2000) 2, 2000, para. 18; Poland State Report, ACFC/SR (2002) 2, 2002, paras. 24 and 25, Estonia State Report, ACFC/SR (99) 16, 1999, para. 35.

[46] Advisory Committee Opinion on the United Kingdom, ACFC/INF/OP/I (2002) 006, 2002, paras. 57 and 116.

[47] See Committee of Ministers, Resolution ResCMN (2002) 9 on the implementation of the Framework Convention for the Protection of National Minorities by the United Kingdom, 799th meeting, 2002, Art. 3(1).

prohibition of advocacy of religious hatred and incitement to religious intolerance.[48]

Further, with a view to promoting religious tolerance, the parties have an obligation to take effective measures to encourage mutual respect and understanding among different religious groups living on their territory.[49] As some states have noted, effective implementation may require the establishment of specific channels for dialogue between state authorities and religious communities.[50] It may also require specific measures to promote tolerance and understanding, in particular in the fields of education, culture, and the media, as foreseen in Article 6(1) FCNM.[51]

While horizontal measures to ensure the protection of persons belonging to national minorities against interference by private persons in their religious activities are an indispensable part of obligations under Article 8, the principal responsibility of the parties is to ensure that minorities are able to pursue their religious beliefs and customs, establish places of worship and religious institutions, and organize their internal religious affairs. As discussed in greater detail below, this may require taking steps to ensure that the legislative framework allows minority communities to practise their religion and conduct their affairs through their institutions and associations. It is common practice among the states parties to have specific legislation providing rules for how religious organizations can acquire legal personality and establishing a basis for relations between the state and religious groups.[52]

Article 8 specifically ties the right to manifest one's religion to persons belonging to national minorities. This link, as well as the overall context of the protection provided by the FCNM, indicates that the states parties should take steps to ensure that persons belonging to national minorities are able to observe and practise their religion and beliefs without discrimination, and on an equal footing with others residing in the state. Indeed, this is the key to the full implementation of the obligations under Article 8. Consequently, the Advisory

[48] See Art. 20(2) ICCPR; Declaration on the Elimination of All Forms of Intolerance and of Discrimination Based on Religion or Belief, UNGA Res. 36/55, 36 UN GAOR, Supp. (No. 51) at 171 (1981), UN Doc. A/36/684. Art. 4(2); and the European Commission against Racism and Intolerance (ECRI) General Policy Recommendation No. 5: Combating Intolerance and Discrimination against Muslims, CRI (2000) 21, 2000, Strasbourg.

[49] Bulgaria State Report, ACFC/SR (2003) 001, 2003, para. 70.

[50] Azerbaijan State Report, ACFC/SR (2002) 1, 2002, para. 37; Moldova State Report, ACFC/SR (2000) 2, 2000, para. 18; Norway State Report, ACFC/SR (2001) 1, 2001, para. 32.

[51] For a more detailed discussion on the measures required to encourage tolerance, mutual respect, and intercultural dialogue see the chapter on Article 6 in this commentary.

[52] See, for example, Austria State Report, ACFC/SR (2000) 3, 2000, para. 45; Moldova State Report, ACFC/SR (2000) 2, 2000, para. 17.

Committee has focused on monitoring state practice with regard to differences in the treatment of various religious entities. Many European states have proclaimed religious neutrality and impartiality, observing the separation of church and state. In their practice, however, some favour religious adherents of the church with historical links to the state or of the majority of the population. The fact that the state declares one particular religion a state religion[53] is not in itself incompatible with freedom of religion. However, exclusive support for such a church would constitute discrimination against adherents of other religions or non-believers. It is clear from the practice of the Advisory Committee that the parties must pay special attention to the situation of national minorities, in particular in cases where the state recognizes a state or official religion, and provides particular support to such a religion, or accommodates some of its religious practices in the public sphere. In this respect, parties are required to provide information on financial or other forms of direct or indirect support from the state to any religious institutions, organizations, or associations. Concerning state support for religious activities, the Advisory Committee clearly stated that having a state church is not in itself contrary to the FCNM, and that Article 8 does not *per se* entail an obligation to fund religious activities. However, if the state makes support available only to one religion, through direct funding from income tax or through a church tax, for example, 'particular attention must be paid to the situation of other religions with a view to guaranteeing all persons belonging to national minorities their rights under the present article [Article 8] as well as their right to equality before the law and equal protection of the law as guaranteed under Article 4 of the FCNM'.[54]

This position is also supported by the authoritative interpretation of Article 18 ICCPR. The Human Rights Committee, in General Comment No. 22 on Article 18, stressed that a state religion should result neither in the impairment of the rights enjoyed under Articles 18 and 27 ICCPR, nor in any discrimination against members of other religions or non-believers. In the view of the Committee certain measures, such as restricting eligibility for government service to members of the predominant religion, or according economic privileges to them or imposing special restrictions on the practice of other faiths, are not in accordance with the prohibition of discrimination based on religion or belief and the guarantee of equal protection.[55] The ECtHR has also issued

[53] Bulgaria State Report, ACFC/SR (2003) 001, 2003, para. 70.

[54] Advisory Committee Opinion on Finland, ACFC/INF/OP/I (2001) 002, 2000, para. 29; Advisory Committee Opinion on Denmark, ACFC/INF/OP/I (2001) 005, 1999, para. 29.

[55] UN Human Rights Committee 'General Comment No. 22' on Freedom of Religion, 48th session (1993), UN Doc. HRI/GEN/1 Rev. 1, para. 9, p. 146.

numerous judgments addressing the discriminatory practices of states affecting minority religious denominations, some of which are discussed in greater detail below.

Full implementation of Article 8 requires both positive and preventive steps to ensure that persons belonging to particular religious groups are not discriminated against. Indeed, a number of states confirmed that their legislation secures the principle of non-discrimination and ensures that all religious denominations are equal before the law and have equal protection of law.[56] In this respect, and as already noted, the Advisory Committee and the Committee of Ministers called for comprehensive legislation to deal with the prohibition of religious discrimination.[57] Further, some states refer to their institutional guarantees to ensure this principle in practice, and mention the adoption of special measures aimed at preventing any religious discrimination.[58]

With regard to specific cases of discrimination in state practice, the Advisory Committee noted that in Croatia there appeared to be differences in how various religious entities were treated with respect to their status in the army and in other contexts. On this point, the Advisory Committee noted that the FCNM does not exclude differences in the treatment of religious entities; however, where such differences exist particular attention must be paid to persons belonging to national minorities.[59] Further, the Advisory Committee welcomed the fact that the Cypriot government had begun to pay the salaries of priests from different religious groups on an equal footing.[60] In considering the Finnish Report, the Committee stressed that where public funding is automatically provided to selected churches only, particular attention must be paid to the situation of other religions, and called upon the government to review its national legislation.[61] In response, the Finnish government acknowledged that there was a need to take steps to ensure greater equality for other religious communities; however, it argued that the privileged positions of the Evangelical Lutheran Church and the Orthodox Church as recipients of automatic funding were justified by the fact that they fulfil important societal duties, such as

[56] See, for example, Azerbaijan State Report, ACFC/SR (2002) 1, 2002, para. 34; Ireland State Report, ACFC/SR (2001) 6, 2001, paras. 65–6.

[57] See the Advisory Committee Opinion on United Kingdom, ACFC/INF/OP/I (2002) 006, 2002, paras. 57 and 116.

[58] Bulgaria State Report, ACFC/SR (2003) 001, 2003, para. 71; Italy State Report, ACFC/SR (1999) 007, 1999, para. 48.

[59] Advisory Committee Opinion on Croatia, ACFC/INF/OP/I (2002) 003, 2002, para. 38.

[60] Advisory Committee Opinion on Cyprus, ACFC/INF/OP/I (2001) 004, 2001, para. 35.

[61] Advisory Committee Opinion on Finland, ACFC/INF/OP/I (2000) 002, 2000, para. 29.

the maintenance of public cemeteries.[62] Lastly, in the case of the United Kingdom the Advisory Committee found that the restriction of the blasphemy law solely to Christians was discriminatory.[63]

Finally, implementation of Article 8 must be reviewed in the light of each state's obligation to take necessary steps to preserve the essential elements of a minority's identity, and specifically its religion.[64] As will be illustrated in sections covering the specific aspects of Article 8, many states provide support to religious communities to enable them to fully enjoy their right to manifest their religion.[65] These measures include: the collection of church taxes from adherents of different religions; the provision of financial support to churches from tax revenues; the payment of priests' salaries; the provision of financial support for the maintenance of church buildings and religious schools; the provision of religious education in schools, as well as higher theological education; and tax relief and exemptions from customs charges for material, objects, and equipment pertaining to religious institutions. These positive measures are not usually adopted specifically with regard to persons belonging to national minorities, but they stem instead from the general state obligation to ensure the right of everyone to manifest his or her religion; nevertheless, persons belonging to national minorities benefit from such policies.

5. *Limitations*

Although the wording of Article 8 does not specifically refer to the right to manifest one's religion or belief in public or private, the provision should be understood in the broadest sense, as encompassing both spheres. In fact, the right to establish religious institutions, provided in the second part of the provision, presumes religious manifestation which extends beyond manifestation in private. Once more, a systematic interpretation based on Article 23 FCNM suggests that the extent of the protection provided in Article 8 should conform with the protection provided under Article 9 ECHR, whose wording explicitly guarantees the right to manifest one's religion in public or private. A similar choice of words is provided in other instruments.[66] The difference between

[62] Comments of the Government of Finland on the Opinion of the Advisory Committee on the Report on the Implementation of the Framework Convention for the Protection of National Minorities in Finland, GVT/COM/INF/OP/I (2001) 002, 2001, Art. 8.

[63] Advisory Committee Opinion on the United Kingdom, ACFC/INF/OP/I (2002) 006, 2002, para. 117.

[64] See Art. 5(1) FCNM.

[65] Lithuania State Report, ACFC/SR (2001) 7, 2001, para. 45.

[66] See, for example, Art. 18 UDHR; Charter of Fundamental Rights of the European Union, Official Journal of the European Communities, 2000, C 364/1, Art. 10; Declaration on the Elimination of All Forms of Intolerance and of Discrimination Based on Religion or Belief, UNGA Res. 36/55, 36 UN GAOR, Supp. (No. 51) at 171 (1981), UN Doc. A/36/684, Art. 1.

private and public religious manifestation has significant legal consequences with regard to the permissibility of limitations, the prohibition of coercive influence, and the extent of state duties in implementing Article 8 FCNM.[67]

The wording of Article 8 FCNM does not expressly provide for any limitations on the manifestation of a religion and belief, in contrast to both the ECHR and the ICCPR.[68] It is, however, of note that a number of drafts of the *travaux préparatoires* foresaw limitations which were not included in the wording of the final text.[69] From the preparatory works, it can be deduced that the freedoms mentioned in Articles 7 and 8 were intended to be a declaration of principles. It was therefore deemed inappropriate to provide specific detail regarding these freedoms.[70] In the end, these limitations were incorporated through the elaboration of Article 19 FCNM, in light of which both Article 7, which guarantees the freedom of religion in general, and the more specific Article 8 must be understood to conform to the corresponding provisions of the ECHR dealing with limitations. Furthermore, the Explanatory Report states that the article combines elements from paragraphs 32(2), 32(3), and 32(6) of the Copenhagen Document.[71] In this respect, paragraph 9(4) of the same document allows for restrictions on exercise of the freedom to manifest one's religion or belief. These limitations must be both prescribed by law and consistent with international standards. In short, the manifestation of religion or belief in Article 8 FCNM is subject to the limitations envisaged in provisions regulating the freedom of religion in other international instruments, *inter alia* Article 9(2) ECHR, which reads, 'Freedom to manifest one's religion or belief shall be subject only to such limitations as are prescribed by law and are necessary in democratic society in the interest of public safety, for the protection of public order, health or morals or for the protection of the rights and freedoms of others.'

Concerning the implementation of Article 8 FCNM, the jurisprudence of the ECtHR is highly instructive, especially with regard to the margin of

[67] Advisory Committee Opinion on Bulgaria, ACFC/SR (2003) 001, 2003, para. 70.

[68] See Art. 9(2) ECHR and Art. 18(3) ICCPR.

[69] Steering Committee for Human Rights (CDDH), Final Activity Report of the CDDH for the Attention of the Committee of Ministers, CDDH (93) 22, 1993, Art. 11(*b*) stipulated: 'Freedom to manifest one's religion or beliefs shall be subject only to such limitations as are prescribed by law and are necessary in democratic society in the interests of public safety, for the protection of public order, health or morals, or for the protection of the rights and freedoms of others.' See also CAHMIN, Proposal concerning the Preliminary Draft Framework Convention for the Protection of National Minorities, CAHMIN (94) 14 Rev., 1994, Art. 7 bis.

[70] European Commission for Democracy through Law (ECDL) on the Set of Principles on National Minorities, Draft Report of the 4th Meeting of the CAHMIN, CD-PV (90) 4 prov., 1990, para. 25; and also CAHMIN, 3rd meeting, CAHMIN (94) 13, meeting report, 1994, para. 36.

[71] Above, n. 14, para. 54.

appreciation of states in assessing the necessity of interference.[72] The consistent practice of the Court requires that limitations pass the following test in order to justify overriding the right to freedom of religion or belief of individuals: the limitation must be 'prescribed by law'; it must pursue one of the enumerated public interests; and the limitation must be 'necessary in democratic society'. In articulating the importance of freedom of religion, the Court stressed that, '[it is] one of the most vital elements that go to make up the identity of believers and their conception of life, but it is also a precious asset for atheists, agnostics, skeptics and the unconcerned. The pluralism indissociable from a democratic society, which has been dearly won over the centuries, depends on it.'[73] In this respect, the Court asserted that in democratic societies, in which several religions coexist within the same population, it may be necessary to place restrictions on this freedom in order to reconcile the interests of the various groups and ensure that everyone's beliefs are respected.[74] With regard to the margin of appreciation in delimiting what is necessary in democratic society, the Court emphasized the need to secure true religious pluralism. Therefore, in assessing whether a restriction is proportionate to the legitimate aim pursued, it maintained that 'very strict scrutiny' should be applied.[75]

This is particularly important for persons belonging to national minorities, as the manifestation of their beliefs, religion, and customs is at the centre of their identity as a group. The maintenance and survival of the group's identity is often dependent on the ability of the minority to transfer their specific features from generation to generation. This factor, as well as the jurisprudence of the ECtHR, speaks in favour of a very narrow margin of appreciation in imposing restrictions on the manifestation of religious beliefs by national minorities.

From the perspective of minority protection and permissible limitations, specific attention should be paid to the interpretation of public morals as one of the grounds of legitimate public interest. There is no universally applicable standard for public morals; they vary from time to time, from place to place, and are characterized by the rapid and far-reaching evolution of opinions. In general, public morals refer to principles that are not always legally enforceable, but which are accepted by a great majority of citizens as general guidelines for their individual and collective behaviour. The morals in countries with a state religion or one dominant religion are often predominantly rooted in the belief system of this religion. Different religious beliefs and traditions are often a hallmark that distinguishes national minorities from the majority of the

[72] *Manoussakis* v. *Greece* (18748/91) (1996), ECHR 41, paras. 37–44.

[73] *Kokkinakis* v. *Greece* (14307/88) (1993), ECHR 20, para. 31.

[74] Above, n. 73, para. 33.

[75] Above, n. 72, para. 44; see also above, n. 55, para. 8, p. 145.

population, and as such their moral precepts can be quite different from those of the majority. In this context, the Human Rights Committee in General Comment No. 22, with respect to Article 18(3) of the ICCPR, permitting restrictions on freedom to manifest religion or belief, observed that 'the concept of morals derives from many social, philosophical and religious traditions; consequently limitations on the freedom to manifest a religion or belief for the purpose of protecting morals must be based on principles not deriving exclusively from a single tradition'.[76] In short, parties to the FCNM trying to impose limitations on the grounds of public morals must apply a very high standard of scrutiny, and they must ensure that any restrictions do not discriminate against persons belonging to national minorities.

Public health presents a different situation. Religious convictions and practices can on occasion conflict with mandatory state health care measures. For instance, some religious traditions forbid blood transfusions or vaccinations. The interpretation of rights in this area is relatively clear when it comes to the protection of the rights of others. For instance, it would be hard to justify refusing vaccinations against an epidemic, since such an action might endanger the health of the rest of the population. Similarly, it would be difficult for parents to defend refusing consent for blood transfusions for their children. However, if the state wants to protect an individual's health against his own religious convictions, such an action might be problematic with regard to his right to freedom of conscience, religion, and belief. In this respect it is interesting to note the case of *Singh Bhinder* v. *Canada*, where the issue of wearing protective headgear in certain workplaces came into conflict with the professed Sikh religious need to wear turbans. In this matter the Human Rights Committee concluded that the rule did not violate Article 18, and such a measure was necessary to protect public health.[77]

Another question regarding the rights of others and public order has recently been discussed extensively across Europe. The French parliament adopted legislation banning all outward displays of religious symbols from French public schools. It is difficult to discuss in the abstract whether such limitations constitute interference in the right to manifest one's religion or belief; however the argument that the French public school system is based on the principle of division of church and state might not in itself be sufficient justification for interfering in what is essentially a private freedom. The rights of others were invoked as

[76] UN Human Rights Committee 'General Comment No. 22' on Freedom of Religion, 48th session (1993), UN Doc. HRI/GEN/1 Rev. 1, para. 8 at 145.

[77] *Karnel Singh Bhinder* v. *Canada*, UN Human Rights Committee, Comm. No. 208/1986 (1989), UN Doc. CCPR/C/37/D/208/1986, paras. 3, 6(2).

grounds for interference in the case of *Karaduman* v. *Turkey*, considered before the Strasbourg organs. In this instance, the European Commission of Human Rights held that a student who chose to pursue her higher education in a secular university must submit to certain university rules, and that regulating the dress of students does not constitute interference with freedom of religion. The Commission accepted the argument of the Turkish state, that the ban on the wearing of headscarves is justified, especially in a country where the majority adheres to a particular religion. In its view, the manifestation of religious symbols, without restrictions of place or form, can constitute a pressure on students who adhere to another religion, or on those who do not practise any religion at all. Further, the Commission accepted the argument that the regulation of headdress is needed so that certain fundamentalist religious currents do not disturb the public order in higher education, and do not negatively impact on the beliefs of others. However, the Commission did not expand its examination to consider whether such a measure was necessary in a democratic society, and whether such a fundamental impairment of an individual's right was proportionate to the aim pursued.[78] The United Kingdom, by comparison, has asserted that the cultural and religious needs of children who attend non-religious schools should be recognized and validated by those schools. For instance, many schools in the United Kingdom with Muslim students arrange for halal food to be part of the school meal, and make adjustments to school uniform policy to take account of sensitivities regarding modesty of dress.[79]

Another example of a balanced approach is the Swiss practice. Swiss national legislation explicitly requires that members of all religions must be able to attend public schools, and that their freedom of belief should not suffer as a consequence. This principle resulted, for instance, in a prohibition on affixing crucifixes to the walls of public classrooms.[80] By the same token, the Swiss Federal Court dismissed a teacher's appeal against the ban on wearing Islamic headscarves. The Court stressed that the preservation of religious peace took precedence over the individual right to wear a religious symbol, and that the ban also protected the rights of pupils and parents. This judgment was later upheld in an appeal before the ECtHR.[81] On the other hand, concerning a request from a Muslim girl for official exemption from having to attend swimming lessons, the Swiss Court held that the refusal to grant such a dispensation was incompatible with the freedom of religion, as there was no public interest

[78] *Karaduman* v. *Turkey* (16278/90) (1993) EHRR, Decision and Report 74, p. 93 at 108–9.

[79] United Kingdom State Report, ACFC/SR (99) 13, 1999, para. 145.

[80] Switzerland State Report, ACFC/SR (2001) 2, 2001, para. 193.

[81] *Dahlab* v. *Switzerland* (42393/98) (2001) ECHR.

that would prevail over the private interest of the girl.[82] It is indeed a fine balancing act that states must perform when trying to secure on the one hand general public interests, such as ensuring the principles of tolerance and integration of society, and on the other hand the rights of religious communities to maintain their distinct religious identity. In this respect, Advisory Committee monitoring under Article 8 could play a positive role by providing guidance to states with regard to acceptable limitations on religious pluralism in a public system.

C. The Right to Manifest one's Religion and Belief

In contrast with similar provisions guaranteeing freedom of religion in other international standards, Article 8 does not put emphasis on any specific form of manifestation. The *travaux préparatoires*,[83] and systematic interpretation, suggest that Article 8 FCNM encompasses the specific forms of manifestation mentioned in Article 9 ECHR and other instruments. The relevant provisions state that the right involves freedom 'either alone [individually] or in community with others and in public or private' to manifest one's religion in four broad areas vital to religious experience, namely 'worship, observance, practice and teaching'. There are no obvious definitions for these forms of manifestation, but they clearly cover a broad range of acts which, given the diversity of religions and belief, would be difficult to spell out in detail. However, international supervisory bodies have provided some indication as to their meaning, as well as the scope of protection offered to manifestations of faith and beliefs. As regards worship, the concept is usually identified with prayers and preaching. General Comment No. 22 on Article 18 extends worship to include 'ritual and ceremonial acts giving direct expression to belief, as well as various practices integral to such acts, including the building of places of worship, the use of ritual formulae and objects, the display of symbols, and the observance of holidays and days of rest'.[84] There is often no clear-cut distinction between the forms of manifestation specified in these instruments. For instance, the General Comment on Article 18 ICCPR groups observance and practice into one category, while enumerating different acts constituting the observance and practice of religion or belief. It affirms that observance and practice may also include, besides ceremonial acts, such customs as the observance of dietary

[82] Switzerland State Report, ACFC/SR (2001) 2, 2001, para. 194.

[83] ECDL, Explanatory Report to the Proposal for a European Convention for the Protection of National Minorities, CDL-MIN (93) 6, 1993, Art. 10; as well as above n. 18, para. 11.

[84] Above, n. 55, para. 4.

regulations, the wearing of distinctive clothing or head coverings, participation in rituals associated with certain stages of life, and the use of a particular language customarily spoken by a group. Under the heading of practice activities, the Comment further includes activities that are integral to the conduct by religious groups of their basic affairs, such as religious teaching, the freedom to choose their religious leaders, priests, and teachers, the freedom to establish seminaries or religious schools, and the freedom to prepare and distribute religious texts or publications.[85]

The UN Declaration on the Elimination of All Forms of Intolerance provides an extensive list of freedoms pertaining to manifestation of religion and belief. Article 6 includes, *inter alia*, the freedoms:

(a) To worship or assemble in connection with a religion or belief, and to establish and maintain places for these purposes; (b) To establish and maintain appropriate charitable or humanitarian institutions; (c) To make, acquire and use to an adequate extent the necessary articles and materials related to the rites or customs of a religion or belief; (d) To write, issue and disseminate relevant publications in these areas; (e) To teach a religion or belief in places suitable for these purposes; (f) To solicit and receive voluntary financial and other contributions from individuals and institutions; (g) To train, appoint, elect or designate by succession appropriate leaders called for by the requirements and standards of any religion or belief; (h) To observe days of rest and to celebrate holidays and ceremonies in accordance with the precepts of one's religion or belief; (i) To establish and maintain communications with individuals and communities in matters of religion and belief at the national and international levels.

In the regional context, the Vienna Document adopted by the Organization for Security and Co-operation in Europe provides the most extensive enumeration of the obligations of the state to protect acts related to the manifestation of religion or belief.[86]

Considering the implementation of Article 8 FCNM by parties, emphasis should be on the comprehensive coverage of the exercise of the right to manifestation of religion and belief. Nevertheless, not every action of an individual or a group based on spiritual convictions and beliefs is considered to be a manifestation of religion or belief. Jurisprudence of the ECtHR has provided limitations on what is to be considered a manifestation of religion or belief, reiterating in a number of cases that 'manifestation' does not cover each act that is motivated or influenced by a religion or belief, and that actions which do not actually express a belief cannot be considered to be protected by Article 9 ECHR. For instance, an expression of religion or belief must be 'closely' linked

[85] Above, n. 84. [86] Above, n. 10, para. 16.

to a person's or a group's religion or belief,[87] and the expression should be in a generally recognizable form. One specific case concerning a member of an ethnic minority is of interest in this context. In *Tsarknias* v. *Greece* the applicant, a priest of the Greek Orthodox Church, and a member of the Macedonian ethnic minority in Greece who demanded that his church support the advocacy of greater cultural rights for Macedonian Greeks, disrupted a congregation and mass held by the bishop of the church, inciting violent disorder. The applicant claimed that judgments against him for disrupting the service had undermined his position as a priest and infringed his right to manifest *his* religion in worship and practice. The Court found the application ill-founded with respect to Article 9, as the applicant had been prosecuted and convicted for 'having disrupted a religious congregation and a mass conducted by the bishop of the region on whom depended *his* church'.[88] The Court's practice shows that whether or not a person or a group is considered to be manifesting spiritual convictions is connected with the perceived external expression, which in turn is then assessed on the basis of *objective criteria*. From the perspective of national minorities, this approach can, in theory, create some problems as regards recognition of lesser known forms of expression of belief by small groups.[89] However, Article 4(2) FCNM obliges states to adopt measures to promote full and effective equality between persons belonging to national minorities and those belonging to the majority, and therefore to take due account of the specific conditions of persons belonging to national minorities. This principle requires that states give special consideration to the particular characteristics of national minorities, including as regards expression of their religion or belief.

Perhaps more importantly from the perspective of national minorities, which often apply their own system of rules or customs based on their beliefs and tradition, Article 9 does not confer the right to refuse to abide by legislation on the basis of one's convictions, when the operation of that legislation is provided for by the Convention, and when it applies neutrally and generally in the public sphere, without impinging on the freedoms guaranteed by Article 9.[90]

87 In *Arrowsmith* v. *United Kingdom*, the Commission established that the leaflets encouraging soldiers not to serve in Northern Ireland distributed by Ms Arrowsmith did not express pacifist views and therefore they did not in fact manifest her belief in the sense of Art. 9; See *Arrowsmith* v. *United Kingdom* (7050/75) (1978) ECHR, especially para. 19.

88 *Tsarknias* v. *Greece* (45629/99) (1999) EHRR, Decision on Admissibility ref. 4556.

89 P. van Dijk, and G. J. H. van Hoof, *Theory and Practice of the European Convention on Human Rights*, 3rd edition (Kluwer Law International, The Hague, 1998), 550.

90 The jurisprudence refers for instance to cases of conscience objections for participating in tax systems which subsidize the military or for participation in their pension schemes. See *C.* v. *United Kingdom* (10358/83) (1984) EHRR, p. 142 at 147; *Vereniging Rechtswinkels Utrecht* v. *The Netherlands* (1986) EHRR 293, p. 200 at 202.

The extent to which such rules, although neutral, might constitute direct or indirect discrimination against minority groups trying to profess their religion is discussed later in this chapter.

One specific aspect of the right to manifest one's religion or belief which is of particular relevance to national minorities is the right of parents to have their children educated in accordance with their beliefs. This right, expressed in a number of international instruments,[91] does not in itself impose a positive obligation to provide or to fund religious education in accordance with parents' wishes. Indeed, many states follow the principle of separation of church and state, and do not include religious instruction in the public school curriculum. However, education is often connected with the transmission of ideas that touch upon religious or other philosophical convictions. In fact, a number of states include the teaching of ethics and the history of religion in their curricula. In these cases such instruction must not be indoctrinating, but objective and pluralistic.[92] It is worth noting that in Article 12(1), the parties to the FCNM have undertaken a specific obligation in the field of education to foster knowledge of the culture, history, language, and religion of their national minorities and of the majority. Such measures should also be assessed in light of the state's general obligation under Article 6(1) to foster tolerance, mutual respect, and understanding, *inter alia*, in the field of education.[93] The Advisory Committee has welcomed the effort of the Norwegian government to adapt the syllabus in public schools to reflect the religious pluralism of the country. Significantly, the Advisory Committee also called for ongoing review of such syllabuses.[94] In this respect, some states have established permanent commissions for harmonization of religious instruction, with the participation of representatives from different religious communities.[95] Ensuring that the views of religious minority communities are reflected in school curricula is extremely important, a point also supported by the Lund Recommendations on the Effective Participation of National Minorities in Public Life (the Lund

[91] European Convention for the Protection of Human Rights and Fundamental Freedoms (ECHR), ETS No. 9, 1952, Protocol No. 1, Art. 2; Art. 18(4) ICCPR; Convention on the Rights of the Child (entered into force 2 September 1990), GA Res. 44/25 annex, 44 (1989), UN Doc. A/44/49, Art. 14(2); Declaration on the Elimination of All Forms of Intolerance and of Discrimination Based on Religion or Belief, UNGA Res. 36/55, 36 UN GAOR, Supp. (No. 51) at 171 (1981), UN Doc. A/36/684, Art. 5(1),(2),(6); above, n. 10, para. 16(7).

[92] See *Kjeldsen, Busk Madsen & Pedersen* v. *Denmark* (5095/71, 5920/72, 5926/72) (1976) ECHR 6, para. 53; The UN Committee on Economic, Social, and Cultural Rights General Comment No. 13, 21st session (1999), UN Doc. HRI/GEN/Rev. 5, 2001, para. 28, at p. 80.

[93] For more detailed discussion see chapters on Art. 6 and Art. 12 in this commentary.

[94] Advisory Committee Opinion on Norway, ACFC/INF/OP/I (2003) 003, 2002, paras. 40 and 85.

[95] Serbia and Montenegro State Report, ACFC/SR (2002) 003, 2002, para. 64.

Recommendations).[96] Recommendations 12 and 13 encouraged states to establish advisory or consultative bodies within appropriate institutional frameworks, to serve as channels for dialogue in addressing issues such as education.

Furthermore, in those systems where public schools provide religious instruction, especially if such instruction is rooted in the religious beliefs of a dominant state religion, or the religion of the majority, parents have the right to withdraw their children from such classes. In reviewing Croatia's report, the Advisory Committee expressly welcomed the fact that attendance in religious classes is optional.[97] This practice has been confirmed in a large number of other state reports.[98] In this respect the UN Committee on Economic, Social, and Cultural Rights, in General Comment No. 24 on Article 13(3) of the International Covenant on Economic, Social, and Cultural Rights (ICESCR), noted that 'public education that includes instruction in a particular religion or belief is inconsistent with Article 13(3) unless provision is made for non-discriminatory exemptions or alternatives that would accommodate the wishes of parents and guardians'.[99] Furthermore, if state funds were allocated to particular religious schools, unless there was reasonable and objective justification for the difference in treatment, such support would clearly amount to discrimination. Respect for the liberty of parents to educate their children according to their beliefs includes the right to choose schools other than those established by public authorities, in line with their religious and moral convictions. This would require parties to the FCNM to recognize privately funded minority schools, provided they meet the general educational standards of the state, something which is also specifically required by Article 13 FCNM.[100] Such practice is widely applied in a large number of states.[101]

A number of states also provide positive support for religious education, in schools or for classes carried out by churches, through their support for the education of priests of different religious denominations.[102] In this respect, it is important from the perspective of Article 8 that the situation of persons belonging to national minorities is also taken into account. In their reports,

[96] OSCE, Lund Recommendations on the Effective Participation of National Minorities in Public Life, The Hague, 1999, Recommendation No. 8.

[97] Croatia State Report, ACFC/INF/OP/I (2002) 003, 2002, para. 39.

[98] Bulgaria State Report, ACFC/SR (2003) 001, 2003, para. 72.

[99] The UN Committee on Economic, Social, and Cultural Rights General Comment No. 13, 21st session (1999), UN Doc. HRI/GEN/Rev. 5, 2001, para. 53.

[100] For more detailed discussion of this subject see the chapter on Art. 13 in this commentary.

[101] Albania State Report, ACFC/SR (2001) 5, 2001, para. 39; Romania State Report, ACFC/SR (99) 11, 1999, para. 31.

[102] Azerbaijan State Report, ACFC/SR (2002) 1, 2002, para. 35.

some states have pointed to the lack of educators or priests who can provide such education in a minority language.[103] In this context, it is of note that paragraph 32(3) of the Copenhagen Document, which served as an inspiration for establishing the scope of the protection guaranteed in Article 8, explicitly guarantees the right of persons belonging to national minorities to conduct religious education activities in their mother tongue.[104] However, as already noted there is no general obligation on the part of the state to provide particular religious education in accordance with parents' wishes. The right refers rather to the 'freedom' of persons belonging to national minorities to conduct such education through private schools or through teaching offered by churches.[105] In this context, Bulgaria expressly stated that in the public curriculum teaching of the subject 'Religion-Islam' is carried out in Bulgarian, which is the official language of instruction in public schools.[106] However, given the principle of Article 5(1), it would be desirable if states that provide special religious education to national minority pupils could arrange for such education to be carried out in a minority language.

Another important element connected with the manifestation of religion is the freedom to use a minority language during religious ceremonies and in religious writings. As the primary responsibility of the state is not to interfere in the religious life of national minorities, public authorities may not impose undue restrictions on the use of any language in public worship, whether it is the mother tongue of persons belonging to a national minority or the liturgical language of a religious community.[107] In their state reports, a number of states have noted that they do not interfere with the use of language by religious congregations.[108] On the other hand, religious institutions may carry out certain public functions connected with civil status, such as weddings or funerals, where they may also legitimately be required to use the official language in administrative proceedings.[109] Some states go further in facilitating the freedom

[103] Hungary State Report, ACFC/SR (99) 10, 1999, para. 83.

[104] See also the commitment of the Vienna Document, which requires that the participating states 'respect the right of everyone to give and receive religious education in the language of his choice, whether individually or in association with others'. Above, n. 10, para. 16(6).

[105] Romania State Report, ACFC/SR (99) 11, 1999, para. 31.

[106] Bulgaria State Report, ACFC/SR (2003) 001, 2003, para. 73.

[107] OSCE, Oslo Recommendations Regarding the Linguistic Rights of National Minorities, The Hague, 1998, Recommendation 4: 'in professing and practicing his or her own religion individually or in community with others, every person shall be entitled to use the language(s) of his or her choice'.

[108] Romania State Report, ACFC/SR (99) 11, 1999, para. 30.

[109] The Oslo Recommendations suggest that it would be legitimate to require use of the official language in addition to minority languages in certificates and documents, as well as registers of religious communities, which pertain to civil status. See above, n. 107, Recommendation 5.

to use a minority language in religious ceremonies by providing subsidies to religious communities which carry out services in a minority language.[110]

Observation of religious holidays in accordance with the precepts of one's religion or belief is another issue where positive measures might be required on the part of the state with respect to national minorities. It is quite common for a state's holidays to correspond to the religious holidays observed by the dominant faith in the country. In light of Article 4(2) FCNM, it would be desirable for parties to allow national minorities, where possible, to choose alternative days in accordance with their religious beliefs, a practice already pursued by some states.[111]

Finally, the financing of religious institutions plays an important role in the enjoyment of the right to manifest one's religion by minority religious communities. Paragraph 32(3) of the Copenhagen Document stipulates a right for persons belonging to national minorities to seek voluntary financial, and other contributions, as well as public assistance. In this respect, the states parties should refrain from applying undue restrictions which might prevent religious communities from professing or practising their religion. On this point, it is of interest that the practice of Armenia, which prohibits financing of religious organizations from centres abroad, has not given rise to any specific observations by the Advisory Committee.[112] Regarding the right to seek public assistance, Article 8 does not impose a positive obligation to grant financial subsidies to the religious institutions of national minorities. However, a large number of states parties have reported that they provide financial subsidies to religious institutions in order to ensure the spiritual, cultural, and social heritage of religious communities.[113] In this regard, the Advisory Committee held that Article 8 does not entail an obligation to fund religious activities *per se*. However, if the state provides subsidies only to specific churches, it is necessary to review such policies in the light of the principles set out in Article 4 FCNM.[114]

D. The Right to Establish Religious Institutions, Organizations, and Associations

Many aspects of religious life have an associational dimension and as such are also covered by the right to freedom of association, as expressly mentioned by

[110] Lithuania State Report, ACFC/SR (2001) 7, 2001, para. 45.

[111] Serbia and Montenegro State Report, ACFC/SR (2002) 003, 2002, para. 62(1.3); Moldova State Report, ACFC/SR (2000) 2, 2000, para. 17; Poland State Report, ACFC/SR (2002) 2, 2002, para. 26.

[112] Armenia State Report, ACFC/SR (2001) 004, 2001, para. 70.

[113] Bulgaria State Report, ACFC/SR (2003) 001, 2003, para. 72; Hungary State Report, ACFC/SR (99) 10, 1999, paras. 82; United Kingdom State Report, ACFC/SR (99) 13, 1999, paras. 143, 144.

[114] Denmark State Report, ACFC/INF/OP/I (2001) 005, 1999, para. 29.

the European Court of Human Rights.[115] Indeed the intent of the drafters of Article 8 FCNM was to provide specific protection to this associational dimension, since there is an intimate connection between religiously motivated association and religious beliefs and practices, which are often the essence of a minority's group identity. To this end, Article 8 expressly binds the parties to recognize the right to establish religious institutions, organizations, and associations. Indeed, as stressed in the Advisory Opinion of the Permanent Court of International Justice on Minority Schools in Albania, it is paramount for a minority to have its own institutions in order to preserve its identity. The Court acknowledged that 'there would be no true equality between a majority and a minority if the latter were deprived of its own institutions, and were consequently compelled to renounce that which constitutes the very essence of its being a minority'.[116] As discussed above, the emphasis is on freedom in this right, as it is primarily of a defensive nature, meaning that it enables national minority groups to ward off impermissible interference from the state or private parties. Persons belonging to national minorities, and their organizational structures, are therefore able to worship together, to assemble in connection with their religion or belief, or to organize themselves for religious purposes without being subject to formal recognition by the state.[117] History is full of examples of the persecution of religious minorities, and of banning outright specific religious organizations and their practices.[118] More subtle forms of

[115] For example, in *Hasan and Chaush* v. *Bulgaria* (30985/96) (2000) ECHR 509, para. 62 the Court stressed that: 'Where the organization of the religious community is at issue, Article 9 of the Convention must be interpreted in the light of Article 11, which safeguards associative life against unjustified State interference. Seen in this perspective, the believers' right to freedom of religion encompasses the expectation that the community will be allowed to function peacefully, free from arbitrary State intervention. Indeed, the autonomous existence of religious communities is indispensable for pluralism in a democratic society and is thus an issue at the very heart of the protection which Article 9 affords. It directly concerns not only the organisation of the community as such but also the effective enjoyment of the right to freedom of religion by all its active members. Were the organisational life of the community not protected by Article 9 of the Convention, all other aspects of the individual's freedom of religion would become vulnerable.' See also *Metropolitan Church of Bessarabia and Others* v. *Moldova* (45701/99) (2001) ECHR 851, para. 118.

[116] *Case Concerning the Minority Schools in Albania* (1935), PCIJ Rep. Series A/B, No. 64, p. 17.

[117] Switzerland State Report, ACFC/SR (2001) 2, 2001, para. 192 expressly referred to the ruling of its Federal Court, which held that 'recognition of a religious community as an official church cannot be a criterion for holding that a collective religious service is permissible. Insofar as the decision to refuse to allow Islamic prisoners to hold their prayers on Friday is based on the fact that the Islamic community does not enjoy any status under public law, it is contrary to Article 15 of the Federal Constitution [which guarantees the right to manifest one's religion]'.

[118] Specific references to the past practice of suppressing the freedom of religion and to legislation which interfered with religious affairs are made in a number of State Reports to the FCNM. See Bulgaria State Report, ACFC/SR (2003) 001, 2003, para. 69; Albania State Report, ACFC/SR (2001) 5, 2001, para. 37; Lithuania State Report, ACFC/SR (2001) 7, 2001, para. 44.

persecution include laws which constrain individual religious practice by denying legal recognition to certain religious organizations. Although, on one hand, religious institutions, organizations, or associations do not require formal state recognition in order to function, on the other hand, as a practical matter, the enjoyment of primary religious rights is often dependent on the religious community having access to suitable legal structures through which to organize their affairs.[119] For instance, it might prove difficult for a religious community without legal status to acquire property, to rent or build a place of worship, to enter into contracts, to bring legal proceedings to protect its assets, or to establish seminaries, schools, or charitable and humanitarian institutions.[120]

As mentioned earlier, the rights in Article 8 FCNM can be effectively implemented by the state only through a combination of forbearance and duties of performance. On one hand the parties to the FCNM must respect the autonomous character of internal religious affairs, and should not without justified reasons interfere in how national minorities organize themselves in pursuing their religious affairs.[121] On the other hand, the wording of Article 8 provides for the right of persons belonging to national minorities to establish religious institutions, organizations, and associations. The parties therefore have a corresponding responsibility to ensure that minority communities will be able to exercise their religious freedom rights through their legal entities. In other words, they have a positive obligation to make legal personality status available to national minorities who wish to practise their faith. Positive measures on the part of states parties are also called for in Article 5 FCNM, which requires states to promote the conditions necessary for persons belonging to national minorities to 'preserve the essential elements of their identity, namely their religion'. A number of states referred to legislation allowing national minorities to obtain legal status in their reports. This is done through laws on association or civil codes, often including basic forms of legal personality that are sufficient to carry out their affairs, but typically lacking in significant additional benefits.[122] A considerable number of states referred to specific laws on religious organizations which provide legal status for religious denominations through registration.[123] Such institutions are

[119] C. Durham, 'Freedom of Religion or Belief: Laws Affecting the Structuring of Religious Communities', OSCE, review conference, ODIHR 1999/4 background paper, 1999, p. 5.

[120] Estonia State Report, ACFC/SR (99) 16, 1999, para. 33.

[121] *Hasan and Chaush* v. *Bulgaria* (30985/96) (2000) ECHR 509, para. 64.

[122] Croatia State Report, ACFC/SR (99) 5, 1999, para. 92.

[123] Armenia State Report, ACFC/SR (2001) 004, 2001, para. 71; Austria State Report, ACFC/SR (2000) 3, 2000, para. 45; Estonia State Report, ACFC/SR (99) 16, 1999, para. 35; Lithuania State Report, ACFC/SR (2001) 7, 2001, para. 44; Russian Federation State Report, ACFC/SR (99) 15, 2002, para. 26; Serbia and Montenegro State Report, ACFC/SR (2002) 003, 2002, para. 64.

often eligible for direct and indirect financial benefits from the state, as well as various other privileges.[124]

The guarantees in other instruments also speak in favour of such a positive duty. The freedom of association standards mentioned above are of significant importance, as the right to form an association is an inherent part of the right to freedom of association. Accordingly, the jurisprudence of the ECtHR confirms that individuals should be able to form a legal entity in order to act collectively in a field of mutual interest.[125] In more general terms, Article 4(2) of the UN Declaration on Minorities requires states to take measures to create favourable conditions to enable persons belonging to minorities to develop their religion. The Vienna Concluding Document is more specific. Paragraph 16(3) expressly commits the participating states '[to] grant upon their request to communities of believers, practicing or prepared to practice their faith within the constitutional framework of their States, recognition of the status provided for them in their respective countries'. Article 27 ICCPR should also be mentioned in this context as it requires that persons belonging to ethnic, religious, or linguistic minorities not be denied the right, in community with other members of their group, to profess and practise their own religion. In fact, if a state denied legal status to religious organizations, it would be in violation of Article 9 ECHR, even in the absence of specific minority protection or non-discrimination provisions. In *Church of Bessarabia and Others* v. *Moldova*, the state's legislation stipulated that only religions recognized by a government decision could practise their religion in Moldova, and only such denominations had legal personality. The Court in this respect noted 'that in the absence of recognition the applicant Church may neither organise itself nor operate. Lacking legal personality, it cannot bring legal proceedings to protect its assets, which are indispensable for worship, while its members cannot meet to carry on religious activities without contravening the legislation on religious denominations'.[126] In conclusion, the Court held that the refusal to recognize the applicants' church had consequences for the applicants' freedom of religion, such that it could not be considered compatible with Article 9 ECHR.[127]

Clearly, the obligation to make legal personality status available to religious associations of national minorities must be distinguished from the compulsory registration of churches and religious associations or organizations, where this

[124] Bulgaria State Report, ACFC/SR (2003) 001, 2003, para. 72; Serbia and Montenegro State Report, ACFC/SR (2002) 003, 2002 para. 62; Sweden State Report, ACFC/SR (2001) 003, 2001, para. 24.

[125] See the landmark case *Sidiropoulos & Others* v. *Greece* (26695/95) (1998) ECHR 55, para. 40.

[126] Above, n. 33, para. 129.

[127] ibid., para. 130.

is required by a state for such minorities' institutions to be able to practise their religion and conduct their affairs. Such authorization requirements for the religious activities of national minorities would be incompatible with Article 8 FCNM. A growing number of cases from the ECtHR have dealt with the registration of religious denominations and these help to clarify the obligations of parties to the FCNM in implementing Article 8. In particular, the question of registration was extensively reviewed in *Manoussakis* v. *Greece*.[128] In this case, Jehovah's Witnesses were prosecuted and convicted by the local courts for having operated a place of worship without having obtained a house of prayer permit first. In fact, the religious community had been trying for years to obtain such a permit, but the government continued to maintain that they were not in a position to grant them the authorization. The Court, in conclusion, observed that the government tended to use the authorization requirements to impose rigid, or indeed prohibitive, conditions on the practice of religious beliefs by certain non-Orthodox movements.

The European Court of Human Rights has not directly addressed the question of whether legislation requiring the prior authorization of religious associations is incompatible with Article 9 *per se*.[129] However, it held that the right of religious association excludes 'any discretion on the part of the State to determine whether religious beliefs or the means used to express such beliefs are legitimate',[130] and that the authorization is compatible only insofar as it is intended to allow the authorities to verify whether the formal conditions required by law have been satisfied. In other words, a formal review of statutes or charters and so forth may be permissible, but only if there is no substantive assessment of the beliefs and practices involved.

In the recent case of *Canea Catholic Church* v. *Greece*, the question of acquiring and maintaining legal personality was disputed. Although the case involved particular facts, it still provides some guidance on the issue of compulsory registration as a condition for acquiring legal personality. The church in question had functioned in the country for many years without any formal registration and had used and freely transferred, moveable and immoveable property, concluded contracts, and taken part in notarial transactions. It also enjoyed tax exemptions provided to

[128] *Manoussakis* v. *Greece* (18748/91) (1996) ECHR 41.

[129] Above, n. 128, para. 6. In a concurring opinion in *Manoussakis* v. *Greece*, Judge Martens expressed a view that prior authorization for the construction of a place of worship may raise serious public order questions and, therefore, such prior authorization could not be dismissed out of hand as incompatible with Art. 9. However, the requirement of prior authorization may in no way enable the authorities to evaluate the tenets of the applicant community, and as a matter of principle the requested authorization should always be given unless very exceptional, objective, and insuperable grounds of public order make that impossible. See para. 6.

[130] Above n. 128, para. 47.

charitable institutions. In other words, its legal personality was clearly recognized and had never been disputed by the authorities. When the church was trying to bring its neighbours to court for destroying a church wall, it was claimed that the church did not possess legal personality because it was not formally registered, and therefore did not possess the right to institute legal proceedings. In light of Article 6(1) ECHR, the Court did not accept the government's argument that the applicant church should have carried out the formalities necessary to acquire one or other form of legal personality provided for in the Civil Code, as there was nothing to suggest that it would one day be deprived of access to a court in order to defend its civil rights.[131] It is therefore possible to assert that an institution can enjoy legal personality even without complying with any formalities required for the registration of religious institutions.

Turning to statutory schemes that govern the formal granting of legal personality, it is important that the formalities, however neutral, should not penalize minorities nor impair the functioning of their religious communities. This principle also extends to state conduct in applying such legislation, and, as was mentioned, under no circumstances may the state misuse such legislation to repress the religious life of national minorities. This is of particular importance for persons belonging to national minorities in countries that have a state church, but also concerns those in states that support the separation of church and state, but apply complex church financing schemes that tend to benefit dominant religions more than smaller or newer minority groups. Indeed, it is crucial that the parties to the FCNM ensure that any formal conditions imposed for obtaining legal status do not result in the impairment of the functioning of a religious community, and that any such conditions are prescribed by law and are necessary in a democratic society in the interests of public safety; for the protection of public order, health, or morals, or for the protection of the rights and freedoms of others, in accordance with Article 9(2) ECHR. Lastly, such conditions, as well as state practice, must not be discriminatory.

When it comes to granting legal status, equality of treatment was taken up by the ECtHR in the *Canea* case. Under Greek law, both the Greek Orthodox Church and the Jewish community in Greece appeared to have automatic and functional access to entity status, and did not have to apply formally for such status, as the Catholic Church was required to do. The Court noted that the Greek court's denial of legal personality violated Article 14 when taken together with Article 6(1).[132] In another instance where legal personality was at issue,

[131] *Canea Catholic Church* v. *Greece* (25528/94) (2001) ECHR 100, paras. 39–47.
[132] Above, n. 131, para. 47.

the Estonian Apostolic Orthodox Church (EAOC, under canonical jurisdiction of the Constantinople Patriarchy) and the Estonian Orthodox Church of Moscow Patriarchy (EOCMP) were in dispute over naming and property rights. As a result the Ministry of Interior had refused to register the EOCMP. In this case, and with regard to Article 8 FCNM, the Advisory Committee called upon Estonia to increase its efforts to resolve the dispute.[133]

From the perspective of national minorities, imposing conditions such as a minimum number of adherents of the religion or a minimum number of church-goers in order to register the religion or place of worship, might disadvantage some national minority groups.[134] In this context, the ECtHR held that the discretion of the state 'to assess whether there is a "real need" for the religious community in question to set up a church' was substantively objectionable in the *Manoussakis* case.[135] In the same case the Court also noted that requiring permit approval to be conditional on favourable review by clergy of another church would be clearly impermissible.[136] Evidently, in the case of any difference in approach to the treatment of different groups in the implementation of Article 8, the parties to the FCNM would have to show that there are reasonable and objective criteria for such differential treatment.

Another important element of the right to maintain religious institutions is the right to the peaceful enjoyment of possession.[137] Some states have confirmed in their state reports that religious denominations have the right to manage their own affairs and to own, acquire, and administer moveable and immoveable property.[138] In this regard, the appropriation of church property, without public interest justifications and compensation, would constitute a violation of the right to enjoyment of possession.[139] A number of states have informed the Advisory Committee that they are in the process of restituting property to churches whose land or buildings were confiscated during Communist rule.[140] In this respect, the Advisory Committee has stressed that

[133] Advisory Committee Opinion on Estonia, ACFC/INF/OP/I (2001) 005, 2001, para. 34.

[134] Czech Republic State Report, ACFC/SR (99) 6, 1999, para. 27; for more information on the state practice see above, n. 119, pp. 47–9.

[135] Above, n. 128, para. 45.

[136] ibid.

[137] European Convention for the Protection of Human Rights and Fundamental Freedoms (ECHR), ETS No. 9, 1952, Protocol No. 1, Art. 1 guarantees that 'Every natural or legal person is entitled to peaceful enjoyment of its possessions. No one shall be deprived of his possessions except in the public interest and subject to the conditions provided for by law and by the general principles of international law.'

[138] Serbia and Montenegro State Report, ACFC/SR (2002) 003, 2002 para. 62; Ireland State Report, ACFC/SR (2001) 6, 2001, para. 66.

[139] ibid.

[140] Bulgaria State Report, ACFC/SR (2003) 001, 2003, para. 71; Hungary State Report, ACFC/SR (99) 10, 1999, para. 82; Poland State Report, ACFC/SR (2002) 2, 2002, para. 26.

states should continue the process of restitution of church property, and that this process should be carried out without discrimination against persons belonging to national minorities.[141] Further, in cases where the state has granted public land to certain churches, it must take into account the principles of equality and prohibition of discrimination set out in Article 4 FCNM. In this regard, and in response to a complaint by the Tartar community of Moldova that despite repeated requests they had not received any support from state authorities in finding a suitable location for a Muslim cemetery, the Advisory Committee called upon the Moldovan authorities to consult with those concerned and identify an appropriate solution.[142]

Finally, members of national minority communities are often members of a church that has its headquarters in the country of their historic origin. In this respect, the right to establish religious associations would also entail the right to establish and maintain free contact across frontiers. In fact, in Article 17(1), the FCNM provides a specific obligation for parties not to interfere with contacts across frontiers, especially those with whom minorities share an ethnic, cultural, linguistic, or religious identity. This transborder dimension is also applicable to religious associations of national minorities holding membership and participating in activities of religious organizations and associations at the international level. Article 17(2) specifically requires states to respect this freedom. In this regard, many state reports confirm that religious communities whose mother churches are abroad are free to maintain their contact with those institutions.[143] This is of particular significance when the clergy of a religious minority can only receive the education they require in another country, for example the country in which the mother church is based. It is also relevant when, as is often the case, priests of the mother church from other countries are able to provide services in the native minority language and are invited to serve in the congregations of national minorities.[144]

III. Conclusion and Outlook

The inclusion of the specific right to manifestation of religion or belief among the substantive provisions of the Framework Convention highlights the essential role that the profession of religion plays in preserving a minority group's

141 Advisory Committee Opinion on Albania, ACFC/INF/OP/I (2003) 004, 2002, paras. 43, 96.
142 Advisory Committee Opinion on Moldova, ACFC/INF/OP/I (2003) 002, 2003, paras. 50, 108.
143 Serbia and Montenegro State Report, ACFC/SR (2002) 003, 2002 para. 64.
144 Hungary State Report, ACFC/SR (99) 10, 1999, para. 82.

identity and existence. Indeed, recognition of the importance of the associational dimension of this right also found expression in the right of persons belonging to national minorities to establish their own religious institutions, organizations, and associations. In this respect Article 8 provides an explicit standard which, although recognized in the jurisprudence of European Court of Human Rights, is not expressly articulated in Article 9 ECHR, or other legally binding human rights standards.

The true value of Article 8, however, lies in its promotion of full and effective equality for persons belonging to national minorities in the enjoyment of their religious freedoms. Although most European states follow the principle of separation of church and state in their constitutional design, very often the state is involved in religious affairs, either through its duty to facilitate free and peaceful exercise of the right to manifest one's religion, or through its tacit support for traditional religion which is often the religion of the majority. In this context, monitoring of the implementation of Article 8 has highlighted the obligation of states to pay particular attention to the situation of national minorities in their activities involving religious communities living on their territories, and to ensure that persons belonging to national minorities are not subject to discrimination in their enjoyment of this right. The Advisory Committee has called for adjustments to legislation and to the administrative practices of states to ensure that national minorities are treated on an equal footing in instances where the state provides support for religious communities, or accommodates religious beliefs or practices in the public system.

A review of FCNM state reports reveals extensive state practice in securing the free and peaceful exercise of the manifestation of religion. Although Article 8 does not elaborate the right to the manifestation of religion or belief in detail, this has not prevented states from providing comprehensive protection for the enjoyment of this right. The general terms of the provision are gradually being filled with concrete meaning through the monitoring process. In this context, guarantees for protection of the manifestation of religion or belief to all are well established in the domestic legal order of states parties, and have been the subject of judicial review by international human rights supervisory bodies for a long time. Indeed, as the drafters of the Convention pointed out, there is a close connection between Article 9 ECHR and the content of Article 8 FCNM. This fact has been clearly demonstrated, and explicitly acknowledged by the states parties in reporting on the implementation of Article 8. The scope of the measures secured by states parties under this article ranges from horizontal protection directed at peaceful enjoyment of the manifestation of religion or belief, to the facilitation of the right to establish religious institutions and associations in state legislative and administrative practice, to more positive measures that assist religious communities in preserving their religious traditions. Although the states parties provide wide-ranging positive measures, state support is typically mentioned in the context of the general assistance that these states provide to all religious denominations. It is to be hoped that the ongoing monitoring of Article 8 will encourage states parties to focus their attention on the specific needs of national minorities regarding the preservation and maintenance of their religious practice and tradition, and that positive measures by states will address those specific areas which are of particular importance for the maintenance of the distinct identity of national minorities.

ARTICLE 9

John Packer and Sally Holt

1. The Parties undertake to recognise that the right to freedom of expression of every person belonging to a national minority includes freedom to hold opinions and to receive and impart information and ideas in the minority language, without interference by public authorities and regardless of frontiers. The Parties shall ensure, within the framework of their legal systems, that persons belonging to a national minority are not discriminated against in their access to the media.
2. Paragraph 1 shall not prevent Parties from requiring the licensing, without discrimination and based on objective criteria, of sound radio and television broadcasting, or cinema enterprises.
3. The Parties shall not hinder the creation and the use of printed media by persons belonging to national minorities. In the legal framework of sound radio and television broadcasting, they shall ensure, as far as possible, and taking into account the provisions of paragraph 1, that persons belonging to national minorities are granted the possibility of creating and using their own media.
4. In the framework of their legal systems, the Parties shall adopt adequate measures in order to facilitate access to the media for persons belonging to national minorities and in order to promote tolerance and permit cultural pluralism.

I. Background

A. Issues

Consistent with the FCNM instrument as a whole, Article 9 seeks to address a number of problems of disadvantage and unequal opportunity. The underlying challenge is to ensure the necessary space and facilities for the breadth of ideas, opinions, and cultures existing throughout society, including of persons belonging to minorities, to be expressed and enjoyed freely. In this respect, the media has special importance as both a vehicle of communication and a carrier of culture. Depending upon the situation, minorities may face obstacles to equal access to the media especially in their own language. This is particularly so where minorities are small in numbers or live geographically dispersed and struggle to maintain their identities. In some situations, minorities also contend with state policies which promote one language (usually the majority's) over others, including through restrictive quotas and similar devices. In the spirit of pluralism, the essence of Article 9 is to require states parties to remove such obstacles (especially those of their own making) and to take concrete steps to create opportunities for equal access to the media.

An important element of Article 9 is its final stipulation that the measures states parties are obliged to adopt should 'promote tolerance and permit cultural pluralism'. This provision recognizes that there often exist majoritarian attitudes and contexts which are effectively inhospitable to minorities and constrain their cultures. In a democratic society, the media can contribute to pluralism by positively reflecting existing diversity and promoting social attitudes of respect. This is not only important for persons belonging to minorities, but is a matter of the wider public interest and good.

B. History

While media regulation is informed by international instruments and jurisprudence guaranteeing the freedom of expression generally and free communication between persons, including the exchange of information and ideas between persons belonging to national minorities (in particular in their own languages), the elaboration of Article 9 of the Framework Convention represents the first attempt to address directly and comprehensively the question of access to the media for persons belonging to national minorities.

A number of aspects of freedom of information were identified in the early stages of the drafting process and it was clear that persons belonging to national minorities should have the opportunity both to access the mainstream media as well as to create, use, and enjoy their own media, without discrimination.

What was less clear was the extent to which the state is obliged to provide support for the latter, with the consequence that this is not directly addressed in the final provision. In this regard, early references to the adoption of special measures, including the provision of adequate public resources to promote such use by minorities, were not retained.[1] It should also be noted that the term 'access' was not defined, although the Opinions of the Advisory Committee have subsequently provided some clarification.[2]

C. Context

Article 9 is not intended as a panacea, but should be understood and applied together with other provisions of the instrument. In this regard, the location of Article 9 within the Framework Convention continues the logic of further specification, following provisions on the importance of promoting conditions for the maintenance and development of identity and culture (Article 5), tolerance and intercultural dialogue (Article 6), and freedom of expression (Article 7). Article 9 also includes some ideas which are themselves given further specification in subsequent provisions, such as the rights to effective participation in economic, social, and cultural life (Article 15) and to maintain contacts across frontiers (Article 14). Other important references within the Convention of direct relevance to Article 9 include the provisions of Article 19 (on permissible limitations) and 23 (on the European Convention on Human Rights); like the freedom of expression itself, the rights within Article 9 are not unlimited and must be carefully assessed and applied with full attention to both possibilities and effects especially insofar as interethnic relations are concerned.[3] In this, considerable guidance may also be derived from the Preamble to the Convention.

II. Analysis

A. Structure of Article 9

Article 9 contains more detailed rules for the protection of the freedom of expression than Article 7,[4] specifically as it pertains to the free expression and reception

[1] See further below under Section II. D. 1.   [2] See below under Section II. E. (*b*).

[3] Essentially, this caution has been recently voiced by a leading commentator; see Concluding Plenary, Conclusions of the Conference by the General Rapporteur, Patrick Thornberry, Professor of International Law, University of Keele, at the Conference 'Filling the Frame' to mark the 5th anniversary of the entry into force of the Framework Convention, Strasbourg, 30–1 October 2003, **www.coe.int/T/E/human_rights/minorities/5._5_anniversary/PDF_Conclusions_Thornberry** 28 August 2004.   [4] FCNM Explanatory Report, para. 55.

of information and ideas by persons belonging to national minorities through the printed and broadcast media in their language of choice. The right of persons belonging to national minorities to receive and impart information in this way depends in great part on their access to media outlets.[5] As such, Article 9 has four substantive provisions expressed in separate sub-paragraphs. Article 9(1) stipulates an undertaking to ensure that persons belonging to national minorities are not discriminated against in their access to the media. Moreover, while the need for regulation of the broadcast media and cinema enterprises through licensing is explicitly recognized in Article 9(2), any distinctions in the provision of access must be without discrimination and based on objective criteria, without prejudice against a minority group or a particular language.

Under Article 9(3), states have both a negative obligation not to hinder the creation and use of media and a positive obligation to ensure that persons belonging to national minorities are granted 'as far as possible' the possibility to create and use their own media. The more flexible wording of the latter acknowledges that technical limitations, namely the number of frequencies available for broadcasting, may affect the ability of the state to grant such possibilities to persons belonging to national minorities.[6] Recognition of states' need to regulate this area is further reflected in their legitimate requirement that the creation and use by minorities of their own media is undertaken within the framework of applicable broadcasting law.

The positive obligations on the state to facilitate access for persons belonging to national minorities to public media as well as the possibility to create and use their own private media are further articulated in Article 9(4). States parties thus undertake to adopt adequate measures in order to promote full and effective equality for persons belonging to a minority, taking into account their specific conditions, in line with the principles of equality and non-discrimination as provided in Article 4 of the Convention. The same provision recognizes the link between ensuring minority access to the media, and the goals of promoting tolerance and ensuring cultural pluralism in the media.

B. Article 9(1): The Right to Receive and Impart Information

1. *Interpretation*

The first sentence of Article 9(1) is modelled on Article 10(1) of the European Convention on Human Rights and Fundamental Freedoms (ECHR), which protects the right to freedom of expression, including the right to seek, impart,

[5] OSCE HCNM, Report on the Linguistic Rights of Persons Belonging to National Minorities (The Hague, 1999), 31.

[6] See above, n. 5, citing FCNM Explanatory Report, para. 61.

and receive information and ideas, without interference by public authorities, and regardless of frontiers.[7] The scope of protection of Article 9(1) as identified by the drafters includes the following four aspects of the freedom of information: the freedom of expression; the freedom to disseminate information in the minority language; the right of access to the public media; and the right of a minority to have its own media.[8] The second sentence of Article 9(1) contains an explicit undertaking by states parties to ensure that there is no discrimination against persons belonging to national minorities in their access to the media.[9] Express reference to access by various groups in society to the media, as well as journalistic and editorial freedom and copyright, were not included in this provision, since the CAHMIN considered it preferable to establish certain objectives through programme-type provisions without going into technical details.[10]

(a) *Forms of Communication*

Obviously, the imparting and reception of ideas through the media is only possible where the language of communication is understood. In this respect, Article 9(1) explicitly recognizes the free choice of language as a vehicle of communication to be a constituent part of the freedom of expression, protected by international law. Early proposals in the drafting history confirm that the right to freely use one's own language applies to both print and audiovisual media.[11] While Article 9(1) refers specifically to minority languages, majority and other languages are also implicitly protected.[12]

As already noted, the freedom of expression is guaranteed 'regardless of frontiers'. While Article 9 does not directly address access by minority groups to broadcasts from other states in the minority language, the free reception of

[7] In this respect, the Ad Hoc Committee for the Protection of Minorities (CAHMIN) recalled the conclusions of a previous discussion regarding the inclusion in the FCNM of elements of rights laid down in the ECHR. CAHMIN, 1st meeting, CAHMIN (94) 5, meeting report, 25–8 January 1994, paras. 29, 38.

[8] Steering Committee for Human Rights (CDDH), Final Activity Report of the CDDH for the Attention of the Committee of Ministers, CDDH (93) 22, 8 September 1993; and CAHMIN, 1st meeting, CAHMIN (94) 5, meeting report, 25–8 January 1994, paras. 36–40.

[9] See CDDH, Final Activity Report, CDDH (93) 22, 8 September 1993 referring to 'the right to access, without discrimination, to the State-owned media as well as to use their own means of communication'. See also CAHMIN, 2nd meeting, CAHMIN (94) 9, meeting report, 14–18 March 1994, at Appendix III, A., Art. 3; CAHMIN, 1st meeting, CAHMIN (94) 5, meeting report, 25–8 January 1994, para. 40; and Federal Union of European Nationalities (FUEN), Fundamental Rights of Persons Belonging to Ethic Groups in Europe, Draft for an Additional Protocol to the ECHR (revised FUEN draft) 1994, Article 10(2).

[10] CAHMIN, 1st meeting, CAHMIN (94) 5, meeting report, 25–8 January 1994, paras. 37.

[11] Draft Protocol (Austria), CDHH (91) 46, 20 December 1991; and Recommendation 1201, 1 February 1993, Art. 7.

[12] FCNM Explanatory Report, para. 56.

broadcasts across borders may be considered as an aspect of the right of persons belonging to national minorities to establish and maintain free and peaceful contacts across frontiers, as stipulated in Article 17(1) of the Convention.[13]

(b) Legitimate Limitations on the Freedom of Expression

Pursuant to Article 23 of the Convention, the meaning and scope of the right to freedom of expression protected under Article 9(1) is the same as that guaranteed by Article 10 of the ECHR.[14] In accordance with Article 19 of the Framework Convention, this right is subject only to those limitations, restrictions, or derogations provided in equivalent provisions of other international legal instruments, particularly the ECHR.[15] Limitations may not, therefore, exceed those stipulated in Article 10(2) of the ECHR, according to which any restrictions imposed by the public authorities may only be such as are in the public interest (i.e. pursue a legitimate aim), are provided by law, and are necessary in a democratic society.[16] This is true for communications originating both within the state and across frontiers. The medium of expression—including language—is not *per se* a legitimate basis to restrict the freedom of expression of persons belonging to national minorities under ECHR Article 10(2).[17] While the content of any media programming may be subject to interference on the grounds listed, minority media may not be censored or interfered with by virtue of the fact it is produced by or for persons belonging to national minorities.

2. *Practice of the Advisory Committee*

The freedom of expression as provided under Article 9(1) is generally enshrined in the constitutions and (usually) the legislation of Council of Europe member

[13] The revised FUEN draft is more explicit that '. . . the right of information shall include the freedom to receive television and radio programmes broadcast from foreign countries in which the same mother tongue is spoken'.

[14] For a discussion of the relationship between interpretation of provisions of the Framework Convention and the interpretation given to the corresponding provisions of the ECHR by the European Court of Human Rights, see the commentary on Art. 23.

[15] See further the commentary on Art. 19.

[16] Under ECHR Art. 10(2) the freedom of expression may be subject to conditions, restrictions, or penalties in the interests of: national security; territorial integrity or public safety; for the prevention of disorder or crime; for the protection of health or morals; for the protection of the reputation or rights of others; for preventing the disclosure of information received in confidence; or for the maintaining of the authority of the judiciary. NBA proposal made in the drafting process to reproduce the text of Art. 10(2) was not maintained; CDDH, Final Activity Report, CDDH (93) 22, 8 September 1993.

[17] The Ad Hoc Committee for the Protection of National Minorities confirmed in its considerations that the right to disseminate information in the minority language precludes state interference; the only legitimate restrictions in that area concern the preconditions for the issuing of licences to broadcast radio and television; CAHMIN, 1st meeting, CAHMIN (94) 5, meeting report, 25–8 January 1994, para. 39.

states. State reports confirm that such constitutional provisions apply to all forms of media,[18] without discrimination and regardless of the language of expression.[19] Any interference with the right to freedom of expression must be in accordance with the law, be in the legitimate public interest, and be necessary in a democratic society.[20] The fact that it is a national minority that is communicating or that communications are made in a minority language cannot in themselves form the basis of interference.[21] Broadcasting-specific legislation frequently further defines and develops the right to free dissemination of information in the mother tongues of national minorities,[22] and their access to the media.[23] Concerning the right to receive information, some states articulate in their constitutions or legislation a duty on the part of the authorities to provide accurate information relating to public policy and matters of concern to the general population,[24] in conjunction with a duty to ensure that 'important social and political groups' have access to the relevant services.[25]

The reception and relay of broadcasting from other countries is specifically protected in the domestic legislation of some states in compliance with the requirements of international agreements.[26] Advisory Committee opinions not only confirm the right of persons belonging to national minorities to the free reception of broadcasting across frontiers in their own language, but also establish that positive action from the state may be required in order to improve the quality of reception from abroad.[27]

3. *Link to Developments outside the FCNM*

The right to freedom of expression encompassing not only the right to impart information and ideas of all kinds, but also the freedom to seek and receive them regardless of frontiers, is a cornerstone of international human rights protection and is enshrined in universal and regional instruments.[28] According to these provisions, not only the substance of the information and ideas expressed, but

[18] See, for example, Croatia State Report, ACFC/SR (99) 5, 16 March 1999.

[19] See, for example, Italy State Report, ACFC/SR (99) 7, 3 May 1999.

[20] See, for example, Estonia State Report, ACFC/SR (1999) 16, 22 December 1999.

[21] As noted in the Denmark State Report, ACFC/SR (99) 9, 6 May 1999.

[22] See, for example, Bulgaria State Report, ACFC/SR (2003) 1, 9 April 2003.

[23] See, for example, Italy State Report, ACFC/SR (1999) 7, 3 May 1999.

[24] See, for example, Moldova State Report, ACFC/SR (2000) 2, 29 June 2000.

[25] See Romania State Report, ACFC/SR (1999) 11, 24 June 1999.

[26] See, for example, Lithuania State Report, ACFC/SR (2001) 7, 31 October 2001, concerning the relay of TV programmes broadcast from EU member states and others that have ratified the European Convention on Transfrontier Broadcasting.

[27] See further below under Section II. E (*a*).

[28] See Art. 19 of the 1948 Universal Declaration of Human Rights (UDHR), Art. 19 of the 1966 International Covenant on Civil and Political Rights (ICCPR), and Art. 10 of the 1950 European Convention for the Protection of Human Rights and Fundamental Freedoms (ECHR).

also the medium in which they are conveyed (including language), is protected.[29] Documents of the Conference for Security and Co-operation in Europe (CSCE) and (later) Organization for Security and Co-operation in Europe (OSCE) explicitly protect the rights of persons belonging to national minorities to disseminate, have access to, and exchange information in their mother tongue,[30] as an aspect of their right to freely express, preserve, and develop their cultural and linguistic identity without discrimination.[31] They also emphasize the importance of communication and the free flow of information and exchange of ideas for persons belonging to national minorities and recall that any restrictions on such rights must be prescribed by law and be consistent with international standards.[32]

The principle of non-discrimination—including on the basis of language—is a bedrock of all key human rights instruments.[33] Under Article 5(*d*)(viii) of the International Convention on the Elimination of All Forms of Racial Discrimination (CERD), states parties specifically undertake to guarantee the enjoyment of the right to freedom of expression to everyone without distinction. Concerning access to the media specifically, OSCE participating states have affirmed explicitly that they will not discriminate against anyone in access to the media on ethnic, cultural, linguistic, or religious grounds, nor will they discriminate against independent media with respect to information, material, and facilities.[34]

Communication across borders (especially where there is a kin state) can be important for persons belonging to national minorities in the maintenance and development of their identity. The right to establish and maintain unimpeded contacts among themselves within their country as well as across frontiers is protected in OSCE documents in similar terms to those stipulated in Article 17

[29] See UN Human Rights Committee, General Comment 10, Art. 19 (19th session, 1983), para. 2; and the judgments of the European Court of Human Rights in the cases of *Oberschlick* v. *Austria*, judgment of 22 May 1991, Series A, No. 204, para. 57, and *Autronic AG* v. *Switzerland*, judgment of 22 May 1990, Series A, No. 178, para. 47.

[30] See 1990 Document of the Copenhagen Meeting of the Conference on the Human Dimension of the CSCE (Copenhagen Document), para. 32.5; and the 1989 Concluding Document of the Vienna Follow-up Meeting 1986–9 of the CSCE, para. 45.

[31] As enshrined in: the Copenhagen Document, para. 32; the 1990 CSCE Charter of Paris for a New Europe; and the 1991 Report of the CSCE Meeting of Experts on National Minorities in Geneva (Geneva Document), Chapter II, para. 4.

[32] Geneva Document, Chapter VII, para. 1.

[33] See, for example, UDHR, Art. 2; ICCPR, Arts. 2(1) and 26; ICESCR, Art. 2(2); UN Declaration on Minorities, Art. 2(1); ECHR, Art. 14 and Art. 1 of Protocol 12; and the European Union Charter of Fundamental Rights, Art. 21.

[34] See, respectively, Geneva Document, Chapter VII, para. 2; and 1991 Document of the Moscow Meeting of the Conference on the Human Dimension of the CSCE (Moscow Document), para. 26.2.

of the FCNM.[35] OSCE standards also reaffirm that persons belonging to national minorities will not be subject to sanctions for having had contacts within or outside their own country simply because they belong to a minority.[36] Unrestricted access by print and broadcast media to foreign news and information services and by the general public to foreign publications and broadcasts should be enjoyed subject only to those restrictions which are provided by law and in accordance with international standards.[37] In this respect, Article 4 of the European Convention on Transfrontier Television (ECTT) guarantees the freedom of reception as well as unrestricted retransmission on states parties' territories of programme services which comply with the terms of the Convention. Specifically with regard to language, direct reception of radio and television broadcasts from neighbouring countries in a language used in identical or similar form to a regional or minority language is guaranteed by the European Charter for Regional or Minority Languages (European Language Charter).[38] The rulings of the European Court of Justice regarding the use of language in the provision of services—including the language of electronic media transmission—confirm the protection of services that come to a linguistic community from foreign stations based in third countries (regardless of whether their language is even spoken to any degree in that country).[39]

C. Article 9(2): Regulation (Including through Licensing)

1. *Interpretation*

Echoing the third sentence of Article 10(1) of the ECHR, Article 9(2) confirms the possibility for states to regulate the media through licensing. According to this provision, the freedom of expression protected by Article 9(1) shall not prevent the licensing of sound radio[40] and television broadcasting, and of cinema enterprises, provided it is carried out on a non-discriminatory basis. Although non-discrimination does not have to be interpreted as meaning

[35] Copenhagen Document, para. 32.4; and Geneva Document, Chapter VII, para. 3.

[36] Geneva Document, Chapter VII, para. 1.

[37] Moscow Document, para. 26.1.

[38] European Charter for Regional or Minority Languages, ETS 148, 5 November 1992, Art. 11(2).

[39] In the case of ECJ, case C-211/91, *Commission of the European Communities* v. *Kingdom of Belgium*, judgment of 16 December 1992, [1992] ECR 6757, Belgian government regulations prohibiting cable TV companies from broadcasting on their network programmes from radio or TV broadcasting stations in other EU member states which were not in (one of) the language(s) of the member states in which the station is established, were found to be in breach of Art. 59 of the EEC Treaty. For a discussion of this ruling in the Latvian context, see L. Raihman, 'Media Legislation, Minority Issues, and Implications for Latvia', p. 15, **www.policy.hu/raihman/PolicyPaper.htm** 27 August 2004.

[40] Although the term 'sound radio', which is also used in FCNM Art. 9(3), does not appear in the corresponding sentence of Art. 10 of the ECHR, according to para. 60 of the FCNM Explanatory Report, it is used only to reflect modern technology and does not imply any material difference in meaning.

identical treatment,[41] any distinction between persons belonging to national minorities and others in their access to the media must be based on objective criteria. The inclusion of these requirements, which are not expressly mentioned in the corresponding provision of the ECHR, was considered by the drafters to be important for an instrument designed to protect persons belonging to national minorities.[42]

Acknowledgement of the need for states to regulate in this area is further reflected in the requirement in Article 9(3) that the creation and use by minorities of their own media be undertaken within the state's broadcasting framework. However, state control may only be exercised within certain limits, and it was in order to ensure respect for constitutional provisions which in some states limit the extent to which a party can regulate access to the media that the proviso 'within the framework of their legal systems' was added specifically to the non-discrimination provision in Article 9(1).[43]

2. *Practice of the Advisory Committee*

The Advisory Committee has drawn attention to the need to regulate through legislation to guarantee access to the media for persons belonging to national minorities[44] and has provided clear and specific guidance for states with regard to their regulatory frameworks. Legislation should be sufficiently clear in order to ensure certainty in implementation[45] and avoid allowing too much discretion to the authorities concerned.[46] Where legal provisions lack the necessary specificity and clarity, the Advisory Committee recommends a flexible approach which makes the most of the possibilities provided by law—in some cases pending amendments to the relevant legislation.[47] Independent regulatory bodies should be responsible for the implementation and enforcement of legislation and policy and for ensuring media independence.[48]

[41] CAHMIN, 1st meeting, CAHMIN (94) 5, meeting report, 25–8 January 1994, para. 40.

[42] FCNM Explanatory Report, para. 59.

[43] Above, n. 42, para. 57.

[44] See, for example, Advisory Committee on the Framework Convention for the Protection of National Minorities, Opinion on Italy, ACFC/INF/OP/I (2002) 7, 13 July 2002, para. 45, noting the vulnerability of radio and television spots in Sardinian, Franco-Provençal, or Friulian which lack legal basis.

[45] See, for example, Advisory Committee Opinion on Estonia, ACFC/INF/OP/I (2002) 5, 12 April 2002, para. 35; Slovakia, ACFC/INF/OP/I (2001) 1, 22 September 2001, paras. 34–5; and Austria, ACFC/INF/OP/I (2002) 9, 7 November 2002, paras. 39, 87.

[46] See, for example, Advisory Committee Opinion on Ukraine, ACFC/INF/OP/I (2002) 6, 27 November 2002, para. 45.

[47] See, for example, ibid., para. 44; and Italy (n. 44 above), para. 46.

[48] See, for example, Advisory Committee Opinion on Armenia, ACFC/INF/OP/I (2003) 1, 15 January 2003, paras. 53, 54 regarding general difficulties affecting the independence of all media (not just minority).

When changes to the media legislative framework are proposed, the Advisory Committee encourages adequate consultation with all concerned persons, including persons belonging to national minorities, in order to ensure that any support a state provides will be sufficient to meet their needs and to strike an appropriate balance among the various national minorities in terms of media access and presence.[49] The effective participation of persons belonging to national minorities in regulatory bodies charged with control or oversight of the media can also contribute to implementation of the principles contained in Article 9.[50] A number of states report making provision for such in order to guarantee appropriate access and coverage for respective national minorities.[51]

Licensing is a common tool employed by states in order to regulate the media without discrimination and based on objective criteria.[52] States report that the relevant authorities are obliged in their allocation of licences to take into account the diversity of interests and needs represented within their populations, including those of persons belonging to national minorities.[53] This is in accordance with respect for democracy and human rights[54] and the principles of plurality, equality, and non-discrimination, and in order to permit cultural pluralism, as provided in FCNM Article 9(4). Licensing is also a useful tool to promote access for persons belonging to national minorities to the broadcast media, whether public or private.[55]

[49] See, for example, Advisory Committee Opinion on Albania, ACFC/INF/OP/I (2003) 4, 18 February 2003, para. 45; and Armenia (n. 48 above), para. 54. See, more generally, the commentary on Art. 15, Section C, for an elaboration of institutions and mechanisms for consulting minorities when contemplating legislation or administrative measures likely to affect them directly.

[50] See Advisory Committee Opinion on Croatia, ACFC/INF/OP/I (2002) 3, 6 February 2002, para. 40.

[51] See, for example, Advisory Committee Opinion on Austria (n. 45 above), paras. 39, 87; Albania (n. 49 above), para. 49; Slovenia State Report, ACFC/SR (2000) 4, 29 November 2000, para. 62; and Hungary State Report, ACFC/SR (1999) 10, 21 May 1999, with respect to arrangements for representation of persons belonging to national minorities on various bodies with monitoring, advisory, and/or decision-making powers.

[52] Germany State Report, ACFC/SR (2000) 1, 24 February 2000, and Serbia and Montenegro State Report, ACFC/SR (2002) 3, 16 October 2002, provide descriptions of transparent and non-discriminatory licensing procedures.

[53] See, for example, Finland State Report, ACFC/SR (1999) 3, 16 February 1999; and Germany State Report, ACFC/SR (2000) 1, 24 February 2000.

[54] See Cyprus State Report, ACFC/SR (99) 2 Rev., 1 March 1999, Section H on Art. 9.

[55] For example, by requiring licensees to allocate a certain amount of time to programmes intended for minorities and/or in minority languages or by laying down 'stimulation criteria to encourage such programming'. See Advisory Committee Opinion on Albania (n. 49 above), para. 49; Lithuania State Report, ACFC/SR (2001) 7, 31 October 2001; and Bulgaria State Report, ACFC/SR (2003) 1, 9 April 2003. See further below under Section II. D.

(a) Proportionality of Regulation

According to the Advisory Committee, the need to promote the common or state language can be one factor to be taken into account in the legitimate licensing of broadcasting enterprises.[56] Any regulation should, however, fully respect the freedom of expression and should hinder neither the creation and use of media by persons belonging to national minorities nor their access to the public media.[57] This raises questions regarding the point at which regulation to promote one language may become unduly restrictive for others.

The Committee has identified a number of factors concerning the nature of the media and the wider social environment to be considered when assessing the proportionality of any language-related (or other) regulation of the broadcast media including the size and dispersal of the minority population, audience needs and aspirations, and the availability of other services (such as broadcasting from abroad) to meet those needs.[58]

Advisory Committee Opinions regarding the legitimacy (or not) of states' limitations on the use of minority language(s) as a medium of expression in broadcasting help to define the parameters of what is proportional. In this respect, an overall exclusion of the use of the languages of national minorities in the nationwide public service and private broadcasting sectors is considered overly restrictive and incompatible with Article 9.[59] This is so even where possibilities for minority language broadcasting exist at regional or local level (taking into account, *inter alia*, the size of the population concerned and their dispersal).[60] With regard to quotas (affecting public and/or private broadcasters) which stipulate either a maximum time allowed for broadcasting in one or more minority languages or a certain percentage for broadcasting in one (usually the state) language, thereby effectively limiting broadcasting time in minority language(s), the Advisory Committee considers that 'excessive quotas may impair the implementation of the rights contained in Article 9 of the Framework Convention'.[61] Thus, while the prescription of language quotas *per se* is not automatically incompatible with Article 9 of the Framework

[56] See, for example, Advisory Committee Opinion on the Russian Federation, ACFC/INF/OP/I (2003) 5, 10 July 2003, para. 76; and Ukraine (n. 46 above), para. 43.

[57] See, for example, Advisory Committee Opinion on Ukraine (n. 46 above) concerning the registration system for the print media.

[58] See further below under Section II. E (*a*).

[59] See Advisory Committee Opinion on Azerbaijan, ACFC/INF/OP/I (2004) 1, 22 May 2003, para. 50.

[60] See Advisory Committee Opinion on the Russian Federation (n. 56 above), paras. 76, 144; and Ukraine (n. 46 above), paras. 43, 97.

[61] Advisory Committee Opinion on Ukraine (n. 46 above), para. 47, regarding the (Ukrainian) language-related quotas imposed by the National Television and Radio Council when taking its licensing decisions.

Convention, care should be taken in their implementation to ensure that they do not result in 'excessive limitations of the right of persons belonging to national minorities to impart or receive information in minority languages'.[62] In practice, an Armenian law limiting broadcasting time in minority languages on public radio and television to a maximum of one hour per week for all national minorities on television and one hour per day on radio has been considered too restrictive.[63] Similarly, in Estonia, while there are no specific legislative provisions for public service broadcasting for persons belonging to national minorities, the time allocated for minority language broadcasting on public service TV in practice—approximately one hour in Russian and no regular broadcasting in the languages of other minorities—'appears limited' in relation to the needs and size of the population concerned, regardless of the availability of foreign broadcasting.[64]

The imposition of rigid translation requirements is also considered to mar the implementation of Article 9 by causing undue difficulties for persons belonging to a national minority in their efforts to create their own media.[65] The Advisory Committee points out in this connection that, while subtitling of minority languages in the state language 'is often advisable and fully in the spirit of the Framework Convention', as far as private broadcasting is concerned, this goal should be principally pursued through incentive-based voluntary methods.[66]

3. *Link to Developments outside the FCNM*

As noted above, licensing regimes are expressly permitted under the ECHR in the third sentence of Article 10(1).[67] European Court case law confirms states' ability (and indeed obligation) to regulate the way in which broadcasting is organized on their territory (including through licensing regimes). They may do so for technical reasons, namely the maintenance of order in the broadcasting frequencies (in light of the limited nature of the radio spectrum),[68] as well as to protect and promote diversity in accordance with principles of

[62] See, for example, Advisory Committee Opinion on Moldova, ACFC/INF/OP/I (2003) 2, 15 January 2003, paras. 54, 55, 109 regarding the (since amended) 65% state language stipulation for public and private broadcasters (with exceptions for satellite and TV broadcasts and foreign stations broadcasting in areas compactly populated by ethnic minorities).

[63] Advisory Committee Opinion on Armenia (n. 48 above), paras. 47, 99.

[64] Advisory Committee Opinion on Estonia (n. 45 above), para. 37.

[65] Above, n. 45, para. 38. [66] ibid.

[67] While Art. 19 ICCPR lacks a similar proviso, licensing for the orderly control of the broadcasting frequencies is considered to fall under the permissible restriction aimed at the protection of public order in Art. 19(3).

[68] See ECtHR, *Groppera Radio AG and Others* v. *Switzerland*, judgment of 28 March 1990, Series A, No. 173, para. 61.

pluralism and democracy (including the individual right to access information from a diversity of sources).[69] The latter obligation is confirmed and elaborated in a number of Council of Europe documents.[70]

However, any state control may only be exercised within certain limits and must be in accordance with the principle of non-discrimination as enshrined in ICCPR Articles 2 and 26, and ECHR Article 14, which includes a duty to treat differently those persons whose situations are different so that effective equality can be achieved. Accordingly, distinctions in access to the media through licensing or other forms of regulation will not be considered discriminatory provided they are based on reasonable and objective criteria.[71] Licensing and other forms of regulation are, moreover, subject to the requirements of ECHR Article 10(2) and ICCPR 19(3)—as confirmed by the case law of the European Court of Human Rights regarding the object, purpose, and scope of application of the third sentence of Article 10(1).[72] Consequently, restrictions on transmissions cannot be founded on licensing power alone, but must be necessary for one of the purposes specified. In order for a restriction on the freedom of expression to be justified under one of the public interest grounds listed, it must be in pursuit of a legitimate aim and the measures taken must be necessary for, and proportionate to, the aim pursued and must not act to undermine the right to freedom of expression itself.

With respect to the proportionality of regulation, the European Court has identified a number of considerations, other than technical, for appropriate licensing (largely corresponding with those identified by the Advisory Committee for consideration in determining the proportionality of any regulatory measure). These include 'the nature and objectives of a proposed station, its potential audience at national, regional or local level, the rights and needs of the specific audience and the obligations derived from international legal instruments'.[73] More specifically, the size of the target audience and their ease of access to alternative broadcasts (e.g. through cable television) are

[69] See ECtHR, *Informationsverein Lentia and Others* v. *Austria*, judgment of 24 November 1993, Series A, No. 276, paras. 30–3.

[70] See, for example, Committee of Ministers Recommendation No. R (99)1 on measures to promote media pluralism, adopted 19 January 1999. The appendix holds that 'national bodies responsible for awarding licenses to private broadcasters should pay particular attention to the promotion of media pluralism in the discharge of their mission'. See further below under Section II. F. for a discussion of diversity and pluralism.

[71] For a discussion of this principle, see UN Human Rights Committee General Comment on Non-discrimination (1989), para. 13; and ECtHR, *Belgian Linguistics* case, judgment of 13 July 1968, Series A, No. 6.

[72] ECtHR, *Groppera Radio AG and Others* v. *Switzerland*, judgment of 28 March 1990, Series A, No. 173, para. 61, reiterating *Lentia* (n. 69 above), para. 29.

[73] *Lentia* (n. 69 above), para. 32.

also relevant.[74] According to the European Commission of Human Rights, a licensing system not respecting the requirements of pluralism, tolerance, and broad-mindedness 'without which there is no democratic society' would infringe Article 10(1) of the ECHR; the Commission identified cultural and linguistic pluralism in addition to 'a balance between lowland and mountain regions and a balanced federalist policy' as factors for consideration in assessing the proportionality of regulation.[75] Clearly, licensing decisions should not be allowed to impair the enjoyment of minority language broadcasting rights:

> . . . Refusal to grant a broadcasting licence may raise a problem under Article 10, in conjunction with Article 14 of the [European] Convention . . . if the refusal . . . resulted directly in a considerable proportion of the inhabitants of the area concerned being deprived of broadcasts in their mother tongue.[76]

The inclusion of persons belonging to national minorities on independent regulatory bodies (including those responsible for awarding licences) is explicitly recognized in the European Language Charter as a way to ensure that their interests are represented and taken into account in the regulatory process.[77] This is consistent with Article 15 of the FCNM which reiterates the undertakings of OSCE participating states in Chapter IV of the Geneva Document with respect to the effective participation of persons belonging to national minorities in public life. The importance of consulting with persons belonging to national minorities and their representation in decision-making or consultative bodies as an aspect of effective participation is also recognized in Chapter III of the Geneva Document and in paragraph 33 of the Copenhagen Document.

D. Article 9(3): Minorities' Own Media

1. Interpretation

As illustrated above in Section B, the freedom of expression, including the right to impart and receive information, is inextricably linked to the possibility to create and use one's own media. Under Article 9(3), states have a twofold obligation with regard to the right of persons belonging to national minorities to their own means of communication. The first sentence, referring specifically to printed media, contains an essentially negative undertaking not to hinder

[74] ECtHR, *Tele 1 Privatfernsehgesellschaft MBH* v. *Austria*, App. No. 32240/96, judgment of 21 September 2000, paras. 39–40.

[75] European Commission of Human Rights decision on admissibility of 16 October 1986 in the *Case of Verein Alternatives Lokalradio Bern* v. *Switzerland*, App. No. 10746/84.

[76] Above, n. 75.

[77] See European Language Charter, Art. 11(3); see also Oslo Recommendations on the Linguistic Rights of National Minorities, February 1998.

its creation and use.[78] The more flexibly worded second sentence emphasizes a positive obligation in the field of broadcasting to ensure 'as far as possible' that persons belonging to national minorities are granted the possibility to create and use their own media. This distinction between negative and positive obligations reflects the scarcity of available frequencies and the consequent need for states to regulate in this field.[79] The phrase 'as far as possible' reflects the reality that states may be affected by these technical factors in their ability to grant the possibility to minority groups to create and use their own media; it is not meant to be read as meaning as far as the state may wish.[80] In other words, within the range of technical possibilities of limits, states must ensure the possibilities for persons belonging to national minorities to create and use their own media. In any case, procedures for the allocation of frequencies—as for licensing regimes and other forms of regulation—must respect the principles of freedom of expression and non-discrimination as articulated in Article 9(1).

The wording of states' obligations under Article 9(3) to ensure that persons belonging to national minorities are 'granted the possibility' to create and use their own media, implies an obligation to create the conditions conducive to a diversity of opportunities for expression in which such media can flourish. This follows from the Preamble to the FCNM, according to which a pluralist and genuinely democratic society should not only respect the cultural and linguistic identity of each person belonging to a national minority, but should 'also create appropriate conditions enabling them to express, preserve and develop this identity'. Article 5(1) explicitly places an obligation on states parties to promote the conditions necessary for persons belonging to national minorities 'to preserve the essential elements of their identity', including their language.

The extent of states' obligations to provide financial and/or other forms of support for minorities' own media is not directly addressed—either in this paragraph or in 9(4) (which requires parties to adopt special measures to facilitate access to the media for persons belonging to national minorities). A proposed formulation whereby the parties would 'undertake to adopt, where necessary, special measures, for the purpose of promoting access to the media and the use of their own means of communication' was not retained in paragraph 3.[81] While opinions in the process of drafting paragraph 4 diverged as to states' obligations to adopt special measures in favour of minorities in connection with their right to establish and

[78] Although some experts preferred a positive wording for this sentence such as 'The parties shall encourage . . . '; CAHMIN, 3rd meeting, CAHMIN (94) 13, meeting report, 11–15 April 1994, point 9.

[79] The allocation of frequencies is specifically cited in the FCNM Explanatory Report, para. 61, as one such positive obligation.

[80] Ibid.

[81] See CAHMIN, 2nd meeting, CAHMIN (94) 9, meeting report, 23 March 1994, Art. 3(2).

maintain their own media, the current wording of Article 9(4) does not preclude the interpretation (according to evolving state practice) of an obligation on states to take adequate measures in this respect both for the purposes of facilitating access for persons belonging to national minorities to the state owned and/or public media, as well as for the establishment and use of their own communications.[82] Certainly, it would be in the spirit of the Convention to do so.

Article 9 does not provide express reference to the right of persons belonging to a national minority to *seek* funds for the establishment of their own media (which is taken as read),[83] or to the extent of states' obligations to provide financial support for the establishment and promotion of such media.[84] However, the principle of non-discrimination in any event requires that minority broadcasters receive an equitable proportion of public funding—or other forms of public support—provided to the media in general.[85]

2. *Practice of the Advisory Committee*

With respect to the obligation not to hinder the creation and use of minorities' own media, Advisory Committee Opinions regarding the proportionality of regulation (discussed above in section II. C. 2.(a)) should be recalled. Accordingly, stipulations regarding the language of broadcasting or translation requirements affecting private broadcasters may be prescribed only to the extent that they do not interfere with efforts by persons belonging to national minorities to create and use their own media.

Reports of state practice and Advisory Committee Opinions confirm that states do have an obligation to act not only to promote access to the public media for persons belonging to national minorities, but to take active measures to support minority (language) media, including through support for the creation of private media companies. Where assistance to minority printed media is limited, the authorities should examine how this may be strengthened.[86] Greater state support for the establishment of private broadcast media by

[82] See CAHMIN, 2nd meeting, CAHMIN (94) 9, meeting report, 23 March 1994, draft Art. 3(2), p. 18, which specifically mentions these two aspects.

[83] Various proposals prohibiting the hindrance of persons belonging to national minorities in their enjoyment of this right were therefore not included in the final draft. See CAHMIN, 3rd meeting, CAHMIN (94) 13, meeting report, 15 April 1994, point 10; and FCNM Explanatory Report, para. 61.

[84] A reference in Art. 10 of the revised FUEN draft to the right to adequate public subsidies for the purpose of ensuring equal access to public media as well as the right to their own means of communication for persons belonging to national minorities was not retained.

[85] See in this connection the revised FUEN draft, referring to the right to 'adequate public subsidies' for the purpose of ensuring equal access to the state's or other public mass media, as well as minorities' own means of communication.

[86] See, for example, Advisory Committee Opinion on Albania (n. 49 above), paras. 46, 97.

persons belonging to national minorities is also recommended.[87] In some instances the Advisory Committee has considered that the authorities should not only support such efforts, but should themselves establish facilities to be run by the minority in question and provide them with the necessary training to do so.[88] Certainly, the possibilities for persons belonging to national minorities to create and use their own media should not be reduced.[89] There are a number of ways in which states may and do create favourable conditions (financial or otherwise) to encourage private minority broadcasting.

In allocating frequencies, certain channels among those set aside and placed at the disposal of the authorities may be allocated specifically for minorities.[90] Where there are technical limitations on the number of frequencies available and/or groups do not have sufficient resources to sustain their own services, the sharing of channels can cater for the needs of a number of minorities, including those that are numerically small or otherwise lack capacity.[91] In Denmark, for example, it is considered practical for several licensees to share a transmission facility.[92] In Germany, 'open channels' are used for local and regional dissemination of non-commercial broadcasting items (although there are no definitive findings as to the extent these channels are used by groups protected under the Framework Convention).[93] Broadcasting on a different frequency band can also be used to increase coverage of minority broadcasting.[94]

[87] See, for example, Advisory Committee Opinion on Armenia (n. 48 above), Executive Summary and paras. 50, 100; and Committee of Ministers Resolution on Armenia, ResCMN (2003) 2, 15 January 2003.

[88] An upcoming Advisory Committee Opinion will propose the setting up of a radio station for Roma. Financial support for some radio programmes broadcast for Roma by certain local radio stations were not considered adequate in this regard.

[89] In Austria, for example, where the transition between old and new arrangements intended to open up new prospects for private radio stations in co-operation with the public service broadcaster has seen a cut in financial aid for private broadcasting companies, the Advisory Committee has cautioned that this should not jeopardize existing programmes; Advisory Committee Opinion on Austria (n. 45 above), paras. 40, 87.

[90] This is the reported intention of the Italian authorities: Comment by the State of Italy, GVT/COM/INF/OP/I (2002) 007. See also Comment by the State of Hungary GVT/COM/INF/OP/I (2001) 004 re the granting of an independent frequency to the only independent Romani radio in Hungary for a seven-year period.

[91] In Estonia, for example, the Advisory Committee has noted with approval the existence in Estonia of one public service radio channel devoted to broadcasting in a number of minority languages and catering increasingly to the needs of persons belonging to all national minorities, including the numerically small ones; Advisory Committee Opinion on Estonia (n. 45 above), para. 36.

[92] Denmark State Report, ACFC/SR (1999) 9, 6 May 1999.

[93] It is reported that the Roma and Sinti minorities experience difficulties in accessing these channels for practical and economic reasons; FCNM Report by Germany on Article 9(3), ACFC/SR (2001) 24 February 2001, at paras. 3, 3.4.

[94] In Poland, for example, some local TV programmes produced by the public service broadcaster and addressed to national minorities are broadcast (or repeated) not only in the regional band, but in a separate frequency band from other transmitters, increasing their coverage; Poland State Report, ACFC/SR (2002) 2, 10 July 2002.

The creation of favourable/preferential licensing regimes, including through selected licensing tenders,[95] has been welcomed by the Advisory Committee as 'appropriate and constructive'.[96] The Advisory Committee has, furthermore, indicated that it would support measures aimed at ensuring broadcasters the possibility to introduce minority language programming also after gaining a concession.[97] As with any licensing stipulation, it is important that these conditions are enforced and that complaints alleging failure to respect licence obligations be investigated.[98] Exemptions from competition legislation or special regimes to relieve minority media from administrative or financial burdens are another effective tool.[99] This is the case in Poland where 'social broadcasters' (a category into which persons belonging to national minorities may fall) are exempt from fees for the granting or changing of licences.[100]

A shortage of financial resources is recognized by the Advisory Committee as a dominant factor preventing persons belonging to national minorities from establishing and/or thereafter maintaining their own private media.[101] This is often the case especially with respect to the media of numerically small as well as dispersed minorities. In such cases, authorities are urged to consider the situation and increase their efforts to address this issue.[102] Where financial (and other resources) offered to national minorities to set up private broadcast or print media are insufficient, the authorities should consider this situation and increase their support to persons belonging to national minorities in this field.[103] In this respect, particular attention should be focused, via consultation

[95] The Hungarian Public Foundation for Minorities, for example, encourages the establishment of local minorities' media and the preparation and transmission of cable TV native language minority programming by the use of selected tenders and also guarantees funds in support of this; Hungary State Report, ACFC/SR (1999) 10, 21 May 1999.

[96] See Advisory Committee Opinion on Hungary, ACFC/INF/OP/I (2001) 4, 14 September 2001, para. 32.

[97] See Advisory Committee Opinion on Croatia (n. 50 above), para. 42.

[98] Advisory Committee Opinion on Hungary (n. 96 above), para. 32.

[99] In Hungary, for example, non-profit organizations owned by local national self-governments may be entitled to make programmes without tender 'if the satisfaction of native language information demands of the minorities are not ensured in the reception area'; Hungary State Report, ACFC/SR (1999) 10, 21 May 1999. See also Comments by Armenia, GVT/COM/INF/OP/I (2003) 1, 15 January 2003, referring to a type of licence that can be obtained at a competitive rate (although it is noted that candidates from national minorities have yet to participate in these competitions) as well as the intention to provide a licence with discounts for representatives of national minorities in areas where they 'reside compactly'.

[100] Poland State Report, ACFC/SR (2002) 2, 10 July 2002.

[101] See, for example, Advisory Committee Opinion on Ukraine (n. 46 above), para. 48; and Azerbaijan (n. 59 above), para. 52 (concerning the print media).

[102] See, for example, Advisory Committee Opinion on the Russian Federation (n. 56 above), para. 75; and Ukraine (n. 46 above), para. 98.

[103] See, for example, Advisory Committee Opinion on Armenia (n. 48 above), para. 54.

with those concerned, on matching aid to needs, and striking a balance between the various national minorities.[104] Authorities are urged to pay particular attention to the needs of numerically small minorities and to provide increased support where necessary.[105]

Many states do, in fact, create the conditions for the provision of financial support for minority media. Support may be provided through the relevant ministries or through specialized government bodies concerned with national minority issues either directly to the press or broadcaster, or indirectly through public associations which aim to support minorities.[106] The practice of subsidizing the printed media (including newspapers, specialist journals, periodicals and magazines, etc.) in particular—and at various levels—is reported in many states[107] and is commended by the Advisory Committee.[108] However, some states have expressed caution in supporting and subsidizing the private media for fear of impinging on their freedom and independence.[109] Provision of funding to foundations which support minority media is recognized by the Advisory Committee as a good method of providing indirect support and thereby avoiding difficult questions regarding media independence which direct funding can raise.[110] Other methods of indirect support include the licensing procedures described above with 'discounts' for persons belonging to national minorities.

A lack of trained personnel is frequently cited as one of the obstacles to the establishment and functioning of minority media.[111] States are encouraged

[104] Ibid., para. 100. See also Advisory Committee Opinion on Norway, ACFC/INF/OP/I (2003) 3, 13 February 2003, paras. 43 and 44; and Sweden, ACFC/INF/OP/I (2003) 6, 25 August 2003, which notes the importance that the distribution subsidy scheme for newspapers is designed in a manner that takes into account the *specific situation* of minority language newspapers (emphasis added).

[105] See, for example, Advisory Committee Opinion on Lithuania, ACFC/INF/OP/I (2003) 8, 25 September 2003, para. 52.

[106] For various avenues of support, see Slovenia State Report, ACFC/SR (2000) 4, 29 November 2000, para. 65; Hungary State Report, ACFC/SR (1999) 10, 21 May 1999; and Russian Federation State Report, ACFC/SR (1999) 15, 8 March 2000.

[107] See, for example, Poland State Report, ACFC/SR (2002) 2, 10 July 2002.

[108] See, for example, Advisory Committee Opinion on Italy (n. 44 above), para. 43, regarding financial support by state, regional and local authorities for the printed press.

[109] See, for example, the Comment by the State of Albania.

[110] This is the case in Germany, for example, where constitutional and legal limits prevent the federal authorities from directly financing broadcasting specially for national minorities, but where the Sorbian People's Foundation—to which the federal authorities and *Länder* directly contribute—can support Sorbian media. The Advisory Committee suggests this solution could be replicated for other minorities; Advisory Committee Opinion on Germany, ACFC/INF/OP/I (2002) 8, 1 March 2002, para. 45.

[111] See Austria State Report, ACFC/SR (2000) 3, 15 November 2000; and Slovenia State Report, ACFC/SR (2000) 4, 29 November 2000, para. 64.

to increase production and broadcasting capacity for persons belonging to national minorities through opportunities for special training and promotion for minority media professionals.[112] Development of the technical infrastructure necessary for publishing or broadcasting by persons belonging to national minorities is another valuable form of support.[113]

3. *Links to Other Developments*

The FCNM is the only multilateral instrument directly addressing the right of persons belonging to national minorities to establish their own media in their own languages.[114] However, Article 11 of the European Language Charter specifies options which states may pursue in order to realize such possibilities for linguistic minorities—in recognition of the vulnerability of regional and minority languages (which represent a small cultural market) and the consequent need for public support.[115] Given that the media often plays a key role in the promotion and preservation of language, culture, and identity, the media may also constitute entities of the kind foreseen in, *inter alia*, paragraph 32.2 of the Copenhagen Document which provides for the right of persons belonging to national minorities to 'establish and maintain their own cultural and religious institutions, organisations or associations'.[116]

The duty of the state not only to protect but also to encourage the conditions for the promotion of the linguistic (and other) identity of persons belonging to national minorities is entrenched in a number of international instruments. Under Article 4(2) of the 1992 UN Declaration on the Rights of Persons Belonging to National or Ethnic, Religious, and Linguistic Minorities, states undertake to 'take measures to create favourable conditions to enable persons belonging to national minorities to express their characteristics and to develop their culture [and] language'. OSCE participating states are also committed to protect and create conditions for the promotion of the identities of persons belonging to national minorities and to take

[112] See, for example, Advisory Committee Opinion on Armenia (n. 48 above), paras. 50, 100.

[113] Slovenian law, for example, stipulates state support for non-commercial mass media intended to inform the Italian and Hungarian national communities and to develop the technical infrastructure necessary for their publishing or broadcasting; Slovenia State Report, ACFC/SR (2000) 4, 29 November 2000, para. 61.

[114] A parallel provision protecting the rights of indigenous peoples is to be found in Art. 17 of the UN Draft Declaration on the Rights of Indigenous Peoples. Futhermore, states' obligations to provide support for the creation of indigenous radio stations and other media are reflected in the Proposed American Declaration on the Rights of Indigenous Peoples, approved by the American Commission on Human Rights, 26 February 1997, Art. VIII, entitled Philosophy, Outlook and Language, at para. 2.

[115] Explanatory Report to the European Language Charter, para. 107.

[116] Explanatory Note to Oslo Recommendation 8.

measures to that effect, in accordance with the principles of equality and non-discrimination.[117]

Concerning forms of state support, under the European Language Charter, undertakings include the necessary allocation of frequencies to those broadcasting in minority languages. Beyond this, the Charter also identifies an important distinction in states' undertakings proposed for the benefit of regional and minority languages in the media according to whether or not they carry out a public service mission. Accordingly, where broadcasting is conceived as a purely private sector function, the state approach should be one of encouragement and/or facilitation.[118]

Regarding funding, only the Central European Initiative's Instrument for the Protection of Minority Rights, in Article 19, specifically refers to the right of persons belonging to a national minority to avail themselves of the media in their own language 'with possible financial assistance'. The requirement that minority language broadcasters receive an equitable proportion of state support for the media is reflected in Article 11(1)(*f*) of the European Language Charter, which provides that states parties must either 'cover the additional costs of those media which use regional or minority languages, wherever the law provides for financial assistance in general for the media', or 'apply existing measures for financial assistance also to audiovisual production in the regional or minority languages'. The requirement to build capacity of minority language broadcasters is also explicit in the European Language Charter, which requires states parties to support the training of journalists and other staff.[119]

Regardless of the extent to which states are obliged to provide support for minorities' own media, they nevertheless have an obligation not to hinder communication between persons belonging to national minorities, including through their own print and broadcasting media. In this respect, the Parliamentary Assembly of the Council of Europe has urged member states 'to abolish restrictions on the establishment and functioning of private media broadcasting in minority languages'.[120] OSCE participating states have also confirmed the importance of refraining from hindering the production of cultural materials concerning or by persons belonging to them[121] and, as mentioned above, have committed themselves not to discriminate against independent media.[122]

117 Geneva Document, Chapter IV; Vienna Document, Principles, para. 19; Copenhagen Document, para. 33.

118 Explanatory Report to the European Language Charter, para. 110.

119 Article 11(1)(*g*).

120 Recommendation 1589 (2003) on Freedom of Expression in the Media in Europe, para. 17(vi).

121 Geneva Document, Chapter IV, para. 3.

122 Moscow Document, para. 26.2.

E. Article 9(4): Facilitating Access

1. *Interpretation*

Article 9(4) emphasizes the need for special measures with the dual aim of facilitating access to the media for persons belonging to national minorities and promoting tolerance and cultural pluralism.[123] The terminology 'adequate measures' mirrors that of Article 4(2) whereby special measures aimed at promoting and achieving de facto equality for persons belonging to national minorities must respect the principle of proportionality in order to avoid discrimination or a violation of the rights of others. This principle requires that the measures take into account the specific conditions of the persons concerned and do not extend in scope or time beyond what is necessary to achieve the goal of full and effective equality.[124] Article 9(4) thus complements the undertaking laid down in the last sentence of Article 9(1) concerning states' obligations to ensure that persons belonging to national minorities are not discriminated against in their access to the media.[125] As illustrated in the previous section, the obligation to take adequate measures in order to facilitate access to the media applies to both the mainstream public media and minorities' own forms of communication.

Funding for minority broadcasting or for programme productions dealing with minority issues is one such facilitative measure specifically envisaged by this paragraph.[126] Encouraging editors and broadcasters (subject to editorial independence) to allow national minorities access to their media as well as offering opportunities for dialogue between groups (in order to promote tolerance) are also envisaged in the Explanatory Report.[127]

2. *Practice of the Advisory Committee*

(a) What is Adequate? Assessing Proportionality

State Reports and Advisory Committee Opinions provide clear guidance as to the specific conditions which should be taken into account by authorities when taking measures aimed at achieving *de facto* equality for persons belonging to national minorities. These considerations apply equally to public and private media.

Audience interests, needs, and desires

In ensuring adequate access to, and presence in, the media for persons belonging to national minorities, the Advisory Committee considers that the authorities

[123] FCNM Explanatory Report, para. 62. [124] Above, n. 123, para. 39.
[125] ibid., para. 62. [126] ibid. [127] ibid.

should examine the expressed interests, needs, and desires of those persons and try and meet their expectations—including through the possibility of support.[128] In doing so, states must assure a proper balance is struck and maintained not just between the interests, needs, and desires of minority and majority groups, but also between those of different national minorities.[129] However, a purely responsive approach is insufficient bearing in mind that, for one reason or another, different minority groups may not come forward with demands.[130] The dynamics, commitment, and financial potential of the minority community concerned all affect the extent to which minorities either take the initiative themselves or demand a response from the state in terms of their media needs.[131] Frequently, they lack the economic and practical resources in order to take advantage of available opportunities such as licensing regimes. Where no requests have been made to the appropriate bodies for licences to establish, for example, local radio or television stations on the part of persons belonging to national minorities, this may reflect less a lack of interest, than a lack of prospective funding and other support.[132] A lack of request does not therefore mean that no support from the state is required.[133] Where they are not already established, the onus is on the state to seek to define the interests, needs, and desires of persons belonging to national minorities in consultation with

[128] Concerning the authorities' need to react to the expressed interests of minority groups, see, for example, Advisory Committee Opinion on Austria (n. 45 above), paras. 41, 88; Germany (n. 110 above), para. 83; and Italy (n. 44 above), para. 44.

[129] See, for example, Advisory Committee Opinion on Germany (n. 110 above), para. 46, regarding the lack of public radio and TV services offered to the Danish minority compared to the wide-ranging provision for the Sorbian minority. In considering Germany's implementation of Art. 6 of the Convention, the Advisory Committee, in para. 35, also encourages the authorities to consider further support for media for 'other groups, including non-citizens' in addition to the Sorbian, Danish, Frisian, and Roma/Sinti minorities.

[130] Advisory Committee Opinion on Austria (n. 45 above), paras. 42, 88.

[131] As observed in the Serbia and Montenegro State Report, ACFC/SR (2002) 3, 16 October 2002, on Article 9(3) with regard to the printed press, at para. 1.1: 'In practice, the creation and utilization of the press depends on economic power and is more developed in economically more prosperous areas. Persons belonging to different national minorities create and use the press to differing extents.' This observation can be said to apply also to the broadcast media.

[132] Advisory Committee Opinion on Albania (n. 49 above), para. 48. See also Advisory Committee Opinion on Armenia (n. 48 above), paras. 50, 100.

[133] As the Advisory Committee has pointed out in the context of German language programming in the framework of the regional public broadcasting system in Denmark; Advisory Committee Opinion on Denmark, ACFC/INF/OP/I (2001) 5, 31 October 2001, para. 30. For a discussion of the notion of demand more generally, see the proceedings of the Conference 'Filling the Frame' to mark the fifth anniversary of the entry into force of the Framework Convention, Strasbourg, 30–1 October 2003, in particular the observation of the General Rapporteur, Prof. Patrick Thornberry, that 'Inaction by State authorities is not an adequate response to minority rights in general, nor indeed is passivity on the part of minority groups.' Above, n. 3.

those concerned and to seek to respond, where appropriate, particularly so that numerically small or otherwise vulnerable groups (e.g. those not politically organized) do not miss out.[134] Such consultation is important in ensuring that the real interests, needs, and desires of those concerned are catered for both in terms of the language and the content of the media. The latter should be varied and wide, ranging beyond the provision of information to include cultural and educational programming.[135] These obligations can be fulfilled through programming targeting one minority or, as is the case in Lithuania, one programme devoted to the 'cultural, linguistic, educational and everyday problems of all the national communities in Lithuania'.[136] The participation of persons belonging to national minorities in editorial and other processes is beneficial in ensuring both the independent nature of the media and its responsiveness to the communities served.[137]

With respect to the broadcast media in particular (and associated technical limitations on available frequencies) it is important to note that measures taken to remedy uneven distribution and to secure a more proportionate distribution of broadcasting time for one minority group do not justify a reduction in time for others.[138] Where a more equitable allocation of resources is required, this should be achieved, where possible, through increasing the overall broadcasting time available to minorities.[139] This principle is explicitly recognized in the legislation and practice of some states.[140]

[134] See, for example, Advisory Committee Opinion on Italy (n. 44 above), para. 47, concerning the Roma who do not receive any broadcast in their own language or specifically intended for them; and Advisory Committee Opinion on Switzerland, ACFC/INF/OP/I (2003) 7, 21 August 2003, para. 50, encouraging consultation with Travellers' representatives concerning their needs.

[135] An example of a good content range is provided by the public service broadcasting programme produced for the Sorbian minority in Germany devoted to the fields of information, culture, and education; see Germany State Report, ACFC/SR (2000) 1, 24 February 2000, on Art. 9(3), at para. 3.2.

[136] Lithuania State Report, ACFC/SR (2001) 7, 31 October 2001.

[137] In Denmark, for example, public service radio transmits weekly and monthly programmes with topics relevant to, and profiles of, the border region, including on the German minority in South Jutland and the Danish minority in Schleswig-Holstein, and with their participation; Denmark State Report, ACFC/SR (1999) 9, 6 May 1999. In Lithuania, a regular show on national radio devoted to the cultural, linguistic, educational, and everyday problems of all the national communities, conducted in a variety of languages, is produced by journalists who belong to national minorities themselves; Lithuania State Report, ACFC/SR (2001) 7, 31 October 2001.

[138] See, for example, Advisory Committee Opinion on Romania, ACFC/INF/OP/I (2002) 1, 10 January 2002, para. 46.

[139] See, for example, Advisory Committee Opinion on Hungary (n. 96 above), para. 29.

[140] According to the Comment by the State of Hungary, for example, the Hungarian 1996 Act on Radio and Television Services clearly stipulates that the broadcasting time allocated to minority programmes cannot be reduced.

Audience size and concentration

The size of the audience is frequently cited as one factor to be considered in determining proportionate access for persons belonging to national minorities to the media generally and to broadcasting time on public media in particular. It can be argued that a large audience (as a proportion of the whole population) can justify greater access.[141] Frequently, however, it is the numerically smallest minorities that lack finances or practical capacity and are therefore most in need of support, leading the Advisory Committee in several cases to direct the relevant authorities to pay special attention to supporting the establishment of minority media for numerically small minorities.[142] Larger minorities, despite their size, may nevertheless remain disadvantaged and may also require special attention in order to strike a proper balance between the needs of different groups.[143]

Support for creation of media at regional or local level particularly in areas where there are large concentrations of persons belonging to national minorities has been identified as an excellent means to support such minorities and ensure a balanced use of existing opportunities.[144] While provisions for meeting the needs of regional/local populations must be regarded in themselves as positive, problems arise where legislation/practice extends support to minority broadcasting *only* in those areas of geographical concentration. In this respect, some states prescribe the use of the state language at national level, but make exceptions in areas where persons belonging to national minorities 'live compactly' and where the languages of the numerically prevalent national minorities in those areas may be used.[145] However, the existence of regional or

[141] See, for example, the Advisory Committee Opinion on Croatia (n. 50 above), para. 41, where the time devoted to programming on minorities and/or programming in minority languages in the public service television is considered much too limited in both time and substance 'taking into account the number of persons belonging to national minorities in Croatia'.

[142] See, for example, Advisory Committee Opinion on Moldova (n. 62 above), paras. 57, 110. See also Committee of Ministers Resolution on the Czech Republic, ResCMN (2002) 2, 6 February 2002, identifying the need for supplementary measures to improve access to the media for persons belonging to numerically small minorities, as well as the State Comment of the Czech Republic reporting on the preparation of a government decree on the provision of such state support for both printed and broadcast media.

[143] See, for example, Advisory Committee Opinion on Moldova (n. 62 above), paras. 56, 100, with respect to the Ukrainian minority.

[144] Ibid., paras. 57, 110. See also the Hungary State Report, ACFC/SR (1999) 10, 25 May 1999, describing the duty of the public service broadcasters vis-à-vis national and ethnic minorities which is carried out in national or, taking into account the geographical location of the minority, regional or local broadcasting.

[145] According to Ukraine State Report, ACFC/SR (1999) 14, 2 November 1999, for example, '[i]n Ukraine's regions where considerable groups of the national minorities representatives reside in a compact manner, specialized editorial boards have been established on the basis of state radio and TV corporations and permanently function in national minorities' languages'.

local media catering to the needs of and/or in the languages of persons belonging to national minorities does not negate the need for such provision at national level.[146] As noted above (section II. C. 2.(a)), the Advisory Committee considers the situation in Ukraine, where provision for both public and private minority language broadcasting is made only in areas of 'compact residency', but where a large number of persons belonging to national minorities live outside those areas, to be incompatible with Article 9.[147] Support for the needs of only one group within a designated area is also problematic. In relation to the Russian Federation, the Advisory Committee has noted that the legitimate goal of protecting the language of the 'titular nation' alongside that of Russian in the subjects of the Federation is not suitable for regions where a large number of residents have other minority languages as their mother tongue.[148] As a result, persons belonging to national minorities who find themselves outside their territorial formation or who do not have a specific formation within the Russian Federation face widespread difficulties in ensuring access to electronic media in their own language—shortcomings which the Advisory Committee considers that the Russian authorities should address.[149]

Available services: character, geographical reach, and quality

For some persons belonging to national minorities, especially those living in border regions, the reception of broadcasting in their own language from abroad may be one available option in accessing mass media. Where the quality of reception from abroad is inadequate, positive action from the state (such as the installation of 'repeater facilities' in order to relay and amplify transfrontier broadcasting) may be required.[150] The need for quality reception extends likewise to domestically produced broadcasting (where terrain or other physical/technical obstacles may present themselves).[151] The Advisory Committee has advised a number of states to remedy problems with regard to the quality of, or indeed the possibility at all for, reception of minority language

146 See, for example, Advisory Committee Opinion on Croatia (n. 50 above), para. 41, where the Committee recognizes the programming in minority languages on public service radio at local level to be important, but notes that provision of such at state level is 'quite limited'.

147 Advisory Committee Opinion on Ukraine (n. 46 above), paras. 43, 97.

148 Advisory Committee Opinion on the Russian Federation (n. 56 above), para. 77.

149 Above, n. 56, paras. 76, 78.

150 This is the case in Albania where such provision is made in the south of the country to facilitate the transmission of Greek and other foreign television broadcasts; Advisory Committee Opinion on Albania (n. 49 above), para. 50.

151 In this regard, see Slovenia State Report, ACFC/SR (2000) 4, 29 November 2000, para. 63, reporting on the authorities' support for development of the technical infrastructure necessary for broadcasting and signal distribution on the territory where the two national minorities live.

broadcasting.[152] Significantly, the Opinions of the Advisory Committee also confirm that the availability of foreign broadcasting in the language of a national minority does not obviate the need for, and importance of, domestically produced broadcasting in that language.[153]

While the development of broadcasting technology potentially opens up new opportunities for minority broadcast media (the use of which should be encouraged),[154] its availability to persons belonging to national minorities should be taken into account. In Sweden, for example, the authorities are advised to bear in mind that digital radio is currently used by persons belonging to national minorities only to a limited extent.[155]

(b) Measures to Facilitate Access to the Media

Since state obligations with regard to facilitating access for persons belonging to national minorities to their own media have been dealt with above in section D, the focus here is on the facilitation of access to state owned and controlled and/or public media.

In this respect, Advisory Committee Opinions clarify that facilitating access to the broadcast media for persons belonging to national minorities implies a general obligation to produce and/or broadcast programmes intended for persons belonging to national minorities in the public broadcast media.[156] Where access by persons belonging to national minorities to the public media is limited (and/or there has been a downward trend in programmes or media in minority languages) the onus is on the government to take appropriate steps to increase the broadcasting time made available to them.[157] These provisions should extend to meeting the needs of all minorities including small ones.[158] In many cases, the Advisory Committee calls for 'review' of the current situation.[159]

Many states do ensure that persons belonging to national minorities are provided with broadcasting time in the framework of public television and radio and at different levels—whether state owned and run, or provided by an

[152] See, for example, Advisory Committee Opinion on Slovenia (not yet public), paras. 52, 94; Italy (n. 44 above), para. 44; and Ukraine (n. 46 above), paras. 48, 98.

[153] Advisory Committee Opinion on Estonia (n. 45 above), para. 37; Albania (n. 49 above), para. 50; and Germany (n. 110 above), paras. 46, 83.

[154] Advisory Committee Opinion on the United Kingdom, ACFC/INF/OP/I (2002) 6, 22 May 2002, para. 69.

[155] Advisory Committee Opinion on Sweden (n. 104 above), para. 43.

[156] Advisory Committee Opinion on Croatia (n. 50 above), Proposal for Conclusions and Recommendations by the Committee of Ministers.

[157] See, for example, Advisory Committee Opinion on Armenia (n. 48 above), para. 48.

[158] Advisory Committee Opinion on Estonia (n. 45 above), para. 36.

[159] See, for example, Advisory Committee Opinion on Czech Republic, ACFC/INF/OP/I (2002) 2, 25 January 2002, paras. 53–4.

independent public service broadcaster (PSB). The prescription of appropriate requirements for PSBs with regard to the provision of programming in minority languages is one of the most effective ways in which states meet their obligations with respect to minority broadcast media. By their nature, they are required to reflect diversity and to meet the interests, needs, and desires of different groups, including those of persons belonging to national minorities.[160] While it has been argued (by the Czech authorities, for example) that respect for the independence of PSBs (as is the case for any broadcaster) precludes interference in their programming, it is nevertheless within the scope of the authorities to influence or make stipulations as to the proportion (and quality) of minority (language) broadcasting time in the context of licensing or other forms of agreement between the authorities and the PSB.[161] State authorities are urged to monitor the PSBs in their obligations and take appropriate measures where they are not honoured.[162]

Further considerations in the guarantee of appropriate broadcast coverage for persons belonging to national minorities by public broadcasters include not only the amount of time allotted to minority broadcasting, but the timing of that programming within the broadcasting schedule. The time slots allotted to minority language programming should be such as to ensure that persons belonging to national minorities can enjoy programming in their own language in a meaningful way (i.e. that they are transmitted at reasonable times of the day)[163] and that they reach the greatest number of the target audience.[164] Where this is not the case, the authorities should examine the situation and find ways of improving it.[165] The Advisory Committee, therefore, considers that not only the ratio of programmes for persons belonging to national minorities, but the time and timing of these programmes, should be kept under review

160 On the role of the PSB in reflecting cultural diversity by providing a balanced selection of programmes responding to the needs of all sectors of the population, including persons belonging to national minorities in various states, see for example: Comments by the Czech Republic, GVT/COM/INF/OP/I (2002) 2, 25 January 2002; Denmark State Report, ACFC/SR (1999) 9, 6 May 1999; Italy State Report, ACFC/SR (1999) 7, 3 May 1999; Serbia and Montenegro State Report, ACFC/SR (2002) 3, 16 October 2002.

161 In this connection, the Advisory Committee has commended Sweden's request to the public broadcasting companies to increase their efforts to take into account the interests of persons belonging to national minorities and pay particular attention to the position of the languages of national minorities in this context; Advisory Committee Opinion on Sweden (n. 104 above), para. 41.

162 See, for example, ibid., paras. 41–3.

163 In this respect, see Advisory Committee Opinion on Moldova (n. 62 above), para. 52, welcoming the advantageous time slots on Moldova's public radio and television services of programmes broadcast for persons belonging to national minorities.

164 Advisory Committee Opinion on Hungary (n. 96 above), para. 31.

165 Advisory Committee Opinion on Romania (n. 138 above), para. 47.

in order to guarantee appropriate coverage for respective minorities.[166] Where changes are made, these should not result in a reduction in the amount of broadcasting time reserved for national minorities on public services and/or movement of programmes to less advantageous time slots—a trend considered 'regrettable' by the Advisory Committee.[167] While the need for media outlets to independently consider reforms in their programming profile is recognized, it is essential that reforms do not lead to negative developments in terms of the quality and volume of broadcasting for minorities, thereby negatively impacting on the implementation of Article 9.[168] As noted above under section II. E. 2 (*a*), where there is a disproportionately uneven allocation of resources between minority groups in terms of broadcasting time, attempts to achieve a more equitable situation should, where possible, result in an increase in the overall amount of broadcasting time available to minorities (i.e. an increase for one should not result in a diminution for others).[169]

While Jacubowicz has noted a certain ambiguity in the term 'access' to the media, both in the Convention and Advisory Committee Opinions, it is clear from state reports as well as the scope of the Opinions that this implies both a passive receptive element and an active participatory one.[170] In line with the principle of equality and non-discrimination, the composition of public institutions—including the public media—should be reflective of the populations they are designed to serve. In this respect, FCNM Article 15 states that '[t]he Parties shall create the conditions necessary for the effective participation of persons belonging to national minorities in cultural, social and economic life and in public affairs, in particular those affecting them'.[171] Minority participation in the creation, editing, etc. of public media programming, as well as their

[166] See, for example, Advisory Committee Opinion on Albania (n. 49 above), para. 49; and the Czech Republic (n. 159 above), paras. 53, 54.

[167] See, for example, Advisory Committee Opinion on Lithuania (n. 105 above), para. 51; and Ukraine (n. 46 above), para. 48.

[168] Advisory Committee Opinion on Sweden (n. 104 above), para. 42, concerning marked cuts in broadcasting time for one of the most important media sources of information for Swedish Finns.

[169] See, for example, Advisory Committee Opinion on Hungary (n. 96 above), para. 29.

[170] For an elaboration of the various forms of passive and active access, see further 'Persons Belonging to National Minorities and the Media', Report prepared by Prof. Karol Jacubowicz for the Conference 'Filling the Frame' to mark the fifth anniversary of the entry into force of the Framework Convention, Strasbourg, 30–1 October 2003, **www.coe.int/T/E/human_rights/minorities/5._5_anniversary/PDF_Report_media_Jakubowicz.asp#** 27 August 2004. See also, for example, the Swedish report which considers it important to facilitate *entry* and *access* to the media for persons belonging to national minorities. The Bulgarian authorities also recognize that, while there are no provisions in law that restrict access to mass media for persons belonging to national minorities, their broader presence is required—including on Bulgarian National Radio and TV—with the state playing a more effective role in support of minority media; Report of Bulgaria on Art. 9(4).

[171] See further the commentary on Art. 15.

presence on PSB management bodies, can help to ensure that such programming meets real audience needs.[172] As already noted in section II. D, special training and promotion of media professionals belonging to minorities can help increase capacity.

3. Link to Developments outside the FCNM

The possible use of special and concrete measures aimed at accelerating and achieving de facto equality for persons belonging to national minorities is firmly rooted in universal human rights instruments.[173] Such measures shall not be deemed to amount to racial discrimination, provided that they do not, as a consequence, lead to the maintenance of separate rights for different racial groups and that they are not continued after the objectives for which they were taken have been achieved.[174] OSCE commitments expressly provide for the adoption of such measures for the purposes of ensuring full equality for persons belonging to national minorities.[175] As noted by the UN Human Rights Committee, 'positive measures' taken by states may also be necessary to protect the identity of a minority and the rights of its members to enjoy and develop their culture and language, in community with the other members of the group. Such measures, which may be necessary to correct conditions which prevent or impair the enjoyment of the rights of minorities guaranteed under Article 27 of the ICCPR—i.e. including the rights 'to enjoy their own culture . . . or to use their own language'—may constitute a legitimate differentiation under the Covenant, provided that they are based on reasonable and objective criteria.[176]

In providing meaningful access for persons belonging to national minorities to broadcast time in their own language(s) on publicly funded media on a non-discriminatory basis, states should take account of the factual situation including the 'situation of each language'.[177] More specifically, Oslo Recommendation 9 states that broadcast time and quality should be 'commensurate with the

[172] See, for example, Croatia State Report, ACFC/SR (1999) 5, 16 March 1999; Slovenia State Report, ACFC/SR (2000) 4, 29 November, para. 60; and Romania State Report, ACFC/SR (1999) 11, 24 June 1999, concerning arrangements for the participation of persons belonging to national minorities in producing and/or editing programmes broadcast by the PSB. See also Advisory Committee Opinion on Albania (n. 49 above), para. 49, re the presence of persons belonging to minorities on management bodies.

[173] See CERD, Arts. 1(4) and 2(2); and CEDAW, Arts. 3 and 4.

[174] ibid.

[175] Copenhagen Document, para. 31.

[176] Human Rights Committee, General Comment 23 on Art. 27 (50th session, 1994), para. 6.2. More specifically, Art. 7(2) of the European Language Charter provides that measures aimed at promoting the equality of minority languages should not be considered discriminatory.

[177] European Language Charter, Art. 11(1).

numerical size and concentration of the national minority and appropriate to its situation and needs'. The Explanatory Note to the Oslo Recommendations confirms the Advisory Committee's view that, while the numerical size of a national minority has a bearing on the share of broadcast time on public radio and/or television to be enjoyed by the minority in question, numerical strength and concentration are not the only criteria to be considered. In judging the amount of time allocated to any minority, consideration must be given to the viable minimum of time without which a smaller minority would not be able to avail itself of the media.[178] A non-discriminatory approach to quality of time allocated to minority programming so that such programming can be enjoyed in a meaningful way is also endorsed by the Oslo Recommendations.[179]

The important role of broadcasters with a public service mission in providing a broad range of programmes catering to the tastes, interests, and needs of all members of society, including persons belonging to national minorities, is well established in European Court case law.[180] The European Language Charter provides a number of programmatic options for states to undertake in this regard (including the encouragement and facilitation of the creation of radio stations and television channels as well as adequate provision for minority language programmes).[181] In the framework of the EU, the June 1997 Protocol on the System of Public Broadcasting in the Member States to the Treaty of Amsterdam establishes that 'the system of public broadcasting in the Member States is directly related to the democratic, social and cultural needs of each society and to the need to preserve media pluralism'. Declarations and Recommendations of the Council of Europe's Committee of Ministers also reaffirm and elaborate upon the important role of public service broadcasting in democratic and plural societies, especially in the light of the potential impact of new media technologies on the respect for cultural diversity.[182]

The Explanatory Report to the European Language Charter confirms that undertakings to guarantee freedom of reception from neighbouring countries relates not only to deliberate obstacles, but to the failure of competent authorities to act to ensure such.[183] The principle that free reception of transfrontier broadcasting does not justify a diminution in domestic broadcasting for persons belonging to national minorities is articulated in Oslo Recommendation 11.

[178] Explanatory Note to the Oslo Recommendations, para. 9. [179] ibid.

[180] See, for example, *Lentia* (n. 69 above), para. 33. [181] Art. 11(1)(*a*).

[182] See, for example, Recommendation No. R (96) 10 on the Guarantee of the Independence of Public Service Broadcasting.

[183] Explanatory Report to the European Language Charter, para. 110.

F. Article 9(4): Tolerance and Cultural Pluralism

1. *Interpretation*

Under Article 9(4), states undertake to act in order to promote tolerance and cultural pluralism in the public media.[184] The drafting process reveals the extent of support among the experts for the inclusion of such a provision reflecting the principle of pluralism—especially in the light of the importance attached to that principle by the Council of Europe.[185] Indeed, several experts expressed the wish that this principle be reflected in a separate provision. The importance of a reference to tolerance and the obligation of states in this regard—particularly in terms of broadcast coverage relating to persons belonging to national minorities—was also raised in the drafting process, hence its reflection in the final provision.[186] In addition, the drafters considered that questions relating to tolerance in the media may also be examined in the context of the Preamble and/or the general principles of the Framework Convention.[187] In this respect, the Preamble to the Convention recognizes the creation of a climate of tolerance and dialogue as 'necessary for enabling cultural diversity to be a source and factor, not of division, but of enrichment within society'.[188] Under Article 2, the provisions of the Convention should be applied 'in a spirit of understanding and tolerance'. More specifically, Article 6 identifies the media as a particularly relevant field in which states should act to promote mutual respect, understanding, and co-operation among all persons living on their territory.

2. *Practice of the Advisory Committee*

A number of state reports explicitly acknowledge the importance of actively supporting opportunities for the freedom of expression of persons belonging to national minorities in a culturally pluralistic society.[189] In this respect, the special role of broadcasters with a public service mission in reflecting and responding to cultural diversity within society and so enabling cultural pluralism is generally recognized.[190]

[184] CAHMIN, 1st meeting, CAHMIN (94) 5, meeting report, 25–8 January 1994, para. 40.

[185] CAHMIN, 3rd meeting, CAHMIN (94) 13, meeting report, 11–15 April 1994, para. 8.

[186] See CAHMIN, 2nd meeting, CAHMIN (94) 9, meeting report, 14–18 March 1994, G. Proposal by the Hungarian expert, p. 19; and CAHMIN (94) 14 rev., 10 June 1994, Proposal by the Portuguese delegation concerning the preliminary draft of the FCNM CAHMIN (94) 12, p. 12).

[187] CAHMIN, 1st meeting, CAHMIN (94) 5, meeting report, 25–8 January 1994, para. 40.

[188] See further the commentary on the Preamble for a discussion of the notion of tolerance.

[189] See, for example, Norway State Report, ACFC/SR (2001) 1, 2 March 2001; and Serbia and Montenegro State Report, ACFC/SR (2002) 3, 16 October 2002.

[190] See also Serbia and Montenegro State Report, concerning the role of the PSB in 'securing diversity'. In Germany, furthermore, private broadcasters may be obliged in their licensing conditions

In relation to the promotion of tolerance, the Advisory Committee encourages the training and sensitization of journalists and media professionals to increase the level and quality of coverage of minority issues in the media in general and to avoid negative stereotyping.[191] The Committee has drawn attention in this connection to the wide personal scope of Article 6 of the FCNM, which extends to asylum seekers and persons belonging to other groups not traditionally residing in the country concerned.[192] Where unbalanced, prejudicial, and stereotypical reporting on any group persists, states are encouraged to impress on the media (without encroaching on their editorial independence) the need to report fairly on minorities.[193] States should also encourage the media to follow their own rules of professional ethics to the letter and to review the effectiveness of complaints procedures they have established.[194] A number of states report improvements or examples of good practice in seeking to achieve more balanced and non-prejudicial reporting on minority groups.[195]

Exposure of different groups to the languages, cultures, and concerns of others, generally, and increased coverage reflecting the cultures and concerns of persons belonging to national minorities in the public mainstream media, specifically, is recognized as an important instrument for the promotion of tolerance, intercultural understanding, and peaceful coexistence.[196] Persons belonging to national minorities often seek such coverage for themselves in the hope that it will lead to non-prejudicial and more balanced reporting.[197] Co-operation and interactivity between the media of majority and minority

to 'reflect the essence of the plurality of opinions in the contents of their programmes', including those of minorities.

[191] See, for example, Advisory Committee Opinion on Albania (n. 49 above), paras. 51, 98; and Ukraine (n. 46 above), para. 39.

[192] See, for example, Advisory Committee Opinion on Austria (n. 45 above), para. 32.

[193] Ibid. See commentary on Art. 6 for a fuller analysis of the role of the media in terms of their coverage (or lack thereof) of minority groups.

[194] Advisory Committee Opinion on Germany (n. 110 above), para. 34.

[195] For example, in its Opinion on Moldova (n. 62 above), para. 55, the Advisory Committee has welcomed the initiative of Moldovan public service television to produce and broadcast a special programme aimed at cultivating an interethnic relations culture based on tolerance, understanding, and acceptance of differences and respect for diversity. In Ireland, a considerable development of media consciousness concerning reportage in relation to racism and discrimination is reported; Ireland State Report, ACFC/SR (2001) 6, 13 November 2001, on Art. 9(3).

[196] See, for example, Advisory Committee Opinion on Cyprus, ACFC/INF/OP/I (2002) 4, 21 February 2002, para. 30. See also Slovenia State Report, ACFC/SR (2000) 4, 29 November 2000, para. 67, concerning radio programmes in the Romani and Slovene languages intended for 'the education and informing of the Roma and for the presentation of their culture, as well as informing the wider society of their problems and thereby fostering tolerance and coexistence'.

[197] This is reportedly one of the current aims of the umbrella organizations of the minorities in Germany; Germany State Report, ACFC/SR (2000) 1, 24 February 2000, on Art. 9(3), para. 4.

groups (as opposed to the development of separate parallel services for different groups) is therefore important.[198] Subtitling, rather than dubbing, is recognized as a useful method of ensuring that the general public receives exposure to the languages and cultures of others.[199] Increased involvement of persons belonging to national minorities in the media can also contribute to improved overall communication and understanding of cultural diversity.[200] In situations where the general public, as far as it does not access minority media, receives only limited information about the cultural life of national minorities and events and problems affecting them, the Advisory Committee has drawn attention to the Committee of Ministers Recommendation No. 97 (21) on the media and the promotion of a culture of tolerance and encouraged states in its active pursuit.[201]

3. Link to Developments outside the FCNM

The fundamental role of the principle of pluralism with respect to the enjoyment of the right to freedom of expression (as a basic element of open and democratic societies) and the role of the mass media—and the broadcast media, in particular—in that respect, is well established in the jurisprudence of the European Court of Human Rights.[202] OSCE participating states also recognize independent and pluralistic media as being essential to a free and open society[203] and have undertaken to ensure the freedom of the media as a basic condition for pluralistic and democratic societies.[204] The importance

[198] In Estonia, for example, the state integration programme aims to 'create and expand the common element of Estonian and increase the interactivity of the Russian-language media system'; Comment of the State of Estonia. Efforts to promote intercultural understanding through programming are also described.

[199] See, for example, Advisory Committee Opinion on Sweden (n. 104 above), para. 45; and Estonia (n. 45 above), para. 38, in which the Committee 'agrees that it is often advisable, and fully in the spirit of the Framework Convention, to accompany minority language broadcasting with sub-titles in the State language'.

[200] In Ireland, the communication programme of the Citizen Traveller Campaign aims to involve the Traveller community further by increasing their access to, and making them more effective in their dealings with, the media and thereby promote greater understanding between Travellers and the settled community; Ireland State Report, (2001) 6, 31 November 2001, on Art. 9(4).

[201] See, for example, Advisory Committee Opinion on Hungary (n. 96 above), para. 33; and Norway (n. 104 above), paras. 45, 88.

[202] See *Lentia* (n. 69 above), para. 38, in which the Court observed that the public's entitlement to receive information and ideas of general interest 'cannot be successfully accomplished unless it is grounded in the principle of pluralism, of which the State is the ultimate guarantor. This observation is especially valid in relation to audio-visual media, whose programmes are often broadcast very widely.'

[203] See 1994 Document of the Budapest Summit, Towards a Genuine Partnership in a New Era, Chapter VIII The Human Dimension, provision 36; and Moscow Document, para. 26.

[204] 1999 Istanbul Summit Declaration, provision 27.

of safeguarding media pluralism is also reflected in the Charter of Fundamental Rights of the European Union and in the European Convention on Transfrontier Television.[205]

Media pluralism is considered essential for the reflection and expression of cultural and linguistic diversity.[206] States have an obligation to ensure that the media duly reflect existing diversity within society—the objective being to achieve 'the existence of a wide variety of independent and autonomous media, permitting the reflection of diversity of ideas and opinions'.[207] In this respect, particular attention to the need to sustain and promote cultural diversity is required.[208] In this connection, OSCE participating states have expressed their conviction that a diversity of means of dissemination 'helps to ensure pluralism and the freedom of artistic and cultural expression'.[209] They have furthermore undertaken to support the electronic mass media by making available information to them so they take into account, in their programmes, aspects of the identity (including linguistic) of national minorities.[210] Article 17 of the UN Convention on the Rights of the Child likewise recognizes the importance of ensuring children access to information and material from a diversity of mass media sources and to 'encourage the mass media to disseminate information and material' in accordance with the Convention's educational goals, including the development of respect for the child's own cultural identity and language as prescribed in Article 29.

European Court of Human Rights jurisprudence also confirms tolerance and broad-mindedness to be fundamental to democratic societies.[211] A number of instruments recognize the role of the PSB as an important vehicle for the promotion of a culture of tolerance and understanding in this connection.[212]

[205] See 2000 Charter of Fundamental Rights of the European Union, Official Journal of the European Communities C 364/1, Art. 11(2); and Preamble and Art. 10bis of the 1989 (amended 2002) European Convention on Transfrontier Television.

[206] See the Preamble of the Council of Europe Committee of Ministers' Declaration on Cultural Diversity, 7 December 2000; and Arts. 2 and 6 of the UNESCO Universal Declaration on Cultural Diversity, adopted by the 31st Session of UNESCO's General Conference, Paris, November 2001, on the relationship between freedom of expression, media pluralism, and cultural diversity.

[207] See Council of Europe Committee of Ministers' Declaration on the Freedom of Expression and Information, adopted 29 April 1982, Art. II(*d*).

[208] Council of Europe Committee of Ministers' Declaration on Cultural Diversity, 3.2. See also Art. 17 of the Draft Declaration on the Rights of Indigenous Peoples according to which states have an obligation to take effective measures to ensure that state owned media duly reflect indigenous cultural diversity.

[209] 1991 Document of the Cracow Symposium on the Cultural Heritage of the CSCE Participating States, para. 6.2.

[210] Geneva Document, Chapter VII., para. 2.

[211] See *Handyside* v. *United Kingdom*, judgment of 7 December 1976, Series A, No. 24, para. 49.

[212] See, for example, Appendix to Recommendation No. R (97) 21 to Member States on the Media and the Promotion of a Culture of Tolerance, item 5.

The importance of maintaining links, including through broadcasting, between groups using identical or similar regional or minority languages within states (particularly for dispersed minorities), as well as the establishment of cultural relations with groups in the state using different languages, is reflected in Article 7(1)(*e*) of the European Language Charter. In Article 7(3), the parties undertake to encourage the mass media to promote 'mutual understanding between all the linguistic groups of the country'. In this respect, the same instrument, in Article 7(1)(*g*), also underlines the importance of the provision of facilities enabling non-speakers of a regional or minority language living in the area where it is used, to learn it if they so desire. Accordingly, an appropriate level of minority language broadcasting should be encouraged at the nationwide level. States parties are required, in Article 12, to foster access to works produced in regional and minority languages by aiding and developing, *inter alia*, translation and subtitling.

III. Conclusion and Outlook

There seems little doubt that Article 9 has captured a substantial range of concrete matters of interest to minorities and for society more generally, and that this is reflected in the practice under the Framework Convention. Notwithstanding the often technical aspects of the media, the essence of the protection to be afforded by the Article has found robust expression in considerations of its effective application which offer practical guidance for state policy, if not always specific solutions or resolutions to underlying tensions. The accumulated and evolving discourse has alone contributed much to this field of increasing social importance in our 'media age'. More specifically, for example, the promotion of a spirit of tolerance and intercultural dialogue has received substantial attention from the Advisory Committee with specific and concrete suggestions as to the various ways of achieving this goal while reconciling competing interests with related international obligations.[213]

The practice under the Framework Convention has also been advanced consistent with the work of other international regimes and institutions, including the United Nations and OSCE systems for the protection of human rights and the protection of minorities. Notable in this regard has been the work of the OSCE High Commissioner on National Minorities under whose auspices Guidelines on the Use of Minority Languages in the Broadcast Media were

[213] See further the report by Prof. Karol Jacubowicz, above, n. 170, for an analysis of Advisory Committee Opinions and Committee of Ministers' Resolutions in this area.

elaborated in 2003.[214] The essence of these Guidelines is to complement and reinforce the efforts of those (including the High Commissioner) seeking real equality for minorities in this field by providing guidance as to appropriate action by and support from the state and other relevant bodies (including those under the Framework Convention) for minority (language) broadcasting.

While much has been achieved in clarifying the standards and suggesting specific and concrete courses of action in this complex and important field, much more remains to be done to give full effect to the provisions for the benefit of all concerned. To this end, two issues stand out. First, it seems clear that it is vital to ensure the effective participation of minorities in all aspects of the media. Indeed, the first President of the Advisory Committee, Professor Rainer Hofmann, has identified the interconnected issues of participation and the media as being amongst the main challenges that states face in implementing the FCNM[215] and it has been suggested that both areas might benefit from particular normative developments or general recommendations made by the Advisory Committee.[216] The second issue upon which the Advisory Committee could further reflect and seek more precision is in grading the various forms of access in terms of the benefits they bring to minorities—in light of the comparative benefits of empowering minorities through their 'active' access.[217] Of course, such further clarifications may only help matters if they are taken into consideration and actively pursued by governments and others as part of good faith efforts to fulfil the letter and spirit of Article 9 and of the Framework Convention as a whole.

[214] For the text of the Guidelines and an Explanatory Note (including references to the Framework Convention), see **www.osce.org/documents/hcnm/2003/10/2242_en.pdf** 27 August 2004. For further materials including a background paper and reports and contributions from an intergovernmental conference on the subject, see the *Mercator Media Forum*, 8, (2005).

[215] Presentation by Prof. Rainer Hofmann, President of the Advisory Committee on the Framework Convention for the Protection of National Minorities, Opening Plenary: The Framework Convention at the End of the First Cycle of Monitoring, at the conference 'Filling the Frame' to mark the fifth anniversary of the entry into force of the Framework Convention, Strasbourg, 30–1 October 2003, **www.coe.int/T/E/human_rights/minorities/5._5_anniversary/PDF_Final_presentation_Hofmann.asp#** 27 August 2004.

[216] Concluding Plenary: Conclusions of the Conference by the General Rapporteur, Patrick Thornberry, above, n. 3.

[217] This has been suggested recently by Prof. Karol Jacubowicz; see above, n. 170.

ARTICLE 10

Fernand de Varennes

1. The Parties undertake to recognise that every person belonging to a national minority has the right to use freely and without interference his or her minority language, in private and in public, orally and in writing.
2. In areas inhabited by persons belonging to national minorities traditionally or in substantial numbers, if those persons so request and where such a request corresponds to a real need, the Parties shall endeavour to ensure, as far as possible, the conditions which would make it possible to use the minority language in relations between those persons and the administrative authorities.
3. The Parties undertake to guarantee the right of every person belonging to a national minority to be informed promptly, in a language which he or she understands, of the reasons for his or her arrest, and of the nature and cause of any accusation against him or her, and to defend himself or herself in this language, if necessary with the free assistance of an interpreter.

I. Background

A. Issues

In general, Article 10 of the Framework Convention for the Protection of National Minorities (FCNM) touches upon the use of national minority languages. This is significant because it directly addresses what other provisions of the Framework Convention only skirt: the extent to which a state must put aside its own exclusive language preferences and permit, or even require public authorities to use a national minority language in addition to an official one.

Article 10 also confronts the often-held belief that a state must be united by a common, or in extreme views, exclusive, working language used by public authorities. This stance has led many states to actively suppress, discourage, or ignore national minority languages and, to this day, some states maintain repressive attitudes and practices premissed on the belief that an official language requires an exclusive linguistic approach.[1]

B. History

In some respects, this provision of the Framework Convention is also a trail-blazer in terms of legal recognition of language rights for national minorities. While other, non-binding instruments suggest that states should not intervene in the private use of a language, or propose that a national minority language ought to be used by public authorities in certain situations, they are not treaties and thus do not of themselves constitute legal obligations. In this category, one can refer to: the UN Declaration on the Rights of Persons Belonging to National or Ethnic, Religious, and Linguistic Minorities; the Organization for Security and Co-operation in Europe (OSCE) Document of the Copenhagen Meeting of the Conference on the Human Dimension; and the Oslo Recommendations regarding the Linguistic Rights of National Minorities. There is one other Council of Europe treaty that deals with minority languages: the European Charter for Regional or Minority Languages. However, the Council of Europe and signatories to this Charter see this document as creating neither individual nor collective rights.

In other ways Article 10 is significant as it gives a clearer legal form to what was beginning to crystallize in various other instruments and a growing number of international decisions. These range from the right of private parties to use a national minority language under freedom of expression, the entitlement to claim the use of a minority language by state officials by the application of non-discrimination in some circumstances, or the use of an individual's language by court and other justice officials when an accused or detainee does not understand the official language in use, or the nature, content, and extent of all of these. All of these rights are increasingly understood. Article 10 incorporates much of this growing legal appreciation of the human rights dimension of

[1] See for a clear example the view of the dissident members of the UN Human Rights Committee in *Ballantyne, Davidson, McIntyre* v. *Canada*, (No. 359/1989) and (No. 385/1989), UN Doc. CCPR/C/47/D/359/1989 and 385/1989/Rev. 1 (1993).

language rights into a tangible form. Because it attempts to bring together a variety of rights which, together, can be generically described as 'language rights' in the sense that they have a considerable impact on language preferences of the state and individuals, this article eventually had to be divided into a number of distinct paragraphs to reflect the distinct origins of the rights involved, and the various debates and consensus or disagreements affecting each.

C. Context

While Article 10 deals with language rights in a general sense, it does not do so exclusively. Other provisions in the treaty address language matters in more specific fields (Article 9 for the media, Article 12 for education, and Article 11 for language use for names, signs, for example). Article 10 may thus be seen as setting out the general approach of the Framework Convention in the two main areas of language rights: the use of a national minority language in private contexts; and the use of a minority language by officials and state institutions.

In this regard, Article 10 appears to indicate how states are to give form to their own rule in terms of language rights according to the solemn declaration in the Preamble that 'a pluralist and genuinely democratic society should not only respect the ethnic, cultural, linguistic and religious identity of each person belonging to a national minority, but also create appropriate conditions enabling them to express, preserve and develop this identity'.

II. Analysis

A. Structure of Article 10

The structure of this provision underlines some of the difficulties raised by the issue of language use. Two of the article's paragraphs were without much controversy at the time of drafting. These were the first paragraph, dealing with the right of a member of a national minority to use his or her language with others (Article 27 of the International Covenant on Civil and Political Rights (ICCPR)), and the third paragraph, dealing with the use of a national minority language in criminal proceedings or contacts with the police and courts when the accused or detained does not understand the language of proceedings (Articles 5 and 6 of the European Convention on the Protection of Human Rights and Fundamental Freedoms (ECHR) and Article 14 ICCPR). Both deal with subject matters long established in European and international treaties, but because they have been generally seen as involving different types of rights, they were recognized in different sections. The first paragraph, for example, deals with what is generally perceived as a strictly 'minority right', whereas the third paragraph does not go beyond the safeguards contained in and normally associated with fair proceedings.

The second paragraph, however, is completely different and was the subject of much more debate at the time of drafting. It is, perhaps, the one section of the Framework Convention which is not only the most challenging, but also contributes the most in both theory and practice for European states. It sets out the conditions under which a state's administrative authorities have an obligation to use a national minority language in contact with members of the public. That individuals may claim such a right from public authorities is novel from the point of view of international and European law, since it is not explicitly recognized in either the ECHR or the ICCPR. It is, perhaps, this paragraph which most directly constitutes a rejection of—or at the very least a qualification of—the concept of *un état, un peuple, une langue*, which can be said to have characterized some views of the nature of European nation-states from a theoretical point of view. Designating a language as 'official' or 'national' does not mean it can or must be exclusive. Given the appropriate context, other languages must also be used by administrative authorities in 'areas inhabited by persons belonging to national minorities traditionally or in substantial numbers' or traditionally inhabited by them.

Because of the structure of this provision, and the various substantive issues that the three paragraphs involve, the drafting background and context for each one will be examined separately in the following section.

B. Article 10(1)

1. Interpretation

Recognition of the right of every person belonging to a national minority to use his or her minority language freely is particularly important and was relatively well established before the adoption of the Framework Convention.

Article 10(1) of the Framework Convention appears largely based on the wording used in Article 27 ICCPR,[2] though most acknowledge that its content may also involve freedom of expression.[3] Other documents reiterate

[2] International Covenant on Civil and Political Rights (ICCPR) (adopted 16 December 1966, entered into force 23 March 1976) 999 UNTS 171, Art. 27 reads: 'In those States in which ethnic, religious or linguistic minorities exist, persons belonging to such minorities shall not be denied the right, in community with the other members of their group, to enjoy their own culture, to profess and practise their own religion, or to use their own language.'

[3] F. de Varennes, *Guide to the Rights of Minorities and Language* (COLPI, Budapest, 2001), 8–11.

that individuals who belong to national (or linguistic minorities) are free to use their language with other members of their group.[4]

Early in the drafting history of this paragraph a wide consensus emerged on the general wording of this segment of Article 10(1). Indeed, except for some minor concerns, the final provision changed very little from an initial proposal in 1990, which read: '[a]ny person belonging to a linguistic minority shall have the right to use his language freely, in public as well as privately.'[5] Essentially, this wording was readopted when the Steering Committee for Human Rights (CDDH) took various texts into account and finalized its report to the Committee of Ministers on 8 September 1993.[6]

While the wording did move away from the actual text of Article 27 ICCPR, it seemed to have been influenced by the then recently approved Document of the Copenhagen Meeting of the Conference on the Human Dimension of the Organization for Security and Co-operation in Europe (OSCE), which stated that persons belonging to national minorities have the right 'to use freely their mother tongue in private as well as in public', and by the work which was being done during the same period on the UN Declaration on the Rights of Persons Belonging to National or Ethnic, Religious, and Linguistic Minorities.

In its wording and content, therefore, Article 10(1) was quite consistent with the developments within other international organizations and instruments by the 1990s, and did not present any significant challenge for its Council of Europe drafters. Perhaps the main issue of concern during its preparation was to ensure an understanding that 'the paragraph concerned the use of a minority language in private relationships, in private and public places, and not in relations with the authorities.'[7]

In and of itself, Article 10(1) does not appear to present any groundbreaking content. Nonetheless, the Framework Convention's own explanatory document does interestingly underline that the provision is closely connected to freedom of

[4] See the Document of the Copenhagen Meeting of the Conference on the Human Dimension of the CSCE, CSCE Second Human Dimension Conference, Copenhagen, 1990, para. 32(1) and the UN Declaration on the Rights of Persons Belonging to National or Ethnic, Religious, or Linguistic Minorities, UNGA Res. 47/135, 1992 amongst others.

[5] Preliminary Draft Convention on the Protection of Minorities, European Commission for Democracy through Law, [DAJ.SC.DEMOCRACY]CONV.MIN., 21 May 1990.

[6] Steering Committee for Human Rights (CDDH), Final Activity Report of the CDDH for the Attention of the Committee of Ministers, CDDH (93) 22, 8 September 1993. Art. 6 reads: 'Every person belonging to a national minority shall have the right to use his/her minority language in private and in public, both orally and in writing. This right shall also apply to the use of the minority language in publications and in the audio-visual sector. This provision does not concern relations between persons belonging to the national minority and the public authorities.'

[7] The Ad Hoc Committee for the Protection of Minorities (CAHMIN) (94) 16, 4th meeting, 1994, Meeting Report, p. 5.

expression rather than Article 27 ICCPR, since Article 10(1) 'enables [national minorities] to exercise their freedom of expression'.[8]

2. *Practice of the Advisory Committee*

That persons belonging to national minorities have the right to use their language in private freely and without interference would appear not to have been highly contentious in terms of its content and its acceptance as a legally enforceable norm. There were few comments or recommendations by the Advisory Committee of Experts dealing specifically with this aspect of Article 10.[9] This might be expected, given that Article 10(1) FCNM is hardly original.

The relative silence of the Advisory Committee on the application of Article 10(1) may also be due to the proximity of this provision's content with that of freedom of expression, a closeness that the Explanatory Report of the Framework Convention acknowledges as well. This means that, on occasion, issues that could be dealt with under Article 10(1) might instead be referred to in Article 7 (under freedom of expression generally). This has occurred in the cases of Liechtenstein and Malta, for example.

There have been, however, a few matters that have raised some concern. One involved national legislation with language provisions, which were interpreted to restrict and prohibit the free use of a national minority language in a private context.

After considering the report from the government of Lithuania, the Advisory Committee pointed out that 'authorities should ensure that . . . provisions are properly implemented in practice, in such a way that the mandatory use of the State language is not extended beyond the public sphere'.[10] It also expressed similar reservations to proposed Russian legislation that could interfere with the use of minority languages in private, especially if it affected private organizations or commercial enterprises.[11] Though not immediately or

[8] CAHMIN Explanatory Report on the Framework Convention for the Protection of National Minorities (1995), Art. 10 para. 1(63).

[9] This has only occurred, usually quite briefly, in the Advisory Committee on the Framework Convention for the Protection of National Minorities, Opinion on Armenia ACFC/INF/OP/I (2003) 001, 2002, Art. 10, para. 55; Opinion on Hungary ACFC/INF/OP/I(2001) 004, 2000, Art. 10, para. 34; Opinion on Lithuania ACFC/INF/OP/I (2003) 008, 2003, para. 53; Opinion on Moldova ACFC/INF/OP/I/ (2003) 002, 2002, Art. 10, para. 58; Opinion on the Russian Federation ACFC/INF/OP/I (2003) 005, 2002, paras. 79–81, 83, and 145; Opinion on Ukraine ACFC/INF/OP/I (2002) 010, 2002, paras. 49–50 and 99; and Opinion on the United Kingdom ACFC/.INF/OP/I (2002) 006 paras. 70 and 119.

[10] Advisory Committee Opinion on Lithuania, ACFC/INF/OP/I (2003) 008, 2003, paras. 55 and 98.

[11] Advisory Committee Opinion on the Russian Federation, ACFC/INF/OP/I (2003) 005, 2002, Art. 10, para. 80.

obviously involving a breach of Article 10(1), the Advisory Committee did signal the unnecessary dangers that poorly drafted or unclear legislation could cause in this regard.

Another matter debated was whether states had to adopt precise legislation to enshrine this right. The Advisory Committee has, on a number of occasions, welcomed the presence of legislation or constitutional provisions unambiguously spelling out that persons belonging to a national minority could freely use their language in private. In the example of a law that does not 'regulate the use of languages in inter-personal unofficial relations or in the activities of non-governmental and religious associations',[12] the Advisory Committee has not gone as far as to state that this, in itself, would constitute a breach of the treaty. It would seem, since Article 10(1) deals with 'linguistic freedom' only and not the provision of public services in a national minority language, that specific legislation might be highly desirable, but not absolutely necessary as long as there were no restrictions on the private use of language.

In addition, there was some useful guidance in areas constituting definite breaches of Article 10(1) (and probably also freedom of expression): some dealt with restrictions affecting the private use of a language, and others with public authorities decreeing an obligation to use a particular alphabet. Specifically, the Advisory Committee's comments on Ukraine's compliance with Article 10 contained the following:

> 49. The Advisory Committee notes that the existing legislation in Ukraine, notably the Law on National Minorities and the Law on Languages, provides for the right of persons belonging to national minorities to use their languages orally and in writing. There have however been certain initiatives, notably at the local level, to introduce norms that would limit this right, including in the private sphere. These include e.g. an unsuccessful attempt by local authorities in Lviv to introduce restrictions on the use of the Russian language in 2000. The Advisory Committee urges the authorities to underline the importance of honouring the right in question and to ensure that no such initiatives are implemented in so far as they would not be compatible with Article 10 or other provisions of the Framework Convention.

Emphasizing that states were perfectly entitled to promote the use of an official language and to ensure its protection,[13] the Advisory Committee added that such a legitimate objective did not authorize a breach of Article 10(1), if it prevented persons belonging to a national minority from using their language freely and without interference 'in private and in public'.

[12] Advisory Committee Opinion on the Russian Federation, ACFC/INF/OP/I (2003) 005, 2002, Art. 10, para. 79.

[13] Advisory Committee Opinion on Ukraine, ACFC/INF/OP/I (2002) 010, 2002, Art. 10, para. 50.

Similarly, while admitting that the situation was 'exceptional', the Advisory Committee concluded that municipal regulations in parts of Switzerland, with the effect of banning private signs not in Romanche, were inconsistent with the state's obligations under the Framework Convention:

> The Advisory Committee *finds* that certain limitations of an exceptional nature to the right to display in a minority language signs, inscriptions and other information of a private nature visible to the public exist in a few municipalities in Graubünden with a view to preserving the Romanche language, whose survival is under threat in some regions. The Advisory Committee *considers* that Romanche could be protected just as well by an obligation to put up bilingual private signs, and encourages the competent authorities to look into this possibility.[14]

Thus, the Advisory Committee has indicated that authorities cannot simply interfere with the use of a national minority language for reasons of policy, protection, or promotion of an official or state language, even if the Constitution itself provides for such measures. While not common in Europe, this line of argument was not unknown. The Advisory Committee has therefore, though in a slightly subdued way, rejected the validity of such considerations as constituting a sufficient ground for restricting the rights contained in Article 10(1), and freedom of expression.

The other specific breach of the Framework Convention, identified by the Advisory Committee, involved the choice of written alphabet. The Advisory Committee was concerned that legislation in the Russian Federation might restrict the private use of language because of legislation decreeing that a language such as Tatar had to be written in a particular alphabet: 'the Advisory Committee is of the opinion that in cases where the use of a language does not concern relations with public authorities, the choice of alphabet should as a rule be left to the discretion of the individuals concerned and not be subject to any normative limitations'.[15]

This is an issue that has arisen in a few other countries, including Moldova and Kazakhstan. Though tentatively, since Article 10 makes no reference to the use of alphabets (whereas Article 11 does), the Advisory Committee has established a connection between 'alphabet' and 'language' *per se*. It has ruled that an alphabet can constitute an integral part of one's language, and, as such, its private use would be covered by provisions, such as Article 10(1), which deal specifically with an individual's right to use a language without restriction

[14] Advisory Committee Opinion on Switzerland, ACFC/INF/OP/I (2003) 007, 2003, para. 96.
[15] Advisory Committee Opinion on the Russian Federation, ACFC/INF/OP/I (2003) 005, 2002, Art. 10, para. 83.

'orally and in writing'. This is one clarification that was greatly needed in international law when considering freedom of expression issues. Consequently, the work of the Advisory Committee is gradually beginning to provide some useful and practical guidance.

3. Overall Interpretation and Future Developments

In its approach to Article 10(1), the Advisory Committee has been fairly clear and consistent in its examination of country reports. There do not appear to be any discrepancies in its opinions on the nature or extent of the obligations under this provision. Its conclusions generally correspond with applicable international human rights laws in the context of Article 10(1) and, in particular, with the inclusion of private language use under the protection of freedom of expression.

Additionally, the Advisory Committee has begun to address how parties should strike the difficult balance between a government's desire to unite its population with an official language and the need to maintain individual liberties in private matters. Thus, even in the case of a legitimate objective such as the protection of the status and even survival of an official language that is 'threatened', as in the case of Romanche in Switzerland, the Advisory Committee has warned that restricting the rights contained in Article 10(1) is not warranted. This is a matter which could be further clarified so as to ensure a greater understanding and consistency, as many states still appear to operate on the mistaken belief that the protection and promotion of an official language is sufficient enough reason to cast aside rights which would fall under Article 10(1), and even the freedom of expression.

C. Article 10(2)

1. Interpretation

The right to have public authorities use a national minority language in 'appropriate circumstances' as far as is possible is one of the most challenging, and perhaps even controversial, provisions of the Framework Convention. As indicated earlier, it directly confronts the issue of whether an official language must necessarily be exclusively favoured and used by the state's apparatus and officials.

It is also a provision that is not widely enshrined in international legal instruments, and thus not generally the subject of international decisions to delimit its boundaries and content. In addition to Article 10 FCNM, only Article 10 of the European Charter for Regional or Minority Languages sets forth a similar type of legal obligation in a treaty. In the latter, however, it is not presented as an individual right, but as an obligation on the part of the state.

It is nevertheless a direction that is referred to, in broadly similar terms, in an increasingly large number of resolutions, declarations, and other documents in the Council of Europe, the European Union (where respect for minority rights is now part of the political criteria for admission of new states to the EU), the OSCE, and the United Nations.[16]

It should also be pointed out that in a limited, though increasing number of cases, the use of a minority language by public authorities has been acknowledged to be a legal obligation under traditional human rights approaches in situations where it was deemed unreasonable or unjustified to use official language exclusively, this involving discrimination on the basis of language. The UN Human Rights Committee has asserted that states cannot, without any justification, unreasonably reject a request for services and information in a minority language,[17] and the European Court of Justice (ECJ) has also recognized language as a 'service' or 'benefit' for citizens of the European Union and that it cannot be withheld in a discriminatory way.[18]

What the above shows, therefore, is that a minority's 'right' to have its language used by public authorities is not yet a well-entrenched entitlement in legal terms at the international level. This also implies that the exact context where such a right can arise is not always clear from its scattered presence in various instruments.

The *travaux préparatoires* of the Framework Convention dealing with Article 10(2) confirm these difficulties, and indeed suggest a great degree of unease in incorporating this provision in the treaty. A number of early Council of Europe attempts to circumscribe the right to have public officials use minority languages were fairly straightforward, referring, for example, to situations where 'a minority reaches a high percentage of the population of a region or of the total population' before the right to have that minority's language used by administrative and other authorities could be activated.[19]

[16] Among these numerous non-binding instruments are the Declaration on the Rights of Persons Belonging to National or Ethnic, Religious, and Linguistic Minorities, Recommendation 1134 (1990) on the Rights of Minorities, Recommendation 13 of the Oslo Recommendations regarding the Linguistic Rights of National Minorities, and the OSCE Document of the Copenhagen Meeting of the Conference on the Human Dimension.

[17] *Diergaardt* v. *Namibia*, (No. 760/1997), UN Doc. CCPR/C/69/D/760/1997 (2000).

[18] Case 137/84 *Ministère public* v. *Mutsch* [1985] ECR 2681 and Case C-275/96 *Bickel and Franz* v. *Italy* [1998] ECR I-7637.

[19] European Commission for Democracy through Law, Set of Principles on National Minorities, Draft Report of the 4th Meeting, CD-PV(90) 4 PRO, 1990, para. 11.

As the draft treaty started to take definite shape, some of the drafters felt it necessary to qualify this right. In February 1993, the provision was still rather unambiguous with few limitations: '[w]henever a minority reaches a substantial percentage of the population of a region or of the total population, its members shall have the right, as far as possible, to speak and write in their own language to the political, administrative and judicial authorities of this region or, where appropriate, of the State.'[20] The limitation to situations of 'substantial numbers' and 'as far as possible' was, as explained in the Explanatory Report of the European Commission for Democracy through Law, necessary 'given the difficulties involved in recognising the right of a minority to use its own language in its relations with the administrative authorities', and in particular 'when the financial means of the State concerned are insufficient or when the number of persons belonging to the minority concerned is too small'.[21]

The absence of a specific percentage or number at which the right to have public officials use a minority language crystallizes difficulties in the interpretation of Article 10(2), but this was a deliberate decision that was made early on. On this the *travaux préparatoires* are quite clear, since the exact point where individuals would be entitled to have their language used by administrative authorities would depend, to a large degree, on the particular context and a multitude of factors at work in the state involved:

> The proposal for a Convention deliberately avoids specifying the percentage above which people belonging to a minority shall be entitled to address administrative authorities in their own language. It seemed preferable to opt for flexible wording to take account of the individual circumstances of the State concerned, including its financial resources.[22]

One consistent element in the drafting process that should be emphasized is the requirement for states to act 'as far as possible'; according to the conditions set out in what has become Article 10(2). As indicated in other chapters, it would seem to show that states must act to the maximum of their abilities and resources in using a minority language, consistent with the overall object and intent to protect national minorities as shown in the Preamble.

By 1994, a number of conditions to the exercise of this right had been added with a number of drafters expressing a 'certain lack of enthusiasm' for any provision on the use of minority languages by public institutions. The price for

[20] European Commission for Democracy through Law, Proposal for a European Convention for the Protection of National Minorities, CDL-MIN(93) 6, 1993, Art. 8.

[21] European Commission for Democracy through Law, Explanatory Report to the Proposal for a European Convention for the Protection of National Minorities, CDL-MIN(93) 7, 1993, para. 32.

[22] Above, n. 21, para. 34.

agreeing to incorporate Article 10(2) was to permit 'restrictions leaving a wide margin of appreciation to the Parties',[23] including the adoption of phrases such as 'parties shall endeavour' and other softening terms.

Because of administrative, financial, and even technical concerns, it was therefore agreed that there ought to be a flexible approach taking two broad categories of conditions into account: (1) 'significant number/proportion' or traditional areas; as well as (2) demand and the actual need for the use of the minority language.[24] Subsequent drafts involved some adjustments in the exact wording, but the basic substantive elements of the provision were in place by this point. There were attempts to heighten the impact of what was to become Article 10(2), most notably by the Austrian delegation,[25] but the draft would not change in any fundamental way overall. It is currently characterized by a large number of 'escape clauses', from earlier compromises owing to 'a certain lack of enthusiasm'.

To facilitate the interpretation of Article 10(2), the drafters of the Framework Convention decided to use the Explanatory Report extensively, describing in greater detail than for other provisions how its legal obligations should be understood. It clearly explains, for example, that Article 10(2) only extends to administrative authorities, though this must be broadly interpreted.[26] Similarly, it repeats the results of the *travaux préparatoires*: the provision must be, because of 'possible financial, administrative, in particular in the military field, and technical difficulties', understood to leave parties 'a wide measure of discretion'.[27]

Despite the wide discretion of the parties, once they have met the conditions in paragraph 2, they have the obligation to 'endeavour to ensure the use of a minority language in relations with the administrative authorities as far as possible',[28] with the 'real need' criterion to be assessed objectively.

Two other points are emphasized in the Explanatory Report. One deals with the impact of these language rights on the status of a state's official language, while the other considers geographical area in determining the application of Article 10(2):

66. The Parties' obligations regarding the use of minority languages do not in any way affect the status of the official language or languages of the country concerned. Moreover, the framework Convention deliberately refrains from defining 'areas

[23] CAHMIN, Preparatory Work (94) 13, 3rd meeting 1994, Meeting Report, para. 17.

[24] Above n. 23, para. 18.

[25] CAHMIN, Proposals concerning the Preliminary Draft Framework Convention for the Protection of National Minorities (94) 12 Rev., 1994.

[26] CAHMIN, Explanatory Report on the Framework Convention for the Protection of National Minorities (95) 010, 1995, Art. 10, para. 2(64).

[27] Above, n. 26.

[28] ibid., Art. 10, para. 2(65).

inhabited by persons belonging to national minorities traditionally or in substantial numbers'. It was considered preferable to adopt a flexible form of wording that will allow each Party's particular circumstances to be taken into account. The term 'inhabited . . . traditionally' does not refer to historical minorities, but only to those still living in the same geographical area (see also Article 11, paragraph 3, and Article 14, paragraph 2).[29]

In other words, Article 10(2) must not be interpreted so as to diminish the status of an official language: Article 10(2) simply indicates a number of situations where an official language cannot be the exclusive language of administrative authorities.[30] As for the aspect of geographical area covered by Article 10(2), together with Framework Convention Articles 11(3) and 14(2), the Explanatory Report offers useful guidance on the interpretation of the expression 'inhabited traditionally'. Although it sometimes appears that parties assume the Framework Convention is limited to 'historical minorities', the Explanatory Report suggests this is not necessarily the case. The term used in the treaty is better understood as referring to areas where one usually finds minorities geographically concentrated, but this concentration does not necessarily need to be a historical one.

From the *travaux préparatoires* and Explanatory Report, it would seem that the Advisory Committee has to involve itself in a balancing act between the 'demand' and 'supply' sides of Article 10(2). On the demand side, an area inhabited by persons belonging to traditional national minorities, from which there is a request corresponding to a real need, has to be present. On the supply side, as far as is possible given the state's circumstances (financial resources, for example), a party to the treaty has to make efforts to ensure the possibility of using the minority language in contacts with administrative authorities.

While the wording of Article 10(2) initially appears to be cautious and even restrictive in comparison to the wording of other similar instruments, particularly non-binding ones, overall it remains broadly consistent: where justified and reasonable to do so, a state must, to the limit of its abilities, respond in a proportionate way to the language preferences of its population.

2. *Practice of the Advisory Committee*

The more controversial evolution and content of Article 10(2), including the numerous conditions and vague terms used in its final form and the possible

[29] CAHMIN, Explanatory Report on the Framework Convention for the Protection of National Minorities (95) 010, 1995, Art. 10, para. 2(65).

[30] See also the Advisory Committee Opinion on Ukraine, ACFC/INF/OP/I (2002) 010, 2002, Art. 10, para. 50: 'while the aim to protect the official language is a legitimate one, it is instrumental that this protection is carried out in a manner that fully protects the rights contained in Articles 10'.

linkage between this type of right and the prohibition of discrimination on the ground of language, help to explain the extensive observations of the Advisory Committee. Broadly, these can be divided into two categories: observations and recommendations on the need for clear legislation setting out the circumstances where an individual could seek to have his or her language used by administrative authorities; and opinions of the Advisory Committee as to a party's compliance with the specific legal obligations under Article 10(2).

In the first case, the need for clear legislation needs to be explained. In the case of linguistic freedom involving private parties, the absence of legislation has not necessarily been a major concern since individuals are generally free to conduct their affairs as they wish, including in the use of a national minority language. The absence of clear guidelines explaining the relationship between administrative authorities and individuals is different, however. State employees without legal obligations to respond to an individual's language preference can simply choose to ignore any request, leaving individuals with no effective entitlement. The Advisory Committee acknowledged this in Armenia where:

> 101. The Advisory Committee *finds* that there is a lack of precision in Armenian legislation on the right to use minority languages in relations with the administrative authorities and notes that, according to the authorities, such a possibility exists in areas inhabited by a sufficient number of persons belonging to national minorities. The Advisory Committee *considers* that this possibility should not be left solely to the discretion of the authorities concerned and that appropriate measures should be taken, including at legislative level, to ensure the effective application of this right.[31]

The absence of legislative clarity is, in the view of the Advisory Committee, 'not in full conformity' with the legal obligations of the Framework Convention.[32] This has not been consistently the case, however, since it has remained oddly tolerant and even inconsistent in the face of other parties lacking clear legislation.[33] This lack of consistency obscures the legal obligations of the parties under the treaty, especially as there are no objective criteria on which the parties can rely as a guide.

[31] Advisory Committee Opinion on Armenia, ACFC/INF/OP/I (2003) 001, 2002, para. 101.

[32] Advisory Committee Opinion on Albania, ACFC/INF/OP/I (2003) 003, 2002, para. 99. See also Advisory Committee Opinion on the Czech Republic, ACFC/INF/OP/I (2002) 002, 2001, Art. 10, para. 55, and Advisory Committee Opinion on Slovakia ACFC/INF/OP/I (2001) 001, 2000, Art. 10, para. 36.

[33] Advisory Committee Opinion on the United Kingdom, ACFC/INF/OP/I (2002) 006, 2001, para. 119 concerning the Irish language in Northern Ireland.

The significance of having legislation guaranteeing the use of a minority language by administrative authorities was further elaborated in the report on the situation in Estonia. Here, the Advisory Committee went to some length to explain why clear legislation was needed, in addition to constitutional guarantees:

40. While welcoming the fact that the use of minority languages in relations between persons belonging to national minorities and the administrative authorities is recognised even at the constitutional level, the Advisory Committee considers that the current legislative framework relating to this issue lacks clarity. This stems partially from the fact that it is unclear to what extent the restrictive definition of the term national minority provided in other contexts (see related comments under Article 3) applies to the provisions that pertain to the use of minority languages, in particular in the Constitution and in the Language Act.[34]

Some Estonian officials did not interpret the law in a restrictive sense in the case of the Russian language, meaning that many minorities could use their own language with administrative authorities. This was not very helpful for speakers of other languages, however.[35] The Committee of Ministers agreed that such a situation remained a potential breach of the treaty and adopted a resolution calling for Estonia to address the remaining 'shortcomings' in its relevant legislation.[36]

Acknowledging that this type of legislation cannot operate in a vacuum, the Advisory Committee has occasionally clarified that once such legislation is in place, authorities have the further obligation to ensure that it is properly applied, and that sufficient resources are in place, including appropriate measures to recruit staff and provide language training.[37]

The second broad category of comments addresses the conditions under which administrative authorities need to use a minority language consequent to specific obligations emanating from Article 10(2). Unfortunately, a number of inconsistencies and vague observations continue to cloud the Advisory Committee's view and application of Article 10(2). As indicated earlier, the right to have a minority language used by administrative authorities is not absolute and is subject to two conditions: '1. The demand for minority language use must emanate from "areas inhabited by persons belonging to

[34] Advisory Committee Opinion on Estonia, ACFC/INF/OP/I (2002) 005, 2001, Art. 10, para. 40.

[35] Above, n. 34, Art. 10, para. 41.

[36] Resolution on the Implementation of the Framework Convention for the Protection of National Minorities by Estonia, Adopted by the Committee of Ministers at the 799th meeting of the Ministers' Deputies, ResCMN (2002) 8, 2002.

[37] Advisory Committee Opinion on Romania, ACFC/INF/OP/I (2002) 001, 2001, Art. 10, para. 50.

national minorities traditionally or in substantial numbers"; and 2. Only when persons in this area request the service and it corresponds to a real need.' Once these two conditions have been satisfied, parties must try to ensure, as far as possible, that conditions facilitating communication between persons in need and the administrative authorities in the minority language are put in place.

The first condition specific under Article 10(2) is less demanding than in the case of Article 11(2). Even if there are not 'substantial numbers' in a given area, it is sufficient that the demand come from an area traditionally inhabited by persons belonging to a national minority for a state to have an obligation to have administrative authorities use the minority language. The second, but lesser, focus on the demographic importance of national minorities may appear initially surprising. It is, however, quite understandable since, for the purposes of Article 10(2), it is sufficient for an area to be traditionally inhabited by a national minority group for persons belonging to a national minority to claim this right. They do not have to be present in 'substantial numbers': meeting one of the criteria, either 'substantial numbers' *or* an area traditionally inhabited by a national minority, is sufficient.

For this reason the Advisory Committee has not been overly concerned with the 'numbers game'. As long as one is dealing with an area traditionally inhabited by a national minority, there is no reason to be entirely focused on whether or not their numbers are or have been 'substantial' enough:

> As concerns Article 10 paragraph 2, the Advisory Committee notes that the use of minority languages in relations with administrative authorities is rather limited. The German authorities explain . . . that this state of affairs is often due, *inter alia*, to the relatively small percentage of persons belonging to national minorities in administrative districts where they reside traditionally. However, the Advisory Committee observes that Article 10 paragraph 2 also applies to such situations provided persons belonging to national minorities traditionally inhabit the areas concerned, if there is a request by such persons and if such a request corresponds to a real need.[38]

This might explain for example that when state legislation did refer to 'substantial numbers', as in the case of Croatia,[39] where persons belonging to a national minority had to be in a majority in order to qualify for the use of their language by administrative authorities, the Advisory Committee indicated that this numerical requirement was too high, advising the Croatian government to 'take measures aimed at obtaining a maximum level of implementation of the

38 Advisory Committee Opinion on Germany, ACFC/INF/OP/I (2002) 009, 2002, Art. 10, para. 48.

39 Advisory Committee Opinion on Croatia, ACFC/INF/OP/I (2002) 003, 2001, Art. 10, para. 44.

law'.[40] Though the Advisory Committee might have explained more clearly its reasons for such a conclusion, it presumably meant that Croatian legislation was more restrictive than what individuals are able to claim under the numerical thresholds under Article 10(2) for the use of a minority language by administrative authorities.

The Advisory Committee has, on other occasions, not always clearly or consistently explained some of its views, especially since the wording of Article 10(2) is accommodating in terms of what it requires as a threshold of minority language use. In the case of Austria, the Advisory Committee seemed to go out of its way to examine the threshold closely under various treaty and legislative provisions and even court cases dealing with the use of national minority languages, mainly Croatian, Slovenian, and Hungarian. It welcomed, for example, an October 2000 ruling of the Constitutional Court concluding that a municipality with at least 10 per cent Slovene speakers 'should be considered an administrative district with mixed populations within the meaning of a treaty provision . . . thus enabling its use in official dealings'.[41] The Advisory Committee did not explain why the 10 per cent threshold was significant if the Slovenes were living in a traditional area. This same failure to explain the relevance of percentages of minorities living in a traditional area, applicable under Article 10(2), occurred in other opinions. In its findings on Estonia, Moldova, and Ukraine however, the Advisory Committee unambiguously confirmed that requiring a minority to constitute the majority of inhabitants in a municipality in order to be entitled to use their language with administrative authorities was too high a bar, and did not fully comply with Article 10(2).[42]

The Advisory Committee's desire to be positive, rather than constantly critical, in its efforts to have states comply with the Framework Convention helps to account for what may initially be seen as inconsistencies or contradictions in its rulings. Thus, in the case of Slovakia, the Advisory Committee described a law as 'a positive step in terms of the implementation of Article 10 of the Framework Convention' when it allowed for minority language use by authorities if a national minority constituted 20 per cent of the population of a municipality.[43] The Advisory Committee did not state that Slovakia fully complied with the

[40] Advisory Committee Opinion on Croatia, ACFC/INF/OP/I (2002) 003, 2001, Art. 10, para. 44.

[41] Advisory Committee Opinion on Austria, ACFC/INF/OP/I (2002) 003, 2001, Art. 10, para. 45.

[42] Advisory Committee Opinion on Estonia, ACFC/INF/OP/I (2002) 005, 2001, Art. 10, para. 40; Advisory Committee Opinion on Moldova, ACFC/INF/OP/I (2003) 002, 2002, Art. 10, para. 62, and Advisory Committee Opinion on Ukraine, ACFC/INF/OP/I (2002) 010, 2002, Art. 10, para. 51.

[43] Advisory Committee Opinion on Slovakia, ACFC/INF/OP/I (2001) 001, 2000, Art. 10, para. 36; see similar comments in Advisory Committee Opinion on Romania, ACFC/INF/OP/I (2002) 001, 2001, Art. 10, para. 49.

treaty, or even that this threshold of 20 per cent was acceptable in terms of Article 10(2). It simply acknowledged that it was taking a step in the right direction. Indeed, if one assumes that many national minorities in Slovakia live in traditional areas, and that the Advisory Committee has made similar statements when dealing with Sami in Nordic countries for example, it becomes clear that setting a high percentage risks creating a breach of Article 10.

Another disappointing ambiguity appears in the case of the opinion on Finland, where the Advisory Committee seemed to comment on whether the state was properly applying its own internal legislation, rather than directly and clearly addressing the content of its obligations under the Framework Convention as is the Advisory Committee's mandate. Furthermore, when pointing out 'implementation difficulties' in the use of the Swedish language in criminal proceedings, the Advisory Committee failed to clarify how these difficulties involved any breach of Article 10, thus offering no useful understanding of a state's actual obligations.[44] Similarly, in the case of Sami language use, the Advisory Committee noted that Finland had to address problems in the implementation of Finnish legislation dealing with the use of these languages, such as the lack of interpretative services in meetings of municipal authorities, without explaining which provision of the Framework Convention this comment applied to.[45] The same criticism could be made when the Advisory Committee referred to the need to fully implement legislation or another treaty such as the European Charter for Regional or Minority Languages, without explaining how and where, or even if, Norway had failed to meet its own obligations on dealing with Sami languages under Article 10(2),[46] which is where its mandate rightly falls.

The Advisory Committee also made general observations on the situation in a number of other states. In relation to Estonia, it merely stated that protecting and promoting the Estonian language was an important and legitimate function without excusing possible violations of Articles 10 and 11 FCNM.[47] Such imprecise 'warnings' are not helpful as they imply that Estonia is in breach of the treaty, yet they do not specify where and how violations occur, or how this could be avoided in the future. Similar comments have been made in a number of other opinions.[48] Such observations, once again, are in a general sense 'relevant', but not helpful legally speaking since they do not expressly clarify the content and extent of state obligations under Article 10(2). In the

44 Advisory Committee Opinion on Finland, ACFC/INF/OP/I (2001) 002, 2000, Art. 10, para. 33.
45 Above, n. 44, Art. 10, para. 34.
46 Advisory Committee Opinion on Norway, ACFC/INF/OP/I (2003) 003, 2002, Art. 10, para. 46.
47 Advisory Committee Opinion on Estonia, ACFC/INF/OP/I (2002) 005, 2001, Art. 10, para. 39.
48 Advisory Committee Opinion on Germany, ACFC/INF/OP/I (2002) 009, 2002, para. 93.

interests of better practice, one would hope that the Advisory Committee would explain the objective approach that it has adopted more precisely, so that parties can implement the Framework Convention more effectively.

There are, nevertheless, a few important matters where the Advisory Committee has determined the proper implementation of Article 10(2). It pointed out, for example, that the linguistic rights guaranteed under Article 10 appear unaffected by the ability of persons belonging to a national minority to use the state's official language.[49]

Though not explicitly stated, the requirement of a 'real need' for the use of a national minority language under Article 10(2) is not, therefore, dependent on lack of proficiency in the official language used by administrative authorities. Even if members of a minority are able to use and understand the official language perfectly, they are still entitled to seek the use of their own language, 'as far as possible', by administrative authorities. Disappointingly, there is no further guidance as to how exactly 'a real need' is to be understood.

Another interesting advancement that the Advisory Committee has tentatively introduced is that states have an obligation of 'active offer' under Article 10 of the Framework Convention. While not consistent in its opinions corresponding to this obligation, on a number of occasions the Advisory Committee seemed to imply that it is not sufficient for states to make it possible to use a national minority language where there are substantial numbers or in a traditional area. States must actively ensure that individuals can in practice exercise this right.[50] This is a controversial point, however. For Germany, the Advisory Committee went beyond the letter of the law in its view of the Framework Convention obligations, and thus the government stated:

> Putting up of notices on office doors stating that staff have knowledge of the Sorbian language is viewed with some reserve. The objective [of Article 10(2)] is to meet the already existing demand for use of the Sorbian language in dealings with administrative authorities, but not to create a demand that is not there in the first place. The obligations arising from the Framework Convention are understood to mean that the relevant needs of the population should be met and people who have mental barriers should be encouraged to use the Sorbian language wherever necessary, but that the aim should not be to create a demand that does not exist in the first place.[51]

[49] Advisory Committee Opinion on Germany, ACFC/INF/OP/I (2002) 009, 2002, Art. 10, para. 49: 'the fact that persons belonging to national minorities also have a command of the German language is not decisive as the effective use of minority languages remains essential to consolidate the presence of those languages in the public sphere.'

[50] Above, n. 49, para. 85.

[51] Comments of the Government of Germany on the Opinion of the Advisory Committee on the Implementation of the Framework Convention for the Protection of National Minorities in Germany, GVT/COM/INF/OP/I (2002) 008, 2002.

The German reading and reaction to the treaty is not necessarily correct, however. Given the principles and objectives of the Framework Convention in the Preamble, as well as a state's obligation to have administrative authorities use a minority language 'as far as possible', where certain conditions are met (as in the case of the Sorbian-speaking minority), it would not seem inappropriate to take steps to ensure that persons belonging to a national minority are informed of when, where, and how they are entitled to use their language with administrative authorities. In other words, it would be difficult for a demand to exist in the use of a national minority language unless individuals know that they are entitled to ask, and potentially obtain, this service from administrative authorities. It is not enough, therefore, to have legislation in place that conforms to the letter and spirit of Article 10(2). States need to actively 'ascertain that persons belonging to national minorities are really able to enjoy and exercise their rights'.[52] It would seem that, as far as possible, persons belonging to a national minority must not only 'not be discouraged'[53] in using their language with administrative authorities, but all reasonable steps should be taken to 'examine to what extent there exists demand for the use of minority languages' and 'to what extent such demands have been met in practice', signalling the need for proactive state behaviour.[54]

What remain disappointing are the Advisory Committee's vague opinions. While it seems to uphold the obligation of 'active offer' by administrative authorities, it does not actually elaborate as to what this is or what form it should take. Furthermore, and for this reason the German reaction is perhaps understandable, the Advisory Committee does not always appear consistent in its interpretation of the Framework Convention. While 'castigating' Germany for not being proactive enough in relation to the Sorbian language issue, even in the face of an apparently low level of demand, the Advisory Committee appeared oddly silent and arguably docile in not similarly commenting in a comparable case in its report on the United Kingdom. At issue there was the United Kingdom's lack of active offer, and lack of legislation governing the use of the Irish language in Northern Ireland. Here however, the Advisory Committee commented that 'the use of minority languages in private and in public and with administrative authorities is significantly less developed in Northern Ireland'.[55] Despite this lack of consistency, it is foreseeable that, in

[52] Advisory Committee Opinion on Hungary, ACFC/INF/OP/I (2001) 004, 2000, Art. 10, para. 35.

[53] Advisory Committee Opinion on Italy, ACFC/INF/OP/I (2002) 007, 2001, Art. 10, para. 48.

[54] Advisory Committee Opinion on Norway, ACFC/INF/OP/I (2003) 003, 2002, Art. 10, para. 47.

[55] Advisory Committee Opinion on the United Kingdom, ACFC/INF/OP/I (2002) 006, 2001, para. 119.

future opinions, the matter of active offer will probably be further addressed by the Advisory Committee. This should provide a clearer understanding of how this relates to the proper implementation of Article 10(2).

A final issue where the Advisory Committee has provided some guidance is over what constitutes an appropriate 'area' for the purposes of Article 10(2). Perhaps surprisingly this is not a matter that is simply left to a state's determination or discretion. The Advisory Committee noted with interest 'that the procedure for demarcating the areas in which the measures [for the use of minority languages] are to apply can be initiated, in particular, at the call of at least 15% of citizens registered as voters and resident within the boundaries of the municipalities concerned.'[56] While not actually stating that this was a requirement for compliance with the specific obligations under Article 10(2), the Advisory Committee seemed to be indicating what was 'highly desirable' in light of the Framework Convention, and the need to be as flexible and generous as possible in this regard, including in the process of determining the parameters of what constitutes an area for administrative authorities corresponding to 'coherent protection perimeters for the linguistic minorities concerned'.[57]

3. *Overall Interpretation and Future Developments*

The clarity and consistency of the Advisory Committee's comments in relation to Article 10(2) have been somewhat disappointing. As it is the first specific international legal standard that recognizes an individual's right to claim the use of a minority language by public authorities, one would expect interpretative challenges. Nevertheless, one would also have hoped that the Advisory Committee could have been more precise and concrete in explaining how to understand and interpret the various conditions for the application of Article 10(2).

For example, its monitoring of Article 10(2) would benefit from clearer distinctions in its opinions on how conditions such as 'if those persons so request and where such a request corresponds to a real need' ought to be interpreted. In most of its opinions, the Advisory Committee has only broadly indicated what it feels is appropriate in relation to a state's use of minority languages by administrative authorities. Unfortunately, these broad indications have not been linked to the actual wording of Article 10(2). As the Advisory Committee is working with a legally binding instrument, rules of treaty interpretation would warrant, from a purely legal point of view, a more methodical approach to interpreting the treaty's obligations. Clarifications on this basis would ensure that parties are given unambiguous and precise direction regarding their obligations.

[56] Advisory Committee Opinion on Italy, ACFC/INF/OP/I (2002) 007, 2001, Art. 10, para. 49.
[57] Above, n. 56, Art. 10, para. 50.

One unfortunate consequence of this lack of clarity and consistency is the uncertainty and frustration that could result. It is difficult to reconcile the Advisory Committee's criticisms of Germany's legislative and other measures in relation to the use of the Sorbian language by administrative authorities with its diffident comments to the United Kingdom, despite the latter having essentially no legislation for the use of the Irish language in Northern Ireland. The omission, or lack of clear legislation, setting out how and when a minority language can be used by administrative authorities has been interpreted as inconsistent with other articles of the Framework Convention for other states. Unclear interpretations will continue, however, as the case of the UK has not been ruled in conjunction with related case law founded on Article 10(2).

On the more constructive side, the Advisory Committee has provided useful clarifications as to a state's obligations under Article 10(2), emphasizing that states must attempt to ensure that, 'as far as is possible', administrative authorities use minority languages. Given the objectives and nature of the Framework Convention as indicated in the earlier part of this book, it needs to be accentuated that the treaty ought to be interpreted in the spirit of tolerance and respect of linguistic and cultural diversity, consistent for democratic societies and in a maximalist yet faithful way.

In this regard, the Advisory Committee has already contributed to an improved understanding of Article 10(2)'s obligations by explaining that the 'numbers game' is not a central one for the purposes of this provision. Since a national minority living in a traditional area is entitled to have its language used by administrative authorities as far as is possible, if those persons so request and where this request corresponds to a real need, the question whether they are in sufficient—read substantial—numbers becomes secondary. Although the Advisory Committee has not stated it explicitly, it would appear that the determination of what is possible for administrative authorities to provide and of what constitutes a real need may require an examination of the numbers of potential users of a minority language. This explains why the Advisory Committee continues to examine the validity of any numerical or percentage threshold in legislation covering the use of minority languages by administrative authorities.

The Advisory Committee has also provided useful guidance in proposing that states parties are responsible for taking proactive measures to ensure individuals are not just provided with a legal framework, but using the minority language in question is possible in practice should they choose to freely exercise this right. In other words, it would seem that there is an obligation of active offer on the part of authorities, which pushes states to act 'as far as is possible' in implementing their obligations under Article 10(2).

Overall, the Advisory Committee has begun to uphold the need for flexibility and the accommodation of linguistic differences with respect to a state's linguistic preferences and policies. Given the diversity of languages, populations, and contexts, the Advisory Committee must also be mindful of the legitimacy of an official language's special position and unifying potential when attempting to strike a balance between the two sides.

D. Article 10(3)

1. Interpretation

Article 10(3) is another rather uncontroversial section of the Framework Convention which was not the subject of any substantial disagreement at the time of its drafting. It reflects the widely acknowledged right of an individual facing arrest, detention, or trial not to be subjected to Kafkaesque dealings which would occur if he or she did not understanding the language used by police or court officials.

This may be the least contentious part of the Framework Convention since, according to the Council of Europe's Explanatory Report: '[t]his paragraph is based on certain provisions contained in Articles 5 and 6 of the European Convention on Human Rights. It does not go beyond the safeguards contained in those articles.'[58] Indeed, when the Steering Committee for Human Rights (CDDH) presented its final report and wording for what was to become Article 10(3), one expert considered the right quite unnecessary in view of the existing provisions of the European Convention on Human Rights.[59]

In this regard, the right of every accused person to an interpreter in criminal proceedings, including the translation of court documents if he or she does not understand the language used in the proceedings, and the right to be informed of the reasons for the arrest and/or detention, and of the nature and cause of any accusation in a language he or she understands, are well established in international human rights treaties. This is clearly indicated in treaty provisions such as Article 14(3)(*f*) ICCPR; and Article 6(3)(*a*) ECHR, amongst others.[60]

[58] CAHMIN, Explanatory Report on the Framework Convention for the Protection of National Minorities (95) 010, 1995, Art. 10 para. 3(67).

[59] Steering Committee for Human Rights (CDDH), Final Activity Report for the Attention of the Committee of Ministers (93) 22, 1993, p. 16.

[60] See Art. 14(3)(*a*) ICCPR; European Convention for the Protection of Human Rights and Fundamental Freedoms (ECHR), ETS 5, 1950, Art. 5(2); and Art. 10(3) FCNM. It is also contained in the Oslo Recommendation 17 regarding the Linguistic Rights of National Minorities, which is not a legally binding document.

A number of European Court of Human Rights (ECtHR) and UN Human Rights Committee decisions and views also confirm this right, indicating its possible scope and limitations.[61]

It should be underlined that Article 10(3) does not actually refer to any right in relation to the use of a national minority language, as such. It only guarantees that an individual must receive certain information and proceedings in 'a' language he or she understands. This might be neither his or her language of preference, nor necessarily a minority language. The limits of this guarantee are consistent with the nature of the rights in this particular section, dealing with traditional concepts and guarantees for fair trials in general.[62]

In the drafting, one point of contention was whether individuals should be able to use a national minority language before judicial authorities 'in areas inhabited by persons belonging to national minorities traditionally or in substantial numbers'. In such a case it would not matter if an individual knew the language of the proceedings, since observing this right would justifiably require the courts to use a national minority language if there were a sufficient number of persons belonging to a national minority present in the relevant area.

This possibility was eventually rejected, though not without some strong divisions among the Council of Europe's experts:

> 19. The Committee discussed the right to use minority language in penal proceedings. A majority was of the opinion that this should not be included in the framework Convention, arguing that such a right would offer little to promote the identity of national minorities. An important minority of experts however was in favour of including a text that would not go beyond the guarantee of Article 6 ECHR. It was therefore decided not to reject this idea at this stage, but to prepare a draft text on a provisional basis. Several experts felt that this right could not stand alone, without any reference to the general fair trial guarantee.[63]

In light of the drafting history and wording of Article 10(3), it would appear that persons belonging to national minorities do not have a right to have their language used by 'judicial' authorities in areas they inhabit traditionally or in substantial numbers. Article 10(3) only requires the use of 'a' language understood by certain court or law officers if a person who belongs to a national minority does not understand the language they use.

[61] See *Isop* v. *Austria*, Application No. 808/60, (1962): 108 YBECHR 5; *Dominique Guesdon* v. *France*, Comm. No. 219/1986 (1990), UN Doc. CCPR/C/39/D/219/1986; *Kamasinski* v. *Austria* No. 9783/82 (1989) ECHR 24; *Brozicek* v. *Italy* Series A, No. 167, 1096/84 (1989) ECHR 23.

[62] CDDH, Final Activity Report for the Attention of the Committee of Ministers, (93) 22, 1993, pp. 6–7.

[63] Above, n. 23, paras. 6–7.

However, as pointed out in the examination of Article 10(2), it would seem that the concept of 'administrative authorities' is broad enough to include the judicial process. This means that where persons belonging to a national minority inhabit a traditional area of that minority and are present in substantial numbers, they may be entitled to claim their right to be heard and use their language under Article 10(2) instead of 10(3).

2. *Practice of the Advisory Committee*

Because of the uncontroversial nature of Article 10(3)'s content and its widespread and long-standing recognition as a fundamental human right already guaranteed under the ECHR and the ICCPR, among others, there were very few observations or recommendations made in respect to this section. Instead, a number of governments went to some length to indicate their complete compliance with this right.[64]

While there have been no difficulties in reaching agreement on the right's content and its recognition, some practical difficulties resulted in countries with a lack of interpreters. In the case of the Czech Republic, the government itself admitted that this was a problem it was trying to address in some circumstances. The Advisory Committee had no choice but to concur that these problems had to be dealt with in a timely fashion in order to avoid a breach of Article 10(3): '[i]n addition, [the Czech Government] notes the difficulties that arise in this area because of a shortage of interpreters of the Roma language. The Advisory Committee encourages the Czech authorities to take any measures likely to improve this situation.'[65]

A similar problem was identified in Moldova, where the Advisory Committee was made aware of financial resource shortages in that country. In order to comply with the obligations of the Framework Convention, authorities had to 'take all necessary measures to ensure that this right is fully safeguarded'.[66]

3. *Overall Interpretation and Future Developments*

The interpretation of Article 10(3) put forward by the Advisory Committee follows the approach consistently applied by the ECtHR and other international bodies when a person faces arrest or court proceedings in a language

[64] See as examples the Report Submitted by Albania Pursuant to Article 25, Paragraph 1 of the Framework Convention for the Protection of National Minorities, ACFC/SR (2001) 5, para. 44; the Report Submitted by Armenia Pursuant to Article 25, Paragraph 1 of the Framework Convention for the Protection of National Minorities, ACFC/SR (2001) 004, para. 81.

[65] Advisory Committee Opinion on the Czech Republic, ACFC/INF/OP/I (2002) 002, 2001, Art. 10, para. 57.

[66] Advisory Committee Opinion on Moldova, ACFC/INF/OP/I (2002), Art. 10, Para. 64.

that he or she does not understand, and is consonant with this widely acknowledged basic human right.[67] One could still criticize the guidance that the Framework Convention has provided in its recommendations to states, however. While it is not in the Advisory Committee's mandate to provide exact details as to what measures or programmes need to be put in place to redress breaches of the Framework Convention, it is no more helpful to state that states must take 'necessary measures' without determining what 'necessary' entails.

III. Conclusion and Outlook

The Advisory Committee has been largely successful in setting out how to reconcile the unique and legitimate status of a state's official language(s) with complementary obligations to use minority languages in the contexts provided for under Article 10. Its approach is maximalist, inclusive, and accommodative in a general sense, and is consistent with the objectives of the Framework Convention to respect 'the ethnic, cultural, linguistic and religious identity of each person belonging to a national minority' where parties have accepted the need to 'create conditions enabling them to express, preserve and develop this identify' as announced in the treaty's Preamble.

Perhaps if there is another common thread in the Advisory Committee's opinions on the implementation of Article 10, it is that a state's official language should never be mistaken for permission to establish an exclusive state language policy. However legitimate it may be to have measures supporting and spreading knowledge of the official language, this must not be at the expense of the rights to use a minority language as outlined in Article 10. This is especially true in cases where these rights are, in fact, linked to the exercise of fundamental rights such as freedom of expression and non-discrimination.

The Advisory Committee has generally pointed out that clear legislation or constitutional provisions are required to ensure that persons belonging to a national minority may, in fact and in law, enjoy the rights they are entitled to under the Framework Convention. Put more simply, the absence of clear laws is to be avoided, as it could potentially lead to breaches of Article 10, or to the inability of individuals to freely exercise the rights to which they are entitled.

While the opinions of the Advisory Committee have been fairly clear and consistent with international human rights standards in the less controversial aspects of Article 10 (such as the first and third paragraphs), the Committee's

[67] For a general approach of the European Court of Human Rights generally, see *Brozicek* v. *Italy* above, n. 61.

handling of the second paragraph has not been as straightforward. There have been some surprising gaps, and even contradictory approaches, which have led to confusion as to what Article 10(2) precisely mandates. This indicates the need for specific legislation, as well as clarification as to what constitutes a request corresponding to a real need for minority language usage by administrative authorities.

The Advisory Committee has, nevertheless, clarified a number of important aspects of Article 10(2), which should assist in the future implementation of the Framework Convention. It has also pointed out that Article 10(2) must be read and applied generously—as far as is possible—in light of the treaty's objectives, and that it is not necessary to have substantial numbers for the use of a minority language by administrative authorities since the involvement of a 'traditional area' can be sufficient. The Advisory Committee has also made the suggestion of active offer on a number of occasions, which is likely to be more fully developed in future opinions. It would then appear that the Committee's view is that states have a proactive role to play and need to take steps to facilitate the use of a minority language, ensuring that, in practice, individuals may be able to seek and obtain the use of a minority language without any obstacle where the conditions of Article 10(2) are met.

One could, however, criticize the lack of clarity or specific explanations in many opinions as to why and how certain state practices are in breach of Article 10, if it is the case. Some of the Advisory Committee's opinions appear to be vague impressions rather than strict and clear interpretations of specific treaty obligations.

It would be useful in its monitoring if the Advisory Committee were to spell out what a state's obligations were in a general comment on language rights under Article 10. This would be particularly helpful in the case of Article 10(2) to dispel the apparent inconsistencies in some of its opinions, and could provide greater legal clarity and certainty in its approach.

More generally, the Advisory Committee clearly needs to discuss the implications of Article 10 on a paragraph-by-paragraph basis. An overly general approach that simply refers to Article 10 does not assist in understanding exactly where a state's obligations originate, or even what its precise obligations are in some cases.

ARTICLE 11

Fernand de Varennes

1. The Parties undertake to recognise that every person belonging to a national minority has the right to use his or her surname (patronym) and first names in the minority language and the right to official recognition of them, according to modalities provided for in their legal system.
2. The Parties undertake to recognise that every person belonging to a national minority has the right to display in his or her minority language signs, inscriptions and other information of a private nature visible to the public.
3. In areas traditionally inhabited by substantial numbers of persons belonging to a national minority, the Parties shall endeavour, in the framework of their legal system, including, where appropriate, agreements with other States, and taking into account their specific conditions, to display traditional local names, street names and other topographical indications intended for the public also in the minority language when there is a sufficient demand for such indications.

I. Background

A. Issues

Article 11 of the Framework Convention for the Protection of National Minorities (FCNM) touches upon specific, and in some ways symbolic, aspects of the protection of minorities. It focuses on guarantees that were, if not necessarily controversial, at least worthy of special attention because of their significance for minorities themselves. Though involving three distinct and seemingly disparate paragraphs dealing with the names of individuals, displays which may be visible to members of the public, and the names of localities and other topographical descriptions respectively, all acknowledge that visible manifestations of a minority language cannot be prohibited.

B. History

Article 11 of the Framework Convention solidifies, in a number of respects, what has begun to be understood as flowing from a number of human rights widely recognized in international and regional instruments. Until recently, it was widely, and mistakenly, assumed that 'linguistic rights' were distinct from traditional individual rights, and that they properly belonged to emerging cultural or minority rights.

This has been demonstrated to be incorrect in the last ten years as the UN Human Rights Committee, the UN Committee on the Elimination of Racial Discrimination, and the European Court of Human Rights among others, have issued a number of decisions, views, and comments that contradict this widespread conception. Particularly, in considering issues of an individual's name or surname and public displays in a minority language, these international bodies have pointed out that the right to private life and/or non-discrimination in the former case, and freedom of expression in the latter, protect an individual's linguistic preferences, at least in their private manifestations.[1]

Article 11 FCNM, on the one hand, thus contains a clarification on what has increasingly been acknowledged as protected under existing individual human rights standards. On the other hand, it also gives a legal form to what has only started to appear in non-binding documents as specific linguistic or minority rights, such as the UN Declaration on the Rights of Persons Belonging to National or Ethnic, Religious, and Linguistic Minorities, and the Oslo Recommendations regarding the Linguistic Rights of National Minorities.

C. Context

Whereas Article 10 FCNM covers the right to language use in general, both by state authorities and individuals, Article 11 appears to raise matters which have been deemed sensitive, or warranting some form of distinct treatment from the more general formulation of the use of a minority language envisaged in Article 10.

[1] See for a general discussion of these issues, F. de Varennes, 'A Guide to the Rights of Minorities and Language', Constitutional and Legal Policy Initiative (COLPI), Budapest, 2001, pp. 8–16. **www.eumap.org/library/static/libr0/l/6/se56p2w.pdf** 2 August 2004.

II. Analysis

A. Structure of Article 11

The three-paragraph structure of this provision points to quite divergent influences. Article 11(1) refers to the right of persons belonging to national minorities to use their first name and surname in their own language, and to have these officially recognized by state authorities, a right now understood in human rights terms to be based on the right to private life.[2]

Article 11(2) is completely different however, as it refers to the right to the public display of signs, inscriptions, and other visual forms of a private nature written in a national minority language. It is a right usually associated with freedom of expression, itself protected in the Framework Convention under Article 7, as well as under Article 10(1), which refers to the writing of a national minority language.

The third section of Article 11 deals with another distinct obligation, which has little connection to the previous two, but may be understood to emphasize a particular application of the general principles in Article 10. It indicates that 'in areas traditionally inhabited by substantial numbers', parties should have local, street, and topographical names in the national minority language. While its wording suggests a close affinity with Article 10(2) FCNM, there are a number of differences between the two, which indicate that the drafters of the treaty envisioned a more restrictive application for the right contained in Article 11(3).

None of these sections can be described as revolutionary, yet their presence in a separate provision would appear to have been an attempt to link the importance of language within the identities of individuals and communities, and the need to address this in a more direct and precise way. Because of the different substantive issues that the three paragraphs involve, the drafting background and context for each one will be examined separately.

B. Article 11(1)

1. Interpretation

The drafting history for Article 11(1) shows there was never any disagreement over its inclusion or general wording. Indeed, it was admitted early on that 'the right to bear one's own name in the minority language . . . was of great importance',[3] and the only concern was over the practicalities involved in

[2] *Coeriel and Aurik* v. *Netherlands*, United Nations Human Rights Committee, Comm. No. 453/1991 (1994), UN Doc. CCPR/C/52/D/453/1991; *Burghartz* v. *Switzerland* (16213/90) (1994) EHRR 101.

[3] Preparatory Committee of the Ad Hoc Committee for the Protection of National Minorities (CAHMIN), 3rd meeting, CAHMIN (94) 13, meeting report, 1994, para. 20.

upholding this right. At one point, it was thought that there should be specific reference to a possible paragraph with respect to the changing of one's own name, 'particularly to cover those situations where family names other than the minority name have been imposed by the public authorities'.[4] This additional paragraph was not included in the end, it being preferable to explain such detailed implementation of the paragraph in the Explanatory Report.[5]

Though not emphasized in the drafting history of Article 11(1), the right to have one's name in a minority language has now been widely admitted to flow from the notion of private life under current human rights treaties:

> ... the sphere of a person's life in which he or she can freely express his or her identity, be it by entering into relationships with others or alone. The Committee is of the view that a person's surname [and name] constitutes an important component of one's identity and that the protection against arbitrary or unlawful interference with one's privacy includes the protection against arbitrary or unlawful interference with the right to choose and change one's own name.[6]

This idea is also contained in an increasing number of international and regional treaties and other documents.[7]

2. *Practice of the Advisory Committee*

Because of the largely uncontroversial and specific nature of Article 11(1), as well as its now acknowledged link to the right to private life under the European Convention for the Protection of Human Rights and Fundamental Freedoms (ECHR) and the International Covenant on Civil and Political

[4] Steering Committee for Human Rights (CDDH), Final Activity Report of the CDDH for the Attention of the Committee of Ministers, CDDH (93) 22, 1993.

[5] CAHMIN, Explanatory Report to the Framework Convention for the Protection of National Minorities, CAHMIN H(1995) 010, 1995: '68. In view of the practical implications of this obligation, the provision is worded in such a way as to enable Parties to apply it in the light of their own particular circumstances. For example, Parties may use the alphabet of their official language to write the name(s) of a person belonging to a national minority in its phonetic form. Persons who have been forced to give up their original name(s), or whose name(s) has (have) been changed by force, should be entitled to revert to it (them), subject of course to exceptions in the case of abuse of rights and changes of name(s) for fraudulent purposes. It is understood that the legal systems of the Parties will, in this respect, meet international principles concerning the protection of national minorities.'

[6] *Coeriel and Aurik* v. *Netherlands*, above, n. 2, para. 10(2).

[7] See, for example, Central European Initiative, Instrument for the Protection of Minority Rights, Turin, 1994, Art. 11; Council Recommendation 1201/1993/EC of 1 February 1993 on an Additional Protocol on the Rights of National Minorities to the European Convention on Human Rights [1993], Art. 7(2), Resolution of the European Parliament on the Languages and Cultures of Regional and Ethnic Minorities [1987], para. 6 and Foundation on Interethnic Relations, Oslo Recommendations Regarding the Linguistic Rights of National Minorities, The Hague, 1998, Recommendation 1. This last document, in its explanatory section, also makes the connection with the right to private life.

Rights (ICCPR) among others, there has been little debate or area of disagreement when the Advisory Committee of Experts has examined country reports to determine how parties have been implementing this right. As with other uncontroversial provisions, a number of parties to the Framework Convention went to some length in their reports to demonstrate that members of national minorities are entitled to use and have their name and surname recognized in their own language.

The Advisory Committee in general has not made any comment on these points unless a definite problem appears to have arisen. Its focus on Hungary's situation was exceptional in this regard. Without saying that the Hungarian authorities were in breach of the treaty, the Advisory Committee referred to the apparently small number of individuals who actually sought to have their names or surnames used and recognized in their minority language.[8] The Committee of Ministers also picked up on this observation, perhaps going even further than the Advisory Committee's report in indicating that Hungary had to ensure that individuals were truly and completely free from obstacles or pressure on the use and recognition of their names in their own language in compliance with its legal obligations:

> The Committee of Ministers *concludes* that the actual use made of legal possibilities for the use and the official recognition of the patronym and first names in the minority language, for bilingual signs with the names of settlements, streets, public offices and companies undertaking public services seems rather limited. It *recommends* that Hungary review this situation in order to ascertain whether this practical state of affairs is the result of the exercise of free choice or whether there are other impediments.

Additionally, there are three specific issues of breaches, or potential breaches which the Advisory Committee of Experts dealt with in some detail. These were: changed spelling, transliteration, and alphabet difficulties; cultural differences and surnames; and corrections by public authorities after forced changes to an individual's name or surname. On the first issue, in some countries the actual spelling of names or surnames in a minority language may cause some difficulties in the implementation of the Framework Convention. For the most part, this problem appears to be related to transliteration, the use of different alphabets, and how a person's name ought to be transcribed from one alphabet to another. Countries like Albania appear to have adopted an approach accepted by the Advisory Committee, since it officially attempts to recognize and register names 'according to their phonetic pronunciation on the

[8] Advisory Committee on the Framework Convention for the Protection of National Minorities, Opinion on Hungary, ACFC/INF/OP/I (2001) 004, 2000, para. 37.

basis of the orthography of [its] alphabet'.[9] Thus, while acknowledging the practical necessity for authorities to use a single alphabet for official documentation as opposed to private documents,[10] this does not obviate the treaty obligation to respect a person's name or surname in their minority language, if it were to be transcribed in a different script for official documentation purposes as far as possible.

While the Albanian approach to following phonetic pronunciation in transliteration sufficiently complied with the requirements of Article 11(1), the Advisory Committee also noted individual complaints in incidents where some members of a national minority were forced to use an Albanian version of their patronym by local authorities. Despite their apparent isolation, such incidents constituted non-compliance with the obligations of the Framework Convention. Thus, the Albanian authorities had to take steps to 'ensure that all civil servants [were] aware of the need to respect this right to use, and have official recognition of, one's patronym in the minority language'.[11]

A slightly different problem arose in relation to the use and recognition of Polish names and surnames in Lithuania. The Polish alphabet contains a few characters that are not present in the Latin alphabet used in the Lithuanian language. In issuing passports, Lithuanian authorities have phonetically transcribed these characters according to their pronunciation. While expressing regrets that no solution has been found to this matter, the Advisory Committee did not actually suggest that the practice breached Article 11(1) FCNM. It would seem, therefore, that as long as a transcription is phonetically accurate, Article 11(1) does not require authorities to adopt characters from an alphabet not officially used by public authorities.

One unresolved aspect of this issue is whether it might be possible to write names or surnames in minority languages with absolute accuracy, given that new technologies make it increasingly simple to add and use other characters. While a literal reading of Article 11(1) does not automatically lead to the conclusion that this is a strict requirement—there would after all be huge practical difficulties if administrative authorities in one country had to simultaneously use for official purposes the Georgian, Cyrillic, Latin, Greek, and Arabic alphabets—an argument in favour of this possibility could be made if only minor adjustments were needed. Thus, in the case of the addition of a few Polish language characters to Lithuanian transcriptions, one could certainly say that if administrative authorities had easy access to computer software or keyboards

[9] Advisory Committee Opinion on Albania, ACFC/INF/OP/I (2003) 004, 2002, para. 54.

[10] This is implied in the Advisory Committee Opinion on Azerbaijan, ACFC/INF/OP/I (2004) 001, 2003, para. 58, among others.

[11] Above, n. 9, para. 55.

that could reproduce these characters, there would really be no sufficient, practical reasons for the administrative authorities not to respect the particular linguistic form of a person's name or surname. This would also seem consistent with the general approach to the Framework Convention, that states have an obligation to comply positively to their obligations as far as is practical.

A clearer breach of the Convention occurred in the Ukraine, where persons belonging to national minorities were forced to use a Ukrainian language version of their names, with authorities using this version for official records and documents, such as passports, without the prior approval of the person concerned.[12] According to the Advisory Committee, this action fell short of the obligations the government of Ukraine had consented to in ratifying the Framework Convention, and had to be corrected if they were still occurring.

One unresolved, yet related matter, is the extent to which authorities must not only permit and use a person's name or surname in a particular language, but also the extent to which minority language versions of names are prominent in official uses. While stating that recording only the Ukrainian version of the names of persons of national minorities in official records and documents, without explicit prior approval of the person concerned was 'particularly disconcerting' and needed to be changed, the Advisory Committee did not provide any clear guidance as to which exact measures in the Convention had been breached. Specifically, it is not clear whether this breach was related only to the use of the Ukrainian form of the name for official purposes without the individual's approval, and whether the Framework Convention's obligations would have been satisfied with the dual use and recognition of both languages for official purposes; or whether the obligations under Article 11 required the exclusive use of a person's name or surname in the minority language. Given the wording of Article 11(1), which clearly refers to one's name and surname 'in the minority language and the right to official recognition of them', and the links between this provision and the right to private life, it would appear that state authorities must recognize and use the name of a person in their minority language.[13]

Without clarifying whether Article 11(1) actually prohibits 'double entries', having state authorities use a person's name in their language and the official

[12] Advisory Committee Opinion on Ukraine, ACFC/INF/OP/I (2002) 010, 2002, para. 55.

[13] See the similar opinion of the Advisory Committee on Azerbaijan where it noted that Azerbaijani authorities had written the names of all citizens 'in the state language' and added that the authorities had to respect the right to the official recognition of names in minority languages 'fully', without elaborating on what needed to be addressed, if anything. Advisory Committee on the Framework Convention for the Protection of National Minorities, Opinion on Azerbaijan, ACFC/INF/OP/I (2004) 001, 2003, para. 58.

language of the state, it would nevertheless seem clear from the wording of the provision that officials must privilege the use of names and surnames in the minority language. Strictly speaking, it seems the only qualification to this right would be in cases where there are spelling variations because of differences of script used by state authorities and a national minority. Even here, and consistent with the Framework Convention's Preamble, it is clear that authorities must respect a person's name and surname as far as they can, approximating their spelling as closely as possible to the spelling used in the minority language.

The second main issue mentioned at the start of this section deals with the effects of the cultural practices and traditions of administrative officials as they affect minority rights under Article 11(1). It seems that even when legislation appears to conform to the requirements of Article 11(1), the Advisory Committee has noted that there could be breaches of the right to use and have one's name and surname recognized in one's own language due to the practices of public officials.

This occurred in the case of the Slovak Republic where, despite legislation protecting the right of persons belonging to national minorities to use their names and surnames in a minority language and the right of official recognition of them, some officials forced minority women to add the traditional Slavic ending for women to their surnames. This action did not conform to the obligations under Article 11(1), and the Advisory Committee found it 'important that the Government review the situation and, where necessary, take measures against the imposition of the Slovak form of surnames and to ensure that such practices are not tolerated in the public sector'.[14] The Committee of Ministers reached the same conclusion and recommended that Slovakia take the measures suggested by the Advisory Committee.

The Czech Republic found itself in a situation somewhat similar to that of Slovakia, but pre-empted a finding that it had breached the Framework Convention by indicating that changes to its legislation would end the practice of imposing Slavic forms to the surnames of women from national minorities:

> An unresolved issue is inscription of feminine surnames in registers (and subsequently in all official documents). The existing law specifies that registration of a feminine surname must be in accordance with the rules of Czech grammar. This means that most feminine surnames are changed according to gender (usually by adding suffixes '-ova' or by changing 'y' to 'a'). The requirement to change the surnames of persons belonging to national minorities against the way they perceive their languages (this does not apply to the Slovak national minority and some other Slavic minorities) is considered to be a discriminating restriction of their linguistic rights. The Government has drafted

[14] Advisory Committee Opinion on Slovakia, ACFC/INF/OP/I (2001) 001, 2000, para. 37.

a new law on registries and names and surnames which deals with this issue in the sense of paragraph 1 of this Article. The law is expected to enter into effect in 2000. The law will allow alternate manner of inscription of feminine surnames in registries, that is without the feminine suffix, upon the request of the person, regardless of whether she is a foreigner or belongs to a national minority or not.[15]

This declaration met with the approval of the Advisory Committee, as being in compliance with the requirements of Article 11(1).[16]

The final issue concerns situations where an individual's name was changed by the public authorities because of restrictions on the use of a minority language, and the right to have such a change corrected. As indicated earlier, Article 11(1) does not specifically refer to the right to change one's name or surname to a minority language, but the paragraph's drafting history and the Framework Convention's explanatory document indicate that such an entitlement is indeed an obligation which flows from the implementation of Article 11(1), especially where a person's name or surname had been forced upon them by state authorities.

Since it is not explicitly detailed in the Framework Convention, it is perhaps understandable that this issue arose in the contexts of a few countries, and that the Advisory Committee had to explain the nature and extent of the Framework Convention's obligations under Article 11(1) more thoroughly in this regard. The Advisory Committee went to some lengths when considering Norway's implementation of Article 11(1) to explain that where the ancestors of persons belonging to national minorities were pressured to 'Norwegianize' their surnames, 'those persons belonging to national minorities who have been forced to give up their original name should be entitled to revert to them'.[17]

The Advisory Committee added two further clarifications regarding the extent of the legal obligations under Article 11(1). First, it specified that the right to have one's name or surname 'corrected' applied not only to someone who had been forced to change his or her name directly, but also to situations where the forced change occurred to their ancestors sometime in the past.[18] Secondly, it held that administrative restrictions or discretionary powers which

[15] Czech Republic State Report, ACFC/SR (99) 6, 1999, para. 32.

[16] Advisory Committee Opinion on the Czech Republic, ACFC/INF/OP/I (2002) 002, 2001, para. 58.

[17] Advisory Committee Opinion on Norway, ACFC/INF/OP/I (2003) 003, 2002, para. 48.

[18] Above, n. 17. It is interesting to note the possible limits to this right. In *Stjerna* v. *Finland* (18131/91) (1994) EHRR 43, for example, authorities changed the surname of a member of the Swedish-speaking minority and this altered form was in use for more than two centuries. The European Court of Human Rights did not consider it a breach of the right to private life that the person's surname was not changed by authorities to the form used two and a half centuries previously

'placed undue obstacles for persons belonging to national minorities attempting to revert to the old surnames of their families' did not conform to the Framework Convention's obligations.[19] It would appear that Norway has been addressing these lacunae in its legislation and practice, with the Norwegian parliament's adoption of a new Law on Personal Names on 7 June 2002, though authorities will still need to ensure that this new legislation fully complies with Article 11(1) in practice.[20]

In its examination of the Ukraine's report, the Advisory Committee acknowledged the difficulty faced by formerly deported people whose original names were often distorted as a result of the deportation, and indicated once again that persons whose names were changed forcibly were entitled to have these returned 'as close to their original form as possible'.[21] While administrative and even linguistic problems were bound to occur in the process of making these changes, parties still had the obligation to make efforts to facilitate these corrections.

3. Overall Interpretation and Future Developments

With its comments on this provision, the Advisory Committee has provided fairly clear indications as to the content of the protection of a person's name or surname. While the link between this issue and the right to respect of private life has been more recently acknowledged by the UN Human Rights Committee and the European Court of Human Rights, until recently there had not been much detailed discussion on the exact limits of such a right, especially in its linguistic aspects.

Thus the Framework Convention specifically guarantees that a person's name or surname includes the language in which it takes form. In light of the comments made in cases such as *Stjerna* v. *Finland* and others, this guarantee would also be covered under the right to private life. Generally, authorities cannot change or refuse to recognize a person's identity through his or her name simply because it is not in a prescribed or official language. On the contrary, it would seem that Article 11(1) clearly demands a strict compliance with the linguistic form and particularities of a minority's name and surname, and that states must officially acknowledge and use these.

because 'the last ancestor who bore that name died more than two hundred years before the applicant applied to acquire the name. Notwithstanding the applicant's own feelings about being a descendant of the ancestors in question, the latter lived so far back in time that no significant weight can be given to those links for the purposes of paragraph 1 of Article 8' (para. 43). It should also be noted that his name could still be considered Swedish. Presumably, had there been a more recent connection, the European Court could have concluded there had been a breach of the right to private life.

[19] Advisory Committee Opinion on Norway, ACFC/INF/OP/I (2003) 003, 2002, para. 49.

[20] Above, n. 19, para. 50.

[21] Above, n. 12, para. 56.

Thus, the Advisory Committee has gone some way towards explaining that in order to comply with the wording and expressed intent of Article 11(1), states must accommodate particular spellings used. Therefore, in the case of a transliteration from one form of orthography to another, state authorities must be as faithful as possible to the phonetic pronunciation of a person's name and surname. While nothing in Article 11(1) actually requires authorities to use a particular script when dealing with a person's name or surname for official purposes,[22] the Advisory Committee's comments, consistent with the Preamble as well as the object and intent of the Convention, indicate the need to recognize and respect the integrity of a minority's identity. This includes the symbolic, yet culturally important issue of a person's own name, and any particularities associated with this, such as names that may vary according to the gender of the individual.

Similarly, authorities must also do all in their power, and without imposing any burdensome requirements, to correct changes to a minority's name or surname, particularly when these were forced upon individuals by state authorities in conjunction with measures to assimilate minorities or strengthen the 'integration' of linguistically and culturally diverse populations, though not exclusively. Despite the practical difficulties this may involve, especially when the changes in question occurred a number of generations ago, and with records being destroyed or lost, as would have seemed to have happened in the Ukraine with formerly deported minorities, members of minorities are still entitled to have their names reverted to their original linguistic forms.

Even if the changes were made some time in the past, the general approach of the Advisory Committee, the direction of the Framework Convention, and the clarifications contained in the Explanatory Report suggest that the time factor should not restrict an individual's right to have authorities correct, recognize, and use his or her name in the linguistically appropriate form.[23]

While these examples represent useful interpretations on the right to have one's name recognized and used in a minority language, and indeed one could say the Advisory Committee has effectively set the broad guidelines on the content and limits of Article 11(1), there are still areas where the Advisory Committee will need to focus and improve on the consistency of its approach. In its opinion on Azerbaijan, among other examples, the Advisory Committee failed to help the authorities understand whether they are fully respecting the

22 The private use of a particular script, whether Latin, Cyrillic, Greek, or Arabic, for example, would be protected under freedom of expression and Art. 11(2) FCNM.

23 While *Stjerna* v. *Finland* (above, n. 18) would suggest that not all changes to a name in the distant past would necessarily breach the right to private life as it affects an individual's name, one should remember that the change had not only occurred more than two centuries previously, it did not actually alter the linguistic form of the name, in that it remained Swedish in its sense.

obligations of Article 11(1), and if not, what precisely they ought to amend since they only use the Latin alphabet for official purposes and writing the names of persons belonging to national minorities.

There are other nagging issues, such as whether authorities should only recognize a person's own name or surname in their own language, or whether authorities can make 'double entries'. That is, in addition to recognizing a minority's proper name, can authorities use a person's 'official language name' simultaneously in official documentation?

Article 11(1) does not specifically prohibit double entries, though significantly it excludes any reason detailing why such a procedure should be followed, since authorities must officially recognize the name of a member of a minority group in his or her minority language. To recognize a minority name for official purposes, but then to use a different name in the official language would seem rather confusing, and impractical at the very least, as well as suspect in light of the general approach and wording of Article 11(1).

C. Article 11(2)

1. *Interpretation*

The right of an individual to display signs and other information of a private nature visible to the public in the language of his or her choice is well understood today to be a basic human right, since it is inherent in the application of freedom of expression.[24] It is also enshrined as a distinct 'minority protection right' under Article 11(2) of the Framework Convention. The drafting history shows some initial hesitation as to how to deal with publicly visible signs in a minority language, and especially on how to distinguish between the use of minority languages by public authorities as opposed to private parties. The two were both treated as occurring 'in the regions in which substantial numbers of a national minority are settled' by the Steering Committee for Human Rights (CDDH).[25] However, because of the distinct nature of both, the paragraph on

[24] As the UN Human Rights Committee clearly stated in *Ballantyne, Davidson and McIntyre* v. *Canada*, UN Human Rights Committee, 359/1989 and 385/1989 (1993), UN Doc. CCPR/C/47/D/359/1989 and 385/1989/Rev. 1. This right would therefore be protected in provisions dealing with freedom of expression generally, such as the International Covenant on Civil and Political Rights (ICCPR) (adopted 16 December 1966, entered into force 23 March 1976) 999 UNTS 171 ICCPR, Art. 19, and the European Convention for the Protection of Human Rights and Fundamental Freedoms (ECHR), ETS 5, 1950, Art. 10. Also, it would be similarly protected under the Second Conference on the Human Dimension of the CSCE, Document of the Copenhagen Meeting of the Conference on the Human Dimension of the CSCE, Copenhagen, 1990, para. 32(5).

[25] Steering Committee for Human Rights (CDDH), Final Activity Report of the CDDH for the Attention of the Committee of Ministers, CDDH (93) 22, 8, 1993.

the private use of a national minority language linked this usage to the freedom of expression, eliminating the need for a 'substantial numbers' requirement in this article and removing it from Article 11 FCNM,[26] whereas the use of a national minority language by public authorities in signs and other displays publicly visible was seen as logically more consistent with the general provisions dealing with language in Article 10 FCNM. Subsequently, there was no disagreement during the drafting process, though some slight changes in wording did occur to accentuate the point that Article 11(2) is limited to signs and other displays of a private nature only.[27]

The drafting history of Article 11(2) also highlights that while the Framework Convention pertains to the protection of national minorities, it does not mean that the rights it contains are limited to the use of a national minority language alone. As admitted by the Ad Hoc Committee for the Protection of National Minorities (CAHMIN), individuals are entitled to freely use any language of their choice, consistent with the 'freedom of expression' origins of this right: '[t]he explanatory report should clearly state that it is self-evident that the right dealt with in this paragraph implies the right to display . . . in the language of the majority or of another minority.'[28]

Additionally, as both the Explanatory Report and the drafting history emphasize, 'this does not . . . exclude persons belonging to national minorities from being required to use, in addition, the official language and/or other minority languages'.[29] This is also consistent with the UN Human Rights Committee's views on the application of freedom of expression and an individual's choice of language on signs and other private displays in public view.[30]

2. *Practice of the Advisory Committee*

State reports have tended to reflect the widespread acknowledgement of the obligations under Article 11(2), in the sense that most governments

[26] CAHMIN (94) 13, 15 April 1994, 3rd meeting 11–15 April 1994, Meeting Report, paragraph 21: 'During the discussion on the right to display in public signs, inscriptions and other private information in the minority language, it appeared that there were no major obstacles to guaranteeing such a right. It was felt that this right should apply generally, ie. (1) without any qualification as to the number of persons belonging to a national minority living in a particular region and (2) it should not be limited to the use of signs etc in the minority language only.'

[27] CAHMIN, 6th meeting, CAHMIN (94) 28, meeting report, 1994, para. 42.

[28] CAHMIN, 4th meeting, CAHMIN (94) 16, meeting report, 1994, para. 23.

[29] CAHMIN, Explanatory Report to the Framework Convention for the Protection of National Minorities, CAHMIN H(1995) 010, 1995, para. 69, and CAHMIN, 4th meeting, CAHMIN (94) 16, 1994, meeting report, para. 23.

[30] *Ballantyne, Davidson and McIntyre* v. *Canada*, above, n. 24.

have suggested they do not restrict displays of a private nature in a minority language.[31] As in the case of Article 11(1), the rather uncontroversial nature of the second paragraph of Article 11, and its association with freedom of expression, has not led to obvious fundamental disagreements between most states parties' reports and the responses of the Advisory Committee on the implementation of the FCNM. In almost all state reports, governments have clearly accepted that persons belonging to a national minority have the right to use their language on signs and other displays that can be seen by the public. By extension, it would also seem uncontroversial that that 'language' in this right also includes a particular script used by a national minority.[32] There is one important qualification to make to this general statement. States parties have not always been clear on the distinction between private displays in a national minority language as expressed in Article 11(2), and the use of a minority language in displays by public officials as set out in Article 11(3). In some cases, these two distinct matters and paragraphs have been discussed as if they were almost one and the same.[33]

Nonetheless, there have been a few challenges to the uncontroversial nature of this provision. In its opinion relating to Azerbaijan, for example, the Advisory Committee expressed its disquiet at the Law on the State Language which, because of overly vague and general wording, could be interpreted to 'prevent a person belonging to a national minority from displaying signs and other information of a private nature visible to the public'.[34] Similarly in Serbia and Montenegro, the Law on the Official Use of Script and Language in Serbia was found to be ambiguous and could 'be interpreted as preventing persons belonging to a national minority from displaying certain information of a private nature visible to the public also in a minority language that is not in official use'.[35]

It would therefore appear that in both Azerbaijan and Serbia and Montenegro, legislation which might have an impact on the right to freely use a minority language for signs and other displays of a private nature had to be revised to dispel any possibility of preventing the right of persons

[31] Albania State Report, ACFC/SR (2001) 5, 2001, para. 42; Austria State Report, ACFC/SR (2003) 3, 2000, para. 61.

[32] Advisory Committee Opinion on Serbia and Montenegro, ACFC/INF/OP/I (2004) 002, 2004, para. 149: 'The Advisory Committee finds that the right of persons belonging to national minorities to use their language *and script* in private . . .' [emphasis added].

[33] Azerbaijan State Report, ACFC/SR (2002) 001, 2001, para. 41.

[34] Advisory Committee Opinion on Azerbaijan, ACFC/INF/OP/I (2004) 001, 2003, para. 59.

[35] Advisory Committee Opinion on Serbia and Montenegro, ACFC/INF/OP/I (2004) 002, 2004, para. 81.

belonging to national minorities to use their language and script in private and in public.[36]

Of a more controversial nature has been the disagreement involving Estonia. In Estonia's report to the Advisory Committee, the government had initially insisted that private signs and displays were unregulated and, therefore, that there were no restrictions on the languages used. As will be discussed in the next section, however, the Advisory Committee indicated it was 'seriously concerned', with this finding and pointed out that existing Estonian legislation (Article 23 of the Language Act, which provides that public signs, signposts, announcements, notices, and advertisements shall be in Estonian) was so wide that it could threaten the guarantees of Article 11(2), and implicitly freedom of expression.

The Advisory Committee explained the extent of the right contained in Article 11(2) quite clearly:

> Bearing in mind that the expression 'of a private nature' in Article 11 of the Framework Convention refers to all that is not official, there should not be a prohibition to use a minority language for example in a sign, poster or an advertisement of a private enterprise by a person belonging to a national minority.[37]

The Committee of Ministers also forcefully concluded that Estonian legislation was 'not compatible' with Article 11 of the Framework Convention, to the extent it prevented the display of signs and other information of a private nature visible to the public in a minority language. The matter should have ended there and have amounted to a misunderstanding by Estonian authorities of the general content of Article 11(2). Rather disturbingly, however, it would appear that a more fundamental disagreement exists that will have to be resolved at a later date. For Estonia, it would seem that Article 11(2) does not apply in situations of 'public interest':

> The provisions of the Language Act are therefore interpreted bearing in mind the general principles enshrined in Article 2(1) determining the scope of the Act. Article 2(1) clearly states that the use of Estonian language in the private sphere is regulated only in cases where it is in the public interest, i.e. public security, public order, public administration, public health, health protection, consumer protection and occupational safety. It further specifies that the respective requirement must be justified and necessary in a democratic society and may not distort the essence of the rights and freedoms being restricted.

[36] Advisory Committee Opinion on Azerbaijan, ACFC/INF/OP/I (2004) 001, 2003, para. 111; Advisory Committee Opinion on Serbia and Montenegro, ACFC/INF/OP/I (2004) 002, 2004, para. 149.

[37] Advisory Committee Opinion on Estonia, ACFC/INF/OP/I (2002) 005, 2001, para. 43.

It follows therefore that the state does not interfere with the right of persons to display information of a private nature visible to the public unless it is necessary in the public interests listed above.[38]

These conflicting views may perhaps be partially explained by the fact that neither the government of Estonia, nor the Advisory Committee, fully described the precise kind of interventions that would affect the use of language on private signs and other displays.

At the more general level, and given the foundations of Article 11(2) in freedom of expression, it should be noted that the above statement by Estonian authorities that 'a' public interest is sufficient reason to restrict Article 11(2) (and the freedom of expression) as long as it is justifiable and 'necessary in a democratic society' is wrong. From a purely legal point of view, and this also appears to be the position of the Advisory Committee, Article 11(2) does not prohibit or prevent the use of a minority language in private activities for the sake of 'public interest'. Nor would a ban on the use of a minority language on private signs and other displays be permitted because of 'public interest' as it relates to freedom of expression. Preventing an individual from using a minority language in private displays is only permitted under the ECHR and the ICCPR in situations where they are absolutely necessary for reasons such as public order, safety, or morality. Indeed, this is exactly the conclusion that the UN Human Rights Committee arrived at in one case concerning private commercial signs.[39]

Another explanation may be that the Estonian authorities may have been under the impression that requiring the simultaneous use of the Estonian language on signs and displays of a private nature is inconsistent with the obligations of Article 11(2). This appears a possible explanation because of the party's insistence that 'Article 2(1) clearly states that the use of Estonian language in the private sphere is regulated only in cases where it is in the public interest.'[40] These words suggest an unstated concern that authorities must be allowed to require the use of the Estonian language in private signs and displays for some purposes. While the point could have been made in a clearer and more precise way, the qualms of the Advisory Committee in relation to Estonia's compliance with Article 11(2) had nothing to do with requiring the use of the

[38] Comments of the Government of Estonia on the Opinion of the Advisory Committee on the Implementation of the Framework Convention for the Protection of National Minorities in Estonia, GVT/COM/INF/OP/I (2002) 005, 2002, para. 43.

[39] Above, n. 30.

[40] Comments of the Government of Estonia on the Opinion of the Advisory Committee on the Implementation of the Framework Convention for the Protection of National Minorities, GVT/COM/INF/OP/I (2002) 005, 2002, para. 43. Emphasis added.

official language, but was actually limited to the possibility of Article 23 of the Language Act being used in a way that prevented the use of a minority language in private displays. The Explanatory Report, and the wording of Article 11(2) itself, ought to have been clear. A requirement to use an official language in conjunction with an individual's preferred language of choice in private signs and displays is not a breach of the Framework Convention, nor presumably of freedom of expression, as long as public authorities do not prevent the free and effective use of one's language in private displays: '[t]he obligation in this paragraph . . . does not . . . exclude persons belonging to national minorities from being required to use, in addition, the official language and/or other minority languages.'[41]

While the possibility of a misunderstanding is not to be excluded, on the more negative side, Estonia also seemed to imply that it had the imprimatur of the Office of the High Commissioner on National Minorities, the European Union, and the Council of Europe in this regard, mainly because of 'statements' from unnamed individuals in these organizations. Be that as it may, the latter are not charged with ensuring the implementation of the Framework Convention, and it seems to signal something of a rejection by Estonia of the very authority of the Advisory Committee of Experts. This is all the more surprising as the Committee of Ministers shared the same views as the Advisory Committee. Indeed, the last word on this matter would appear to have been from the Committee of Ministers: '[the] protection of national minorities is not always addressed in an adequate manner in the legislative process and administrative practice. Despite certain recent improvements in the relevant legislation, there remain shortcomings with respect to the use of minority languages, including as regards the private signs visible to the public.'[42]

3. *Overall Interpretation and Future Development*

Largely uncontroversial since it was disentangled from the official use of a minority language for signs and other public displays, Article 11(2) of the Framework Convention has not been the subject of a great deal of interpretation since most states parties appear to readily acknowledge that they do not limit the right of persons belonging to national minorities to use their language on signs and other displays in the public view. At least partly, this may also be due to the increasing recognition that this right is also protected under freedom of expression.

[41] Above, n. 5, para. 69.

[42] Committee of Ministers, Resolution ResCMN (2002) 8 on the implementation of the Framework Convention for the Protection of National Minorities by Estonia, 799th meeting, 2002.

Among the few areas where the Advisory Committee needed to issue findings was the need for clarity in legislation in order to avoid laws that might in some way be interpreted as prohibiting displays of a private nature, which were not in an official language. Beyond this, the main Advisory Committee clarification related to the use of script or alphabet, so that the reference to language in Article 11(2) also incorporated scripts. The result of this measure was that individuals were free to use the script in which their national minority language is written on signs and other displays of a private nature.

Nevertheless, one contentious matter which will probably recur is the dispute that arose when Estonia seemed to argue that 'public interest' could be used as grounds to circumvent the obligations of Article 11(2), and restrict the right of individuals to use a minority language in displays of a private nature. While the Advisory Committee, and indeed the Committee of Ministers, appears to have rather firmly rejected this contention, it is by all means not a completely closed debate since there are a number of other states in Europe with similar legislation.

D. Article 11(3)

1. Interpretation

The drafting history of Article 11(3) FCNM, and even its separation from both Articles 11(2) and 10(2) with which it shares affinities, indicate that its inclusion was met with some strong reservations and disagreements. As will be shown later, its final wording was only agreed upon on the addition of a number of restrictions and 'escape clauses', making this paragraph one of the 'language' provisions of the Framework Convention with the most limitations. Part of the hesitation, and even resistance, to the incorporation of such a provision may be connected to its novelty from a legal point of view, as few treaties recognize such an obligation on the part of public authorities.[43]

The extent of the divisions during the drafting process can be seen early on with a number of the experts involved being opposed to any recognition of a right to have traditional local names, street names, and other topographical indications displayed in a minority language because of political sensitivity:

> Some experts voiced objections to the inclusion of a principle from which such a right, politically very sensitive, could be derived, whilst others stated that they were in favour of a provision on this subject. The Committee did not reject the idea out of hand.

[43] See Council of Europe (CoE), European Charter on Regional or Minority Languages, ETS No. 148, 1993, Art. 10(2)(*g*); and Central European Initiative, Instrument for the Protection of Minority Rights, Turin, 1994, Art. 14. Another influential, though non-binding document, which contains a similar provision is to be found in Foundation on Interethnic Relations, Oslo Recommendations Regarding the Linguistic Rights of National Minorities, The Hague, 1998, Recommendation 3.

A text would therefore be drafted on a provisional basis. This text should be very flexible ('States will facilitate/encourage' . . . 'States will not prevent the putting up of signs . . .') and be limited to areas where such a practice would meet a certain need, in particular where substantial numbers of a national minority are settled.[44]

Opposition to the inclusion of this type of provision did not diminish during the drafting process, with some experts 'strongly opposed to the inclusion of any provision on the subject in the framework Convention'.[45] Three variants (i, ii, and iii)[46] were subsequently considered, but even these were deemed to be too generous or difficult in terms of implementation 'due to complex historical and legal conditions' as some of the experts put it.[47] The variant which was to form the basis for Article 11(3), (variant iii), was still a compromise, since it was approved 'with a view to making the provision more acceptable for the experts who had expressed objections'.[48] This more acceptable amendment was one that added a number of qualifications—a less generous view would be to describe them as 'escape clauses'—to the obligations of this paragraph, since variant iii now added that the obligation to take such actions would only arise 'in the framework of [the parties'] legal system and taking into account their specific conditions'.[49]

Even at this late stage, some of the experts involved in the drafting were still unable to wholeheartedly accept the inclusion of a paragraph dealing with the use of a national minority language in local names and other topographical indications by public authorities. Unfortunately, a fuller explanation of the experts' reasons for such strong opposition is not part of the public record, though it can be extrapolated from some of the comments made during the drafting process. This absence of a clear consensus may also help to explain why

[44] CAHMIN, 3rd meeting, CAHMIN (94) 13, meeting report, 1994, para. 22.

[45] CAHMIN, 5th meeting, CAHMIN (94) 19, meeting report, 1994, Art. 11, para. 14.

[46] Above, n. 45, Appendix IV:

'Variant i: In regions inhabited by national minorities traditionally or in substantial numbers, if those minorities so request and where such a request corresponds to a real need, the Parties shall endeavour to display local names, street names and other topographical indications intended for the public also in the minority language.

Variant ii: In [administrative] areas [traditionally] inhabited by substantial numbers of persons belonging to a national minority, the Parties shall endeavour, in the framework of their legal systems, to display local names, street names and other topographical indications intended for the public also in the minority language, taking into account the request of persons belonging to such a minority and the special conditions of these areas.

Variant iii: In areas traditionally inhabited by substantial numbers of persons belonging to a national minority, Parties shall endeavour to display traditional local names, street names and other topographical indications intended for the public also in the minority language when there is a sufficient demand for such indications.'

[47] CAHMIN, 6th meeting, CAHMIN (94) 28, meeting report, 1994, para. 7.

[48] Above, n. 47, para. 8.

[49] Above, n. 47, pp. 31–2.

Article 11(3) is so much 'weaker' than Article 10(2) with which it is the most closely connected, since both address the use of a national minority language by public officials. There was continued reference to 'strong political connotations' in having public officials use a national minority language in naming localities and other topographical locations, though the drafting record never explains what exactly these connotations were.[50]

One possible explanation is that by using the traditional names of localities and topography in a minority language for official purposes, the region may in fact be seen as 'owned' by, or at least associated with, a community distinct from the majority, perhaps resurrecting unwanted historical or even 'separatist', claims in some countries. This would constitute the amorphous 'political' or 'historical' conditions mentioned during the drafting process. Be that as it may, Article 11(3) was finally incorporated into the Framework Convention, though with restrictions and conditions which make it a seemingly less demanding provision for authorities than most others in the document.

2. *Practice of the Advisory Committee*

Article 11(3) is different from most of the other provisions in the Framework Convention since it does not involve a right which individuals can claim under this agreement, but rather an obligation for states parties ('the Parties shall endeavour, in the framework of their legal system'). Additionally, the Explanatory Report emphasized that Article 11(3) does not involve an official 'recognition' of local or topographical designations in a national minority language in any way:

> This article aims to promote the possibility of having local names, street names and other topographical indications intended for the public also in the minority language. In implementing this principle the States are entitled to take due account of the specific circumstances and the framework of their legal systems, including, where appropriate, agreements with other States. In the field covered by this provision, it is understood that the Parties are under no obligation to conclude agreements with other States. Conversely, the possibility of concluding such agreements is not ruled out. It is also understood that the legally binding nature of existing agreements remains unaffected. This provision does not imply any official recognition of local names in the minority languages.[51]

[50] CAHMIN, 6th meeting, CAHMIN (94) 28, meeting report, 1994, para. 8.

[51] CAHMIN, Explanatory Report to the Framework Convention for the Protection of National Minorities, CAHMIN H(1995) 010, 1995, para. 70; also: '68. In view of the practical implications of this obligation, the provision is worded in such a way as to enable Parties to apply it in the light of their own particular circumstances. For example, Parties may use the alphabet of their official language to write the name(s) of a person belonging to a national minority in its phonetic form. Persons who have been forced to give up their original name(s), or whose name(s) has (have) been changed by force, should be entitled to revert to it (them), subject of course to exceptions in the case of abuse of rights and changes of name(s) for fraudulent purposes. It is understood that the legal systems of the Parties will, in this respect, meet international principles concerning the protection of national minorities.', para. 70.

Like Article 10(2), Article 11(3) involves the use of a national minority language by public officials, but it is not worded as an individual right. It merely outlines that states parties ought to 'endeavour', it is not even drafted in a way which clearly states that parties have a legal obligation to take specific measures. Parties must, therefore, make earnest attempts to ensure the use of national minority languages in the name of localities and topographical locations when the other conditions of Article 11(3) are met. It is here, however, that the content of Article 11(3) and how it is to be implemented encounter difficulties. Parties to the Framework Convention need only make earnest attempts to use national minority languages: (*a*) in areas traditionally inhabited by substantial numbers of persons belonging to a national minority; (*b*) in the framework of their legal system, including, where appropriate, agreements with other states; (*c*) taking into account their specific conditions; and (*d*) when there is a sufficient demand for such indications. Article 11(3) is thus subject to greater restrictions than Article 10(2), since all four of these requirements must be met simultaneously. For the former there needs to be a 'sufficient demand', while for Article 10(2) a 'real need' suffices. Article 10(2) can also be invoked in areas inhabited by persons belonging to national minorities traditionally or in substantial numbers, one or the other situation being sufficient. Article 11(3), however, is more demanding in its requirements for application: parties only need to make earnest efforts in areas that are simultaneously traditional and still inhabited by substantial numbers of persons belonging to a national minority. Additionally, Article 11(3) is further qualified by requiring consideration of a state's 'specific conditions' and of 'the framework of its legal system'; both are requirements that do not appear in Article 10(2).

All of these conditions leave much more leeway for parties, increasing the number of contexts where they would not be obliged to make earnest efforts to display traditional local names, street names, and other topographical indications in national minority languages. Also, given the vagueness and uncertainty as to the exact meaning of some of these conditions, a much less onerous and more malleable 'right' is suggested in comparison with most other provisions of the Framework Convention. This malleability may lead to stronger disagreements as to the extent of the obligations of parties under Article 11(3).

One point that is worth underlining in terms of the general content of this paragraph: it is clear that parties have no obligation to use a national minority language exclusively. Article 11(3) only guarantees that parties must make earnest efforts to have such indications 'also in the minority language', meaning in addition to that state's official language. The Advisory Committee's approach to the interpretation of Article 11(3) has, however, blurred the lines, and in some regards perhaps has not been as helpful as it could have been by not approaching the legal requirements of this provision in a clear and forthright way. There are, however, a few areas where the Advisory Committee has clarified a number of issues. One of the first and clearest indications is the identified need for legislation to implement the obligations of a state party under Article 11(3) effectively.

In the opinion of the Advisory Committee, the absence of legislation setting out the situations where public authorities would use a national minority language in local names and other topographical indications does not conform to a party's obligations under Article 11(3). This was the most frequent concern expressed by the Advisory Committee. While in some cases such as Albania, states parties suggested that in practice there was a general use of local names and other topographical indications in national minority languages, this was not enough to discharge completely the 'earnest efforts' required by Article 11(3):

> [T]he Advisory Committee is concerned by the lack of clear criteria concerning the display of traditional local names, street names and other topographical indications in minority languages intended for the public. The Advisory Committee therefore considers that the Government should examine the need for an adequate legal and administrative framework to govern the display of names and topographical indications in minority languages and adopt appropriate legislation in full conformity with Article 11 paragraph 3 of the Framework Convention. The Advisory Committee notes in this respect the comment of the Government in the State Report that 'a complete legal improvement of all the matters treated in this Article remains an issue to be dwelt upon in the future'. . .[52]

Thus, the Advisory Committee was of the opinion that to comply fully with Article 11(3), specific legislation setting out the conditions where the use of national minorities for locality names and topographical indications would be required from public authorities, and therefore that 'the Government should examine the need for an adequate legal and administrative framework to govern the display of such names and topographical indications and adopt appropriate legislation'.[53]

Even where there were no actual complaints, the Advisory Committee concluded that in light of the content of Article 11(3) not providing legislation to ensure the protection of national minorities in relation to the use of their language for purposes of locality, street and topographical names was remiss:

> The Advisory Committee *finds* that there is a lack of precision in Armenian legislation concerning the possibility of using minority languages in topographical indications.

[52] Advisory Committee Opinion on Albania, ACFC/INF/OP/I (2003) 004, 2002, para. 47.

[53] Above, n. 52, para. 101.

The Advisory Committee *considers*, despite the fact that there have been no complaints from the persons concerned, that the authorities should supplement their legislation so as to ensure that the relevant provisions of the Framework Convention may be effectively implemented.[54]

Even when there is fairly clear and generous legislation in place, there may still be insufficient compliance with the Framework Convention. Such a situation arose in Serbia and Montenegro, where full implementation of the practice of significant legislative guarantees in that country's Law on the Official Use of Language and Script in Serbia were not always apparent. In other words, while the Advisory Committee commended Serbia and Montenegro for its legislation and practices concerning the use of a minority language for official topographical indications in general, it noted that practical problems remained 'in relation to the street names in areas inhabited by a substantial number of Romanians and Croats respectively'.[55]

In addition, national legislation would not comply with Article 11(3) if those who were entitled to the use of their national minority language were unaware of their entitlement. In Estonia, for example, the Advisory Committee noted that almost no municipality had availed itself of the legal possibility to introduce place names and to display topographical indications in a minority language. Thus, it recommended that the government examine the extent to which municipalities were 'aware of the existing possibility to introduce minority language place names and topographical indications and support, as appropriate, the implementation of the provisions at issue'.[56] The Committee of Ministers also made a recommendation to the same effect.

As the Advisory Committee concluded in relation to Italy, it would seem that 'a clear legal basis at national level enabling local authorities to adopt topographical indications in accordance with local traditions and customs, in addition to the official names'[57] would satisfy the requirements of Article 11(3). Indeed, it would seem that simply having clear and unambiguous legislation is insufficient. A more proactive role might be warranted in order for a state party to discharge its obligations, since the Advisory Committee determined that state authorities should monitor 'developments in this field carefully and, where necessary, take measures to encourage the introduction of minority language place names'.[58]

[54] Advisory Committee Opinion on Armenia, ACFC/INF/OP/I (2003) 001, 2002, para. 103.

[55] Advisory Committee Opinion on Serbia and Montenegro, ACFC/INF/OP/I (2004) 002, 2004, para. 83.

[56] Advisory Committee Opinion on Estonia, ACFC/INF/OP/I (2002) 005, 2001, para. 42.

[57] Advisory Committee Opinion on Italy, ACFC/INF/OP/I (2002) 007, 2001, para. 52.

[58] Advisory Committee Opinion on Norway, ACFC/INF/OP/I (2003) 003, 2002, para. 91.

A slightly different problem, which the Advisory Committee also sought to address, involved situations where legislation was in place, which at first glance appeared to conform to Article 11(3), but it might not have been implemented because of conflicts with other legislation. In such a case, and when minority languages were not being used as envisaged in Article 11(3), the Advisory Committee did not hesitate to conclude that this constituted a breach of the international obligations agreed to under the Framework Convention:

> . . . whereas the law on national minorities in force authorises bilingual public signs in areas inhabited by persons belonging to national minorities in substantial numbers, the law on the State language authorises the use of minority languages only for the names and signs of organisations representing national minorities. According to the latter law, the State language must be used for all other public signs. The Advisory Committee finds that the lack of clarity resulting from such conflicting provisions gives cause for concern. It notes that in practice the law on the State language often prevails over the law on national minorities. The Advisory Committee considers that this situation is not compatible with the Framework Convention and calls upon the authorities to take all necessary steps, including legislative, in order to ensure that the legislation, and the relevant practice, is compatible with Article 11 paragraph 3 of the Framework Convention. . . . [59]

From the outset, all states parties must have clear legislation setting forth conditions for when public authorities have to display traditional local names, street names, and other topographical indications intended for the public in a minority language under Article 11(3). As for clarifying the exact conditions under which states parties must make 'earnest efforts' and endeavour to have authorities display local, street names, and topographical indications in minority languages, the Advisory Committee has faced a much more daunting challenge, and in some respects the Committee has not succeeded. Possibly the single most important requirement under Article 11(3), for example, is the reference to the obligations of this provision being limited to 'areas traditionally inhabited by substantial numbers of persons belonging to a national minority'. What then constitutes a substantial number of persons becomes a determining factor.

A number of states parties had legislation or policies in place which equated 'substantial' with more than half of the population of a municipality or area. While neither the drafting history of Article 11(3) nor the Explanatory Report of the Framework Convention suggest specific numerical thresholds for this provision, so as to be flexible and permit consideration of all relevant

[59] Advisory Committee Opinion on Lithuania, ACFC/INF/OP/I (2003) 008, 2003, para. 58.

considerations,[60] the Advisory Committee has clearly indicated that such a high percentage is too onerous and not in keeping with the obligations, nature, or objectives of the Framework Convention. Thus, in the case of the Ukraine, laws which only permitted the use of a national minority language in conjunction with the Ukrainian language, if the majority of the population in a locality where persons belonging to a minority, were deemed to be too stringent:

> The Advisory Committee *finds* that the numerical threshold for the introduction of place names in a minority language is such that it constitutes an obstacle with respect to certain minority languages in areas traditionally inhabited by substantial numbers of persons belonging to a national minority.[61]

Similarly, the Advisory Committee was of the view that to limit the use of a national minority language for locality and topographical designations only where 'necessary' would also appear not to conform to Article 11(3). It found that this could be interpreted too restrictively, since this paragraph of the Framework Convention refers to situations involving traditional areas and substantial numbers, rather than any kind of necessity. Forthcoming legislation imposing such a criterion appears to be doubtful. With such a law in place in Russia, the Advisory Committee recommended that the government 'ensure that . . . envisaged amendments of the Law on the Languages of the Peoples of the Russian Federation do not curtail further the scope of this provision or negatively affect other guarantees furthering the implementation of Article 11 of the Framework Convention'.[62]

While the upper limits as to what constitutes a 'substantial' number has been relatively straightforward, what might not be substantial enough for the purposes of Article 11(3) has not been clearly described by the Advisory Committee so far. In a general sense, the Advisory Committee seems to have adopted an 'as generous as possible' interpretation towards the need to make earnest efforts to use national minority languages. Even in cases where the actual numbers of persons belonging to a national minority have not been particularly high, the Advisory Committee seemed satisfied with the application of Article 11(3) in circumstances where members of minorities inhabited their traditional areas. For example, the Advisory Committee would 'note with approval', without citing any requirements under Article 11(3), practices in

60 'The relatively flexible wording of this provision stemmed from a desire to be able to take due account of the specific circumstances prevailing in the various State Parties . . . ', in Advisory Committee Opinion on Austria, ACFC/INF/OP/I (2002) 009, 2002, para. 49.

61 Above, n. 60, para. 102.

62 Advisory Committee Opinion on Russia, ACFC/INF/OP/I (2003) 005, 2002, para. 149.

countries like Finland, Norway, Italy, and others where even when dealing with groups that can be quite small in traditional areas, signs are to be bilingual. Furthermore, it noted that in Finland a municipality is considered bilingual if more than 8 per cent of the population or 3,000 inhabitants speak the Swedish language.

While these practices were seen as positive examples, they were not clearly described as required under Article 11(3) of the Framework Convention. There was no clear indication by the Advisory Committee that the figures cited were 'substantial numbers'. If one were to try to find some consistent numerical threshold as to what would be sufficiently 'substantial' for the purposes of Article 11(3), there have been favourable suggestions from the Advisory Committee when considering areas where persons belonging to a national minority constituted 25 per cent and even 10 per cent of a local population. Thus, the Advisory Committee responded very favourably to the conclusion of Austria's Constitutional Court that the Law on Ethnic Groups was unconstitutional, having imposed a minimum threshold of 25 per cent for entitlement to the display of topographical indications in minority languages, because it was too high to satisfy the requirements of the Convention in some parts of the country. According to the Constitutional Court, it was sufficient to have a national minority form more than 10 per cent of the total population in an area over a long period to entitle the inhabitants to display bilingual topographical indications. Indirectly, and in light of the conditions in Austria, the Advisory Committee seemed to be of the belief that a lower threshold of 10 per cent provided a good basis for determining 'substantial numbers': '[t]his interpretation, which is entirely in keeping with Article 11, paragraph 3 of the Framework Convention, represents a major improvement in the rights of persons belonging to national minorities.'[63] With regard to Article 11(3) however, the Advisory Council has not always been coherent or consistent. In contrast to its findings in the case of Austria, it seemed to approve a threshold of 20 per cent in the context of the Czech Republic as consistent with that country's obligations under Article 11(3):

> The Advisory Committee also notes that a provision of the new Act on municipalities (No. 128/2000) that entered into force in May 2000 authorises bilingual signs for topographical indications. Two conditions are laid down with regard to the bilingual signs: at least 20% of the citizens residing in the municipality must consider themselves as persons belonging to the national minority concerned . . . The Advisory Committee

[63] 'The relatively flexible wording of this provision stemmed from a desire to be able to take due account of the specific circumstances prevailing in the various State Parties . . . ', in Advisory Committee Opinion on Austria, ACFC/INF/OP/I (2002) 009, 2002, para. 50.

welcomes this development and expresses the hope that the new provisions will operate satisfactorily in practice.[64]

The Advisory Committee similarly favoured the introduction of legislation that authorized bilingual signs in localities where a minority represents over 20 per cent of the population in Romania.[65]

As such, it seems clear that the Advisory Committee has approached this provision using a 'carrot and stick' strategy because of its controversial genesis and undoubtedly sensitive impact on 'ownership'. In the case of more blatant breaches of Article 11(3), the Advisory Committee has indicated fairly clearly where a state's obligations under the Convention have not been met, opting for the 'stick' approach. A 'carrot' would, however, seem to be adopted in cases where the state party has been improving the protection of national minorities with increasing official topographical indications and local names in a national minority language where there are substantial numbers in traditionally inhabited areas; this ought to be welcomed as encouraging further progress.

From a strictly legal point of view, the Advisory Committee has been applying a double standard. Objectively speaking, there have to be concrete reasons for finding that 10 per cent of a national minority in an area is 'substantial enough' for Austria to have met its legal obligations under Article 11(3) for example, but that double this percentage would be needed in the neighbouring Czech Republic for this government to have any legal obligation under Article 11(3). In the absence of any attempt from the Advisory Committee to explain its reasoning, the Austrian authorities would be entitled to question the Committee's approach and conclusions since the mandate of the Advisory Committee is to deal with the interpretation of the legal obligations under the Framework Convention after all, and not be influenced by other considerations which could result in inconsistent and unpredictable approaches, as is apparently the case here.

Even more disconcerting from a legal point of view are some, though very few, cases where the Advisory Committee appears to have completely disregarded a literal reading of the Framework Convention. In its examinations of reports from Albania[66] and Germany, for example, the Advisory Committee does not appear to have closely considered whether traditional areas are still inhabited by substantial numbers of persons belonging to a national minority.

[64] Advisory Committee Opinion on the Czech Republic, ACFC/INF/OP/I (2002) 002, 2002, para. 59.

[65] Advisory Committee Opinion on Romania, ACFC/INF/OP/I (2002) 001, 2001, para. 51.

[66] Advisory Committee Opinion on Albania, ACFC/INF/OP/I (2003) 004, 2002, para. 56.

In fact, it seemed to demand active measures from the German authorities consistent with Article 11(3), despite the absence of substantial numbers:

The Advisory Committee *finds* that despite legal requirements to display topographical indications in the Sorbian language in areas traditionally inhabited by Sorbians, notably in the *Land* of Brandenburg, monolingual signs are only being replaced by bilingual ones at a very slow rate so that the whole operation could take several more years. The Advisory Committee *considers* that the German authorities should step up their efforts to speed up the full implementation of the legal provisions on bilingual signposting in areas traditionally inhabited by Sorbians.[67]

Oddly, while Article 11(3) itself is quite clear that the obligation to have official displays of traditional local, street, and other topographical indications is only required if there are substantial numbers of persons belonging to a national minority in an area, at no point did the Advisory Committee concern itself with whether or not the Sorbian population was present in 'substantial numbers'.

The legal interpretation of the Advisory Committee as to the other 'numerical' requirement of Article 11(3), that there be a 'sufficient demand' from persons belonging to a national minority in addition to 'substantial numbers', is also one of the most unsatisfactory of the Committee's monitoring activities. In fact, the Committee's actions in this regard are almost completely arbitrary and difficult to explain other than by referring to the earlier 'carrot and stick' analogy.

In describing what constitutes 'sufficient demand' in areas traditionally inhabited by substantial numbers of a national minority, the report from the Czech Republic explained that new legislation for municipalities permitted bilingual signs for topographical indications where national minorities represent at least 20 per cent of the population and where there is a demand from at least half (50 per cent) of them.

The Advisory Committee seemed to accept that unless there was a demand from more than half of the members of a national minority in an area, there was no need for Czech municipal authorities to provide bilingual signs:

The Advisory Committee also notes that a provision of the new Act on municipalities (No. 128/2000) that entered into force in May 2000 authorises bilingual signs for topographical indications. Two conditions are laid down with regard to the bilingual signs: at least 20% of the citizens residing in the municipality must consider themselves as persons belonging to the national minority concerned and, of these, at least 50% must request these signs. The Advisory Committee welcomes this development and expresses the hope that the new provisions will operate satisfactorily in practice.[68]

[67] Advisory Committee Opinion on Germany, ACFC/INF/OP/I (2002) 008, 2003, para. 86.

[68] Advisory Committee Opinion on the Czech Republic, ACFC/INF/OP/I (2002) 002, 2001, para. 59.

This apparent determination, that there is no obligation under Article 11(3) unless more than half the persons belonging to a national minority request it, is odd and even more difficult to explain in light of the object and intent of the Convention, since the Advisory Committee has generally emphasized that states parties must protect national minorities and their rights as much as possible.

Thus, when dealing with a number of reports, such as the German one, the Advisory Committee has not hesitated to castigate authorities even though there was no evidence of a demand of 50 per cent or more of members of national minorities for the bilingual display of signs and other topographical indications. Similarly, the Advisory Committee did not hesitate in the case of Serbia and Montenegro to note the need for that country to make additional efforts to have 'street names in areas inhabited by a substantial number of Romanians and Croats',[69] but without any reference whatsoever to the need for a 'sufficient request' threshold, or any indication of what this might be.

Unless one accepts that there are some states parties that the Advisory Committee tends to treat more harshly than others for no obvious reason, the Committee's inconsistent approaches will need to be addressed if states parties are to treat their obligations under Article 11(3) seriously.

One situation which one might have suspected to create difficulties in the interpretation of the requirement for a 'traditionally inhabited area' under Article 11(3) has surprisingly not occurred. Neither the Advisory Committee nor any state party has raised the traditional occupation of an area as an issue, even when dealing with national minorities such as the Roma that may have historically moved frequently through borders. It could possibly have been raised in relation to Russian-speaking minority groups of Estonia where, despite the presence in those countries of long-standing historical Russian communities, many of the present day populations arrived after the period of Soviet occupation or are descendants of these migrants. However, when discussing the issue of topographical indications in countries where these matters might have been raised, such as Romania, Slovakia, Hungary, or Estonia, the Advisory Committee has not provided any guidance or examined these matters in any direct way.

The closest treatment of this matter was only in passing and in relation to an opinion on Estonia's compliance, where the Advisory Committee referred to the 1997 Place Names Act, which limited the use of place names and topographical indications in a minority language on the basis of the language of the permanent residents in 1939.[70] In this matter, the Advisory Committee

[69] Advisory Committee Opinion on Serbia and Montenegro, ACFC/INF/OP/I (2004) 002, 2004, para. 83.

[70] Advisory Committee Opinion on Estonia, ACFC/INF/OP/I (2002) 005, 2001, para. 41.

did not comment as to whether the reference to the year 1939 in the Estonian legislation was a determination of what constituted a 'traditionally inhabited area' for the purposes of Article 11(3), but neither did it indicate that this type of requirement was inconsistent with the provision.

Though tentative, it could be possible to interpret this absence of comment to mean that the determination of what constitutes a traditionally inhabited area is not an onerous one, and that as long as a minority can show some 'long-standing' link with an area, perhaps even as brief as fifty years, then this would be sufficient to satisfy this requirement under Article 11(3).

Finally, one last issue that has been highlighted by the Advisory Committee is the pace at which topographical indications are provided in national minority languages. In its opinion on Germany, it noted that topographical indications in the Sorbian language in areas traditionally inhabited by the Sorbian minority might take a number of years:

> . . . it appears that the aforementioned legal provisions have not yet been entirely put into practice, particularly by the local authorities. The situation seems less satisfactory in the *Land* of Brandenburg where the Advisory Committee's attention was drawn to the fact that monolingual signs were only being replaced by bilingual ones at a very slow rate and that the whole operation could take several more years.[71]

Noting that some municipalities were possibly hesitant to put up bilingual signposts because of the costs involved, the Advisory Committee indicated that the slow pace and reluctance of local authorities due to the expense was not sufficient reason to disregard obligations under Article 11(3): '[t]he Advisory Committee does not accept this financial argument as appropriate and considers that the German authorities should ensure the full implementation of the legal provisions on bilingual signposting in areas traditionally inhabited by Sorbians.'[72]

It would therefore seem that unless there are practical difficulties in the use of topographical indications, financial inconveniences are not valid considerations for delaying the implementation of a state party's obligation under Article 11(3), and that authorities are to proceed 'as quickly as possible wherever it is still necessary'.[73]

3. *Overall Interpretation and Future Development*

From the various comments on specific issues considered by the Advisory Committee, it would seem that despite its timid wording and numerous requirements, Article 11(3) still imposes tangible legal obligations on states

[71] Advisory Committee Opinion on Germany, ACFC/INF/OP/I (2002) 008, 2003, para. 52.
[72] ibid., para. 53. [73] ibid., para. 54.

parties to: (*a*) have legislation in place that clearly sets out the criteria that would, given a state's specific conditions, provide for the use of a national minority language in local names and other topographical indications in traditional areas where there is a sufficient demand from a substantial population; (*b*) take steps to promote the use of a national minority language in local names and other topographical indications where 'substantial numbers' are present. While not suggesting that a single percentage can be applied to extremely different situations in various countries, less than 25 per cent and perhaps even as low as 10 per cent of the population could be 'substantial' enough to require states parties to make earnest efforts to have bilingual designations; (*c*) be as generous as possible, rather than rigid and dogmatic, in determining how many individuals use a minority language and whether they are present in substantial numbers in a given area. To require that persons belonging to a national minority must speak the minority language in their daily life would probably be inappropriate and exclude individuals who should be considered to be part of a national minority, for example; and (*d*) introduce topographical indications in minority languages as quickly as possible where warranted under Article 11(3). Reasons of administrative or financial convenience are not sufficient for a state party to delay this action.

Thus, while not disputing that states parties have a degree of flexibility in applying Article 11(3) in light of 'specific conditions', and even political and historical considerations if we are to believe the drafting history of this paragraph, the Advisory Committee has nevertheless opted for an interpretation which proposes fairly clear guidelines on the type of conduct expected, as well as the type of conduct that would fall short of expectations.

Undoubtedly, there are some troublesome aspects of the Advisory Committee's approach to monitoring the compliance of states parties with Article 11(3) that will need to be addressed in the future. While its approach has broadly followed the obligations described above thus far, the Advisory Committee has been erratic at times, and clearly inconsistent and contradictory in the way it has handled Article 11(3).

From even the most generous of views, the Advisory Committee's treatment of Germany and the Czech Republic for example, in terms of what constitutes a sufficient demand for the provision of topographical indications in a national minority language under Article 11(3), makes no sense. The absence of any rational explanation as to why 50 per cent of a national minority in one traditional area must request such indications in their language for a state (the Czech Republic) to have the obligation to provide them, while for another state (Germany) no evidence of any demand at all from the national minority seems to have been needed, is completely unsatisfactory from a legal point of view.

The role of the Advisory Committee is to monitor state compliance with the rights and obligations provided for in a legally binding document, and not to decide issues according to subjective or changing views of what is desirable. Therefore, the inconsistencies as to what constitutes a sufficient demand for the purposes of Article 11(3) will eventually need to be ironed out to ensure that states parties have a sufficiently clear understanding of situations where they will need to provide minority language indicators, as quickly and as far as is practical and possible.

Additionally, there are a number of other requirements that the Advisory Committee will need to clarify to ensure that the obligations under Article 11(3) are well understood and, therefore, will be complied with more readily. It would be helpful for states parties to understand that their obligations arise in traditionally inhabited areas only, but that this concept is to be interpreted in a broad and generous sense, and not be held as applicable only to 'ancient' population groups that have been established in the same localities for centuries. Similarly, the Advisory Committee should be more consistent in what is required in terms of sufficiency of numbers and to demand this sufficiently in line with the explanation outlined above.

III. Conclusion and Outlook

The Advisory Committee has had mixed success in providing clear guidelines and in assisting our understanding of the distinct provisions of Article 11. For the first two paragraphs dealing with what is, in effect, specific aspects emanating from the private use of a minority language—a person's name or surname also being linked to the right to private life, while private signs and displays is associated with freedom of expression—the Advisory Committee has set out the broad outlines and content of both rights fairly clearly. At least as regards its handling of these two provisions, it could be said that it has maintained an approach that is maximalist, inclusive, and accommodating, all of which are quite clearly consistent with the objectives of the Framework Convention. On a number of occasions, it has referred to the principle that states parties should comply with Article 11 obligations 'as far as is possible'. This could be understood to mean that since the object of the FCNM is to ensure respect for 'the ethnic, cultural, linguistic and religious identity of each person belonging to a national minority', it is for states parties to make a case as to why they have not established the maximum conditions and opportunities for minorities to preserve and develop their identities.

Thus, one can find a common thread in the Advisory Committee's opinions in its handling of Article 11(1) and Article 11(2): broadly speaking, states parties cannot impinge on an individual's free choice of language in the form of their names and in the private displays of their language. Furthermore, in the case of a person's name and surname, this free choice must not only be tolerated, it must be recognized and used by states parties for official purposes.

Although perhaps somewhat hidden away in the content of its monitoring reports, it is here that the Advisory Committee has, for one of the first times in international law, provided some precise indications as to what the free choice of language for the purpose of one's name and surname and private displays entails. The Advisory Committee unhesitatingly concluded that considerations regarding private displays in a minority language should also include the script used for that particular language, or more accurately, the script freely chosen by an individual. While this right can be said to emanate from the freedom of expression, until now no international body had made the clear link between language of choice and script as a constituent element of language.

In the case of names and surnames, international law has more clearly established that these were covered by the right to private life. Under the Framework Convention and the monitoring reports and conclusions of the Advisory Committee, however, it is now clear that this right extends to the linguistic forms of names and surnames. In addition, a number of opinions of the Advisory Committee have clarified that Article 11 must be understood to accommodate changing forms of a person's surname due to cultural traditions. In the case of some Slavic surnames, for example, these forms will vary depending on whether the person is male or female, with the endings -yj or -ij for the masculine and -a or -ia for the feminine, for example. Thanks to the Advisory Committee's opinions, it is indubitable that this gender differentiated spelling is protected and must not only be permitted, but also recognized by authorities. Defining the link between this right and the right to private life may also assist other international courts and decision-making bodies in their dealings with issues of linguistic and cultural diversity.

As with Article 10, the Advisory Committee has generally pointed out that clear legislation or constitutional provisions are required to ensure that persons belonging to a national minority may, in fact and in law, enjoy the rights they are entitled to under the Framework Convention. This is especially true in the case Article 11(3), which deals with the use of a minority language for official purposes by public authorities, and to Article 11(2) to a more limited extent when involving recognition and use of a person's name in a minority language.

While the opinions of the Advisory Committee have been fairly clear and consistent with international human rights standards in the less controversial aspects of Article 11, such as the first and second paragraphs, the Committee's handling of the third paragraph leaves many uncertainties, contradictions, and seemingly arbitrary results. While it must be acknowledged that the challenges were greater with regard to this paragraph as only one other international treaty, the European Charter for Regional or Minority Languages, deals with the obligation to use a minority name for topographical indications and the *travaux préparatoires* of the FCNM show a series of difficult and even controversial compromises in this respect, the Advisory Committee has not provided the sort of clear guidance one might have hoped or expected. Especially in relation to what constitutes substantial numbers and a sufficient demand for a state party to have the obligation to put up topographical indications in a minority language under Article 11(3), the Advisory Committee's opinions have been not very helpful, as they do not appear to have any consistency or obvious objective basis. While the Committee has generally required states parties to do 'as much as is possible' to implement their treaty obligations, this has not always been the case with Article 11(3). The Advisory Committee has deemed legislation 'acceptable for now', imposing unusually burdensome statistical thresholds before authorities are required to respond to demands for bilingual signage in the case of some states, while for others it has deemed it necessary for a state to comply with this regulation, even in the absence of any significant demand from national minorities. In the absence of any justification or explanation in the written opinions of the Advisory Committee, these apparent double standards will need to be remedied in the coming years to avoid uncertainty and confusion as to the extent of a state party's obligations under this provision.

In spite of these shortcomings, the Advisory Committee has clarified a number of important aspects of Article 11(3), which should assist in the future implementation of the Framework Convention, even if it has not been consistent in their application. On this point, it has generally indicated that Article 11(3) must be read and applied generously, 'as far as is possible' to repeat the words used in a number of its opinions, in light of the Framework Convention's objectives.

The determination of what constitutes a traditionally inhabited area, substantial numbers of persons belonging to a national minority, or the nature of the efforts required by states parties when they 'endeavour' to have topographical indications in a minority language ought not be approached in a restrictive way. This may explain why in a number of cases the Advisory Committee has not overly concerned itself with the 'numbers game', but seemed to focus more on whether it was dealing with a traditionally inhabited area, though again not always consistently.

Finally, from a practical point of view, the Advisory Committee has not been very receptive to arguments of administrative or financial inconvenience as a means to avoid implementing the obligations of Article 11. Particularly in the application of Article 11(3), delays caused by municipal authorities unwilling to set aside the funding necessary for bilingual signs in areas satisfying the conditions of this provision were deemed to be inconsistent with the obligations of the Framework Convention.

As with some of the other parts of the FCNM, a lack of clarity or specific explanation as to why and how certain state practices are in breach of Article 11 remains in many opinions. Yet again, some of the Advisory Committee's opinions do not always appear to be clear interpretations of specific FCNM obligations. These practices should be avoided in the future to give states parties firmer and clearer guidelines as to their legal commitments.

ARTICLE 12

Patrick Thornberry

1. The Parties shall, where appropriate, take measures in the fields of education and research to foster knowledge of the culture, history, language and religion of their national minorities and of the majority.
2. In this context the Parties shall *inter alia* provide adequate opportunities for teacher training and access to textbooks, and facilitate contacts among students and teachers of different communities.
3. The Parties undertake to promote equal opportunities for access to education at all levels for persons belonging to national minorities.

I. Background

A. Issues

The provisions of the Framework Convention for the Protection of National Minorities (FCNM) on education represent a fresh chapter in a complex history of instruments and principles, some of which reach back into the era before the advent of universal human rights. Thus the minority treaties and declarations under the aegis of the League of Nations were typically concerned with education and the use of language in education.[1] Evidence from the period also indicates that the education provisions of the League instruments were a matter of primary concern to all parties to the system, including petitioners to the League authorities.[2] The emotional entanglement of minority communities in educational issues suggests that deep intergenerational impulses are at work; education will appear to many members of minority groups as a vital safeguard for their continued existence as distinct communities. The provisions of the Framework Convention address key questions in a form that manifests elements of the League approach within a human rights framework. In essence, Article 12 addresses questions of cultural knowledge in the area of minority rights, the 'human capital' necessary to deliver this curriculum, and the right of access to it. In addition, Article 13 addresses the specific issue and implications of the right of minorities to establish their own educational and training establishments, and Article 14 partially deals with the vexed issue of minority languages in education. The 'individualist' Convention terminology of 'persons belonging to minorities' invests the three articles, but is not rigorously maintained. Thus in its call for knowledge of the history and culture of minorities, the language of Article 12 properly refers to its collective aspect, that is knowledge of the community, not simply its individualized components. The provisions on education are to be read in the light of the instrument as a whole. The other specific reference to education in the Framework Convention is in Article 6, according to which the parties shall encourage 'a spirit of tolerance and intercultural dialogue and take effective measures to promote mutual respect and understanding and co-operation among all persons living on their territory . . . in particular in the fields of education, culture and the media'. The formative role of the education system in the maintenance of identity is widely understood, as is its role as an agency of socialization for democratic citizenship. International law favours the notion that education should contribute to the integration of minorities into general society, while disapproving of policies of assimilation against the will of those who belong to minorities, a principle reflected in Article 5(2) of the Framework Convention. Assimilation essentially involves the disappearance of a culture through absorption into another, usually larger and more dominant group. Assimilation *per se* is not 'forbidden' by international norms.[3] On the contrary, it allows individuals a choice as to whether they wish or do not wish

[1] P. Thornberry, *International Law and the Rights of Minorities* (Clarendon Press, Oxford, 1991), ch. 2.

[2] Above, n. 1.

[3] CAHMIN, Explanatory Report to the Framework Convention, H(1995) 010, Strasbourg, 1995, para. 45, according to which Art. 5, para. 2 'does not prohibit voluntary assimilation'.

to embrace minority rights.[4] On the other hand, if assimilation is not contrary to the will of individuals, conditions in the state, including the institutions of education, should be adequate to facilitate the maintenance of minority distinctiveness. Neglect of minority rights is not an acceptable policy.

B. History

A number of general human rights texts address issues of content and access in the field of education. The human right to education was one of the first fruits of the human rights movement. Article 26 of the Universal Declaration of Human Rights (UDHR) provides that everyone has the right to education, which shall be free, 'at least in the elementary and fundamental stages', and that elementary education shall be compulsory. Furthermore, education 'shall be directed to the full development of the human personality and to the strengthening of respect for human rights and fundamental freedoms. It shall promote understanding, tolerance and friendship among all nations, racial or religious groups, and shall further the activities of the United Nations for the maintenance of peace'. No linguistic medium of education is specified, but there is a content and purpose for education in the encouragement of mutual understanding, tolerance, and friendship between nations, religions, and races.[5]

The International Covenants on Human Rights carry forward the inspiration of the UDHR and add elements relevant to our study. Article 27 of the International Covenant on Civil and Political Rights (ICCPR) sets out a basic standard of minority rights in terms of culture, religion, and language, but does not specifically account for education.[6] The article has produced a respectable amount of case law but little on education; the most substantive case on education relates primarily to Article 26 of the Covenant rather than Article 27.[7]

[4] Framework Convention for the Protection of National Minorities (FCNM), Art. 3, para. 1 protects the right of persons belonging to a minority to choose to be treated, or not to be treated, as such. The choice is expressed as one belonging to those already 'belonging' to minorities. Second Conference on the Human Dimension of the CSCE, Document of the Copenhagen Meeting of the Conference on the Human Dimension of the CSCE, Copenhagen, 1990, para. 32 delves deeper in that it visualizes choice as governing the initial question of belonging to a group.

[5] For observations on the drafting of the article, see J. Morsink, *The Universal Declaration of Human Rights: Origins, Drafting and Intent* (University of Pennsylvania Press, Philadelphia, 1999), 212–17.

[6] 'In those states where ethnic, religious or linguistic minorities exist, persons belonging to such minorities shall not be denied the right, in community with the other members of their group, to enjoy their own culture, to profess and practise their own religion, or to use their own language', International Covenant on Civil and Political Rights (adopted 16 December 1966, entered into force 23 March 1976) 999 UNTS 171 (ICCPR), Art. 27.

[7] UN Human Rights Committee, *Waldman* v. *Canada* (1999) Comm. No. 694/1996, UN Doc. CCPR/C/67/D/694/1996, 1999, pp. 86–102.

Article 13 of the International Covenant on Economic, Social, and Cultural Rights (ICESCR) reiterates Article 26 UDHR on the purposes of education, adding that 'education shall enable all persons to participate effectively in a free society'.[8] The commitment of the international community to raise the general level of education in society is evidenced by the references in Article 13 to the provision of free and compulsory primary education for all, to the provision of secondary and higher education equally accessible to all, and to the progressive introduction of free secondary education and higher education.[9] Article 13 ICESCR is the subject of the extensive General Comment No. 13 by the Committee on Economic, Social, and Cultural Rights.[10] According to this Comment, 'education in all its forms and at all levels shall exhibit the following interrelated and essential features',[11] those of availability; accessibility, which incorporates 'overlapping dimensions' of non-discrimination; physical accessibility and economic accessibility; acceptability; and adaptability.[12] Of these essential features, some have specific significance for minority groups, notably the emphasis on non-discrimination in access to education, and the notion of acceptability. On acceptability, the Comment explains that education must be 'relevant, culturally appropriate and of good quality'.[13] The approach in the Comment is an important validation of the contemporary sensitivity of international law to cultural diversity. Instruments on minority rights are not rendered redundant by this general affirmation of culturally appropriate education; on the contrary, while binding in their own right, they supply essential guidance for the content of the Covenant, giving further expression to the interrelationship of human rights instruments.

The Convention on the Rights of the Child (CRC) deals extensively with education in Articles 28 and 29.[14] Furthermore, the article is the focus of the

[8] International Covenant on Economic, Social, and Cultural Rights (ICESCR) (adopted 16 December 1966, entry into force 3 January 1976), UNGA Res. 2200 A (XXI) (1966), UN Doc A/6316, Art. 13, para. 1.

[9] Above, n. 8, Art. 13, para. 2.

[10] Committee on Economic, Social, and Cultural Rights 'General Comment No. 13' in 'The Right to Education', 21st session (1999), UN Doc. E/2000/22, E/C.12/1999/11, pp. 111–27.

[11] Above, n. 10, para. 6.

[12] The '4-A scheme'—see UN Commission on Human Rights, Preliminary Report of the Special Rapporteur on Education of the UN Commission on Human Rights, 55th session (1999), UN Doc. E/CN.4/1999/39 for a seminal elaboration of the scheme.

[13] Above, n. 10, para. 33.

[14] Office of the High Commissioner for Human Rights, Convention on the Rights of the Child, UNGA Res. 44/25 (1989), Art. 29 prescribes that education should be directed to, *inter alia*: '(c) The development of respect for the child's parents, his or her own cultural identity, language and values, for the national values of the country in which the child is living, the country from which he or she may originate, and for civilizations different from his or her own. (d) The preparation of the child for responsible life in a free society, in the spirit of understanding, peace, tolerance, equality of sexes, and friendship among all peoples, ethnic, national and religious groups and persons of indigenous origin.'

first General Comment by the Committee on the Rights of the Child, entitled 'The Aims of Education', issued in 2001.[15] The Comment insists that the child's right to education is not only a matter of access, but also of content. It recognizes, while not elaborating explicitly on culture, that tensions may exist between the global and the local, between efforts to promote tolerance among all peoples, and the provisions on respect for identity, observing that:

> in fact, part of the importance of this provision lies precisely in its recognition of the need for a balanced approach to education and one which succeeds in reconciling diverse values through dialogue and respect for difference. Moreover, children are capable of playing a unique role in bridging many of the differences that have historically separated groups of peoples from one another.[16]

The Comment also underscores the importance of reading the Convention as a whole, including Article 30,[17] a provision on the children of minorities and the indigenous, which employs a formulation that closely follows Article 27 ICCPR. Other relevant instruments include the International Convention on the Elimination of All Forms of Racial Discrimination (CERD), which refers to 'the right to education and training' as among the rights to be protected against discrimination in Article 5(*e*)(v); additionally, Article 7 CERD calls for anti-racist education, and the promotion of tolerance and friendship among national and racial or ethnic groups and human rights education in general.[18]

In the European sphere, the European Convention for the Protection of Human Rights and Fundamental Freedoms (ECHR), has spawned a number

The text integrates respect for minority identity and values with respect for the values of the national community, and value systems beyond the national community. The purpose of education is understood as cosmopolitan and particular, with a pronounced intercultural aspect.

[15] Committee on the Rights of the Child, General Comment No 1, The Aims of Education, 26th session (2003), UN Doc. CRC/GC/2001/1.

[16] Above, n. 15, para. 4.

[17] CRC, Art. 30 reads: 'In those States in which ethnic, religious or linguistic minorities or persons of indigenous origin exist, a child belonging to such a minority or who is indigenous shall not be denied the right, in community with the other members of his or her group, to enjoy his or her own culture, to profess and practise his or her own religion, or to use his or her own language'.

[18] Committee on the Elimination of Racial Discrimination (CERD), General Recommendation V, Reporting by State Parties, 15th session (1977), UN Doc. A/32/18 at 75, Chapter VIII, Decision 3 (XV) drew the attention of the states parties to the fact that, in accordance with Art. 7 of the Convention, the information to which the preceding paragraph refers should include information on the 'immediate and effective measures' which they have adopted, 'in the fields of teaching, education, culture and information', with a view to: (*a*) 'combating prejudices which lead to racial discrimination'; (*b*) 'Promoting understanding, tolerance and friendship among nations and racial or ethnical groups'; (*c*) 'Propagating the purposes and principles of the Charter of the United Nations, the Universal Declaration of Human Rights, the United Nations Declaration on the Elimination of All Forms of Racial Discrimination' as well as the International Convention on the Elimination of All Forms of Racial Discrimination.

of key cases on education, founded on the rather negatively phrased Article 2 of Protocol 1.[19] The provisions may be appraised in terms of several articles of the Framework Convention, but were interpreted by the European Court of Human Rights (ECtHR) in a rather limiting manner, regarding access to a specific form of education in the *Belgian Linguistics* case,[20] an influential statement on the system of unilingual regions in Belgium.[21] However, in the special circumstances in *Cyprus* v. *Turkey*, the Court invested the right with greater weight in relation to Greek-Cypriot parents who wished to continue the Greek language primary education of their children in the north of Cyprus through to the level of secondary education. The lack of such continuing provision by the authorities of the 'TRNC' was deemed a denial of the substance of the right at issue.[22] The meaning of 'philosophical convictions' has also been an issue under the Convention, with case law favouring a pluralist and non-indoctrinating approach to education, without a specific commitment to interculturalism or equivalent philosophy.[23] Further questions of language in education are considered below.

The UN Declaration on the Rights of Persons Belonging to National or Ethnic, Religious, and Linguistic Minorities[24] sets a basic global standard in the field of minority rights. Article 4(4) provides that, 'States should, where appropriate, take measures in the field of education in order to encourage knowledge of the history, traditions, language and culture of the minorities existing within their territory. Persons belonging to minorities should have adequate opportunities to gain knowledge of the society as a whole.'[25] According to the Eide commentary on the Declaration:

> The overall purpose of Article 4.4 is to ensure egalitarian integration based on non-discrimination and respect for each of the cultural, linguistic or religious groups which

[19] 'No one shall be denied the right to education. In the exercise of any functions which it assumes in relation to education and teaching, the state shall respect the right of parents to ensure such education and teaching in conformity with their own religious and philosophical convictions' in European Convention for the Protection of Human Rights and Fundamental Freedoms (ECHR), ETS No. 5, Protocol to the Convention for the Protection of Human Rights and Fundamental Freedoms, 1950, Art. 2.

[20] *Belgian Linguistics Case*, Series A, No. 6 (1968), EHRR 252.

[21] Where the essence of the 'access' point was that Art. 2 does not oblige a state party to establish at its own expense, or to subsidize, education of any particular type or at any particular level, but that the article safeguarded access to schools once they were established.

[22] *Cyprus* v. *Turkey* (25781/94) (2001) EHRR 327, judgment, para. 278.

[23] See, in particular *Kjeldsen, Busk Madsen and Pedersen* v. *Denmark* (5095/71) (1976) EHRR 6, Series A, 23; also *Skender* v. *Former Yugoslav Republic of Macedonia* (62059/00) (2001) EHRR.

[24] A. Eide, Commentary to the UN Declaration on the Rights of Persons Belonging to National or Ethnic, Religious, and Linguistic Minorities (2001), UN Doc. E/CN.4/Sub.2/AC.5/2001/2, paras. 64–70.

[25] These provisions are also common in frequently 'stronger' texts on indigenous peoples: International Labour Organization (ILO) Convention No. 169 Concerning Indigenous and Tribal

together form the national society. The formation of more or less involuntary ghettos where the different groups live in their own world without knowledge of, or tolerance for, persons belonging to the other parts of the national society would be a violation of the purpose and spirit of the Declaration.[26]

This paragraph of the Declaration coheres with the line of principles leading to Article 12 of the Framework Convention, acting as a source of inspiration for the latter.

At the European regional level, Article 7 of the Charter for Regional or Minority Languages includes, among its 'objectives and principles', the promotion of 'mutual understanding between all the linguistic groups of the country and in particular the inclusion of respect, understanding and tolerance in relation to regional or minority languages among the objectives of education'. Article 8 includes reference to making arrangements 'to ensure the teaching of the history and the culture which is reflected by the regional or minority language'. Paragraph 34 of the 1990 Conference on Security and Co-operation in Europe (CSCE) (now the Organization for Security and Co-operation in Europe (OSCE)) Document of the Copenhagen Meeting of the Conference on the Human Dimension (the Copenhagen Document) provides, *ex facie*, a more generous statement in paragraph 32(2) of an 'institutions' right in the same field as Article 13 FCNM, and a slightly more elaborate provision on language in education. In paragraph 34, the Copenhagen Document focuses on history and culture, providing that, in 'the context of the teaching of history and culture in educational establishments, the [participating states] will also take account of the history and culture of national minorities'. This is reinforced by paragraph 40(4) whereby the states are to 'endeavour to ensure that the objectives of education include special attention to the problem of racial prejudice and hatred and to the development of respect for different civilizations and cultures'.[27] The above basic principles are subsumed in the Hague Recommendations, paragraph 19 of which provides that, in view of 'the importance and value that international instruments attach to intercultural education and the highlighting of

Peoples in Independent Countries (adopted 27 June 1989, entry into force 5 September 1989), 76th session, Art. 31 provides that: 'Educational measures shall be taken among all sections of the national community, and particularly those that are in most direct contact with the peoples concerned, with the object of eliminating prejudices that they may harbour in respect of these peoples. To this end, efforts shall be made to ensure that history textbooks and other educational materials provide a fair, accurate and informative portrayal of the societies and cultures of these peoples.'

[26] A. Eide, Commentary to the UN Declaration on the Rights of Persons Belonging to National or Ethnic, Religious, and Linguistic Minorities (2001), UN Doc. E/CN.4/Sub.2/AC.5/2001/2, para. 69.

[27] Second Conference on the Human Dimension of the CSCE, Document of the Copenhagen Meeting of the Conference on the Human Dimension of the CSCE, Copenhagen, 1990, para. 40(4) regarding remarks on Roma education issues.

minority histories, cultures and traditions, State educational authorities should ensure that the general compulsory curriculum includes the teaching of the histories, cultures and traditions of their respective national minorities'. The intercultural aspect of the Recommendations is further strengthened in the proposition that '[e]ncouraging members of the majority to learn the languages of the national minorities within the State would contribute to the strengthening of tolerance and multiculturalism within the State'.[28]

C. Context

The broad textual scheme of the education rights in the Framework Convention has already been described in the introduction to this chapter. As stated in the General Comment on the right to education by the Committee on Economic, Social, and Cultural Rights, education 'is both a human right and an indispensable means of realizing other human rights'. The same sentiment may be applied to the normative scheme of the Framework Convention. In the particular context of minority rights, the possibilities to enjoy these rights are severely reduced in the absence of a coherent education strategy. The different elements of the Convention 'hang together', so that minority empowerment in education leads to empowerment in other areas. Conversely, educational disempowerment leads to disadvantage. The chances of political and social participation; effective equality; success in economic and cultural life; and the realization of freedom of expression through minority media, are reduced by a lack of attention to education. The consequences of this deficiency are seen notably in the case of the Roma, for whom educational deprivation connects with cumulative, systemic discrimination against them.[29]

II. Analysis

A. Structure of Article 12

The structure of Article 12 is complex and is addressed below in interconnected sections dealing with curriculum; intercommunal educational contacts; and educational access. The special section on the educational situation of the Roma ties together all strands of Article 12, and, additionally, cuts across the main education articles in the Framework Convention. The Convention

[28] Foundation on Interethnic Relations Recommendations, The Hague Recommendations regarding the Education Rights of National Minorities and Explanatory Note No. 12, 13, 1996, para. 19.

[29] By 'systemic', I do not mean to suggest deliberate discrimination, but rather the interconnected nature and resultant policies in various fields, with disparate impact on Roma communities.

organs have devoted a great deal of attention to the educational situation of Roma in particular, revealing a spectrum of national conditions from unsatisfactory to severely deficient.

Key terms in debates on educating mixed populations are: 'multiculturalism' and 'interculturalism'. 'Multiculturalism' reflects the coexistence of cultures in the same society and is usually understood as a programme or policy to recognize cultural differences expressed through the education system and elsewhere, in order that individuals may 'know' their own culture. 'Interculturalism', or intercultural dialogue, is referred to in Article 6 of the Framework Convention,[30] and for example, in the Council of Europe's European Charter for Regional or Minority Languages, and in essence denotes reciprocity of learning among cultural groups.[31] Article 12 of the Framework Convention appears to have elements of both approaches. Specifically, Article 12(1) suggests a benign social reciprocity associated with general society's knowledge of their minorities, and vice versa; meanwhile Article 12(2) is in part explicitly intercultural in its references to 'contacts among students and leaders of different communities'. Finally, Article 12(3) emphasizes the importance of access to education for minorities without specifying content. The point on education 'at all levels' illustrates not only the importance of education for individuals to succeed in the particular society, but also the group need to increase its survival capacity through the education of its members. The Framework Convention's account of intercultural education implies that the general population should be aware of minority presence, history, and culture; and equally that minorities should not retreat into psychological ghettos where they take no interest in fellow citizens. The aim, in the words of the Explanatory Report, is to 'create a climate of tolerance and dialogue'.[32] The provisions of Article 12 have a potential impact on many elements of educational curricula. For minorities and majorities, negative stereotypes of 'the Other' should be avoided, and incitement of hostility between populations even more so.[33] Education in formal and less formal

[30] Ad Hoc Committee for the Protection of National Minorities (CAHMIN), Explanatory Report on the Framework Convention for the Protection of National Minorities, H(1995) 010, 1995, para. 48.

[31] Council of Europe (CoE), European Charter on Regional or Minority Languages, ETS No. 148, Explanatory Report, 1993, para. 14 does not define the term 'interculturalism', but provides some illumination in its observation that the approach 'corresponds fully to the values traditionally upheld by the Council of Europe and its efforts to promote closer relations between peoples, increased European co-operation and a better understanding between different population groups within the State on an intercultural basis'.

[32] Above, n. 30, para. 71.

[33] Above, n. 8, Art. 20: '(1) Any propaganda for war shall be prohibited by law. (2) Any advocacy of national, racial or religious hatred that constitutes incitement to discrimination, hostility or violence shall be prohibited by law.'

senses is enhanced by intercommunal contacts. Prejudice is often strongest where there are few contacts between groups.

B. The Curriculum

1. Travaux préparatoires *of Article 12*

The following account of the progress of the *travaux préparatoires* takes the various elements in Article 12 all together. In drafting the article, the Steering Committee of Human Rights (CDDH) drew heavily on the UN Declaration on Minorities under the general rubric of 'cultural freedoms',[34] combining its norms on general participation, cultural development, and education. The Ad Hoc Committee for the Protection of National Minorities (CAHMIN) report on its third meeting referred to intercultural learning, and textbooks, as points raised in discussion; points which have generally been subsumed into the text of the Framework Convention.[35] On the other hand, a suggestion that minority pupils 'be required' to learn the official language of the country does not figure in the final text. The 1994 CAHMIN Preliminary Draft Convention is explicit on the intercultural thrust of the education provisions, with its Article 10(1) referring to school teaching as favouring 'mutual understanding and a spirit of tolerance',[36] while Article 10(2) provided that '[t]he Parties shall endeavour to include in school curricula the teaching, not only of the culture and history of the majority, but also of their national minorities'. Article 10(3) added that '[f]or these purposes, the parties shall promote the publication of the appropriate school textbooks, if possible also in the minority language, and adequate teacher training'. Furthermore, state proposals feeding into the drafting process did not greatly deviate from the general thrust of the Preliminary Draft. The suggestion by Turkey to add 'solidarity' to phrases on mutual understanding and tolerance is an exception and[37] a suggestion which would have shifted the balance of the text away from minority history and culture, towards a greater emphasis on education within a broader framework of national citizenship. A Council for Cultural Co-operation (CDCC) proposal sought to make the intercultural perspective more explicit by adding the words, 'in an intercultural perspective', to the Draft, explaining that this

[34] Steering Committee, Final Activity Report, Doc. CDDH (93) 22, 8 September 1993.

[35] CAHMIN, 3rd meeting, CAHMIN (94) 13, meeting report, 1994.

[36] CAHMIN, Preliminary Draft Framework Convention on the Protection of National Minorities, CAHMIN (94) 12, 1994.

[37] CAHMIN, Proposals Concerning the Preliminary Draft Framework Convention, CAHMIN (94) 14 Rev., 1994, p. 24.

concept implied 'not only respect for identities, but also the notion of interaction and synthesis between cultures as opposed to segregation'.

Further CAHMIN processing produced a text which moved towards its present shape by changing 'to encourage' knowledge, to the formula 'to foster' knowledge, the latter verb being slightly stronger and signifying in this context an obligation to promote the growth of knowledge. There is also a shift in the final CAHMIN versions from referring to knowledge of the culture and history of national minorities as an add-on, or lexically secondary, to knowledge of the culture and history of the majority; to placing the minority element first. The Draft Convention suggestion that textbooks were to be published in minority languages does not appear in the final text, and the notion of 'publication' of textbooks was changed to 'access to textbooks', 'it being understood that the former was covered by the latter',[38] in the sense that 'access' included the publication of textbooks and their purchase in other countries.[39] The processing of suggestions on the final version of Article 12(3) also involved juggling with the term 'access', wherein 'equal access to education at all levels' became 'equal opportunities for access to education at all levels', a change which *ex facie* results in a less demanding text.[40] The reference to equality was highlighted by the delegation of Norway as an important derivative of the general principle of equality.[41]

(a) *Article 12(1)*

The text of Article 12(1), as it stands, incorporates the modest but firm injunction '*shall* . . . take measures' to foster knowledge[42] of minorities and the majority 'where appropriate'. It is difficult to visualize cases where it would not be appropriate. As noted, there is no explicit reference to 'interculturalism', but the concept encapsulates the thrust of the paragraph. The absence of the requirement to inculcate principles of 'solidarity' through the educational process keeps the paragraph within the liberal ethos of minority rights and its concern for diversity.[43] It is implicit in the text that the necessary 'knowledge' to be fostered should be critical and fair-minded, avoiding ideological

[38] CAHMIN, 6th meeting, CAHMIN (94) 28, meeting report, 1994, p. 9.

[39] CAHMIN, 7th meeting, CAHMIN (94) 32, meeting report, 1994, p. 47.

[40] Compare the 4th and 5th Meeting Reports of CAHMIN—CAHMIN, 4th meeting, CAHMIN (94) 16, 1994, p. 26, and CAHMIN, 5th meeting, CAHMIN (94) 19, 1994, p. 28, respectively, with CAHMIN, 6th meeting, CAHMIN (94) 28, 1994, p. 32.

[41] Above, n. 37, pp. 10–11.

[42] Emphasis added.

[43] Compare Arts. 10 and 29 of the African Charter on Human and Peoples' Rights, setting out an obligation of solidarity and employing it as a potential restriction on freedom of association. African Charter on Human and Peoples' Rights (adopted 27 June 1981, entered into force 21 October 1986) (1982) 21 ILM 58 (Banjul Charter).

manipulation or propaganda and racist and xenophobic ideas, and presented with full respect for human rights.[44]

2. *Practice*

(a) *Disseminating Knowledge of Minority Cultures*

The Advisory Committee has been frequently engaged with Article 12, though its interpretations of the article's requirements have not produced a great deal of contestation on the part of reporting states. The report of the Russian Federation is not untypical in its statement that, 'all-Russia textbooks . . . coexist with education programmes developed and regional textbooks published in all constituent entities of the Russian Federation, where the historical past of the native peoples, their culture and their religious beliefs, customs and traditions have received a fairly complete coverage.'[45] In some cases, governments deliver a critique of their national performance, which may strengthen the norm in question. Thus, the government of the Czech Republic observed that:

> Education of the majority population about the culture, history, language and religion of national minorities has traditionally been neglected. In spite of a certain progress made during the last ten years, Czech instruction books remain largely textbooks of the Czech ethnic nation, its history, culture, its fight for ethnic autonomy and later state sovereignty . . . It is as though the Czech lands have not traditionally been the home of various ethnic, cultural and religious communities, especially the German and Jewish national minorities, and the perpetually disregarded Romanies.[46]

The Committee favours the teaching of intercommunal tolerance in general curricula for the population as a whole, in addition to any specific education afforded to members of minorities; otherwise the point of the article would be blunted. Hence, the Committee recommended that Albania consider including the teaching of tolerance in schools as a means of reducing discrimination against Roma and Egyptians in the country.[47] In the case of Slovakia, the Committee welcomed plans to introduce a multicultural component in

[44] See the language employed in Committee of Ministers, Recommendation Rec. (2001)15 on History Teaching in Twenty-first-Century Europe, CoE, 771st meeting, 2001.

[45] Russian Federation State Report, ACFC/SR (99) 15, 2000. Similarly, in the case of Sweden, 'The government considers it important that all children in Sweden, whether they belong to a minority or majority, already learn in school about the history of the national minorities in Sweden and their culture, language and religion, and also their part in society': Sweden State Report, ACFC/SR (2001) 003, 2001. See also Switzerland State Report, ACFC/SR (2001) 2, 2001, para. 227.

[46] Czech Republic State Report, ACFC/SR (99) 6, 1999.

[47] Advisory Committee on the Framework Convention for the Protection of National Minorities, Opinion on Albania, ACFC/INF/OP/I (2003) 004, 2002, paras. 39–40.

the core curriculum of schools.[48] Similarly, for Italy, the Committee expressed the wish that the authorities will take advantage of a new law 'to increase the multicultural and multiethnic component of school syllabi and . . . facilitate purchase and/or publication of textbooks. More generally, the . . . Committee hopes that efforts to increase knowledge about minority cultures will be enlarged for the benefit of the majority as well as the minority.'[49]

In cases where states have reported that they provide multicultural education in minority areas, but not elsewhere, the Committee has recommended that the authorities extend the content of such curricula to areas other than those inhabited by national minorities.[50] In addressing another type of pedagogical limitation, the Opinion on Armenia noted that 'culture, history, religion and the traditions of persons belonging to minorities are only taught in special Sunday classes, not as part of the general teaching curriculum', and advised Armenia to eliminate this and other shortcomings.[51] The point seems to be that 'sidelining' such education is a limiting factor, resulting in an inadequate response to the demands of the Convention. The Advisory Committee conceives the implementation of Article 12 in broad, socially and culturally inclusive terms, linking it to a general concept of social integration. Hence, in the case of Estonia and in relation to reforms involving reduction of instruction in Russian, the Advisory Committee commented that 'the implementation of the reform must be carried out in a manner that contributes to the integration of persons belonging to national minorities but not their assimilation'. The Committee also emphasized that education should receive attention in the framework of the national integration programme 'in a manner that covers all national minorities of Estonia'.[52]

While the main Convention provisions on language are set out in Articles 10, 11, and 14, the simple and generalized reference to 'language' in Article 12(1) has brought forward information from governments, and comment by the

[48] Advisory Committee Opinion on Slovakia, ACFC/INF/OP/I (2001) 001, 2000, para. 41.

[49] Advisory Committee Opinion on Italy, ACFC/INF/OP/I (2002) 007, 2001, para. 53.

[50] Advisory Committee Opinion on Austria, ACFC/INF/OP/I (2002) 009, 2002, para. 56; Advisory Committee Opinion on Germany, ACFC/INF/OP/I (2002) 008, 2002, para. 55. Germany reported very frankly that 'as part of school education, knowledge of the culture and language of these [listed] minorities in Germany is passed on to a much greater extent in the respective traditional settlement area than in other parts of the national territory' in Germany State Report, ACFC/SR (2000) 1, 2000 on Art. 12.

[51] Advisory Committee Opinion on Armenia, ACFC/INF/OP/I (2003) 001, 2002, para. 65, 104, and Resolution ResCMN (2003) 2 on the Implementation of the Framework Convention for the Protection of national Minorities by Armenia, 2003: 'The authorities should show greater commitment . . . to promote awareness of the culture, history, languages and traditions of both the minorities and the majority.'

[52] Advisory Committee Opinion on Estonia, ACFC/INF/OP/I (2002) 005, 2001, para. 44.

Advisory Committee, connected with the role of language in fostering integration, mutual respect among groups, and social solidarity. Most of this is 'buried' in remarks on culture and history. *Ex facie*, the function of the language element in Article 12(1) is, as elsewhere in the paragraph, to implicate not just the language education of members of national minorities, but also education about minority languages for the benefit of the majority populations and the whole society. These remarks on 'spreading the message' relating to minority culture, may be adapted, *mutatis mutandis*, to minority languages.

It may be observed that there are relatively few references in the canon of reports and comments to the question of 'research', implicated as well as 'education' in Article 12(1). Positive evaluations of the contributions of research are made in most of the reports under the Convention, while they rarely elicit comment from the Advisory Committee. The importance of research arguably increases in the case of vulnerable, small communities in particular countries; hence the commendation to Norway for research into national minorities, including numerically small groups.[53]

(b) Curriculum Content

In addition to questioning the range of the dissemination of educational materials on minorities, the Committee has been concerned about the adequacy of their content. The Committee has responded to comments on the adequacy of information concerning minority cultures, and has drafted a recommendation for the Committee of Ministers in the case of Finland to the effect that Finland should ensure 'that textbooks, and the educational system in general, provide adequate information on minorities, including on their culture and language'.[54] In addition, the Norwegian report made a very useful statement on Article 12 to the effect that '[t]eaching must aim at enhancing the self-confidence of pupils belonging to national minorities, while presenting the idea of a culturally pluralist Norway in a positive light to the majority population'. Norway also advanced an opinion on the purposes of research in terms of self-knowledge for members of minority groups, an aspect of Article 12 touched on to a lesser extent than others.[55] The Committee, however, responded to representations by national minorities that textbooks did not contain adequate information on national minorities in

[53] Advisory Committee Opinion on Norway, ACFC/INF/OP/I (2003) 003, 2002, para. 52.

[54] Advisory Committee Opinion on Finland, ACFC/INF/OP/I (2001) 002, 2000, proposals in respect of Art. 12.

[55] 'The minority groups express a need for more knowledge about themselves. Historical knowledge, knowledge of the recent past and better knowledge of their language and its development are other key topics. Several of the groups have demanded the right to participate in determining the basic criteria for research projects concerning them' in Norway State Report ACFC/SR (2001) 1, 2001.

Norway, and advised the government to monitor the situation, especially as the system of national registration of textbooks had been abolished, making it difficult to provide information.[56] In the case of the Ukraine, while praising Ukraine for placing multiculturalism and mutuality at the centre of the curriculum, the Committee took the view that the 'principles are not fully reflected in practice and that, *inter alia*, the contents of history textbooks do not always adequately portray the roles played and the positive contributions made by national minorities'.[57]

The teaching of history is implicated in the Committee's critiques of curriculum content. The Advisory Committee has taken the view that history taught in schools should reflect a country's ethnic diversity,[58] and that education materials that contain negative stereotypes of minorities should be revised.[59] The Committee has commended states for withdrawing history textbooks that do not conform to these requirements.[60] The report by Romania under the Framework Convention states that the Law on Education of 1995 provides that 'textbooks on general history and Romanian history are required to reflect the history and traditions of the national minorities in Romania'. However, the Committee was concerned by 'reports from various sources that history teaching does not sufficiently reflect Romania's ethnic diversity', although a 1999 national law provided for this. Accordingly, it considered that 'the Romanian authorities should explore, in consultation with representatives of the national minorities, approaches to the teaching of history more designed to enhance the intercultural dialogue promoted by the Framework Convention'.[61] The government did not demur from the Committee's observations, commenting merely that possibilities for improvement were being examined and that specific measures had been taken in connection with Holocaust education. The Advisory Committee has also taken the opportunity to recommend that states draw on the principles contained in the Committee of Ministers' Recommendation No. 15 (2001), on history teaching in twenty-first century Europe.[62]

[56] Advisory Committee Opinion on Norway, ACFC/INF/OP/I (2003) 003, 2002, para. 53, 93; Norway responded by referring to a white paper on how schools could improve the teaching of culture. Comments by Norway on the Opinion of the Advisory Committee on the Framework Convention on the Protection of National Minorities, GVT/COM/INF/OP/I (2003) 003, 2003.

[57] Advisory Committee Opinion on the Ukraine, ACFC/INF/OP/I (2002) 010, 2002, para. 58, 103.

[58] Advisory Committee Opinion on Finland, ACFC/INF/OP/I (2001) 002, 2000, para. 36; Advisory Committee Opinion on Norway, ACFC/INF/OP/I (2003) 003, 2002, para. 53; Advisory Committee Opinion on Romania, ACFC/INF/OP/I (2002) 001, 2001, para. 54.

[59] Advisory Committee Opinion on Albania, ACFC/INF/OP/I (2003) 004, 2002, para. 57; Advisory Committee Opinion on Croatia, ACFC/INF/OP/I (2002) 003, 2001, para. 47.

[60] Advisory Committee Opinion on Slovakia, ACFC/INF/OP/I (2001) 001, 2000, para. 38.

[61] Advisory Committee Opinion on Romania, ACFC/INF/OP/I (2001) 001, 2001, para. 54.

[62] See, for example, the Advisory Committee Opinion on Ukraine, ACFC/INF/OP/I (2002) 010, 2002, para. 58.

(c) Resources/Participation

Among the persistent questions addressed by the Committee, in addition to the above, are those of resources and minority input into curriculum processes. Dissemination of educational material requires, as with all human rights, the allocation of adequate resources. The importance of adequate resources for the achievement of educational objectives is stressed in a number of observations by the Committee,[63] which has adopted a pragmatic approach in the case of countries whose resources are enlarged through links with kin states of their national minorities. Thus, in the case of Moldova, the Advisory Committee noted the support in educational resources given by kin states of the minorities, and at the same time encouraged the authorities 'to ensure that all the national minorities, particularly those that are numerically smaller or do not enjoy the support of a kin-State, benefit equitably from the special government programmes for national minorities in the field of education'.[64] This sentiment is echoed in the corresponding resolution of the Committee of Ministers.[65] The kin-state support should ideally be seen as a supplement to state resources, and not as a substitute for adequate provision, even within limited budgets. Otherwise, issues of discrimination and state responsibility could well arise, with some minorities, on account of the 'accident' of possessing kin states, being placed in a more favourable position than others. Almost inevitably, the Roma would lose out in such a calculation, as would other vulnerable groups.

The Convention does not comment on input into the drafting of curricula which particularly concern minorities, including the general curriculum to the extent that minority cultures are represented. However, the participation provisions of Article 15 suggest, at least that minorities should have input, making education more responsive to their interests and concerns. Thus, in its opinion on Albania, the Advisory Committee, commenting favourably on Albania's plans to review the school curriculum and textbooks, considered it important 'that attention is given to national minorities in these changes, and that persons belonging to minorities are consulted in the revision process'. Such changes had a double dimension to improve understanding about national minorities; and to 'ensure that stereotypes of national minorities are removed from all

[63] Advisory Committee Opinion on Finland, ACFC/INF/OP/I (2001) 002, 2000 and proposals for conclusions and recommendations by the Committee of Ministers in respect of Article 12. Advisory Committee Opinion on Hungary, ACFC/INF/OP/I (2001) 004, 2000, para. 39, and proposals, etc., for the Committee of Ministers in respect of Art. 12.

[64] Advisory Committee Opinion on Moldova, ACFC/INF/OP/I (2003) 002, 2002, para. 76.

[65] Resolution ResCMN (2003) 4 on the Implementation of the Framework Convention for the Protection of National Minorities by Moldova, 2003.

educational materials'.[66] The Committee observed the self-critical nature of the report advising that it was necessary 'to redouble efforts in this area'.[67]

3. *Overall View*

Practice overall suggests a widespread awareness of the importance of intercultural education, as the self-critical stance of some governments indicates. There is also awareness that, in a complex society, the complexity of history, culture, and traditions should be appropriately reflected in educational syllabuses. As with all human rights, adequate resources should be devoted to education for the good of society as a whole, including its minority components. To fulfil the requirements of Article 12(1), the mere removal of offensive stereotypes from textbooks is not enough. What is required is a more active policy of presenting minority culture in a fair and balanced fashion, highlighting the contribution of the group to the cultural richness of the nation as a whole.

C. Article 12(2): Teachers, Textbooks, Contacts

1. Travaux préparatoires *and Text*

The second paragraph of Article 12 is tolerably clear and did not produce a great deal of discussion in the drafting process, except for a brief flurry in relation to 'access' to textbooks. The demands of this paragraph are light, although the *inter alia* reference suggests that the authorities should interpret the educational strategy for the achievement of the aims of the first paragraph in broader terms than teacher training, access to textbooks, and facilitation of contacts. It specifies that opportunities should be 'adequate' to achieve the aims of the article as a whole, while 'facilitation' implies the easing of obstacles, such as unnecessary bureaucratic conditions impeding intercommunal contacts. The term 'different communities' suggests the facilitation of inter-minority contacts on account of shared experiences, as well as contacts between 'majority' and minorities; the relevant 'communities' are not restrictively described in the text.

2. *Convention Practice*

The second paragraph of Article 12 begins with the phrase 'in this context', which refers to the preceding paragraph and suggests that its provisions on teacher training and intercommunal student and teacher contacts are 'tied' to the objectives of intercultural education in Article 12(1). Accordingly, the

[66] Advisory Committee Opinion on Albania, ACFC/INF/OP/I (2003) 004, 2002, para. 57. The government agreed with the Committee, and pointed to the practice of including 'authors belonging to minorities' in the revision process.

[67] Above, n. 66, para. 60.

report of Germany observes that, 'teacher training and development of appropriate educational materials are important prerequisites for information on the history and culture of the groups protected under the Framework Convention'.[68] The Committee Explanatory Report was fairly unilluminating on this paragraph, observing merely that '[t]he list in the second paragraph is not exhaustive whilst the words "access to textbooks" are understood as including the publication of textbooks and their purchase in other countries.'[69] Moreover, information relayed by states in the area of teacher training has not been a particular focus for the opinions of the Advisory Committee. Nevertheless, Germany made a rather full statement on the paragraph:

> In . . . Germany, there are no governmental impediments whatsoever as regards contacts among pupils and teachers from different communities; instead, various efforts are made to intensify such contacts. Governmental measures for teacher training, and government-supported promotion of such measures taken by other parties, are adjusted to the respective requirements of the various minorities, and these are different for the various languages of the groups protected . . . under the Convention.

Attention to the situation of language recalls the methodology of the European Charter for Regional or Minority Languages, with its emphasis on the condition of the language as such.[70] All the same, this cannot be 'the whole story' for the Framework Convention which, unlike the Charter, is a framework for minority rights. The German statement also refers to the positive effect of the system of transfrontier co-operation entailed by the Bonn–Copenhagen Declarations of 1955. There is also extensive reference to the situation of the Roma and Sinti, whose General Council is, according to the report:

> against the introduction of the Romani language in publicly maintained schools, and, in particular, against the development of a written form of this language; the Council also opposes the idea of teaching the language by non-Roma/non-Sinti teachers. The Council's preferred alternative is cultivation of the language within family and clans, passing it on to future generations; there is however a division of opinion reported within the Roma community on the role of the state system. The . . . Council also objects to separate schools or classes for Roma or Sinti only.

States report on their support for programmes of teacher training, admit to shortcomings,[71] and emphasize, as does Germany, the positive role of international agreements.[72] The Advisory Committee does not tend to individuate

[68] Germany State Report, ACFC/SR (2000) 1, 2000.
[69] Above, n. 3, para. 71.
[70] Above, n. 31, Art. 7, para. 1.
[71] Norway State Report, ACFC/SR (2001) 1, 2001.
[72] Poland State Report, ACFC/SR (2002) 2, 2002; Serbia and Montenegro State Report, ACFC/SR (2002) 003, 2002.

comments on the second paragraph of Article 12; the implications of Article 12(2) are generally considered with Article 12 as a whole. Consequently, various shortcomings have been identified: the lack of training officers and qualified teachers;[73] the shortage of textbooks;[74] and the limited contacts between pupils attending minority language schools and those attending schools where the state or official language is the medium of instruction.[75] A not untypical compendium of difficulties in implementing Article 12 appears from the Committee's Opinion on Moldova identifying 'shortcomings' on the basis of government information. The list included: a shortage of teachers; the difficulties in finding teachers versed in both state and minority languages; a lack of textbooks; the higher costs of textbooks for pupils belonging to national minorities; the difficulty of ensuring continuity of minority education through different levels; and a general lack of financial resources.[76] In some Committee assessments, it seems fairly clear that the 'distribution of shortcomings' is unequal among the various minorities, so that some are more disadvantaged than others.[77] The issue of separation of minority pupils and others in society is a specific focus of this paragraph.[78]

3. *Overall View*

The second paragraph of Article 12 also suggests the need for positive proactive measures to achieve its objectives. The provisions on contacts, especially for the young, supply an essential basis for positive intercommunal relations with the potential to endure. The provision encourages the growth of broad and generous affiliations and personal relationships across communal divides.

[73] Advisory Committee Opinion on Armenia, ACFC/INF/OP/I (2003) 001, para. 65; Advisory Committee Opinion on Finland, ACFC/INF/OP/I (2001) 002, 2000, para. 40 and 'Proposals for the Committee of Ministers'; Advisory Committee Opinion on Romania, ACFC/INF/OP/I (2002) 001, 2001, para. 53.

[74] Advisory Committee Opinion on Austria, ACFC/INF/OP/I (2002) 009, 2002, paras. 55, 91; Advisory Committee Opinion on Croatia, ACFC/INF/OP/I (2002) 003, 2001, para. 48, and 'Proposals for the Committee of Ministers'; Advisory Committee Opinion on Hungary, ACFC/INF/OP/I (2001) 004, 2000, para. 39 and 'Proposals': in reply, Hungary stressed the 'substantial support' for teacher training and the role of support from kin states; Advisory Committee Opinion on Romania, ACFC/INF/OP/I (2002) 001, 2001, para. 53.

[75] Advisory Committee Opinion on Estonia, ACFC/INF/OP/I (2002) 005, 2001, para. 46, and 'Proposals for the Committee of Ministers'.

[76] Advisory Committee Opinion on Moldova, ACFC/INF/OP/I (2003) 002, 2002, para. 74.

[77] Advisory Committee Opinion on Romania, ACFC/INF/OP/I (2002) 001, 2001, para. 53, and 'Proposals'; and, for example, Advisory Committee Opinion on Ukraine, ACFC/INF/OP/I (2002) 010, 2002, para. 59.

[78] See remarks above and recall, for example, Advisory Committee Opinion on the United Kingdom, ACFC/INF/OP/I (2002) 006, 2001, paras. 84, 123.

Insofar as there is community resistance to such contacts and familiarization programmes, educational means are more likely to overcome barriers in the long run than 'top-down' exhortations to associate.

D. Article 12(3): Equality and Access

1. Travaux préparatoires *and Text*

As noted, the *travaux préparatoires* reveal the shift from 'equal access' to 'equal opportunities for access' to education at all levels, softening the obligation. This obligation is further relaxed by requiring that access only be 'promoted' instead of 'provided'. Human rights instruments on education, including the ICESCR, take progressively qualified stances as they advance along the age range, whereas the Framework Convention addresses 'all levels' in one succinct paragraph. It may be noted that 'equal opportunities' is without a comparator—equal to whom? Presumably, this means equal with the population at large, otherwise 'equality among minorities' could be read in some cases as equality in inferiority. 'Equality' is subject to its normal meaning in international minority rights law: equality in fact, not merely in law: equality, not uniformity.[79]

2. Practice

The Framework Convention makes no comment on levels of education beyond the reference in Article 12(3).[80] Questions of access to education infuse many comments of the Advisory Committee, and outstandingly so in the case of the Roma,[81] including the case of the so-called 'special schools' which is a key Article 12(3) issue. The 'levels' of education addressed in reports and opinions of the Advisory Committee implicate facets of education from pre-school[82] to higher education. The Committee interprets the access requirement to mean that governments should engage in a policy of supporting access for all national minorities according to their different requirements and demands. In this respect, the responsibility of governments is to implement equality as a genuine right requiring an active governmental contribution and strategy.[83] 'Access'

[79] *Case concerning the Minority Schools in Albania*, Advisory Opinion, PCIJ Rep. Series B No. 15, 1928; *Thlimmenos* v. *Greece* (34369/97) (2000) EHRR 161.

[80] In which respect, see CoE, Parliamentary Assembly, ETS No. 148, Recommendation 1353 on the Access of Minorities to Higher Education, Strasbourg, 1998.

[81] See the section below on particular issues for Art. 12 as a whole.

[82] See, for example, Advisory Committee Opinion on Estonia, ACFC/INF/OP/I (2002) 005, 2001, para. 48; Advisory Committee Opinion on Finland (above, n. 73), para. 38; Advisory Committee Opinion on Slovakia, ACFC/INF/OP/I (2001) 001, 2000, para. 40.

[83] See, for example, Advisory Committee Opinion on Armenia, ACFC/INF/OP/I (2003) 001, 2002, paras. 63–9.

includes addressing the question of absenteeism among members of national minorities, pre-eminently among Roma children and pupils of other vulnerable minorities.[84] 'Access' implicates the question of school exclusions, which can have a differential impact on members of minority groups. In the case of the UK, the Committee shared the concern of the state government regarding exclusions and 'the continuing over-representation of African and African-Caribbean pupils amongst those excluded'. Correspondingly, it encouraged the government 'to continue to give priority to this issue'.[85]

The position of national minorities at the primary school level is perhaps one of the lesser concerns of the Committee, in that this right is generally secured, though questions of curriculum content and various shortcomings in the education offered may cloud the picture for particular groups.[86] The Advisory Committee appears to consider that any under-representation of minorities in institutions of secondary education and higher education to be contrary to the right to equal opportunities in access to education at all levels as set out in Article 12(3). Cost and transportation issues also figure among the impediments recognized by the Committee in relation to access to secondary education.[87] Once again, in the case of the UK, the Committee noted that 'the government has recognised that while certain ethnic groups are well represented in higher education, other groups . . . remain seriously under-represented. The . . . Committee considers that the Government should examine the issue further in order to redress this imbalance.'[88]

Changes in language policies for university instruction with the potential to disadvantage minority language students may suggest a need for targeted assistance to the students concerned.[89] The injunction to extend education in minority languages to the university level is a staple recommendation of the Committee.[90] Under certain circumstances, the Convention may require the creation of multicultural universities where languages other than the state language are used as the medium of instruction, and initiatives to set up such institutions are to be pursued through consultation with the groups

[84] The differential position of minorities receiving support from kin states and those without kin states crops up in this connection. See, for example, the Advisory Committee Opinion on Armenia, ACFC/INF/OP/I (2003), 001, 2002, paras. 63–9, in connection with the Assyrians and the Yezidis.

[85] Advisory Committee Opinion on the United Kingdom, ACFC/INF/OP/I (2002) 006, 2001, para. 80, 132.

[86] See comment above on Art. 12, para. 1.

[87] Advisory Committee Opinion on Italy, ACFC/INF/OP/I (2002) 007, 2001, para. 55.

[88] Advisory Committee Opinion on the United Kingdom, ACFC/INF/OP/I (2002) 006, 2001, para. 85.

[89] Advisory Committee Opinion on Estonia, ACFC/INF/OP/I (2002) 005, 2001.

[90] Advisory Committee Opinion on Albania, ACFC/INF/OP/I (2003) 004, 2002, para. 105—in response to which the government raised the issue of differential motivation on the part of different ethnic groups to avail themselves of higher-level education.

concerned.[91] Reserving places for Roma students at institutions of higher education, for example, has been noted and welcomed by the Committee as a method of securing national minority access.[92] In the case of Romania, the Committee added that, in addition to reserving places, 'it is important that the authorities launch information campaigns to help ensure that they are filled'.[93]

3. *Overall Interpretation*

In Convention practice on access to education, there appears to be a general understanding of the concept of equality, to mean that attention must be paid to the situation of particular communities and persons belonging to them, as opposed to a mechanical, uniform approach. The importance of educational access for minorities at all levels, including university, is rightly stressed: minorities need their intellectuals and skilled people so that their 'culture' is not infantilized or stunted in growth. Proactive strategies by various governments are in evidence, including, where appropriate, the reservation of university places for particular communities where appropriate, an approach that can be justified not only by calling on the notion of 'special measures', but also by the broad minority rights commitment to provide means for cultures to survive and flourish.

E. Educational Issues and the Roma

1. *A Spectrum of Disadvantages*

The early history of Roma education policy is largely about assimilation, a policy vividly portrayed in the 'Report on The Situation of Roma and Sinti in the OSCE Area' of the OSCE High Commissioner on National Minorities:

> Early modern policies . . . attempted to change Roma into 'Christians', 'new citizens' and 'new farmers' by removing them from Romani families, placing them with non-Romani ones, and sending them to schools to have their difference educated out of them. These strategies were echoed in CEE countries after World War II as governments used schools to enforce policies of assimilation—Roma were forcibly settled, expected to conform closely to rigid standards of sameness, and display a demonstrative loyalty to the ethnic majority. Romani children were to learn such norms by having their Romaniness removed in school, and their culture itself was viewed as a package

[91] Advisory Committee Opinion on Romania, ACFC/INF/OP/I (2002) 001, 2001, para. 55; Advisory Committee Opinion on Ukraine, ACFC/INF/OP/I (2002) 010, 2002, para. 61.

[92] Advisory Committee Opinion on Moldova, ACFC/INF/OP/I (2003) 002, 2002, para. 72; Advisory Committee Opinion on Romania, ACFC/INF/OP/I (2002) 001, 2001, para. 57.

[93] ibid.

made up of social disadvantage and deviance which a tide of systematic schooling would cleanse.[94]

Such policies are forceful; demeaning to all concerned, not just the victims; and are disfavoured by contemporary standards of human rights. Regrettably, traces of old attitudes and practices linger, and assimilation may have given way to more exclusionary practices. On the basis of state reports, the Advisory Committee has made many critical observations on Roma education, the situation of which appears to be dire in many states, despite some improvements, plans, and prospects. A gamut of educational issues implicates the whole of Article 12 of the Framework Convention in the Advisory Committee reports. Leading questions include: absenteeism;[95] low completion and achievement rates for various levels of education;[96] the bullying of Roma children;[97] the lack of sensitivity to lifestyle and traditions;[98] the lack of recognition or use of the Romani language in schools[99]—including the complete absence of education in mother tongue to Roma pupils;[100] low income of Roma families impeding access to schools; and even lack of food for Roma children, inhibiting school attendance.[101] Among many recommendations to remedy situations, we may note the suggestion to the government of the United Kingdom to 'dovetail' the education provisions for Roma/Gypsy and Traveller children with the provision of suitable stopping places for families in order to avoid evictions, thus helping to address the educational requirements of a nomadic Roma/Gypsy population.[102] The itinerant culture of some Roma groups was also a matter of

[94] OSCE High Commissioner on National Minorities, Report on the Situation of Roma and Sinti in the OSCE Area, The Hague, 2000, p. 69, citing C. Cahn et al., 'Roma in the Educational Systems of Central and Eastern Europe', *Roma Rights*, (Summer 1998).

[95] Advisory Committee Opinion on Italy, ACFC/INF/OP/I (2002) 007, 2001, para. 55; Advisory Committee Opinion on Albania, ACFC/INF/OP/I (2003) 004, 2002 para. 60; Advisory Committee Opinion on Moldova, ACFC/INF/OP/I (2003) 002, 2002, para. 77; Advisory Committee Opinion on Romania, ACFC/INF/OP/I (2002) 001, 2001, para. 57.

[96] Advisory Committee Opinion on the Czech Republic, ACFC/INF/OP/I (2002) 002, 2001, para. 63; Advisory Committee Opinion on Slovakia, ACFC/INF/OP/I (2001) 001, 2000, para. 40; Advisory Committee Opinion on the Ukraine, ACFC/INF/OP/I (2002) 010, 2002, para. 105.

[97] Advisory Committee Opinion on Albania, ACFC/INF/OP/I (2003) 004, 2002, para. 59.

[98] ibid., para. 60; Advisory Committee Opinion on Romania, ACFC/INF/OP/I (2002) 001, 2001, para. 58.

[99] Advisory Committee Opinion on Albania, ACFC/INF/OP/I (2003) 004, 2002, para. 60; Advisory Committee Opinion on Croatia, ACFC/INF/OP/I (2002) 003, para. 49; Advisory Committee Opinion on Finland, ACFC/INF/OP/I (2001) 002, 2000, para. 40; Advisory Committee Opinion on Hungary, ACFC/INF/OP/I (2001) 004, 2000, para. 39.

[100] Bulgaria State Report, ACFC/SR(2003) 001, 2003.

[101] Advisory Committee Opinion on Romania, ACFC/INF/OP/I (2002) 001, 2001, para. 57.

[102] Advisory Committee Opinion the United Kingdom, ACFC/INF/OP/I (2002) 006, 2001, para. 82.

Committee concern in the case of Norway, in terms of promoting access to education at all levels.[103]

2. *Special Schools/Special Classes*

In the work of the Committee, one issue in particular stands out as engaging the most elaborated suggestions of the Committee: that of the segregation of Roma children in 'special schools' or 'special classes'. The Committee has been particularly critical of the placing of Roma children in special schools designed for mentally handicapped students, sometimes misleadingly described as 'special schools' for Roma, and has welcomed 'news' that Roma children are no longer treated in this way. In the case of Austria, the Committee welcomed that fact that, 'as a result of the determined efforts of the authorities in recent years, there are no longer any Roma attending special schools for mentally disabled children in the main autochthonous settlement area of this minority . . . It is of the opinion that other regions could draw inspiration from this achievement'.[104] It might be added that this could also occur in other countries. A clear statement of the Committee's position appears from its comments with respect to the Czech Republic:

> The system of so-called 'special' schools has recently been the subject of much attention. While these schools are designed for mentally handicapped children, it appears that many Roma children who are not mentally handicapped are placed in these schools due to real or perceived language and cultural differences between Roma and the majority. The Advisory Committee considers that such practice is not compatible with the Framework Convention. The . . . Committee stresses that placing children in such special schools should take place only when it is absolutely necessary and always on the basis of consistent, objective and comprehensive tests.[105]

The Czech Republic's response to these comments included a note on moves towards the use of the Romani language in communications with Roma children, and a Bill to abolish 'special schools'. In a supplementary comment, the government took the view that, '[t]he problem does not reside in the very existence of remedial schools but in the fact that many Roma children are, for objective reasons, unable to cope with the demands . . . in ordinary elementary schools,' adding that it was recommended 'that only those children from the Romani community who have a proven mental disability should be included in remedial schools'.

[103] Advisory Committee Opinion on Norway, ACFC/INF/OP/I (2003) 003, 2002, para. 54, 94.

[104] Advisory Committee Opinion on Austria, ACFC/INF/OP/I (2002) 009, 2002, para. 57, 93.

[105] Advisory Committee Opinion on the Czech Republic, ACFC/INF/OP/I (2002) 001, 2001, para. 61. The Committee added that both the government and civil society agreed on the need for a major reform, but disagreed on its precise nature and the resources required to implement it.

In general, the Committee, while respecting principles of parental choice, urges states to find ways of combating de facto segregation,[106] including on the one hand, dealing with the reluctance of Roma parents to send their children to regular schools, and on the other, addressing the phenomenon where non-Roma parents withdraw their children from schools attended by Roma. In the case of Hungary, the Committee took the view that, whereas 'the Hungarian authorities obviously should pay due respect to the principle of parental choice, they must at the same time not remain passive before these undesirable developments and take measures to counteract them'.[107] As with 'special schools', the Committee regarded the placing of Roma in segregated special classes to be retrograde. In the case of Croatia, moreover, the Committee was 'highly concerned' about reports that Roma children were:

> . . . placed in separate classes and [that] school facilities are organised and operated in a manner that appears to stigmatise Roma pupils. The . . . Committee stresses that placing children in special classes should take place only when it is absolutely necessary and always on the basis of consistent, objective and comprehensive tests.[108]

The Committee adverted to the complexity of the segregation question in noting the reservations expressed by some Roma on pupil enrolment in 'regular' classes. According to the Committee, the key to remedying the current situation was to ensure 'that the education system reflects and takes fully into account the language and culture of the minority concerned'.[109] Croatia did not fundamentally disagree with the Committee on the matter of 'complexities'. It did, however, add in phrases that appear to shift some 'responsibility' from the state to the Roma minority, that the education of Roma 'is a serious problem caused by their way of life and their attitude towards the system, laws, rights and obligations of citizens and requires particular efforts and solutions'.[110] In this last respect, the Croatian response to the Committee highlighted a dual-track programme of educational integration, coupled with

106 The provision of separate education is a Committee concern, irrespective of the controversies on 'special schools'. In the case of the UK, for example, the Committee took the view that 'the placing of Irish traveller children in a separate school gives rise to concern from the point of view of Article 12', further recommending that traveller and settled children be educated in an integrated environment. Advisory Committee Opinion on the United Kingdom, ACFC/INF/OP/I (2002) 006, 2001, para. 84.

107 Advisory Committee Opinion on Hungary, ACFC/INF/OP/I (2001) 004, 2000, para. 43.

108 Advisory Committee Opinion on Croatia, ACFC/INF/OP/I (2002) 003, 2001, para. 49.

109 Above, n. 108. In this respect, the Committee regularly cites Committee of Ministers, Recommendation No. (2000) 4 on the Education of Roma/Gypsy Children in Europe, 2000. See also the Advisory Committee's Proposal to the Committee of Ministers regarding Croatia.

110 Comments of the Government of Croatia on the Opinion of the Advisory Committee on the Report of the Implementation of the Framework Convention for the Protection of National Minorities in Croatia, GVT/COM/INF/OP/I (2002) 003, 2002 in relation to Arts. 12 and 14.

the exercise of minority rights aimed at preserving mother tongue and culture. The Committee has favourably responded to government efforts enabling Roma children to be taught in regular classes, including, in the case of Finland individualized teaching programmes. In this vein, the government of Finland has stressed that 'the same tests and criteria are applied to all children whose placement into special or adapted education is being considered. Irrespective of the type of education envisaged, consultations with the parents or custodians of the child as well as sufficiently comprehensive tests are required.'[111] Elsewhere, the Committee has warned of the dangers of 'culturally biased testing'.[112]

III. Conclusion and Outlook

Article 12 makes specific reference to culture, history, language, and religion. The aspect of religion in the Article will require further elaboration in future practice, in the light of the *Welfare Party* case before the ECtHR,[113] which included a sweeping rejection of Sharia law as incompatible with human rights. The judgment in *Welfare Party* reads human rights as an essentially secular product which, *ex facie*, is difficult to reconcile with legal and cultural pluralism. The thrust of the judgment is also about values: rights of women; criminal law and procedure; the failure to distinguish public from private, and so on, that the Turkish authorities would, in the Court's view, have failed to respect. Irrespective of the substantive human rights debate on the scope of normative incompatibilities, the judgment appears to commit itself to a double essentialization of the 'Human Rights are X; Sharia is Y' variety. An alternative psychology might avoid this double closure and, certainly from the human rights 'end', reflect further on the partial or incomplete quality of the human rights project.[114] The approach to non-traditional European legal systems and

[111] Comments of the government of Finland on the opinion of the Advisory Committee on the Report of the Implementation of the Framework Convention for the Protection of National Minorities in Finland, GVT/COM/INF/OP/I (2001) 002, 2001, paras. 37–40. In the case of Hungary, the government stressed that 'aptitude testing of children may happen only at the request and with the consent of the parents, who have legal remedies in case of an unfavourable decision': Comments of the Government of Hungary on the Opinion of the Advisory Committee on the Report of the Implementation of the Framework Convention for the Protection of National Minorities in Hungary, GVT/COM/INF/OP/I (2001) 004, 2001 relating to minority education.

[112] Advisory Committee Opinion on Hungary, ACFC/INF/OP/I (2001) 004, 2000, para. 41.

[113] *Refah Partisi (The Welfare Party) and Others* v. *Turkey* (41340/98) (2003) EHRR 87, judgment.

[114] M. Mookherjee, 'Exclusion, internalization, harm', *Ethnicities*, 3 (2003), 345–68.

practices is already capable of challenging the limits of cultural self-expression in the context of the Framework Convention. In view of its greater solicitude for 'culture', the Convention organs need not necessarily follow the European Court's sweeping approach and instead develop their own strategy. 'Cultural' challenges have knock-on effects in education processes because they respond to the question of how the traditions and customs of particular communities are represented. In other areas, the treatment of women members of minorities from within and without the communities may ostensibly give rise to a 'double discrimination', as well as specifically affecting their education opportunities.[115] Within its mandate, the Advisory Committee will be required to plot strategies which at once, respect cultural authenticity, but also address the elements of common humanity and dignity reflected in the Convention as a whole, with all its partiality and incompleteness.

In Article 12, taking measures to foster knowledge of majority and minority cultures is envisaged as a duty of states parties 'where appropriate'. It would seem that, in practice, encouraging this mutuality is always 'appropriate', assisting our increasingly diverse societies to achieve a measure of solidarity. In the gaze of the Convention, diversity, cultural self-knowledge, and mutuality run together as underpinning motifs of educational processes in the wider 'social', as well as the narrower 'curricular' senses. It would appear from Convention practice that many states make genuine efforts to promote solidarity through education, but that these efforts are patchy and halting. Particular issues are raised when education processes are dominated by top-down philosophies and practice, and where the curriculum is 'emancipated' only with great difficulty from the ethos of a 'founding nation' or 'dominant nation' which may invest curricula with culturally limiting perspectives. A related issue in practice is the limitation of multicultural approaches in education to minority areas. This, in itself, may be a manifestation of a dominant nation ethos, where the 'mutuality of knowledge' paradigm, favoured in the Framework Convention, is not fully realized. Relatively speaking, it would appear that majority populations often have inadequate knowledge of minority cultures and the contribution of minorities to society in general. Mainstreaming knowledge of minorities is perhaps the essence of what is required. In all this, the teaching of history appears to raise particular problems. On the history component of education, Edward Said has written, '[d]efensive, reactive and even paranoid nationalism is, alas, frequently woven into the very fabric of education, where children as well as older students

[115] European Monitoring Centre on Racism and Xenophobia, Breaking the Barriers: Romani Women and Access to Public Health Care, Council of Europe, 2003, pp. 79 ff.

are taught to venerate and celebrate the uniqueness of *their* tradition (usually and invidiously at the expense of others).'[116] Since history teaching is a natural forum for evoking national memories,[117] it is widely accepted that texts should be drafted with special sensitivity to the historical role of minorities. This is the essence of the approach of the Advisory Committee, which draws upon a wider repertoire of practice from the Council of Europe and elsewhere.

Current practice also strongly suggests that it is incumbent on states parties to make the enjoyment of the right in Article 12 a realistic possibility, through adequate provision of resources, including the adequate supply of personnel, the indispensable 'human capital' of educational systems. The Advisory Committee visualizes the rights encompassed in Article 12 as requiring sustained and consistent attention by state authorities, including attention to all manifestations of exclusion from and lack of access to schools. In the latter respect, the situation of many Roma communities is dire. The lack of attention to Romani language and culture in educational processes leads to the situation where many Roma communities are deprived of a means to develop cultural self-confidence through cultural and linguistic self-knowledge, as well as of the basic skills and knowledge needed to succeed in the general society. The emergence of so-called special schools is a symptom of a wider failure to address Roma education. This issue is not an 'Article 13 issue' of a minority's right to their own schools, but an issue of placement by state authorities, and what that implies for the community in terms of inequality, stereotyping, and banishment to the margins of society.

In minority affairs, educational issues are often delicately balanced between integration and separation. If integration is pushed too far, the result is assimilation and the disappearance of the minority as a distinct culture. A policy of separation, on the other hand, can lead to a ghetto culture of withdrawal from society. The Framework Convention suggests ways and means through which a balance is to be achieved between the separate domain reserved for the flourishing of minority culture, and the common domain of shared rights and responsibilities.[118] The Framework Convention's premisses are that identity is shaped through interaction with others and that identity is multiple or hybrid.[119] It proposes that each person may be touched by a complex of

[116] E. W. Said, *Culture and Imperialism* (Vintage, London, 1994), p. xxix.

[117] Alternatively, it contributes to the construction of a national identity through the selection of 'events', personalities, and principles.

[118] A. Eide, Possible Ways and Means of Facilitating the Peaceful and Constructive Solution of Problems involving Minorities (1993), UN Doc. E/CN.4/Sub.2/1993/34, section II.

[119] C. Taylor, *The Ethics of Authenticity* (Harvard University Press, Cambridge, Mass., 1991).

influences, from family to neighbourhood, through ethnic group and the wider society of the state, as well as the cosmopolitan ideals of human rights. The education and other provisions should be seen as opening up possibilities of individual self-authorship in conjunction with community survival, and the aspirations of states for a coherent and functioning democratic polity.

ARTICLE 13

Patrick Thornberry

1. Within the framework of their education systems, the Parties shall recognise that persons belonging to a national minority have the right to set up and to manage their own private educational and training establishments.
2. The exercise of this right shall not entail any financial obligation for the Parties.

I. Background

A. Issues

Article 13 of the Framework Convention for the Protection of National Minorities (FCNM) is a contemporary expression of the freedom of minorities to establish their own educational institutions as an alternative or supplement to public provision. The right coheres with the general right recognized in 'undifferentiated' human rights instruments to establish private institutions for specific purposes, including the furtherance, in the terminology of the European Convention for the Protection of Human Rights and Fundamental Freedoms (ECHR), of education according to one's 'religious and philosophical convictions'.[1] In the sphere of minority rights, this freedom to set up and

[1] European Convention for the Protection of Human Rights and Fundamental Freedoms (ECHR), ETS No. 5, Protocol to the Convention for the Protection of Human Rights and Fundamental Freedoms, 1950, Art. 2.

manage institutions may be looked upon as a necessary 'defence mechanism' in the face of the potential of state institutions to develop public systems of education that neglect the interests of minorities. As elsewhere in education matters, there is a tension between state control and personal freedom; between the desideratum of enabling and facilitating social participation on the one hand and, on the other, recognizing a community's right to choose its own means of securing the protection and development of its ethnic, linguistic, and religious identity. While there is an element of 'separatism' in all this, the element of freedom to choose is the essence of the right: this is an exercise in minority rights and not an exercise in state creation of segregated systems of education. The exercise of this freedom is capable of raising complex questions in increasingly complex societies, including the relationship between general and specific educational systems, and between the treatment of the freedom of one group compared to others—both of which raise questions of discrimination. The general ethos of such schools raises other difficult questions, whether the school is established for reasons of religion or is more 'secular' in orientation.

B. History

The principles reflected in Article 13 have a long history in international law. The ancestry of the present provision may be traced back at least to the League of Nations, and the standard formula reflected in the Polish Treaty and others, to the effect that the minorities were to 'enjoy the same treatment and security in law and in fact as the other Polish nationals', and that, in particular, they would '[have] an equal right to establish, manage and control at their own expense charitable, religious and social institutions, schools and other educational establishments, with the right to use their own language and to exercise their religion freely therein'.[2] To this were added provisions on 'adequate facilities' in the public educational system at the primary school phase for education in minority languages, and for an 'equitable share' in any sums that may be provided from the public purse for educational, religious, and charitable purposes.[3] The League treaties and declarations linked the educational and other freedoms with a promise of equitable dealing with regards to public funds. These institutional and resource aspects were subsumed under an overall concept of equal treatment and security in law and in fact, for members of minority groups as compared with nationals of the majority or titular nation,

[2] Treaty between the United States of America, the British Empire, France, Italy, Japan, and Poland signed at Versailles, 1919, cited in League of Nations, Protection of Linguistic, Racial, and Religious Minorities, IB Minorities, 1927.

[3] Above, n. 1, Art. 9; see also Art. 10 on provision for Jewish schools.

a concept explained by the Permanent Court of International Justice: '[e]quality in law precludes discrimination of any kind; whereas equality in fact may involve the necessity of different treatment in order to attain a result which establishes an equilibrium between different situations.'[4]

Further 'institutional' references in the canon of general human rights include Article 13(3) of the Covenant on Economic, Social, and Cultural Rights which refers to the liberty of parents and others to choose schools other than those established by the public authorities, which ensure the religious and moral education of their children in accordance with their own convictions. Article 13(4) respects the liberty of 'individuals and bodies' to establish and direct educational institutions subject to the rule that such institutions conform to minimum standards laid down by the state. General Comment 13 of the Committee on Economic, Social, and Cultural Rights observes apropos Article 13(4) that 'everyone, including non-nationals, has the liberty to establish and direct educational institutions', emphasizing that this includes all types of educational institutions.[5] Further, bearing in mind 'the principles of non-discrimination, equal opportunity and effective participation in society for all, the State has an obligation to ensure that the liberty set out in Article 13(4) does not lead to extreme disparities of educational opportunity for some groups in society'.[6] The question of disparities of opportunity referred to here relates primarily to costly systems of private schooling which privilege certain sectors of society, and not to schools established for linguistic or religious reasons. On funding obligations, the Comment draws the conclusion that a state party 'has no obligation to fund institutions established in accordance with . . . paragraphs 3 and 4; however, if a State elects to make a financial contribution to private educational institutions, it must do so without discrimination': a determination against which the provisions of Article 13 may be measured.[7] Further important points in General Comment 13 are made on academic freedom,[8] even though it is not explicitly mentioned in the article, and on the basis of the argument that the right to education can only be enjoyed if accompanied by the academic freedom of staff and students. The so-called 4A scheme of availability, accessibility, acceptability, and adaptability frames the General Comment. All of the elements have relevance for

[4] *Case Concerning the Minority Schools in Albania*, Advisory Opinion, PCIJ Rep. Series A/B No. 64, 1928, p. 19.

[5] Committee on Economic, Social, and Cultural Rights, General Comment 13 on the Right to Education (Art. 13), Report on the Twentieth and Twenty-First Sessions, (1999), UN Doc. E/2000/22 E/C.12/1999/11, Annex VI, para. 30.

[6] Above, n. 5.

[7] ibid., para. 54.

[8] ibid., paras. 38, 39.

minorities, while particular note may be taken on cultural acceptability and the ability of educational systems to respond to the needs of changing societies and communities.[9] In relation to private educational provision, we may also note Articles 28 and 29 of the Convention on the Rights of the Child (CRC) on the structures and aims of education, with Article 29(2) providing that the generality of these articles shall not be construed 'so as to interfere with the liberty of individuals and bodies to establish and direct educational institutions', subject to observance of the principles or aims of education[10] in Article 29, and to minimum standards established by the state. Article 30 CRC, on children of minorities and indigenous peoples, may be assimilated to Article 27 of the International Covenant on Civil and Political Rights (ICCPR).

The UN Declaration on Minorities does not contain a specific provision on education 'institutions', in addition to its provisions on languages in education and educational content. However, Article 2(4) provides that persons belonging to minorities 'have the right to establish and maintain their own associations', a formulation that is wide enough to include educational and religious institutions, bearing in mind that 'associations' was chosen as the widest term available.[11] The provisions are much clearer on the institutional side in the case of general instruments on indigenous peoples. Thus, Article 27(3) of the International Labour Organization (ILO) Convention 169 on Indigenous and Tribal Peoples combines institutional and resource elements in providing that 'governments shall recognize the right of these peoples to establish their own educational institutions and facilities, provided that such institutions meet minimum standards established by the competent authority in consultation with these peoples. Appropriate resources shall be provided for this purpose.' Article 15 of the UN Draft Declaration on Indigenous Peoples would go further towards the development and control of specific group institutions imbued with their own values: 'Indigenous children have the right to all levels and forms of education of the State. All indigenous peoples also have this right and the right to establish and control their educational systems and institutions providing education in their own languages, in a manner appropriate to their cultural methods of teaching and learning.'[12]

[9] Above, n. 5, para. 6.

[10] See commentary on FCNM, Art. 12.

[11] A. Eide, Final Text of the Commentary to the Declaration (2001), UN Doc. E/CN.4/Sub.2/AC.52001/2, para. 51.

[12] This article is under examination by a working group of the UN Commission on Human Rights along with all the other articles in the draft declaration, although it is relatively uncontroversial within the context of the drafting process. For the latest discussions, see Commission on Human Rights, Report of the Working Group Established in Accordance with Commission on Human Rights Resolution 1995/32, 59th session (2003), UN Doc. E/CN.4/2003/92.

In terms of European regional instruments, as observed in relation to Article 12 of the Framework Convention, Article 2 of Protocol 1 ECHR uses a negative formulation to encapsulate the right to education:[13] '[n]o person shall be denied the right to education. In the exercise of any functions which it assumes in relation to education and teaching, the State shall respect the right of parents to ensure such education and teaching in conformity with their own religious and philosophical convictions.' It is not absolutely clear from this provision if the state is entitled to prohibit the establishment of private schools. The structure of the second sentence of the Article, referring to state functions, suggests that it does not create a right to establish private education; so that any such right would be better argued in the context of the general right to education in the first sentence.[14] The case law on the issue is somewhat indirect, and is mostly directed towards encouraging the state authorities to provide the necessary education, rather than supporting the establishment of private schools.[15] European texts on minority rights have generally taken a clear stance on the institutions aspect of minority protection, and its resource implications. Paragraph 32(2) of the Organization for Security and Co-operation in Europe (OSCE) Copenhagen Document provides simply that persons belonging to national minorities have the right 'to establish and maintain their own educational, cultural and religious institutions, organizations or associations, which can seek voluntary financial and other contributions as well as public assistance, in conformity with national legislation'. The OSCE Geneva Meeting of Experts in July 1991 added an important element to the last formula: '[t]he participating States reaffirm, *and will not hinder the exercise of*, the right of persons belonging to national minorities to establish and maintain their own

[13] Despite this negative formulation, the European Court of Human Rights (ECHR) has clarified that there is 'no doubt that Article 2 does enshrine a right'—*Belgian Linguistics Case*, Series A. No. 6 (1968), EHRR 252, pp. 30–1. The exiguous nature of the right is attested to by the Court's statement that the state party was not obliged to establish or subsidize education of any particular type or at any particular level at its own expense.

[14] J. G. Merrills and A. H. Robertson, *Human Rights in Europe: A Study of the European Convention on Human Rights* (Manchester University Press, Manchester, 2001), 248. In *Kjeldsen, Busk Madsen and Pedersen* v. *Denmark* (5095/71) (1976) EHRR 6, Series A, 23, para. 50, the Court found that the *travaux* of the European Convention 'indisputably demonstrate . . . the importance attached by many members of the Consultative Assembly [of the Council of Europe] and a number of governments to freedom of teaching, that is to say freedom to establish private schools'.

[15] See, for example, *Cyprus* v. *Turkey* (25781/94) (2001) EHRR 327, judgment. In *Kjeldsen, Busk, Madsen and Pedersen* v. *Denmark* (above, n. 14) the Court found that the second sentence of Art. 2 of Protocol 1 'aims in short at safeguarding the possibility of pluralism in education which possibility is essential for the preservation of the "democratic society" as conceived by the Convention. In view of the power of the modern State, *it is above all through State teaching that this aim must be realised*'. Emphasis added.

educational, cultural and religious institutions, organizations and associations'.[16] The 'non-hindrance' element is taken up in The Hague Recommendations regarding the Education Rights of National Minorities:

(8) In accordance with international law, persons belonging to national minorities, like others, have the right to establish and manage their own private educational institutions in conformity with domestic law. These institutions may include schools teaching in the minority language.

(9) Given the right of persons belonging to national minorities to establish and manage their own educational institutions, States may not hinder the enjoyment of this right by imposing unduly burdensome legal and administrative requirements regarding the establishment and management of these institutions.

(10) Private minority language educational institutions are entitled to seek their own sources of funding without any hindrance or discrimination from the State budget, international sources and the private sector.[17]

As might be expected from such a lengthy pedigree, the basic 'institutions' aspect of the article figures in all of the principal drafting exercises predating the Convention, including in this the work of the Venice Commission, the Parliamentary Assembly of the Council of Europe, and the Austrian draft Protocol to the ECHR guaranteeing the protection of ethnic groups. The provision on financial obligation, or the absence of obligation, became more pronounced as the work of the Ad Hoc Committee for the Protection of National Minorities (CAHMIN) progressed.

C. Context

The provisions of Article 13 complement the education principles in Articles 12 and 14, and the 'identity' and freedom from forced assimilation provisions of Articles 5 and 6, as well as the 'association' principles of Articles 7 and 8. The provision on financial obligations in the second paragraph of the article brings into play the equality and non-discrimination principles of Article 4.

[16] OSCE, Commission on Security and Co-operation in Europe (CSCE) Meeting of Experts on National Minorities, Geneva, 1991, V, para. 2, emphasis added.

[17] Foundation on Interethnic Relations, The Hague Recommendations Regarding the Education Rights of National Minorities and Explanatory Note No. 12, 13, 1996 according to which, 'The right of national minorities to establish and maintain their own institutions, including educational ones, is well grounded in international law and must be recognized as such. Although the State has the right to oversee this process from an administrative perspective and in conformity with its own legislation, it must not prevent the enjoyment of this right by imposing unreasonable administrative requirements which might render it practically impossible for national minorities to manage their own educational institutions. Although there is no formal obligation for States to fund these private establishments, these institutions should not be prevented from seeking resources from all domestic and international sources.'

II. Analysis

A. Structure of the Article

As is apparent from the arrangement of principles, there is a clear presentation of two issues in Article 13: the freedom of establishment, followed by the consequences of such a freedom for the resources of the state. The present analysis will take the two together as they emerged from the *travaux préparatoires* in view of their essential interconnection. Nowhere else in the Convention is there such a clear coupling of a right with the negation of a particular form of obligation which might otherwise flow from the exercise of that right. The issues are individuated to some degree later in the analysis, bearing in mind that there is only a minor degree of 'practice' to report from the Framework Convention organs.

B. Issues

1. Travaux préparatoires

Awareness of general provisions under the UNESCO Convention and other instruments permitting the setting up of private schools for religious and linguistic and other reasons filtered in to the large number of drafts of Article 13. The institutional teaching of minority languages was a particular focus of drafting concerns. The Venice Commission's preliminary draft of a Convention on the Protection of Minorities provided that '[c]hildren shall have the right to receive obligatory schooling in their mother tongue. When the State is not in a position to provide such teaching in State schools, it must allow children who so wish to attend private schools; the State may prescribe that the language spoken by the majority also be taught in such schools';[18] in relation to state schools a later Venice draft added that, '[a]s far as possible, all or part of the schooling shall be given in the mother tongue of pupils belonging to the minority'.[19] On state schools and the provision relating to the situation where the minority had reached a 'substantial percentage of a region or the total population', the private school alternative was to take effect where the state was unable to so provide. The Commission explained that '[t]he drafters of the proposal for a Convention regard either of these solutions as sufficient to ensure schooling in the language of the minority. The State concerned will

[18] European Commission for Democracy through Law (ECDL), Preliminary Draft Convention on the Protection of Minorities [DAJ.SC.DEMOCRACY]CONV.MIN, 1990, Art. 10. See also ECDL, Set of Principles on National Minorities Drawn up by the European Commission for Democracy through Law, Draft Report of the 4th Meeting, CD-PV (90) 4 PROV, 1990.

[19] ECDL, Proposal for a European Convention for the Protection of National Minorities, CDL-MIN (93) 6, Art. 9.

choose between the two options depending on its particular circumstances and financial resources.'[20] It seems clear from the Committee of Venice drafting that in the case of private schools, and under the above conditions, 'the State shall have the right to prescribe that the official language or languages also be taught in such schools'.[21] The Explanatory Report on the Convention distils the essence of the provisions of Article 13(1) as:

> The Parties' obligation to recognise the right of persons belonging to national minorities to set up and manage their own private educational establishments is subject to the requirements of their educational system . . . The establishments covered by this paragraph may be subject to the same forms of supervision as other establishments . . . Once the required standards are met, it is important that any qualifications awarded are officially recognised. The relevant national legislation must be based on objective criteria and conform to the principle of non-discrimination.[22]

A hint of the financial implications of such moves came from the Parliamentary Assembly of the Council of Europe: national minorities were to have the right to maintain their own educational, religious, and cultural institutions, and for this purpose, 'they shall also have the right to solicit voluntary financial and other contributions including public assistance.'[23] The 1993 Steering Committee for Human Rights (CDDH) report for the attention of the Committee of Ministers was more 'parsimonious' on financial aspects: minority schools could be set up, 'without any (financial) obligation on the part of the State'.[24] Views in CAHMIN on the financial aspects of private minority schools were not unanimous. A 1994 Meeting Report notes that:

> Views diverged as to the financial contributions of the State. While some thought that the social function of the creation of these establishments was adequate justification for a financial contribution by the State, the majority of experts thought that there should be no obligation of the State in this respect, or that it should at least be limited by the financial resources available to the State.[25]

There is considerable difference between these two alternatives: the first amounts to the recognition of a right coupled with a disinclination to support it with material resources from the state; the second would situate the right

[20] ECDL, Explanatory Report to the Proposal for a European Convention, CDL-MIN (93) 7, 22, 1993, para. 36.

[21] Above, n. 19, Art. 9.

[22] Above, n. 20, para. 72.

[23] Parliamentary Assembly of the Council of Europe, Recommendation 1990/1134/EC of 1 October 1990 on the Rights of Minorities, 42nd Ordinary Session, (1990), para. 11(iii).

[24] Steering Committee for Human Rights (CDDH), Final Activity Report of the CDDH for the Attention of the Committee of Ministers, CDDH (93) 22, 1993.

[25] CAHMIN, Meeting Report, CAHMIN (94) 13, 3rd Meeting, 1994, para. 31.

within essentially the same framework as human rights in general, since the achievement of human rights almost inevitably consumes state resources. The CAHMIN Preliminary Draft Convention softens the blow just a little in adding to the 'no financial obligation' formula a rider that 'in the regions where mandatory schooling is exclusively or essentially ensured by these private establishments, the Parties shall endeavour to finance them, as far as possible, in whole or in part'.[26] The Romanian delegation responded with the proposal that the rider 'should be dropped, the hypothesis envisaged being exceptional, moreover, a majority of experts did not support this approach.'[27] The minimalistic suggestion that the state should 'endeavour, as far as possible' to finance minority schools was duly dropped, leaving the Convention with its negation of any obligation to support such establishments. On the other hand, the CAHMIN added that, while the paragraph 'does not entail any financial obligation for the Party concerned . . . neither does it exclude the possibility of such a contribution', a formula in essence repeated in the Explanatory Report on the Convention.[28]

2. *Right to Set up Private Minority Schools*

As noted, there is relatively little Convention practice on the implementation of either paragraph of Article 13. A number of countries report that they have no private schools specifically for national minorities.[29] In most cases, the right is stated as one granted to members of national minorities to the same extent as to other citizens. A smaller number of states appear to have supplemented general provisions with specific minority rights provisions, facilitating the establishment of private institutions for members of national minorities.[30] An even more limited number of examples of private universities specifically for national minorities appear in the reports,[31] though higher level religious training institutions are also accounted for.[32]

[26] European Commission for Democracy through Law (ECDL), Preliminary Draft Convention on the Protection of Minorities [DAJ.SC.DEMOCRACY]CONV.MIN, 1990, Art. 11, para. 2.

[27] CAHMIN, Proposals on the Preliminary Draft Convention, CAHMIN (94) 14 Rev., 1994, p. 18.

[28] Above, n. 20, para. 73.

[29] Albania State Report, ACFC/SR (2001) 005, 2001; Bulgaria State Report, ACFC/SR (2003) 001, 2003; Poland State Report, ACFC/SR (2002) 002, 2002; Slovenia State Report, ACFC/SR (2000) 004, 2000.

[30] Austria (Treaty of St Germain, Art. 67), Estonia (National Minorities Cultural Autonomy Act), Hungary (the Minorities Act), Russian Federation (Law on National and Cultural Autonomy), Serbia and Montenegro (Law on the Protection of the Rights and Freedoms of National Minorities), Ukraine (draft laws).

[31] See, for example, Romania State Report, ACFC/SR (1999) 011, 1999; and Ukraine State Report, ACFC/SR (1999) 014, 1999.

[32] Bulgaria State Report, ACFC/SR (2002) 001, 2003.

3. Financial Support

Despite the bleak wording of Article 13(2), that there is no financial obligation for states parties in respect of private minority schools, most states parties do provide subsidies to such schools.[33] In the case of Austria, with reference to the Komensky School in Vienna, the only school to provide a full bilingual education for the Czech and Slovak minority, the Committee welcomed the fact that the authorities covered the cost of the education, though the legislation did not require them to do so. Since funding difficulties remained, the Committee urged the authorities to continue their discussions with representatives of the minorities to identify funding solutions, especially in view of the historical importance of the school for the minorities in question.[34] The Committee also encouraged further subsidies for the schools of other minorities.[35] In the case of Germany, the Committee noted that the education system for the Danish minority is entirely private, and, in welcoming the fact that the *Land* of Schleswig-Holstein pays for the education of each Danish minority pupil, it expressed the hope that this form of financial support could also be used to benefit other national minorities.[36] However, in view of the fact that the average cost per pupil was higher for minority pupils than for others, the Committee again encouraged dialogue to find appropriate funding solutions.

III. Conclusion and Outlook

The importance of the basic freedom of establishment principle in Article 13 should not be underestimated. For some minority groups the best guarantee of maintaining their distinct identities resides in the development of their own educational institutions. In general terms, this freedom goes some way toward facilitating the expression of cultural and religious pluralism. On the other hand, the line between 'own institutions' and a separatist policy is a fine one. The proliferation of private establishments makes state control of educational

[33] The position is made clearer in some reports than in others. See in particular Austria State Report, ACFC/SR (2000) 003, 2000; Cyprus State Report, ACFC/SR (1999) 002 Rev., 1999; Czech Republic State Report, ACFC/SR (1999) 009, 1999; Denmark State Report, ACFC/SR 1999) 009, 1999; Germany State Report, ACFC/SR (2000) 001, 2000; Hungary State Report, ACFC/SR (1999) 010, 1999; Italy State Report, ACFC/SR (1999) 007, 1999; Norway State Report, ACFC/SR (2002) 001, 2001; Slovakia State Report, ACFC/SR (1999) 008, 1999; Sweden State Report, ACFC/SR (2001) 003, 2001; and the United Kingdom State Report, ACFC/SR (1999) 013, 1999.

[34] Advisory Committee Opinion on Austria, ACFC/INF/OP/I (2002) 009, 2002, paras. 58, 59, 94.

[35] Above, n. 34, paras. 60, 95.

[36] Advisory Committee Opinion on Germany, ACFC/INF/OP/I (2002) 008, 2002, para. 56.

systems difficult to maintain, and may go against the interculturalism reflected in the Convention. Private schools for minority groups will not necessarily escape the social censure associated with schools for the financially privileged, even if this is neither their basis nor their remit. Issues of general equality and non-discrimination will inevitably be raised in the context of privatization programmes in education. The equality/non-discrimination principle works in the interface between the general population and minority groups, as well as in that between minority groups themselves. While there are states with apparently no private educational institutions, the broad freedom to establish such institutions does not appear to be challenged by states. Nor do they appear to greatly 'hinder' this right, though questions of curriculum control or oversight may loom larger in the perspective of the Advisory Committee in the course of time, especially if forms of religious or political 'fundamentalism' continue to attract adherents, and private institutions move towards separation on the basis of both gender and ethnicity.

If the challenge to the state presented by the establishment principle of Article 13(1) is essentially one of social solidarity or national ethos, the challenge of the second paragraph is to the cost of this particular human rights commitment. The draconian statement in Article 13(2), that the right to set up private institutions 'shall not entail any financial obligation' for the parties, may lead to an incorrect reading of state obligations in many practical situations. As the Explanatory Report notes in respect of the first paragraph, the principle of non-discrimination enters the equation when considering minority education.[37] In conformity with this principle, it can be argued that if states subsidized the education of some groups, they would be obliged to consider subsidizing others. A clear instance of this principle emerges from the case of *Waldman* v. *Canada* before the Human Rights Committee,[38] where the author of the complaint, who was of the Jewish faith, paid for Jewish schools for his children out of household funds, whereas Catholic schools received public funding from the authorities in the Province of Ontario. The Committee observed that he had sent his children to private schools not because he wished for private education but because the publicly funded system made no provision for his denomination.[39] The Committee found a violation of the equality article, Article 26, observing that while the ICCPR 'does not oblige States parties to fund schools which are established on a religious basis . . . if a State party chooses to provide public funding to religious schools, it should make

[37] Above, n. 20, para. 72.

[38] *Waldman* v. *Canada*, Comm. No. 694/1996, views (1999), UN Doc. A/55/40, CCPR/ C/67/ D/694/1996, pp. 86–101.

[39] Above, n. 38, para. 10(5).

this funding available without discrimination'.[40] In a concurring opinion, Committee member Scheinin observed that in the scheme of the Covenant, public funding for religious or other minorities was not discriminatory. On the contrary, the minority rights provision in Article 27 imposed positive obligations to promote religious instruction (for religious minorities) and public funding was a means to that end. Furthermore, the operation of this principle could also apply to the Jewish community, and in the circumstances, the funding disparity amounted to discrimination.[41] So, while a state may not be obliged to fund private minority schools, if they fund the private schools of one group, this may raise the question of funding for others. The non-discrimination principle does not of course oblige states to treat all groups uniformly; the underlying principle of equality is more nuanced. Much depends on issues such as group demand, the amount and feasibility of funding, and perhaps curriculum issues, before moving to any determination that the principle of non-discrimination has been breached. The Advisory Committee appears to have sensed this principle in recommending or encouraging governments to provide subsidies for other minorities. In this respect, state practice in many cases has been more generous than the minimalist second paragraph of Article 13. In the practice of the Committee, issues such as the historical importance of the school or institution for the identity of the minority in question have weight in recommending 'funding solutions' to particular problems. Nevertheless, the provisions of the article contrast unfavourably with the provisions of Article 27 of ILO Convention 169 for example, which presents a more attractive proposition for indigenous groups. Clearly they do not cohere well with more 'positive' aspects of the Framework Convention in Articles 4 and 5, for example. Article 13 FCNM, as with others, requires a contextual reading in the light of the instrument as a whole, and should not be read in a manner that undermines what is offered by kindred international instruments.

[40] *Waldman* v. *Canada*, above, n. 38, para. 10(6).

[41] Above, n. 38, pp. 100–1.

ARTICLE 14

Fernand de Varennes and Patrick Thornberry

1. The parties undertake to recognise that every person belonging to a national minority has the right to learn his or her minority language.
2. In areas inhabited by persons belonging to national minorities traditionally or in substantial numbers, if there is sufficient demand, the Parties shall endeavour to ensure, as far as possible and within the framework of their education systems, that persons belonging to those minorities have adequate opportunities for being taught the minority language or for receiving instruction in this language.
3. Paragraph 2 of this article shall be implemented without prejudice to the learning of the official language or the teaching in this language.

I. Background

A. Issues

The first paragraph of Article 14 addresses the broadest aspects of language learning, without specific reference to educational systems. The second paragraph contains the third reference in the Convention to minority 'areas', wherein certain, more specific rights are to be enjoyed by members of minorities subject to the fulfilment of certain triggering conditions. The paragraph adds further normative dimensions to this concept; it is also specific to educational systems, although the term 'schools' is not used. The Explanatory Report states in this connection that the Framework Convention 'deliberately refrains from defining "areas inhabited by persons belonging to national minorities traditionally or in substantial numbers". It was considered preferable to adopt a flexible form of wording which will allow each party's particular circumstances to be taken into account.'[1] In this case, it may be observed that, since the areas in question need not be 'traditionally inhabited',[2] they will include areas where there is a substantial minority presence, such as quarters of large cities into which minorities have migrated in substantial numbers. In cases of traditional or substantial inhabitation, the ruling idea is the demarcation of local space. The minorities do not 'own' the space—this is not autonomy, let alone self-determination—but their presence is manifested through a series of public permissions and possibilities set out in the Convention. The concepts recognize attachment and historical presence in 'traditional' areas, and force of numbers, demands, and needs in traditional and other areas of substantial presence. Especially in the case of the traditionally inhabited areas, enjoyment of these spatially conditioned and demarcated rights is the Convention's 'substitute' for a 'full-blown' concept of territorial autonomy. If Article 14(2) projects an area of 'enhanced', territorially bounded rights, it is not illogical to surmise that they must add something to the general language learning right in 14(1). According to the third paragraph of Article 14, the implementation of the second paragraph is, as elsewhere in the language provisions of the Convention, to be made without prejudice to the position of the official language. In all cases, a balance needs to be struck which respects a twin-track approach: equipping the members of minorities with sufficient language skills to succeed in the broader society, while facilitating the preservation and development of their own language(s). The education process is critical to the success of any such social strategy. Remarks on paragraphs 1 and 3 of Article 14 apply, *mutatis mutandis*, to 14(2), in addition to the general remarks essayed in this volume on education, in general and with reference to Articles 12 and 13.

B. History

As pointed out in the commentary to Article 13 of the Framework Convention, the League of Nations system of minority protection explicitly addressed the

[1] Ad Hoc Committee for the Protection of National Minorities, CAHMIN, Explanatory Report on the Framework Convention for the Protection of National Minorities, H(1995) 010, 1995, Art. 10, para. 2(66).

[2] 'Traditional inhabitation' and 'substantial numbers' are *alternative* conditions for the enjoyment of the rights in Art. 14(2) and Art. 10(2); both conditions are required in order to engage the rights in Art. 11(3).

question of private minority educational institutions that permitted the free use of language and practice of religion; additionally, in the public education system, at least in the primary schools, education was to be provided 'through the medium of' the language of the minorities. Compared to the League of Nations, UN instruments have been somewhat reluctant to address the question of language, despite the basic non-discrimination formula set out in the Charter itself, that there shall be no discrimination in the enjoyment of human rights on grounds of 'race, sex, language or religion'. The formulation of the right to education in the Universal Declaration of Human Rights (UDHR) does not make specific reference to language in education, and this is also true of the right set out in Article 13 of the International Covenant on Economic, Social, and Cultural Rights (ICESCR). As observed in relation to Article 13 of the Framework Convention, in the UNESCO Convention against Discrimination in Education, the establishment of schools for 'religious or linguistic reasons' is exempted from the general condemnation of discrimination in education under specified conditions;[3] further, the right of national minorities to carry on their own educational activities, includes, 'depending on the educational policy of the State, *the use or the teaching of their own language*'.[4] In contrast to the UDHR and the ICESCR, Article 27 of the International Covenant on Civil and Political Rights (ICCPR) makes specific reference to the use of language but not to education; as does Article 30 of the Convention on the Rights of the Child. General Comment No. 23 of the UN Human Rights Committee—on the rights of minorities—does not elaborate an educational dimension. In the sphere of language, the Comment refers, rather, to the distinctive nature of the right of individuals belonging to a linguistic minority to use the language among themselves and how this differs from other rights in the Covenant.[5] This may reflect the paucity of educational questions in the 'case law' of the Committee,[6] although linked issues of language and education surface more frequently in the Committee's Concluding Observations on particular countries.[7] The latter is also true of the Committee on the Elimination of Racial Discrimination (CERD); the Convention

[3] UNESCO, Convention against Discrimination in Education, 1960, 429 UNTS 93, Art 2(*b*).

[4] Art. 5(1)(*c*) Convention against Discrimination in Education, emphasis added.

[5] UN Human Rights Committee, General Comment No. 23: The Rights of Minorities, 1994, UN Doc. CCPR/C/21/Rev.1/Add.5, Art. 27, para. 5(3).

[6] CAHMIN, Commentary on the Provisions of the Framework Convention for the Protection of National Minorities, H(1995) 010, 1995, Art. 13.

[7] For examples, see D. Wilson, Minority Rights into and through Education, paper prepared for the Council of Europe Conference to mark the 5th anniversary of the coming into force of the Framework Convention, Strasbourg, 2003.

contains only a general reference to a right to education and training, without an express language component,[8] and to anti-racist education.[9] In practice, however, the CERD makes frequent references to language education issues.[10]

The UN Declaration on Minorities addresses both language and education in Article 4, providing that, 'States should take appropriate measures so that, wherever possible, persons belonging to minorities may have adequate opportunities to learn their mother tongue or to have instruction in their mother tongue.' The Eide commentary to the Declaration reflects some of the ethos of the Framework Convention in remarking that learning the mother tongue is the minimum, and that further steps to be taken will depend on various factors including the size of the minority group and the nature of its settlement. Echoing the provisions of Article 14 of the Framework Convention, Eide expresses the view that in cases 'where the language of the minority is a territorial language traditionally spoken and used by many in a region of a country, states should to the maximum of their available resources ensure that linguistic identity can be preserved'.[11]

The 'institutional' aspects of International Labour Organization (ILO) Convention 169 on Indigenous and Tribal Peoples have already been discussed in relation to other articles of the Convention. On language, the first paragraph of Article 28 provides that indigenous children 'shall, wherever practicable, be taught to read and write in their own indigenous language or in the language most commonly used by the group to which they belong'. The second paragraph adds that, '[a]dequate measures shall be taken to ensure that these peoples have the opportunity to attain fluency' in the national language or in one of the official languages of the country. The provisions reflect the importance of bicultural and bilingual education for indigenous people, based on the problems faced by many indigenous groups who 'have commonly suffered from two different problems in connection with education: in the first place they are often not allowed access to the educational facilities to which other members of the national population have access; and second, when they do have access, their own traditions, cultures and languages, are usually ignored or even denigrated.'[12]

[8] Committee on the Elimination of Racial Discrimination (CERD), International Convention on the Elimination of all Forms of Racial Discrimination, UNGA Res. 2106 (XX), 1965, Art. 5(*e*)(v).

[9] Art. 7 CERD.

[10] CERD, 2002, UN Doc. A/57/18, 60th and 61st sessions, Reports on Liechtenstein, paras. 152–3, Lithuania, para. 172, Moldova, para. 214, Armenia, para. 280, and Estonia, para. 350; CERD, 2003, UN Doc. A/58/18, Reports on Albania, paras. 301 and 310, Latvia, para. 452, which include points on education and language.

[11] A. Eide, Commentary to the UN Declaration on the Rights of Persons Belonging to National or Ethnic, Religious, and Linguistic Minorities, UN Doc. E/CN.4/Sub.2/AC.5/2001/2, para. 61.

[12] M. Tomei and L. Swepston, *Indigenous and Tribal Peoples: A Guide to ILO Convention 169* (International Labour Office, Geneva, 1996), 24.

The educational 'balance' to be struck in the case of indigenous groups may be a matter of great delicacy: educational systems imposed by states have done as much to damage indigenous cultures as to protect them.

As for European instruments, the European Convention for the Protection of Human Rights and Fundamental Freedoms (ECHR) does not advance the case for minority language education to any great extent. The Convention is directed to human rights in general, and although it has in practice done a great deal to advance minority interests at every level, it is not a minority rights instrument as such. The reticence of the Convention organs to find a strong base for language rights through, for example, imaginative interpretations of provisions on freedom of expression, is mirrored in the approach to minority language education. Taking the right to education set out in Article 2 of Protocol 1 to the Convention,[13] in the *Belgian Linguistics* case, the applicants argued that 'philosophical convictions', in the second sentence of the article, should be interpreted to include the cultural and linguistic preferences of parents. However, the European Commission on Human Rights, followed by the Court, was unanimous that the second sentence of Article 2 was not intended to guarantee respect for preferences or opinions in cultural or linguistic matters.[14] The term 'philosophical convictions' was explained by the Court in *Campbell and Cosans* v. *the United Kingdom*[15] as relating to 'such convictions as are worthy of respect in a democratic society . . . and are not incompatible with human dignity'.[16] In this case, the views of the applicant on the practice of corporal punishment in schools related to 'a weighty and substantial aspect of human life and behaviour'.[17] Based on the reading of 'philosophical convictions' in *Campbell and Cosans*, one author commented that 'the desire of parents, based on cultural and linguistic association with an ethnic group, to have their children educated in their mother tongue also has to be recognised as such a conviction.'[18] This approach to the meaning of 'philosophical convictions' was doubted in the admissibility decision in *Skender* v. *the Former Yugoslav Republic of Macedonia*. In this case, the Third Section of the Court revisited the *Belgian Linguistics* case, and pointed out that, 'a right to education in a particular language or a right to obtain from the State the creation of a particular kind of educational establishment cannot be derived from Article 2 of Protocol 1'; further, to interpret 'religious' and 'philosophical' as covering linguistic preferences 'would amount to

[13] See chapters on Arts. 12 and 13 in this commentary.

[14] *Belgian Linguistics Case*, Series A, No. 6 (1968), EHRR 252, para. 3, p. 32.

[15] *Campbell and Cosans* v. *the United Kingdom*, Series A, No. 48 (7511/76) (1982) EHRR 3.

[16] Above, n. 15, p. 16.

[17] Above, n. 15.

[18] Blum cited in C. Hillgruber and M. Jestaedt, *The European Convention on Human Rights and the Protection of National Minorities* (Verlag Wissenschaft und Politik, Cologne, 1994), 26, n. 64.

a distortion of their ordinary and usual meaning and read into the Convention something which is not there'.[19] Some shift away from the limiting ECHR approach may be discerned in *Cyprus* v. *Turkey*, where the Court, in supporting the finding of a violation of Article 2 of Protocol 1 by the Commission,[20] in relation to schools in northern Cyprus that were open to Greek Cypriots and offered classes in English or Turkish, observed that:

> the option available to Greek-Cypriot parents to continue their children's education in the north is unrealistic in view of the fact that the children in question have already received their primary education in a Greek-Cypriot school there. The authorities must no doubt be aware that it is the wish of Greek-Cypriot parents that the schooling of the children be completed through the medium of the Greek language. Having assumed responsibility for the provision of Greek-language primary schooling, the failure of the TRNC authorities to make continuing provision for it must be considered in effect a denial of the substance of the right at issue. It cannot be maintained that the provision of secondary education in the south in keeping with the linguistic tradition of the enclaved Greek Cypriots suffices to fulfil the obligation . . . in Article 2 of the First Protocol, having regard to the impact of that option on family life.[21]

The result of the case was heavily conditioned by the facts, including the prior existence of the schools and their abolition by the Turkish authorities, and by the denial of the rights of Greek Cypriot children, particularly male children over 16, to return to the north of Cyprus if they went to the southern part for their education.[22]

The most extensive normative reflection on minority languages is that contained in the European Charter for Regional or Minority Languages, Article 8 of which addresses education. The application of provisions depends on the condition of the language—illustrating the fact that the Charter is an instrument designed to protect the European linguistic heritage rather than minority rights—and is to be 'without prejudice to the teaching of the official language(s) of the State'.[23] The provisions relate to the use of language at all levels of

[19] *Skender* v. *'the former Republic of Macedonia'* (62059/00) (2001) EHRR. The Court further recalled that the *travaux* of the article confirm 'that the object . . . was in no way to secure respect by the State of a right for parents to have education conducted in a language other than that of the country in question', an affirmation which begs the question of what exactly is 'the language of the country' in question, when there may be many, including the languages of national minorities.

[20] *Cyprus* v. *Turkey* (25781/94) (2001) EHRR 327, report adopted on 4 June 1999.

[21] Judgment of 10 May 2001, para. 278. See also, *Cyprus* v. *Turkey*, above, n. 20, paras. 273–7 and 279–80.

[22] For comment, see G. Gilbert, 'The Burgeoning Minority Rights Jurisprudence of the European Court of Human Rights', *Human Rights Quarterly*, 24 (2002), 736–80.

[23] Council of Europe (CoE), European Charter for Regional or Minority Languages, ETS No. 148, Strasbourg, 1992, heading to Art. 8(1).

education; the provisions on secondary levels are conditioned by demand and a 'sufficient numbers' formula, reminiscent of the Framework Convention.

C. Context

The education provisions of Article 14 link naturally with those for Articles 6, 12, and 13. The overall identity-enhancing philosophy and purpose of the Convention as expressed in the Preamble, and particularly Articles 4 and 5, should also be borne in mind. The approach of the Convention organs to questions of traditional inhabitation, numbers, and demand also implicates that terminology in Articles 10 and 11.

II. Analysis

A. Structure of the Article

The structure of Article 14 is complex due to the disagreements and controversies surrounding the extent to which states parties should be involved in and support linguistic rights in education. Its three-paragraph structure once again points to the divergent influences that led to their incorporation into the Framework Convention. Article 14(1) refers to the right of persons belonging to national minorities to learn their own language and is straightforward in its wording. Article 14(2) is the exact opposite: it imposes on states an obligation to take measures for the teaching of, or instruction in, a national minority language. It is, however, full of limitations which could be seen as escape clauses or the watering down of state obligations. Concurrent with the rights identified in the Framework Convention, the third section of Article 14 deals with the recognition that individuals must not be prevented from learning the official language in the exercise of these rights, a right also consistently acknowledged in international treaties and other instruments.[24]

Because of the different substantive issues that the three paragraphs involve, the drafting background and substantive content for each one will be examined separately.

[24] Conference for Security and Co-operation in Europe (CSCE), Document of the Copenhagen Meeting of the Conference on the Human Dimension of the OSCE, 2nd Conference, Copenhagen, 1990, para. 34; Foundation on Interethnic Relations, The Hague Recommendations Regarding the Education Rights of National Minorities and Explanatory Note No. 12, 13, 1996, Art. 8(1) of the European Charter for Regional or Minority Languages; UNESCO, Convention against Discrimination in Education, 11th Session, Art. 5(1), 1962.

B. Article 14(1)

1. Travaux préparatoires

To understand both the potential as well as the limits of Article 14(1), the background of the negotiations that led to its convoluted wording is particularly illuminating. The *travaux préparatoires* show an early controversy as to whether there should be an unqualified right for individuals to be educated in or learn their own language in state establishments. Initial documents generally seemed to approve that, '[w]hen the State is not in a position to provide such teaching in State schools, it must allow children who so wish to attend private schools.'[25] However, quickly there was disagreement between those with a more generous view who wished to grant the right to schooling in a national minority language in all cases where a state was in 'a position to provide such schooling',[26] and those opposed to 'proclaiming a right for children to receive a certain type of education'.[27] These conflicting views were to result in division of Article 14 into three paragraphs instead of a single one as early documents demonstrated. The final wording of Article 14(1), and indeed of the two other paragraphs, reflects the compromises that were made to reconcile both positions to a certain degree.

A 1993 draft seemed to support the right of individuals to be entitled to learn their national minority language in public schools and to receive instruction in their language 'as far as possible':

> Whenever the conditions of Article 8 are fulfilled, in State schools, obligatory schooling shall include, for pupils belonging to the minority, study of their mother tongue. As far as possible, all or part of the schooling shall be given in the mother tongue of pupils belonging to the minority.[28]

This principle was, however, subject to satisfying a demographic requirement, 'whenever a minority reaches a substantial percentage of the population of a region or of the total population'.[29] Furthermore, its wording presented states with a choice between two alternatives, 'either to organise in State schools, schooling in the mother tongue of the minority, or to allow children belonging to the minority to attend private schools in which schooling is given

[25] European Commission for Democracy through Law (ECDL), Preliminary Draft Convention on the Protection of Minorities [DAJ.SC.DEMOCRACY]CONV.MIN, 1990.

[26] ECDL, Set of Principles on National Minorities Drawn up by the European Commission for Democracy through Law, Draft Report of the 4th Meeting, CD-PV (90) 4 PROV, 1990, para. 12.

[27] Above, n. 26, para. 11.

[28] ECDL, Proposal for a European Convention for the Protection of National Minorities, CDL-MIN (93) 6, 1993, Art. 9.

[29] ibid., para. 35.

in their mother tongue',[30] depending on a state's circumstances and financial resources. Later drafts clarified that 'every person belonging to a national minority has the right to learn his/her minority language and to be instructed in that minority language'.[31]

In early 1994, there was still general agreement among the drafters that every person belonging to a national minority had the right to learn the minority language,[32] but the wording of the draft was to change in the June 1994 draft. It indicated that parties should recognize that this right existed rather than stating that individuals had such a right.[33] During this period, a proposal from the Austrian delegation that this right also extend to being taught in a national minority language, in general, was not retained.[34]

Article 14(1) in its final form thus appears to enshrine, as stated in the Explanatory Report, one of the principal means by which national minorities can assert and preserve their identity. Yet at the same time the report explains that 'without prejudice to the principles mentioned in paragraph 2, this paragraph does not imply positive action, notably of a financial nature, on the part of the State'.[35] It would then seem that Article 14(1) is more of a declaration of the broad principle recognizing the centrality of language for national minorities, particularly in the field of education. An examination of the Advisory Committee views provides insight on both the use and limits of this provision.

2. *Recognition*

Article 14(1) recognizes the right to learn a national minority language, without explicitly stating that parties have an obligation to enshrine this recognition in legislation or in the constitution. A number of states parties referred to such legislative or constitutional provisions,[36] and the Advisory Committee has favourably noted these in passing, but at no point has the Advisory Committee suggested that the absence of any provision to this effect involved a breach of a state's obligations under Article 14(1). Instead, the Advisory Committee has

30 ibid., para. 36.

31 Steering Committee for Human Rights (CDDH), Final Activity Report of the CDDH for the Attention of the Committee of Ministers, CDDH (93) 22, 1993, Art. 7.

32 Preparatory Work of the Ad Hoc Committee for the Protection of National Minorities (CAHMIN), Meeting Report, CAHMIN (94) 13, 1994, 3rd Meeting, p. 7.

33 CAHMIN, Preliminary Draft Framework Convention for the Protection of National Minorities, CAHMIN (94) 12, 1994, p. 6.

34 CAHMIN, Proposals concerning the Preliminary Draft (94) 14 Rev., 1994; CAHMIN, Framework Convention for the Protection of National Minorities, CAHMIN (94) 12, 1994, Proposals by the Austrian Delegation, p. 3.

35 CAHMIN, Explanatory Report on the Framework Convention for the Protection of National Minorities, H(1995) 010, 1995, Art. 14, para. 1(74).

36 Including Albania, Armenia, Romania, and many others.

looked at whether or not national minorities were able to learn their own language, and if there were obstacles to the exercise of this right in practice.[37]

In some cases, there has been criticism over the lack of clear legislation dealing with national minority education; however, this has generally been with respect to situations involving numerical thresholds for entitlement to state-provided schools rather than the recognition of the right to learn one's own language.[38] One difficulty occurred in Slovakia where legislation seemed to limit the constitutional right to learn one's language to a specific number of national minority languages, while excluding the Roma language. Despite the absence of any reference to Article 14(1), one could argue that the Advisory Committee's criticism of this non-recognition of the Roma language falls within the ambit of this provision when it concluded that:

> . . . the scope of the School Act is limited to the languages enumerated in the above paragraph and, consequently, no school in Slovakia offers instruction in the Roma language. The Advisory Committee is therefore of the opinion that it needs to be examined to what extent the current legal and practical status of the Roma language in the education system of Slovakia meets the demands of the said population. Such an examination would help to establish whether further measures are needed to ensure adequate opportunities for being taught the Roma language or for receiving instruction in this language.[39]

3. Right to Learn Minority Language

Most of the Advisory Committee comments have skirted Article 14(1) and usually addressed various issues of education of or in a national minority language by focusing on the implementation of Article 13 or 14(2). It found, for example, that in Albania there was 'a lack of education in and of minority languages for the Aromanian/Vlach and the Roma minorities' and considered 'that the Albanian authorities should discuss with these minorities how best to cater for their needs',[40] without precisely indicating how or even if Article 14(1) was at stake. This is a pattern often repeated in other state reports.[41]

In a number of cases, there is still a clear, if implicit, indication that while states may not have a financial obligation to support each individual's right to

[37] Advisory Committee on the Framework Convention for the Protection of National Minorities, Opinion on Armenia, ACFC/INF/OP/I (2003) 001, 2002, para. 72.

[38] Above, n. 37, para. 71.

[39] Advisory Committee Opinion on Slovakia, ACFC/INF/OP/I (2001) 001, 2000, para. 44.

[40] Advisory Committee Opinion on Albania, ACFC/INF/OP/I (2003) 004, 2002, para. 107.

[41] See, for example, the similar approach of the Advisory Committee when it dealt with the state report of Romania in relation to the Roma minority in the Advisory Committee Opinion on Romania, ACFC/INF/OP/I (2002) 001, 2001, para. 63.

learn his or her national minority language under Article 14(1), they certainly ought to 'discuss with the minorities concerned how best to cater for these needs', as befits a democratic society.[42] Similarly, when some national minorities found it difficult to learn their own language in practice, even without neglect on the part of public authorities, the Advisory Committee has tended to 'encourage' authorities to find measures 'so as to help [national minorities] protect and affirm their linguistic identity'.[43]

While the Explanatory Report clearly does not imply any positive state obligation to provide resources to learn a national minority language under Article 14(1), some ambiguity remains in the way the Advisory Committee has dealt with this issue. It has, for instance, often recommended greater financial assistance for the teaching of national minority languages in its reports to a number of States (Armenia, Estonia, Germany, Moldova, Norway, Slovak Republic, etc.), but has more often than not anchored these concerns using Article 14(1). Nonetheless, it has occasionally linked the right to learn a national minority language with effective equality:

> 119. The Advisory Committee notes with concern the shortcomings in the field of education, notably with regard to the teaching of or in minority languages. It considers that the authorities should show greater commitment in this area, in order to enable persons belonging to national minorities to enjoy equal access to education and to promote awareness of the culture, history, languages and traditions of both the minorities and the majority. Increased attention is needed in this field with respect to the Assyrians and the Yezidis.[44]

Even this linkage is problematic however, as the European Court of Human Rights indicated in the *Belgian Linguistics* case,[45] that equality and non-discrimination did not guarantee education in one's language of choice. The UN Human Rights Committee, too, was of the view that the lack of funding or financial support for a minority school could constitute a breach of equality and be discriminatory, but only where other minority schools were supported in ways that were unreasonable and unjustified.[46] None of these considerations was advanced by the Advisory Committee, making its approach towards defining educational linguistic rights under Article 14 seem particularly hesitant. Instead of specifically identifying the positive legal obligations of public authorities under this article, it made vague references to the need for public

42 Above, n. 41, para. 66.

43 Advisory Committee Opinion on Armenia, ACFC/INF/OP/I (2003) 001, 2002, para. 76.

44 Above, n. 43.

45 *Belgian Linguistics Case*, above, n. 14.

46 UN Human Rights Committee, *Waldman* v. *Canada*, (1999) Comm. No. 694/1996, UN Doc. CCPR/C/67/D/694/1996, 1999.

authorities to be supportive and consultative.[47] Indeed, and perhaps surprisingly, the Advisory Committee appears to use this vague approach to interpret rights under Article 14(1) as a means of expanding the scope of the Framework Convention to persons belonging to the majority, even when the treaty theoretically deals with the rights of minorities alone.[48]

C. Article 14(2)

1. Travaux préparatoires

In early drafts and discussions of this provision, a distinction was drawn between relevant principles for private schools and those for state schools. It was clear from the outset that, in view of the common opinion that the state would not be obliged to subsidize private minority schools, minority language teaching in state schools would be subject to various kinds of conditionality, including: traditional minority presence in certain areas; sufficient proportion of the population; and demand for such teaching.[49] In consequence, a suitably flexible wording was from the outset regarded as desirable.[50] Accordingly, the Preliminary Draft Framework Convention introduced the formula, 'if those minorities so request and this request corresponds to a real need' to govern this aspect of education.[51] In this context, the phrase 'if the overwhelming majority of these persons so request', preferred by the delegation of Turkey as it 'triggered' the language education right, did not find favour in the CAHMIN. Education *in* the minority language and study *of* the minority language both appear in the Preliminary Draft Convention, and the CAHMIN envisaged that the Explanatory Report on the Convention would state that these two elements of minority language learning were not mutually exclusive, a principle specifically endorsed in Article 14 of the draft resulting from the fifth meeting in June/July 1994.[52] In the drafting process, the provisions of the third paragraph of Article 14 were 'detached' from 14(2) and references to the need

[47] See, for example, the treatment of the right of Roma to learn their language in Italy in the Advisory Committee Opinion on Italy, ACFC/INF/OP/I (2002) 007, 2001, para. 60. It is never explained from which provision of the Framework Convention this obligation emanates, nor under what conditions, if any.

[48] Advisory Committee Opinion on Finland, ACFC/INF/OP/I (2001) 002, 2000, para. 46, examining the Finnish-speaking majority living in the province of Åland. The present situation over there may involve an issue of discrimination that is quite distinct from the issue of what constitutes a minority.

[49] CAHMIN, Report of the Third Meeting, CAHMIN (94) 13, 1994, para. 24.

[50] Above, n. 49, para. 27.

[51] CAHMIN, Preliminary Draft Framework Convention for the Protection of National Minorities, CAHMIN (94) 12, 1994, Art. 12, 13.

[52] CAHMIN, Report of the 5th meeting, CAHMIN (94) 19, 1994.

and the importance of learning the official language[53] were deleted in favour of the milder formula in the current 14(3). In the report of the seventh CAHMIN, interpretative points were drafted on the flexible wording of the provision, its linkage with available state resources, the lack of definition of 'sufficient demand' in favour of a contextual, country-specific approach to implementation, and the observation that the 'in/of' language education formulae are not mutually exclusive.[54] These principles now inform the Explanatory Report on the Convention.[55]

2. *The Area*

The paragraph is replete with qualifying phrases, which, if interpreted restrictively, could reduce its effectiveness. Accordingly, this has led the Committee to give attention to the restrictive phrases in the course of its examination of country reports. In terms of 'traditional' inhabitation, or inhabitation in substantial numbers, the Committee has cited the need for accurate statistical information in order to 'demarcate' the relevant areas and target national policy effectively.[56] In this respect, the 'areas' for the application of the provision may be found in both rural and urban areas, and that the minority in question may be a 'dispersed' minority.[57] The linguistic education provision in Article 14(2) is also prefaced by the qualification 'if there is sufficient demand'. It would appear that the Committee is not necessarily impressed by arguments that there is little demand for language education services. After all, demand for particular services may be related to community awareness of the existence of services, and confidence that they will be delivered if requested. Thus, in cases like the UK, where there is, *ex facie*, demand from the large immigrant population, the Committee encouraged a more proactive approach to minority language education, particularly in areas 'where there are substantial numbers of ethnic minorities'.[58] While it is true that contemporary capitalist economies propel themselves forward in part through stimulation of demand, the Committee, in calling for a 'proactive' approach, may be more appropriately referring to information and awareness-raising campaigns than to any 'stimulation' of demand. Whatever the

[53] CAHMIN, Report of the 6th meeting, CAHMIN (94) 28, 1994.

[54] CAHMIN, Report of the 7th meeting, CAHMIN (94) 32, 1994, paras. 75–7.

[55] CAHMIN, Explanatory Report on the Framework Convention for the Protection of National Minorities, H(1995) 010, 1995, paras. 75–7.

[56] Advisory Committee Opinion on Albania, ACFC/INF/OP/I (2003) 004, 2002, para. 65.

[57] Advisory Committee Opinion on the Russian Federation, ACFC/INF/OP/I (2002) 007, 2002, paras. 96–8, 155.

[58] Advisory Committee Opinion on the United Kingdom, ACFC/INF/OP/I (2002) 006, 2001 para. 91.

parameters of the 'proactive' approach, it is clear that a purely 'passive' approach on the part of governments is not an adequate response to the demands of the paragraph. Further, the Advisory Committee, in what is effectively a 'reasonable foreseeability/rule of law' issue, has called for clear 'demand' thresholds to trigger the introduction of minority language education.[59] Thus, in the case of Croatia, the Committee regretted that the relevant law did 'not stipulate clear numerical or other criteria that would trigger the introduction of instruction in a minority language even though in practice such criteria, which may cater also to the needs of numerically small and dispersed minorities, have reportedly been established'.[60] In a similar vein, the Committee has observed that the introduction of bilingual education was too exposed to the exercise of discretion on the part of the authorities and schools. Consequently, it has called for legislative guarantees to buttress the legal status and thresholds of such education.[61] In addition, the Committee has called for legislation to be supplemented by implementing regulations and teaching practice.[62]

The Committee's concern for clarity in the guarantee of minority language education extends to clarity in the definition of language programmes,[63] and a preference for co-ordinated national programmes.[64] The shortage of teachers with relevant qualifications to teach minority languages is a frequent Committee concern, as is the shortage of appropriate textbooks.[65] In general, it may be said that in many countries the teaching of (some) minority languages at the primary/basic level is satisfactory, but that possibilities at secondary and upper levels may be restricted. Bearing in mind the educational importance of developing a mature knowledge of minority languages at post-primary levels,[66] and having regard for the degree of satisfaction on the part of some minority groups when minority education is available up to and including tertiary level,[67] the Committee has made recommendations to continue education at

[59] Advisory Committee Opinion on Croatia, ACFC/INF/OP/I (2002) 003, 2001, para. 51; Advisory Committee Opinion on Armenia, ACFC/INF/OP/I (2003) 001, 2002, para. 71; Advisory Committee Opinion on the Russian Federation, ACFC/INF/OP/I (2002) 007, 2002, paras. 94, 154.

[60] Advisory Committee Opinion on Croatia, ACFC/INF/OP/I (2002) 003, 2001, para. 51.

[61] Advisory Committee Opinion on Estonia, ACFC/INF/OP/I (2002), 005, 2001, paras. 51, 52; the views are restated in the Committee's Draft Recommendations for the Committee of Ministers.

[62] Advisory Committee Opinion on Italy, ACFC/INF/OP/I (2002) 007, 2001, para. 58; Advisory Committee Opinion on Romania, ACFC/INF/OP/I (2002) 001, 2001, and Recommendations for the Committee of Ministers, para. 62.

[63] Advisory Committee Opinion on the Czech Republic, ACFC/INF/OP/I (2002) 002, 2001, para. 66.

[64] Advisory Committee Opinion on Italy, ACFC/INF/OP/I (2002) 007, 2001, para. 58.

[65] Advisory Committee Opinion on Armenia, ACFC/INF/OP/I (2003) 001, 2002, paras. 74, 75.

[66] See chapter on Art. 12 in this commentary.

[67] Advisory Committee Opinion on Cyprus, ACFC/INF/OP/I (2002) 004, 2001, para. 39.

the post-primary phase, building on acquired linguistic knowledge.[68] Furthermore, it has recommended that the authorities consider extending minority language education into the sphere of higher education in a number of cases.[69]

3. Threshold Numbers

The Committee has also taken a stance on appropriate and inappropriate numbers of pupils to justify classes.[70] In the absence of categorical statements by the Advisory Committee on what is 'sufficient', in practice the Committee has tended to commend lower numerical thresholds for the setting up of minority classes, though its approach is broadly contextual.[71] A reading of Committee practice on this issue suggests that, the 'mechanical' application of numerical criteria would not do justice to the nuances of individual cases: that the 'numbers game' is a game played in particular contexts where there are different demands, needs, and possibilities. In the case of the network of Sorbian schools in Germany, the Committee's solicitude for the fate of the schools and the numerical criteria for the continuation of classes was strongly conditioned by circumstances such as the historical significance of the schools for the Sorbian identity and that the schools had not only an educational function, but were also an expression of Sorbian identity.[72] In this respect, the Committee has encouraged governments to take a less rigid approach to minimum numbers of pupils for minority classes than for the 'regular' or 'mainstream' classes, an approach that would appear to be in keeping with encouragement for the normativization of 'proactivity' or 'special measures' in the wider field of minority rights.[73] The Advisory Committee points to the generality of the provision in Article 14(2), and its application in principle to all groups satisfying

[68] Advisory Committee Opinion on Austria, ACFC/INF/OP/I (2002) 009, 2002, para. 98; Advisory Committee Opinion on Estonia, ACFC/INF/OP/I (2002) 005, 2001, paras. 51–2, and Recommendations to the Committee of Ministers; Advisory Committee Opinion on Germany, ACFC/INF/OP/I (2002) 008, 2002, para. 59, 87; Advisory Committee Opinion on Russian Federation, ACFC/INF/OP/I (2001) 007, 2002, para. 97; Advisory Committee Opinion on the United Kingdom, ACFC/INF/OP/I (2002) 010, para. 92.

[69] Advisory Committee Opinion on Albania, ACFC/INF/OP/I (2003) 004, 2002, para. 61; Advisory Committee Opinion on Romania, ACFC/INF/OP/I (2002) 001, para. 55.

[70] In one case, the Committee considered that a minimum requirement of twenty pupils to run a class offering minority language teaching was very high. Advisory Committee Opinion on Germany, ACFC/INF/OP/I (2002) 008, 2002, para. 60.

[71] Advisory Committee Opinion on the Ukraine, ACFC/INF/OP/I (2002) 010, 2002, paras. 63.

[72] Advisory Committee Opinion on Germany, ACFC/INF/OP/I (2002) 008, 2002, paras. 59, 60.

[73] Advisory Committee Opinion on Austria, ACFC/INF/OP/I (2003) 001, 2002, para. 96.

the provisions, including the 'minority within a minority'.[74] Consequently, it encourages discussion with members of minority groups as to how their needs in this sphere are to be accommodated.[75] In terms of the span of minority groups in a particular country, the Committee appears to favour 'a balanced response to the specific language needs of all national minorities, bearing in mind their particular situations and the need for existing resources to be shared out equitably'.[76] This 'balance' is achieved to varying degrees in different states with varying levels of consistency, except in the case of Roma language education, where 'consistency' appears to reside in the lack of such education rather than in its provision by the authorities.[77] It seems clear from the Committee's general practice that approaches which incorporate participatory strategies for the relevant minorities are preferred to 'top-down' approaches.[78]

4. *Teaching 'in' and 'of' Minority Languages*

Apart from the general right 'to learn his or her minority language' in paragraph 1 of Article 14, the specific 'minority areas' right in 14(2) is to be implemented according to 14(3) without prejudice to learning of or teaching in the official language.[79] The Advisory Committee has made it clear that adequate resources must be dedicated by the state to the teaching of the state language for national minorities.[80] The wording of the minority language learning provision in 14(2) appears to visualize either being taught the minority language in the same way as any other language, as a curriculum subject; or being taught through the medium of the minority language. These are the alternatives discussed in the implementation practice, even if the term 'instruction in' (the minority language) does not make for great clarity if it is attempting to convey the notion

[74] Thus in the case of the mostly Swedish-speaking province of Åland, the Committee observed that there was no provincial legal provision for instruction in Finnish, though it was taught in the public school system as a subject, and while recognizing the specific constitutional status of the province, thought that 'it would be useful to examine to what extent the current situation concerning the status of the Finnish language in the education system of the Åland islands meets the demands of the Finnish-speaking population of the province': Advisory Committee Opinion on Finland, ACFC/INF/OP/I (2001) 002, 2000, para. 46.

[75] Advisory Committee Opinion on Albania, ACFC/INF/OP/I (2003) 004, 2002, paras. 66, 107.

[76] Advisory Committee Opinion on Moldova, ACFC/INF/OP/I (2003) 002, 2002, para. 83. Advisory Committee Opinion on Norway, ACFC/INF/OP/I (2003) 003, paras. 57–9, 96.

[77] See the chapter on Art. 12 in this commentary.

[78] Advisory Committee Opinion on Albania, ACFC/INF/OP/I (2003) 004, 2003, paras. 65, 66, 106, 107; Advisory Committee Opinion on Armenia, ACFC/INF/OP/I (2003), 2002, para. 74.

[79] Art. 14(2) and Art. 14(3) FCNM. The Explanatory Report (para. 78) observes that 'knowledge of the official language is a factor of social cohesion and integration'. The Advisory Committee has made it clear that the state must dedicate adequate resources to the teaching of the state language for national minorities in its Opinion on Armenia, ACFC/INF/OP/I/ (2003) (004), 2002, para. 74.

[80] Advisory Committee Opinion on Armenia, ACFC/INF/OP/I (2003) 001, 2002, para. 74.

of education 'through the medium of' a minority language. Assuming that both alternatives are indicated, there appears to be no Convention obligation to support education in the latter sense, although the Explanatory Report observes that there is nothing to prevent a state from implementing both alternatives,[81] perhaps through the medium of bilingual instruction. It is however possible to construct an argument favouring the obligation to provide education through a minority language. Thus, the fact that there is a general provision on language learning in paragraph 1 of Article 14 suggests that the provisions in paragraphs 2 and 3 of that article, which are restricted to minority areas, must add something to the basic right in paragraph 1. This could mean the right to have education (instruction) through the medium of the minority language, subject to the conditions in paragraphs 2 and 3. The Explanatory Report does not draw the strong conclusion in respect of paragraphs 2 and 3, though it conceded that bilingual education may be a means of fulfilling Convention requirements.[82] The Committee does not confine itself to comments on the 'minimalist' obligation to the teaching *of* the minority language,[83] but addresses many governments in the framework of a preference for bilingual approaches, in which context it has observed that the alternatives in Article 14(2) 'are not mutually exclusive'.[84] It does, however, comment unfavourably on further 'conditionality' for triggering minority language education such as lack of sufficient knowledge of a state language. In other words, the paragraph is minimalist enough, and should not be hedged in by further restrictions.[85]

D. Article 14(3)

1. Travaux préparatoires

Article 14(3) was, in many respects, the least controversial segment of this provision during the drafting process. It follows what could be described as a widely recognized international standard, that individuals must be entitled to learn the official language at school. This principle is contained in a wide-ranging

[81] Ad Hoc Committee for the Protection of National Minorities, CAHMIN, Explanatory Report on the Framework Convention for the Protection of National Minorities, H(1995) 010, 1995, Art. 14, para. 2(77).

[82] Above, n. 81.

[83] Emphasis added.

[84] Advisory Committee Opinion on Sweden, ACFC/INF/OP/I (2003) 006, 2003, para. 60.

[85] Thus, the Committee has commented: 'The existing regulations envisage bilingual basic education, as a maximum for minorities other than Sami and Kven-Finnish . . . only when they have acquired a sufficiently good knowledge of Norwegian to be able to follow the ordinary teaching programme. Bearing in mind that the guarantees of Article 14 are not conditioned upon lack of knowledge of the State language, the . . . Committee considers that the authorities should examine to what extent there is demand amongst the national minorities . . . to receive instruction in and of their language': Advisory Committee Opinion on Norway, ACFC/INF/OP/I (2003) 003, 2002, para. 59.

number of instruments, notably the UNESCO Convention against Discrimination in Education,[86] the UN Declaration on the Rights of Persons Belonging to National or Ethnic, Religious, or Linguistic Minorities,[87] and others.[88]

Neither do the *travaux préparatoires* reveal any hesitancy or controversy among drafting parties in including this provision. Rather, there was repeated emphasis on the compatibility of protecting and promoting the use of national minorities in education and of acquiring fluency in the official language(s) of the state. Thus, the history of Article 14(3) shows frequent reference to this linguistic duality and the need for it to be upheld. Probably this was to alleviate any concerns parties might have as to the status of a country's official language: '[i]t should also be mentioned in this provision that instruction in a minority language should not prejudice the right of the State to stipulate that the official language(s) of the country should also be taught, as part of its policy of integration.'[89] Indeed, the *travaux préparatoires* show no strong debate or dissent over the final wording of this provision of the Framework Convention. The only difficulty that arose was over how to address the situation where a state had more than one official language. As indicated in the Explanatory Report, there was no agreed formula to address this point, so it was left for states 'to settle the particular questions which the implementation of this provision shall entail'.[90]

2. *Teaching of Official Language*

Given its uncontroversial nature, it is perhaps to be expected that Article 14(3) is hardly ever considered explicitly. Indeed, it is difficult to distinguish between cases where the Advisory Committee dealt specifically with Article 14(3) from situations where it gave consideration to Article 14 in its entirety. The Advisory Committee did not find any case where it could be said that a state denied members of a national minority the right to learn the official language under Article 14(3). There were, however, a number of reports, including ones on Estonia and Ukraine, where the Advisory Committee had concerns that an

[86] Art. 5, Convention against Discrimination in Education.

[87] Declaration on the Rights of Persons Belonging to National or Ethnic, Religious, or Linguistic Minorities, UNGA Res. 47/135 (18 December 1992), annex 47 UN GAOR 49, 210, UN Doc. A/47/49, Art. 4(3).

[88] Including Foundation on Interethnic Relations Recommendations, The Hague Recommendations Regarding the Education Rights of National Minorities and Explanatory Note No. 12, 13, 1996, Conference on Security and Co-operation in Europe (CSCE), Document of the Copenhagen Meeting of the Conference on the Human Dimension of the OSCE, 2nd Conference, Copenhagen, 1990.

[89] CAHMIN, 3rd meeting, CAHMIN (94) 13, 1994, Meeting Report, p. 6.

[90] Ad Hoc Committee for the Protection of National Minorities, CAHMIN, Explanatory Report on the Framework Convention for the Protection of National Minorities, H(1995) 010, 1995, Art. 10, para. 79.

emphasis on the teaching of the official language seemed to exclude the use of minority languages in education, in a way that was inconsistent with the other rights under Articles 13 or 14 of the Framework Convention. It found that such a practice could lead to assimilation rather than integration.[91] As it explained in the following observations on Estonia:

54. The Advisory Committee notes that in the basic schools with a minority language as the main language of instruction the teaching of Estonian is obligatory. This principle is fully in line with the Framework Convention. The Advisory Committee also notes that Estonian is being increasingly introduced to persons belonging to national minorities through voluntary 'language immersion' programmes. While recognising the results that may be achieved through such programmes in some circumstances, the Advisory Committee considers it essential that the voluntary nature of participation in such initiatives is fully maintained and that the decision to allocate substantial resources to these programmes does not hamper the availability or quality of minority language education in the areas concerned.[92]

Similarly when examining the report of the Ukraine, the Advisory Committee acknowledged the importance of reforms that set about changing the linguistic regime imposed during the Communist era and it therefore accepted the validity of protecting and strengthening teaching practices both of and in the official language. Nevertheless, it emphasized that this should 'not result in undue limitation of the rights of persons belonging to national minorities under Article 14 of the Framework Convention'.[93]

Only in the cases of Moldova and Serbia and Montenegro did the Advisory Committee express concerns over the teaching of a state's official language. In the case of Moldova, this was to ensure that whatever measures were taken in the teaching of minority languages, especially in relation to the use of Russian, they would 'be taken without prejudice to the learning of or the teaching in the state language',[94] especially since acquisition of the official language was a slow process for many. In the case of Serbia and Montenegro, there were instances where Serbian was taught in schools, where the language of instruction was a national minority language, but outside normal teaching hours. According to the Advisory Committee, this did not sit well with the right enshrined in Article 14(3) since:

While it is fully legitimate to ensure that the Serbian language is taught to all pupils, the Advisory Committee finds it important that the teaching of the Serbian language is introduced in a manner that does not discourage pupils from opting for minority

[91] Advisory Committee Opinion on Estonia, ACFC/INF/OP/I (2002) 005, 2001, at para. 50.
[92] Above, n. 91.
[93] Advisory Committee Opinion on Ukraine, ACFC/INF/OP/I (2002) 010, 2002, para. 65.
[94] Advisory Committee Opinion on Moldova, ACFC/INF/OP/I (2003) 002, 2002, para. 83.

language teaching. In this respect, the Advisory Committee is concerned about the reports that such Serbian language teaching has been introduced as an addition to, rather than part of, the regular school work of the pupils concerned. The Advisory Committee believes that such classes should be a truly integral part of the regular education of the pupils concerned and it calls on the authorities to review the situation and to introduce improvements where necessary.[95]

Here, the Advisory Committee was concerned that Serbian language instruction was offered and made available in an 'either/or' way: if students were to choose to be educated in their national minority language, as they were entitled, they would forfeit their chances to acquire any degree of fluency in the official language. This kind of choice was unacceptable in the view of the Advisory Committee. It recommended that a balance be achieved so that education in a national minority language and teaching of the Serbian language were offered as part of the regular educational programme, and not as an addition to the regular schoolwork of the pupils receiving instruction in a minority language.

III. Conclusion and Outlook

The Advisory Committee has specifically dealt with Article 14(1) on only a few rare occasions, and for this reason there are perhaps not as clear guidelines and understanding provided as to its content and impact as with other provisions. This was probably to be expected in light of the less controversial origins and nature of the right involved, since this provision, as indicated in the Explanatory Report, does not entail a positive obligation to support all activities linked to learning a national minority language financially. Nevertheless, in the future the Advisory Committee will have to clarify the potential significance of Article 14(1) more accurately, since in practical terms it has intimated that authorities should still take steps to consult with national minorities so as to address the needs and availability of opportunities to learn their language. One tension which will need to be addressed in a more straightforward fashion in the future is if and how states parties have positive obligations flowing from Article 14(1), perhaps even financial ones, when the *travaux préparatoires* and the Explanatory Report to the treaty would both initially suggest this is not necessarily the case. While it is logical, given the Framework Convention's objectives, for such assistance to be provided to give effect in some situations to the right enshrined under Article 14(1), this would need to be specified more clearly so that states parties understand the basis for the seeming contradiction.

[95] Advisory Committee Opinion on Serbia and Montenegro, ACFC/INF/OP/I (2004) 002, 2004, para. 97.

Paragraph 2 of Article 14 echoes the hesitations of equivalent paragraphs elsewhere in the Convention, and, as elsewhere, the Convention organs try to make sense of them. If the qualifying conditions were interpreted restrictively, they would make the right in question almost impossible to exercise, stripping it of practical effect. In this respect, it is noteworthy and appropriate that the Advisory Committee does not countenance further restrictions on the application of this 'minimalist' paragraph, and that it seeks to address the uncertainties it produces by calling for clear demand thresholds and other criteria for language education. In general, the Committee has also expressed a preference for lower numerical thresholds, so that the exercise of the right is a real possibility where concentrations of minority groups are to be found. States have not been ungenerous in this respect and are also likely to go beyond the minimal requirement of teaching minority languages as they would foreign languages. Many states offer instruction through the medium of minority languages in some subjects or for a sufficient percentage of the curriculum, where this makes pedagogic sense. The Committee appears to prefer bilingual approaches to education, even if it has not articulated a clear normative perspective on this.

The hesitant provisions of Article 14(2) mirror hesitations elsewhere in the canon of international human rights law on the question of language in education, although provisions in the area of indigenous rights tend to be more strongly committed to the promotion of education for indigenous groups through indigenous languages. The 'own institutions' element in ILO Convention 169 is as strong as the 'state institutions' element[96] and indigenous participation in decisions affecting them is a conspicuous theme running through that text as a whole. Although Convention 169 does not employ the vocabulary of autonomy, the overall institutional aspect of the Convention, including provisions on collective entitlements to lands and territories, may produce equivalent or stronger protective effects than the 'area' concept in the Framework Convention. Furthermore, the provisions in 169 are not hedged in with the types of qualifications incorporated in Articles 10, 11, and 14.

Authors have been critical of the Advisory Committee's approach to Article 14, suggesting that its recommendations are uncommonly weak, even where there are clear violations of rights. Article 14(2) does not provide a strong basis for action, at least when taken alone. Nonetheless, the overall normative structure of the Framework Convention does permit some 'firming up' of the provisions in 14(2), despite the proliferation of qualifying phrases. Thus, we may argue in favour of better integration of the positive culture-promoting aspects of the text with the

[96] See chapter on Art. 13 in this commentary.

specific and narrow language of Article 14(2). Points have been made above on the interrelationship between the first two paragraphs of Article 14, lending more strength and bite to the second paragraph; this approach can be extended outwards to include the principles of Articles 4, 5, and 6, which articulate the importance of states proactively devising ways and means to make the survival and flourishing of minority cultures and languages a realistic proposition. State provision of educational services in minority languages is an essential element of this project and does not, in itself, implicate elements of institutional separatism, though governments are concerned, at times, by the hermetic 'ethos' that such an approach to education may generate. Perhaps what is required in this case is further reflection on the article-by-article approach to interpreting Framework Convention norms, moving towards a general comment on the education rights as a whole, or the language rights as a whole. Such a comment might include an account of the normative relationship between official/state languages and minority languages, which to some extent stand opposed in the Framework Convention, whereas the Hague recommendations attempt to demonstrate that education in minority languages and in the state language can be better understood in a relationship of complementary and mutual necessity.

As for Article 14(3), an article-by-article approach would also be beneficial in clarifying the few matters which may still need to be addressed in relation to the right to learn a state's official language, such as that this right must not be enforced in such a way as to limit the rights of persons belonging to national minorities to learn or be instructed in their own language.

Overall, and given the centrality of eduction in preserving a national minority's language and culture heritage, one can conclude that the Advisory Committe has been both practical and forceful in ensuring compliance with the Framework Convention's objectives. From a practical point of view it has acknowledged the vast diversity of situations and needs that exists in very different contexts by indicating that states parties must consult with and respond to the linguistic rights of national minorities in education. At the same time, it has attempted to give substance to the various paragraphs by pointing out that there is an entitlement to the learning of a national minority language and, in appropriate contexts, to having instruction provided in such a language by public authorities by emphasizing that this right must be put in place where the conditions set out in the Framework Convention are met. There nevertheless remains the criticism of inconsistencies, lack of clarity or specific explanations in its treatment of states reports under Article 14 which still needs to be dealt with more effectively in the future in order for states parties to have a better grasp of the nature and extent of their legal obligations under the Framework Convention.

ARTICLE 15

Marc Weller

The Parties shall create the conditions necessary for the effective participation of persons belonging to national minorities in cultural, social and economic life and in public affairs, in particular those affecting them.

I. Background

Article 15 of the FCNM[1] is a key and foundational provision. It represents a vision for governance and life in modern, diverse societies. In the initial phase of their development, minority rights addressed diversity through provisions aimed at precluding destruction, displacement, or discrimination of minorities. This, one might say, was an attitude of protection. The individual was to be

[1] The commentary to this Article represents a further development of the author's study on political participation commissioned by the Council of Europe on the occasion of the 5th anniversary of the entry into force of the FCNM.

preserved from active interference and mistreatment by the state on account of his or her appurtenance to a minority. During the second phase of development, toleration and promotion was added to protection. In addition to pledging to refrain from persecution and discrimination, the state undertook to recognize and respect diversity. In a negative sense, this implies an obligation not to interfere in the cultural and other practices on which minority identity is based. In a positive sense, the state was obliged to generate the space necessary for the full expression of minority identities and to proactively support their development.

Article 15 adds a further element—that of genuine integration and co-governance. The right to full and effective participation in public affairs and in cultural, social, and economic life grants access to the state and the society it serves in all its aspects. In fact, the right to effective participation is inherent in our view of the modern, democratic, and constitutional state. All segments of society must have a sense of inclusion in the processes of democratic decision making. This need is particularly pronounced in relation to non-dominant groups that might otherwise experience a sense of structural disenfranchisement—after all, democracy implies majoritarianism. At least where public decisions within the state (for instance elections) are taken according to identity, rather than diverse interests, minorities are at risk of being turned into objects, rather than subjects of the state.

A. Issues

In terms of political participation, one may distinguish three layers of entitlement. The first relates to a voice in governance of the state as a whole. This implies not only equal chances in electoral terms, including unhindered registration for minority parties. There may also be a more far-reaching, positive entitlement on the part of minorities, requiring the state to arrange political decision-making in a way that ensures full representation of minorities in decision-making processes where they would otherwise be excluded due to their non-dominant position. Secondly, there is the entitlement of minorities to the auto-determination of issues that are of particular relevance to them. On the one hand, this includes the right to arrange issues that are of direct relevance to the expression and development of minority identity—cultural autonomy. On the other, it is claimed that minorities must also have the right to organize and maintain political processes in areas where they are a local majority—territorial autonomy. The former is more widely accepted, although not always practised by states. The latter is at times disputed as a genuine entitlement.

However, it is increasingly accepted that minorities should be given control over regions where they may be a majority through the concepts of subsidiary and enhanced local self-government. Hence, it may be more the use of the term territorial autonomy, rather than the actual concept that underpins it, that causes the dispute.

A third aspect relates to the internal democracy of minority communities. Little or no attention has been devoted to this issue thus far. However, members of minorities are entitled to genuine representation through organizations and institutions of their choice. Hence, there are two aspects to this issue: on the one hand, the state must permit minority communities to arrange for their own decision-making processes. Minority organizations, on the other hand, are also under certain obligations, including ensuring accountability and transparency of minority governance arranged according to genuinely democratic principles.

In addition to political participation, there is the right to effective access to opportunities in cultural, social, and economic life. This includes the right of members of minorities to enjoy on equal terms cultural or social benefits, and to compete for economic opportunities. In addition, additional opportunities specifically for members of minorities may be generated, especially through functional self-administration in parts of these sectors.

Full and effective participation is, of course, related to the other branches of minority rights—protection, toleration, and promotion. Minorities could not participate effectively in a state that persecutes them, and they would not be able even to approach the chances offered by Article 15 if they were subjected to structural discrimination within the state. Positive measures may be required to enable members of minorities to achieve these benefits. For instance, where minorities have suffered disadvantages over a longer time, it may not suffice suddenly to launch a new, advanced system of minority participation in decision making. This may need to be flanked with educational and other offerings to ensure that genuine opportunities for participation arise. Similarly, members of minorities could not participate in governance and in the economic and social life of the state *as members of their respective minority* in the absence of a flourishing minority cultural environment.

B. History

To place the references to the drafting history that follow in context, it is convenient to review the general evolution of the Article at the outset. The Venice Commission Proposal of 1990 contained only a very general affirmation of the right to 'real' participation of persons belonging to minorities in the state's affairs.[2] However, there was an additional express reference to a requirement of parliamentary representation in proportion to the size of the respective minority.[3] This provision was later removed, having been found to be 'difficult to implement'.[4] However, the Venice Commission instead added a requirement for effective participation in relation to decisions affecting regions where the respective minorities live or matters affecting them. When the reference to the regional dimension was removed in the Preliminary Draft Framework Convention for the Protection of National Minorities, some governments objected, arguing that at least such an indirect reference to decentralization and local autonomy should be retained.[5] While this turned out not to be possible, the Explanatory Report does refer to decentralized or local forms of government.[6] In a draft protocol to the ECHR proposed by Austria to the Steering Committee for Human Rights (CDDH), a democratic process for the election of minority representatives would have been envisaged.[7] This suggestion was not taken up.

C. Context

The International Covenant on Civil and Political Rights (ICCPR) provides for a broad range of democratic entitlements. However, there is no specific provision addressing political participation of persons belonging to minorities. Instead, Articles 2 and 26 establish a prohibition of discrimination on grounds including race, colour, language, or religion. Article 27 of the ICCPR precludes the denial of the rights of persons belonging to ethnic, religious, or linguistic minorities, in community with other members of the group, to enjoy their own culture, to profess and practise their own religion, or to use their own language. However, there is no reference to political, or economic, cultural and social participation.

The 1992 UN General Assembly Declaration on the Rights of Persons Belonging to National or Ethnic, Religious, and Linguistic Minorities confirms, in Article 2(2), the right of persons belonging to minorities to participate effectively in cultural, religious, social, economic, and public life.[8] Article 4(5) adds, almost uniquely, that states should consider appropriate measures to enable

[2] European Commission for Democracy through Law (ECDL), Preliminary Draft Convention on the Protection of Minorities, CONV.MIN, 21 May 1990, para. 8.

[3] Above, n. 2.

[4] ECDL, Explanatory Report to the Proposal for a European Convention for the Protection of National Minorities, CDL-MIN (93) 22, 22 February 1993, para. 42.

[5] Proposals concerning the Preliminary Draft Framework Convention for the Protection of National Minorities, CAHMIN (94) 12, 10 June 1994, Hungary, Norway, Portugal, with reference to the then Art. 14.

[6] FCNM Explanatory Report, para. 80.

[7] Steering Committee for Human Rights, CDHH (91) 46, 20 December 1991.

[8] UN General Assembly Resolution 47/135 of 18 December 1992.

persons belonging to minorities to participate fully in the economic progress and development in their country. This is complemented by Article 5(2), which invites states to plan and implement international assistance programmes with due regard for the legitimate interests of persons belonging to minorities.

ILO Convention No. 169 of 1989 applies the principle of effective participation in a very meaningful way, although it is restricted in application to indigenous and tribal peoples. There are significant requirements for consultation of the peoples concerned when the government or parliament is proposing to take measures affecting them directly. Indigenous and tribal peoples are also guaranteed representation at all levels of decision-making in the state. Moreover, there is a very strong emphasis on self-governance as it relates to development, beliefs, institutions, land use, and economic development. Given the special situation of indigenous and tribal peoples on account of their quasi-colonial disenfranchisement, it is not necessarily the case that these provisions can simply be transferred to the area of minority rights. Nevertheless, many of the principles of Convention No. 169 can be usefully employed to help understand what the legal elements of full and effective participation ought to be.

At the European regional level, the Document of the Copenhagen Meeting of the Conference on the Human Dimension of the CSCE of 29 June 1990 (Copenhagen Document) marks an increasing interest in minority issues generally, and in effective participation in particular. The Copenhagen Document affirms the need to respect the rights of persons belonging to national minorities to effective participation in public affairs, including participation in the affairs relating to the protection and promotion of the identity of such minorities.[9] In this context, the declaration refers to the possibility of establishing appropriate local or autonomous administration corresponding to the specific historical and territorial circumstances of minorities.[10]

The OSCE has also generated relatively detailed recommendations that may over time acquire the status of soft law. Of principal relevance for Article 15 are the Lund Recommendations on the Effective Participation of National Minorities in Public Life of 1999. These address the areas of participation in decision making, self-governance, and guarantees. Other OSCE recommendations, for instance on linguistic rights, education, or access to broadcast media, also include references to good practice in relation to minority representation in these areas.

The European Charter for Regional or Minority Languages offers extensive provisions seeking to ensure access of minorities to public life through the

[9] Copenhagen Document, para. 35.

[10] Above, n. 9, para. 36.

medium of minority languages. Moreover, Article 7(4) of the Charter makes provision for minority participation in the determination of language policy within the state. At the sub-regional level, the Central European Initiative Instrument for the Protection of Minority Rights guarantees full and effective participation and obliges the state to take steps to promote the exercise of this entitlement. There is also an express right of persons belonging to a national minority to establish political parties. While not endorsing autonomy or local self-governance as a means of achieving effective participation, there is provision for enhanced local decision-making processes.

In the FCNM itself, there are a number of overlapping provisions affecting full and effective participation. Much of the practice under the FCNM concerning issues of social and economic participation is in fact treated—and treated extensively—under Article 4(2) and is not dealt with here. Similarly, steps to enhance the cultural identity of minorities are addressed at length under Articles 5(1) and 12(1). Here, only the issue of cultural self-administration will be addressed as part of functional autonomy. Finally, attention should be drawn to Article 7, in the context of freedom of assembly and association.

When considering the individual aspects of full and effective participation that are part of Article 15 itself, this analysis will consider, first, issues of state construction. This includes the constitutional design of the state, electoral processes and procedures, and mechanisms designed to enhance a minority voice in decision making. The analysis will then turn to steps taken to enhance the representation of persons belonging to national minorities in executive agencies and the judiciary. Finally, the analysis will consider cultural, social, and economic participation.

II. Analysis

A. Effective Political Participation and State Construction

Effective political participation of members of minorities can be facilitated in a number of ways. These relate to the constitutional design of the state, electoral representation, and the establishment of institutions and practices to ensure national minority input.[11]

[11] For general surveys, see Minority Unit of the Director of Human Rights of the Council of Europe, *Overview of Forms of Participation of National Minorities in Decision-Making Processes in Seventeen Countries* (Council of Europe, Strasbourg, 1998); J. Frowein and R. Bank, *The Participation of Minorities in Decision-Making*, E/CN.4/Sub.A.C.5/2001/CRP.6; Y. Ghai, *Public Participation of Minorities*, Minority Rights Group International Report (2001).

1. *A State for All Citizens*

When introducing Article 15, one of the drafting bodies involved, the Ad Hoc Committee for the Protection of National Minorities (CAHMIN) emphasized that the principal aim of this provision is to generate a real sense of equality between persons belonging to national minorities and those forming part of the majority.[12] Virtually all states have reported to the Advisory Committee on the formal equality of all citizens (and in relation to local government, at times non-citizens) in terms of voting in elections, and the right to stand for office or to form, or participate in, political parties. One might argue that such equality should be evident in the very designation and design of the constitutional system. For instance, the designation in the constitution of the state as the state of a particular nation or ethnic group, rather than as the state of all its citizens, could give rise to concern.[13] Where particular national or ethnic groups are so nominated, the Advisory Committee has requested particular steps to enhance effective participation for other groups as well.[14]

More substantively, the layering of public authority in ways to accommodate members of national minorities is at issue. This can be achieved through a transfer of authority to territorial units, or through the functional assignment of special rights of participation.

2. *Territorial Layering of Public Authority*

Initial drafts for what was to become Article 15 referred not only to an especially strong right of effective participation in relation to matters particularly affecting members of national minorities. Such a right would also exist in relation to 'decisions affecting the regions where they live'.[15] This formulation would have pointed towards an acknowledgement of a special right of consultation or participation in decision-making of persons belonging to national minorities living in territorially compact areas.

[12] Ad Hoc Committee for the Protection of Minorities (CAHMIN), 7th meeting, CAHMIN (94) 32, Draft Explanatory Report of the Framework Convention for the Protection of National Minorities, 10–14 October 1994, Appendix V, para. 80, subsequently adopted by the Committee of Ministers as ETS 157, H (95) 10, February 1995.

[13] This debate has been prominent in relation to the states that emerged from the former Socialist Federal Republic of Yugoslavia. The Ohrid Agreement of August 2001 expressly avoided such a designation and instead determined that the Former Yugoslav Republic of Macedonia is a state of its citizens.

[14] Advisory Committee on the Framework Convention for the Protection of National Minorities, Opinion on Croatia, ACFC/INF/OP/I (2002) 003, para. 62.

[15] ECDL, Proposal for a European Convention for the Protection of National Minorities, CDL-MIN (93), 22 February 1993, Art. 14. See also the Commentary to this article, ibid., at para. 44, emphasizing that '[t]he word "region" must be understood in this article and throughout the Convention in its geographical meaning of an entity of national territory rather than its political, judicial or administrative meaning'.

Of course, regional layering of authority can range from a confederal system to a federal or a devolved state structure.[16] This may include autonomy arrangements for areas where national minorities constitute a local majority. However, among some governments, this is considered a rather sensitive area. Nevertheless, the CSCE Copenhagen Document provides:[17]

> The participating States note the efforts undertaken to protect and create conditions for the promotion of the ethnic, cultural, linguistic and religious identity of certain national minorities by establishing, as one of the possible means to achieve these aims, appropriate local or autonomous administrations corresponding to the specific historical and territorial circumstances of such minorities and in accordance with the policies of the State concerned.

The OSCE High Commissioner on National Minorities has expanded on this issue in detail in the Lund Recommendations.[18] Autonomy has also occupied the Working Group on Minorities of the Sub-Commission of the UN Commission on Human Rights for some time.[19] Yet, in the context of the FCNM, the situation is different. The final version of Article 15 as adopted does not fully reflect the emphasis on local self-governance found in other documents. In contrast to the corresponding provision in the UN Declaration on the Rights of Persons Belonging to National or Ethnic, Religious, and Linguistic Minorities, the rather cautious reference to decisions specially affecting 'regions where they live' was struck from the final version of Article 15 of the FCNM.[20] Nevertheless, when addressing Article 15, the official FCNM

[16] Indeed, one state emphasizes that its strong federalist structure provides for maximum participation of minorities; Switzerland State Report, ACFC/SR (2001) 2, para. 237. The Advisory Committee pronounced itself highly satisfied with this arrangement, ACFC/INF/OP/I (2003) 007, para. 74. The Advisory Committee has also acknowledged the importance of devolution in relation to effective participation of the persons concerned in Scotland, Wales, and Northern Ireland; Advisory Committee Opinion on United Kingdom, ACFC/INF/OP/I (2002) 006, para. 93.

[17] Copenhagen Document, para. 25. See also the CSCE Meeting of Experts on National Minorities, 1–19 July 1991, IV., para. 7.

[18] Lund Recommendations, paras. 19–21, where the word 'autonomy' is mostly avoided and instead reference is made to 'self-government'.

[19] The UN Working Group on Minorities has for some years had the issue of autonomy on its agenda, as has the UN General Assembly, which has addressed autonomy as a means of avoiding self-determination disputes. For instance, in the Report of the Working Group on Minorities on its Fifth Session, UN Doc. E/CN.4/SUB.2/1999/21, 24 June 1999, it is stated at para. 82(*g*): 'Decentralization of powers based on the principle of subsidiarity, whether called self-administration or devolved power, and whether the arrangements are symmetrical or asymmetrical, would increase the chances of minorities to participate in the exercise of authority over matters affecting themselves and the entire societies in which they live.' See, for example, F. de Varennes, 'Towards Effective Participation and Representation of Minorities', UN Doc. E/CN.4/Sub.2/AC5/1998/WP4.

[20] Proposals to include a reference to subsidiarity were opposed in CAHMIN as these 'would touch upon the constitutional systems of the Parties'. CAHMIN, 1st meeting, CAHMIN (94) 13, meeting

Explanatory Report encourages governments to consider, for instance, decentralized or local forms of government as a means of achieving effective participation.[21] This is fully in accordance with Article 4(3) of the European Charter of Local Self Government, which emphasizes that 'public responsibilities shall generally be exercised, in preference, by those authorities which are closest to the citizens'.

In subsequent practice before the Advisory Committee, autonomy has been addressed expressly in several types of circumstances.[22] First, there are instances of historically well-established autonomy regimes, at times triggered by previous conflicts and border changes. Paradoxically, the historically based examples tend to feature more advanced and broad autonomy provisions than those that have been more recently created. These tend to be established in treaties and/or be constitutionally entrenched. There are broad powers of decision-making for autonomous parliamentary assemblies and executive institutions. This is matched by local judicial structures.

While the functioning of the two principal instances of historically based autonomies has been acknowledged by the Advisory Committee, some difficulties have emerged in relation to other cases. For instance, one more recently negotiated autonomy arrangement was noted with approval by the Advisory Committee.[23] However, in the end, that arrangement was not fully implemented and is now under review in the context of general constitutional restructuring.[24] Another instance highlights the difficulties involved in attempting to restore a former provincial autonomy regime after a period of unilateral abrogation.[25] This experience suggests the need to ensure firm constitutional entrenchment of autonomy where it has been granted, and the need for mechanisms to redress claims of hesitant implementation of newly agreed autonomy settlements.

report, 25–8 January 1994, para. 46. A stronger regional dimension was proposed by Hungary, Norway, and Portugal. CAHMIN, Proposals Concerning the Preliminary Draft Framework Convention for the Protection of National Minorities, CAHMIN (94) 12 Rev., 10 June 1994, pp. 11–14. On Art. 2 of the UN Declaration, see the Commentary provided by the Chairman of the UN Working Group, Asbjørn Eide, E/CN.4.Sub.2/AC.5/2001/2, 2 April 2001, paras. 38 et seq.

[21] FCNM Explanatory Report, para. 80.

[22] Finland State Report, ACFC/SR (1999) 3, p. 28; Italy State Report, ACFC/SR (1999) 007; Moldova State Report, ACFC/SR (2000) 2, pp. 82–3; Russian Federation State Report, ACFC/SR (1999) 15, from p. 44; Slovenia State Report, ACFC/SR (2000) 4, p. 56, para. 108.

[23] Advisory Committee Opinion on Moldova, ACFC/INF/OP/I (2003) 002, para. 92.

[24] A constitutional commission is at present addressing the complex political situation in the territory of Moldova. An interesting feature of the Gagauz autonomy is, however, the provision establishing the head of the regional government as a member of the central government.

[25] Serbia and Montenegro State Report, ACFC/SR (2002) 003, and Advisory Committee Opinion on Serbia and Montenegro, ACFC/INF/OP/I (2004) 002, para. 111.

One instance features a very complex system of regional layering of public authority. Some of these layers have been established specifically with certain national or ethnic populations in mind, essentially providing ethnically based governance at the local or regional level. It should be noted, however, that often regions of autonomous government that form part of this system may themselves include significant minority populations of their own.[26] These may, in turn, require particular provisions guaranteeing effective participation within the autonomous entity.

While the number of express autonomy regimes noted above is not small, the regional layering of authority has been mainly addressed through the related notion of devolved local governance. The link between local governance and territorial autonomy is drawn expressly by one state.[27] In another instance, enhanced local self-governance has been advanced as being 'equal' to regional autonomy.[28] The Advisory Committee itself has recalled 'that decentralized or local forms of government are often an important factor in creating necessary conditions for effective participation of persons belonging to national minorities in decision-making,' adding that the issue is of particular significance where national minoritries are 'concentrated in certain areas'.[29]

It is one of the most consistent features of the state reports submitted thus far that they consistently focus on structures of locally devolved governance as a means of satisfying the requirements of Article 15.[30] Mostly states note the number of local councils and other bodies that are filled by representatives of persons belonging to national minorities. Areas of difficulty appear to relate principally to the adequate resourcing of local minority self-governance. There are also issues of genuine local minority representation that will be considered below.

In the context of local administrative reform, it has been emphasized that governments should design such measures in a manner that contributes also to the effective participation of persons belonging to national minorities.[31] This would imply an obligation not to implement reforms that would have a detrimental effect on effective participation—or even to engage in such reform with the aim of demographic or electoral manipulation.

[26] Russian Federation State Report, ACFC/SR (1999) 15, from p. 44.

[27] Slovenia State Report, ACFC/SR (2000) 4, p. 56, para. 108.

[28] Hungary State Report, ACFC/SR (1999) 10, p. 126.

[29] Advisory Committee Opinion on Azerbaijan, ACFC/INF/OP/I (2004) 001, para. 76.

[30] One might distinguish 'devolved' from 'decentralized' governance. In cases of devolved governance, actual competence is transferred to the regional or local level. In the case of decentralized governance, decisions may be taken by officials who are based locally, but who operate within the overall national framework and in the exercise of nationally established competences.

[31] Advisory Committee Opinion on the Slovak Republic, ACFC/INF/OP/I (2001) 001, para. 48.

3. *Functional Layering of Public Authority*

As was noted above, Article 15 emphasizes the need to generate the conditions necessary for the effective participation of persons belonging to national minorities, in particular in relation to issues 'affecting them'. Hence, it is logical to expect an emphasis on mechanisms enhancing participation in areas where cultural, social, economic, or political issues are at stake that have a particular relevance to members of national minorities. Mainly, this will be achieved through the institutions and processes of consultation that will be addressed in Section C below. However, at the level of state construction, one may perhaps expect a specific design that preserves space for such enhanced involvement in policy making. One such design would rely on the functional devolution of powers of decision and administrative functions to persons belonging to national minorities.

This model is applied in instances where a national minority is endowed with a formal legal status. As opposed to the usual emphasis on individual rights collectively exercised, in these cases, the minority itself is recognized as a legal subject, or as a 'public legal person', exercising functions of decision making and administration.[32]

In this context, some states have pioneered a very interesting mechanism of co-decision between representative institutions of persons belonging to national minorities and national legislative and executive bodies.[33] In another instance, 'self-government' in the fields of the use of language and script, education, information and media, and culture is provided for through the election of 'National Councils'. These Councils are to have a membership of fifteen to thirty-five representatives, depending on the total number of persons belonging to the national minority.[34] The way of choosing the representatives for the Councils is regulated by law, drawing upon members of parliament or regional assemblies representing persons belonging to a national minority, local councillors, persons nominated by prominent minority organizations, etc.[35] There are also somewhat less institutionally developed mechanisms relating principally to cultural affairs, although economic, social, and language issues may also be included.[36] Finally, the special case of functional autonomies for indigenous peoples may be noted.[37]

[32] Slovenia State Report, ACFC/SR (2000) 4, para. 106.

[33] Hungary State Report, ACFC/SR (1999) 10, pp. 126–7.

[34] Serbia and Montenegro State Report, ACFC/SR (2002) 003, pp. 103–4, para. 2, although financing and implementation have remained problematic; Advisory Committee Opinion on Serbia and Montenegro, ACFC/INF/OP/I (2004) 002, para. 108.

[35] Also Slovenia State Report, ACFC/SR (2000) 4, p. 57, para. 110.

[36] For example, Estonia State Report, ACFC/SR (1999) 16, p. 62.

[37] Sweden State Report, ACFC/SR (2001) 003, p. 37.

While some of the functions and powers of these bodies come close to consultative mechanisms, it is envisaged, at least in theory, that they also perform executive roles and attract appropriate state funding for these purposes. However, a full assessment of the effectiveness of this type of design by the Advisory Committee is not yet available.

B. Electoral Representation

In the Explanatory Report accompanying the FCNM, states are encouraged to promote the 'effective participation of persons belonging to national minorities in the decision-making process and elected bodies both at national and local levels'.[38] The Parliamentary Assembly of the Council of Europe required in its Recommendation 1201 (1993) of 1 February 1993 that this should include the right of persons belonging to national minorities to set up their own political parties.[39] The European Commission for Democracy through Law, in its Draft Convention on the Protection of Minorities of 1990 had gone even further, contemplating a provision requiring that 'minorities must be represented in Parliament in proportion to their size'.[40] This proposal was subsequently dropped, given the difficulties in implementing such a mechanical formula.[41] Nevertheless, adequate representation of minorities both at the parliamentary and at the local level has been repeatedly raised in the implementation dialogue following the first round of state reports.

1. Registration of Parties and Candidates

One issue concerns the registration of parties or candidates that profess to represent members of national minorities. Direct restrictions on 'minority parties' remain controversial. At times, governments have argued that persons belonging to national minorities are able to seek representation through the other principal parties,[42] hence no special minority parties are required.[43] Such an attitude is, however, not consistent with standards within the Council of Europe or, indeed, universal human rights law.[44] Moreover, the Advisory

[38] FCNM Explanatory Report, para. 80. Also see the important OSCE ODIHR 'Guidelines to Assist National Minority Participation in the Electoral Process' (2001).

[39] Art. 6.

[40] ECDL, Preliminary Draft Convention on the Protection of Minorities, DAJ.SC.DEMOCRACY, Conv. Min, 21 May 1990, Draft Art. 8(2).

[41] ECDL, Draft Report of the 4th Meeting, 25–6 May 1990, CD-PV-(90) 4, para. 19.

[42] Comment by Albania, GVT/COM/INF/OP/I (2003) 004.

[43] Such criticism has led Albania to abolish one such restriction. On this issue, see also Bulgaria State Report, ACFC/SR (2003) 001, although this has not yet been subjected to opinion from the Advisory Committee.

[44] Parliamentary Assembly of the Council of Europe, Recommendation 1201 (1993), Art. 6: 'All persons belonging to a national minority shall have the right to set up their own organizations, including political parties.'

Committee has opposed language requirements for candidates in parliamentary and local elections.[45] In some instances, states parties have formally revoked such restrictions.[46] It should be noted, however, that disguised restrictions may exist that may not be specifically targeted at excluding representatives of one or more minorities, but that are, in practice, applied in this way. For instance, a requirement for all parties to have a branch in more than half the subjects of a federal state may make the establishment of a minority party representing persons living in a territorially compact area impossible.[47] Hence, it is prudent not only to scrutinize the legislative framework for the registration of parties and candidates, but also the practice and outcomes.

Where elections are concerned, the issue of citizenship is of particular concern. It is now widespread practice that non-citizens who are long-term residents can participate in local elections—a fact commended by the Advisory Committee.[48] While non-citizens would ordinarily be excluded from national elections, the situation may be more complex where large segments of a population have been excluded from citizenship due to extraordinary developments.[49]

2. *Proportionate Representation and Quotas*

Quotas for the representation of persons belonging to national minorities are a comparatively rare phenomenon, mainly, but not exclusively, in evidence in states that have recently suffered from ethnic tension or conflict. Croatia, for instance, provides for proportional representation of national minorities with a share of the population exceeding 8 per cent in the lower chamber. Pending a new census, it is specified that there are eight members to represent persons belonging to national minorities, three of whom represent the largest of these. This is matched by representation in the upper house. Smaller national minorities are guaranteed at least one seat in the upper chamber.[50] However, the Advisory Committee had to note in that instance that these provisions were not, in fact, implemented, the relevant legislation having been suspended.

45 Advisory Committee Opinion on Estonia, ACFC/INF/OP/I (2002) 005, para. 50(1); see also, for instance, Latvia in CCPR, Comm. No. 884/19999, CCPR/C/72/D/884/1999; Advisory Committee Opinion on Russian Federation, ACFC/INF/OP/I (2003) 005, para. 106.

46 Advisory Committee Opinion on Albania, ACFC/INF/OP/I (2003).

47 Advisory Committee Opinion on Russian Federation, ACFC/INF/OP/I (2003) 005, para. 105.

48 Advisory Committee Opinion on Estonia, ACFC/INF/OP/I (2002) 005, para. 50(5). See also the Final Text of the Commentary to the Declaration on the Rights of Persons Belonging to National or Ethnic, Religious, and Linguistic Minorities, E/CN.4/Sub.2/AC.5/2001/02, 2 April 2001, para. 50: 'Forms of participation by resident non-citizens should also be developed, including local voting rights after certain period of residence and inclusion of elected non-citizen observers in municipal, regional and national legislative and decision-making assemblies.'

49 Above, n. 48.

50 Croatia State Report, ACFC/SR (1999) 5, p. 154.

Moreover, not all persons belonging to sizeable minorities were included in the minimum representation of at least one seat.[51] Happily, this situation has now been addressed through a new constitutional law and other provisions, and remains to be addressed anew in the next monitoring cycle.

In Romania, the constitution provides a saving clause, guaranteeing a right to one parliamentary representative for persons belonging to national minorities that have failed to obtain sufficient votes.[52] Slovenia reserves one seat each for two sizeable national minorities, elected through separate lists, without precluding, of course, the election of persons belonging to or representing national minorities through the ordinary electoral process.[53]

In one case, it was noted that the establishment of special electoral district with the aim to ensure that a minority candidate will achieve a mandate could raise concerns relating to the rights of persons not belonging to that minority; moreover, there might also be an issue of inequality in relation to groups that are not offered the same benefits in similar circumstances elsewhere.[54]

Where the absence of special provisions to ensure effective participation of persons belonging to minorities in parliament has been noted, the Advisory Committee has encouraged the government to devise and implement measures to create conditions conducive to the views of such persons being heard more clearly during the decision-making process, especially when decisions are likely to affect them directly.[55] This appears to be a rather cautious suggestion, possibly offering to trade direct representation of what are in fact sizeable minority populations for more consultation.

In another instance, the Advisory Committee has noted that the question of establishing electoral arrangements for parliamentary representation is a domain where, from the point of view of international standards, states enjoy a broad margin of appreciation. 'Clearly, the Advisory Committee cannot and would not wish to trespass thereon.'[56] In that instance, the Committee nonetheless considered itself entitled to criticize the relevant government for having failed to achieve appropriate representation of persons belonging to national minorities in parliament in view of that government's own standards in this field. In the case of Croatia already noted above, the Advisory Committee took a rather robust view when standards that provide for minimum representation of persons belonging to national minorities were left

[51] Advisory Committee Opinion on Croatia, ACFC/INF/OP/I (2002) 003, para. 61.

[52] Romania State Report, ACFC/SR (1999) 11 Prov., p. 53.

[53] Slovenia State Report, ACFC/SR (2000) 4, para. 113.

[54] Advisory Committee Opinion on Russian Federation, ACFC/INF/OP/I (2003) 005, para. 105.

[55] Advisory Committee Opinion on Czech Republic, ACFC/INF/OP/I (2002) 002, para. 70.

[56] Advisory Committee Opinion on Hungary, ACFC/INF/OP/I (2001) 004, para. 49.

unimplemented.[57] The withdrawal of such provisions, once granted, even through ordinary legal processes, has also given rise to concern. Hence, in relation to the Autonomous Republic of Crimea, the Advisory Committee regretted the reduced representation of Crimean Tatars in the regional legislature caused by the removal of reserved seats.[58]

In a number of instances, however, the Advisory Committee has been more forthright, measuring governments not only according to whether or not they have complied with their own targets and provisions, but according to the level of representation that has been achieved in relation to the population balance.[59] In these cases, the Advisory Committee has expressly called for authorities to devise and implement measures to create conditions for increased participation by persons belonging to national minorities in the decision-making process and in elected bodies, at both a national and a local level.[60]

3. *'Small' and Dispersed Minorities*

The representation of members of 'smaller' national minorities poses particular difficulties. The same applies to territorially dispersed members of national minorities, especially Roma.[61] While larger groups may manage to obtain parliamentary representation through ordinary processes, others may be structurally unable to achieve this, given the demographic situation. State reports will generally focus only on the larger groups in claiming adequate representation.[62] Nevertheless, the Advisory Committee has also insisted on adequate provision for persons belonging to non-territorial minorities, for instance travellers.[63] The Advisory Committee has emphasized that it would be permissible to give special consideration to ways of achieving representation in spite of demographic obstacles.[64] Such mechanisms may include the removal of a national threshold of minimum votes for parliamentary representation in relation to representatives of persons belonging to smaller national

[57] Advisory Committee Opinion on Croatia, ACFC/INF/OP/I (2002) 003.

[58] Advisory Committee Opinion on Ukraine, ACFC/INF/OP/I (2002) 010, para. 70, relating to Autonomous Republic of Crimea.

[59] Advisory Committee Opinion on United Kingdom, ACFC/INF/OP/I (2002) 006, para. 126: '. . . finds that the representation of ethnic minorities in legislative bodies is low and considers that the United Kingdom should examine the legal, procedural and institutional barriers that may hinder ethnic minority representation in these legislative bodies.'

[60] Advisory Committee Opinion on Czech Republic, ACFC/INF/OP/I (2002) 002, para. 70; Advisory Committee Opinion on Lithuania, ACFC/INF/OP/I (2003) 008, para. 76.

[61] For instance, Advisory Committee Opinion on Germany, ACFC/INF/OP/I (2002) 008, para. 66.

[62] For example, Bulgarian Helsinki Committee, Report of September 1999, at 63, but note the example of Croatia given above.

[63] Advisory Committee Opinion on Switzerland, ACFC/INF/OP/I (2003) 007, para. 76.

[64] Advisory Committee Opinion on Albania, ACFC/INF/OP/I (2003), para. 73.

minorities.[65] The Advisory Committee has noted that the maintenance of a 5 per cent threshold in one instance reportedly reduced the chances of members of national minorities to be represented in parliament.[66] The insistence on a registration of minority parties in more than half the number of federal units of the state was also seen to have a likely negative impact on electoral chances.[67]

In another instance, the requirement for registration of candidates by the collection of signatures was waived for candidates representing persons belonging to national minorities.[68] Such steps are more urgent where there is no minority representation in parliament at all, despite the possible absence of any factors that actively preclude such representation.[69] To this proposal, some governments have answered that such action might infringe upon the rights of the majority.[70] However, as was noted above, the Advisory Committee has nevertheless increasingly required that targets for actual representation should be met, irrespective of obstacles of this kind.

Where parliamentary representation is indeed impossible because of small numbers of persons belonging to a national minority, governments are encouraged to seek other means to take account of minority interests.[71] Presumably this refers to consultative mechanisms, which will be addressed below.

4. Regional and Local Representation

There are also examples of enhanced chances of representation of persons belonging to national minorities at the regional or local level. For instance, the statute for one autonomous province requires that the composition of the regional parliament must be consistent with the size of the linguistic groups present in the territory.[72] Another example provides for minimum representation of members of national minorities in local councils in ethnically mixed

[65] Germany and the German *Land* of Schleswig-Holstein, Advisory Committee Opinion on Germany, ACFC/INF/OP/I (2002) 008, para. 63. Serbia and Montenegro notes that its own failure to remove a 5 per cent threshold in such instance is 'not affirmative towards national minorities—if they do not form a coalition, parties rallying persons belonging to national minorities cannot easily win seats in parliament'. Serbia and Montenegro State Report ACFC/SR (2002) 003, para. 102. See also Slovak Republic State Report, ACFC/SR (1999) 8, para. 38.

[66] Advisory Committee Opinion on Lithuania, ACFC/INF/OP/I (2003) 008, para. 75.

[67] Above, n. 66.

[68] Denmark State Report, ACFC/SR (1999) 9, p. 46.

[69] Advisory Committee Opinion on Armenia, ACFC/INF/OP/I (2003) 001, para. 77; Austria State Report, ACFC/SR (2000) 3, pp. 102–3.

[70] Comment by Armenia, GVT/COM/INF/OP/I (2003) 001; Denmark State Report, ACFC/SR (1999) 9, p. 45.

[71] Advisory Committee Opinion on Armenia, ACFC/INF/OP/I (2003) 001, para. 77.

[72] Italy State Report, ACFC/SR (1999) 007, p. 84, concerning not only the German and Italian language groups, but also the Ladin speakers.

local areas. This is coupled with safeguards against the simple mechanical outvoting of representatives of persons belonging to national minorities.[73] A notable problem has arisen where candidates stand in election for a slot reserved for candidates representing persons belonging to national minorities without actually representing these.[74]

With respect to local government, most governments report on minority representation in areas where persons belonging to a national minority live in larger numbers, claiming that there is adequate representation at regional or district level, and at the level of village or town councils and majors. In some instances, there are formal commitments to the proportionate representation of population segments, or minimum quotas, at the local level.[75] However, certain groups, in particular Roma, remain excluded in a number of instances.[76]

5. Electoral Districts, Rules, and Practices

In some instances, electoral districts could have been designed to offer a more realistic chance for representatives of persons belonging to national minorities. In others, it was noted that certain rules on registration (say, minimum numbers of signatures for a party or candidate to enter the elections) do not assist in encouraging effective participation. Moreover, specific provisions and guarantees to ensure that the drawing up of electoral districts should be adopted to take account of the need to represent persons belonging to national minorities have been requested by the Advisory Committee.[77] To help avoid conflicts over such issues, it is good practice to include minority representation in electoral commissions and other bodies concerned with the preparation and conduct of elections.[78]

6. Parliamentary Working Practices

Where minority representatives constitute significant parliamentary groups, it is good practice to assign significant parliamentary positions to all of these, including the right to representation in parliamentary committees, the right to chair these, and even the right to occupy the post of Vice-President of the parliament.[79] For smaller groups, or individual parliamentary representatives of persons belonging to national minorities, the waiver of certain restrictions relating

[73] Slovenia State Report, ACFC/SR (2000) 4, para. 111.
[74] Advisory Committee Opinion on Hungary, ACFC/INF/OP/I (2001) 004, para. 52.
[75] Croatia State Report, ACFC/SR (1999) 5, p. 155.
[76] Advisory Committee Opinion on Germany, ACFC/INF/OP/I (2002) 008, para. 66.
[77] Advisory Committee Opinion on Ukraine, ACFC/INF/OP/I (2002) 10, para. 69.
[78] Azerbaijan has reported such a process; Azerbaijan State Report, ACFC/SR (2002) 1, p. 45.
[79] Bulgaria State Report, ACFC/SR (2003) 001, p. 103.

to parliamentary working practices (in particular committee representation) is encouraged.

C. Institutions and Mechanisms for Effective Participation

The FCNM Explanatory Report proposes a number of ways of ensuring effective participation outside parliamentary representation. The establishment of representative institutions of persons belonging to national minorities that can be consulted when 'contemplating legislation or administrative measures likely to affect them [members of national minorities] directly' has been encouraged.[80] There are two elements that need to be fulfilled here: first, persons belonging to national minorities must be able to set up their own organizations to articulate and defend their interests. Secondly, such bodies must be given a means of influencing relevant decisions. The FCNM Explanatory Report notes that persons belonging to national minorities may be directly involved in the 'preparation, implementation and assessment of national and regional development plans and programmes likely to affect them directly', and in the preparation of studies on the impact of projected development activities.[81]

1. Ministries, National Offices, or Officers for Minorities

Virtually all states parties have set up special offices to address minority issues. Where this has not yet occurred, the Advisory Committee has pointed out that such a body can be most useful to develop a 'coherent policy' in this field.[82] At times, special ministries have been proposed or established towards this end. In one instance, the Advisory Committee and Committee of Ministers criticized the termination of such a ministry after only a very short period and invited the state concerned to consider re-establishing that body.[83]

Where a ministerial appointment is not available, other options to ensure high level interest in minority issues have been established.[84] For instance, a presidential commissioner may be established to raise minority concerns at the highest levels of policy-making.[85]

Another variant, often established in parallel with national offices for minority issues, is the creation of focal points for minority issues within the principal ministries that are of relevance (for instance, education, central ministries of

80 FCNM Explanatory Report, para. 80.

81 Above, n. 80.

82 Advisory Committee Opinion on Armenia, ACFC/INF/OP/I (2003) 001, para. 79.

83 Advisory Committee Opinion on Albania, ACFC/INF/OP/I (2003), para. 68.

84 The establishment of a 'Special Department of Interethnic Relations' in Moldova may be noted in this context; Advisory Committee Opinion on Moldova, ACFC/INF/OP/I (2003) 002, para. 86.

85 Noted with approval by the Advisory Committee in its Opinion on Cyprus, ACFC/INF/OP/I (2002) 004, para. 42—however, this institution has since been suppressed by the authorities.

local government and administrative affairs). Ministries may also use advisory boards to help inform them of the concerns of persons belonging to national minorities.[86] In this way, minority concerns can be 'mainstreamed' in the most relevant areas of public policy. This kind of provision is combined in some examples with a national office for minority affairs that can ensure co-ordination of policy across ministries.

An interesting development also relates to the appointment of officials with special responsibility for minority affairs in local authorities.[87]

2. *Consultative Bodies*

In some instances, persons belonging to national minorities may be represented directly in the principal decision-making bodies, for instance through a second chamber of parliament, or through other mechanisms that may be endowed with delaying or blocking powers on the part of national or religious 'communities'.[88] However, more often there is provision for softer forms of participation through consultation. Generally, this is facilitated through national minority advisory or consultative councils.[89] These can function at a national but also at a regional level and will facilitate consultation between the legislature or government in relation to a variety of issues.[90] These may include:[91]

- participation in the preparation of governmental strategies and measures addressing issues of concern to persons belonging to national minorities;
- commenting on draft legislative measures, decrees, etc.;
- monitoring the situation of persons belonging to national minorities and issuing reports;
- providing a forum for co-ordination among different minorities;

[86] Finland State Report, ACFC/SR (1999) 3, p. 28, in relation to Sami and Roma, with the Advisory Committee requesting a similar mechanism for Russian speakers; Advisory Committee Opinion on Finland, ACFC/INF/OP/I (2001) 002, para. 49.

[87] Advisory Committee Opinion on Moldova, ACFC/INF/OP/I (2003) 002, para. 86.

[88] Mostly, such designs can be found in states that have been subjected to ethnic conflict or tension, for instance Bosnia and Herzegovina after the Dayton accords. In Cyprus, such blocking powers exist in principle for the Turkish community, but are not applied, in view of their small number outside Northern Cyprus, according to the Comment of the Government on the Advisory Committee Opinion, GVT/COM/INF/OP/I (2002) 004, para. 7. With reference to the autonomous Province of Bolzano, Italy State Report, ACFC/SR (1999) 007, p. 84.

[89] An interesting example falling between representation and consultation is furnished by Cyprus, providing for co-representation of representatives of religious groups in the House of Representatives, but without legislative powers.

[90] On the regional level, for example, Russian Federation State Report, ACFC/SR (1999) 14, pp. 44–5; Slovenia State Report, ACFC/SR (2000) 4, para. 114.

[91] For example, Austria State Report, ACFC/SR (2000) 3, pp. 102–3; Czech Republic State Report, ACFC/SR (1999) 6, pp. 40–1.

- providing a forum for exchange with governmental and parliamentary officers;
- issuing policy guidance for public authorities;
- co-ordination of minority policy across public agencies;
- co-ordination of minority policy across regions and units of local governance;
- support for the external representation of persons belonging to national minorities on the part of the government, including engagement with international monitoring bodies.

In addition to such consultative functions, these bodies may also fulfil executive functions in their own right. For instance, it is good practice that such bodies take a prominent role in the distribution of resources directed towards cultural activities of organizations serving persons belonging to national minorities.

While the range of activities enunciated here is broad, practice under the Convention shows that the competence and working practices of such bodies, especially as they relate to legislative scrutiny, need to be clearly established to ensure effectiveness.[92] In principle, this should take the form of legislative entrenchment.[93] On occasion, the Advisory Committee has questioned whether a purely advisory function of consultative bodies is sufficient.[94] The status of such councils (a state organ, an NGO, a mixture of the two) also needs clarification in some instances.[95]

At times, the question of which minorities are represented in the consultative body may be at issue—the Advisory Committee has taken an expansive view, emphasizing the need to also include 'small' minorities and perhaps also moving beyond so-called traditional or autochthonous minorities. When establishing consultative bodies, it is important to take account of organizations that may already exist to articulate the interests of persons belonging to national minorities. In one instance, the Advisory Committee noted the problems of a lack of co-ordination or even competition that may otherwise ensue.[96]

The personal membership of such councils is also a matter of interest. One may expect nomination of members from established parties and organizations representing persons belonging to national minorities, from church organizations

[92] Advisory Committee Opinion on Armenia, ACFC/INF/OP/I (2003) 001, para. 79.

[93] Estonia State Report, ACFC/SR (1999) 16, pp. 61–2; Advisory Committee Opinion on Lithuania, ACFC/INF/OP/I (2003) 008, para. 78.

[94] Advisory Committee Opinion on Cyprus, ACFC/SR (1999) 2 Rev., p. 59, para. 1(*e*).

[95] Croatia, for instance, reports that its Council is established as an NGO. Croatia State Report, ACFC/SR (1999) 5, p. 162. However, important changes in legislation and practice since that time should be noted.

[96] Advisory Committee Opinion on Armenia, ACFC/INF/OP/I (2003) 001, para. 79.

and similar bodies. A balance in political/ideological orientation among groups representing the same national minority population is desirable. Due account must also be taken to ensure that the organizations chosen are indeed genuinely and widely representative. Where the government appoints representatives, it appears prudent to provide a means of redress for these organizations. This may even involve access to courts.[97] An overemphasis on just one of several representative organizations has been criticized.[98]

In some instances, consultative bodies may include a sizeable representation of governmental officers or junior ministers—indeed, at times these may be chaired by senior officials who will not normally be representatives of persons belonging to national minorities.[99] This practice has generally not been directly questioned in the published opinions of the Advisory Committee. Still, one may infer from a set of opinions that the Advisory Committee is not satisfied with the fact that some consultative bodies are made up of a majority (or even exclusively) of public officials.[100] One may also ask whether it would be better practice to enhance control over the proceedings on the part of representatives of persons belonging to national minorities. Moreover, the Advisory Committee has commended one state for changing the majority in its Council of National Minorities and Ethnic Groups to ensure a majority of representatives of persons belonging to national minorities.[101]

In one instance, the Advisory Committee noted that the governing body of an institution intended to support the interests of persons belonging to a particular national minority was composed of only six members representing persons belonging to national minorities out of fifteen.[102] However, this institution was a grant-giving foundation, rather than a mechanism principally devoted to consultation.[103]

Of course, the mere establishment of consultative bodies is insufficient. The government must ensure that these bodies can effectively function by providing for timely contact with parliamentary committees and government

[97] An instructive example on all of these points is furnished by Austria State Report, ACFC/SR (2000) 3, pp. 120–3, and the Advisory Committee Opinion on Austria, ACFC/INF/OP/I (2002) 009, para. 68.

[98] Advisory Committee Opinion on Romania, ACFC/INF/OP/I (2002) 001, para. 67.

[99] Czech Republic State Report, ACFC/SR (1999) 6, pp. 41 ff.

[100] Advisory Committee Opinion on Switzerland, ACFC/INF/OP/I (2003) 007, para. 77; Advisory Committee Opinion on Norway, ACFC/INF/OP/I (2003) 003, para. 61; Advisory Committee Opinion on Lithuania, ACFC/INF/OP/I, 008, para. 79; Advisory Committee Opinion on Ukraine, ACFC/INF/OP/I (2002), para. 69.

[101] Advisory Committee Opinion on Slovak Republic, ACFC/INF/OP/I (2001) 001, para. 46.

[102] Advisory Committee Opinion on Germany, ACFC/INF/OP/I (2002) 008, para. 65.

[103] Comment by Germany, GVT/COM/INF/OP/I (2002) 008.

departments, providing early consultation on legislative and other projects and furnishing adequate resources to these bodies.[104] This includes regular consultation and the offering of explanations by government or parliament for failing to respond to the recommendations of consultative bodies.[105] Where the government retains an influence on the working practices of such councils (not a practice to be encouraged) it bears responsibility for the effectiveness of their functioning.[106]

In addition to general consultative bodies, specialist bodies also exist which only address the concerns of persons belonging to one particular national minority, for instance Roma, or other persons belonging to minorities who are in a unique position.[107]

Similarly, functional consultative bodies may be established within individual ministries covering issues of particular concern for persons belonging to national minorities.[108] The Advisory Committee has, however, had occasion to remind governments that consultation should not be limited only to narrow functional areas, such as culture.[109]

Finally, consultation can be facilitated in the absence of standing consultative bodies. In Finland, the Parliament Act provides generally for a right of representatives of a national minority to be heard by parliament and negotiate in relation to matters of special consequence to them. Similar provisions exist at the level of state and municipal authorities.[110] The Advisory Committee, however, found that the ad hoc nature of such arrangements leads to uncertainty and proposed the establishment of guidelines clarifying the obligation to negotiate.[111] In relation to Norway, the Advisory Committee suggested that ad hoc consultative structures should be transformed into permanent bodies and processes.[112]

3. *Remedies*

In some instances, petition bodies of parliaments will be available to persons belonging to national minorities, or specialized parliamentary petitioning

[104] This was found to be lacking, for instance in Advisory Committee Opinion on Lithuania, ACFC/INF/OP/I (2003) 008, para. 79.

[105] Advisory Committee Opinion on Romania, ACFC/INF/OP/I (2002) 001, para. 66.

[106] Advisory Committee Opinion on Croatia, ACFC/INF/OP/I (2002) 003, para. 63.

[107] For example, Czech Republic State Report, ACFC/SR (1999) 6, p. 41; Sweden State Report, ACFC/SR (2001) 003, p. 36; on non-Roma, see for instance the Liaison Committee Concerning the German Minority in Denmark, Denmark State Report, ACFC/SR (1999) 9, p. 47.

[108] Czech Republic State Report, ACFC/SR (1999) 6, p. 42; on the Estonian Cultural Council of National Minorities, Estonia State Report, ACFC/SR (1999) 16, p. 62.

[109] Advisory Committee Opinion on Moldova, ACFC/INF/OP/I (2003) 002, para. 88.

[110] Finland State Report, ACFC/SR (1999) 3, p. 27, para. 113.

[111] Advisory Committee Opinion on Finland, ACFC/INF/OP/I (2001) 002.

[112] Advisory Committee Opinion on Norway, ACFC/INF/OP/I (2003) 003.

bodies may be contemplated.[113] Provision may be made for specialized Ombudspersons, who may also engage in consultative functions themselves. The good practice in this respect pioneered by Hungary is now also being adopted in a number of other instances. Where no specialized Ombudsperson is available specifically for members of national minorities, it can be noted that more general human rights Ombudsperson institutions are developing sections dealing particularly with minority issues.[114] Overall, however, state reports tend to offer few insights into remedies that may be available.

D. Effective Participation and Executive Representation

A previous Austrian draft proposal relating to a proposed Protocol to the ECHR suggested that members of an ethnic group should have the right to access to public offices. In regions inhabited by ethnic groups, public offices 'have to be filled with due consideration to the principle of proportional representation'.[115] The principle of executive representation is not directly addressed in Article 15, but dialogue between governments and the FCNM, and the findings of the Committee of Ministers, confirm that this is indeed an important element of effective participation.

1. National

At the national level, executive representation relates to ministerial posts at the top level. At times, attempts will be made to reserve certain portfolios for representatives of persons belonging to national minorities. However, minority representatives will normally only achieve a ministerial appointment if they are affiliated with a party that has joined a governing coalition.[116] Exceptions relate to post-conflict settlements in the Western Balkans, which have, however, not yet been subject to review by the Advisory Committee, and to regional autonomous governments.[117] There are also instances where informal arrangements operate to ensure minority representation at a high level of government, or where care is taken to ensure that the post of Minister for Ethnic or National Questions (where it exists) is filled by a representative of persons belonging to a minority.[118]

[113] Czech Republic State Report, ACFC/SR (1999) 6, pp. 41 ff., and Comment by the Czech Republic, GVT/COM/INF/OPI/I (2002) 002.

[114] Advisory Committee Opinion on Lithuania, ACFC/INF/OP/I (2003) 008, para. 79.

[115] Steering Committee for Human Rights (CDHH), Draft Protocol to the European Convention on Human Rights Guaranteeing the Protection of Ethnic Groups, CDHH (1991), 46, 20 December 1991, Draft Art. 6.

[116] Slovak Republic State Report, ACFC/SR (1999) 8, pp. 37–8.

[117] Italy State Report, ACFC/SR (1999) 007.

[118] Serbia and Montenegro State Report, ACFC/SR (2002) 03.

While representation at senior governmental levels remains rare, provision must be made for equal representation of public servants in public agencies serving central governmental functions. In exceptional instances, states have committed themselves to achieving proportional representation in public service, but the Advisory Committee had to note the disconcerting situation of having failed to meet such targets.[119] In relation to several states parties, the Advisory Committee has noted that no adequate provision has been made in this respect.[120] While it has been answered that there exists a level playing field and candidates for such posts are not excluded due to their appurtenance to a given minority, it has been clarified that governments should adopt special measures to remedy such a situation.[121]

Most governments do report on the number of minority appointees in certain sectors of government. However, very rarely is there a comprehensive listing that could be placed in relation to the demographic composition of the state in question. Often, minority representation is particularly difficult in public offices connected with law, order, and security.[122]

The Advisory Committee has pronounced itself quite clearly where it has found that members of minorities have suffered from systematic exclusion from public service. In such instances, it not only required the adoption of special measures to remedy the situation, but also an individual remedy for victims of this practice.[123] Where, on the other hand, formal provision exists for proportionate representation of members of minorities in public service, it has been noted that such provision might only apply for some groups while others remain disadvantaged.[124]

2. *Regional or Local*

While it may be difficult to achieve roughly proportionate representation of persons belonging to national minorities at the national level, this tends to be an even more important aim at the regional and local levels. Generally, a review of state reports indicates that virtually all states profess to making efforts in this respect, although the results have not always been impressive. At times, it is argued that the process of appointment is an objective one, where minority

119 Croatia State Report, ACFC/SR (1999) 5, p. 157—a pledge not yet fulfilled, especially in relation to ethnic Serbs.

120 Advisory Committee Opinion on Albania, ACFC/INF/OP/I (2003), para. 68.

121 Advisory Committee Opinion on Ireland, ACFC/INF/OP/I (2004) 003, para. 97.

122 Advisory Committee Opinion on Serbia and Montenegro, AVFC/INF/OP/I (2004) 002, para. 103.

123 Advisory Committee Opinion on Croatia, ACFC/INF/OP/I (2002) 003, paras. 56–7.

124 Italy State Report, ACFC/SR (1999) 007.

applicants are neither advantaged nor disadvantaged. The need for special measures in such circumstances has been consistently emphasized, however.

In this context, one may note that several governments report on the numbers of mayors or councillors belonging to national minorities. However, it is not easy to see these examples in relation to the overall picture throughout these states, including demographic factors in regions where minorities may be concentrated.

It is also an interesting phenomenon that devolution of public authority to territorial units can, in certain instances, have an adverse effect on representation of persons belonging to national minorities.[125]

3. *Functional*

Generally, there has been little comment on the failure to achieve adequate representation of persons belonging to national minorities in particular sectors of public administration. Rather, criticism tends to concern the exclusion of specific groups of persons belonging to national minorities. However, once more, on occasion the absence of such representation in the areas of justice, policing, and the military has been particularly noted and requests have been made for the enhancement of programmes of special measures, even where they already exist.[126]

E. Effective Participation in Cultural, Social, and Economic Life

The Steering Committee for Human Rights (CDHH) included in its report to the Committee of Ministers of 1993 a specific provision within a draft article on cultural freedoms that emphasized the right of persons belonging to national minorities to 'participate effectively in cultural life'.[127] In the FCNM, this principle is now included in Article 15. It was already noted above that some states have provided functional consultation bodies attached to specialist ministries. This applies particularly to cultural affairs.[128]

In one instance, formal cultural autonomy has been accorded to persons belonging to a specific national minority—although this group would also qualify as an indigenous people.[129] The other special 'cultural autonomies'—

[125] Advisory Committee Opinion on United Kingdom, ACFC/INF/OP/I (2002) 006, para. 93.

[126] Advisory Committee Opinion on Romania, ACFC/INF/OP/I (2002) 001, para. 71; Advisory Committee Opinion on United Kingdom, ACFC/INF/OP/I (2002) 006, para. 96.

[127] CDHH, Final Activity Report to the CDDH for the Attention of the Committee of Ministers, CDHH (93) 22, Art. 8(*a*), 8 September 1993.

[128] Estonia State Report, ACFC/SR (1999) 16, p. 62.

[129] Finland State Report, ACFC/SR (1999) 3, p. 27.

in fact ranging beyond purely cultural matters—have already been referred to above.

Several governments report on support given to cultural associations and activities relating to persons belonging to national minorities, often down to the level of individual small project grants. This does not always facilitate an understanding of the impact of such programmes, especially when set against general expenditure in this area. A per capita formula might assist in making such comparisons.

While some governments report on the involvement of organizations representing persons belonging to national minorities in funding decisions, actual accountability to the interests of minority stakeholders remains difficult to fathom.

In some instances, governments report on special programmes adopted to support the cultural life of members of communities of Travellers—for example, Ireland has a noteworthy initiative aimed at researching and documenting their history, and enhancing their cultural identity and skills.[130]

Social and economic participation has also been addressed on several occasions. It was noted that in some instances, members of national minorities enjoy an advantageous position in the economic sector, in part due to economic links with an ethnic kin state.[131] However, in other instances, governmental agencies have engaged in economic surveys and found that in areas of compact minority population, economic and quality of life indicators are inferior.[132] Such surveying and reporting by governments appear to be an enormously important first step in addressing such inequalities, especially if followed by a concrete governmental action plan designed to remedy the situation.[133] More often than not, however, there has been insufficient data available, inhibiting an assessment of the situation by the Advisory Committee.

In relation to a number of states, the Advisory Committee has noted shortcomings in the participation of minorities in economic life,[134] in one instance

130 Ireland State Report, ACFC/SR (2001) 6, p. 91.

131 Comment by Albania, GVT/COM/INF/OP/I (2003) 004.

132 Bulgaria State Report, ACFC/SR (2003) 001, p. 102. In the case of Bulgaria, reference is made to the annual reports on human development of the UNDP. The findings in the Danish report are also interesting, indicating that no economic differences can be detected in relation to persons belonging to the German national minorities, Denmark State Report, ACFC/SR (1999) 9, p. 45.

133 Bulgaria State Report, ACFC/SR (2003) 001, p. 103; Advisory Committee Opinion on Lithuania, ACFC/INF/I (2003) 008, para. 81.

134 Advisory Committee Opinion on Estonia, ACFC/INF/OP/I (2002) 005, para. 15(9).

reaching the point of discrimination.[135] The objection of governments that economic divergences may be due to lagging regional development, rather than national, ethnic, religious, or linguistic factors, are not likely to persuade in this respect.[136] The Committee has had to acknowledge that certain factors, such as urban development vs. development in rural regions (the latter often inhabited by persons belonging to national minorities) may pose a challenge in generating equal economic opportunities. Nevertheless it has requested that governments endeavour to develop measures capable of limiting the effects of such structural differences.[137] Hence, the Advisory Committee has endorsed and encouraged active and decisive measures to address economic opportunities for persons belonging to national minorities especially in economically depressed regions.[138] Even where governments may have presented advanced programmes to engage economic and social exclusion, the Advisory Committee has not hesitated to propose an extension of such measures until the intended result has been achieved.[139]

In virtually all reports, the exclusion of Roma from economic opportunities has been noted.[140] Some governments have responded by referring to programmes of action in this respect, although this issue remains one of considerable difficulty and lack of actual significant progress has been a source of great concern to the Advisory Committee in a significant number of its opinions. Hence, it has requested greater emphasis on measures designed to give access to such disenfranchised communities, including also Travellers, to the labour market.[141]

At times, the Advisory Committee has had occasion to resist unnecessary restrictions on access to economic activity. For instance it was found that language requirements for the delivery of certain services did not appear to be required to protect a specific public interest.[142] The Committee also noted that cumbersome residency registration procedures might have an adverse effect on minority economic activity.[143]

135 Advisory Committee Opinion on Croatia, ACFC/INF/OP/I (2002) 003, para. 65.

136 Comment by Estonia, GVT/COM/INF/OP/I (2002) 005.

137 Advisory Committee Opinion on Switzerland, ACFC/INF/OP/I (2003) 007, paras. 75 and 103.

138 Advisory Committee Opinion on Ukraine, ACFC/INF/OP/I (2002) 010, para. 73.

139 Advisory Committee Opinion on United Kingdom, ACFC/INF/OP/I (2002) 006, para. 95.

140 Advisory Committee Opinion on Albania, ACFC/INF/OP/I (2003), para. 75; Advisory Committee Opinion on Croatia, ACFC/INF/OP/I (2002) 003, para. 65; Advisory Committee Opinion on Finland, ACFC/INF/OP/I (2001) 002, para. 93.

141 Advisory Committee Opinion on Ireland, ACFC/INF/OP/I (2994) 003.

142 Advisory Committee Opinion on Azerbaijan, ACFC/INF/OP/I (2004) 001, para. 79.

143 Above, n. 142.

III. Overall Contribution of Article 15

A. Consolidated Review of Practice

A number of commentators have criticized Article 15 as a provision that is too general to offer any legal substance. This review tells a different story. States have generally reported seriously and in most instances extensively on their efforts to encourage effective participation, either in relation to Article 15 alone, or in conjunction with other related provisions, including Articles 3, 4, and 7. They have done so against the background of quite specific expectations of achievement in discrete areas of public policy. These expectations have been further refined and shaped through the review process of the Advisory Committee. In view of this extensive practice, there can be no doubt that all states parties regard effective participation of persons belonging to national minorities as an essential (and mandatory) component of a peaceful and democratic society.[144]

One might also note that the Committee of Ministers, too, has directly and expressly engaged in the issue of effective participation at all levels. It has recommended equal participation in the electoral process,[145] adequate representation in parliament and other elected bodies,[146] the establishment of effective consultative mechanisms,[147] the general participation of members of certain communities in cultural, social, and economic life,[148] as well as in public affairs,[149] and the enhancement of economic opportunities of persons belonging to national minorities.[150]

Of course, Article 15 is phrased in quite general terms, lacking the breadth and depth of other standards, in particular the far more lengthy Lund Recommendations. However, virtually all of the solutions offered in the Lund document are visible in the state practice that have been reported, and have been commented upon by the Advisory Committee, in the context of

[144] This is the formulation used in the General Principles of the Lund Recommendations.

[145] Committee of Ministers Resolution on Cyprus, ResCMN (2002) 3, 21 February 2002.

[146] Committee of Ministers Resolution on Hungary, ResCMN (2001) 4, 21 November 2001.

[147] Committee of Ministers Resolution on the Russian Federation, ResCMN (2003) 9, 10 July 2003; Committee of Ministers Resolution on Norway, ResCMN (2003) 6, 8 April 2003; Committee of Ministers Resolution on Armenia, ResCMN (2003) 2, 15 January 2003.

[148] Committee of Ministers Resolution on Ukraine, ResCMN (2003) 5, 5 February 2003.

[149] Committee of Ministers Resolution on Moldova, ResCMN (2003) 4, 15 January 2003; Committee of Ministers Resolution on Estonia (although somewhat indirectly), ResCMN (2002) 8, 13 June 2002.

[150] Committee of Ministers Resolution on the United Kingdom, ResCMN (2002) 9, 13 June 2002; Committee of Ministers Resolution on Croatia, ResCMN (2002) 1, 6 February 2002.

Article 15 and related provisions of the FCNM.[151] Of course, not all possible approaches or solutions are evident in relation to each individual state. Many states do not even address all the principal issue areas through some form of mechanism (i.e. full equality, democratic and executive representation, equal chances). The challenge, therefore, remains to encourage states to develop provisions for the effective participation of persons belonging to national minorities in a fully comprehensive way. A review of action across states after five years of the operation of the FCNM can only assist in identifying patterns of best practice relating to each of the principal areas of concern.

Obviously, there does not exist one single specific model of performance that must be applied by all states parties in all circumstances. This applies with particular force to issues of state construction and political system design. However, even if states may dine *à la carte* when implementing Article 15, there must emerge a full and satisfying dinner at the end of the day. In other words, there may be a range of options for the achievement of the individual aspects of effective participation, but ultimately Article 15 is indeed a provision of hard law—and it is an obligation of result.

In its early practice, the Advisory Committee has addressed Article 15 issues with some initial caution. Often, it has couched its suggestions in fairly general terms. Very specific requests have at times only been made in cases of evident discrimination, or where a state has failed to comply with its own, already existing provisions for effective participation. Of course, the Advisory Committee will continue to be mindful of the fact that states enjoy a margin of appreciation where effective participation is concerned. But increasingly, it has raised the level of expectation, covering all major issues of relevance to effective participation.

In relation to general full equality, it is now clear that the overall state structure must not be such as to exclude persons belonging to national minorities from the democratic process. As it is now fashionable to say, 'ownership' of the state must not appear to appertain to a titular or dominant group. In this area, the Advisory Committee has found a clear voice concerning the need of 'ensuring that the necessary structural guarantees—electoral or consultative—exist to allow for effective participation of all persons belonging to national minorities in the political process'.[152]

[151] For a review of state practice according to the Lund Recommendations, see the very useful Kristian Myntti, Commentary on the Lund Recommendations on the Effective Participation of National Minorities in Public Life (Institute for Human Rights, Åbo Akademi University, Turku, 2001).

[152] Advisory Committee Opinion on Albania, ACFC/INF/OP/I (2003), para. 72.

In terms of parliamentary representation of persons belonging to national minorities, the Committee has now gone beyond an insistence that governments only meet the targets they themselves have established.[153] While remaining mindful of the concern of governments to avoid inequality to the detriment of majority populations, the Advisory Committee has in its more recent practice unambiguously noted the need of 'facilitating access by [persons belonging to national minorities] to parliament or, more generally bringing them into the various branches of power'.[154] This may require special measures in terms of electoral systems design or electoral procedures, at least where there are a significant number of persons belonging to specific national minorities. While there is no formal requirement of strict proportionality of members of parliament to segments of the population, states will now need to demonstrate that there is adequate representation in elected bodies, both local and national. Where this is not possible, there will be even greater pressure upon the state to demonstrate that it is balancing this deficiency through particularly well-developed consultative mechanisms.

Indeed, representation in elected bodies must generally be flanked by formally established consultative mechanisms where the numbers of persons belonging to minorities so warrant. Best practice indicates that these should be established in law. Composition of these councils should be genuinely representative, taking account of a wide range of interests among persons belonging to national minorities. Appointments should be made in consultation with representative institutions or based on elections within minority organizations. Ordinarily, one would expect that representatives of persons belonging to national minorities would constitute the majority of the members of these councils and that they are in a position to control or guide its proceedings.

The functions and powers of consultative councils should be made evident in the legislation establishing them. This includes in particular the formal requirement of timely and substantive consultation relating to legislation of special interest to persons belonging to national minorities. The exercise of decision-making functions of such councils, also in relation to the expenditure of funds dedicated to the enhancement of minority culture and social life, is noteworthy. However, it is also clear that the purview of consultative councils should not only be restricted to cultural affairs.

One issue that has not been fully addressed by the Advisory Committee as yet concerns the quality of representation of persons belonging to national

[153] For example, Advisory Committee Opinion on Hungary, ACFC/INF/OP/I (2001) 004; Advisory Committee Opinion on Croatia, ACFC/INF/OP/I (2002) 003.

[154] Advisory Committee Opinion on Armenia, ACFC/INF/OP/I (2003), para. 77.

minorities. While it is clear that the government is under certain obligations in establishing mechanisms for effective participation, organizations claiming to represent persons belonging to national minorities might also need to demonstrate their genuine representativeness and the transparency of their democratic and financial practices. Consultative councils might be ideal bodies to propose relevant codes of conduct.

In terms of minority self-government, it would be premature or perhaps even wrong to note that there has been a recognition of territorial autonomy as a mandatory requirement for areas mainly inhabited by persons belonging to national minorities. However, there is no doubt that subsidiarity in decision making and an emphasis on genuinely representative local government are now to be expected. While many governments offer partial statistics of the representation of persons belonging to national minorities at the local level, a more comprehensive review of these figures in relation to local population balances would need to be encouraged. In this way, the success of measures aiming to enhance effective participation can be better assessed.

Functional autonomies or minority self-government also furnish interesting examples in relation to states featuring sizeable minority populations. These should be carefully evaluated in order to establish whether such designs could also be deployed in other states. In nearly all instances, the Advisory Committee has had to note deficiencies in executive representation of persons belonging to national minorities. Indeed, on this issue, the stories told in the state reports may not always correspond to reality. Often, information is provided in an anecdotal way, picking out positive examples from individual municipalities, without presenting the overall picture. Where such problems exist, the practice of the Advisory Committee would indicate that one would now expect the development of specific targets and action plans by governments on how they intend to meet these. Such action plans would cover access to education, specific training for applicants from under-represented groups, recruitment drives, appointment procedures, and advancement and retention programmes, etc.

It is particularly noteworthy that there appear to be instances of exclusion from positions in areas connected with justice and security (police and military). When considering the urgency of the need to redress this deficiency, one might bear in mind that exclusion from precisely these functions tends to enhance a sense of overall disenfranchisement and alienation of minority communities within the state.

Disenfranchisement and exclusion is of course not only relevant in relation to elected and appointed public offices. As Article 15 makes clear, full and effective participation has a strong cultural, social, and economic dimension. While the cultural dimension has been addressed elsewhere in this commentary, one may note that once again the state reports tend to employ an anecdotal technique of presentation, often providing a listing of individual cultural projects or activities that have attracted state funding. A more structured review of such state programmes has been encouraged by the Advisory Committee.

This applies with even greater vigour where economic and social exclusion are concerned. It is by no means the case that all minorities everywhere suffer from economic disadvantage and social relegation. Nevertheless, persons belonging to national minorities tend to be at special risk of slipping into this category. Indeed, there may exist structural factors contributing to the de facto exclusion of entire minority populations. This applies especially, although not exclusively, to Roma. Here, only a few governments have as yet treated Article 15 as a substantive obligation of the first order. This is partially explained by an analysis of this phenomenon through Article 4. However, another problem lies in the absence of reliable statistical data. The Advisory Committee has now requested states to present figures on social and economic exclusion and, in some instances, the creation of action plans to address exclusion.

B. Link to Other Developments

The emerging practice surrounding Article 15 is not mirrored in other international standards, or in jurisprudence. Article 15 remains one of the very few provisions covering effective participation in a legally binding instrument at the regional or the universal level. Consequently, there are also very few pronouncements from implementation bodies on this issue. The European Court of Human Rights has considered the issue of electoral systems, including 'ethnic votes'.[155] It has also addressed the issue of language requirements for parliamentary candidates in a way that is fully consistent with the views of the FCNM Advisory Committee.[156] This has also been reflected in the ruling of the Human Rights Committee.[157] In relation to the establishment of minority political parties and also their possible dissolution, the European Court of Human Rights has perhaps advanced beyond the pronouncements of the Advisory Committee.[158]

[155] *Mathieu-Mohin and Clerfayt* v. *Belgium*, Case No. 9267/81, judgment of 2 March 1987, paras. 57 ff.

[156] *Podkolzina* v. *Latvia*, Case No. 46726/99, 9 April 2002, paras. 36 ff.

[157] *Antonina Igantane* v. *Latvia*, Comm. No. 884/1999, CCPR/C/72/D/884/1999, paras. 7.4 ff.

[158] *Selim Sadak and Others* v. *Turkey*, Cases No. 25144/94, 26149/95–26154/95, 17100/95, 27101/95, judgment of 16 June 2002.

With respect to consultative mechanisms or procedures, the Human Rights Committee has addressed a number of cases, mainly touching upon economic co-decision. However, these cases have tended to concern indigenous groups that have claimed particular rights in relation to land use on the basis of this status.[159]

C. Overall Conclusion

Article 15 has served as a focal point for the crystallization of legal obligations concerning effective participation of minorities. The rather general terms of the Article are beginning to be filled out with concrete legal meaning. This is certainly the case in relation to the overall structure of the state, the need for adequate parliamentary representation, consultative processes, and executive representation. In other, sensitive areas, debates will continue. These concern claims for territorial autonomy and issues of party registration. The latter are of course often connected with the question of the 'recognition' of minorities addressed under Article 3. Finally, it is noteworthy that Article 15 has also served to highlight the obligation of states to go beyond the combating of discrimination when considering cultural, social, and economic opportunities of persons belonging to minorities. Overall, implementation practice on this article has been considerable. The better understanding of the principle of effective participation derived from the study of this state practice provides a useful point of reference when considering this issue outside the context of the FCNM.

[159] *Ilmari Laensman et al.* v. *Finland*, Comm. No. 511/1992, CCPR/C/52/D/11/1992, from para. 9.2; *Apirana Mahuika et al.* v. *New Zealand*, Comm. No. 547 /1993, CCPR/C/70/D/547/1993, from para. 9.5.

ARTICLE 16

Jennifer Jackson-Preece

The Parties shall refrain from measures which alter the proportions of the population in areas inhabited by persons belonging to national minorities and are aimed at restricting the rights and freedoms flowing from the principles enshrined in the present framework Convention.

I. Background

A. Issues

Article 16 of the Framework Convention for the Protection of National Minorities (FCNM) addresses those circumstances in which policies of demographic change or territorial reorganization are used to deny minority rights. Such policies may include: expropriation; eviction; expulsion; and the redrawing of administrative boundaries (gerrymandering).

Practices like these have historically featured in state policies of oppression towards minorities, owing to the important relationship between territories and peoples reflected in the principle of self-determination. As Theodor Meron notes, self-determination is a right of 'cohesive national groups ("peoples") to choose for themselves a form of political organisation and their relation to other groups'.[1] Evidence of cohesiveness as demonstrated by demographic size and territorial concentration thus becomes a crucial element in identifying those

[1] See T. Meron, *Principles of Public International Law* (Oxford University Press, Oxford, 2001), 599.

groups to whom self-determination might reasonably be applied. The international protection of minorities within states is controversial precisely because it is feared that such recognition could become the pretext for minority claims to self-determination in the form of secession or irredentism. For this reason, it is now general international practice to deny any specific claims and actions contrary to the principle of territorial integrity of existing states within minority rights guarantees, as evident in Article 21 FCNM.[2]

Nevertheless, the criteria of demographic size and territorial concentration continue to be associated with minority protection, particularly with respect to provisions for minority language use, minority language education, and minority participation in cultural, social, economic, and political affairs. Thus, for example, the minority language provisions enshrined in Article 14(2) FCNM apply only to those areas inhabited by minorities either 'traditionally' or 'in substantial numbers'.[3] Accordingly, the temptation to manipulate demographics with a view to limiting or avoiding state obligations towards minorities persists, notwithstanding the now conventional interpretation of the principle of self-determination to exclude minority demands for political independence. Article 16 is intended to protect against precisely this sort of deliberate political manipulation of minority populations by states.

B. History

The post-Cold War period saw a resurgence in those practices aimed at the deliberate displacement of peoples to secure the continued rule of the dominant ethnic group over contested territories as, for example, in Bosnia, Croatia, Armenia, Azerbaijan, Somalia, Rwanda, and Kosovo. Needless to say, the brutality and loss of life associated with notorious instances of this kind, such as ethnic cleansing in the former Yugoslavia and the genocide in Rwanda, were a shocking reminder that the politics of ethnic exclusiveness can take the form

[2] Art. 21 of the Framework Convention on the Protection of Minority Rights (FCNM), 1997 reads: 'Nothing in the present framework Convention shall be interpreted as implying any right to engage in any activity or perform any act contrary to the fundamental principles of international law and in particular of the sovereign equality, territorial integrity and political independence of states.'

[3] Art. 14(2) FCNM reads: 'In areas inhabited by persons belonging to national minorities traditionally or in substantial numbers, if there is sufficient demand, the Parties shall endeavour to ensure, as far as possible and within the framework of their education systems, that persons belonging to those minorities have adequate opportunities for being taught the minority language or for receiving instruction in this language.' This is very similar to the wording of Art. 8(4) UN Declaration on the Rights of Persons Belonging to National or Ethnic, Religious, and Linguistic Minorities, UNGA Res. 47/135, 1992 which states: 'Nothing in the present Declaration may be construed as permitting any activity contrary to the purposes and principles of the United Nations, including sovereign equality, territorial integrity and political independence of States.'

of policies intended to redraw the ethnic map through demographic manipulation. As UN Special Rapporteurs A. S. Al-Khasawneh and R. Hatano noted in their 1993 report, The Human Rights Dimensions of Population Transfer: '[a]s much as population transfer [and by extension other practices aimed at demographic manipulation] has prevailed as an instrument of State-craft in every age in recorded history, ours could be distinguished as the century of the displaced person.'[4] One could add that in the vast majority of cases such displaced persons belong to minority groups.

As a direct response to events like those noted above, by the early 1990s a number of Council of Europe bodies were considering proposals to prohibit measures specifically intended to alter demographics in areas inhabited by minorities. The European Commission for Democracy through Law included such a provision in its Preliminary Draft Convention on the Protection of Minorities (1993). Article 13 of the Draft Convention called upon states to 'refrain from pursuing or encouraging policies aimed at the assimilation of minorities or aimed at intentionally modifying the proportions of the population in the regions inhabited by minorities'.[5] While Article 14 required that 'as far as possible, States shall take minorities into account when dividing the national territory into political and administrative sub-divisions, as well as into constituencies.'[6]

Both the Steering Committee for Human Rights (CDDH) Draft Protocol to the ECHR Guaranteeing the Protection of Ethnic Groups (1991), and the Parliamentary Assembly of the Council of Europe Recommendation 1201 (1993) on an Additional Protocol on the Rights of National Minorities to the ECHR also included protective measures against deliberate changes to the demographic composition. Article 5 of the CDDH Draft (1991) stipulated that: 'ethnic groups and their members may neither be expelled from the territory nor forced into resettlement, deliberate changes in the demographic composition of an ethnic group region at the expense of the ethnic group is inadmissible'.[7] In a similar vein, Article 5 of Parliamentary Assembly Recommendation 1201 (1993) prohibited 'deliberate changes to the demographic composition of the region in which a national minority is settled, to the detriment of that minority'.[8]

Ultimately, preparatory work for what became the Framework Convention for the Protection of National Minorities was assigned to the Ad Hoc Committee for the Protection of National Minorities (CAHMIN). Initial

4 UN Doc. E/CN.4/Sub.2/1993/17 (1993), para. 5.

5 European Commission for Democracy through Law, DAJ/SC/DEMOCRACY/CONV/MIN, 1990.

6 Above, n. 5.

7 Steering Committee for Human Rights (CDDH) (91) 46, 1991.

8 Parliamentary Assembly of the Council of Europe, Recommendation 1201 (1993), Art. 5.

drafts combined protection against forcible assimilation with prohibitions against policies aimed at modifying demographics in regions inhabited by minorities. Thus, for example, Article 3 of the CDDH Working Paper, dated 1 February 1994, stated that: 'the Parties shall refrain from pursuing or encouraging policies aimed at such assimilation, in particular by [intentionally] modifying the proportions of the population in regions inhabited by minorities'.[9] In May, the proposed Article 3 was reorganized and the practice of deliberate demographic change was given its own dedicated article.[10] The final version of October 1994 thus incorporated a separate Article 16. In its present wording: '[t]he parties shall refrain from measures which alter the proportions of the population in areas inhabited by persons belonging to national minorities and are aimed at restricting the rights and freedoms flowing from the principles enshrined in the present Framework Convention'.[11]

No explicit reason is given in the *travaux préparatoires* for this organizational restructuring. One can assume it reflected a growing realization that while both assimilation and policies of demographic change are intended to improve the majority's position relative to the minority population, these practices are, nevertheless, sufficiently distinct to warrant separate treatment.

C. Context

Article 16 seeks to secure the preservation and promotion of minority communities in territories where they have historically resided, by protecting them from policies of demographic change or administrative redistricting whose *raison d'être* is contrary to the rights and freedoms enshrined in the FCNM. In so doing, Article 16 reinforces those provisions guaranteeing minority equality and non-discrimination (Article 4(1), 4(2), and 4(3)), the right to identity (Article 5(1)), freedom from unwanted assimilation (Article 5(2)), and the right to effective participation in cultural, social, and economic life, and in public affairs (Article 15). Broadly speaking, in order to satisfy the provisions of Article 16, state policies of demographic change or redistricting must neither discriminate against nor deliberately target members of minorities. Accordingly, legal and administrative procedures relating to such policies must guarantee

[9] Ad Hoc Committee for the Protection of National Minorities (CAHMIN/GR) (94) MISC. 1, 1994, Preliminary Draft Preamble and opening provisions containing certain principles of the Framework Convention, Working Paper.

[10] CAHMIN (94) 12, 1994, Art. 16 reads: 'The Parties shall refrain from measures which alter the proportions of the population in areas inhabited by persons belonging to national minorities, and are aimed at restricting the rights and freedoms which flow from the principles enshrined in the present Convention.'

[11] CAHMIN (94) 32, 7th meeting, 1994, Meeting Report.

equality of treatment and the right of individual review. Similarly, there is an expectation that members of minorities or their representatives will participate in the decision-making processes with respect to determining such policies.

II. Analysis

A. A Duty to Refrain

Article 16 creates an obligation for states parties to *refrain* from measures that alter the proportions of the population in areas inhabited by persons belonging to minorities. Thus, this provision is phrased as a *negative* requirement. In the first instance the onus is on states to avoid or abjure from particular practices or policies that are detrimental to minority demographics. In practice, however, this negative requirement translates into a *positive* obligation for the state to ensure that relevant legal procedures are fair and objective, include a right of individual review, and that minorities are able to participate fully and effectively in political and administrative decision-making processes.

B. Measures that Alter the Proportions of the Population

The CAHMIN Explanatory Report which accompanies the Framework Convention specifically identifies four examples of measures which could potentially be intended to alter minority demographics in ways contrary to the rights and freedoms codified within it: expropriation; eviction; expulsion; and the redrawing of administrative boundaries (gerrymandering).[12] Expropriation, eviction, and expulsion all refer to practices associated with the forced movement of persons. Where such actions are directed at minority populations, physical relocation becomes an instrument to change demographics within a particular territory. In contrast, redrawing administrative boundaries (gerrymandering) seeks to alter demographics by changing the juridical map; minority populations remain *in situ*, but the relevant juridical units to which they belong are rearranged in ways unfavourable to minority interests. This list of examples is intended to be illustrative rather than exhaustive. Accordingly, there may be other measures not identified within the CAHMIN Explanatory Report that reflect a calculated effort to change demographics in ways counter to the rights and freedoms contained in the Framework Convention. These too would be contrary to Article 16. Colonization or settlement by rival ethnic groups within territories traditionally

[12] CAHMIN Explanatory Report on the Framework Convention for the Protection of National Minorities (1995) Art. 16, para. 81.

occupied by minorities, as per Israeli policy in the West Bank, is an obvious example of such a practice.

1. Expropriation

Expropriation is the taking of private property by a state. The right to property is recognized in Article 17 of the Universal Declaration on Human Rights (UDHR), which affirms both that 'everyone has the right to own property alone as well as in association with others' and 'that no one shall be arbitrarily deprived of his property'. A similar, albeit somewhat more muted, recognition of property rights can be found in Protocol 1(1) to the European Convention on Human Rights (ECHR) and in Article 21 of the American Convention on Human Rights (ACHR). Nevertheless, expropriations are permissible under international law (as under the municipal law right of eminent domain) provided that they are done for a legitimate public purpose and the state pays prompt, adequate, and effective compensation.[13] This standard of conduct is apparent in Protocol 1(1) to the ECHR, which specifically allows for the abrogation of property rights 'in the public interest' and 'subject to the conditions provided for by law and by the general principles of international law'. However, if the taking is regarded as unlawful then it is sometimes referred to as confiscation. Furthermore, there is a general expectation that such measures shall be in keeping with the principle of non-discrimination.

Problems arise with respect both to what constitutes legitimate public purpose or adequate and effective compensation. It has been suggested, for example, that where overriding national interests are at stake, expropriation is lawful even if compensation is less than fair market value. This would appear to be the rationale of the European Court of Human Rights, which has tended to give an allegedly offending state a wide margin of appreciation by applying the so-called 'fair balance' test, which seeks to stress the greater good arising from the state being allowed to interfere with the property of the individual.[14] Similarly, the recent UN General Assembly request for an International Court of Justice (ICJ) opinion on the legal consequences arising from the construction of the wall being built by Israel as the occupying power in the Palestinian Territory, has highlighted further ambiguities regarding justifiable acts of expropriation under international law. One of several points of controversy in this referral is the extent to which Article 23 of the Hague Convention of 1907 provides a legal basis for Israeli expropriation of Palestinian property in the West Bank. Specifically, it prohibits the destruction or seizure of any enemy's

[13] See Meron, above, n. 1, pp. 533–42.

[14] See *James and Others* v. *UK* (8793/79) (1986) ECHR.

property 'unless such destruction or seizure may be imperatively demanded by the necessities of war'. The Israeli government has contended that this security barrier is an immediate and necessary response to the continued and pervasive threat of Palestinian terrorism and is thus justifiable in the interests of national security. The ICJ opinion of 9 July 2004 found that the Israeli security fence violates certain international and humanitarian laws and that Israel must compensate Palestinians who lost land or property as a result of the construction of the fence. Moreover, the ICJ categorically stated that these infringements could not be justified on the grounds of Israeli national security.[15]

As regards minority questions, it is perhaps the question of intent (legitimate purpose) that is most significant. In certain circumstances, expropriation has been used to encourage the movement of minorities considered undesirable by the state. In such circumstances, members of minority communities are specifically targeted by expropriation measures with a view to depriving them of those resources (homes, businesses, community institutions, etc.) that are necessary to sustain their continued existence on the territory of the state. The so-called 'Benes Decrees', enacted by the Czechoslovak government in exile from 1940 to 1945, and retroactively ratified by the Czechoslovak Parliament in 1946, are a classic example of expropriation for such purposes.[16] In this case, property belonging to members of the German-speaking minority in the Sudetenland was collectively confiscated and nationalized as part of a larger post-war programme of forced population transfer. The perceived threat to Czechoslovak national security in the aftermath of German aggression and occupation was considered a reasonable justification for such measures. Here it is perhaps important to recall that the 1945 Potsdam Protocol concluded between Churchill, Truman, and Stalin authorized the forced transfer of ethnic Germans from east of the Oder–Neisse line.[17] More recently, policies of expropriation have been directed at minority communities in the former Yugoslavia as part of what is now referred to as 'ethnic cleansing'. Thus, for example, in 1994 the UN General Assembly, in Resolution 1994/223 'Situation of Human Rights in Kosovo', called upon the government of Yugoslavia (now Serbia and Montenegro) to halt its expropriation of Albanian property in Kosovo. Lacking economic resources and adequate accommodation, many ethnic Albanians were effectively forced into exile in neighbouring states.

[15] International Court of Justice, Advisory Opinion on Israel's Security Barrier, 9 July 2004, **www.adl.org/Israel/Israel_Security_Fence_ICJ.pdf** 17 August 2004.

[16] 'The Benes Decrees: A Spectre over Central Europe', *The Economist*, 15 August 2002.

[17] Protocol of the Potsdam Conference, 17 July–2 August 1945, Art. 13, **www.yale.edu/lawweb/avalon/decade/decade17.htm** 17 August 2004.

It is the clear purpose of Article 16 to prohibit expropriations for purposes like those noted above. In this context, any public expropriations with the express aim of depriving members of minorities of their property are unlawful prima facie. However, expropriations intended for legitimate purposes, such as economic development, which disproportionately affect persons belonging to minorities, would still be permissible. This qualified provision is consistent with the general ECHR approach to property rights, which tends to view these as limited rather than absolute.

To date, no concerns with respect to current acts of expropriation have arisen under the FCNM monitoring process; nevertheless, the consequences of prior expropriation were considered as part of the Opinion on Croatia of 6 April 2001.[18] The Advisory Committee thus noted that the 1991–5 conflict in the region (the Yugoslav war of secession) substantially altered the proportion of the population in a number of areas inhabited by persons belonging to national minorities. This prior experience of 'ethnic cleansing', whether as cause or consequence, included acts of expropriation and resettlement which resulted in cases of double occupancy and other housing-related concerns that remained outstanding in 2001. The Advisory Committee drew attention to these cases and called upon the government of Croatia to resolve these property and housing issues in order to facilitate a sustainable process of refugee return. Clearly therefore, the responsibilities of states, arising with respect to expropriation under Article 16, are ongoing. As such they are not exclusively limited to current acts of expropriation *per se*, but they also extend to the consequences of prior policies.

2. *Forced Eviction*

Forced eviction is 'the permanent or temporary removal against their will of individuals, families and/or communities from the homes and/or land which they occupy, without the provision of, and access to, appropriate forms of legal or other protection'.[19] Such practices arguably violate a number of universal human rights, including *inter alia* the right to liberty and security of the person (International Covenant on Civil and Political Rights (ICCPR) Article 9(1)), the right to freedom of movement and residence (ICCPR Article 12(1)), the right to be free from arbitrary interference with one's privacy, family, and home

[18] Advisory Committee Opinion on Croatia, adopted on 6 April 2001, ACFC/INF/OP/I (2001), para. 66.

[19] Committee on Economic, Social, and Cultural Rights, General Comment 3, The Nature of States Parties Obligations (Article 2(1), para. 9 of the Covenant, UN Doc. HRI/GEN/1/Rev. 1 at 45 (1994)).

(ICCPR Article 17(1)), and the right to an adequate standard of living, including housing (International Covenant on Economic, Social, and Cultural Rights (ICESCR) Article 11(1)).

Of these provisions, the right to freedom of movement is particularly significant with respect to forced eviction since it is generally understood to include a free choice of residence. Such choice is clearly stipulated in Article 12 ICCPR, Article 2 Fourth Protocol to the ECHR, Article 22 ACHR, and Article 12 of the African Charter on Human and People's Rights (Banjul Charter). These provisions do allow for certain restrictions to the freedom of movement, but only where necessary to protect national security or public safety, and as provided for by law.[20] Moreover, Article 5 of the International Convention on the Elimination of All Forms of Racial Discrimination stipulates that freedom of movement applies to everyone without distinction as to race, colour, or national or ethnic origin. Accordingly, instances of forced eviction are generally considered to be prima facie illegal, and can only be justified in the most exceptional circumstances and in accordance with the relevant principles of international law.[21]

As with expropriation, the criteria of legitimate purpose and due process are essential in distinguishing between a 'legal eviction' and evictions deemed 'forced', 'arbitrary', 'unfair', and 'illegal'. Legitimate evictions are those aimed at individuals who have actively reneged on their legal or contractual duties towards fellow tenants, and/or residents, or the persons or entities owning residential properties or lands. Here too, there is a presumption in favour of non-discrimination on grounds of race, religion, ethnic, or national origin. Moreover, any such evictees should have full recourse to due process of law and/or other remedies to protect their human rights. Indeed, the UN Commission on Human Rights has recommended that 'all Governments provide immediate restitution, compensation and/or appropriate and sufficient alternative accommodation or land . . . to persons and communities which have been forcibly evicted . . . .'[22]

'Illegal evictions' are frequently a necessary precursor to policies of forced relocation, forced resettlement, forced expulsion, and population transfer or exchange. In such cases, persons to be evicted are often singled out because they

[20] See Art. 12 of the International Covenant on Civil and Political Rights (ICCPR), Art. 2 of the Fourth Protocol to the European Convention on the Protection of Human Rights and Fundamental Freedoms (ECHR), Art. 22 of the American Convention on Human Rights (ACHR), and Art. 12 of the African Charter on Human and People's Rights (Banjul Charter).

[21] Committee on Economic, Social, and Cultural Rights, General Comment 4, The Right to Adequate Housing, Art. 11(1), para. 8(*a*) of the Covenant, UN Doc. HRI/GEN/1/Rev. 1 at 53 (1994).

[22] UN Commission on Human Rights Res. 1993/77.

possess identities, beliefs, or political opinions at odds with the majority of the population or that are contrary to the aims and interests of the government.[23] The use of force in such evictions, whether by agents of the state such as police or military officials or by paramilitaries or vigilante mobs, is commonplace and often disproportionate. It is not uncommon for illegal acts of eviction to be followed by the irreparable destruction of the homes and property of the evictees. In these circumstances, the persons affected generally have few or no legal remedies available to them, while compensation is ad hoc and usually inadequate.

Israeli practices in the Occupied Territories are representative of illegal eviction. Since the start of Israel's occupation in 1967, some 10,000 Palestinian families have been served with eviction and demolition orders.[24] Most home demolitions occur when Israel confiscates Palestinian land to expand settlements, build bypass roads or, most recently, to construct the so-called 'security fence'. However, evictions and demolitions also occur when Palestinians 'illegally' build on the land that they own because they fail to satisfy what has been criticized as a deliberately obstructivist system of building permits.[25] The UN Human Rights Committee has stated that Israeli policy violates the obligation of a state party to ensure, without discrimination, the right not to be subjected to arbitrary interference with one's home, the freedom to choose one's residence, and the right to equality of all persons before the law.[26]

In a similar vein, the European Court of Human Rights has found forced eviction to violate a number of ECHR provisions. In *Cyprus* v. *Turkey* (1982),[27] the forcible eviction of persons from their homes, the refusal to let them return, and the separation of families were recognized as clear infractions of Article 8, which guarantees respect for private and family life including the home. While the court acknowledged that Article 8(2) did provide for derogations in limited circumstances, subject only to such interference from public authorities as is necessary to protect national security, public safety, economic well-being, disorder or crime, health or morals, or the rights and freedoms of others and in accordance with the law, it further found that this provision could never justify the forced displacement of civilians. This interpretation was affirmed in

[23] UN Sub-Commission on Prevention of Discrimination and Protection of Minorities Res. 1991/12.

[24] The Israeli Center for Human Rights in the Occupied Territories (B'TSELEM), **www.btselem.org/English/Statistics/index.asp** 19 August 2004.

[25] 'Israeli Policy of House Demolitions', *B'TSELEM*, February 2002.

[26] Concluding Observations of the Human Rights Committee: Israel, 18/08/98, CCPR/C/79/Add. 93, para. 12.

[27] *Cyprus* v. *Turkey* 4 EHRR 482 (1982).

Akdivar and Others v. *Turkey* (1996),[28] *Mentes and Others* v. *Turkey* (1997),[29] and *Selcuk and Asker* v. *Turkey* (1998).[30]

Often, of course, the distinction between legal and illegal eviction may become blurred. This is especially the case in those circumstances where persons or groups do not have legal access to housing resources, thus unavoidably becoming illegal occupants or squatters. For example, in many parts of Europe the Roma live in accommodations that are not legally sanctioned. Such illegal occupancy has made the Roma especially vulnerable to eviction. At the same time, widespread hostility towards the Roma can severely limit their opportunities for resettlement.[31] In circumstances like these, it has been suggested by the United Nations Committee on Economic, Social, and Cultural Rights, that states exercise caution, respecting their existing obligations relating to the right to adequate housing.[32]

The particular vulnerability of persons belonging to minorities with respect to state practices of forced eviction, especially as precursors to forced relocation, forced resettlement, and forced expulsion, was recognized by both the International Labour Organization (ILO) and the Organization for Security and Co-operation in Europe (OSCE) prior to the drafting of the FCNM. Article 16 of ILO Convention 169 Concerning Indigenous Peoples and Tribal Populations in Independent Countries (1991) stipulates that such peoples shall not be removed from the lands which they occupy except where considered necessary as an 'exceptional measure'. Even in these circumstances, movement should take place only with their 'free and informed consent', and where such consent cannot be obtained, relocation will take place 'only following appropriate procedures established by national laws and regulations, including public inquiries . . . which provide the opportunity for effective representation of the peoples concerned'. Whenever possible, such peoples 'shall have the right to return to their traditional lands as soon as the grounds for relocation cease to exist'. Moreover, 'persons thus relocated shall be fully compensated for any resulting loss or injury'. In a similar vein, the 1992 Helsinki Document VI (27), calls upon states to 'refrain from resettling and condemn all attempts, by the threat or use of force, to resettle persons with the aim of changing the ethnic

28 *Akdivar* v. *Turkey* (21893/93) (1996), ECHR 35.

29 *Mentes and Others* v. *Turkey* (23186/94) (1997), ECHR 98.

30 *Selcuk and Asker* v. *Turkey* (23184/94) (1998), ECHR 36.

31 Report on the Situation of Roma and Sinti in the OSCE Area, OSCE High Commissioner on National Minorities, 2000, p. 1.

32 General Comment No. 4: The Right to Adequate Housing, Art. 11(1) 6th session, 1991, Report of the Committee on Economic, Social, and Cultural Rights on the right to adequate housing, para. 3.

composition of areas within their territories'. The provisions of Article 16, insofar as they apply to the practice of forced eviction, are thus a continuation of this prior trend in minority rights protection; their effect is to render prima facie unlawful forced eviction specifically directed against persons belonging to minorities. As with expropriation, however, there is some leeway for interpretation arising out of the distinction between aims and effects.

Germany's state report of 24 February 2000 provides an interesting example of a potential infringement under Article 16, with respect to the legally regulated dissolution of Horno Gemeinde and, as a corollary, the resettlement of the German-Sorbian population of this community to facilitate lignite mining.[33] The German government justified this resettlement on the basis of economic necessity, as lignite mining is a key industry of the *Land* of Brandenburg, which substantially contributes to the economic development of this region. According to the state report, there are no economically exploitable lignite beds or deposits outside built-up areas; thus the problem of resettlement is unavoidable. The German government claimed that the inhabitants of these areas were resettled without regard to their ethnic origin and identity; therefore, the aim of this policy was in no way contrary to provisions of the FCNM. Moreover, it was claimed that the decision-making processes involved under the Town and Country Planning Act of 20 July 1995 and the Brandenburg Act on Lignite Mining Policy of 7 July 1997 stipulated that Sorbs (Wends) should take part in all decision making by the institution responsible for regional planning. Accordingly, representatives of Domowina (the umbrella organization of Sorbian/Wendish associations) were included as advisory members of the Regional Assembly of the Lusatia-Spreewald Regional Planning Association.

Under the relevant national law, Horno Gemeinde was dissolved and was incorporated in Jänschwalde Gemeinde on 27 September 1998 under local government law. The Act on Lignite Mining Policy, Article 2 of which regulates the dissolution of Horno Gemeinde, was the subject of five legal proceedings before the *Land* of Brandenburg Constitutional Court. The five proceedings: an avoidance petition for judicial review of statutes or administrative acts submitted by a parliamentary group of the Brandenburg *Landtag*; and constitutional complaints filed by Domowina; by the Council for Sorbian (Wendish) Affairs established at the Brandenburg *Landtag*; by Horno Gemeinde; and by an inhabitant of Horno. In its decision of 18 June 1998, the *Land* Constitutional Court found that, in view of the special importance of lignite

[33] Germany State Report, ACFC/SR (2000) 1, 2000, para. 2.

mining for structural improvements, job security and energy supply, the legislator's decision to dissolve the Horno Gemeinde and to use its area for open-cast lignite mining was constitutional. The Court's decision was made in light of the state's aim as stipulated in Article 25 (paragraph 1, first sentence) of the *Land* Constitution, namely the protection, preservation, and cultivation of the Sorbs' (Wends') settlement area.[34] The Court's decision took special account of the supplementary provisions of this Act, calling for a maximum of considerate treatment for the inhabitants of the community and, in particular, for resettlement within the Sorbian populated area. The subsequent AC Opinion described the dissolution of Horno Gemeinde and, as a corollary, the resettlement of the German-Sorbian population of this community in Lower Lusatia in Brandenburg to make way for lignite mining as a matter of 'deep concern'.[35] Despite this official apprehension, the dissolution and resettlement was nevertheless considered to be a legal action on the part of the German authorities. The Opinion ruled that the motivation of the authorities was economic and not intended as a deliberate effort to deprive the Sorbian minority of its rights. Thus, the explanatory report's emphasis on aims over effects was maintained with respect to this case, primacy being given to the declared purpose as distinct from any possible negative consequences. At the same time, however, it is significant that the German authorities felt obliged to justify their actions with respect to the dissolution of Horno Gemeinde. Their lengthy submission on this case would suggest that practice arising under Article 16 puts the onus on states to demonstrate that their actions are not contrary to the principles enshrined in the Framework Convention. Moreover, it would appear that such justification must demonstrate due regard for both the effective participation of the minority in the relevant decision-making process and the right of individual appeal in accordance with domestic legal provisions. This finding is consistent with the AC Opinion on Germany under Article 5, where the Advisory Committee noted that the forced dissolution of municipalities where members of national minorities traditionally reside should be taken 'only as a last resort, when there is no alternative'.[36] With respect to the dissolution of Horno, where all the legal channels of appeal were exhausted, the Advisory Committee stipulated that it 'expects that the German authorities will pay due heed to the legitimate aspirations of the Sorbian people to maintain their culture and preserve their identity when determining the public interest'.[37]

[34] Germany State Report, ACFC/SR (2000) 1, 2000, para. 2.

[35] Advisory Committee Opinion on Germany, ACFC/INF/OP/I (2002) 008, 2002, para. 96.

[36] Above, n. 35, para. 32. [37] Above, n. 36.

3. *Expulsion*

Expulsion is '[a]n act or failure to act, by an authority of a State with the intention and with the effect of securing the removal of a person or persons against their will from the territory of the State'.[38] Consequently, deportation is the 'factual execution of the expulsion order'.[39] The act of crossing an international frontier distinguishes the practice of expulsion and, by extension, deportation, from similar actions associated with forced relocation, forced resettlement, and other forms of internal displacement. Where expulsion/deportation is provided for under international agreement and is subject to, orderly and humane, criteria, as was accepted practice during the interwar period and the immediate aftermath of the Second World War, it is often referred to as population transfer or population exchange. Broadly speaking, international standards relevant to expulsion may be found both in international criminal law and human rights law. Since the latter half of the nineteenth century it has been generally recognized that there are acts or omissions for which international law imposes criminal responsibility on individuals and for which punishment may be imposed either by properly empowered international tribunals, or by national courts and military tribunals.[40]

Article 5(1) of the Rome Statute of the International Criminal Court defines such criminal acts to include: war crimes (violations of humanitarian law); crimes against humanity; the crime of genocide; and the crime of aggression. The Nuremberg Tribunal ruled that '[mass] deportations were contrary to the international conventions . . . [and] the laws and customs of war'.[41] Several of the accused at Nuremberg were found guilty of having committed the crime of mass deportation. The prohibition of mass deportations in warfare was further strengthened and clarified in Article 49 of the Geneva Convention IV Relative to the Protection of Civilian Persons in Time of War (1949) and its Additional Protocols I and II (1977). Article 49 of the Geneva Convention, concerning the protection of civilians in enemy territory, states that 'individual or mass forcible transfers, as well as deportations of protected persons from occupied territory . . . are prohibited, regardless of their motive'. Exceptions are permissible only if the 'security of the population or imperative military reasons so demand'.

[38] J. M. Henckaerts, *Mass Expulsion in Modern International Law and Practice* (Nijhoff, The Hague, 1995), 4.

[39] K. Doehring, 'Aliens, Expulsion and Deportation', 1 *European Journal of International Law* 109 (1992) cited in Henckaerts, above, n. 38, p. 5.

[40] I. Brownlie, *Principles of Public International* Law (Oxford University Press, Oxford, 1998), 565.

[41] A. de Zayas, 'International Law and Mass Population Transfers', *Harvard International Law Journal*, 207 (1975), 215.

Even then, persons must be returned home as soon as hostilities in the area have ended. From this Article, Theodor Meron concludes that 'although it was less clear that individual deportation was already prohibited in 1949, I believe that this prohibition has by now come to reflect customary law'.[42]

Mass expulsion/deportations are also prohibited within the meaning of 'crimes against humanity'. These differ from war crimes as crimes against humanity may be committed in peace as well as in war, and against a state's own citizens (as for instance when the majority ethnic group in a state targets its minority citizens). Moreover, the fact that a particular action was sanctioned in domestic law prevailing at the time it was committed, or was authorized in military orders, is not a defence where crimes against humanity are concerned. This concept, then, extends protection against mass expulsion to domestic, peacetime circumstances, such as those pertaining in Germany during the 1930s, or in Bulgaria during the 1980s, removing the legitimacy of domestic laws sanctioning it. Article 6 of the London Charter of the International Military Tribunal (IMT Charter), adopted to assist in the prosecution of Nazi war criminals, defined 'crimes against humanity' as 'murder, extermination, enslavement, deportation and other inhuman acts committed against any civilian population before or during the war'. Ultimately, the UN General Assembly and the Convention on the Non-applicability of Statutory Limitation to War Crimes and Crimes against Humanity (1968) affirmed the principles of international law recognized in the IMT Charter and the judgment of the Nuremberg Tribunal, further confirming 'crimes against humanity' and the inclusion of mass expulsion/deportation under this rubric as customary law. Most recently, Article 7 of the Rome Statute of the International Criminal Court has specified that 'crimes against humanity' include 'deportation or forcible transfer of population' which refers to 'forced displacement of the persons concerned by expulsion or other coercive acts from the area in which they are lawfully present, without grounds permitted under international law'.

There are a number of international human rights texts that also provide indirect protection against expulsion/deportation. It has been suggested, for example, that indirect protection may arise from provisions concerning *inter alia* the right to self-determination, protection against genocide and discrimination, freedom of movement, freedom of assembly, freedom of expression, cultural identity, and protection against forced labour. All of these provisions pertain to acts within categories of practice that are associated with direct or

[42] T. Meron, *Human Rights and Humanitarian Norms as Customary Law* (Oxford University Press, New York, 1989), 48–9.

indirect expulsion/deportation. Such provisions may be found in a number of international texts including: the UN Charter (1945); the Universal Declaration of Human Rights (1948); the Convention on the Prevention and Punishment of the Crime of Genocide (1948); the International Convention on the Elimination of All Forms of Racial Discrimination (1966); the International Covenant on Civil and Political Rights (1966); the International Covenant on Economic, Social, and Cultural Rights (1966); and the Declaration on the Rights of Persons Belonging to National or Ethnic, Religious, or Linguistic Minorities (1992). The explicit prohibition of expulsion/deportation has occurred far less frequently, however. Indeed, such provisions are noticeably absent from both the Universal Declaration on Human Rights (1948) and the European Convention on Human Rights (1950). Presumably this absence took place in the context of immediate post-war population transfer, most notably the expulsion of approximately fourteen million ethnic Germans from east of the Oder–Neisse as provided for in the Potsdam Protocol of 1945.[43]

An express prohibition against expulsions was included in the Fourth Protocol to the European Convention for the Protection of Human Rights (1963). Significantly, the Explanatory Report indicates that the Committee of Experts responsible for drafting the protocol '[t]hought it desirable to insert . . . a provision by which collective expulsions . . . of the kind which have already taken place [presumably a reference to the transfer of ethnic Germans] would be formally prohibited'.[44] On this basis, Protocol Four represents a deliberate rejection of prior European policies of mass expulsion and population transfer.[45] Article 3 of the Protocol states: '[n]o one shall be expelled by means either of an individual or of a collective measure from the territory of a state in which he is a national.' Article 4 goes on to prohibit 'collective expulsion of aliens'. The European Court of Human Rights has interpreted the prohibition of expulsion under Articles 3 and 4 as a procedural criterion such that a legitimate expulsion must be decided on the basis of an 'objective and reasonable' (that is to say, a real rather than a merely formal) case-by-case review.[46] Thus, mass expulsions are prima facie illegal under the

[43] A. Bell-Fialkoff, 'A Brief History of Ethnic Cleansing', *Foreign Affairs*, 72/1 (1993), 115.

[44] Explanatory Reports on the Second to Fifth Protocols to the European Convention for the Protection of Human Rights and Fundamental Freedoms, Council of Europe, Doc. H (71) 11 (1971), 50.

[45] For a discussion of European practices with respect to population transfer and mass expulsion, see J. Jackson-Preece, 'Ethnic Cleansing as an Instrument of Nation-State Creation: Changing State Practices and Evolving Legal Norms', *Human Rights Quarterly*, 20/4 (1998), 817–42.

[46] Above, n. 38, pp. 12–13. See also *Becker* v. *Denmark, Year Book of the European Convention on Human Rights* (1976), 416.

ECHR until a state can demonstrate due process for each and every case.[47] This interpretation was confirmed and codified in Article 1 of Protocol 7 to the ECHR (1984), which states that 'an alien lawfully resident in the territory of a State' shall not be expelled 'except in pursuance of decisions reached in accordance with the law', and shall be allowed: (1) 'to submit reasons against his expulsion'; (2) 'to have his case reviewed'; and (3) 'to be represented for these purposes before the competent authority'. The fulfilment of these rights is limited by Article 15, which allows for derogation in 'time of war or other public emergency threatening the life of the nation' and such restrictions are reiterated in Article 2 Protocol 7. It remains to be seen, therefore, how effective a protection these provisions would provide against expulsion/deportation in circumstances of war or civil unrest, which are precisely the situations when expulsion is most likely to occur, as recent events in former Yugoslavia demonstrate.

Article 13 ICCPR, adopted three years after the Fourth Protocol to the ECHR in 1966, also restricts the legal expulsion (in this case) of aliens. Expulsion of an individual is permitted only:

> in pursuance of a decision reached in accordance with law and shall, except where compelling reasons of national security otherwise require, be allowed to submit the reasons against his expulsion and to have his case reviewed by and be represented for the purpose before, the competent authority or a person or persons especially designated by the competent authority.

Once again, the key distinction between a legal act of expulsion and a prohibited expulsion is based upon the procedural requirement of fair and objective individual review.

Similar provisions are contained in the ACHR. Article 22(5) guarantees that 'no one can be expelled from the territory of the state of which he is a national', while Article 22(9) prohibits the 'collective expulsion of aliens'. Here, the distinction between legal and prohibited expulsion is largely predicated upon the right to individual review as per the findings of the Inter-American Commission on Human Rights with respect to decree 233 of 13 June 1991, in which President Balaguer of the Dominican Republic authorized the expulsion of large numbers of Haitians.[48] According to the Commission, the provisions

[47] J. M. Henckaerts, *Mass Expulsion in Modern International Law and Practice* (Nijhoff, The Hague, 1995), 14. See also G. Goodwin-Gill, 'Mass Expulsion: The Legal Aspects', Working Group of Experts on the Problem of Mass Expulsion, Institute of Humanitarian Law, San Remo, Italy, October 1984.

[48] Above, n. 38, p. 15. See also Annual Report 1991, Inter-American Commission on Human Rights, OEA/Ser.L/V/II.81 Rev. 1, Doc. 6, 14 February 1992, pp. 258–9.

of Article 22, in conjunction with Article 8 on the right to a fair trial, obliged the Dominican government to 'consider the individual situation of persons accused of violating the Immigration Law and to grant them the right to present their defence in the framework of a formal hearing'.[49]

Article 12 of the Banjul Charter is worded somewhat differently, and with seemingly greater emphasis on the predicament of minorities. Article 12(2) guarantees the right of every individual to leave and return to his own country subject only to such restrictions as provided for by law. Article 12(4), on the other hand, ensures that non-nationals legally admitted to a state may only be expelled by virtue of a decision taken in accordance with the law; the emphasis here is on due process as the determinant of legitimate expulsion. Uniquely, Article 12(5), which prohibits the mass expulsion of non-nationals, defines expulsion in this context to be 'that which is aimed at national, racial, ethnic or religious groups'. As a result, the Banjul Charter is immediately concerned with problems of discrimination more likely to be encountered by minorities than either the ECHR or the ACHR, both of which are more generally oriented towards arbitrariness *per se*. It has been suggested that this difference is one of emphasis rather than quality since: '[t]he absence of an individual assessment necessarily entailed an element of discrimination based on nationality, race, ethnicity or religion.'[50] Nevertheless, this difference may form part of the rationale behind the inclusion of Article 16 in the Framework Convention since the more general requirements of the ECHR are not specifically concerned with minority predicaments, in contrast to the Banjul Charter, for instance.

The provisions of Article 16 thus have the effect of making any expulsion directed at members of national minorities prima facie illegal. In such circumstances, the onus would likely rest upon the state to demonstrate that the aim of its expulsion/deportation order was not contrary to the provisions of the Framework Convention. This condition would apply in addition to the usual procedural rule of objective and reasonable case-by-case review as per ECHR requirements. As of July 2004, no concerns with respect to expulsion/deportation have arisen under the FCNM monitoring process.

4. Redrawing Administrative Boundaries (Gerrymandering)

Gerrymandering is the practice of arranging electoral or administrative boundaries so that one political party or ethnic group has more power than another

[49] Annual Report 1991, Inter-American Commission on Human Rights, OEA/Ser.L/V/II.81 Rev. 1, Doc. 6, 14 February 1992, p. 277.

[50] Above, n. 38, p. 19.

or others by diluting the other's voting strength.[51] Explicit prohibitions against gerrymandering *per se*, or indeed its particular relevance to minorities, are not usually incorporated into any human rights texts. However, guarantees in favour of participation, and in particular the participation of members of minorities, do feature in several key standard-setting documents and should, in principle, provide some degree of protection against such measures.

Article 21 of the Universal Declaration of Human Rights recognizes the individual's right to take part in government and have equal access to public services. It further stipulates that the will of the people should be the basis of government, and that this should be expressed in periodic and genuine elections with free voting procedures. Similarly, Article 25 ICCPR guarantees every citizen the right and the opportunity, without any distinction arising from race, colour, sex, language, religion, political or other opinion, national or social origin, property, birth or status—as per Article 2 requirements—to take part in the conduct of public affairs, to vote and be elected in genuine periodic elections, and to have access to public services in his or her country. The practice of gerrymandering, in as much as it is intended to create inequalities between citizens with respect to their participation in public affairs would appear to be a violation of these provisions.

More specifically, the European Charter of Local Self-Government recognizes the 'right and the ability of local authorities, within the limits of the law, to regulate and manage a substantial share of public affairs under their own responsibility and in the interests of the local population' [Article 1]. Furthermore, Article 5 stipulates that '[c]hanges in local authority boundaries shall not be made without prior consultation of the local communities concerned, possibly by means of a referendum where this is permitted by statute'. Since gerrymandering is unlikely to be welcomed by the population it is directed against, this provision would seem to provide an indirect attempt to preclude such measures. In addition, a number of existing provisions and recommendations specific to persons belonging to minorities provide protection against gerrymandering. Article 2 of the 1992 UN General Assembly Declaration on the Rights of Persons Belonging to National or Ethnic, Religious and Linguistic Minorities recognizes the right of minorities to participate effectively in cultural, religious, social, economic, and public life. In a similar vein, the OSCE High Commissioner on National Minorities states, in the Lund Recommendation on the Effective Participation of National

[51] Gerrymandering definition in **www.legal-definition.com/G/gerrymandering.htm** 17 August 2004.

Minorities in Public Life, that the electoral system should facilitate minority representation and influence (Article 9), and that geographic boundaries of electoral districts should facilitate the equitable representation of national minorities (Article 10). Finally, Article 15 of the Framework Convention stipulates that 'Parties shall create the conditions necessary for the effective participation of persons belonging to national minorities in cultural, social and economic life and in public affairs, in particular those affecting them.' Since gerrymandering alters the proportion of the population as defined by administrative boundaries with a view to limiting the effectiveness of minority participation in public affairs, it is clearly excluded by the requirements of Article 15. Consequently, the provisions of Article 16 reinforce the right to effective participation outlined in Article 15, as this applies to the creation or alteration of administrative boundaries.

A number of state reports discuss domestic practices with respect to electoral and/or administrative redistricting, these include: Denmark, Croatia, Estonia, Slovenia, Slovakia, Hungary, Switzerland, and the United Kingdom. In discussing redistricting, states tend to emphasize provisions for public consultation and accountability. Thus, for example, the report submitted by Estonia in 1999 notes that the Territory of Estonia Administrative Division Act requires consultation with the residents of the rural municipality or city to be affected by any such measures.[52] Statements like this would appear to suggest that states are cognizant of the potential implications for compliance in this area, regarding both their undertakings under Articles 15 and 16 of the Framework Convention and, where applicable, the European Charter for Regional or Local Self-Government.

Nevertheless, the only Advisory Opinion that makes reference to redistricting practices is the 2002 report on Moldova. The Administrative-Territorial Organization Act of 12 November 1998 had caused concern amongst the mostly ethnic Bulgarian population of the district of Taraclia who believed their identity was threatened by a proposed incorporation into a larger geographical unit.[53] In December 2001, the Moldovan government further revised the administrative-territorial system, largely restoring the geographical divisions that existed prior to the controversial 1998 Act.[54] In their opinion, the Advisory Committee found it necessary to remind the Moldovan authorities of the

> need to consult with those concerned by the administrative-territorial changes adopted, in order to ensure that these measures do not infringe the rights and freedoms enshrined in the Framework Convention, including with respect to participation in

[52] Estonia State Report, ACFC/SR (99) 16, 1999.

[53] Advisory Committee Opinion on Moldova, adopted on 1 March 2002, ACFC/INF/OP/I (2002), para. 94.

[54] Above, n. 53, para. 95.

the decision-making process. Such an obligation is included in Article 9 of the [Moldovan] National Minorities Act.[55]

The official response from Moldova disputed these findings of the Advisory Committee, but not the general expectations on minority participation in the redistricting process. Accordingly, Moldova claimed that the new Act of 2001 had been formulated with a view to promoting the identity of persons belonging to national minorities and that communities likely to be affected by the proposed changes had been consulted.[56]

C. Limitations and Restrictions

The provisions of Article 16 are deliberately limited to state actions aiming to restrict the rights and freedoms flowing from the Framework Convention. This wording confines the scope of protection afforded by Article 16 in two key respects: (1) it does not apply to non-state actors; and (2) policies which limit the rights and freedoms of minorities, but do not intend such purposes, are permissible.

1. State versus Non-state Actors

The role of the state with respect to non-state actors was the subject of some disagreement during the drafting of Article 16. Thus, for example, one expert claimed that Article 16 provisions probably did not cover ethnic cleansing since that practice is often carried out by groups within the state rather than by the state itself.[57] This raises the broader question of tacit versus explicit state involvement in measures that alter the composition of a population in areas inhabited by persons belonging to minorities.

Here it is perhaps useful to recall the jurisprudence of the European Court of Human Rights with respect to its interpretation of mass expulsion. In *Becker* v. *Denmark*[58] mass expulsion was defined as 'any measure of the competent authority'. The Council of Europe's Explanatory Report to Protocol 7 contains an identical definition.[59] Acts by non-state actors were thus excluded from this definition in the same way that they were excluded from the wording of Article 16 of the Framework Convention.

55 Advisory Committee Opinion on Moldova, adopted on 1 March 2002, ACFC/INF/OP/I (2002), para. 96.

56 Comment by Moldova on the Advisory Committee Opinion adopted on 1 March 2002.

57 CAHMIN Meeting Report (94) 9, 1994, para. 19.

58 *Becker* v. *Denmark, Year Book of the European Convention on Human Rights* (1976), 416.

59 Explanatory Report on Protocol No. 7 to the Convention for the Protection of Human Rights and Fundamental Freedoms, Council of Europe (1985), para. 10, ETS no. 117, **http://conventions.coe.int/Treaty/en/Reports/HTML/117.htm** 17 August 2004.

However, it has been suggested by Jean Marie Henckaerts and others that: '[s]ituations in which the government tolerates or even abets . . . indirect measures by private persons or groups would also impose a liability on a government for not having prevented a mass expulsion'.[60] A similar reasoning could be applied to Article 16: any state that did not actively try to prevent or, having failed to do so, to prosecute private perpetrators of ethnic cleansing, and by extension other actions intended to alter the proportions of the population in areas inhabited by national minorities, would be in violation of the Framework Convention. At present, however, it remains to be seen whether or not the Advisory Committee will adopt this more expansive interpretation in their compliance decisions.

2. *Aims versus Effects*

The distinction between those measures aimed at restricting the rights and freedoms of minorities and those that do restrict them was also controversial during the drafting process. A significant minority of CAHMIN members felt that unintentional or implicit effects should also be included within the scope of protection afforded by the proposed article on demographic changes inimical to national minorities.[61] The prevailing view, however, was that measures effectively restricting rights and freedoms could sometimes be justified and, therefore, legitimate.[62] This view is explicitly endorsed in the CAHMIN Explanatory Report accompanying the final draft of the Framework Convention.[63] In this report, the resettlement of a village to build a dam is cited as an example of a measure whose aim is not contrary to the principles of the Framework Convention, and thus permissible, even though the effect of such action might be inimical to minority demographics.[64] Consequently, the Advisory Committee's position on the dissolution of Horno Gemeinde and, as a corollary, the resettlement of the German-Sorbian population, suggests a similar rationale.[65] Nevertheless, this limitation is likely to remain controversial in the monitoring process since it is often difficult to distinguish between deliberate and unintended consequences. Accordingly, the potential for state misuse of the distinction between aims and effects persists and will require careful observation by the Advisory Committee and Council of Ministers.

[60] Above, n. 38, p. 109.

[61] CAHMIN Meeting Report (94) 9, 1994, para. 18.

[62] Above, n. 61.

[63] CAHMIN Explanatory Report on the Framework Convention for the Protection of National Minorities (1995), para. 82.

[64] Above, n. 63.

[65] Advisory Committee Opinion on Germany, ACFC/INF/OP/I (2002) 008, 2002, para. 96.

III. Conclusions and Outlook

Article 16 is a direct response to problems of ethnic cleansing and other actions designed to alter existing demographics in ways inimical to the legitimate rights and interests of national minorities. As such, this article represents an important development in minority rights standards since it is the first general prohibition of measures intended to alter the proportion of the population in areas inhabited by national minorities to be incorporated into a multilateral convention of this kind.[66] Established practices complying with Article 16 remain scarce, largely owing to the fact that the most recent examples of these actions predated the Framework Convention's coming into effect.[67] Therefore, on the basis of information currently at its disposal, the Advisory Committee has found in the vast majority of cases that the implementation of Article 16 does not call for any specific observations. Nevertheless, state reports with respect to Article 16 obligations would suggest that the following criteria are widely recognized as essential for compliance: state policies of demographic change (1) must not discriminate against, nor deliberately target members of national minorities; (2) legal and administrative procedures relating to such policies must guarantee equality of treatment and the right of individual review; and (3) members of minorities or their representatives must be able to participate in the decision-making process with respect to such policies.

66 Both ILO Convention No. 169 Concerning Indigenous Peoples and Tribal Populations in Independent Countries (1991) and the Helsinki Document (1992) prohibit forcible resettlement but stop short of including a general prohibition against all measures intended to alter existing demographics.

67 Ethnic cleansing in Croatia and Bosnia during 1992–5 and electoral and administrative redistricting in Slovakia during 1995–6 predated the entry into force of the Framework Convention in 1998, while ethnic cleansing in Kosovo between March and June 1999 occurred prior to Serbia and Montenegro's ratification of the Framework Convention in 2002.

ARTICLE 17

Jennifer Jackson-Preece

1. The Parties undertake not to interfere with the right of persons belonging to national minorities to establish and maintain free and peaceful contacts across frontiers with persons lawfully staying in other States, in particular those with whom they share an ethnic, cultural, linguistic or religious identity, or a common cultural heritage.
2. The Parties undertake not to interfere with the right of persons belonging to national minorities to participate in the activities of non-governmental organisations, both at the national and international levels.

Article 17(1)

I. Background

A. Issues

Article 17(1) of the Framework Convention for the Protection of National Minorities (FCNM) addresses those circumstances wherein members of the same ethnic, cultural, religious, linguistic, or cultural group are divided by existing international frontiers. Such an ethnic group may constitute a minority in more than one state. Such groups are also sometimes referred to as 'dispersed minorities',[1] as in the case of the Basques who exist as minorities in both Spain and France, or indeed the Roma who exist as minorities in several European states. Alternatively, the same ethnic group may form a minority in one state and a majority in another, usually neighbouring, state. They are sometimes referred to as 'kin minorities' because they possess a kin state where their ethnic group comprises the majority. The ethnic Hungarian minority in Slovakia and Romania inhabiting areas adjacent to the border with Hungary fall under this category. Transfrontier minorities are the consequence of prior historical developments involving the creation or consolidation of states. In general, the minorities in question have remained within their historic homelands, but over the course of time political boundaries have moved around them through war, conquest, purchase, or succession, such that the minority in question has either failed to achieve its own independent nation-state, as for example the Basques, or has been cut off from their kin state, as in the case of the Hungarian minority in Slovakia and Romania. The term transfrontier minorities could also represent scattered populations that are at odds with the territorially defined character of the modern nation-state.

Article 17(1) seeks to ameliorate those deleterious consequences arising from such political divisions by facilitating free and peaceful transfrontier contacts on the part of minorities particularly, although not exclusively, with those persons with whom they share an ethnic, cultural, linguistic, or religious identity, or a common cultural heritage. It should, however, be stressed that in this process Article 17(1) takes existing international frontiers as a given. Its application is not, therefore, intended to support the secessionist or irredentist claims of either transfrontier minorities or kin minorities.

[1] Committee of Experts on Issues Relating to the Protection of National Minorities (DH-MIN), Final Activity Report on 'Dispersed Ethnic Minorities' (DH-MIN) (99) 7 Rev. 3, 1999.

B. History

The provisions of this article are largely based on Paragraph 32(4) of the Copenhagen Document of the Conference on Security and Co-operation in Europe (CSCE), which guarantees minorities the right to, 'establish and maintain unimpeded contacts among themselves within their country as well as contacts across frontiers with citizens of other States with whom they share a common ethnic or national origin, cultural heritage or religious beliefs'.[2] During the early 1990s, a number of Council of Europe bodies including the European Commission for Democracy through Law, the Steering Committee on Human Rights (CDDH), and the Ad Hoc Committee for the Protection of National Minorities (CAHMIN) were considering proposals along these lines. Accordingly, there was a general consensus on the importance of this right, and the desirability of including it in the Framework Convention.[3] Eventually, it was decided that the provision should be drafted along the lines of the CDDH text,[4] with one significant difference: it should not refer to the 'territorial integrity of the State'. Instead, CAHMIN took the view that such a limitation was already covered by draft Article A, which later became Article 21 of the Framework Convention.[5] Finally, CAHMIN made a clear distinction between the right to transfrontier contact and the issue of co-operation between states, since the former would be conferred upon individuals and the latter upon states parties to the Convention.[6]

C. Context

Article 17(1) seeks to preserve and promote minority identities by facilitating free and peaceful contacts across international frontiers, in particular on the part of those who share a common ethnic, cultural, linguistic, or religious

[2] Ad Hoc Committee for the Protection of National Minorities (CAHMIN), Explanatory Report on the Framework Convention for the Protection of National Minorities, H(1995) 010, 1995, para. 84. See also the Second Conference on the Human Dimension of the CSCE, Document of the Copenhagen Meeting of the Conference on the Human Dimension of the CSCE, Copenhagen, 1990, Art. 32, para. 4.

[3] CAHMIN, 3rd Meeting, CAHMIN (94) 13, Meeting Report, 1994, para. 38.

[4] Steering Committee for Human Rights (CDDH), Final Activity Report of the CDDH for the Attention of the Committee of Ministers, CDDH (93) 22, 1993. Art. 12 of this draft includes the following: 'a) States must not prevent persons belonging to a national minority from associating, establishing and maintaining free and unimpeded contacts, while duly respecting the territorial integrity of the State, with the citizens of another country with whom this minority shares ethnic, religious or linguistic features or a cultural identity; b) No restrictions shall be placed on the exercise of this right other than such as are prescribed by law and are necessary in a democratic society, taking into account notably the requirements of provisions relating to the crossing of borders.'

[5] Above, n. 3, para. 40. [6] Above, n. 3, para. 39.

identity, or a common cultural heritage. In so doing, Article 17(1) reinforces those provisions guaranteeing the right to identity (Article 5) and the right to freedom of assembly and association (Article 7). Such contacts are, however, constrained by the principles of sovereign equality, territorial integrity, and the political independence of states (Article 21), and cannot therefore be used in support of minority claims to secession or irredentism.

II. Analysis

A. A Duty not to Interfere

Article 17(1) creates a duty on states parties not to interfere with free and peaceful transfrontier contacts by persons belonging to minorities. Stated in this way, this provision is a *negative* requirement. In the first instance, therefore, the onus is on states to avoid or abjure from particular practices or policies detrimental to such interaction. In practice, however, this negative requirement translates into a *positive* obligation on the part of the state to ensure that relevant legal procedures, such as visa requirements, are fair and objective and do not create unreasonable or unnecessary impediments to transfrontier contacts.

B. The Right to Establish and Maintain Contacts across Frontiers

Contacts across frontiers may take one of two forms: free movement of persons; or the free communication of thoughts, ideas, opinions, cultural and artistic expression, and social and scientific knowledge.

1. Freedom of Movement across Frontiers

The right to freedom of movement within states is recognized in a number of international standard-setting documents including: Article 13 of the Universal Declaration on Human Rights (UDHR); Article 12 of the International Covenant on Civil and Political Rights (ICCPR); Article 2 of Protocol No. 4 of the European Convention for the Protection of Human Rights and Fundamental Freedoms (ECHR); Article 22 of the American Convention on Human Rights (ACHR); Article 12 of the African Charter on Human and People's Rights (Banjul Charter); and even Article 7 of the Framework Convention. It is universally accepted that such provisions include a right of mobility within the boundaries of the state for all those legally staying on its territory. Thus, Article 13

UDHR guarantees that 'everyone has the right to freedom of movement within the borders of each State'. Meanwhile, Article 12(1) ICCPR limits this right to those 'lawfully within the territory of the state', and adds a further restrictive qualification in Article 12(3), 'which are provided by law, are necessary to protect national security, public order (*ordre public*), public health or morals, or the rights and freedoms of others'. Similarly qualified interpretations of freedom of internal movement may be found in the ECHR, the ACHR, and the Banjul Charter.

Nonetheless, there is considerably less agreement on the extent to which such provisions may give rise to a right of transfrontier movement between states. Each of the provisions cited also includes the guarantee that everyone has the right to leave any country, including his own, and to return to his country. While the right of exit from a state is broadly defined however, the right of entry is limited to those citizens returning to the state in which they are nationals. Consequently, a state can legitimately impose a visa requirement for non-citizens (aliens) crossing its borders, and can deny them the right to enter its territory. By the same token, while visa requirements do not constitute a limitation on the freedom of movement *per se*, they can have significant practical and political consequences for persons seeking to maintain free and peaceful contacts across frontiers.

The European Agreement on Regulations Governing the Movement of Persons between Member States of the Council of Europe (1957) aims to facilitate transfrontier movement by providing for reciprocal visa-free tourist entry for nationals of participating states, subject to the presentation of valid travel documents, such as a passport. This type of entry applies to tourist visits of not more than three months' duration, and excludes both longer stays, and all entry for the purpose of gainful employment. Nevertheless, under the terms of the agreement each state signatory reserves the option, on grounds relating to *ordre public*, security or public health, to order the temporary suspension of these provisions (Article 7). Moreover, these undertakings in no way prejudice the laws and regulations governing visits by non-citizens (aliens) to the territory of state signatories (Article 3).

The free movement of persons between member states, including both residency and employment, is one of the fundamental rights guaranteed to European Union (EU) citizens. Article 2 of the Treaty on European Union (TEU) identifies one of the core objectives of the Union as the development of, 'an area of freedom, security and justice, in which the free movement of persons is assured in conjunction with appropriate measures with respect to external border controls, asylum, immigration and the preventing and combating of crime'.[7] Similarly, Article 18 of the Treaty Establishing the European Community (TEC) guarantees that, '[e]very citizen of the Union shall have the right to move and reside freely within the territory of the Member States, subject to the limitations and conditions laid down in this Treaty and by the measures adopted to give it effect'.[8]

The right to freedom of movement in the specific context of the European Union thus includes transnational movement. Nevertheless, this right is linked to citizenship status and does not extend to all persons within the territory of EU member states. Instead, Article 62 TEC gives the Council of Ministers of the European Union the power to determine 'the conditions under which nationals of third countries shall have the freedom to travel within the territory of Member States'.

Moreover, not all EU citizens are immediately eligible for full mobility rights. In the context of EU enlargement, the citizens of new member states qualify for full rights of movement, including residency and employment, only after an initial transitional period.[9] In both the 1981 Greek and the 1986 Spanish/Portuguese accessions, seven-year transitions were stipulated before citizens of the new member countries could work in other EU member states. Similarly, the 2004 East European enlargement arrangements have specified a transition of up to seven years before citizens of the former Communist states can acquire full mobility rights within the European Union, although curiously such restrictions do not apply to citizens of newly admitted Cyprus or Malta, presumably because of their small population size. During this seven-year period, it is up to the EU countries that were members prior to 2004 to decide when citizens from the new member states are permitted to enter their job markets. By 2011 at the latest, there will be complete freedom of movement including residence and employment for citizens of all new member states. The rationale for such transitional arrangements is to ensure that labour migration from one EU member state to another does not have a sudden and adverse impact on the economies of either. While there are no automatic restrictions on the mobility rights of citizens of the pre-2004 member states, the new members may choose to impose equivalent limitations on a quid pro quo basis.

While such qualifications may be justifiable on economic grounds, they remain highly controversial both inside and outside the European Union.

[7] Consolidated Version of the Treaty on European Union, *Official Journal of the European Communities*, C325/11, 2002.

[8] Above, n. 7, C325/45.

[9] Worker Mobility and Free Movement of Persons, **www.eurunion.org/legislat/agd2000/agd2000.htm** 20 July 2004.

Amongst pre-2004 EU member states this controversy centres upon the uncertainty surrounding the number of possible migrants from the newly admitted East European states and how such migration might impact upon social services and labour markets. Thus, for instance, Sir Andrew Green, Chairman of MigrationWatch UK, recently raised the spectre of a UK population increase of seven million by 2031 and queried where the new roads, rail, hospitals, schools, and houses would come from.[10] More specifically as regards persons belonging to minorities, there tends to be disproportionate concern regarding the likelihood and desirability of specific ethnic groups embarking upon westward migration in response to problems of economic or social exclusion in their countries of origin, the Roma being a classic case in point. As *The Economist* magazine noted in January 2004:

> Central Europe's Roma minorities—about 9% of the population in Slovakia, 5% in Hungary and 3% in the Czech Republic—are a particular cause for concern. The poorest Roma villages, especially in eastern Slovakia, are among the most desperate places in Europe, with no work and little schooling. A flow of Roma migrants claiming political asylum led Britain to reintroduce temporary visas for Slovaks a few years ago. Such barriers will be illegal after EU enlargement . . .[11]

However, such restrictions are permissible during the initial seven-year transition period commencing on 1 May 2004.

Meanwhile, the Council of Europe has voiced misgivings with respect to the citizens of those states that remain outside the enlarged European Union. A 2004 report by the Parliamentary Assembly thus noted a

> real risk of 'segregation' in Europe between the European Union member States . . . and the other countries of Central and Eastern Europe which are member states of the Council of Europe. The citizens of the latter, who will be denied the freedom of movement in the future EU member states [those East European states acceding to the European Union in 2004] which they enjoyed hitherto, are liable to feel like the 'oddments' of European integration. . . . In some cases, the consequence of closing these frontiers will be to reduce contacts between members of the same ethnic group living on either side.[12]

The provisions of Article 17(1) of the Framework Convention are intended to limit precisely this sort of deleterious effect upon minorities resulting from

[10] See, for example, A. Green, 'Blunkett has failed to wake up to the immigration nightmare', *Daily Telegraph*, London, 24 February 2004.

[11] 'Migration in the European Union: The Coming Hordes', *The Economist*, 15 January 2004.

[12] Council of Europe Parliamentary Assembly Report, Consequences of European Union Enlargement for Freedom of Movement between Council of Europe Member States, Doc. 10025, 2004.

the existence of borders and by extension also border controls, including visa requirements and other entry restrictions between states. The clear implication of Article 17(1) insofar as it applies to transnational movement, is that border controls should not place undue limitations upon the mobility of persons belonging to minorities. Accordingly, while Article 17(1) does not preclude entry restrictions such as visa requirements, these should in no way discriminate against persons belonging to minorities. For example, the Advisory Committee Opinion on Albania noted that:

> the Albanian authorities should continue to facilitate contacts across frontiers, including through efforts to ensure with its neighbours that visa requirements are implemented in a manner that does not cause undue restrictions on the right of persons belonging to national minorities to establish and maintain contacts across frontiers, and that these efforts should be ensured, not just for minorities with a kin-state, but for all persons belonging to national minorities, including the Roma.[13]

The emphasis here is not so much on Albania's right to enforce visa requirements *per se*, which is clearly recognized as legitimate, but on the particular effect such requirements have on persons belonging to minorities. Following this line of reasoning, the Roma should not be disproportionately affected by visa requirements as compared with members of other national or ethnic groups. A similar view of proportionality with respect to visa requirements is apparent in the AC Opinions on Estonia, Finland, Hungary, Romania, Slovakia, and Ukraine.[14]

Such an interpretation of Article 17(1) of the Framework Convention is consistent with the International Convention on the Elimination of All Forms of Racial Discrimination, guaranteeing equality 'without distinction as to race, colour, or national or ethnic origin' and 'equality before the law', notably in the enjoyment of specific rights including the 'right to leave any country, including one's own, and to return to one's country'. It is also in keeping with Article 2(5) of the UN Declaration on the Rights of Persons Belonging to National or Ethnic, Religious, and Linguistic Minorities, which states that, '[p]ersons belonging to minorities have the right to establish and maintain, without any

[13] Advisory Committee Opinion on Albania, ACFC/INF/OP/I (2003), 004, 2002, para. 113.

[14] Advisory Committee Opinion on Estonia, ACFC/INF/OP/I (2002), 005, 2001, para. 63; Advisory Committee Opinion on Finland, ACFC/INF/OP/I (2000) 002, 2000, para. 17; Advisory Committee Opinion on Hungary, ACFC/INF/OP/I (2001) 004, 2000, para. 56; Advisory Committee Opinion on Romania, ACFC/INF/OP/I (2001) 001, 2001, para. 73; Advisory Committee Opinion on Slovakia, ACFC/INF/OP/I (2000) 001, 2000, para. 50; Advisory Committee Opinion on Ukraine, ACFC/INF/OP/I (2002) 010, 2002, paras. 77–8.

discrimination, free and peaceful contacts with other members of their group and with persons belonging to other minorities, as well as contacts across frontiers with citizens of other States to whom they are related by national or ethnic, religious or linguistic ties.'

2. *Freedom of Communication across Frontiers*

Freedom of communication, more commonly referred to as the right to freedom of expression, is one of the core civil liberties and is incorporated within all of the main human rights standard-setting documents: Article 19 UDHR; Article 19 ICCPR; Article 10 ECHR; Article 13 ACHR; and Article 9 of the Banjul Charter. Significantly, the application of this right is not confined to communication within the boundaries of a state but extends to transfrontier communication. As Article 19(2) of the ICCPR points out, 'this right shall include freedom to seek, receive and impart information and ideas of all kinds, *regardless of frontiers* [emphasis added], either orally, in writing or in print, in the form of art, or through any other media of his choice'. Similar recognition of transfrontier communication may be found in the ECHR and the ACHR, although not in the Banjul Charter whose provisions for freedom of expression are comparatively limited.

The right to freedom of expression is plainly important for the preservation and development of language, culture, identity, religion, political opinion, and social and scientific knowledge not only for persons belonging to minorities, but for all individuals. Since at least the end of the seventeenth century, this freedom has been closely associated with the struggle for popular sovereignty and representative government, and it remains one of the core foundations of every free, open, and democratic society. However, that said, freedom of communication is not an absolute right and may be derogated from in certain circumstances as stipulated within the standard-setting documents. As Article 19(3) ICCPR outlines:

> The exercise of the rights provided for in . . . this article carries with it special duties and responsibilities. It may therefore be subject to certain restrictions, but these shall only be such as are provided by law and are necessary: 1) For respect of the rights or reputations of others; 2) for the protection of national security or of public order (*ordre public*), or of public health or morals.

Article 10(2) ECHR includes similar restrictions with additional conditions for territorial integrity, the prevention of disorder or crime, the protection of the reputation or the rights of others, for preventing the disclosure of information received in confidence, or for maintaining the authority and impartiality of the judiciary. Meanwhile, Article 13(5) ACHR prohibits communication intended as,

> . . . propaganda for war and any advocacy of national, racial, or religious hatred that constitute incitements to lawless violence or to any other similar action against any person or group of persons on any grounds including those of race, color, religion, language, or national origin shall be considered as offenses punishable by law.

Needless to say, there is extensive jurisprudence not only from the European Court of Human Rights (ECtHR) in Strasbourg, but also from the supreme or constitutional courts of many states relating to these restrictions and limitations on the freedom of expression. In all of these cases, a common standard of proportionality is apparent, such that limitations on the freedom of communication are only justifiable where they could lead to some clear and imminent public danger, be it in the interest of national security, or to compensate someone who has been unjustly defamed.[15] Accordingly, Chapter VII, Paragraph 1 of the CSCE Report on the Geneva Meeting of Experts on National Minorities points out, 'no one belonging to a national minority, simply by virtue of belonging to such a minority, will be subject to penal or administrative sanctions for having had contacts within or outside his/her own country'. Such a discriminatory restriction of the right to freedom of communication would be inconsistent with prevailing international standards.

The provisions of Article 17(1), insofar as they apply to freedom of communication, thus reinforce the general right to freedom of expression as defined in Article 7 of the Framework Convention by underscoring its transfrontier applicability. With this phrasing, Article 17(1) further underscores the application of rights to freedom of expression and association as already guaranteed in the ECHR, the ICCPR, and the constitutions of many states parties to the Convention regarding the particular circumstances of minorities. Persons belonging to minorities have a right to communicate freely both within and across international frontiers subject only to those reasonable limitations consistent with prevailing international standards. Thus, for example, the United Kingdom (UK) noted in its 1999 state report that during consultation on its self-reporting obligations concern was expressed by one organization

[15] As in the often cited example of the man who falsely shouted 'fire' in a theatre and caused a panic, and the corresponding judgment of US Supreme Court Justice Oliver Wendell Holmes in *Schenck* v. *United States*, US Supreme Court, 249 US 47, 1919. Cited in P. Sieghart, *The Lawful Rights of Mankind* (Oxford University Press, Oxford, 1986), 142–3.

that Article 17 of the Framework Convention might not be compatible with the Criminal Justice (Terrorism and Conspiracy) Act 1998.[16] In defence of its position, the UK government argued that the Act in question was compatible with prevailing standards under the ECtHR, which provide for derogations from the right to freedom of expression in the interest of national security. The conspiracy provisions of the Act were directed against those who organize terrorist and other crimes abroad, and did not therefore affect the general right to freedom of expression across frontiers. According to the UK, the conspiracy provisions of this Act were not designed for use against any specific groups in the UK. Evidently, the Advisory Committee found this justification of the UK position persuasive, as the government's implementation of Article 17(1) did not give rise to any specific observations from the Advisory Committee.[17] While to date (July 2004), the Advisory Committee has not found any state party to be in violation of its undertakings with respect to transfrontier communication arising under Article 17(1), prevailing expectations such as those noted above will no doubt provide the standard against which potential infractions or derogations can be assessed.

C. Limitations and Restrictions

1. Persons (not States)

Article 17(1) applies to contacts between *persons*, where '*persons* belonging to national minorities' have the right to maintain contacts with '*persons* lawfully staying in other States' [emphasis added]. The provisions of Article 17(1) thus exclude contact between persons belonging to national minorities and the governments of their kin states or indeed any other state for that matter. Such a limitation is in keeping with the view that international relations regarding minority questions are best dealt with through bilateral or multilateral arrangements between states, rather than unilateral extraterritorial actions on the part of any particular state. As preliminary discussion within the European Commission on Democracy through Law on the viability of a minority rights instrument highlighted, these provisions were 'not aimed at assuring the international relations of minorities'.[18] According to one member of the Commission, to act otherwise was 'liable to prove irrelevant

[16] United Kingdom State Report, ACFC/SR (99) 13, 1999, Notes.

[17] Advisory Committee Opinion on the United Kingdom, ACFC/INF/OP/I (2001) 006, 2001, para. 102.

[18] European Commission for Democracy through Law (ECDL), Draft Report of the 4th Meeting, CD-PV (90), 1990, para. 118.

and perhaps even dangerous', and it was 'highly unlikely that governments would accept it'.[19]

2. *Lawful versus Unlawful Staying in a State*

Similarly, it is only contact between persons '*lawfully* staying in . . . States' [emphasis added] which is protected by Article 17(1). Those persons *unlawfully* staying in a state in contravention of that state's usual immigration procedures are not accorded rights under this provision. Such a limitation is consistent with the view that states have a legitimate power to enforce border controls and entry requirements, provided that these arrangements satisfy the usual international standards with respect to non-discrimination and due process.

3. *Free and Peaceful Contacts*

Finally, the scope of Article 17(1) is limited to 'free and peaceful contacts'. This wording is identical to that of Article 2(5) of the Universal Declaration on the Rights of Persons Belonging to National, Ethnic, Religious and Linguistic Minorities.[20] According to Asbjørn Eide, Chairperson of the Working Group on Minorities of the Sub-Commission on the Promotion and Protection of Human Rights, this limitation has two aspects, 'it must not involve the use of violent means or preparation of the use of such means; secondly, the aims must be in conformity with the Declaration and generally with the purposes and principles of the Charter of the United Nations, as set out also in Article 8(4) of the Declaration.'[21]

A similar interpretation is warranted with respect to Article 17(1) of the Framework Convention. The stipulation in favour of 'free and peaceful contacts' should thus be read as a restriction clause which reinforces the provisions of Article 21 that, '[n]othing in the present framework Convention shall be interpreted as implying any right to engage in any activity or perform any act contrary to the fundamental principles of international law and in particular

[19] European Commission for Democracy through Law (ECDL), Draft Report of the 4th Meeting, CD-PV (90), 1990, para. 118.

[20] Art. 2(5) of the Universal Declaration on the Rights of Persons Belonging to Minorities reads: 'Persons belonging to minorities have the right to establish and maintain, without any discrimination, free and peaceful contacts with other members of their group and with persons belonging to other minorities, as well as contacts across frontiers with citizens of other States to whom they are related by national or ethnic, religious or linguistic ties.' Universal Declaration on the Rights of Persons Belonging to Minorities, UNGA Res. 47/135 (18 December 1992), annex, GAOR Supp. 49 at 210, UN Doc. A/47/49 (1993).

[21] A. Eide, Final Text of the Commentary to the Declaration on the Rights of Persons Belonging to National or Ethnic, Religious and Linguistic Minorities, Un Doc. E/CN.4/Sub.2/Ac.5/2001/2, 2001, para. 52.

of the sovereign equality, territorial integrity and political independence of States.'[22]

III. Conclusion and Outlook

Article 17(1) addresses the circumstances of those ethnic, cultural, religious, or linguistic groups who exist in the territory of more than one state. In so doing, it builds upon prior efforts within the Organization for Security and Co-operation in Europe (OSCE) and the United Nations to protect dispersed and kin minorities. The ability to maintain regular contact with their co-ethnics across state jurisdictions is an essential element of efforts designed to preserve and promote the distinct identity of such transfrontier minorities and the persons belonging to them. Consequently, international initiatives to provide for such minority contact constitute a noteworthy standard-setting innovation of the post-Cold War period.

The right to transfrontier contacts has two distinct components: it guarantees free movement of persons between states; and it provides for free communication of thoughts, ideas, opinions, cultural and artistic expression, and social and scientific knowledge across borders. This right operates within the confines of prevailing international standards with respect to existing boundaries and those domestic legal and administrative arrangements designed to enforce border controls and entry requirements. Such arrangements are therefore legitimate under the terms of Article 17(1), provided they allow for due process and do not discriminate on the basis of race, colour, religion, or national or ethnic origin. Similar constraints also apply to communications across frontiers. These may be curtailed in the interests of territorial integrity, the prevention of disorder or crime, the protection of the reputation or the rights of others, the non-disclosure of information received in confidence, or for the maintenance of judicial authority and impartiality.[23]

In addition to these general limitations arising from prevailing international practice regarding freedom of movement and freedom of expression, Article 17(1) contains three additional restrictions: it applies to persons and not states; it only applies to those persons 'lawfully residing' on the territory of a state; and its scope is limited to 'free and peaceful contacts' thus excluding actions contrary to the provisions of Article 21.

22 The drafting report refers to this provision explicitly as a 'restriction clause' along these lines. See above, n. 3, para. 40.

23 ECHR restrictions regarding the right to freedom of expression must be adhered to in the case of judicial authority and impartiality, but only where these restrictions are proportionate and non-discriminatory.

Article 17(2)

I. Background

A. Issues

Article 17(2) aims to protect the communal life of persons belonging to national minorities by guaranteeing their right to participate in the activities of non-governmental organizations (NGOs). These organizations are widely recognized as vital both for the preservation and promotion of minority identities, and the general development of civil society and democratic values within states. Paradoxically, it is precisely in those circumstances where the institutions of civil society and democratic government are comparatively weak, and where minorities tend to be most vulnerable, that NGOs are likely to be both of the greatest assistance and the most likely to encounter public hostility. This hostility can take different forms. It may involve direct attacks by state or non-state actors upon individuals who belong to NGOs, or the operational premises of these organizations. Alternatively, the government concerned may introduce legislation or administrative requirements designed to limit or prevent the activities of NGOs. In either case, the ability of persons belonging to minorities to form their own associations and institutions, or to engage constructively with internationally based NGOs, may be compromised. Article 17(2) is intended to protect against such infringements of the freedom to associate.

B. History

Article 17(2) is the result of a proposal from the Portuguese delegation to the CAHMIN.[24] Its provisions are largely based upon paragraph 32(6) of the Copenhagen Document of the CSCE, which guarantees the right of minorities to 'establish and maintain organizations or associations within their country and to participate in international non-governmental organizations'.

C. Context

Article 17(2) reinforces those provisions guaranteeing the right to freedom of assembly and association (Article 7) and the right to effective participation in cultural, social, and economic life, and in public affairs (Article 15). Moreover,

[24] Ad Hoc Committee for the Protection of National Minorities (CAHMIN), 4th Meeting, (CAHMIN) (94) 14 Rev., meeting report, 1994.

concerning the activities of minority NGOs, an international dimension is added to these rights so that the participation of persons belonging to national minorities in these bodies is not confined to the territory of the state, but may legitimately transcend state frontiers. This kind of provision is important for a number of reasons: it is a necessary component to ensure that transfrontier minorities are able to maintain contacts with their co-ethnics in other states; it facilitates NGO monitoring of state compliance with minority rights standards; and it encourages international dialogue and co-operation on minority issues.

II. Analysis

A. A Duty not to Interfere

Article 17(2) creates a duty for states parties not to interfere with the participation of persons belonging to minorities in the activities of NGOs, whether this is at the domestic or international level. In the first instance, and as it is phrased as a negative requirement, the onus is on states to avoid or abjure from particular practices or policies detrimental to such participation. In practice, however, this negative requirement may translate into a *positive* obligation on the part of the state to protect the participation of minorities in NGO activities from interference by non-state actors. The possibility of such positive obligations has been recognized by the ECtHR with respect to those provisions of the ECHR relating to freedom of assembly and association. Accordingly, it seems reasonable to assume that a similar interpretation may be given to Article 17(2).

B. The Right to Participate in the Activities of Non-governmental Organizations, both at the National and International Level

The minority right to participate in NGOs may be derived from the general right to freedom of association. Freedom of association is one of the core civil liberties, and as such features within all of the main human rights standard-setting documents: Article 20 UDHR; Article 22 ICCPR; Article 11 ECHR; Article 16 ACHR; Article 10 of the Banjul Charter; and Article 7 of the Framework Convention. Article 5 of the UN Declaration on the Right and Responsibility of Individuals, Groups and Organs of Society to Promote and Protect Universally Recognized Human Rights and Fundamental Freedoms has interpreted these general provisions for freedom of association to include the right to 'form, join and participate in non-governmental organizations, associations or groups' and 'to communicate with non-governmental or international organizations'.

In the first instance, the right to freedom of association as defined in the leading human rights treaties cited above is an individual right.[25] What has been less clear, however, is whether or not organizations created by individuals exercising their right of association might also claim protection under these provisions. Early references under the Optional Protocol to the ICCPR, which provides for a right of individual review by the UN Human Rights Committee once all domestic remedies have been exhausted, were not supportive of such a wide interpretation.[26]

Nevertheless, recent judgments under the ECHR have now established that, once formed, organizations are themselves entitled to broad legal protections. In *United Communist Party of Turkey and Others* v. *Turkey* (1998), the ECtHR took the view that freedom of association not only concerned the right to form a political party but also guaranteed the right of such a party, once formed, to carry on its political activities freely. Accordingly, it ruled that Turkey could not dissolve a political party that had not engaged in illegal activities simply because the national authorities regarded it as undermining the constitutional structures of the state:

> [T]he Convention [the ECHR] is intended to guarantee rights that are not theoretical or illusory, but practical and effective . . . The right guaranteed by Article 11 would be largely theoretical and illusory if it were limited to the founding of an association, since the national authorities could immediately disband the association without having to comply with the Convention. It follows that the protection afforded by Article 11 lasts for an association's entire life and that dissolution of an association by a country's authorities must accordingly satisfy the requirements of paragraph 2 of that provision. . . . [27]

Freedom of association is not an absolute right and can be limited in certain circumstances. Article 22(2) ICCPR permits limitations, 'which are prescribed

[25] Trade unions are a notable exception. Under International Labour Organization Convention (ILO) No. 87 Concerning Freedom of Association and Protection of the Right to Organize, 1948, individuals have a right to form and join workers' and employers' organizations, and these organizations also have rights (such as the right not to be dissolved, to join federations and confederations of organizations including international organizations, etc.).

[26] See, for example, UN Human Rights Committee, *J.B. et al.* v. *Canada*, Comm. No. 118/1982, 1986, UN Doc. Supp. No. 40 (A/41/40) at 151. Nevertheless, the dissenting opinions of Rosalyn Higgins, Rajsoom Lallah, Andreah Mavrommatis, Torkel Opsahl, and S. Amos Wako argued that the right to freedom of association 'requires that some measure of concerted activities be allowed; otherwise it could not serve its purposes. To us, this is an inherent aspect of the right granted by article 22, paragraph 1.'

[27] *The United Communist Party of Turkey and Others* v. *Turkey* (19392/92) (1998) ECHR 1, 133/1996/752/951, Grand Chamber decision **www.icnl.org** 20 July 2004.

by law and which are necessary in a democratic society in the interests of national security or public safety, public order (*ordre public*), the protection of public health or morals or the protection of the rights and freedoms of others'. Similar restrictive clauses may be found in the ECHR, the ACHR, and the Banjul Charter.[28] The emerging case law under the ECHR has interpreted these restrictions so that limitations must be prescribed by law; they must be justified in accordance with the four aims outlined in the restrictive clause (in the interest of national security or public safety, for the prevention of disorder or crime, for the protection of health or morals, or the rights and freedoms of others); they must be necessary in a democratic society; and they must be proportionate in their response.[29] The onus is on the state to demonstrate that it has complied with these requirements to the satisfaction of the Court.

Freedom of association is a general right and therefore applies universally to all individuals regardless of whether or not they belong to a minority. However, because this universal freedom is considered particularly relevant for the protection of minorities, it is reiterated in the main minority rights standard-setting documents. Article 27 ICCPR augments the general right to freedom of association outlined in Article 22 with the further condition that '[i]n those States in which ethnic, religious or linguistic minorities exist, persons belonging to such minorities shall not be denied the right, in community with the other members of their group, to enjoy their own culture, to profess and practise their own religion, or to use their own language.' Similarly, Article 2(4) of the UN Declaration on the Rights of Persons Belonging to National or Ethnic, Religious and Linguistic Minorities specifically stipulates that, '[p]ersons belonging to minorities have the right to establish and maintain their own associations.' And, as has already been pointed out, Article 32(6) of the Copenhagen Document of the CSCE guarantees minorities the right to 'establish and maintain organizations or associations within their country and to participate in international non-governmental organizations'.

28 Thus, for example: Council of Europe (CoE), European Convention for the Protection of Human Rights and Fundamental Freedoms (ECHR), 1950, Art. 11(2) stipulates that 'No restrictions shall be placed on the exercise of these rights other than such as are prescribed by law and are necessary in a democratic society in the interests of national security or public safety, for the prevention of disorder or crime, for the protection of health or morals or for the protection of the rights and freedoms of others. This article shall not prevent the imposition of lawful restrictions on the exercise of these rights by members of the armed forces, of the police or of the administration of the State;' while Article 16(2) ACHR states that 'the exercise of this right shall be subject only to such restrictions established by law as may be necessary in a democratic society, in the interest of national security, public safety or public order, or to protect public health or morals or the rights and freedoms of others'.

29 See, among others, above, n. 27; *Sidiropoulos and Others* v. *Greece* (26695/95) (1998) EHRR 55, 57/1997/841/1047 and *Freedom and Democracy Party (ÖZDEP)* v. *Turkey* (23885/94) (1999) EHRR 139.

The right to participate in the activities of non-governmental organizations, as enumerated in Article 17(2), adheres in the first instance to persons, and not to the minority group of which they are a member, nor do they apply to any organization they might create or join. Such persons are free to establish any association as they see fit, including those related to their distinct ethnic, cultural, religious, or linguistic identity. However, following the logic enumerated by the ECtHR in *United Communist Party of Turkey and Others* v. *Turkey* (1998), and subsequently in *Freedom and Democracy Party (ÖZDEP)* v. *Turkey* (1999), which extended the same protection to a political party that had the express aim of recognizing the Kurdish minority in Turkey,[30] it seems reasonable to assume that NGOs themselves would receive the same broad legal protection under Article 17(2) of the Framework Convention.

The specific inclusion of an international dimension distinguishes the minority right to participate in NGO activities as per Article 17(2) of the Framework Convention and Article 32(6) of the Copenhagen Document, from both Article 27 ICCPR and Article 2(4) of the Universal Declaration on Minorities, as well as the universal right to freedom of association contained in Article 22 ICCPR, Article 11 ECHR, Article 16 ACHR, Article 10 of the Banjul Charter, and even Article 7 of the Framework Convention. Nonetheless, this extension of the general principle of freedom of association is consistent with recent interpretations of that right according to Article 5 of the UN Declaration on the Right and Responsibility of Individuals, Groups, and Organs of Society to Promote and Protect Universally Recognized Human Rights and Fundamental Freedoms. Such an international dimension is particularly important for transfrontier minorities who wish to maintain regular contact and communication with their ethnic kin in other states, reinforcing the provisions of Article 17(1) for free and peaceful contact across frontiers. This fact is explicitly recognized by the Advisory Committee in its 2001 Opinion on Cyprus. Here the Advisory Committee considers it important:

> that . . . the Turkish Cypriots and the Maronites can maintain free and frequent contacts with members of their community living in the north of Cyprus. It therefore welcomes the fact that freedom of movement has been facilitated in recent years and that reciprocal visits to religious sites continue. The Advisory Committee encourages the Cyprus authorities to continue this policy.[31]

[30] *Freedom and Democracy Party (ÖZDEP)* v. *Turkey* (23885/94) (1999) EHRR 139 **www.icnl.org** 20 July 2004.

[31] Advisory Committee Opinion on Cyprus, ACFC/INF/OP/I (2001), 004, 2001, para. 45.

This international dimension may also contribute to the monitoring of state compliance with minority rights undertakings, by facilitating the work of advocacy NGOs like Minority Rights Group and the European Roma Rights Centre. Similarly, international organizations of this kind are an important medium for encouraging international dialogue and co-operation on minority issues. Until July 2004, no concerns have arisen with respect to Article 17(2) under the Framework Convention monitoring mechanism.

C. Limitations and Restrictions

It is only to be expected that the right of persons belonging to minorities to participate in NGOs will be subject to the same limitations as the universal right to freedom of association, namely those necessary in a democratic society in the interests of national security or public safety, public order, the protection of public health or morals, or the protection of rights and freedoms of others. In the absence of any Advisory Committee opinions determining the legality of limitations to Article 17(2), it seems reasonable to assume that their criteria for making such determinations will follow those established under the ECHR. Presumably, signatory states will be expected to demonstrate that any limitations are prescribed by law; justified in accordance with prevailing international standards; necessary in a democratic society; and proportionate in their response. In addition, such limitations must not discriminate on the basis of race, colour, religion, or national or ethnic origin.[32] In other words, they must apply equally to persons belonging to the majority. Finally, the provisions of Article 17(2) are also subject to the specific restrictions set forth in Article 21 of the Framework Convention.[33]

How might these criteria apply to restrictions arising under the Framework Convention? The jurisprudence of the ECtHR suggests that limitations may be justified where an organization calls for 'the use of violence, an uprising or any other form of rejection of democratic principles'.[34] Moreover, the Court rejected the justification of an interference with the freedom of association on the grounds that the party in question made reference to the rights to self-determination of the 'national or religious minorities' without encouraging

[32] This requirement is contained in the International Convention on the Elimination of All Forms of Racial Discrimination, UNGA Res. 2106 (XX), 1965.

[33] Art. 21 FCNM stipulates that 'Nothing in the present framework Convention shall be interpreted as implying any right to engage in any activity or perform any act contrary to the fundamental principles of international law and in particular of the sovereign equality, territorial integrity and political independence of States.'

[34] Above, n. 30, para. 40.

minority secession in any way.[35] In the end, this conclusion should not be interpreted as a justification for interference in any peaceful activity favouring secession, it merely suggests that such action may be a relevant fact in the review of any restrictive measures taken by a state. In contrast, it is plain that a state may reasonably curtail the activities of any organization that advocates hatred or incites discrimination, hostility, or violence towards a minority.[36]

III. Conclusion and Outlook

Article 17(2) ensures that persons belonging to national minorities will be able to participate in NGO activities both within states and at the international level. In so doing, it builds upon prior efforts within the OSCE and the United Nations to protect the communal life of minorities and those organizations and associations that represent that communal life. While Article 17(2) is formulated as an individual right of persons belonging to national minorities, the effect of this guarantee is likely to confer additional protection on NGOs themselves, because their continued existence is necessary to make this right effective and not merely theoretical or illusory. Although limitations may be applied to the enjoyment of this right in accordance with the provisions set forth in Article 21 of the Framework Convention, and those restrictions attached to the general right to freedom of association under the ICCPR and the ECHR, it is assumed that the onus will be on states to demonstrate that any such limitation is necessary in a democratic society, prescribed by law, proportionate, and non-discriminatory.

[35] *Freedom and Democracy Party (ÖZDEP)* v. *Turkey* above, n. 30, para. 41.

[36] Committee of Experts on Issues Relating to the Protection of National Minorities (DH-MIN), The Participation of Minorities in the Decision-Making Process, (DH-MIN) (2001) 1, 2000, para. 47.

ARTICLE 18

Jennifer Jackson-Preece

1. The Parties shall endeavour to conclude, where necessary, bilateral and multilateral agreements with other States, in particular neighbouring States, in order to ensure the protection of persons belonging to the national minorities concerned.
2. Where relevant, the Parties shall take measures to encourage transfrontier co-operation.

Article 18(1)

I. Background

A. Issues

Article 18(1) of the Framework Convention for the Protection of National Minorities (FCNM), aims to promote interstate relations conducive to the protection of persons belonging to national minorities and, by extension, international peace and stability. Implicit within this provision is the recognition that relations between states may be complicated by the presence of minorities, particularly when the minority ethnic group in one state forms the majority of the population in a neighbouring one. Indeed, a prior attempt to recognize international minority rights during the interwar period failed precisely because minority questions degenerated into political struggles between kin minorities and kin states. The revisionist aims of the treaties of 1919 to set new international boundaries clashed with the objectives of treaty-bound states wishing to preserve the territorial status quo where it was to their advantage. This pitted Germany against Poland, Germany against Czechoslovakia, Poland against Lithuania, Hungary against Romania, Hungary against Czechoslovakia, Austria against Yugoslavia, Bulgaria against Greece, Greece against Turkey, and Greece against Albania.[1] Consequently, in the early post-First World War period, the problem of disgruntled kin minorities and interventionist kin states was blamed as a major causal factor in the outbreak of the Second World War, and was used to justify the forced transfer of kin minorities to their respective kin states.[2] Article 18(1) seeks to avoid this sort of conflict by encouraging dialogue and co-operation in the area of minority protection, especially between neighbouring states with transfrontier minorities.

B. History

From the outset, the Ad Hoc Committee for the Protection of National Minorities (CAHMIN), which was responsible for drafting what was to become the Framework Convention, sought to include a provision signalling the importance of international co-operation on minority issues along the lines of Article 14(*a*) of the European Charter for Regional or Minority Languages

[1] J. Jackson-Preece, *National Minorities and the European Nation-States System* (Clarendon Press, Oxford, 1998), 89–93.

[2] J. Jackson-Preece, 'Ethnic Cleansing as an Instrument of Nation-State Creation: Changing State Practices and Evolving Legal Norms', *Human Rights Quarterly*, 20/4 (1998), 822–32.

and Article 32 of International Labour Organization (ILO) Convention 169 Concerning Indigenous and Tribal Peoples in Independent Countries.[3] This type of provision follows from earlier political recommendations made by the Organization for Security and Co-operation in Europe (OSCE), which encouraged states to make:

special efforts . . . to resolve specific problems in a constructive manner and through dialogue by means of negotiations and consultations with a view to improving the situation of persons belonging to national minorities. They recognise that the promotion of dialogue between States, and between States and persons belonging to national minorities, will be most successful when there is a free flow of information and ideas between all parties. They encourage unilateral, bilateral and multilateral efforts by governments to explore avenues for enhancing the effectiveness of their implementation of CSCE commitments relating to national minorities.[4]

Initial drafts of the Framework Convention described the usefulness of such arrangements for 'settl[ing] questions concerning national minorities', whereas subsequent versions were reworded to emphasize the 'objective of the protection of persons belonging to national minorities'. Similarly, the original plan was to 'give substance to the provision' by including a 'non-exhaustive list of fields in which such co-operation would be particularly appropriate in the context of the protection of national minorities', but this was eventually dropped in favour of a simpler statement.[5]

[3] Ad Hoc Committee for the Protection of National Minorities (CAHMIN), 3rd meeting, CAHMIN (94), meeting report, 1994, p. 11. Article 14(*a*) of the European Charter for Regional or Minority Languages states that 'The Parties undertake a) to apply existing bilateral and multilateral agreements which bind them with the States in which the same language is used in identical or similar form, or if necessary to seek to conclude such agreements, in such a way as to foster contacts between the users of the same language in the States concerned in the fields of culture, education, information, vocational training and permanent education.' Similarly, Art. 32 of International Labour Organization (ILO) Convention 169 stipulates that 'Governments shall take appropriate measures, including by means of international agreements, to facilitate contacts and co-operation between indigenous and tribal peoples across borders, including activities in the economic, social, cultural, spiritual and environmental fields.' Convention Concerning Indigenous and Tribal Peoples in Independent Countries, ILO, Convention No. 169 (adopted 27 June 1989, entry into force 5 September 1991), 72 ILO Official Bull. 59, 1989.

[4] Conference for Security and Co-operation in Europe (CSCE), Meeting of Experts on National Minorities, Geneva, 1991, III, para. 2.

[5] Thus, for example, the CAHMIN draft of 10 May 1994 stated that, 'The Parties shall endeavour to conclude, where necessary, bilateral and multilateral agreements with other States in order to settle questions concerning national minorities, in particular in the fields of information, environmental protection, economy, infrastructure, youth exchanges, culture and education' (CAHMIN, Preliminary Draft Framework Convention for the Protection of National Minorities, CAHMIN (94) 12, 1994, p. 7). By 7 July 1994 this text had been reworded to read: 'The Parties shall endeavour to conclude, where necessary, bilateral and multilateral agreements with other States, in particular neighbouring

C. Context

Article 18(1) of the Framework Convention encourages states to conclude bilateral and multilateral agreements for the protection of national minorities where the circumstances warrant it. Such arrangements may go some way towards facilitating that sort of cross-border minority contact envisioned in Articles 17(1) and 17(2), and thus are particularly relevant with respect to neighbouring states, especially those with transfrontier minorities on their territory. At the same time, this sort of interstate co-operation may also benefit the governments concerned by encouraging dialogue and co-operation on matters of mutual concern. This is consistent with the provisions of both the first and second articles of the Framework Convention, concerning the protection of minorities as it falls within the scope of international relations, and regarding principles of good neighbourliness respectively.

II. Analysis

Article 18(1) is an aspirational clause. Unlike many of the other provisions of the Framework Convention, which prescribe definite guidelines for conduct to be taken or avoided, such as Article 16's provision that 'states shall refrain from measures which alter the proportion of the population in areas inhabited by persons belonging to national minorities', Article 18(1) sets a standard of conduct towards which states should strive. The provisions of Article 18(1) are, therefore, not obligatory but recommended; states are not obliged to enter into bilateral and multilateral agreements with their neighbours, but should 'endeavour to conclude' these 'where necessary'.

A. Bilateral and Multilateral Agreements

It is widely recognized that bilateral and multilateral agreements can play useful roles in the establishment and preservation of friendly relations between states.[6] Reciprocal arrangements of this kind can reassure kin states that their ethnic cousins elsewhere are well protected, while reassuring states administering to

States, in order to assure the protection of persons belonging to the national minorities concerned' (CAHMIN, 5th meeting, CAHMIN (94), meeting report, 1994, p. 30). The draft of 18 August 1994 changed 'assure' to 'ensure' in the English translation, and it is this version which ultimately became enshrined as Art. 18 in CAHMIN, 5th meeting, CAHMIN (94), meeting report, 1994, p. 2.

[6] A. Eide, Final Text of the Commentary to the Declaration on the Rights of Persons Belonging to National or Ethnic, Religious, and Linguistic Minorities, E/CN.4/Sub.2/AC.5/2001/2, 2001.

such kin minorities that these groups will not become a pretext for intervention in their sovereign affairs. Consequently, bilateral and multilateral treaties that include minority provisions not only promote state compliance with human and minority rights standards, but also act as instruments of conflict prevention. To function in this way, however, such arrangements should be reciprocal and not one-sided, consistent with prevailing international standards, avoid preferential treatment for certain groups or individuals, and provide mechanisms for follow-up consultations with respect to these bilateral and multilateral undertakings.[7]

During the Cold War period, bilateral arrangements were the preferred means of resolving minority problems, and a number of successful examples of this sort of arrangement date from that period. The De Gasperi Gruber Agreement of 1946 between Austria and Italy, granting various rights to the German-speaking minority of Bolzano and Trento, is a case in point. Among other tenets of this agreement, the Italian government undertook to provide primary and secondary education in German to members of this national minority, and to ensure parity of German and Italian in the public administration in these regions.[8] Similarly, the 1955 Copenhagen–Bonn Declarations of Denmark and the Federal Republic of Germany respectively guaranteed the German minority in Denmark and the Danish minority in Germany the following rights: equality before the law; the right to establish educational institutions; the right to maintain cross-border religious, cultural, and professional relations; the right to an appropriate share of public broadcasting facilities; and the use of Danish or German in the law courts and public offices of each state.[9]

Subsequent to this experience, the European Council, the principal policy and rule-making body of the European Union, endorsed a pact to promote stability and peace in Europe by encouraging bilateral arrangements to protect minorities, strengthen the inviolability of existing frontiers, and reinforce the democratic transition in formerly Communist states in 1993.[10] The pact, signed in Paris in 1995, sought to create a new set of international commitments and a framework within which signatory states could create a climate of confidence favourable to democracy, respect for human and minority rights, and economic progress and peace. Ultimately three regional round tables were established, one for the Baltic states, another for Central and Eastern Europe, and a third for South-Eastern Europe, with the aim of encouraging neighbouring states to resolve disputes bilaterally, and to explore new forms of co-operation. Several of

[7] M. van der Stoel, Minority Rights, Participation and Bilateral Agreements, OSCE, speech, 2000.

[8] Above, n. 1, p. 116. [9] Above, n. 8. [10] Above, n. 1, p. 51.

these agreements are mentioned in the various state reports on compliance with Article 18(1), including: the Treaty of Friendship, Co-operation, Good Neighbourliness, and Security between the Republic of Albania and the Greek Republic (1996); the Treaty between the Republic of Azerbaijan and Georgia on Strengthening of Friendship, Co-operation and Mutual Security (1996); the Treaty on Friendship, Co-operation, and Mutual Security between the Republic of Azerbaijan and the Russian Federation (1997); the Treaty between the Republic of Hungary and the Republic of Croatia on Amicable Relations and Co-operation (1992); the Treaty between the Republic of Hungary and Federal Republic of Germany on Amicable Co-operation and Partnership in Europe (1992); the Treaty between the Republic of Hungary and Romania on Understanding, Co-operation, and Good Neighbourly Relations (1996); the Treaty between the Republic of Hungary and the Republic of Slovakia on Good Neighbourly Relations and Amicable Co-operation (1995); the Treaty on the Principles of Good Neighbourly Relations and Co-operation between the Republic of Hungary and Ukraine (1991); the Treaty between the Italian Republic and the Republic of Croatia on the Rights of Minorities, concluded in Zagreb (1996); the Treaty between the Republic of Poland and the Federal Republic of Germany on Neighbourliness and Friendly Co-operation (1991); the Treaty between the Republic of Poland and Ukraine on Neighbourliness, Friendly Relations, and Co-operation (1992); the Treaty between the Republic of Poland and the Russian Federation on Friendly and Neighbourly Relations (1992); the Treaty between the Republic of Poland and the Republic of Belarussia on Neighbourliness and Friendly Co-operation (1992); and the Treaty between the Republic of Poland and the Republic of Lithuania on Friendly Relations and Neighbourly Co-operation (1994), to name a few.

B. Advisory Committee Opinions

Given that Article 18(1) is an aspirational clause, it is only to be expected that the Advisory Committee Opinions regarding this provision are also aspirational, rather than directional, in nature. Where criticism is forthcoming, states are not necessarily judged to be in breach of their obligations, but rather encouraged to make better use of existing and possible bilateral and multilateral arrangements, particularly those with neighbouring states to resolve disputes involving minorities in their jurisdiction. Thus, for example, with respect to Armenia the Advisory Committee

> regrets that such [bilateral] co-operation cannot be developed by Armenia with all neighbouring countries [an oblique reference to Azerbaijan]. It expresses the hope that

a fair and lasting political settlement will be secured to solve the existing problems [namely the dispute over Nagorno-Karabakh], *inter alia* in the interests of persons belonging to national minorities.[11]

Similarly, Moldova, Hungary, Romania, and Slovakia have all been encouraged to improve the functioning of their bilateral arrangements. The Advisory Opinion on Hungary, for instance:

welcomes that Hungary is party to numerous bilateral treaties and cultural agreements covering the protection of persons belonging to national minorities and in this context welcomes the attempts to improve the functioning of the joint commissions envisaged in the 1995 Treaty on Good Neighbourliness and Friendly Co-operation between the Slovak Republic and Hungary.[12]

This type of commentary is consistent with a provision intended to encourage, but not to mandate, particular behaviour on the part of signatory states.

C. Limitations and Restrictions

Article 18(1) encourages states to co-operate in order to find constructive solutions to situations involving minorities. In accordance with Article 21 of the Framework Convention, states are expected to adhere to the principle of non-intervention in their bilateral and multilateral relations. States should abstain from any use of force or the threat of force, and should encourage respect for the fundamental principles of international law, especially the sovereign equality, territorial integrity, and political independence of existing states. Accordingly, states should also encourage groups within other states, such as their ethnic kin, to resolve their disputes peacefully, without providing either tacit or explicit support for groups engaged in any illegal activity such as terrorism. Ultimately, the protection of persons belonging to national minorities is the responsibility of the state in which that minority resides. Moreover, it is a basic principle of international law that states can act only within their sovereign jurisdiction, not extraterritorially. Although a kin state may have a particular interest in issues affecting persons of the same ethnicity living in neighbouring states, ties of kinship do not entail a right to exercise jurisdiction over such persons under existing international law.[13] This is why Article 18(1)

[11] Advisory Committee on the Framework Convention for the Protection of National Minorities, Opinion on Armenia, ACFC/INF/OP/I (2002), 001, 2002, para. 86.

[12] Advisory Committee Opinion on Hungary, ACFC/INF/OP/I (2000), 004, 2000, para. 57.

[13] Correspondingly, in recent years, Hungary has come under international pressure to amend its 2001 Act on Hungarians Living in Neighbouring Countries, sometimes referred to as the 'Status Law', which originally sought to grant special rights to ethnic Hungarians abroad. As a result of this external

refers to 'bilateral and multilateral agreements', rather than to unilateral initiatives. Unilateral attempts by a kin state to protect their ethnic cousins elsewhere are thus a clear violation of existing international law, and contrary to the provisions of Article 21 of the Framework Convention.

III. Conclusion and Outlook

Article 18(1) is an aspirational clause, which seeks to promote international relations conducive to the protection of persons belonging to minorities and, by extension, the preservation of international peace and stability. States, and in particular neighbouring states which possess transnational minorities, are thus encouraged to enter into bilateral and multilateral arrangements for the protection of such persons. It is hoped that arrangements like these will help to avoid or ease tensions between states while contributing to state compliance with international standards of human and minority rights.

Article 18(2)

I. Background

A. Issues

Article 18(2) encourages states to engage in transfrontier co-operation with the view to promoting international tolerance, prosperity, stability, and peace. This paragraph recognizes exchanges of information and experience between states as important means to encourage state compliance with the minority rights undertakings contained in the Framework Convention. Such transfrontier co-operation facilitates arrangements specifically tailored to the wishes and needs of the persons immediately concerned and is likely to be useful in implementing the provisions of the Framework Convention, especially as these apply to the circumstances of transfrontier minorities.

criticism, the Hungarian government introduced amendments designed to bring the law in line with minimum international standards. Accordingly, the scope of the amended law now appears to be limited to support for education and culture, and the intended benefits are no longer restricted to ethnic Hungarians. OSCE, 'High Commissioner Warns of Hungarian Status Law Precedent', press statement, The Hague, 2003 **www.osce.org/news/generate.php3?news_id = 3372** 21 July 2004.

B. History

Article 18(2) builds upon prior efforts to encourage transfrontier co-operation on minority issues within the OSCE, as well as the Council of Europe. Thus, for example, Article VII(4) of the OSCE Geneva Report on National Minorities recommended:

> transfrontier co-operation arrangements on a national, regional and local level, inter alia, on local border crossings, the preservation of and visits to cultural and historical monuments and sites, tourism, the improvement of traffic, the economy, youth exchange, the protection of the environment and the establishment of regional commissions.

Similarly, Article 14(*b*) of the European Charter for Regional or Minority Languages calls upon parties to undertake, 'for the benefit of regional or minority languages, to facilitate and/or promote co-operation across borders, in particular between regional or local authorities in whose territory the same language is used in identical or similar form'.

As a result of this experience, the Fundamental Rights of Persons Belonging to Ethnic Groups in Europe (FUEN) Draft for an Additional Protocol to the European Convention for the Protection of Human Rights and Fundamental Freedoms (ECHR) (Revised FUEN Draft, 1994) stipulated in Article 18(4) that, '[t]he right to unimpeded contacts shall also include the right to transfrontier co-operation and to the promotion thereof, in particular in the fields of culture, education, instruction, youth exchange, information, environmental protection, economy and trade'. Article 18(5) further specified that, '[t]ransfrontier co-operation may be realized a) through joint commissions and territorial communities or authorities and b) through non-governmental organizations and working arrangements such as workshops and committees.'

Similarly, the CAHMIN, charged with the task of preparing what ultimately became the Framework Convention, was also quick to recognize the importance of transfrontier co-operation for the protection of persons belonging to national minorities. The Preliminary Draft of the FCNM of 10 May 1994 cautioned that 'if necessary, the Parties shall take measures in particular to encourage transfrontier co-operation in border areas where national minorities reside'.[14] In July 1994, the Committee adopted the abbreviated version of this draft that was eventually incorporated as Article 18(2) of the Framework Convention.[15]

[14] Preliminary Draft Framework Convention for the Protection of National Minorities, Ad Hoc Committee for the Protection of National Minorities (CAHMIN) (94) 12, 1994, p. 7.

[15] CAHMIN, 5th meeting, CAHMIN (94), meeting report, 1994, p. 30. In this version, the provision for what was then referred to as Art. 19 reads as follows: 'Where relevant, the Parties shall take measures to encourage transfrontier co-operation'.

C. Context

Article 18(2) of the Framework Convention encourages states to engage in transfrontier co-operation for the protection of national minorities where the circumstances warrant it. This recommendation is consistent with the principle of good neighbourliness outlined in Article 2 and may provide further opportunities for the transfrontier peaceful contacts envisioned in Articles 17(1) and 17(2).

II. Analysis

Article 18(2), like Article 18(1), is an aspirational clause. Instead of stipulating clear guidelines for state conduct with respect to minorities, it endorses a form of behaviour which states are free to follow as they see fit. The provisions of Article 18(2) are not therefore obligatory, but rather recommended practice; states are not obliged to enter into transfrontier co-operation, but should take measures to 'encourage such cooperation' where they deem it 'relevant' to do so.

A. Transfrontier Co-operation

The principle of transfrontier co-operation is not specifically defined in the Framework Convention; however, it seems reasonable to infer that the type of co-operation envisioned here is similar to the one set forth in Article 1 of the European Outline Convention on Transfrontier Co-operation between Territorial Communities or Authorities (1980). In this context, transfrontier co-operation, 'shall mean any concerted action designed to reinforce and foster neighbourly relations between territorial communities or authorities within the jurisdiction of two or more Contracting Parties and the conclusion of any agreement and arrangement necessary for this purpose'. Such arrangements may be negotiated directly between territorial communities, or authorities within the jurisdiction of signatory states, acting on their own behalf and independent of their respective national governments.[16] Any resulting agreements will be expected to conform with both the national laws of the states concerned and their existing international commitments.[17] However, with respect to the protection of national minorities, such co-operation is not limited to territorial communities or authorities, which are public bodies by definition, but may

[16] Protocol No. 2 to the European Outline Convention on Transfrontier Co-operation between Territorial Communities or Authorities Concerning Interterritorial Co-operation, Council of Europe (CoE), 169, Strasbourg, 1998, Art. 2(3).

[17] Above, n. 16.

also extend to include the activities of non-governmental organizations (NGOs) and informal working arrangements such as workshops and committees.[18] Correspondingly, the concept of transfrontier co-operation would incorporate those peaceful contacts protected in Article 17(1) and 17(2) of the Framework Convention.

Following the end of the Cold War, a number of programmes were established to encourage transfrontier co-operation in Europe. The Council of Europe, for instance, has encouraged the creation of transfrontier 'Euroregions' to promote international understanding and co-operation amongst its members. Euroregions may involve similar levels of authority, such as regions and provinces. A case in point is the 'Carpathian Euroregion', which is made up of Hungarian megyes (counties), Ukrainian oblasts (regions), Polish voivodships (provinces), and Romanian judets (counties), while the Slovak side currently participates with observer status.[19] Alternatively, Euroregions can encompass different levels of authority, as is the case with respect to the 'Euregio Maas-Rhine' where Dutch and Belgian provinces co-operate with 'Regio Aachen', an association of German municipalities, and the German community of Belgium.[20] Euroregions also differ in the type of transfrontier activities they undertake. Some of these activities are limited to exchanges of information, consultation, and commissioned studies, while others have the capacity to manage and implement specific projects.[21] Similarly, the European Union's PHARE Cross Border Co-operation Programme (PHARE CBC), which was originally created to assist Poland and Hungary in 1989, is designed to encourage integration amongst European Union accession states and between these states and the current members of the European Union.[22] Until 2003, PHARE CBC was directed at Central and East European countries, but it has now been extended to cover the Bulgarian border with Turkey and the Bulgarian and Romanian borders with Ukraine, Moldova, Serbia and Montenegro, and the former Yugoslav Republic of Macedonia.[23] Both of these programmes are referenced in the state reports on Article 18(2). Thus Bulgaria's state report of 9 April 2003 cites the 'Danubius Euroregion' between Bulgaria and Romania, the 'Mesta-Nestos Euroregion' between Bulgaria and Greece, and the PHARE transfrontier

[18] FUEN, Fundamental Rights of Persons belonging to Ethnic Groups in Europe, Draft for an Additional Protocol to the ECHR (Revised FUEN Draft), 1994, Art. 18(5).

[19] CoE, Composition of Euroregions, Legal Affairs **www.coe.int/T/E/Legal%5FAffairs/Local%5Fand%5Fregional%5FDemocracy/Transfrontier%5Fco%2Doperation/Euroregions/4Composition.asp#TopOfPage** 22 July 2004.

[20] Above, n. 19.

[21] ibid.

[22] The European Union Online, PHARE, Enlargement **http://europa.eu.int/comm/enlargement/pas/phare** 22 July 2004.

[23] Above, n. 22.

co-operation programme between Bulgaria and Greece, as examples of transfrontier co-operation consistent with the sort of 'best practice' envisioned by the Framework Convention.[24]

B. Advisory Committee Opinions

As of July 2004, there were no Advisory Committee Opinions specific to Article 18(2). The absence of statements is consistent with the aspirational nature of the provision, which recommends but does not require specific state conduct on the issue of transfrontier co-operation.

C. Restrictions and Limitations

Article 18(2) is subject to the restrictions specified in Article 21 of the Framework Convention, which states that efforts to engage in transfrontier co-operation must be consistent with the fundamental principles of international law, including the sovereign equality, territorial integrity, and political independence of states.

III. Conclusions and Outlook

Like the first paragraph of Article 18, Article 18(2) is an aspirational clause. It aims to encourage, but does not mandate transfrontier co-operation between states. The aspirational nature of Article 18 is consistent with the overall approach of the Framework Convention to the protection of persons belonging to minorities. Two sets of considerations inform this provision: the sharing and exchange of knowledge of best practices in the area of minority protection; and the promotion of mutual trust and understanding, particularly between neighbouring states that possess transfrontier minorities.[25]

[24] Bulgaria State Report, ACFC/SR (2003), 001, 2003, para. 1.

[25] A. Eide, Final Text of the Commentary to the Declaration on the Rights of Persons Belonging to National or Ethnic, Religious, and Linguistic Minorities, E/CN.4/Sub.2/AC.5/2001/2, 2001, para. 75.

ARTICLE 19

Lauri Hannikainen

The Parties undertake to respect and implement the principles enshrined in the present framework Convention making, where necessary, only those limitations, restrictions or derogations which are provided for in international legal instruments, in particular the Convention for the Protection of Human Rights and Fundamental Freedoms, in so far as they are relevant to the rights and freedoms flowing from the said principles.

I. Background

A. Issues

Present day international law recognizes the paramount importance of human rights. Therefore, it is no surprise that a number of human rights have been declared 'absolute' in character—being universal and without restrictions or derogations. Other human rights, however, permit limitations and/or derogations that are deemed necessary (in a democratic society). In other words, they are not absolute. With these definitions in mind, minority rights have not been expressly declared absolute, but there are absolute rules giving fundamental protection to minorities; the primary example is the prohibition of genocide.

The rights to culture and religion are among the most essential minority rights. Evidently, a state may have legitimate grounds to prohibit certain minority group cultural or religious practices, if these practices contradict international laws that prohibit discrimination, for example. Furthermore, there are also legitimate grounds to limit the human rights of others to protect minority groups. The use of hostile propaganda against minorities may be prohibited, for instance.

Article 19 deals with the question of making limitations to, or derogations from, the Framework Convention for the Protection of National Minorities (FCNM). It links the Convention to other human rights instruments, bringing its interpretations in line with them. The purpose of this article is clear: only limitations, restrictions, and derogations of the provisions of the Convention having a legitimate source in other human rights instruments are permitted. The European Convention on the Protection of Human Rights and Fundamental Freedoms (ECHR) has been given primacy, in this regard.

The synonymous terms 'limitation' and 'restriction' confine the application of international human rights instruments to a specific human right. Article 11 ECHR on the right to freedom of peaceful assembly and to freedom of association is a typical example. After having provided for the existence of these rights, the article stipulates: '[n]o restrictions shall be placed on the exercise of these rights other than such as are prescribed by law and are necessary in a democratic society in the interests of national security or public safety, for the prevention of disorder or crime, for the protection of health or morals or for the protection of the rights and freedoms of others.' These kinds of limiting provisions have been attached to a number of freedom rights with the following message: there is broad freedom but there are limitations to it. Such limitations can be of a permanent nature, but their extent can vary.

Derogations mean something else, they are limiting measures during public emergency. In exceptional circumstances, a state is temporarily excused from a number of its human rights obligations through their limitation for the purpose of restoring and maintaining order, facilitating early resolution of a crisis situation. During a public emergency, a state may derogate from a number of its human rights obligations, but not from all of them. Nonetheless, few human rights conventions contain provisions for public emergencies, implying that those without specifications for emergencies do not permit derogations *at any time*. This tenet may be difficult to uphold in practice, however.

The starting point in international law is that only those limitations to and derogations from international treaties are permitted, which are provided for in that treaty. Conventions that are especially relevant here are: the ECHR and International Covenant on Civil and Political Rights (ICCPR), both of which include one article on public emergency as well as provisions for the limitation of certain freedom rights. All states parties to the Framework Convention have ratified the ECHR and the ICCPR.

B. History

The European Commission for Democracy through Law proposed a draft framework convention with the inclusion of an article providing for the right to provide limitations to the articles that deal with some freedom rights.[1] This idea was highlighted by the Ad Hoc Committee for the Protection of National Minorities (CAHMIN), which stated that a clause of this type should not be of a general nature applicable to all substantive provisions of the convention, but should only apply to provisions that are expressly mentioned in this clause. CAHMIN soon provided a draft article singling out those provisions applicable to the limitation clause. The draft article accounted for the freedoms of expression, peaceful assembly and association, and movement.[2]

The Swiss delegation had a different idea, however. Its alternative proposal was a short draft article stating that the rights and freedoms flowing from the principles enshrined in the Convention should be subject to such restrictions only as justified by an overwhelming public interest. The Swiss reasoning went as follows: the restriction clauses in the ECHR could be justified on the ground that its provisions may, in the majority of the ratifying states, be directly invoked against national authorities. These are justiciable human rights. In contrast, in a framework convention which restricted itself to setting aims which states would then undertake to implement with a wide margin of discretion, it would be sufficient to define the essential factors which made it possible to restrict the rights and freedoms flowing from the principles laid down in this instrument. It would be paradoxical to state that an international instrument did not directly confer any rights or freedoms on the persons to whom it applied while, at the same time, referring specifically to restrictions to be placed on their rights and freedoms.[3]

Carefully considering the Swiss reasoning, CAHMIN expressed the view that the entire article on limitations could be left out of the Convention. Due to their general character, principles are not subject to 'limitations', 'restrictions',

[1] European Commission for Democracy through Law (ECDL), Framework Convention for the Protection of National Minorities (FCNM) Explanatory Report to the Proposal for a European Convention for the Protection of National Minorities, CDL-MIN (93) 6, 1993.

[2] Ad Hoc Committee for the Protection of National Minorities (CAHMIN), Preliminary Draft Convention for the Protection of National Minorities (94) 12, 1994.

[3] CAHMIN, Proposals concerning the Preliminary Draft Framework Convention for the Protection of National Minorities (94) 14 Rev., 1994. The Advisory Committee established by the Framework Convention has shown appreciation of the Swiss analysis.

or 'derogations'. In international instruments these terms are usually relevant to rights and freedoms. The obligations contained in Section II (Articles 4–19) of the Framework Convention already allow the parties a rather wide margin of appreciation, calling the need for yet another escape clause into question.[4] The final outcome of this debate was the inclusion of Article 19—a short provision with a fairly general character.

When the final text of the Convention was accepted, CAHMIN released an explanatory report on its interpretation. Regarding Article 19, the report explained that when the concepts included in the Framework Convention had an equivalent in other international legal instruments, 'only the limitations, restrictions or derogations provided for in those instruments [were] allowed'. When the concepts set forth in the Framework Convention had no equivalent in other international legal instruments, 'the only limitations, restrictions or derogations allowed [were] those which, included in other legal instruments (such as the ECHR) in respect of differing undertakings, [were] relevant'.[5]

How should one interpret this last sentence? One obvious answer is that the criteria for legitimate limitations and derogations created in those other legal instruments are to be applied. They answer the question as to whether limitations to, or derogations from, a given provision of the Framework Convention are permissible. So far, no state has made reservations to Article 19.

C. Context

Article 19 refers, in principle, to all articles in the Framework Convention. A reading of the Convention raises the following considerations. First, in the Preamble the most relevant provision is the statement that the parties were 'resolved to define the principles to be respected and the obligations which flow from them' and the statement on the determination of the parties 'to implement the principles set out' in the Convention. These statements confirm that the Convention creates principles that the parties are to implement and these principles create obligations for the parties to respect. The Convention is not meant to create legal rights for persons belonging to minorities or to whole minority groups in the international arena. Secondly, there are a number of provisions in the Convention to which limitations and/or derogations appear to be permissible according to certain other conventions or instruments. A closer look at these is given below.

[4] CAHMIN, Summary of the Main Points raised by the Opinion of the Directorate of Legal Affairs on the Draft Framework Convention (94) 25, 1994.

[5] CAHMIN, Meeting Report (94) 32, 7th meeting, 1994.

II. Analysis

A. Minor Attention to Article 19 in the Monitoring of Respect of the Framework Convention

There is very little relevant practice by the Advisory Committee or the Committee of Ministers regarding Article 19. Some states have reported on their laws that provide for limitations and/or derogations that may be relevant in the field of the Framework Convention. In all cases so far, the Advisory Committee has come to the conclusion that the implementation of Article 19 does not give rise to any specific observations, while the Committee of Ministers has given no comments.

B. Limitations and Restrictions

Besides being listed as a primary source in Article 19, the ECHR is of special significance because of its rich practice and because of its provisions permitting the limitation of certain freedom rights. The European Court of Human Rights (ECtHR), with its sufficient pool of resources, is one of the most prominent human rights organs in the world. A handicap of the ECHR, however, is its lack of any specific article on minorities. In addition, its prohibition of discrimination has been of limited scope and significance. In terms of the latter shortcoming, the future looks better, since a fairly recent protocol, No. 12 (2000), has been dedicated to the prohibition of discrimination—lending more strength and scope to this prohibition. The ICCPR has one specific article on minorities, Article 27: on the right of persons belonging to ethnic, religious, and cultural minorities to enjoy their own culture, religion, and language. This Convention also has a substantial article on the prohibition of discrimination. Its monitoring organ, the Human Rights Committee, has been called the 'world ombudsman against discrimination', but when compared with the resources of the European Court, this Committee has very limited resources. Specific conventions on discrimination, especially the Convention on the Elimination of All Forms of Racial Discrimination and its monitoring organ, play important roles in delineating the boundary between discrimination and lawful differential treatment.

In the ECHR, the most notable provisions on limitations are in the articles providing for the rights to freedoms of thought, conscience, and religion (9), of expression (10), of assembly and association (11), and of movement (Protocol 4, Article 2), as well as the right to respect for privacy, family unity, home, and correspondence (8). Where the other articles previously mentioned include lists of permissible grounds for limitation similar or nearly similar to that of Article 11 quoted above, Article 10 on freedom of expression also includes a longer list of grounds, but they are not of any particular significance here.

These limitations are exceptions to freedom rights. It is a general principle of international law that exceptions to the main rule are to be interpreted narrowly, and this is the European Court's line of argument.[6] The limitations must: (1) be prescribed by law; (2) have a legitimate aim; (3) be necessary in democratic society; and (4) respect the principle of proportionality. The Court has interpreted these requirements in great detail; however, it has also granted states a certain margin of appreciation, varying according to the case in question.

There is a rich jurisprudence from the European Court on several aspects of minority rights. The fact that the ECHR lacks any specific provisions on minority rights and weakly prohibits discrimination, however, has set limits on the Court's handling of complaints by applicants who belong to a minority. Gilbert has concluded that the ECHR is not designed to protect minority rights. Instead, in cases open before the Court, any reference by an applicant referring to minority rights can be declared 'manifestly ill-founded'.[7] On the positive side, the Convention does not deny groups their right to claim them under the ECHR if they prove themselves to be victims.[8]

There have been minority-related cases before the European Court on: the registration of associations formed by persons and groups which regard their group as a minority; freedom of expression; discrimination; educational rights; religious groups and their institutions (with several on the appointment of the leader of an institution of a minority religion by the authorities); participatory rights; and the way of life of a minority (Roma).[9] There have also been cases dealing with the limitation of rights both to the detriment of claimed minority interests and, on the other hand, for their protection.

In the practice of the European Court some cases concerning the rights to freedom of association and of expression of members belonging to minorities are especially relevant in this context, as are some judgments on Article 8. Many cases on freedom of expression have dealt with the rights of the Kurdish people in Turkey, when the Turkish government and courts have regarded them as

[6] See R. Jennings and A. Watts, *Oppenheim's International Law*, i, 9th edn., (Longman, London, 1992), 421; J. Viljanen, *The European Court of Human Rights as a Developer of the General Doctrines of Human Rights Law* (Tampere University, Tampere, 2003), 165–331.

[7] G. Gilbert, 'The Burgeoning Minority Rights Jurisprudence of the European Court of Human Rights', *Human Rights Quarterly*, 24, (2002), 780.

[8] Above, n. 7, p. 740.

[9] Above, n. 7 pp. 737–80; S. Spiliopoulou Åkermark, 'The Limits of Pluralism—Recent Jurisprudence of the European Court of Human Rights with Regard to Minorities: Does the Prohibition of Discrimination Add Anything?', *Journal on Ethnopolitics and Minority Issues in Europe (JEMIE)*, 3 (2002).

threats to Turkey's national unity and territorial integrity. The European Court has found violations in many of those cases.[10] However, Turkey has not ratified the Framework Convention.

Some cases on freedom of association are of particular interest. In the cases of *Sidiropoulos and Others* v. *Greece* and *Metropolitan Church of Bessarabia and Others* v. *Moldova*, the European Court found violations of the freedom of association. In *Sidiropoulos*,[11] the applicants belonged to an association called 'Home of Macedonian Civilization'. At issue was the fact that the Greek authorities refused to register the group on grounds that they caused a threat to territorial unity and to Greek national security. The government interpreted the inclusion of the word 'Macedonian' in their name as a sign of wanting to identify the Greek region of Macedonia with the neighbouring state of the 'Former Yugoslav Republic of Macedonia', and as favouring the annexation of the Greek Macedonia to this neighbouring state. The association claimed that it represented a territorial entity of the Macedonian minority in Greece and spoke for the rights of this suppressed minority. Admittedly, the name of the association is quite grandiose—Home of Macedonian Civilization. One could submit that the neighbouring Former Yugoslav Republic of Macedonia may want to claim this 'Home' as part of its own territory. However, the European Court did not find evidence that the association formed a threat to Greece: its declared aim was to assert minority consciousness and to preserve and develop the traditions and culture of this minority.

In the *Metropolitan Church* case,[12] the authors established a regionally autonomous Orthodox Church in Bessarabia, Moldova, attached to the patriarchate of Bucharest. The founding document of the church emphasized its non-political and Moldovan character and was recognized by all Orthodox patriarchates with the exception of the patriarchate of Moscow. The Moldovan government claimed that the establishment of this church nurtured conflicts not only between Orthodox churches, but also threatened state relations, risking the independence and territorial integrity of the young Republic of Moldova vis-à-vis Russia and Ukraine. According to the government, the members of this new church could be full and active members in the existing Metropolitan Church of Moldova as there was no difference, from a religious point of view, between the two. A claim was also made that the church's activities would foster nationalistic tendencies with negative consequences for the political and social

[10] *Jacobs and White, The European Convention on Human Rights*, 3rd edn., ed. C. Ovey and R. White (Oxford University Press, Oxford, 2003), 281–2.

[11] *Sidiropoulos and Others* v. *Greece* No. 26695/95 (1998) ECHR 55.

[12] *Metropolitan Church of Bessarabia* v. *Moldova* No. 45701/99 (2001) ECHR 2001-XII.

situation in Moldova. The European Court was not convinced by these arguments, however. It noted that the denial of recognition and registration had prevented the new church from defending its interests and that only formal recognition could give it sufficient legal standing. According to the Court, when the authorities recognized other liturgical associations, they did not apply the criteria which they used in refusing to recognize the aspiring church.

On the other hand, the European Court accepted the denial of the right of one ethnic minority association in the case of *Gorzelik and Others* v. *Poland*.[13] The applicant organization was the Union of People of Silesia, whose aim was to awaken and strengthen the national consciousness of Silesians, restore Silesian culture, and protect the ethnic rights of persons of Silesian nationality. One paragraph of the founding document stated that the Union was an organization of the Silesian national minority. In highlighting this passage, the Polish government was able to prove to the European Court that the registration of the Union would mean the recognition of the Silesian ethnic group as a national minority. While Polish law grants specific rights to national minorities, even the Union admitted that it was not seeking formal recognition as a national minority with the aim of benefiting from privileges for minorities granted by Polish law. The government stated that if the Union agreed to delete or alter the term 'national minority' in its founding document, it would be registered without difficulty, but the Union refused to do this. The European Court supported the government's argument and found that with slight modification of its founding document, the Union could secure registration. Since it refused a reasonable compromise, the Court found no violation of Article 11.

Only two of the three cases discussed deal with entities that can be regarded as national minorities, the cases of *Sidiropoulos* and *Gorzelik*. The third case *Metropolitan Church*, can also be of value in the assessment of the extent of legal limitations to the right to freedom of association of national minorities, however.

The ICCPR has many articles similar to the ECHR, including articles on the freedom rights. As such, these two conventions are 'sister' conventions: one is applicable in a universal context and the other in an all-European context. In fact, the Human Rights Committee of the ICCPR has, in many ways, used the practice of the ECtHR as its guide. They do, however, differ in some respects. The reports of the Committee are much shorter and less detailed than those of the European Court, for example, and they are not formally binding, whereas the Court's decisions are. Instead, the Committee can only offer recommendations. Furthermore, the ICCPR permits complaints only by individual victims of violations, not by groups.

[13] *Gorzelik and Others* v. *Poland* No. 44158/98 (2001) ECHR 869.

The ICCPR and Human Rights Committee also have strong monitoring aspects. The Committee not only considers complaints that it receives, but it also deliberates periodic reports by states parties on a regular basis. Furthermore, it gives general comments on the interpretation of various human rights articles of the ICCPR. Interpreting the ICCPR's article on minority rights (Article 27) and its comprehensive article on the prohibition of discrimination (Article 26) have enabled the Committee to take a broader, more inclusive approach to these questions than the European Court has been able to.

The general comments on individual articles by the Human Rights Committee have consolidated essential aspects of the interpretation of these articles. The General Comment on Article 27 includes many interesting statements on the scope of minority rights—but not directly on their limitation,[14] and in its observations on state reports the Committee has been able to specify the content of minority rights.[15] In its comments on individual complaints under Article 27, the Committee has taken a position on: (1) the extent of the rights of persons belonging to minorities vis-à-vis the majority; (2) the limitation of a person's rights vis-à-vis his or her minority group as a whole; or (3) a numerical minority's rights vis-à-vis the numerical majority within a minority group. To give examples, in the *Kitok* v. *Sweden* case[16] the applicant lost his membership to a Sami (indigenous) village in Sweden, because he had left the village for several years and, upon returning, did not retrieve his full rights, specifically his right to herd reindeer. This situation arose because of considerations for the interests of Sami reindeer herders in a broader context. The Swedish government pointed out that the area available for reindeer grazing is limited and therefore only a limited number of Sami can subsist (with additional alternative income) from reindeer herding. According to the government, the conflict here was primarily between Kitok and the Sami village. Kitok had requested the Swedish authorities to grant him admission to the village, despite the villagers' refusal. The Committee accepted the reasoning of the Swedish government begrudgingly. In *Apirana Mahuika et al.* v. *New Zealand*,[17] the applicants who belonged to a numerical minority within the indigenous Maori people lost their case because the Committee recognized the right of the numerical majority of the Maori to negotiate a settlement for the Maori people with the government in fishery matters.

[14] UN Human Rights Committee 'General Comment 23' (1994) (50), GAOR, 1314th meeting (5th session), UN Doc. A/49/40, annex V. Art. 27.

[15] A. Spiliopoulou Åkermark, *Justifications of Minority Protection in International Law* (Uppsala University, Uppsala, 1996), 129–77.

[16] UN Human Rights Committee Comm. No. 197/1985, (1988), 43rd session, GAOR, UN Doc. A/43/40, pp. 221–30.

[17] UN Human Rights Committee Comm. No. 547/1993, (2000), 70th session, GAOR, UN Doc. A/56/40 (vol. ii), pp. 11–29.

Concerning Article 26 ICCPR, the Human Rights Committee has adequately upheld the prohibition of discrimination in its comments on state reports and in individual cases.[18] As with Article 27, there are no comments on the limitations of the rights in Article 26.

When one takes a closer look at various articles of the Framework Convention, limitations appear to be permissible. Article 5, for example, calls upon the state to promote the conditions necessary for persons belonging to national minorities to maintain or develop their culture and to preserve the essential elements of their religion and traditions. While this provision is of general character and permits states quite a wide margin of appreciation in choosing the means of promotion, a state may want to set limitations on the promotion of traditions which, for example, discriminate against women. Limitations of the freedom rights in Articles 7, 8, and 9 FCNM are to be assessed according to the criteria applied within the ECHR and ICCPR.

Article 13 FCNM confirms the obligation of states to recognize that persons belonging to a national minority have the right to set up and manage their own private educational and training establishments. States may set various requirements on the quality and contents of these establishments, if they want national recognition for the degrees that they grant. Framed in this way, these requirements resemble conditions more than limitations; however, they may be seen as limitations by the administrators of minority schools. The 1960 UNESCO Convention against Discrimination in Education permits ratifying states to set qualitative standards on private educational establishments (Article 2), speaking to the importance of good quality education for pupils belonging to national minorities. As such, the limitations of Article 13 protect rather than discriminate.

As set out in Article 17, states are obliged not to interfere with the right of persons belonging to national minorities to maintain free and peaceful contacts across frontiers with persons lawfully staying in other states, in particular those who share common identity or culture with them. In recognizing a state as sovereign, with external boundaries, however, it has a right to set limits on the movements across its international borders.

Finally, it should be noted that Article 4 of the International Covenant on Economic, Social, and Cultural Rights (ICESCR) stipulates limitations on actions that are detrimental to the social well-being of the people residing in a state. This particular clause only permits ratifying states to limit the rights

[18] R. Hanski and M. Scheinin, *Leading Cases of the Human Rights Committee* (Åbo Akademi University, Turku/Åbo, 2003), 325–74; I. Boerefijn, *The Reporting Procedure under the Covenant on Civil and Political Rights, Practice and Procedures of the Human Rights Committee* (Intersentia-Hart, Antwerp, 1999), chs. XIV–XVI.

recognized by the Covenant as long as they remain 'compatible with the nature of these rights and solely for the purpose of promoting the general welfare in a democratic society'. This provision, with its safeguards, was primarily intended to be protective of the rights of individuals rather than permissive on the imposition of limitations by the state, and it has been interpreted accordingly by the monitoring organ of the ICESCR, the Committee on Economic, Social, and Cultural Rights. The clause allows states to impose limitations where an unlimited interpretation of a right would lead to absurd results and/or various rights clashing with each other or with the legitimate interests of the state.[19] Sepúlveda correctly observes that states wanting to impose limitations must interpret Article 4 in a restrictive manner and comply with the protective safeguards contained within it.[20] From a minority rights perspective, the points of interest in the Covenant appear to be the articles recognizing the right of everyone to an adequate standard of living (Article 11), and to education (Article 13). In practice, Article 4 has received only limited attention.

Regarding the criterion of 'general welfare in a democratic society', general welfare is understandably an important notion, but it should not be realized at the cost of minority rights. If, however, a state's economy is having particularly serious problems, a temporary reduction of public funds for the education of members of minorities cannot be legitimately ruled out. The criterion of 'compatible with the nature of these rights' appears to be a legitimate ground of limitation when applied according to the principles presented in the previous paragraph, in other words, that the right of everyone to an adequate standard of living is upheld.

C. Derogations

The ECHR and ICCPR contain similar articles on the right to derogate from human rights obligations during public emergencies. However, as a more recent convention, the ICCPR article on derogation is more detailed and comprehensive. As such, the ICCPR article is treated here as the principal provision, while the article of the ECHR is referred to as a complementary provision.

[19] P. Alston and G. Quinn, 'The Nature and Scope of States Parties' Obligations under the International Covenant on Economic, Social and Cultural Rights', *Human Rights Quarterly*, 9 (1987), 192–206; see also 'The Limburg Principles on the Implementation of the International Covenant on Economic, Social and Cultural Rights', UN Doc. E/CN.4/1987/17, Annex reprinted in *Human Rights Quarterly*, 9/2 (1987), 122–35.

[20] M. M. Sepúlveda, *The Nature of Obligations under the International Covenant on Economic, Social and Cultural Rights* (Intersentia-Hart, Antwerp, 2003), 279 and more generally pp. 277–302.

According to Article 4 ICCPR, during public emergencies that threaten the life of the nation and its public status, parties to the ICCPR may take measures derogating from their obligations under the Covenant. They are, however, required to adhere strictly to derogations as required by the immediate situation without inconsistencies towards their other obligations under international law. In addition, these circumstances do not permit states parties to discriminate solely on the ground of race, colour, sex, language, religion, or social origin. Article 4 points out, however, that no derogation from seven specific articles of the Covenant may be made under any conditions. Article 16 is included on this list and specifies that everyone should have the right to recognition everywhere as a person before the law. Article 18 is also featured on this list and it recognizes the right of everyone to freedom of thought, conscience, and religion. It should be pointed out, however, that Article 18 permits the limitation of freedom to manifest one's religion or beliefs *even in normal circumstances* on the grounds of public safety, order, health, or morals, or the fundamental rights and freedoms of others, making the scope of this non-derogable right quite narrow. In comparison, the ECHR's shorter list of non-derogable rights includes neither of these provisions.

No international instrument or body has declared minority rights to be absolute in character, nor do the lists of non-derogable rights in the ICCPR and ECHR indicate any strong link to the Framework Convention. Moreover, the list of non-derogable rights in the ICCPR *does not include* Article 27, which recognizes the right of persons belonging to minorities to enjoy their culture, profess and practise their religion, or use their language. If there is a violent interethnic conflict in a state, its government may have legitimate grounds to restrict various freedom rights, in order to stem the prolongation of the violence, so that these derogations in fact reduce the right of persons belonging to the involved minority to enjoy their culture, to profess and practise their religion, and to use their language.

Especially important in Article 4 ICCPR are the following regulations and their caveats: (1) Derogations are permitted only to the extent strictly required by the exigencies of the situation. This requires necessity and proportionality and permits derogations only on a temporary basis. After a crisis has subsided, the rights that have been restricted must be fully restored. (2) Article 4 contains a minimum prohibition of discrimination giving fundamental protection to national minorities. (3) There are obligations of states and human rights that can never be derogated—that is to say, they are of absolute character. (4) Other obligations of states may limit their right to derogate from human rights obligations during public emergency. This applies, in particular, to norms of humanitarian law applicable during armed conflicts.

What is regrettable in Article 4 is that it does not adequately regulate national decision-making procedures during public emergencies.[21] Another regrettable aspect is the overly short list of non-derogable rights. It does not include, for example, even the most basic judicial guarantees to persons accused of having committed a crime and put to a trial. The same shortcomings apply to Article 15 ECHR. This is especially peculiar as both conventions include a long and substantial article on judicial guarantees.

In 2001, the Human Rights Committee adopted its General Comment on the interpretation of Article 4. The Committee considered that non-derogable rights are in danger if effective legal remedies guaranteeing the respect of these rights are absent. A person must always have legal means to demand respect for his or her absolute rights. Therefore, the Committee opposes arbitrary deprivations of liberty or deviations from fundamental principles of fair trial during public emergencies.[22]

If there is pressing need to resort to derogations that go beyond the 'normal' limitations permitted during non-emergency situations, it is still more natural to direct those derogations to freedom rights, such as those of movement, assembly, and expression. However, the Moscow Meeting of the Human Dimension Conference of the Conference for Security and Co-operation in Europe (CSCE) in 1991 called upon the parties to uphold the freedom of expression and reporting even during a time of public emergency in order to enable public discussion on respect for human rights and on the termination of the public emergency.[23]

The Human Rights Committee has discussed national laws and policies of states on public emergency in its comments on state reports.[24] The ECtHR has dealt with derogations from human rights during public emergency in

[21] Conference on Security and Co-operation in Europe (CSCE), 3rd Conference on the Human Dimension of the CSCE, Moscow, 1991, para. 28. The document of the Moscow Meeting gives instructions to the participating states on appropriate national procedures in order to avoid dictatorial action.

[22] UN Human Rights Committee, 'General Comment 29' (2001) (72), 1950th meeting, UN Doc. CPR/C/21/Rev.1/Add.11, Art. 4.

[23] Conference on Security and Co-operation in Europe, 3rd Conference on the Human Dimension of the CSCE, Moscow, 1991, para. 28(9).

[24] A. L. Svensson-McCarthy, *The International Law of Human Rights and States of Exception* (Martinus Nijhoff Publishers, The Hague, 1998), and J. Oraa, *Human Rights in States of Emergency in International Law* (Clarendon Press, Oxford, 1992). These monographs deal in different chapters with the views and practice of the Human Rights Committee and the European Court of Human Rights.

a number of cases, especially in the context of conflict in Northern Ireland, and, more recently, regarding Kurdish persons in their home regions in South-East Turkey.[25] In many of these cases the Court found the state concerned guilty of violations, especially in the Kurdish cases.[26] Many of these cases have focused on the authorities' ill-treatment of persons belonging to minorities rather than with their specific minority rights. Mostly, they have addressed their ill-treatment during conflict, or when in detention.

When one looks at the Framework Convention from the perspective of the provisions on public emergency in the ICCPR and the ECHR, it has to be admitted that many provisions of the Framework Convention do not create strict obligations. Instead, it calls for measures to promote state obligations towards minorities. Temporary derogations during public emergency, such as the interruption of promotional work on rights are possible. On the other hand, there are provisions that *hardly permit derogations*. In particular: Article 6(2), where the parties assume responsibilities to protect persons who may be subject to threats, hostility, or violence as a result of their ethnic, cultural, linguistic, or religious identity; Article 10(3), where the parties undertake to inform persons belonging to national minorities promptly, in a language he or she understands, the reasons of his or her arrest, and of the nature and cause of any accusation against him or her, and to defend himself or herself in this language, if necessary with the free assistance of an interpreter. If such a person does not have a command of the language of the majority, Article 10(3) should be applied even during times of public emergency; and Article 16, where a state is obliged not to use a situation of public emergency for the purpose of altering the proportions of the population in areas inhabited by persons belonging to national minorities in order to restrict the rights flowing from the principles enshrined in the Framework Convention.

III. Conclusion and Outlook

Article 19 has played a minor role in the first years of practice of the Framework Convention's monitoring organs. So far, therefore, this article appears to be adequate in its content. The provisions of certain other conventions and the work

[25] A. L. Svensson-McCarthy, *The International Law of Human Rights and States of Exception* (Martinus Nijhoff Publishers, The Hague, 1998), and J. Oraa, *Human Rights in States of Emergency in International Law* (Clarendon Press, Oxford, 1992). These monographs deal in different chapters with the views and practice of the Human Rights Committee and the European Court of Human Rights.

[26] New judgments will come on the alleged violations of the rights of Chechen applicants in Russia.

of their monitoring organs do not necessarily provide for a full interpretation of Article 19; however, they give sufficient guidance to the monitoring organs of the Framework Convention.

A provision like Article 19 does not typically play a major role in the international application of conventions. Article 19 uses other international instruments as a measuring stick for legal limitations of, and derogation from, the Framework Convention. The most prominent international legal organs dealing with limitations and derogations are the European Court of Human Rights and the Human Rights Committee. The European Court, especially, has created a comprehensive set of interpreting principles on limitations to the freedom rights in the ECHR. If a state party to the ECHR extends the scope of limitations in disregard of the Court's principles, that state can expect to be challenged by individual applicants. As regards derogations during public emergencies, the Human Rights Committee has dealt with them quite comprehensively in its comments on state reports.

Article 19 may be referred to occasionally in the comments of the monitoring organs of the Framework Convention. If a crisis were to emerge in a territory populated by a national minority, if the state in question resorted to limitations and/or derogations jeopardizing international standards, and if they were directed to members of this territorial minority in particular, it seems natural that the monitoring organs of the Framework Convention would intervene on their behalf, necessitating the use of Article 19.

Presently, a serious emergency exists in Chechnya, where there have been substantial limitations of, and derogations from, international human rights standards. When commenting on the state report of Russia on its implementation of the Framework Convention, the Committee of Ministers expressed concern for the human rights problems in the Chechen Republic. The Committee pointed out how these problems have hampered efforts to implement a number of the Framework Convention's provisions, principles that should be fully observed during the political settlement in this Republic. The Committee of Ministers did not point to any specific articles in the Convention in this vein,[27] though the Advisory Committee has been more specific. Concerning the situation in Chechnya, it pinpointed implementation problems concerning: Article 4 on non-discrimination; Article 6 on protection against threats and hostility; Article 16 on the prohibition to alter proportions of the population; and Article 7 on the provision of freedom rights. All of these

[27] Resolution of the Committee of Ministers on the Implementation of the Framework Convention for the Protection of National Minorities by the Russian Federation, Committee of Ministers, ResCMN (2003).

provisions have been mentioned previously. Limitations to, and derogations from, the first three articles mentioned appear to be either prohibited altogether or substantially restricted. In its comment on Article 7, the Advisory Committee stated that in Chechnya, and in the areas directly affected by the conflict of Chechnya, a number of limitations of these freedom rights have been reported and therefore the cessation of hostilities and consolidation of a well-functioning administration that fully respects human rights is essential also for the implementation of the provisions of the article. However, the Committee did not refer at all to Article 19 in its discussion.[28]

[28] Advisory Committee of the Framework Convention for the Protection of National Minorities, Opinion on the Russian Federation, ACFC/INF/OP/I (2003) 005, 2002.

SECTION III

ARTICLE 20

Peter Hilpold

In the exercise of the rights and freedoms flowing from the principles enshrined in the present framework Convention, any person belonging to a national minority shall respect the national legislation and the rights of others, in particular those of persons belonging to the majority or to other national minorities.

I. Background

A. Issues

This provision aims to introduce a balance between rights and obligations: members of minorities are not only bearers of rights, but also holders of duties. This is a very sensitive area and, therefore, during the drafting process a great deal of attention was given to the actual wording of this provision. In the past, other documents have made reference to an 'obligation of loyalty', immediately evoking the question of whether members of minorities are subject to greater restrictions than other people, perhaps at the price of the special status they aspire to. This assumption would, however, be dangerous for a modern minority protection system as will be shown below. With regard to the Framework Convention for the Protection of National Minorities (FCNM), a compromise has been found with which minorities will be able to live: the loyalty requested from them towards the state as a whole and towards other groups and people living in the state is neither greater nor lesser than for any other member of the same state community. From a political standpoint, this does not prohibit states from reminding minorities of their obligations towards others, even if minorities are the only groups to be addressed by this exhortation.

B. History

As is known, the question of loyalty became an important issue during both world wars. While the minority treaties concluded after the First World War referred only to rights and not to duties, the League of Nations received requests to balance the concessions for rights with respect for corresponding duties.[1] On 21 September 1921, in a resolution of the Assembly of the League of Nations, the existence of a duty of loyalty for members of minorities was officially proclaimed.[2] The Secretariat was obliged to assist the Council 'in ascertaining in what manner the persons belonging to racial, linguistic or religious minorities fulfil their duties towards their state. The information thus collected might be placed at the disposal of the States Members of the League of Nations if they so desire.' It was rightly remarked[3] that to punish a group for the possible disloyalty of one or several individuals was a legally ill-conceived approach; all the more in a system based on individual rights, as was the system of minority protection administered by the League of Nations. This approach was considered politically unsustainable, as it disregarded that loyalty is a reciprocal issue and did not allow for cases where it was the government that has first disrupted the bond of mutual faith and trust.[4] After the Second World War, allegations of disloyalty constituted one of the main political justifications for the deportation of millions of German-speaking people from the territory of the Republic of Czechoslovakia.[5] The same allegation was also used after the war to call into question the usefulness of minority protection altogether.

Notwithstanding these negative experiences, the concept of loyalty as a precondition for the concession of minority rights has survived in modern

[1] A. Mandelstam, *La Protection internationale des minorités* (Recueil Sirey, Paris, 1931), 131–47.

[2] 'L'Assemblée, tout en reconnaissant le droit fundamental des minorités à être protégées par la Société des Nations contre toute oppression, insiste sur le devoir qui incombe aux personnes appartenant aux minorités de race, de réligion ou de langue de coopérer, en citoyens loyeaux, avec la nation à laquelle ils appartiennent maintenant.'

[3] On the whole issue see O. Luchterhand, *Nationale Minderheiten und Loyalität* (Verl. Wiss. u. Politik. Köln, 1997) (in particular, pp. 35 ff.).

[4] Above, n. 3.

[5] ibid., pp. 43 ff. The so-called Benes decrees which constituted the basis for the mass expulsion and the expropriation of disloyal people were demonstrated through the broad definition of disloyalty and the harsh sanctions related to all the problems inherent in this concept.

human rights. By and large, however, a trend characterized by continuous adaptation and a weakening of this concept to make it compatible with modern conceptions of how the relationship between the majority and the minority should be structured in a liberal democracy can be observed.

Article 16 of the Preliminary Draft Convention on the Protection of Minorities[6] lays out an explicit duty for members of minorities to be loyal to the state. This proposed formulation was later watered down to require any member of a minority to 'fulfil the obligations deriving from his status as a national of his State'. In addition, respect for national legislation and the rights of others, particularly members of the majority and of other minorities, is required.[7] The Explanatory Report to this proposal[8] decided not to lay down any specific obligations of loyalty for the minority member. This statement is probably a little euphemistic as the term 'loyalty', though softened in its phrasing, is still used in the Draft Convention.

The Parliamentary Assembly of the Council of Europe was more prudent when drafting Recommendation 1201 (1993) on an Additional Protocol on the Rights of National Minorities to the European Convention for the Protection of Human Rights and Fundamental Freedoms (ECHR) (1 February 1993). Article 14 of the proposal refers to the possibility of restricting the duties and responsibilities of the citizens of the state, but this may only happen in exceptional circumstances.

The requirement to respect national legislation can also be found in other documents on human rights and minority rights law. This is the case, for example, with Article 17 ECHR and Article 54 of the Charter of Fundamental Rights (on the prohibition of abuse of rights). In some documents, the problem of how to find a balance between the rights and the duties of minorities has been elegantly overcome, either by formulating an obligation to treat members of minorities, and of the majority, alike (Conference for Security and Co-operation in Europe (CSCE) Meeting of Experts on National Minorities, Geneva, 1–19 July 1991, IV, paragraph 4),[9] or by providing the guarantee that the rights set forth in the documents mentioned above should not prejudice the enjoyment by all persons of universally recognized human rights and fundamental freedoms (UN Declaration of 18 December 1992).

[6] European Commission for Democracy through Law (ECDL), Preliminary Draft Convention on the Protection of Minorities [DAJ.SC.DEMOCRACY]CONV.MIN, 1990.

[7] ECDL, Proposal for a European Convention for the Protection of National Minorities, CDL-MIN (93) 6, 1993, Art. 15.

[8] Above, n. 7.

[9] 'The participating States affirm that persons belonging to a national minority will enjoy the same rights and have the same duties of citizenship as the rest of the population.'

The Framework Convention does not contain any reference to loyalty. In the Explanatory Report to this Convention, the 'reference to national legislation does not entitle Parties to ignore the provisions of the framework Convention. Persons belonging to national minorities must also respect the rights of others. In this regard, reference may be made to situations where persons belonging to national minorities are in a minority nationally but form a majority within one area of the State.'[10]

C. Context

Article 20 is closely related to Article 21, which aims to preserve national integrity. It could be argued that Article 21 is superfluous as Article 20 already regulates the principles stated therein. The dangers addressed by Article 21 are, however, seen by many states to be of such a fundamental nature that a specific regulation on this situation was deemed necessary. In a more generic way, Article 20 is also related to Article 2, which requires states to operate in good faith. It could be argued that a similar attitude may also be expected from the members of minorities.

II. Analysis

A. Structure of the Article

Article 20 contains an obligation for members of a minority to respect national legislation and the rights of others. These two obligations do not necessarily coincide and, therefore, have been appropriately kept distinct.

B. Balancing Rights and Duties

There can be no doubt that the primary aim of this Convention is to provide special protection to members of minorities and to grant them particular rights through special measures,[11] though the extent of this second aim has still

[10] Ad Hoc Committee for the Protection of National Minorities (CAHMIN), Explanatory Report on the Framework Convention for the Protection of National Minorities, CAHMIN H(1995) 010, 1995, para. 89.

[11] See, with regard to International Covenant on Civil and Political Rights (ICCPR) (adopted 16 December 1966, entered into force 23 March 1976) 999 UNTS 171, Art. 27 or, respectively, the UN Declaration of 18 December 1992, C. Tomuschat, 'Protection of Minorities under Article 27 of the International Covenant on Civil and Political Rights', in R. Bernhardt (ed.), *Völkerrecht als Rechtsordnung, internationale Gerichtsbarkeit, Menschenrechte, FS Mosler* (Springer, Berlin, 1983), 949–79; P. Hilpold, 'Minderheitenschutz im Rahmen der Vereinten Nationen: Die Deklaration vom 18. Dezember 1992', *Schweizerische Zeitschrift für internationales und europäisches Recht*, 1–2 (1994), 31–54.

to be defined. It should no longer be contested that positive measures do not violate the principle of equality.[12] There are, of course, corresponding duties, but they do not operate on the same level. Members of a minority do not have to be offered compensation for the protection that is granted; they are not the beneficiaries of charity,[13] but of protective measures granted only because they find themselves in a disadvantaged position. For this reason, it would be misleading to say that members of a minority have a duty of loyalty towards the state that would extend beyond the duties of the members of the majority towards this same entity. As shown above, such an attitude was previously expressed particularly during the interwar period, when the rules on the protection of minorities were of an absolute exceptional nature, and had not yet been rooted in a general human rights system. After the Second World War this situation changed. Though they were initially and reluctantly granted over the years, it became clear that minority rights were natural and necessary elements of the human rights protection system, and therefore no special 'compensation' or gratitude was required for these rights to be recognized.[14] The complete integration of minority rights into the human rights concept, opposed by many advocates of the traditional minority protection concept at first,[15] meant that protection could not be made conditional on a certain

[12] As is known, this principle has already been stated by the Permanent International Court in the case of Minority Schools in Albania, Advisory Opinion of Minority Schools in Albania, (1935) PCIJ, Series A/B No. 64, 3, p. 17, although it has taken some time for this principle to find general acceptance. With regard to the relevant modern constitutional law debate see, *inter alia*, P. Hilpold, *Modernes Minderheitenrecht* (Manz et al., Vienna, 2001), 58 ff.; A. Pizzorusso, *Minoranze e maggioranze* (Einaudi, Torino, 1993), 77 ff.

[13] J. Bruegel, 'A Neglected Field: The Protection of Minorities', *Harvard Human Rights Journal*, 4 (1971), 413 ff. at 440 f. See also P. Thornberry, *International Law and the Rights of Minorities* (Clarendon Press, Oxford, 1991), 166 ff. and K. Henrard, *Devising an Adequate System of Minority Protection* (Martinus Nijhoff, The Hague, 2000), 47.

[14] At the beginning, especially in the Sub-Commission on Prevention of Discrimination and Protection of Minorities, there was some reluctance to forgo the condition of loyalty. See F. Capotorti, *Study on the Rights of Persons Belonging to Ethnic, Religious and Linguistic Minorities* (United Nations, New York, 1991), para. 23.

[15] In particular, this approach had many followers in German-speaking countries where it still has some declared, or at least documented, adherents. There are several reasons for this situation. First of all, this is a consequence of the strength minority rights gained in Germany after the First World War when, as a result of the redrawing of the border lines in Europe, large numbers of German-speaking people remained outside the borders of Germany and Austria. As there was not yet any general human rights system available at the time, the minority rights system had to develop autonomously. Secondly, there was also a strong interest for collective minority rights as a result of war-related events, closely related with the aim to keep the minorities intact as a group. This approach was easier to reconcile with a separate protection system than with one which was fully integrated into an individualistic human rights system. Finally, a separate minority protection system is far easier to control with regard to its field of application. As in the German-speaking world, the attempt to distinguish between 'traditional minorities' and 'new minorities' is very accentuated. For those

attitude, but was consequential to the presence of a certain situation. In the way that no compensation has to be offered to be able to take advantage of general human rights, minority rights also apply automatically as long as a member of such a group wishes to be protected. Of course, the national legislation has to be respected, but this obligation applies to members of the majority in the same way. Why, then, was it deemed necessary to include this provision at all? Primarily, this provision is meant to impede an abuse of rights. The balance between rights and duties is, therefore, not of an external nature, that is to say, of a kind where each concession has to be counterbalanced by a corresponding duty. Instead, it is of an internal characteristic. In other words, the rights and privileges awarded have to be exercised in view of the function that minority protection fulfils. These norms do not exempt members of a minority from having to respond to the general law applicable on a certain territory, but they create a special environment where the members of the minority can survive and prosper in the same way as the members of the majority (or the members of other minorities).

Some writers have tried to distinguish between two groups of rights: the prohibition of discrimination and some basic rights on the one hand, and far-reaching positive measures on the other.[16] While the first would apply without any preconditions, the second could be made dependent on the demonstration of a particular form of loyalty.[17] This approach appears to be problematic, as positive measures are considered a necessary component of minority protection. Privileges going beyond what is required in international minority law, such as conditionality, are theoretically conceivable, but are hardly feasible in practice. Nor are they desirable from the viewpoint of a minority policy inspired by modern democratic principles. In fact, privileges of this kind could indirectly constitute discrimination of the members of the majority and would probably not be reconcilable with the principle of equality.[18] This type of policy would also be undesirable for minorities, as this would make them increasingly dependent upon the good will of the government, restricting

opposing specific protection for 'new minorities' it seems advisable to oppose a full integration of minority rights into the human rights system as, according to the human rights approach, the actual need for protection is decisive, unless group belonging pertains to an individual.

[16] See V. Grammatikas, 'The Definition of Minorities in International Law: A Problem still Looking for a Solution', *RHDI* 52 (1999), 321–64 (357 ff.). According to Otto Kimminich, loyalty is not a defining element of the minority concept but, on the other side, it cannot be pretended either that a state protects disloyal groups. See O. Kimminich, *Rechtsprobleme der polyethnischen Staatsorganisation* (Mainz, Munich, 1985), 100.

[17] Above, n. 16, p. 359.

[18] See also the Report submitted by A. Eide, Possible Ways and Means of Facilitating the Peaceful and Constructive Solution of Problems Involving Minorities, Working Paper, UN Doc. E/CN.4/Sub.2/1993/34, 1993.

their ability to act freely in their political choices. On the other hand, it goes without saying that in the search for the best possible minority rights solution, an open and mutually supportive political attitude by all the parties involved would be a great help. This, however, is a political consideration and is something quite different from the requirement of loyalty for the concession of rights.

C. The Rights of Persons belonging to Other Minorities[19]

Article 20 not only refers to the rights of persons belonging to the majority, but also to those of persons belonging to other minorities. This is a remarkable provision that underscores the essence of the Framework Convention as a human rights instrument. Its concrete relevance depends on the factual situation, however. In a situation where 'other national minorities' are of a comparable size and strength, and have a similar influence on politics, this provision does not add much in respect to the pertinent formulation of other instruments where this specific reference is lacking. Different groups of minorities are equal beneficiaries of the norms on minority protection. That they must not hinder each other in the use of their rights is a logical consequence of a protection system with many actual or potential beneficiaries. Vertically granted rights must be protected from any horizontal threat, as otherwise this protection would remain without effect.

Nevertheless, this provision becomes highly relevant when there are stronger and weaker groups that require protection, and particularly in the case of 'minorities in the minority'. What are the main traits characterizing a 'minority in the minority'? Members of these groups find themselves in a disadvantaged position both with respect to the majority as well as with respect to other larger or more influential minority groups. Sometimes the larger minority claims to be the representative of the smaller minority in its interactions with the government. In other cases, especially when a minority in the minority is composed of people belonging to the majority, their status as a minority—as such—is often contested.[20] Understandably, larger minorities fear that this concept could be

[19] See on this issue in general, P. Hilpold, 'Der Schutz der Minderheit in der Minderheit', *Migralex*, 1/1 (2003), 3–12.

[20] Unfortunately, in the case of the UN Human Rights Committee, *Ballantyne, Davidson, McIntyre* v. *Canada* Part II, Comm. No. 385/1989, UN Doc. A/48/40, Rev. 11993, pp. 91–109, the UN Human Rights Committee was not prepared to extend the protection of Art. 27 ICCPR to such groups. In this specific case, it was the members of the majority Anglophone community in Canada who were denied qualification as a minority group within Quebec as this province did not constitute an independent state. See P. Thornberry, 'The UN Declaration on the Rights of Persons Belonging to National or Ethnic, Religious and Linguistic Minorities: Background, Analysis, Observations, and an Update', in A. Phillips and A. Rosas (eds.), *Universal Minority Rights* (MRG & Åbo Akademi, Turku, 1995), 13–76 at p. 22, P. Hilpold, *Modernes Minderheitenrecht* (Schultess, Vienna, 2001), 155 ff.

used as an instrument of abuse by the majority in order to diminish the force of protection for minority interests. Abusively assuming the role of an arbiter between the larger minority and the minority in the minority, the majority may not grant any protection at all, or even privilege people belonging to the majority in the end. It should, however, be possible to identify such strategies and to distinguish situations where a real need for protection exists from those where the call for protection is unwarranted. The mere fear of abuse should not become a pretext to disengage from recognized obligations. It can even be argued that the larger minority stands to gain in adopting a fair attitude towards the smaller, weaker minority group. Acting in a positive manner, the larger minority can make clear that protection does not constitute an unjustified privilege, but is the expression of a general principle residing in the principle of equality.

D. The Issue of Double Discrimination

The words 'the rights of others' also refer to the rights of other members of the same minority group. Minority provisions that create a specific status for the members of a particular group may be associated with the danger that those who want to take advantage of these rights have to accept limitations of other rights. The justification adopted for such measures usually refers to the essential cultural particularities that need to be protected in order to preserve the main traits distinguishing the respective groups. Article 20 of the Framework Convention, however, makes clear that granting minority rights may not be made conditional upon the acceptance of limitations of rights guaranteed by other human rights documents and instruments. The Framework Convention has been created to extend the rights of minority members and not to compromise between divergent needs where the individual could be made worse off with regard to his general human rights position. Otherwise, a member of a minority might find himself in a situation where he is not only the potential subject of discrimination by members of the majority, but also by members of his own group—resulting in double discrimination. In the end, this extension of rights is a natural consequence of the Framework Convention being a human rights instrument whose primary aim is not to find compromises, but aims, first and foremost, to strengthen the position of individuals when they constitute members of a minority.

E. State Practice with Regard to Article 20

The state reports pursuant to Article 25 that have been made public so far, differ in the interpretative approach that they take when considering Article 20.

In many reports, we find no statement on this article at all. In others, the content of this article is merely repeated with some partial emphasis on the general duty to respect national legislation. This kind of interpretation does not make a valuable contribution to an effective system of minority protection. In some state reports, however, a different approach is taken, and even the problem of the minority in the minority is addressed, at least indirectly. In the report presented by Croatia,[21] for example, reference is made to the Croatian Constitutional Law on Human Rights and Freedoms and the Rights of National and Ethnic Communities or Minorities in the Republic of Croatia in which the preamble defines the intent of this law: to 'enable less numerous ethnic and national communities or minorities of the same religion, race and language, a free development of their distinctive characteristics within the majority citizen community or majority communities without abuses by either the majority or the minority'.

The report presented by Moldova is also interesting in this respect. It states that the legislation of Moldova does not offer any one ethnic group privileges at the expense of another, and that persons belonging to ethnic minorities are aware that their rights are closely linked to the obligation to respect these same rights when dealing with persons belonging to other minorities, and particularly persons belonging to the majority ethnic group.[22]

The issue of the 'minority in the minority' has been specifically addressed in the opinion on Finland adopted on 22 September 2000.[23] There the Advisory Committee took the position that the Finnish-speaking population living in the province of Åland can be considered a 'minority in the minority'. Consequently, they could rely on the protection provided by the Framework Convention as far as the issues concerned were within the competence of that Province.[24]

The opinion on Moldova clearly illustrates that the granting of minority rights can involve difficult considerations in balancing the rights of various groups.[25] In this case, the Advisory Committee considered

> that the authorities should ensure that measures in favour of the language of a particular national minority are not taken at the expense of the languages of other national minorities. It believes that, in promoting the linguistic rights in Article 10 of the Framework Convention, the Moldovan authorities

21 Croatia State Report, ACFC/SR (99) 5, 1999.

22 Moldova State Report, ACFC/SR (2002) 2, 2000.

23 Advisory Committee on the Framework Convention for the Protection of National Minorities, Opinion on Finland, ACFC/INF/OP/I (2001) 002, 2000.

24 Above, n. 23, para. 17.

25 Advisory Committee Opinion on Moldova, ACFC/INF/OP/I (2003) 002, 2002.

> should seek a balanced approach to the various languages spoken by persons belonging to national minorities, including those that are disadvantaged or numerically smaller.[26]

On the whole this practice evidences a vision according to which full efficacy can be given to the minority rights enshrined in the Framework Convention only if a broad perspective is adopted that takes into consideration the position of all persons directly or indirectly involved. Of course, the greater the number of groups living on a certain territory, the greater the challenge tends to get for the minority policy.

III. Conclusion and Outlook

As has been shown, the attempt to attach duties to the rights granted by a minority protection instrument has a long tradition, but the nature of this 'balancing' has changed dramatically over the years. When formulated as a 'duty to loyalty', this obligation risks transforming minority rights into a concession deliberately granted by the majority, a concession that can be withdrawn at any time the majority deems the minority group unworthy of it. If this obligation of loyalty by minority groups is accentuated more than is required from the members of the majority, minority group members are more restricted in their political freedoms. On the other hand, if this obligation is conceived as a general rule requiring the balancing of rights and duties in a multi-ethnic state, it could help to enhance the general acceptance of minority protection in a liberal, democratic environment. A special field of application of this principle regards the 'minority in the minority'. Here, in its attitude towards smaller weaker groups, a minority group can demonstrate that it does not insist on being the exclusive beneficiary of privileges, but only wants to take advantage of the general principle binding the members of the majority and those of the minority without placing other minority groups in a position of further relative disadvantage.

[26] Advisory Committee Opinion on Moldova, ACFC/INF/OP/I (2003) 002, 2002, para. 66.

ARTICLE 21

Peter Hilpold

Nothing in the present framework Convention shall be interpreted as implying any right to engage in any activity or perform any act contrary to the fundamental principles of international law and in particular of the sovereign equality, territorial integrity and political independence of States.

I. Background

A. Issues

Article 21 of the Framework Convention for the Protection of National Minorities (FCNM) introduces a safeguard common in human rights instruments and, in particular, in minority rights documents. On the one hand, it constitutes a concession to the fears of states that granting minority rights could constitute a prelude to territorial disruption. Acts contrary to the fundamental principles of international law and, in particular, of the sovereign equality, territorial integrity, and political independence of states cannot be justified for purposes of minority protection. By severing any linkage of this kind, these provisions assure states that minority rights do not constitute a basis for destabilizing demands. Seen positively, this provision emphasizes, on the other hand, the fact that the entire Framework Convention is founded on the understanding that solutions for minority problems have to be arrived at peacefully and constructively. Implicit in this position is the conviction that constructive approaches and instruments are well suited to promote stable solutions that can satisfy all parties involved, and which contribute to peace themselves. If we combine these assumptions, we can come to the conclusion that minority protection, as it is understood by the Framework Convention, is not only unrelated to measures of force or violence, but it may even counter their increasing influence.

B. History

Safeguards of this kind can be found in many international documents on human rights,[1] and within minority rights. The Draft Convention on the Protection of Minorities prepared by the European Commission for Democracy[2] provided the immediate inspiration for this article, as did paragraph 37 of the Copenhagen Document of the Conference on Security and Co-operation in Europe (CSCE).[3] An analogous provision can be found in Article 8(4) of the UN Declaration on the Rights of Persons Belonging to National or Ethnic, Religious, or Linguistic Minorities of 18 December 1992.[4] Discussions on this provision within the Ad Hoc Committee for the Protection of National Minorities (CAHMIN) took place in close connection with discussions on the possible introduction of an obligation of loyalty. As shown

[1] Universal Declaration of Human Rights (adopted 10 December 1948) UNGA Res. 217 A(III) (UDHR), Art. 30; International Covenant on Civil and Political Rights (adopted 16 December 1966, entered into force 23 March 1976), UNGA Res. 2200A (XXI), 1966, (ICCPR), Art. 5; International Covenant on Economic, Social, and Cultural Rights (adopted 16 December 1966, entered into force 3 January 1976) 993 UNTS 3 (ICESCR), Art. 5.

[2] European Commission for Democracy through Law (ECDL), Draft Report of the 4th Meeting [DAJ.SC.DEMOCRACY] CONV.MIN, CD-PV (90) 4 Prov., 1990; ECDL, Set of principles on national minorities drawn up by the European Commission for Democracy through Law; CDL-MIN (93) 6, 1993.

[3] Conference for Security and Co-operation in Europe (OSCE), Document of the Copenhagen Meeting of the Conference on the Human Dimension of the CSCE, Copenhagen, 1990: 'None of these commitments may be interpreted as implying any right to engage in any activity or perform any action in contravention of the purposes and principles of the Charter of the United Nations, other obligations under international law or the provisions of the Final Act, including the principle of territorial integrity of States.'

[4] Declaration on the Rights of Persons Belonging to National or Ethnic, Religious, or Linguistic Minorities, UNGA Res. 47/135 (18 December 1992), annex 47 UN GAOR 49, 210, UN Doc. A/47/49: 'Nothing in the present Declaration may be construed as permitting any activity contrary to the purposes and principles of the United Nations, including sovereign equality, territorial integrity and political independence of States.' See also, for a similar provision, the United Nations Draft Declaration on the Rights of Indigenous Peoples, Commission on Human Rights, Sub-Commission on Prevention of Discrimination and Protection of Minorities, 45th Session, 1994, UN Doc. E/CN.4/Sub.2/1993/29, Annex 1, Art. 45.

in the commentary on Article 20, the CAHMIN abstained from introducing such an obligation, as it was rightly found that an obligation of loyalty applies uniformly to all the members of a society without distinction. This conclusion, in turn, influenced interpretations of Article 21.

C. Context

Article 21 is closely related to Article 2, which expresses an obligation of good faith. Article 21 gives further substance to Article 2 both with regard to the instruments available for the implementation of minority rights, and in relation to the expectations that state-granted minority rights can have with regard to the beneficiaries of these rights. Article 21 also appears to be related to Article 20, in its content and its systematic position in the Framework Convention, as the latter contains a general obligation for any person belonging to a national minority to respect national legislation. An analysis of the systematic relationship between Article 20 and Article 21, both reciprocally and with regard to the other provisions of the Framework Convention described below, will provide further insight into the content of this provision.

Article 21 should also be read in conjunction with Article 18, which invites the parties to conclude co-operation agreements in the field of minority protection; and with Article 17, which allows persons belonging to national minorities to co-operate beyond their own state borders. Read together these three articles demonstrate that international law does not offer any means to disrupt territorial integrity, but to the contrary, provides valuable instruments to reconcile state integrity and transborder minority protection.

II. Analysis

A. Structure of the Article

This article requires the rights mentioned in the Framework Convention to be used in conformity with the fundamental principles of international law. In particular, the sovereign equality, territorial integrity, and political independence of states must be respected. This provision gives rise to questions of who the subjects of these obligations are, and to the ways in which the protection of minority rights and the respect for territorial integrity can be reconciled. It also questions the essence of such a safeguard, and whose interests are protected by it.

B. Subjects of the Obligation

1. General Considerations with Particular Reference to the Relationship of Article 21 with Article 20

It is interesting to note that the language of the provisions of Section III of the Framework Convention differs remarkably from that of the provisions of Section II, which contains the majority of the Convention's provisions. While Section II contains clear interstate obligations ('The Parties undertake . . .'), which have to be implemented by the parties through specific legislation, the provisions of Section III are of a far more general nature. The Framework Convention has not been conceived as an instrument upon which individuals can rely directly, nor does it, in a technical manner, create obligations to bind individuals.

Section III contains general interpretative principles; principles designed both to co-ordinate the various provisions of the Convention, as well as to co-ordinate this Convention with other human rights documents. In this context, it seems acceptable to address the individual directly. This is even more the case if we consider that these provisions contain exhortations, and are of a political nature. Finally, in interpreting these provisions, we have to keep in mind that they have been formulated or taken from documents whose provisions, again at least in part, have given them the character of self-executing norms. This is particularly the case for Article 5(1) of the International Covenant on Civil and Political Rights (ICCPR), which explicitly addresses the individual: '[n]othing in the present Covenant may be interpreted as implying for any State, group or person any right to engage in any activity or to perform any act aimed at the destruction of any of the rights or freedoms recognized herein, or at their limitation to a greater extent than is provided for in the present Covenant.'[5] That said, we can examine the relationship that exists between Article 21 and the previously discussed Article 20. Acts endangering the existence of states are prohibited both by national and by international law, for example. This does not make Article 21 redundant as it has a different scope. To determine and analyse these differences one could take resort to a legalistic, though not to say formalistic, attitude, and proceed accordingly.

In a convention that is meant to regulate interstate obligations, a provision prohibiting certain acts should be interpreted as being directed against states, first and foremost. In this sense, Article 20 should not be approached any differently from Article 21. Article 20, however, does make direct reference to the 'person' as a subject of a specific obligation, while Article 21 lacks any

[5] This provision is worded in exactly the same way as in Art. 5 ICESCR.

reference to 'persons' or 'individuals'. From this perspective, it could be concluded that in order to respect the fundamental principles of international law, only states have binding obligations, and that the acts of individuals do not fall into the purview of this provision. In contrast, individuals are addressed at least in a mediate way in Article 20. According to this narrow interpretation, there is a difference in the way that Articles 20 and 21 should be read, but this difference is limited and related to the position of individuals within the state. In Article 21, the individual is not considered at all; while Article 20 does allude to the rights of individuals, even this is a marginal point.

It can be observed that this restrictive viewpoint does not do justice to these two provisions. While these obligations bind states in a formal sense, they also send clear political signals to minorities and their members. Furthermore, they operate as an inherent limitation of the rights granted to the members of minorities. This should not be interpreted to mean that granting minority rights can be made dependent on submissive behaviour, which introduces a tacit obligation of loyalty. Instead, these provisions have been designed to impede abuses. This has happened not only in the interest of the state and members of the majority, but also in the interests of members of minority groups, whose fate depends on the existence of a peaceful and co-operative environment to an even greater extent.

Consequently, the assertion that the role of the individual in these two provisions does not differ significantly stands firm. More accurately, the main difference lies in the fact that the situation described in Article 20 is of an internal nature, while Article 21 tries to preserve the international subjectivity and capacities of the state as a whole, given its powers, rights, and attributes, within its given boundaries.

2. *The Obligations of States*

As shown above, states are not necessarily the primary subjects of these provisions, if we analyse their content and aims. States are, however, bound by this provision and are the intended focal points. In fact, it should be kept in mind that as an international treaty, the Framework Convention binds its parties, first and foremost. Seen from this perspective, the provisions of Article 21 contain a double obligation. First of all, in their endeavours to fulfil the obligations resulting from this treaty and to promote its general aims, the parties have to abstain from any activity that would violate the sovereign equality, the territorial integrity, and the political independence of other states. This obligation can be relevant when a kin state aims to protect an ethnic group living outside its territorial boundaries, usually in a neighbouring country as a consequence of national borders having been redrawn. In this context, mere interest in the plight of these groups does not constitute a violation of fundamental international legal principles. In fact, the opposite is true.[6]

The overall aim of the Framework Convention is to improve the situation of members of national minorities, and national boundaries should not hinder activities with this objective, as long as they do not intend to infringe upon national sovereignty. The Framework Convention itself explicitly recognizes the necessity of joint action across borders (Article 18), and of allowing persons belonging to national minorities 'to establish and maintain free and peaceful contacts across frontiers with persons lawfully staying in other States' (Article 17). From this perspective, Article 21 aims to impede the abuse of minority protection measures by other parties, if the goals are inconsistent with international law. It can be argued that with this specific interpretation Article 21 will only be relevant in very extreme situations.

Article 21 contains not only an obligation to abstain from the activities mentioned in this provision, but it implicitly contains an obligation to prevent them should private actors become engaged. The obligation of good faith (Article 2 FCNM) requires parties to do their best to fulfil the aims of the Convention. As a consequence, they also have to demonstrate their best efforts to avoid subjects blocking the fulfilment of this aim within their jurisdiction. If, for example, private persons or groups aim to overthrow the neighbouring regime by force, or to carry out military actions from the neighbouring regime, the government of the respective member state has a duty to intervene and to curb these activities.[7]

[6] In Europe, the CSCE process has contributed decisively towards clarifying the interest for human rights in general, and for minority rights in particular, as a common issue of the state community. This community shares the same basic values, in which the principle of non-intervention cannot be opposed. This experience was also an important precedent for the establishment of the monitoring process in the Framework Convention. See H. J. Heintze, *Selbstbestimmungsrecht und Minderheitenrechte im Völkerrecht* (Nomos, Baden-Baden, 1994), 162 ff.

[7] Although Art. 11 of the International Law Commission's Articles on State Responsibility seems to absolve states of responsibility for the acts of private persons, it neither acknowledges nor adopts the view that states have a general obligation to protect individuals and prevent them from being harmed. In *The United States Diplomatic and Consular Staff in Tehran Case (United States* v. *Iran)* [1980] ICJ Rep. 3, the ICJ stated: 'The conclusion just reached by the Court that the initiation of the attack . . . cannot be considered as in itself imputable to the Iranian State does not mean that Iran is, in consequence, free of any responsibility in regard to those attacks; for its own conduct was in conflict with international obligations . . . Iran was placed under the most categorical obligations as a receiving State, to take appropriate steps to ensure the protection of the United States Embassy and Consulates . . . This inaction of the Iranian Government by itself constituted clear and serious violations of Iran's obligations to the United States under the . . . Vienna Convention on Diplomatic Relations . . . ' (p. 29). Aside from specific treaty obligations, it can be argued that each state has an obligation under general customary law to prevent its territory from becoming a base for violent attacks

3. Are the Members of Minorities Themselves Bound by this Provision?

A considerable number of state reports presented pursuant to Article 25 of the Convention give no further discussion regarding this provision. It seems that the scenarios described in this article are considered exceptional, and therefore irrelevant to the everyday functioning of a state.

It is even more interesting that in those cases where the parties actually report on this article, they do not refer to their duties in this field or to the relevant duties of other parties. Instead, they refer to the behaviour of individuals belonging to minorities, or to the activities of the groups themselves.[8] This seems to confirm the position outlined previously, where both the states and the members of the minorities themselves are bound by this provision. If the content of the obligation in force for the member states is interpreted in the way it has been here—that is referring to extreme situations and completely leaving out any form of political intervention in favour of minorities or their individual members brought forward in conformity with international law—then no member state has violated this provision so far. Such a violation would, in any case, invoke the application of a multitude of instruments created to prevent or immediately solve a serious international crisis in Europe.[9]

As far as reference is made in the reports to the activities of the minorities or their members, some technical questions arise, as described above, as an international treaty cannot, as a rule,[10] directly oblige individuals or non-state groups. It could be argued that these reports, in referring to activities of individuals and groups in reality primarily examine whether the respective party has maintained its obligations to impede the disruptive activities previously described. This would be a mere formalistic approach, however. As has already been shown at length, the nature of the Framework Convention, as an international treaty without self-executing provisions, does not prevent the inclusion of minorities, or members of minority groups, within the purview of this

against the territory of other states. This obligation is linked to the duty of co-operation. See also G. Dahm, J. Delbrück, and R. Wolfrum, *Völkerrecht*, 1/3 (2002), 910. On this subject see also G. Sperduti, 'Responsibility of States for Activities of Private Persons', *Encyclopedia of Public International Law*, iv (North-Holland, Amsterdam, 2000), 216–19 and B. Conforti, *Diritto internazionale* (Editoriale Scientifica, Napoli, 2002), 354 f.

[8] See, in particular, Germany State Report, ACFC/SR (2000) 1, 2000.

[9] Within the territory of the European Union, the monitoring and sanctioning mechanism introduced by Art. 7 TEU ranks most prominently. With regard to this mechanism see, *inter alia*, P. Pernthaler and P. Hilpold, 'Sanktionen als Instrument der Politikkontrolle—der Fall Österreich', *Integration*, 23/2 (2000), 105–19; F. Schorkopf, *Die Maßnahmen der XIV EU-Mitgliedstaaten gegen Österreich* (Springer, Berlin, 2001).

[10] The exceptions regulated in international criminal law are not relevant here.

provision. This happens indirectly, as a limitation of the rights granted to them and on a political level.

As the formulation of Article 21 of the Framework Convention has not been drafted especially for this document, but has been taken from other documents, authoritative interpretations with regard to these earlier instruments can be referred to for further elucidation of the content of this provision.

As is known, Article 8 of the Declaration on the Rights of Persons Belonging to National or Ethic, Religious, or Linguistic Minorities[11] contains a nearly equivalent provision.[12] This provision has been interpreted by Asbjørn Eide, Chairperson of the Working Group on Minorities of the Sub-Commission on the Promotion and Protection of Human Rights, in the following way:

As stated in the preamble, the Declaration is based on the principles of the Charter of the United Nations. Note should also be taken of the conviction expressed in the preamble that the promotion and protection of the rights of minorities contribute to the political and social stability of States. Article 8.4 serves as a reminder that nothing in the Declaration can be construed as permitting any activity which is contrary to the purposes of the Charter. Particular mention is made of activities that are contrary to the sovereign equality, territorial integrity and political independence of States. As pointed out above, the rights of persons belonging to minorities are different from the rights of peoples to self-determination, and minority rights cannot serve as a basis for claims of secession of dismemberment of a State.[13]

At this point, some considerations over the relationship between the concept of minority rights and the right to self-determination seem appropriate. In General Comment 23 ICCPR a clear distinction between these two concepts is drawn:

The Covenant draws a distinction between the right to self-determination and the rights protected under article 27. The former is expressed to be a right to peoples and is dealt with in a separate part (Part I) of the Covenant. Self-determination is not a right cognizable under the Optional Protocol. Article 27, on the other hand, relates to rights conferred on individuals as such and is included, like the articles relating to other personal rights conferred on individuals, in Part III of the Covenant and is cognizable

[11] Declaration on the Rights of Persons Belonging to National or Ethnic, Religious, or Linguistic Minorities, UNGA Res. 47/135 (18 December 1992), annex 47 UN GAOR 49, 210, UN Doc. A/47/49, Art. 4(3).

[12] Above, n. 11, Art. 8(4): 'Nothing in the present Declaration may be construed as permitting any activity contrary to the purposes and principles of the United Nations, including sovereign equality, territorial integrity and political independence of States.'

[13] See the Final Text of the Commentary to the Declaration on the Rights of Persons Belonging to National or Ethnic, Religious, and Linguistic Minorities, E/CN.4/Sub.2/AC.5/2001/2, 2 April 2001, para. 84.

under the Optional Protocol. . . . The enjoyment of the rights to which article 27 relates does not prejudice the sovereignty and territorial integrity of a State party. At the same time, one or other aspect of the rights of individuals protected under that article—for example, to enjoy a particular culture—may consist in a way of life which is closely associated with territory and use of its resources. This may particularly be true of members of indigenous communities constituting a minority.[14]

Beneath this distinction lies a specific, although very common misunderstanding of the concept of self-determination. In this context, self-determination is equalized with external self-determination or secession. One of the greatest fears associated with the concession of minority rights concerns the possibility that members of the minority could see these concessions as a first step towards the change of frontier lines or the creation of an autonomous state. In practice, these fears inhibit the development of more extensive minority rights. Therefore, it is both in the interest of the states granting minority rights, and in that of the beneficiaries of these rights, to counter such fears.

It also has to be mentioned, however, that the concept of self-determination goes far beyond external self-determination and secession. The internal aspect of this right, in close connection with the discussion about a right to democracy,[15] probably constitutes the most challenging aspect of this right.[16] It has been shown convincingly that the establishment of a democratic order, which is not based only on the majority rule, but also seeks to guarantee the effective participation of all groups, can decisively contribute to the strengthening of a culturally and ethnically diverse political system.[17] The concept of self-determination, interpreted in this broad sense, is therefore not an alternative or even a threat for minority protection, but rather an important auxiliary instrument.[18]

[14] United Nations Human Rights Committee, ICCPR, 'General Comment 18' in 'The Rights of Minorities', 50th Session, 1994, Art. 27.

[15] See, on this subject, T. Franck, 'The Emerging Right to Democratic Governance', in *American Journal of International Law*, 86 (1992), 46–91; G. H. Fox, 'Self-Determination on the Post-Cold War Era: A New Internal Focus?', *Michigan Journal of International Law*, 16 (1995), 733–81.

[16] P. Thornberry, 'The Democratic or Internal Aspect of Self-Determination with some Remarks on Federalism', in C. Tomuschat (ed.), *Modern Law of Self-Determination* (Nijhoff, Dordrecht, 1993), 101–38; A. Cassese, *Self-Determination of Peoples: A Legal Reappraisal* (Cambridge University Press, Cambridge, 1995); P. Hilpold, 'Sezession und humanitäre Intervention: Völkerrechtliche Instrumente zur Bewältigung innerstaatlicher Konflikte?', *Zeitschrift für öffentliches Recht*, 54 (1999), 529–602.

[17] See, for example, A. Eide, 'In Search of Constructive Alternatives to Secession', in Tomuschat, above, n. 16, pp. 139–76.

[18] Again, it has to be emphasized that a concept of self-determination, interpreted in such a broad sense, does not include any right to secession. On this subject, see other works by P. Hilpold: *Der Osttimor-Fall, eine Standortbestimmung zum Selbstbestimmungsrecht der Völker* (Peter Lang, Frankfurt, 1996); Hilpold, above, n. 16, pp. 529–602.

III. Conclusions and Outlook

As mentioned above, this provision has to be qualified as a safeguard clause, as a guarantee to make sure that the whole Framework Convention is not misinterpreted as a challenge to statehood. The prudence with which this provision is addressed, if at all, in the state reports, reveals how thorny this issue is. What seems to be a limitation of the rights of minorities and a concession to states, at first sight, benefits both in reality. The principle of good faith, as regulated in Article 2, finds specific expression here. If the contents and limits of minority protection are clearly defined in advance, a climate of mutual trust can be created where central authorities and the members of the minorities co-operate in the creation of a state which is not seen as an instrument for oppression and the arbitrary exercise of power, but as the institutional framework of a participative democracy.

ARTICLE 22

Lauri Hannikainen

Nothing in the present framework Convention shall be construed as limiting or derogating from any of the human rights and fundamental freedoms which may be ensured under the laws of any Contracting Party or under any other agreement to which it is a Party.

I. Background

A. Issues

The text of Article 22 may sound surprising to many readers: an international convention pointing out that nothing in the convention shall be construed as limiting or derogating from any of the human rights which may be ensured under the laws of any contracting party. Isn't one of the basic purposes of international conventions to obligate participating states to bring their laws in line with these conventions? Is the Framework Convention for the Protection of National Minorities (FCNM) an exception?

No, it is not. The drafting history of Article 22 makes it clear that it is not intended that states will go below the standards created by the Framework Convention. The Explanatory Report of the Ad Hoc Committee for the Protection of National Minorities (CAHMIN) on the Convention, explains Article 22 as follows: it is based on Article 60 of the European Convention for the Protection of Human Rights and Fundamental Freedoms (ECHR) and sets out a well-known principle. 'The aim is to ensure that persons belonging to national minorities benefit from whichever of the relevant national or international human rights legislation is most favourable to them.'[1] Indeed, Article 22 is virtually a copy of the corresponding article in the ECHR—at the time of the preparation of the Framework Convention it was Article 60 in the ECHR, since its revision, it is now at Article 53 ECHR.

B. History

The European Commission for Democracy through Law, in its proposal for a European convention for the protection of national minorities included Article 17, according to which the Convention shall not prejudice the provisions of domestic law or any international agreement which provides greater protection for minorities or persons belonging to minorities.[2] This proposal followed the example of several existing conventions. The content of this provision was very clear but CAHMIN preferred the model set by the ECHR. Throughout 1994, the text of draft Article 22 remained virtually the same in CAHMIN's various drafts, and became the final text of the Convention.[3]

II. Analysis

Since Article 22 uses Article 53 ECHR as its model and is nearly identical in its wording, one can presume that the interpretation of Article 53 is directly relevant for Article 22. One can safely conclude that the European Court of Human Rights (ECtHR) does not find national legal infringements of the ECHR to be acceptable. Among numerous illustrations one can refer to *Serif* v. *Greece*, a case concerning the autonomy of religious minorities. Greek law provided for the election of Muslim religious leaders (muftis) by members of the Muslim minority in the province of Thrace. When the Mufti of Rodopi died, the law was changed to allow the President of the Republic to appoint muftis. The European Court found that this new law violated Article 9 ECHR on the right to freedom of religion, while the former legal text was in line with ECHR provisions.[4] Article 22 FCNM, like Article 53 ECHR, has a positive purpose. Similar to many other human rights conventions, the Framework Convention is meant to pronounce internationally recognized

[1] Ad Hoc Committee for the Protection of National Minorities, CAHMIN (94) 32, 7th meeting, 1994, Meeting Report.

[2] European Commission for Democracy through Law (ECDL), Explanatory Report to the Proposal for a European Convention for the Protection of National Minorities, CDL-MIN (93) 6, 1993.

[3] See *inter alia* CAHMIN/GR (94) 2 Rev., 1994, Report of the 1st meeting of the CAHMIN Drafting Group; CAHMIN (94), 6th meeting, 1994, Meeting Report.

[4] *Serif* v. *Greece* (38178/97) (1999) EHRR 169.

minimum requirements for states. According to Article 22, the Convention is not meant to limit or derogate from higher standards that may be ensured under national laws of any contracting state or under any other agreement to which it is a party. Higher standards in national laws and bilateral treaties are welcome.

However, it is difficult to regard the text of Article 22 as a good formulation of a legal provision. Its meaning is clear to international human rights experts and to members of leading state organs, but not necessarily to a lower state organ with national legal experts, for example. A person unfamiliar with international human rights law may assume that the Convention is a promotional instrument that does not create legally binding obligations, when this is not the case. The provision proposed by the European Commission for Democracy through Law is much clearer on this point. Inspired by the Convention on the Prohibition of All Forms of Discrimination against Women (CEDAW) (Article 23), the Convention on the Rights of the Child (CRC) (Article 41), the Convention on the Protection of the Rights of All Migrant Workers and Members of Their Families (Article 81), the European Social Charter (Article 32) and the Revised Charter (Article H), and the European Convention on Nationality (Article 26), it provides clearer accommodations for higher standards under national laws or other legal instruments; *e contrario* it should be clear to a reader that lower national standards being in conflict with the Convention are not permitted.[5] The provision proposed by the European Commission for Democracy through Law can be regarded as a standard among human rights conventions. The inclusion of such a text in Article 22 would have prevented any misunderstandings.

The first round of state reports to the Council of Europe on the Framework Convention has not led to critical comments by the Committee of Ministers or the Advisory Committee on states' observance of Article 22. However, at least one statement of a government to the Council of Europe on its observance of the Framework Convention raises initial questions. Bulgaria, in its state report, points out under the title of Article 22 that human rights and fundamental freedoms in Bulgaria are guaranteed by the constitution, and they should not be limited or impaired by the provisions of the Framework Convention.[6] The reader may assume that there is no discrepancy between the Bulgarian constitution and the Framework Convention, even though this is not explicitly

[5] Article 27 of the Vienna Convention on the Law of Treaties pronounces one of the basic principles of international treaty law: a state party may not invoke the provisions of its internal law as a justification for its failure to perform a treaty.

[6] Bulgaria State Report, ACFC/SR (2003) 001, 2003.

stated with reference to Article 22 in the constitution. However, an overall view of the Bulgarian report gives a clear picture that in the Bulgarian view, the constitution is not problematic from the perspective of the Framework Convention. On the other hand, the Moldovan government states in its report that the constitution and certain articles in several named laws will be brought into line with the Framework Convention.[7]

Even though the European states recognize the importance of their international legal obligations, the constitution of a state is the supreme law of the national legal system and it is not easily amended. Many states are reluctant to recognize that their international obligations take precedence over their constitution. This problem has come out in practice in different contexts. However, this is a problem of wider horizons and goes beyond Article 22—even if this article was proposed by the European Commission for Democracy through Law, a body devoted to enhancing constitutional legislation.

The parties to the Framework Convention are welcome to establish minority rights based on higher standards than those spelled out in the Convention, whether by national legislation or bilateral treaties. Since the Convention is a broad framework convention, states have a lot of space to move in this respect. However, states have to be wary that the outcome of such an arrangement is not an infringement of any provisions of the Convention. One potential example would be if a state gave preferential treatment to a particular minority, which had the effect of discriminating against other minorities.

III. Conclusion and Outlook

Notwithstanding the somewhat problematic formulation of Article 22, difficulties in its application by the states parties are not apparent. States parties certainly understand the meaning of this article and can be expected to avoid infringing it with their national laws. Presumably governments of the states parties are able to keep things under control—to see to it that public authorities do not misinterpret Article 22. If such interpretations were to emerge, governments would need to revoke them. However, the monitoring organs of the Framework Convention will no doubt be watching closely for this type of development.

[7] Moldova State Report, ACFC/SR (2000) 2, 2000.

ARTICLE 23

Peter Hilpold

The rights and freedoms flowing from the principles enshrined in the present framework Convention, in so far as they are the subject of a corresponding provision in the Convention for the Protection of Human Rights and Fundamental Freedoms or in the Protocols thereto, shall be understood so as to conform to the latter provisions.

I. Background

A. Issues

This Article specifies the relationship between the Framework Convention for the Protection of National Minorities and the protection system of the European Convention for the Protection of Human Rights and Fundamental Freedoms (ECHR). This latter system is the decisive reference point for the interpretation of the Framework Convention, insofar as corresponding provisions can be found in both documents. Comparable provisions guide similar relationships between other human rights documents. Such a mechanism of co-ordination can be useful in regulating the various interactions of general human rights instruments, as it assures the consistent development of human rights law. In particular, this mechanism can successfully prevent past achievements in this field from being watered down. In the relationship between human rights documents and instruments for the protection of minorities, however, the application of these clauses may cause some problems. In fact, the subject of minority protection instruments is far more restricted and specific than that of general human rights instruments. In this context, the greatest challenge is to determine what these 'corresponding provisions' are.

B. History

In order to understand the meaning of Article 23, a historical and a systematic analysis of the underlying questions is particularly important. Creating a new human rights protection instrument nowadays most often means inserting new provisions into a field that is already densely packed with other norms that will have to give way and be adjusted to accommodate these new provisions. From a technical viewpoint, this situation in the human rights area is not unique in international law, rather a general characteristic of it. As known, there is no central law-making institution in international law, therefore the further development of international legal order largely depends on the conclusion of international bilateral and multilateral treaties. Without the same restrictive environment of national legal instruments, the international legal field is complicated with conflicting norms, lacunae, and a vast array of interpretative problems.[1] In general, awareness of this problem has risen in international legal circles over recent years and discussions now focus on the 'fragmentation of international law'.[2] Besides these parallels between the development of human rights law and general international law, there are also features that are unique to the human rights area. Up to this moment, no international human rights convention has created a 'self-contained regime'.[3] Rather, each relevant document is embedded in a broad network of instruments, which are closely interconnected.

In human rights law, conflicts of norms differ from those in general international law as a result of the widely diverging implementation structure of the norms in these fields.[4] In fact, wide areas of general international law are composed mainly of bilateral obligations where the principle of reciprocity is pivotal to effective implementation. In the field of human rights, however, the

[1] Clarifications with regard to some of these problems have been obtained through the Vienna Convention on the Law of Treaties (VCLT), though not of all. See, in particular, Arts. 30 and 31 of the Convention.

[2] G. Hafner, 'Risks Ensuing from Fragmentation of International Law', UN Doc. ILC(LII)/WG/LT/L.1/Add. 1, p. 24 (2000) (included as annex to UN Doc. A/55/10 (2000)). See also 97 AJIL 2003, pp. 166–7.

[3] B. Simma, 'Self-contained Regimes', *NYIL* (1985), 111–36.

[4] On the 'implementation structure' (*Erfüllungsstruktur*) of international treaties, see B. Simma, *Das Reziprozitätselement im Zustandekommen völkerrechtlicher Verträge* (Duncker & Humblot, Berlin, 1972), 205 ff.

principle of reciprocity is an inadequate means to ensure compliance as the relative obligations are of a so-called 'objective' nature.[5] Therefore, in the ongoing process of creating law, the principle of reciprocity may ensure that state rights are not infringed,[6] but by no means does it provide a guarantee that the overall protection standard will not suffer. The construction of the international human rights protection system is modelled on a building block approach where, after the foundations were laid following the Second World War step-by-step a large and sophisticated edifice has been constructed.[7] Presumably each new contribution helps to strengthen the existing structure as a whole; however care has to be taken to ensure overall compatibility and that new developments do not call past achievements into question. While open derogations of human rights norms in later provisions are unusual, there is a persistent danger that new developments will limit the scope of established standards. It is interesting to note that these fears did not arise during more recent stages in the development of the human rights system, but have existed from its very beginning. The provision that rights granted by previous agreements may not be limited or derogated from can be found in Article 19(8) of the International Labour Organization (ILO) Constitution 1919; in Article 32 of the Social Charter 1961,[8] which was replicated in Article 5(2) of the International Covenant on Civil and Political Rights (ICCPR) and the International Covenant on Economic, Social, and Cultural Rights (ICESCR); in Article 41 of the International Convention on the Rights of the Child 1989; and in Article 23 of the Convention on the Elimination of All Forms of Discrimination against Women (CEDAW) of 1979.[9]

Article 53 ECHR is particularly relevant in our context. Even in 1950 the Contracting Parties wanted to make sure that, '[n]othing in this Convention shall be construed as limiting or derogating from any of the human rights and fundamental freedoms which may be ensured under the laws of any High Contracting Party or under any other agreement to which it is a Party.'[10] This

[5] Meaning that these obligations are owed to the state community as a whole. See the *Barcelona Traction Case* (*Belgium* v. *Spain*), judgment, [1970], ICJ Rep. 4. With respect to a related statement by the European Human Rights Commission, see *Austria* v. *Italy*, D 788/60, Annuaire de la Convention 4, p. 117, spec. 139.

[6] P. Pustorino, 'Commentary to Art. 53 ECHR', in S. Bartole B. Conforti, and G. Raimondi, *Commentario alla Convenzione Europea per la Tutela dei Diritti dell' Uomo e delle Libertà Fondamentali* (CEDAM, Padova, 2001), 741–8 at p. 745.

[7] For a recent account of this development, see C. Tomuschat, *Human Rights: Between Idealism and Realism* (Oxford University Press, Oxford, 2003).

[8] See Art. H of the revised Social Charter of 3 May 1996, ETS 163.

[9] P. Pustorino, 'Commentary to Art. 53 ECHR', in Bartole, Conforti, and Raimondi, above, n. 6, p. 741.

[10] Prior to the amendments established by Protocol no. 11, European Convention for the Protection of Human Rights and Fundamental Freedoms (ECHR), ETS 5, 1950, Art. 60 was the relevant one.

provision guaranteed that the ECHR operated as a minimum standard that could only be derogated from by more favourable provisions. At the same time, this provision gave further expression to the principle of subsidiarity, which characterizes the application of the entire ECHR.[11] As long as the Council of Europe remained the main actor in the human rights law-making process in Europe, consistency and coherence among its component single instruments was relatively easy to arrange as co-ordination took place within the organization itself. This task became more difficult after the European Union entered the field of human rights law, requiring the co-ordination of activities of two otherwise independent organizations. The greatest challenge, in this context, was the elaboration of the Charter of Fundamental Rights. Notwithstanding the many parallels and similarities that originated from both organizations, the creation of a new human rights document threatened to lower the standards that the Council of Europe had already set. It is therefore not surprising that the Council was one of the main proponents of the special safeguards that were eventually included in the Charter of Fundamental Rights.[12]

The resulting provisions, Paragraph 3 of Article 52 and Article 53 of the Charter, seem to provide detailed rules for the co-ordination of both legal orders, although many questions remain open as long as no definitive solution is found to govern the relationship between the ECHR and the Charter of Fundamental Rights.[13] To better understand the tension that exists between the two, it may be interesting to contrast the approaches chosen for the Charter of Fundamental Rights on the one hand, and the Framework Convention on the other. Article 52(3) of the Charter states, for example: '[i]n so far as this Charter contains rights which correspond to rights guaranteed by the Convention for the Protection of Human Rights and Fundamental Freedoms, the meaning and scope of those rights shall be the same as those laid down by the said Convention. This provision shall not prevent Union law providing more extensive protection.' At the same time, Article 53 stipulates that:

[n]othing in this Charter shall be interpreted as restricting or adversely affecting human rights and fundamental freedoms as recognised, in their respective fields of application, by Union law and international law and by international agreements

[11] L. Besselink, 'Entrapped by the Maximum Standard: On Fundamental Rights, Pluralism and Subsidiarity in the European Union', *Common Market Law Review* (1998), 629 ff.

[12] M. Cartabia, 'Commentary to Art. 53 of the Charter of Fundamental Rights', in R. Bifulco, M. Cartabia, and A. Celotto, *L'Europa dei diritti: Commento alla Carta dei diritti fondamentali dell' Unione Europea* (Il Mulino, Bologna, 2001), 360–6 at p. 361.

[13] T. Groppi, 'Commentary to Art. 52 of the Charter of Fundamental Rights', in Bifulco, Cartabia, and Celotto, above, n. 12, pp. 351–60 at p. 360.

to which the Union, the Community or all the Member States are party, including the European Convention for the Protection of Human Rights and Fundamental Freedoms, and by the Member States' constitution.

Together these two provisions ensure that the standard set by the ECHR system operates as a minimum, safeguarding higher national standards and, on the whole, maintaining the plurality of human rights protection systems.[14] By the same token, the last sentence of Article 52(3) makes sure that higher standards are not prevented from being introduced within the European Union, a development that many expect to take place in the future. Finally, the Explanatory Report to the Charter also contains a provisional 'correspondence table' linking the single norms of the ECHR and the parallel provisions of the Charter.

It is interesting to note that problems of co-ordination between general human rights provisions and specific provisions for the protection of minorities have appeared in relation to instruments encompassing both of these kinds of provisions. This problem was highlighted by the UN Human Rights Committee, in its General Comment 23 on the rights of minorities (Article 27) of 8 April 1994, where it stated the following: '8. The Committee observes that none of the rights protected under article 27 of the Covenant may be legitimately exercised in a manner or to an extent inconsistent with the other provisions of the Covenant.' With this statement, the UNHRC underscores that minority rights are human rights and that the overall human rights protection standard must not suffer from the additional guarantee of minority rights. Minority rights must be interpreted in a way that makes them compatible with the general human rights system.

The Framework Convention, as an instrument designed specifically for the protection of minorities, has to look to other human rights instruments to find a reference benchmark that is capable of determining the human rights standard to be used in the application of this instrument. The relevant norms regulating the relationship between this document and other human rights instruments, in particular the ECHR, can be found in two different provisions of the Convention, Article 22 and Article 23. Whilst the first provision aims to ensure that the Framework Convention neither diminishes the existing level of protection guaranteed by other human rights protection instruments, nor precludes the formulation of more progressive regulations, the second

[14] Above, n. 12; M. Borowski, 'Commentary to Art. 53 of the Charter of Fundamental Rights', in J. Meyer, *Kommentar zur Charta der Grundrechte der Europäischen Union* (Nomos, Baden-Baden, 2003), 593–601; above, n. 13.

article states a presumption of absolute conformity between the provisions of the Framework Convention and the related provisions of the ECHR.

The desire to bring interpretations of the Framework Convention in line with ECHR jurisprudence seems to have been the starting point for negotiations in the Ad Hoc Committee for the Protection of National Minorities (CAHMIN).[15] However, the drafting history of Article 23 shows that despite discussions on the content of the provision, the conclusion was somewhat disappointing. In this respect, Article D of the Preliminary Draft Framework Convention for the Protection of National Minorities differs from the final version and merits citation:

> The rights and freedoms flowing from the principles enshrined in the present Convention which are the subject of a corresponding provision in the European Convention on Human Rights or in its Protocols thereto, as well as the restriction clauses contained in Article 20, shall be interpreted in accordance with the European Convention on Human Rights and the case-law of its organs.

In the final version, both the reference to the restriction clause and to the case law of the ECHR organs was deleted, without any notable improvement. With regard to the second change, some discussion has been reported. In particular, both the Austrian and the Romanian delegations argued that the reference to the 'case law' was inappropriate, as it could never act as a source of interpretation. From a narrow and formalistic point of view, this criticism may be correct, but it does not take into account the significant factual importance that the case law of international tribunals, and in particular that of the European Human Rights Court, has generated. Without assuming a Common Law position, it can certainly be said that the case law of the European Human Rights Court is of enormous importance as an interpretative guide for the Framework Convention.[16]

C. Context

With regard to context, the ECHR is explicitly referred to in the Preamble of the Framework Convention.[17] Likewise, Articles 7, 8, and 10(3) are of further

[15] Ad Hoc Committee for the Protection of National Minorities (CAHMIN) (94) 5, 1st meeting 1994, Meeting Report: 'It was indicated that in no case the interpretation of the provisions of the framework Convention should depart from the interpretation given to the corresponding provisions of the ECHR by the European Court of Human Rights.'

[16] On the important role of precedent in the continuing development of the European legal area, see R. Schulze and U. Seif, *Richterrecht und Rechtsfortbildung in der Europäischen Wirtschaftsgemeinschaft* (Mohr Siebeck, Tübingen, 2003).

[17] It is well known that preambles do not create legal commitments *per se*, but according to Art. 31(2) VCLT they are part of the context that one may rely upon for interpretation purposes. See, for example, H. D. Treviranus, 'Preamble', *EPIL* 3 (1997), 1097–8.

relevance. In addition, some claim that a close relationship exists with Article 22 of the Framework Convention, but as will be demonstrated, this argument is not convincing.

II. Analysis

A. Structure of the Article

The following will examine how the way in which the ECHR is interpreted, together with its protocols, may influence the interpretation of the Framework Convention. In this context, it will be shown that Article 23 has a rather problematic structure. If read together with other provisions of this document, however, it may reveal, especially in a future-oriented perspective, an important role within this Convention.

B. Corresponding Provisions of the ECHR

According to Article 23 of the Framework Convention the only provisions of the FCNM that have to be interpreted in conformity with the ECHR are those that correspond to an existing and equivalent ECHR provision. This approach is not unusual, *per se*. It was adopted a few years after the Framework Convention was drafted, to clarify the relationship between the ECHR and the Charter of Fundamental Rights. This reflects the attempts in the Explanatory Report to the Charter to identify specific relationships between the individual articles of these two documents. The Explanatory Report to the Framework Convention, however, does not give such assistance to the interpreter. On closer inspection one may arrive at the following explanation for this situation: the two documents operate on different levels, although their basis is the same. The ECHR is a document concerned with general protection of human rights that, at the same time, does not focus on minority rights in a strict sense. The Framework Convention, on the contrary, deals with a specific field, namely minority rights.

With regard to Article 52(3) of the Charter, this provision has been called a 'transfer norm', which introduces nearly all the material guarantees of the ECHR and its protocols, into the system laid out in the Charter. It comes close to a material accession of the European Union to the ECHR as it lays the basis for close co-operation between the European Court of Justice (ECJ) and the European Court of Human Rights.[18] A transferral of jurisprudence on such an

[18] J. Borowski,, 'Commentary to Art. 52 of the Charter of Fundamental Rights', in J. Meyer, *Kommentar zur Charta der Grundrechte der Europäischen Union* (Note), (Nomos, Baden-Baden, 2003), 577–92 (paras. 34 ff.).

ample and systematic basis cannot take place between the ECHR and the Framework Convention as the nature and the aim of these two instruments is too divergent, nor are their judicial organs linked. Already, the fact that within the Framework Convention respect for individual provisions is guaranteed by a political institution, the Committee of Ministers, rather than an independent judicial organ means that legally derived jurisprudence cannot be transferred 'lock, stock and barrel' into a system which also has to take political considerations into account and is structured accordingly. That said, as the Framework Convention operates on a different basis from the ECHR and has a different orientation, a direct transfer of norms would fail on technical grounds. In spite of this, none of these differences stands in the way of a close connection between the two documents, albeit this connection operates in a somewhat different form than a first glance at the wording of Article 23 may suggest.

If we look for provisions in the Framework Convention with directly 'corresponding provisions' in the ECHR only a few come to mind. These are: Article 7 (freedom of peaceful assembly, of association, of expression and of thought, conscience and religion); Article 8 (the right of every person belonging to a minority to manifest his or her religion or belief and to establish religious institutions, organizations and associations); and Article 10(3) (the right of every person belonging to a national minority to be informed promptly, in a language which he or she understands, of the reasons for his or her arrest, and of the nature and cause of any accusation against him or her, and to defend himself or herself in this language, if necessary with the free assistance of an interpreter). There is a rich jurisprudence on these related rights in the ECHR from which the monitoring bodies of the Framework Convention already heavily draw. Outside of these provisions the interpretation of the Framework Convention gains less from the search for specific, corresponding provisions in the ECHR than from a broader, more generic approach. In this sense, human rights have a role to play in the Framework Convention in two respects. First of all, they form the basis for all minority rights. It was the clear intent of the drafters of this Convention not to create a new category of rights, but to demonstrate that minority rights represent a natural, though specific, aspect of human rights protection. Without this connection, the concept of minority rights would hardly find acceptance, either on a political or on a theoretical ground nowadays.[19]

[19] For further comments on this issue refer to the following publications of this author: *Modernes Minderheitenrecht* (Manz, Vienna, 2001) and 'Der Schutz der Minderheit in der Minderheit', *Migralex* 1 (2003), 3–12. Of course, the need for such a reservation was far more urgent with the Charter, as this document has a scope comparable to that of the ECHR even though, as previously mentioned, the ECHR does not contain provisions on minority rights in a strict sense.

Secondly, when it comes to the concrete application of minority rights instruments (which also regularly contain general human rights provisions), the general human rights order is an important reference point to prevent conflicts in legal interpretation between different human rights in a strict sense, between human rights and minority rights; and between minority rights. The capacity to balance potentially conflicting rights is a traditional characteristic of the human rights system, and minority rights are also human rights in their substance.

C. The Relationship of Article 23 with Article 22 of the Framework Convention

At first glance, it does not seem probable that Article 23 will engender much discussion in the monitoring procedure as neither violations nor progress in its implementation are likely to be reported. So far, no statement relevant to this provision has been made in the reports presented pursuant to Article 25 of the Convention. If violations of Articles 7, 8, or 10(3) are alleged, usually direct reference is made to the corresponding provisions of the ECHR and the relevant jurisprudence without resorting to Article 23, which would technically permit such an approach. Nonetheless, this is not a futile provision, a norm without meaning. If we look beyond its strict wording, this provision, in addition to the Preamble, provides for a strong connection between the Framework Convention and the ECHR. Even if Article 23 seems to require a specific link between a provision of the ECHR and a corresponding provision of the Framework Convention in order for the FCNM clause to be deemed relevant to the interpretation of the latter provision, and even if all references to ECHR case law have been deleted from the final version of Article 23, it is also the general spirit of the ECHR, as expressed in the European Court of Human Rights, which has to be taken into consideration in the interpretation of the provision of the Framework Convention. At the same time, Article 23 should be read in close connection to Article 22. Interpreting the Framework Convention in conformity with the ECHR does not mean that the ECHR would set a maximum standard. Although this principle has not been stated in Article 23 it can be found in Article 22, which refers to 'any other agreement' and therefore includes the ECHR.[20]

[20] In this regard, the text of Art. 52(3) of the Charter of Fundamental Rights gives a far more convincing structure, as the reference to the ECHR for the interpretation of this document is immediately qualified by the reservation that the Union should not be prevented from providing more extensive protection.

III. Conclusions and Outlook

It has been shown that Article 23 of the Framework Convention appears to permit a seamless insertion of the Framework Convention into a normative environment characterized by the presence of a highly recognized and extremely effective international order for the protection of human rights—the ECHR. Though of different nature and aims, these two documents have significant common ground. This is most evident in Articles 7, 8, and 10(3) of the Framework Convention which refer, either directly or through the language used, to corresponding provisions of the ECHR. In the first reporting cycle, broad attention has been given to these references. They have created the basis for detailed monitoring in areas of pivotal importance for the effective protection of minorities. Reliance on the jurisprudence and practice of the Strasbourg organs has allowed for years of precedence-setting case law to assist in the interpretation of these contentious issues.

It can also be argued, however, that the explicit interconnection of these two documents is equally important. Thus, Article 23, together with the relevant provision in the Preamble of the Framework Convention, is a reminder of the fact that minority rights are human rights. At the same time, these provisions indicate that wherever minority rights conflict with general human rights principles, a balancing of the different interests has to be achieved that takes into account the Framework Convention as an important human rights instrument. It is hoped that in future monitoring activities, greater attention will be given to the broader function of Article 23. As such, the possibility of closer ties between practically every minority rights protection norm and general human rights aspects can contribute to a balanced and, ultimately, more effective application of the Framework Convention.

SECTION IV

ARTICLES 24–26

Kyriaki Topidi

Article 24

1. The Committee of Ministers of the Council of Europe shall monitor the implementation of this framework convention by the Contracting Parties.
2. The Parties which are not members of the Council of Europe shall participate in the implementation mechanism, according to modalities to be determined.

Article 25

1. Within a period of one year following the entry into force of this framework Convention in respect of a Contracting Party, the latter shall transmit to the Secretary General of the Council of Europe full information on the legislative and other measures taken to give effect to the principles set out in this framework Convention.
2. Thereafter, each Party shall transmit to the Secretary General on a periodical basis and whenever the Committee of Ministers so requests any further information of relevance to the implementation of this framework Convention.
3. The Secretary General shall forward to the Committee of Ministers the information transmitted under the terms of this Article.

Article 26

1. In evaluating the adequacy of the measures taken by the Parties to give effect to the principles set out in this framework Convention the Committee of Ministers shall be assisted by the advisory committee, the members of which shall have recognised expertise in the field of the protection of national minorities.
2. The composition of this advisory committee and its procedures shall be determined by the Committee of Ministers within a period of one year following the entry into force of this framework Convention.

I. Background

A. Issues

The monitoring mechanism of the Framework Convention for the Protection of National Minorities (FCNM) is laid out briefly in Articles 24–6. More specifically, Article 24 FCNM designates the Committee of Ministers (CoM) as the competent body for monitoring the implementation by states parties of the Framework Convention. The Committee itself is a mainly political body, composed of Foreign Ministers from each of the states parties. In theory, the Committee has the power to control the monitoring process to the extent that it may politicize it.

According to Article 26 FCNM, however, the Committee of Ministers is not the sole body that evaluates the adequacy of measures taken by a state party. It is assisted by an Advisory Committee (AC), which ensures monitoring efficiency. It was left for the Committee of Ministers to determine the rules concerning the composition of the Advisory Committee and its procedure.[1] The monitoring procedure is completed under Article 25 FCNM, requiring states parties to submit a report providing full information on legislative and other measures giving effect to the Framework Convention within one year of its entry into force for each state. In addition, reports are due every five years, complementing

[1] Committee of Ministers, Resolution (97) 10 on the Rules on the Monitoring Arrangements under Articles 24 to 26 of the Framework Convention of the Protection of National Minorities (FCNM), 601st meeting, 1997.

the information included in the first report, and whenever the Committee of Ministers requests one.[2]

These particular provisions of the FCNM raise several important aspects to be taken into consideration when discussing the implementation mechanism of the Framework Convention. The relations between the Advisory Committee and the Committee of Ministers constitute one important component of the monitoring mechanism. The work of the Advisory Committee in its various dimensions is another matter meriting some attention, including considerations for: its access to sources of information and level of contacts with states and NGOs; the composition and procedures which define its work; and the impact that this has on the obligations of the states parties. An examination of these questions will then lead us to compare the FCNM monitoring mechanisms with alternative existing monitoring mechanisms of minority rights, and to discuss the impact of the FCNM monitoring mechanism for the advancement of minority rights standards.

B. History

A number of fundamental elements of the monitoring mechanism deserve historical examination. First, the choice of an appropriate monitoring mechanism for the FCNM was not simple or straightforward. The work of the European Commission for Democracy through Law, between 1990 and 1993, clearly favoured a judicial mechanism, allowing for both individual and state petitions, combined with regular reporting, and the presence of a committee constituted of members serving in their individual capacity.[3]

The Ad Hoc Committee for the Protection of National Minorities (CAHMIN), while negotiating the final text of the FCNM, was faced with three broad possibilities on the question of controlling the implementation of the Convention. The first option consisted of a Committee of Ministers assisted by a consultative committee; while the second was to establish a committee of governmental experts to examine state reports, an option openly preferred by some states such as Austria.[4] The final alternative was to form a Committee

[2] Framework Convention for the Protection of National Minorities (FCNM), Art. 25.

[3] European Commission for Democracy through Law (ECDL), Preliminary Draft Convention on the Protection of Minorities [DAJ.SC.DEMOCRACY] CONV. MIN, 1990, Arts. 18–22. Also, ECDL, Proposal for a European Convention for the Protection of National Minorities, CDL-MIN (93) 6, 1993, Arts. 18–30.

[4] See Appendix I, Ad Hoc Committee for the Protection of National Minorities (CAHMIN), Control of the Implementation of the Framework Convention for the Protection of National Minorities, CAHMIN 94 (17), 1994, pp. 2–5.

of independent experts, which gained the support of most states,[5] and was finalized by the CAHMIN in 1994.[6]

Another important element in the establishment of the monitoring mechanism was the decision relating to the periodic cycle for submitting state reports. Initially, discussions in CAHMIN considered two years to be sufficient for the first state report.[7] The one-year option prevailed, however, in a move that reflected the period fixed for state reporting under Article 15 of the European Charter for Regional or Minority Languages.[8]

It is clear from the stages of preparatory work done by CAHMIN that transparency was a major concern,[9] although only a limited release of reports was discussed.[10] Transparency continued to be a concern for the AC and the CoM, even after the completion of the drafting of the Convention, as will be discussed below.

Finally, follow-up procedures are crucial within any given monitoring mechanism. The experience of the UN Human Rights Committee (HRC), the monitoring body of the International Covenant on Civil and Political Rights (ICCPR), has demonstrated that follow-up success may vary, and it is greatly dependent on the intentions of the state party.[11] The procedure in the case of the FCNM was developed later in the process, during the more detailed set-up

[5] See, for example, CAHMIN, Informal Proposal for Further Discussion in the CAHMIN Submitted by the Delegation of the Netherlands in Co-ordination with Belgium, Germany, Hungary, Norway, and Portugal, CAHMIN 94 (24), 1994, in particular Arts. 21–31.

[6] CAHMIN, 7th meeting, CAHMIN 94 (32), 1994, Art. 22, p. 20.

[7] Above, n. 5, under Art. 25(*a*).

[8] Council of Europe (CoE), European Charter for Regional or Minority Languages, ETS No. 148, Strasbourg, 1992. The period for subsequent reporting was, however, one to three years under the Charter. A similar proposal was also submitted to the CAHMIN for the FCNM, but was not retained. See CAHMIN, Informal Proposal for Further Discussion in the CAHMIN Submitted by the Delegation of the Netherlands in Co-ordination with Belgium, Germany, Hungary, Norway, and Portugal, CAHMIN 94(24), 1994, Art. 25(*b*).

[9] See, for example, CAHMIN, 7th Meeting, CAHMIN 94 (32), meeting report, 1994, pp. 21–2, Art. 21 where the Committee notes: 'The monitoring of the implementation of this Convention shall, insofar as possible, be transparent. In this regard it should be advisable to envisage the publications of the reports and other texts resulting from such monitoring.'

[10] Above, n. 5, Art. 26 includes two alternatives in this direction. Alternative I states that 'Reports submitted pursuant to Article 25 may [shall] be made available [to the public] on request'. Alternative II reads: 'The report pursuant to Article 25, shall be made available [upon request] to organizations competent in the field of the protection of national minorities . . .'.

[11] In the context of the International Covenant on Civil and Political Rights (ICCPR), the state party is expected to report back to the Human Rights Committee (HRC) within 90 days from the issue of the communication that concerns it on the measures it has taken to comply with the recommendation of the Committee. This mechanism has known only limited success. For a lengthier analysis of the mechanism, see M. A. Martin Estabanez and K. Gal, *Implementing the Framework Convention for the Protection of National Minorities*, ECMI Report No. 3, (ECMI, Flensburg, 1999), 37.

of the monitoring mechanism, and was made with particular reference to the enactment of the AC's rules of procedure.

C. Context

This group of articles is relatively autonomous with respect to the other provisions of the FCNM, in the sense that it deals with the implementation of the Convention. Nevertheless, it is linked to the general evaluation of the Convention as an instrument to advance minority rights standards.

II. Analysis

A. Structure

The following sections are devoted to three main topics contained in Articles 24, 25, and 26, and will be presented in reverse order so as to follow the chronological order of the intervention of each actor in the Convention's monitoring process. The first topic will delineate the Advisory Committee, its work, its composition, and its relationship with the Committee of Ministers. The second will cover the monitoring mechanism as realized from the perspective of states parties and their obligations, and the third and final topic will provide commentary and discussion of the role of the Committee of Ministers within the monitoring process.

B. The Role of the Advisory Committee (Article 26 FCNM)

The Advisory Committee is an independent body composed of up to eighteen ordinary experts. The choice of independent experts, not representing of their respective countries of origin, was intentional so as to involve an impartial body, alongside the politically charged Committee of Ministers, thus reducing the danger of politicizing the monitoring process.

The Committee of Ministers selects members of the Advisory Committee from candidates proposed by the states parties. They are required to have 'recognized expertise' in the field of minority protection and, most importantly, they are to be independent and impartial.[12] Their term is four years and it can be renewed only once.[13] As each member is nominated by one state, Advisory Committee members are not allowed to vote on the opinions regarding the

[12] Above, n. 1, Rule 6. [13] ibid., Rule 16.

state that nominated them. The body is led by a President and first and second Vice-Presidents. It meets in camera and decisions are usually taken by majority vote.

In order to perform its monitoring activities more efficiently, the Advisory Committee devised an Outline for State Reports[14] before drafting its own rules of procedure.[15] It also established working groups responsible for establishing and maintaining contacts with governmental and non-governmental actors in a given country, and for drafting the text of an opinion on a specific state. The composition of these country-specific working groups complies with the rule that no member will be appointed to the group dealing with the report of the state that has nominated him or her, or to one dealing with the report of a state that includes a minority with ethnic or other strong ties with the population of the state of which the member is a national.

Article 26 does not address the competencies or the mission of the Advisory Committee. Resolution (97)10 establishing its rules of procedure is more detailed in this respect. According to this resolution, the main duties of the Advisory Committee are to examine the reports submitted periodically by states parties,[16] and to prepare opinions on the measures that states need to take to fully implement the Convention.[17] It may also request additional information from a state party,[18] as well as receive information from other sources such as individuals and non-governmental organizations with the intention of using it in the preparation of its opinions.[19] In brief, the monitoring activities of the AC begin after the Secretariat of the FCNM receives a state report, which is then transmitted to all members of the AC. In a first meeting, following a discussion of issues on the implementation of the FCNM, and when additional information is required from state authorities, a questionnaire is drafted and subsequently adopted by the plenary with the intention of being sent to the state concerned.

The next stage in the process occurs after the completion of the draft opinion within the working group. This opinion is then presented to the plenary of the AC and amendments are discussed. As of September 1999, the opinions include both article-by-article comments of the state's performance, as well as proposals for conclusions and recommendations for the Committee of

[14] Committee of Ministers, Outline for Reports to be Submitted Pursuant to Article 25 Paragraph 1 of the Framework Convention for the Protection of National Minorities, 1st Meeting, CoE, ACFC/INF (98) 1, 1998.

[15] Committee of Ministers, Rules of Procedure of the Advisory Committee on the Framework Convention for the Protection of National Minorities, CoE, ACFC/INF (98) 2, 1998.

[16] Above, n. 1, Rule 20. [17] Above, n. 1, Rule 23. [18] Above, n. 1, Rule 29.

[19] Above, n. 1, Rule 30.

Ministers' attention, but to which the CoM is not bound.[20] Each adopted AC opinion is transmitted to the governments concerned and to the Committee of Ministers.

The Committee further disposes of a series of measures that considerably widen its scope of activities: it may actively seek information from non-governmental sources after having notified the Committee of Ministers;[21] and it may hold meetings with governments or any other person having obtained a specific mandate from the Committee of Ministers for that purpose beforehand.[22] The requirement to obtain an express mandate from the Committee of Ministers was perceived, however, as a form of indirect censorship by some AC members.[23] Nevertheless, according to the Advisory Committee, involving NGOs and minority groups in the process has proved useful,[24] to the extent that the Ministers' Deputies authorized the AC to hold meetings with non-governmental bodies and independent institutions in the context of the visits it conducts upon the invitation of the states parties concerned, at their 708th meeting on 3 May 2000.[25] This authorization was given for the entire initial monitoring cycle. The same regulation provides for the possibility of Advisory Committee involvement in the monitoring and the follow-up of the Committee of Ministers' conclusions and recommendations through an initiative of the latter.[26]

The possibility of performing country visits has evolved to become a tool facilitating and enriching the task of the AC.[27] As a traditional monitoring tool, country visits are also prominent in the work of other international bodies, such as the Committee for the Prevention of Torture (CPT). Given their usefulness, on 17 May 2000 the Committee of Ministers decided to provide the Advisory Committee with a general mandate to conduct such visits. This mandate responded to a clear need to determine whether a violation is

[20] At its meeting on 30 November 2001, the Advisory Committee introduced some changes to the structure of its opinions by inserting a new section IV entitled 'Main Findings and Comments of the Advisory Committee' and discontinuing section V of its earlier opinions on 'Proposal for Conclusions and Recommendations by the Council of Ministers'. See Advisory Committee of the Framework Convention for the Protection of National Minorities, 3rd Activity Report, ACFC/INF (2002) 1, 2002, para. 27.

[21] Above, n. 1, Rule 31.

[22] Above, n. 1, Rule 32.

[23] A. Phillips, *The Framework Convention for the Protection of National Minorities: A Policy Analysis* (Minority Rights Group International, London, 2002), 6.

[24] Advisory Committee on the Framework Convention for the Protection of National Minorities, 1st Activity Report, ACFC/INF (1999) 001, 1999, para. 20; Advisory Committee on the FCNM, 2nd Activity Report, ACFC/INF (2000) 001, 2000, para. 20; and Advisory Committee of the FCNM, 3rd Activity Report, ACFC/INF (2002) 001, 2002, para. 18.

[25] Advisory Committee of the FCNM, 2nd Activity Report, above, n. 24, para. 25.

[26] Above, n. 1, Rule 36.

[27] Above, n. 1, Rule 32, para. 2.

occurring *in situ*.[28] Consequently, such country visits have been evaluated as informative and useful for both states and the AC.[29] In fact, they have provided a better appreciation and understanding of the situation, as well as a framework for dialogue on contentious issues;[30] even more so, given the Committee's developed practice of meeting government representatives, as well as representatives of national minorities and members of civil society. Furthermore, these visits have been successful in targeting regions where minority groups reside in order to inspect their living conditions there.[31]

Over the last five years, the Advisory Committee has become a crucial component of the FCNM monitoring mechanism. Its work has clearly developed beyond the boundaries of Article 26 FCNM and is currently undertaking the core of the monitoring procedure, with the Committee of Ministers receiving its opinions, state comments on the opinions, and adopting resolutions that are based on the Advisory Committee's work, for the most part. The similarities with the European Commission against Racism and Intolerance (ECRI) are noticeable insofar as both monitoring mechanisms followed a step-by-step approach to achieve a fairly independent position that allows them to engage in constructive dialogue.[32] The AC's main task remains the formulation of opinions based on legal criteria, determining the degree of implementation of state party commitments and the fulfilment of their legal obligations under the FCNM. It does not analyse individual petitions, however. This is a result of the FCNM drafters' choice not to opt for a judicial mechanism to monitor the legal obligations resulting from the Convention.

C. The Monitoring Mechanism and the Obligations of States Parties (Article 25 FCNM)

The implementation of the Convention is monitored on the basis of state reports submitted one year after the entry into force of the FCNM in that state, and every five years thereafter.[33] The AC drafted an outline for the state reports, which the Committee of Ministers subsequently adopted on

[28] Martin Estabanez and Gal, above, n. 11, p. 50.

[29] R. Hofmann, 'Review of the Monitoring Process of the Council of Europe Framework Convention for the Protection of National Minorities', *European Yearbook of Minority Issues*, 1 (2003), 435–60, at p. 442.

[30] Above, n. 23, p. 7.

[31] The most recent such country visits of the Advisory Committee to states parties to the Convention are: on 31 March 2003 to Azerbaijan; on 26 September 2003 to Serbia and Montenegro; on 10 November 2003 to Bulgaria; and on 8 December 2003 to the former Yugoslav Republic of Macedonia.

[32] See above, n. 28 at p. 47, for a further comparison between the two bodies, from this angle.

[33] Art. 25(1) and (2) FCNM.

30 September 1998.[34] In most cases, the state reports followed the proposed structure, although the level of analysis varied. The main criticism in this respect reflected the need for additional factual evidence.[35]

The monitoring mechanism of the FCNM subscribes to the model of mechanism that does not provide possibilities for individual complaints. In this sense it can be called non-judicial, as opposed to the ones devised within the European Convention for the Protection of Human Rights and Fundamental Freedoms (ECHR), where the European Court of Human Rights (ECtHR) is principally responsible for the existing implementation of the Convention. Likewise, because the FCNM monitoring mechanism is non-judicial it does not issue judgments that are compulsory for the states parties involved, as is the case for the European Court of Justice of the European Union or for the ECtHR of the Council of Europe.[36] The logic of the FCNM is different, and this is duly reflected in the way its implementation is monitored. Structurally speaking, the monitoring mechanism of the FCNM is closer to the group of treaty-based, non-judicial mechanisms, as its procedure is inquisitive in nature, rather than adversarial.

Nevertheless, the value of this reporting system is not negligible. It clearly allows for a thorough examination of national measures with a view to assessing their conformity with the Convention's standards, despite the lack of legally binding force of its findings. This type of mechanism also distinguishes itself from other non-judicial mechanisms, as it has an exclusive state reporting-based function, whilst the mandates of other human rights mechanisms expand to include interstate complaints: for example, the HRC under Article 41 of the ICCPR; and individual complaints, as for example, the Committee on the Elimination of Racial Discrimination (CERD) under Article 14 of the International Convention on the Elimination of All Forms of Racial Discrimination.

[34] Each report should be divided into two major parts. The first portion should serve as an introduction and should outline the way each state has sought to implement the Convention. The second part should provide a detailed analysis of the measures undertaken in each instance on an article-by-article basis, divided into five categories (narrative, legal, state infrastructure, policy, and factual).

[35] Above, n. 23, at p. 5. See also Advisory Committee on the FCNM, 1st Activity Report, ACFC/INF (1999) 001, 1999, para. 17; Advisory Committee on the FCNM, 2nd Activity Report, above, n. 24, para. 13; and Advisory Committee of the FCNM, 3rd Activity Report, ACFC/INF (2002) 001, 2002, para. 12.

[36] Art. 46(1) ECHR (formerly 53) refers to the mandatory nature of the decisions of the Court specifying that states parties must abide by the final judgment pronounced by the European Court of Human Rights. The supervision of the execution of judgments assigned to the Committee of Ministers of the Council of Europe, according to Art. 46(2) ECHR (formerly 54). See. M. Telalian, 'Mechanisms for Monitoring Compliance with Human Rights within the United Nations and the Council of Europe: Effectiveness and Prospects', in M. Vassiliou and H. Psomiades (eds.), *Human Rights in the 21st Century* (Human Rights Defence Centre, Ant. N. Sakkoulas Publishers, Athens, 2001), 111–58, at p. 135.

The quality of the monitoring process depends on the independence of the monitoring body.[37] In the case of the FCNM, the CoM is assisted by the AC. In this respect, it is worth considering the relationship between the two. Other factors naturally influence the quality of the control, for example: the periodicity of control; NGO involvement in the process; the competence of the monitoring body to issue country-specific comments; and the state of follow-up measures, are some of these factors.[38]

The main deficiency of the current FCNM reporting structure, as witnessed also by the case of the HRC, and very impressively by the Committee against Torture, is the risk that states do not comply with their reporting obligations in due time,[39] which the AC has repeatedly deplored.[40] To date, the AC and the CoM have not managed to address this issue successfully. The possibility of collecting information on a state that has not duly reported remains disputed. As illustrated by paragraph 20 of the UN Convention against Torture, ex officio investigation is possible, but such investigation would have to draw exclusively on non-governmental sources. In a March 2003 decision, the CoM authorized the AC to submit a proposal for the commencement of monitoring the FCNM when the state is delayed in submitting its report by more than twenty-four months.[41] So far, the only country-specific decision taken on this issue by the CoM concerns Bosnia-Herzegovina, which submitted its report subsequent to the threat of an ex officio investigation.[42] Therefore, it appears that this measure has considerable potential with respect to the timely submission of state reports, and may contribute to a stabilization in the duration of the monitoring cycle.

The quality of the submitted state reports is another issue to be addressed. In cases where states do not accurately describe the human rights situation in their territories, bodies such as the HRC have had problems in fully addressing these issues during their dialogues with states parties.[43] The AC has not vocalized any

[37] Telalian, above, n. 36, p. 135. [38] ibid.

[39] Above, n. 28, pp. 32, 43. In the case of the Committee against Torture (CAT), for some states the initial report is more than ten years overdue.

[40] See Advisory Committee on the Framework Convention for the Protection of National Minorities, 1st Activity Report, ACFC/INF (1999) 001, 1999, para. 16; Advisory Committee on the FCNM, 2nd Activity Report, ACFC/INF (2000) 001, 2000, para. 15 and Advisory Committee of the FCNM, 3rd Activity Report, ACFC/INF (2002) 001, 2002, para. 14.

[41] Committee of Ministers, Framework Convention for the Protection of National Minorities—Failure to Comply with the Reporting Obligation, 832nd Meeting, COM (2002) 80/GR-H (2002) 27/GR-H (2003) 1, 2003.

[42] Committee of Ministers, Framework Convention for the Protection of National Minorities—Proposal Regarding the Commencement of the Monitoring of the Framework Convention without a State Report, 850th Meeting, CM/Del/Dec (2003) 832/4.2, 2003.

[43] Above, n. 28, pp. 32–3.

complaints to this effect so far; however the time available for examining reports is limited. In practice, this means that either the discussion of state reports is limited—the HRC devotes on average one day for discussions with a state's delegation, for instance[44]—or the time needed for monitoring is extended, slowing the whole process, as in the case of the FCNM, which requires approximately two years for the completion of the monitoring process for one state party.

The participation of states in the monitoring process does not end with the submission of the initial report, however. States are invited to comment on the AC's opinion within four months of the opinion's distribution to the Committee of Ministers.[45] A variety of reactions within these comments were initially noted, with some states claiming that parts of the AC's opinion are factually inaccurate as occurred with the Slovak report; others merely rejected any criticism, as in the case of Estonia. Some states, such as Italy, complimented the AC's work; and some states, like Denmark, reacted negatively to the opinion as a whole. In general, the current trend has shifted towards a more careful consideration of the AC comments by the states parties.

The duration of the confidential stage of the monitoring cycle is a third matter of concern. In principle, the conclusions and recommendations of the CoM are made public upon their adoption,[46] while the opinion of the AC becomes public once the CoM has made its own conclusions or recommendations public.[47] Gradually, states have received AC opinions more constructively and have also agreed to the early publication of opinions accompanied by their comments. During its 756th meeting from 12–14 June 2001, and pursuant to Rule 27 of Regulation 97(10), the CoM decided to publish AC opinions, comments of states parties, and the conclusions and recommendations of CoM at the same time. A further step was taken when the CoM agreed that states parties may publish the AC's opinion as it concerns them, as well as their written comments before the adoption of the respective CoM conclusions and possible recommendations.[48] Procedurally speaking, the publication of opinions after the submission of state comments has the advantage of avoiding delays before the adoption of a CoM resolution. Unfortunately, a number of governments are not prepared to agree to this new procedure. As of May 2003, the AC opinions for Ireland, Poland, Slovenia, and Spain had not been made

[44] Above, n. 28, p. 33.

[45] Committee of Ministers, Monitoring of the Implementation of the Framework Convention, 740th Meeting, Item 4.3, CM (2000), 2001, pp. 165, 166, 177, 178.

[46] Above, n. 1, Rule 25. [47] Above, n. 1, Rule 26.

[48] Advisory Committee on the FCNM, 3rd Activity Report, ACFC/INF (2002) 001, 2002, para. 29.

public, pending the issuing of the conclusions and recommendations of the Committee of Ministers.[49]

Despite the evolution of monitoring towards a more consensual process, the duration and transparency of the monitoring activities requires further improvement. The monitoring system adopted under the FCNM differs greatly from other systems, such as the one under the UN Convention against Torture where the UN Committee against Torture holds public meetings and engages in public dialogue with each state party delegation on its conclusions and recommendations.[50] Monitoring practice has shown that the mere publication of reports is insufficient. States parties should envisage an even earlier publication of AC opinions, especially since the CoM has decided to allow governments to publicize the AC opinions before the adoption of the relevant resolution. The publication of the AC opinion upon its receipt by the government concerned could, thus, accelerate and clarify the process that currently exceeds two years.[51] The first example of this practice has already taken place in the case of Serbia and Montenegro, setting a precedent for the publication of AC opinions to come.[52]

Once the monitoring cycle of documents—from state reports to CoM resolutions—is completed for a given state, it is the task of this state to provide for further FCNM implementation. Within the framework of this effort, the continuation of dialogue is regained.[53] Follow-up may take various forms including seminars or public awareness initiatives, stimulating further the dialogue between minority and majority groups.[54] States are also invited to inform the AC of measures taken either in response to recommendations of the CoM or to comments emanating from the AC itself on a regular basis.[55] Rule 24 of Regulation (97)10 even allows the CoM to set a time limit for states to

[49] The Advisory Committee opinions were adopted for Ireland on 22 May 2003, for Poland on 27 November 2003, for Slovenia on 12 September 2002, and for Spain on 27 November 2003.

[50] Above, n. 28, p. 34.

[51] R. Hofmann, 'Review of the Monitoring Process of the Council of Europe Framework Convention for the Protection of National Minorities', *European Yearbook on Minority Issues*, 2 (2002/2003), 459.

[52] The AC Opinion on Serbia and Montenegro was adopted on 27 November 2003 and published on 2 March 2004, before the adoption of the CoM Resolution.

[53] Above, n. 1, Rule 36 constitutes the legal basis of the follow-up procedure.

[54] Above, n. 23 at p. 8 explains that in the summer of 2002, Croatia, Finland, Hungary, and Romania convened local conferences involving government officials and civil society. Increasing public awareness at the domestic level through dialogue is another option chosen by Denmark, in Hofmann, above, n. 51, at p. 458. More recently, ACFC follow-up seminars were organized in Cyprus (28 January 2004), in Italy (16 March 2004), and in the Russian Federation (24 March 2004).

[55] Above, n. 51, p. 457.

submit information on the implementation of its recommendations. This rule, if applied, enlarges the obligations of states considerably.

Under the second monitoring cycle, the outline of state reports will follow the same direction and will propose the further institutionalization of follow-up activities, mainly in requiring states to answer specific questions and to indicate steps they have taken in response to CoM resolutions.[56]

D. The Committee of Ministers (Article 24 FCNM)

According to Article 24 FCNM, the Committee of Ministers bears the main political responsibility for monitoring the Convention. It is empowered to evaluate the process, and is assisted in its task by the Advisory Committee.

Despite initial reservations about the potential politicization of the process,[57] these fears have so far proved unfounded. The Advisory Committee does not appear to be dominant to the Committee of Ministers as a result of its composition and working ethics. Rather the AC has managed to remain within its mandate, and in response the CoM has developed confidence in the AC. This confidence has been demonstrated through CoM endorsement of several AC proposals without amendments on, *inter alia*, AC rules of procedure, and the collection of information from sources other than the state concerned.[58]

The Committee's more specific input concerns the final stage of the monitoring process, where it drafts recommendations and conclusions for the states parties. In this task, the Committee has demonstrated that it is guided by the AC's work to a great extent.[59] In this respect, a comparison of the work of the AC and the CoM has revealed agreement on the issues to be raised for each state report. There have been few exceptions to this rule, and those that do exist can be attributed to the different roles of the AC and the CoM within the monitoring mechanism. More specifically, in early CoM resolutions, some omissions in the conclusions were noted in comparison with AC opinions.[60] These divergences do not alter the more general positive trend in relations between the two organs reflecting the will of the AC's independent experts and the representatives of states to reach a consensus, most often with direct

[56] Above, n. 51, pp. 401–33, at 432.

[57] Above, n. 23, p. 5.

[58] Above, n. 23, p. 5 gives a list of such proposals.

[59] Above, n. 51, pp. 444–6 for examples of early reports that reflect this interaction between the two organs.

[60] Above, n. 23, p. 7 for a number of cases where the CoM has omitted elements of the Advisory Committee's concluding remarks. Such was the case in its resolutions on Croatia, Czech Republic, Hungary, and Slovakia.

references in the CoM resolutions to the AC opinions. With a view to contributing towards the advancement of public dialogue on minority issues, the Committee of Ministers has progressed a step further in allowing the publication of AC opinions and state comments before it has adopted its own conclusions and recommendations.[61] Finally, the CoM has entrusted the AC with the follow-up procedure of implementation of the FCNM, a clear sign of its high degree of confidence.

III. Conclusion and Outlook

In 1995, and before the FCNM had been applied and monitored, the Parliamentary Assembly of the CoE was of the opinion that, '[t]he Convention is weakly worded . . . Its implementation mechanism is feeble and there is danger that, in fact, the monitoring procedures may be left entirely to the governments.'[62] The reality of the first, nearly completed monitoring cycle, has not been as discouraging, however. True, the implementation mechanism of the FCNM is characterized by the absence of an individual petition mechanism. But while this fact renders the system less 'judicial' in nature, it has the advantage of addressing minority issues at a more general level, for the benefit of broader communities.[63] Furthermore, states tend to accept the AC opinions more readily as these views do not seem to generate legal effects in a strict sense. Here, a parallel can be drawn with the work of the HRC of the ICCPR and the absence of legal effects for its communications, although state reporting is only one action area in which it is competent. In sum, a non-judicial mechanism does not automatically signify the 'legal irrelevance' of the views of the Committee.[64] Furthermore, the FCNM monitoring system has managed to focus on positive legislative strategies, due to relatively smooth relations developed with states parties, and also between the AC and the CoM. It is the increasing involvement of concerned minority groups and their representatives that will give the monitoring mechanism the extra impetus required to distinguish it from other bodies and treaties that work in the same area.

[61] Hofmann, 'Review of the Monitoring Process of the Council of Europe Framework Convention for the Protection of National Minorities', above, n. 51, p. 443.

[62] Council Recommendation 1995/1255/EC on the Protection of the Rights of National Minorities, CoE (1995), para. 7.

[63] P. Thornberry, 'The Framework Convention on National Minorities', in I. Ziemele (ed.), *Baltic Yearbook of International Law*, 2 (2002), pp. 127–57.

[64] Above, n. 28, see p. 36 for similar arguments.

At the global level, one can see a potential link between the work of the UN Working Group on Minorities and the AC, with respect to the exchange of information on the situation of minorities in certain states. By the same token, the work of the HRC and the AC could also be linked through exchanges of information.[65] Contacts have already been established between the AC and various bodies of the Council of Europe. Through these contacts, the AC can consult with other Council of Europe bodies.[66] Correspondingly, co-ordination of the activities of the various competent international organizations should also be synchronized, though not all of them can respond to the same needs. As Estebanez and Gal have pertinently pointed out, the FCNM could constitute a basis for regular action at the European level, while the OSCE High Commissioner on National Minorities could fundamentally operate as a body for immediate action.[67] Similar proposals for co-ordination could enhance the global advancement of minority rights standards, perhaps even more efficiently than a strong legal text.

[65] Above, n. 28, pp. 51–2.

[66] Advisory Committee on the FCNM, Second Activity Report, ACFC/INF (2000) 001, 2000, para. 32, and Advisory Committee on the FCNM, Third Activity Report, ACFC/INF (2002) 001, 2002, paras. 16, 41–4.

[67] Above, n. 28, p. 52.

SECTION V

ARTICLES 27–32

Matthew Draper

Article 27

This framework Convention shall be open for signature by the member States of the Council of Europe. Up until the date when the Convention enters into force, it shall also be open for signature by any other State so invited by the Committee of Ministers. It is subject to ratification, acceptance or approval. Instruments of ratification, acceptance or approval shall be deposited with the Secretary General of the Council of Europe.

Article 28

1. This framework Convention shall enter into force on the first day of the month following the expiration of a period of three months after the date on which twelve member States of the Council of Europe have expressed their consent to be bound by the Convention in accordance with the provisions of Article 27.

2. In respect of any member State which subsequently expresses its consent to be bound by it, the framework Convention shall enter into force on the first day of the month following the expiration of a period of three months after the date of the deposit of the instrument of ratification, acceptance or approval.

Article 29

1. After the entry into force of this framework Convention and after consulting the Contracting States, the Committee of Ministers of the Council of Europe may invite to accede to the Convention, by a decision taken by the majority provided for in Article 20.d of the Statute of the Council of Europe, any non-member State of the Council of Europe which, invited to sign in accordance with the provisions of Article 27, has not yet done so, and any other non-member State.

2. In respect of any acceding State, the framework Convention shall enter into force on the first day of the month following the expiration of a period of three months after the date of the deposit of the instrument of accession with the Secretary General of the Council of Europe.

Article 30

1. Any State may at the time of signature or when depositing its instrument of ratification, acceptance, approval or accession, specify the territory or territories for whose international relations it is responsible to which this framework Convention shall apply.

2. Any State may at any later date, by a declaration addressed to the Secretary General of the Council of Europe, extend the application of this framework Convention to any other territory specified in the declaration. In respect of such territory the framework Convention shall enter into force on the first day of the month following the expiration of a period of three months after the date of receipt of such declaration by the Secretary General.

3. Any declaration made under the two preceding paragraphs may, in respect of any territory specified in such declaration, be withdrawn by a notification addressed to the Secretary General. The withdrawal shall become effective on the first day of the month following the expiration of a period of three months after the date of receipt of such notification by the Secretary General.

Article 31

1. Any Party may at any time denounce this framework Convention by means of a notification addressed to the Secretary General of the Council of Europe.

2. Such denunciation shall become effective on the first day of the month following the expiration of a period of six months after the date of receipt of the notification by the Secretary General.

Article 32

The Secretary General of the Council of Europe shall notify the member States of the Council, other signatory States and any State which has acceded to this framework Convention, of:

a. any signature;

b. the deposit of any instrument of ratification, acceptance, approval or accession;

c. any date of entry into force of this framework Convention in accordance with Articles 28, 29 and 30;

d. any other act, notification or communication relating to this framework Convention.

I. Background

A. Issues

Section V lays out the mechanisms by which states may accede to the Framework Convention for the Protection of National Minorities (FCNM), denounce it, or limit its territorial scope. The section is based on the Model Final Clauses for Conventions and Agreements Concluded within the Council of Europe (CoE).[1]

Section V consists of six articles. Article 27 limits signature of the Framework Convention to members of the CoE, although it does provide a mechanism for non-members to be invited to join. Article 28 sets out the rules governing when the Framework Convention enters into force and, for CoE members that join subsequently, when they become bound by it. Article 29 describes how non-members of the CoE may be invited to join the Framework Convention by the Committee of Ministers (CoM) and when the Framework Convention enters into force for such states. Article 30 allows states to specify the parts of their territories to which the Framework Convention is to apply. Article 31 provides the manner in which states may denounce, or rather withdraw from, the Framework Convention. Finally, Article 32 requires the Secretary-General of the CoE to notify the states of any signatures, accessions, and ratifications, as well as any other state communication relating to the Framework Convention.

Section V does not explicitly address the issue of reservations or interpretative declarations. As a result, the international law of treaties applies to any

[1] As adopted by the Committee of Ministers, Model Final Clauses for Conventions and Agreements Concluded within the Council of Europe, Council of Europe (CoE), 384th meeting, 1980, **http://conventions.coe.int/Treaty/EN/Treaties/Html/ClausesFinales.htm** 16 August 2004.

reservations or other statements that states attach to their accession to the Framework Convention. The applicable rule appears in Article 19(*c*) of the Vienna Convention on the Law of Treaties (1969) (Vienna Convention),[2] which states that reservations are permitted unless they are 'incompatible with the object and purpose of the treaty'. The major issues confronting states seeking to enter or to object to a reservation to the Framework Convention include: (1) what is meant by the 'object and purpose' of the Framework Convention; and (2) how a reservation is determined to be incompatible with it. Other issues include identifying which treaty bodies and other international actors are competent to decide whether a reservation is incompatible with the Framework Convention, and what effects such a determination has on a reserving state's rights and obligations.

B. History

Section V is based closely on the Model Final Clauses for Conventions and Agreements Concluded within the Council of Europe. Adopted in 1980, the Model Final Clauses were an attempt by the CoE to encourage uniform treaty texts with regard to accession and reservations that were consistent with the 1969 Vienna Convention. Many Council of Europe treaties are similarly modelled after the CoE's Model Final Clauses.[3]

II. Analysis

A. Structure of the Presentation

This chapter first addresses the implications of signature to the Framework Convention, rather than full accession. Next, it discusses the relatively unusual approach that the Framework Convention takes among CoE treaties towards the acceptability of accession by states that are not CoE members. Thirdly, it discusses the implications of the territorial application rule set out in Article 30(1) FCNM. Finally, this chapter addresses the subject of reservations and interpretative declarations to the Framework Convention.

[2] Vienna Convention on the Law of Treaties (adopted on 23 May 1969, entered into force 27 January 1980), 1155 UNTS 331; 8 ILM 679.

[3] Virtually every CoE treaty drafted since 1980 follows this pattern. See, for example, Convention for the Protection of Individuals with Regard to Automatic Processing of Personal Data, CoE, ETS No. 108, 1981, Arts. 22–7; European Convention for the Prevention of Torture and Inhuman or Degrading Treatment or Punishment, CoE, ETS No. 126, 1987, Arts. 18–23.

B. Signature versus Ratification

Article 27 requires signature and 'ratification, acceptance or approval' for a state to be bound by the Framework Convention. To date, forty-two states have signed the Framework Convention and thirty-five have ratified it. The CoE members who have signed, but not ratified, the Framework Convention include: Belgium, Georgia, Greece, Iceland, Luxembourg, and the Netherlands. Although these states are not yet committed to the implemention of the Framework Convention, by signing it they have indicated their intention to become a party and have a good faith obligation under Article 18 of the Vienna Convention not to work to defeat the object and purpose of the treaty prior to its entry into force. The International Law Commission (ILC) has remarked that it is generally accepted that 'an obligation of good faith to refrain from acts calculated to frustrate the object of the treaty attaches to a state which has a signed a treaty subject to ratification'.[4]

C. Ratification by Non-Member States

Article 27 deviates from the Model Final Clauses by allowing non-members of the CoE to join the Framework Convention.[5] This open approach is common among CoE treaties that have been elaborated with the participation of non-members of the CoE.[6] However, the Framework Convention is unusual in that only one other CoE treaty allows for non-members to adhere to it even before it has entered into force.[7] The drafters of the Framework Convention added this sentence to the Model Final Clause for Article 27: 'Up until the date when the Convention enters into force, it shall also be open for signature by any other State so invited by the Committee of Ministers.' The Explanatory Report, referring to the CoE Vienna Declaration (1993, Appendix II), notes that this was understood to include those states participating in the Conference on Security and Co-operation in Europe (CSCE)/Organization on Security

[4] International Law Commission (ILC), Yearbook of the International Law Commission (1966) UN Doc. A/CN.4/SER.A/1995/Add. 1, II, p. 202.

[5] The approach taken in Art. 27 is anticipated by para. 12 of the Framework Convention's Preamble, which also explicitly contemplates the participation of non-CoE member states.

[6] Canada and the United States have been allowed to sign a number of CoE treaties, from the Convention on the Transfer of Sentenced Persons, CoE, ETS No. 112, 1983, to the Criminal Law Convention on Corruption, CoE, ETS No. 173, 1999. Another example is the Convention for the Protection of Individuals with Regard to Automatic Processing of Personal Data, CoE, ETS No. 108, 1985 which, having been drafted with the participation of OECD member states, may be joined by OECD member states.

[7] The only other example of this CoE practice is the Convention on the Preservation of European Wildlife and Habitats, CoE, ETS No. 104, 1982.

and Co-operation in Europe (OSCE).[8] CSCE/OSCE states had taken part in the elaboration of the Framework Convention. Indeed, Appendix II of the Vienna Declaration refers to the CoE's determination to memorialize the CSCE/OSCE's political commitments to protect national minorities, including the Copenhagen Document.[9] The CoE clearly intended the Framework Convention as a legal commitment to which some or all CSCE/OSCE participating states would adhere. This provision in Article 27 was included in order to allow them to join even before the Framework Convention had entered into force.[10] As it happened, both Albania and Armenia signed it before they had joined the CoE and prior to the Framework Convention's entry into force on 1 February 1998. In addition, several non-member states have signed the Framework Convention since its entry into force.

D. Territorial Application

Article 30(1) stipulates that a party may only make declarations regarding the territorial application of the Framework Convention in relation to 'the territory or territories for whose international relations it is responsible'. This is a more robust formulation than appears in the Model Final Clause, which allows states to make declarations with regard to any of their territories. The Framework Convention's formulation follows the example of the European Convention on the Protection of Human Rights and Fundamental Freedoms (ECHR) (ETS No. 005, 1954, Article 56), the only other CoE treaty to contain this specification. This phrase arises out of the intention of the drafters of both treaties to ensure that human rights protections do not depend on the legal status a state may assert applies to a particular territory. The effect of the phrase 'territories for whose international relations it is responsible' is meant to provide a more rigorous definition of a state's territory, making it more difficult for states to evade their responsibilities under the Framework Convention when a state's sovereignty over a particular territory is ambiguous. As a result, under the Framework Convention a state must make a formal declaration to the Secretary-General of the CoE if it wishes to exclude the application of the Framework Convention from part of its territory.

[8] Preparatory Work of the Ad Hoc Committee for the Protection of National Minorities (CAHMIN), Explanatory Report, CAHMIN H(1995) 010, 1995, para. 98.

[9] See also para. 11, Preamble FCNM, which invokes the minority protections of the CSCE/OSCE.

[10] See European Commission for Democracy through Law (ECDL), Proposal for a European Convention for the Protection of National Minorities, CDL-MIN (93) 6, 1993, Art. 32; CAHMIN, 5th Meeting, CAHMIN (94) 19, Meeting Report, 1994, para. 37.

No state has ever explicitly invoked Article 30(1) to limit the territorial scope of the Framework Convention. Denmark is the sole signatory to have entered a declaration that, *inter alia*, purports to limit the Framework Convention's territorial scope. Denmark, in a declaration handed to the Secretary-General upon ratification, stated that the Framework Convention 'shall apply to the German minority in South Jutland of the Kingdom of Denmark'.[11] In effect, Denmark was seeking to exclude the application of the Framework Convention to any territory other than South Jutland. The Advisory Committee found that the result of Denmark's territorial approach was to exclude certain minority groups a priori. Denmark's declaration was not compatible with the Framework Convention since it led to a number of 'arbitrary or unjustified distinctions'.[12] The Advisory Committee's report indicates that the Danish government has retreated from this position and considers the Framework Convention to apply to all Danish territory.[13] Denmark has not, however, withdrawn its original declaration by submitting a notification to the Secretary-General in accordance with Article 30(1). The CoM has passed a resolution urging Denmark to reconsider its position and enter into a dialogue on this matter with the Advisory Committee.[14]

Regardless, it is unclear how a state could ever enter an Article 30(1) territorial declaration without making any 'arbitrary or unjustified distinctions'. The Advisory Committee argues that: '[a]lthough the Framework Convention attaches importance in a number of its provisions to the criterion of traditional inhabitation of certain areas for protection, the majority of its provisions are designed to apply throughout the territory of the state concerned, of course taking into account all relevant circumstances.'[15] The inclusion of Article 30(1) would therefore appear to be superfluous to the operation of the Framework Convention. Whether it was carelessly included amongst much of the rest of the Model Final Clauses or for some other reason, it is now clear that the Framework Convention's implicit rejection of arbitrary distinctions render Article 30(1) virtually impossible to invoke.

[11] CoE, Declaration Contained in a Note Verbale dated 22 September 1997, handed to the Secretary-General at the time of deposit of the instrument of ratification, on 22 September 1997 (Denmark) **http://conventions.coe.int/**.

[12] Advisory Committee on the Framework Convention for the Protection of National Minorities, Opinion on Denmark, ACFC/INF/OPI (2001) 5, 2000, paras. 16–23.

[13] Above, n. 12, para. 12.

[14] Resolution ResCMN (2001) 2 on the Implementation of the Framework Convention for the Protection of National Minorities by Denmark, adopted by the Committee of Ministers, 2001.

[15] Above, n. 12, para. 17.

E. Reservations and Interpretative Declarations

The ILC's definition of the term 'reservation' is based on the Vienna Conventions of 1969, 1978, and 1986:

> 'Reservation' means a unilateral statement, however phrased or named, made by a state or an international organization when signing, ratifying, formally confirming, accepting, approving or acceding to a treaty or by a state when making a notification of succession to a treaty, whereby the state or organization purports to exclude or to modify the legal effect of certain provisions of the treaty in their application to that state or to that international organization.[16]

Declarative interpretations are similar to reservations, except that they do not exclude or modify the legal effect of any provision of the treaty. Rather, they purport to 'specify or clarify the meaning or scope attributed by the declarant to a treaty or to certain of its provisions'.[17] In order to determine whether a statement qualifies as a reservation, declarative interpretation, or something else, one must look beyond the actual term used by the declarant and determine whether the statement indeed modifies its obligations.

The Model Final Clauses contain provisions for restricting the types of reservations states may make to a treaty. Due to opposition from some states, it was not possible for the drafters of the Framework Convention to include any provisions regarding reservations or interpretative declarations. By not including any of the provisions of the Model Final Clauses that address reservations, the Framework Convention by default allows any reservation that is compatible with the object and purpose of the Framework Convention.[18] This approach is consistent with Article 19(*c*) of the Vienna Convention, which states that when a treaty is silent with regard to the formulation of reservations by states, reservations are permitted unless they are 'incompatible with the object and purpose of the treaty'.

1. *The Object and Purpose of the Framework Convention*

The object and purpose of the Framework Convention, according to the Venice Commission, 'is to achieve respect for and afford protection to the ethnic, cultural, linguistic and religious identity of persons belonging to a national minority as well as appropriate conditions enabling them to express, preserve and develop this identity'.[19] The Explanatory Report states that the

[16] ILC, 'Fifth Report on Reservations to Treaties of its 52nd Session' (1 May 2000), UN Doc. A/CN.4/508/Add. 2, Addendum, para. 1(1).

[17] Above, n. 16, para. 1(2).

[18] Above, n. 8.

[19] ECDL, Opinion on Possible Groups of Persons to which the Framework Convention for the Protection of National Minorities could be Applied in Belgium, CDL-AD (2002) 1, 2002, para. 5.

Framework Convention seeks 'to specify the legal principles which States undertake to respect in order to ensure the protection of national minorities'.[20] The report adds that 'the main aim' of the Framework Convention is set out in the penultimate paragraph of the Preamble,[21] which stipulates that the Convention defines 'the principles to be respected and the obligations which flow from them, in order to ensure . . . the effective protection of national minorities and of the rights and freedoms of persons belonging to those minorities, within the rule of law, respecting the territorial integrity and national sovereignty of states'. Whether a particular reservation is incompatible with the object and purpose of the Framework Convention is an objective inquiry to be conducted on a case-by-case basis. The inquiry should determine if, in fact, a reservation arbitrarily denies Framework Convention protections to persons belonging to a national minority.

In addition to the limitations on reservations derived from the Framework Convention's particular object and purpose, the Framework Convention shares limitations common to other multilateral human rights treaties. This derives from the fact that multilateral human rights treaties like the Framework Convention do not resemble contracts, the premiss upon which bilateral treaties—and the rules that govern them—are based. This difference in character means that some types of reservations that might be compatible with ordinary treaties may be incompatible with multilateral human rights treaties. In an advisory opinion on the Convention on the Prevention and Punishment of the Crime of Genocide, another human rights treaty that is broadly adhered to, the International Court of Justice stated that 'in a convention of this type one cannot speak of individual advantages or disadvantages to States, or of the maintenance of a perfect contractual balance between rights and duties. The high ideals which inspired the Convention provide, by virtue of the common will of the parties, the foundation and measure of all its provisions.'[22]

The Human Rights Committee of the International Covenant on Civil and Political Rights (ICCPR) has addressed the differences between human rights treaties and other types of treaties more than any other treaty body. In a General Comment, the Committee argues that reservations are incompatible with the object and purpose of the treaty if they offend peremptory norms of international law: '[a]lthough treaties that are mere exchanges of obligations between States allow them to reserve *inter se* application of rules of general international law, it is otherwise with human rights treaties, which are for the benefit of persons within

[20] Above, n. 8, para. 10. [21] Above, n. 8, para. 28.

[22] International Court of Justice, Advisory Opinion on Reservations to the Convention on the Prevention and Punishment of the Crime of Genocide, ICJ 15, 1951.

their jurisdiction.'[23] Not surprisingly, some states have resisted this interpretation.[24] Indeed, the Committee's approach may go further than international law currently allows. A reservation to a treaty provision which restates a rule of customary international law will not release the reserving state from the operation of the rule, but it may release it from the monitoring or dispute resolution provisions of the treaty that depend on that rule.[25] Indeed, the ILC, reacting to the Committee's comment, states that it considers the Vienna Convention to still fully apply to all treaties, including 'treaties in the area of human rights'.[26]

The Committee argues that there is a 'heavy onus' on states to justify any reservations to the non-derogable rights included in the ICCPR.[27] This would appear to apply equally to the Framework Convention vis-à-vis the rules governing derogations and limitations in the European Convention. Article 19 of the Framework Convention explicitly requires that any derogations or limitations placed by states on its protections must be compatible with rules governing such actions under the European Convention.

Finally, the Committee states that the ICCPR contains important supportive guarantees to the rights it secures which, likewise, may not be the subject of a state's reservation.[28] These guarantees include the enforcement mechanisms of the ICCPR, such as the reporting and monitoring mechanisms. Such reasoning would certainly extend to the Framework Convention. For example, a reservation to Article 26, which establishes an Advisory Committee to the Convention, would not be permitted.

2. *Compatibility of Reservations: Who Decides?*

According to international law, unless a treaty provides otherwise, the permissibility of a reservation is a determination to be made by the states parties to the

[23] UN Human Rights Committee General Comment 24 (52) in General Comment on Issues Relating to Reservations Made upon Ratification or Accession to the Covenant or the Optional Protocols Thereto, or in Relation to Declarations under Article 42 of the Covenant (1994), UN Doc. CCPR/C/21/Rev.1/Add.6, para. 8.

[24] See, for instance, UN Human Rights Committee, Observations of the United States of America on General Comment No. 24, (52) (1995), UN Doc. A/50/40, Annex VI, para. 2: 'It is clear that a State cannot exempt itself from a peremptory norm of international law by making a reservation to the Covenant. It is not at all clear that a State cannot choose to exclude one means of enforcement of particular norms by reserving against inclusion of those norms in its Covenant obligations.'

[25] R. Jennings and A. Watts (eds.), *Oppenheim's International Law* (Longmans, London, 1992), para. 615.

[26] ILC, 'Report of the International Law Commission on the Work of its 49th Session', (12 May–18 July 1997), UN GAOR, 52nd Session, Supp. No. 10, p. 126.

[27] Above, n. 26, para. 10. See also International Covenant on Civil and Political Rights (ICCPR) (adopted 16 December 1966, entered into force 23 March 1976) 999 UNTS 171, Art. 4(2).

[28] Above, n. 26, para. 11.

treaty or the International Court of Justice. In the case of the Framework Convention, there are three other bodies that have authority to consider the validity of reservations. First, the Secretary-General, as the institution charged with receiving instruments of ratification and other communications regarding the Framework Convention, may informally consult with a state that enters a reservation that appears to be incompatible with the object and purpose of the Framework Convention. This is common practice for the Secretary-General with regard to CoE treaties.[29] If the state insists that its accession to the treaty is conditioned on its reservation, however, the Secretary-General will nevertheless register the ratification and notify the parties.[30]

The Framework Convention, like many other normative treaties, establishes independent mechanisms to monitor its implementation. Article 24 states that the CoM should monitor implementation of the Framework Convention. In addition, Article 26 states that the Advisory Committee should assist the CoM in evaluating the adequacy of the measures taken by the parties to give effect to the Framework Convention's principles. Both the CoM and the Advisory Committee possess the competency to express an opinion on the validity of reservations.

By requiring the Advisory Committee to consist of persons with a 'recognized expertise in the field of the protection of national minorities', Article 26 creates an independent body of experts to give the CoM an objective assessment of the measures taken by parties. Furthermore, the power of the Advisory Committee to issue opinions on the validity of reservations is deduced from its mandate to evaluate the adequacy of measures taken by the parties. A reservation limits the scope of the reserving state's commitment, thereby restricting the scope of the Advisory Committee's authority to evaluate that state's minority protections. In order to determine what circumstances it should evaluate and which standards it should apply, the Advisory Committee must be competent to determine whether a statement is a reservation and, if so, whether it is a valid one. The ILC states that where a normative treaty is silent on the subject, 'the monitoring bodies established thereby are competent to comment upon and express recommendations with regard, *inter alia*, to the admissibility of reservations by States, in order to carry out the functions assigned to them'.[31] The Venice Commission addressed the Framework Convention specifically on this subject in a recent opinion:

[T]he implementation of the Framework Convention should not be a source of arbitrary or unjustified distinctions. With a view to preventing any such distinctions from being made, the Committee of Ministers of the Council of Europe, with the

[29] J. Polakiewicz, *Treaty-Making in the Council of Europe* (CoE, Strasbourg, 1999).
[30] Above, n. 29. [31] Above, n. 26.

assistance of the Advisory Committee on the Framework Convention, exercises a supervisory role on the personal scope given by each country to the implementation of the Framework Convention.[32]

However, as the ILC points out, a monitoring body's competence to evaluate reservations does not exclude or affect the traditional forms of control by the contracting parties under general international law.[33]

Finally, the legal force of the Advisory Committee's opinions cannot exceed its mandate as an adviser to the CoM. The Advisory Committee cannot, therefore, require a party to alter or withdraw a reservation that it deems invalid; at most it may recommend to the CoM that a reservation is impermissible and should be declared invalid. In practice, the Advisory Committee has often criticized the substance of a state's statement, but it has yet to declare a statement to be a reservation that is incompatible with the Framework Convention explicitly.

3. *Effect of Incompatible Reservations*

Article 24 of the Framework Convention requires the CoM to monitor implementation. If the CoM were to issue a determination on the inadmissibility of a reservation to the Framework Convention, this could be considered as binding on the reserving party. Any such determination by the CoM would have the added weight of being the result of the votes of the Foreign Ministers representing the states parties to the Framework Convention. Such a vote would inevitably reflect the understanding of states parties regarding the content of the Framework Convention, and provide further evidence of the inadmissibility of the reservation. Alternatively, the states parties to the Framework Convention could conclude that a reservation is inadmissible based on the advice of the Advisory Committee. In either case, the impermissible reservation would become void and the reserving party would continue to be bound by the entire Framework Convention, including the provision(s) from which it had attempted to reserve. This is the 'severability doctrine' adopted by the European Court of Human Rights in the *Belilos* Case.[34] The Framework Convention is arguably governed by this approach given its general human rights character, its comprehensive references to the ECHR,[35] and the aims of the Framework Convention as contained in its text.[36]

[32] ECDL, Opinion on Possible Groups of Persons to which the Framework Convention for the Protection of National Minorities could be Applied in Belgium, CDL-AD (2002) 1, 2002, para.1.

[33] Above, n. 26.

[34] *Belilos* v. *Switzerland* (10328/83) (1988) EHRR 4.

[35] Para. 10, Preamble FCNM; and Art. 19 and 23 FCNM.

[36] J. A. Frowin and R. Bank, 'The Effect of Member States' Declarations Defining "National Minorities" upon Signature or Ratification of the Council of Europe's Framework Convention', *Heidelberg Journal of International Law*, 59 (1999), 672.

In the more likely scenario that the Advisory Committee determines a reservation to be inadmissible, the opinion is not binding on the reserving state. Nevertheless, the ILC urges states:

> to cooperate with monitoring bodies and give due consideration to any recommendations that they may make . . . The Commission also notes that, in the event of inadmissibility of a reservation, it is the reserving State that has the responsibility for taking action. This action may consist, for example, in the State either modifying its reservation so as to eliminate the inadmissibility, or withdrawing its reservation, or forgoing becoming a party to the treaty.[37]

4. State Practice

The majority of states parties to the Framework Convention have not entered any declaration or reservation upon signing it. Fourteen states have entered interpretative declarations, most of which provide a definition for the term 'national minority'.[38] This is not surprising given the fact that the Framework Convention contains no explicit definition for national minority. All the same, most states parties do not stipulate any definition. Two signatories, Belgium and Malta, explicitly call their statements 'reservations'.[39] Finally, Russia's declaration objects to the legality of certain declarations made by other states parties, particularly Estonia's.[40]

(a) Defining 'National Minority'

So far, the statements submitted by states upon ratification that seek to define the term national minority appear to be declarative interpretations, rather than reservations. It is important to note that none of the statements explicitly excludes any groups.[41] Rather, the statements typically identify particular groups to whom the

[37] Above, n. 26, para. 157.

[38] The fourteen states are: Austria, Azerbaijan, Belgium, Bulgaria, Denmark, Estonia, Germany, Liechtenstein, Luxembourg, Poland, Slovenia, Sweden, Switzerland, and the former Yugoslav Republic of Macedonia. Their statements are available at **http://conventions.coe.int/**.

[39] See CoE, Declaration Contained in the Instrument of Ratification, deposited on 6 January 1997 (Estonia); and CoE, Reservation Contained in the Instrument of Ratification, deposited on 10 February 1998 (Malta). Available at **http://conventions.coe.int/**.

[40] CoE, Declaration Contained in the Instrument of Ratification, deposited on 21 August 1998 (Russian Federation). Available at **http://conventions.coe.int/**.

[41] The one exception to this may be the declaration of Slovenia, which clearly excludes the application of the term 'national minority' to the Roma community, although it clearly states that the Framework Convention's provisions would apply to the Roma as well. This clear exclusion could be determined to be an inadmissible reservation to the FCNM. See CoE, Declaration Contained in a Note Verbale from the Permanent Representation of Slovenia, dated 23 March 1998, handed to the Secretary-General at the time of deposit of the instrument of ratification, on 25 March 1998. Available at **http://conventions.coe.int/**.

Framework Convention's protections will apply or provide a list of criteria for determining whether a group, or a member of a group, is a national minority. These declarations can only be considered reservations if they have the de facto effect of denying the Framework Convention's applicability to groups or persons who would otherwise fall under its protections. For example, Denmark's statement, since it appeared to exclude certain groups in fact, could have been determined to be a reservation to the Framework Convention. However, Denmark's subsequent interpretation and practice indicate that its statement has not had a de facto exclusionary effect.

As noted elsewhere in this volume, the text of the Framework Convention itself (for example Article 5), international practice, and the practice of the Advisory Committee all provide important guidance regarding the definition of the term 'national minority'. However, given the lack of a definition for 'national minority' in the text of the Framework Convention itself, only reservations that clearly exclude legitimate national minorities should be considered inadmissible.

(b) Citizenship Limitations

The Estonian declaration provides Framework Convention protections only to those persons who are, *inter alia*, Estonian citizens.[42] Estonian law currently makes it difficult for Russians, who account for as much as 40 per cent of the population, to become citizens. The Estonian declaration, therefore, appears to exclude Russians from the protections of the Framework Convention. In response, the Russian Federation's declaration states that 'attempts to exclude from the scope of the Framework Convention the persons who permanently reside in the territory of States Parties to the Framework Convention and previously had citizenship but have been arbitrarily deprived of it, contradict the purpose of the Framework Convention for the Protection of National Minorities'.[43] The Advisory Committee has found that this statement by Estonia was restrictive, given the 'prevailing situation of minorities in Estonia' and that its citizenship requirement did 'not appear suited' to the situation in Estonia.[44] Importantly, the CoM supports this view.[45] The Advisory Committee's opinion

[42] CoE, Declaration Contained in the Instrument of Ratification, deposited on 6 January 1997 (Estonia). Available at **http://conventions.coe.int/**.

[43] CoE, Declaration Contained in the Instrument of Ratification, deposited on 21 August 1998 (Russian Federation). Available at **http://conventions.coe.int/**.

[44] Advisory Committee Opinion on Estonia, ACFC/INF/OP/I (2002) 005, 2001, para 17.

[45] See Resolution ResCMN (2001) 8 on the Implementation of the Framework Convention for the Protection of National Minorities by Estonia, adopted by the Committee of Ministers, 799th meeting, 2002.

indicates that an objective evaluation of the Estonian statement may conclude it to be an impermissible reservation since the Russian population in Estonia appears to qualify as a national minority for the purposes of the Framework Convention. The Venice Commission, while commenting on a similar situation in Lithuania, argues that the a priori exclusion of non-citizens is inconsistent with the Framework Convention.[46] Some commentators have suggested that a criterion more suited to the situation of newly independent states such as Estonia would be a requirement of 'firm and long-standing ties to the State'.[47] Still, it should be noted that neither the Advisory Committee nor any other body of the Council of Europe has gone so far as to state explicitly that Estonia's reservation is contrary to the object and purpose of the Framework Convention. Given the contradictory statements by Russia and Estonia and the Advisory Committee's reluctance to clearly indicate whether Estonia's statement is a reservation incompatible with the object and purpose of the Framework Convention, the citizenship requirement controversy remains unresolved.

(c) Belgium's Reservation

Upon signing the Framework Convention, Belgium submitted a reservation stating that the Framework Convention 'applies without prejudice to the constitutional provisions, guarantees or principles, and without prejudice to the legislative rules which currently govern the use of languages'. This statement has the effect of making the Framework Convention's language provisions inapplicable to Belgium. Belgium's reservation also states that its government will decide its own notion of national minority at a later date. The Council of Europe's Parliamentary Assembly adopted a strongly worded resolution, which states, *inter alia*, that:

> The Assembly therefore regrets that the Belgian authorities deemed it necessary to accompany the signature of the framework convention by such a broad reservation that it risks undermining most of the convention's provisions. If the Kingdom of Belgium decided to uphold upon ratification of the convention the reservation it made upon signature, it might be considered as a violation of the Vienna Convention on the Law of Treaties which does not allow countries to enter reservations upon ratification of treaties which void them of their meaning.[48]

Regarding Belgium's mode of defining the term 'national minority', the Parliamentary Assembly's resolution states that, depending on how Belgium

[46] ECDL, Opinion on the Draft Law on Amendments to the Law on National Minorities in Lithuania, 237/2003, CDL-AD (2003) 12, 2003. [47] Above, n. 36, p. 678.

[48] Resolution 1301 of the European Parliament on the Protection of Minorities in Belgium, 2002, para. 4.

decides to go about it, '[s]uch a declaration would probably have to be understood as a reservation incompatible with the object and purpose of the framework convention itself.'[49] The Parliamentary Assembly is the only CoE body to reach a determination as to the validity of Belgium's statement.

Since Belgium has yet to ratify the Framework Convention, the Advisory Committee has not had occasion to comment on the reservation in an Opinion. The Parliamentary Assembly is not formally empowered by the FCNM to make binding judgments as to the validity of reservations. Moreover, it is not an objective, expert body like the Advisory Committee, but a political institution. Nor does the Framework Convention specify it as having a supervisory or monitoring role. However, its resolutions should be given appropriate weight as evidence of CoE states' understandings of the legal obligations contained in the Framework Convention. The fact that Belgium has yet to ratify the Framework Convention gives a strong indication as to the weight it assigns to the Assembly's opinions.

III. Conclusion and Outlook

Like numerous other CoE treaties, Section V of the Framework Convention follows the CoE's Model Final Clauses for the most part. Some of the Framework Convention's departures from the Model Final Clauses have been examined above. Notably, the provision that allows states to limit the territorial application of the Framework Convention's protections is more limited than that followed in the CoE's Model Final Clauses. In addition, the Framework Convention does not contain the optional provisions of the Model Final Clauses that address reservations. This omission ensures that international treaty law governs the Convention. Reservations are permitted unless they are incompatible with the object and purpose of the Convention. States' declarations that purport to limit the application of the Framework Convention to particular named groups, or groups that qualify under listed criteria, are permitted so long as they do not create any de facto arbitrary distinctions.

While the Advisory Committee is empowered to determine whether a state's declaration is, in fact, an impermissible reservation, it does not possess the authority to require a state to withdraw or alter its declaration. Only the International Court of Justice, CoE Committee of Ministers, or the other states

[49] Resolution 1301 of the European Parliament on the Protection of Minorities in Belgium, 2002, para. 19.

parties have the power to require a reserving state to do so. The determinations and recommendations of the Advisory Committee should be given particular deference, however. With regard to impermissible reservations, the Framework Convention is governed by the CoE's severability doctrine.

To date, the Advisory Committee has rarely commented on the statements made by states parties upon signature or accession. However, the Committee generally discourages reservations: '[the Advisory Committee] believes that States should exercise great restraint in making reservations/declarations when signing and/or ratifying the text. It also believes that States Parties should be encouraged to reconsider their reservations/declarations periodically with a view to possibly revoking them.'[50] The Advisory Committee would provide a great service to states parties to the Framework Convention if it were to clearly indicate whether it considers a state's statement to operate as an interpretative declaration or as a reservation, and whether that reservation is permissible or not. By providing objective clarity to the obligations of the Framework Convention, all signatories will better understand what is required of them. In addition, this will also allow states that wish to join the Framework Convention to better understand the obligations they will assume upon accession.

[50] Opinion of the Advisory Committee on the Framework Convention for the Protection of National Minorities on Parliamentary Assembly Recommendation 1492 (2001) on the Rights of National Minorities, ACFC 2001, para. 6.

CONCLUSION: THE CONTRIBUTION OF THE EUROPEAN FRAMEWORK CONVENTION FOR THE PROTECTION OF NATIONAL MINORITIES TO THE DEVELOPMENT OF MINORITY RIGHTS

Marc Weller

I. Introduction

This commentary has put the Framework Convention for the Protection of National Minorities to the test. It seeks to establish whether the Convention is a human rights treaty like any other human rights treaty—whether it contains legal obligations that are sufficiently firm to be described as human and minority 'rights'. It also seeks to give meaning to these provisions by advancing their interpretation on the basis of state practice that has accumulated over a period of close to seven years of the operation of the treaty.

As was noted in the Preface, this test has been conducted against the odds. The 'framework' character of the convention, the absence of a clear definition of minorities, the lack of a clear commitment to collective rights, the rather general formulation of some of its provisions, the extensive claw-back clauses, and the lack of judicial enforcement led to not inconsiderable scepticism at the time of its creation exactly a decade ago. After all, the governments of the Council of Europe adopted this convention with all its apparent defects instead of the Protocol to the European Convention on Human Rights that had been put forward by the Council's own Parliamentary Assembly.[1] That Protocol would have placed minority rights in Europe directly within the system of human rights protection, generating coverage of this issue by the powerful European Court of Human Rights.

So, did the people of Europe, represented in the Parliamentary Assembly, demand a Rolex, but receive an imitation Swatch instead?[2] Did the Framework Convention turn out to be a fig-leaf exercise, commenced at a time when the then still mainly Western European institutions were demanding compliance by the states of Eastern and Central Europe with standards they themselves were unwilling to accept as hard legal obligations? In other words, is this a convention on minority rights that is meant to disguise the fact that there are no real minority rights?

To answer this question on the basis of the scholarship assembled in this commentary, it will be convenient to consider, by way of conclusion, the general position of the Convention within the area of minority rights. First, the substance of the Convention will be located within the field. Then, its reach will be considered. Finally, a few words will be said about the legal character of the Convention and about the implementation process.

II. The Development of Minority Rights as Part of Human Rights

Some authors would regard the entire area of human rights with some general scepticism. Philip Allott, for instance, has drawn our attention to the fact that

[1] Council Recommendation 1201/93/EC of 1 February 1993 on an Additional Protocol on the Rights of National Minorities to the European Convention on Human Rights (1993), Parliamentary Assembly of the Council of Europe, 22nd Sitting, Doc. 6742.

[2] This appeared to be the initial view of the Council Recommendation 1255/95/EC of 31 January 1995 on the Protection of the Rights of National Minorities, Parliamentary Assembly of the CoE, 3rd sitting, Doc. 7228, para 7. See G. Gilbert, 'The Council of Europe and Minority Rights', *Human Rights Quarterly*, 18 (1996), 160; G. Alfredsson, 'A Frame an Incomplete Painting [*sic*]: Comparison of the Framework Convention for the Protection of National Minorities with International Standards and Monitoring Procedures', *International Journal on Minority and Group Rights*, 7 (2000), 291. Cf.: F. Steketee, 'The Framework Convention: A Piece of Art or a Tool for Action?', *International Journal of Minority and Group Rights*, 8 (2001).

it should not be necessary for the constituents of the state to struggle for the recognition of basic rights.[3] Why should it be necessary to obtain a guarantee from the state establishing that it is not entitled to exterminate or torture us? Surely we never assigned to the state such powers when we subscribed to the constitutional compact that underpins it.

From this perspective, human rights discourse is an antiquated undertaking that confirms that which it seeks to challenge. In demanding the positive legal assurance that the state will not torture us, we appear to confirm that the state is entitled to exercise whatever powers it claims until and unless it has expressly given up such powers through human rights commitments enshrined in international law. In a way, claims for human rights appear to confirm an absolute view of state sovereignty in the shape of the Lotus principle internally applied: the state is entitled to do anything that is not specifically prohibited.[4]

Of course, one might argue that significant abuses by the state are unlikely, given the fact that it is, or should be, subject to democratic control. However, majoritarian decision-making is no great defence for the interests of those who are a structural minority. In states where decisions are taken not according to cross-cutting interests of diverse constituents, but according to ethnic, religious, linguistic, or related criteria, the non-dominant group will always lose out.[5] Even where a democratic system is coupled with a rule of law society, this in itself is not a sufficient guarantee against majoritarian abuse or dominance. After all, the laws that guide the institutions of such a state are themselves the product of a majoritarian decision-making process. Hence, human and minority rights are still seen as a necessary defence against the otherwise all-powerful state.

A. Sovereignty and Human and Minority Rights

Of course, such a neoclassical view of the absolute state can no longer be maintained. Change has occurred in two ways. First, it is now accepted that the state itself is nothing other than the accumulation of the competences that have been transferred to it by its constituents in a constitutional instrument. The constitutional state is limited in its powers by this grant of authority. Even if the state might claim some residual, or inherent powers that have not been expressly transferred, these need to be constitutionally based. On no account

[3] Generally, P. Allott, *Eunomia: A New Order for a New World* (Oxford University Press, Oxford, 1990).

[4] 'The rules binding upon states therefore emanate from their own free will . . . Restrictions upon the independence of states cannot therefore be presumed.' *Case Concerning the Steamship Lotus (France* v. *Turkey)* PCIJ Rep. Series A, No. 10, pp. 16, 18.

[5] It is of course not necessary for the group to be numerically inferior in order to be non-dominant.

can there be a claim to powers that threaten the existence of segments of the population—of the very constituents from whose collective identity sovereign powers are derived—or that subject them to systematic torture or other abuse.[6]

If state powers need to be positively grounded in a grant of public authority by the constituencies of the state, there is also a negative limitation to be considered. State powers are negatively delimited by guarantees of fundamental rights that can be found in all modern constitutions.

In addition to this internal, constitutional limitation on state power, there exist external limitations. The state exists within the framework of an international constitutional order. For instance, even if the majority population were to constitutionally authorize the state to exterminate or forcibly remove another population group in a way that is entirely in accordance with that state's constitutional order, the state authorities would still lack authority to conduct such an action.

This international constitutional order is organized through the mechanism of general international law, of *jus cogens* status and of *erga omnes* effect. General international law establishes obligations that apply to all states, whether or not one can demonstrate that they have specifically consented to them. Essential human rights obligations are part and parcel of this general corpus of universal law. By virtue of the doctrine of *jus cogens*, no state can contract out of these essential obligations.[7] Even in times of war or public emergency, there exists a non-derogable core of human rights. The doctrine of *erga omnes* obligations ensures that third states have a legal interest in the performance of human rights obligations by other states. This is particularly important, given that human rights establish legal relations between the state and its own constituents. The latter do not always have remedies to ensure compliance.[8] Hence, it is sometimes necessary for other states and international institutions to act as agents of the international constitution in considering issues of compliance on behalf of otherwise disenfranchised constituents. Indeed, in cases of serious violations of peremptory obligations, including core human rights obligations, states

[6] Hence, a state that systematically destroys a constitutionally relevant population segment while denying it the necessary means for survival, or permanently and forcibly displaces it, exposes itself to international action on behalf of that population which it manifestly no longer genuinely represents.

[7] Vienna Convention on the Law of Treaties (entered into force 27 January 1980), 1155 UNTS 331, Art. 53.

[8] '. . . an essential distinction should be drawn between the obligations of a State towards the international community as a whole, and those arising vis-à-vis another state in the field of diplomatic protection. By their very nature the former are the concern of all states. In view of the importance of the rights involved, all States can be held to have a legal interest in their protection, they are obligations *erga omnes*.' *Barcelona Traction Light and Power Company Case* [1970] 2nd Phase, ICJ Rep. 4, para. 33.

are legally committed to opposing these through collective action.[9] Finally, particularly grave violations of human rights also attract individual criminal responsibility. The authors of such crimes can be pursued universally through international judicial mechanisms where available, or through the domestic courts of other states.[10]

It is not disputed that the so-called core human rights are part of general international law, that they are non-derogable and that they are of *erga omnes* character. But how about minority rights? It is no longer a matter of doubt that minority rights are part and parcel of human rights.[11] This being so, minority issues that are covered by minority rights no longer fall exclusively within the domestic jurisdiction of states—they are a matter of international concern. This is stated clearly in virtually all of the applicable standard-setting documents, whether hard or soft law. Indeed, the Framework Convention itself devotes its very first substantive article to a reiteration of the fact that 'The protection of national minorities and of the rights and freedoms of persons belonging to those minorities forms an integral part of the international protection of human rights, and as such falls within the scope of international co-operation.'

But what is the substance, if any, of these human rights of minorities? Hurst Hannum wrote in an article published in 1991 that 'the substantive development since 1945 of international law related to minorities has been minimal'.[12] At the time, he could only point to Article 27 of the International Covenant on Civil and Political Rights as a manifestation of any progress, however limited.

Certainly, the past decade has seen an acceleration in the development of standards on minorities. This development commenced with the adoption of the path-breaking CSCE Copenhagen Document of 1990, followed by a plethora of further OSCE documents and recommendations. In 1992, the UN adopted the Declaration on the Rights of Persons Belonging to National or Ethnic, Religious, and Linguistic Minorities. Interestingly, though, the only hard, legally binding standards that advance upon the venerable and quite conservative Article 27 of the ICCPR have been adopted by the states of the Council of Europe. In fact, outside the specialized European Charter for

9 International Law Commission (ILC), 'Text on Responsibility of States' (2001), 53rd session, UN Doc. A/CN.4/L.602/Rev.1, Art. 40, 41.

10 At the international level, the Rome Statute of the International Criminal Court (ICC), following upon the Yugoslavia and Rwanda Tribunals, is particularly significant. At the domestic level, a number of states have prosecuted individuals alleged to have been involved in 'ethnic' crimes in Yugoslavia, Rwanda, and elsewhere.

11 See the chapter on Article I FCNM in this volume.

12 H. Hurst, 'Contemporary Developments in the International Protection of the Rights of Minorities', *Notre Dame Law Review*, 66 (1991), 1431, 1444.

Regional and Minority Languages, the Framework Convention still remains the only general fully binding treaty on minority rights.[13] A full decade has passed since the adoption of this text by the Council of Europe without any further progress having been made in the setting of binding standards in other parts of the world, or at the universal level. In Europe, the existence of the Framework Convention has also had the effect of justifying the opposition of governments to the adoption of even more advanced instruments.

Thus, the Framework Convention remains the only significant legally binding expression of the substance of minority rights as human rights. Of course, there are additional, very well developed soft law standards or recommendations, at least in the OSCE region. However, in view of the lack of binding quality, and consequently of implementation monitoring mechanisms, there is no implementation practice that can be readily reviewed and can assist in the further development and progressive interpretation of such standards. An enhanced interpretation of the Framework Convention is therefore not only relevant for a better understanding of its own provisions. A clear understanding of its substantive provisions can also add substance to similar obligations expressed in soft law, such as the UN Declaration, that have universal reach.

It will be convenient to consider the contributions of the Framework Convention to the development of minority rights discourse according to the chronological development of minority rights.[14] Initially, minority rights focused on the protection of the existence of minorities. Then there followed provisions relating to toleration and promotion of minority identity. Finally, there is the more fundamental approach of seeking to achieve diversity within a democratic society through full and effective participation in the state.

B. Protection: Existence and Non-discrimination

The right of protection consists of two elements: one relating to existence, the other to non-discrimination.

The right of existence is a negative right. It obliges the state to refrain from exterminating or severely mistreating a group or its members by virtue of their membership of the group. This protection of the group is expressly stipulated in the prohibition of genocide. This prohibition is reinforced through the

[13] One might also consider the often overlooked 1994 Central European Initiative Instrument for the Protection of Minority Rights, although it is a sub-regional instrument and its legal character is somewhat ambiguous.

[14] See generally, G. Pentassuglia, *Minorities in International Law* (Council of Europe Publishing, Strasbourg, 2002).

protection from crimes against humanity. Crimes against humanity cover systematic violations against population segments in time of peace or war even when it is not clear that the victims are targeted exclusively with the aim of destroying the group as such. The list of prohibited acts under the concept of crimes against humanity is also broader than those considered to characterize genocide.[15] In times of armed conflict, whether external or internal, the existence of minority groups is also protected through the generally applicable core of humanitarian law. Moreover, state practice since 1991 has confirmed that the practice of ethnic cleansing is also prohibited under all circumstances. Ethnic cleansing consists of a systematic policy designed to remove permanently one or more national or ethnic, religious, or linguistic population groups from portions of territory through destruction or forced displacement, mainly with a view to subjecting that territory to repopulation by another, preferred population group.

Unquestionably, the prohibitions of genocide, of crimes against humanity, war crimes directed against specific segments of the population and of ethnic cleansing are part of *jus cogens*. According to the ILC document on state responsibility, which in this instance reflects state practice, the gross and systematic failure by the responsible state to comply with these obligations has consequences for third states. These must co-operate to bring to an end through lawful means any such serious breach of obligations under peremptory norms of general international law. Third states must also not recognize as lawful a situation created by a serious breach nor render aid in maintaining that situation.[16]

The second element of the doctrine of protection concerns non-discrimination. Discrimination consists of different and disadvantageous treatment that is not justified by an objective and legitimate public aim, or that is disproportionate to that aim. Initially, within the Council of Europe the discussion of discrimination tended to focus on distinctions in relation to the enjoyment of human rights.[17] That is to say, discrimination would be ancillary to the primary violation of another human right. However, it is now

[15] The Convention on the Prevention and Punishment of the Crime of Genocide, 78 UNTS (1951) 277 (1948), Art. 3 nominates: killing, causing serious bodily or mental harm, deliberately inflicting conditions of life calculated to bring about its physical destruction in whole or in part, imposing measures intended to prevent births within the group or forcibly transferring children of the group to another group. Arguably, these prohibited acts can be interpreted widely to cover some of the more recently recognized elements of crimes against humanity. Nevertheless, the concept of genocide remains a rather technical one that does not always offer coverage to minority situations, even if in the cases of very grave human rights violations.

[16] Above, n. 9, Art. 41.

[17] International Covenant on Civil and Political Rights (ICCPR) (adopted 16 December 1966, entered into force 23 March 1976) 999 UNTS 171, Art. 26; European Convention for the Protection of Human Rights and Fundamental Freedoms (ECHR), ETS 5, 1950, Art. 14.

clear that in general 'no one shall be discriminated against by any public authority on any ground'.[18]

The right to be free from discrimination applies to all persons. That is to say, it is not specifically focused on minorities. Article 26 of the International Covenant on Civil and Political Rights prohibits discrimination on any ground such as race, colour, sex, language, religion, political or other opinion, national or social origin, property, birth or other status. Of course, race, colour, language, religion, and national origin tend to be among the distinguishing features of minorities. Moreover, minorities are particularly threatened by discrimination. Hence the right is particularly apposite to them, protecting persons belonging to ethnic, racial, religious, linguistic, or other groups from arbitrary distinction in treatment on account of their appurtenance to the group.[19]

Initially, this was a negative right, obliging the state to refrain from acting in a discriminatory way. However, already Article 26 of the ICCPR requires that all states 'guarantee' by law to all persons equal and effective protection against discrimination. This requires a proactive attitude of the state to ensure that discrimination cannot occur. Indeed, it is now clear that the state may be obliged to adopt special measures (sometimes called affirmative action) to combat indirect or structural discrimination.[20]

Like the right to existence, the prohibition of discrimination, in particular of racial discrimination (which includes discrimination on account of national or ethnic origin), is of course part of general international law, applying universally to all states, whether or not they have subscribed to the International Covenant on Civil or Political Rights or to the Convention on the Elimination of all Forms of Racial Discrimination.[21] Certainly the negative obligation to prevent discrimination is non-derogable, enjoying *jus cogens* status.[22] The

[18] Protocol No. 12 to the ECHR, ETS No. 177, 2000, Art. 1, para. 2. See S. Spiliopoulou Åkermark, 'The Limits of Pluralism—Recent Jurisprudence of the European Court of Human Rights with Regard to Minorities: Does the Prohibition of Discrimination Add Anything?', *Journal of Ethnopolitical and Minority Issues in Europe*, 3 (2002), **www.ecmi.de** 15 September 2004.

[19] Hence, ECHR, Art. 14 expressly includes 'association with a national minority' as a prohibited ground for discrimination; see also Protocol No. 12 to the ECHR, Art. 1.

[20] See at greater length Art. 4 above.

[21] Above, n. 12, p. 1444; International Covenant on Civil and Political Rights (ICCPR) (adopted 16 December 1966, entered into force 23 March 1976) 999 UNTS 171; United Nations Convention on the Elimination of All Forms of Racial Discrimination, UNGA Res. 2106 (XX) (1965).

[22] Already the *Barcelona Traction Case* noted above considered not only genocide, but also the prohibition of 'racial discrimination' as part of general international law to which an *erga omnes* effect applies, *Barcelona Traction Light and Power Company Case* [1970] 2nd Phase, ICJ Rep. 41970 IJC 4, para. 32. See also J. Packer, 'United Nations Protection of Minorities in Time of Public Emergency: The Hard-Core of Minority Rights', in D. Premont (ed.), *Non-derogable Rights in States of Emergency*

doctrine of serious violations of peremptory norms, requiring the organized international community to react to grave breaches of *jus cogens*, applies in cases of systematic and grave discrimination conducted over a protracted period and directed against whole and defined population segments. While an attempt was made to attach international criminal responsibility to racial discrimination in the extreme case of apartheid, this was not universally accepted.

One may ask whether the Framework Convention measures up to the very strong entrenchment of protection of minorities in general international law. To take existence first: the substantive part of the Convention does not concern itself with existence in terms of genocide, crimes against humanity, or war crimes. This is in line with other minority rights instruments that also address existence in general terms only. The UN Declaration on the Rights of Persons Belonging to National or Ethnic, Religious, and Linguistic Minorities contains a substantive obligation to 'protect the existence' of minorities.[23] Article 3 of the Venice Commission Proposal for a European Convention for the Protection of Minorities would have stated that 'minorities have the right to be protected against any activity capable of threatening their existence'.[24]

As was noted in the discussion of the Preamble, the drafters of the Framework Convention did consider whether they should include a reference to ethnic cleansing in the Preamble.[25] In view of the events occurring at the time in the former Yugoslavia and in the Caucasus region, such a proposal would have appeared quite relevant, but it was not followed.[26] One may presume that the Council of Europe took the view that active threats to the existence of minorities through extermination or forcible displacement are already sufficiently covered elsewhere. Hence the Framework Convention would not be the place to restate these already strongly established legal restrictions. Moreover, the Council of Europe represents a community of values that are meant to be unquestionable in all member states. It was probably not

(Brill, Brussels, 1996), 501, 521: '. . . national or ethnic, religious or linguistic minorities possess non-derogable rights to existence and to non-discrimination'. As opposed to the negative prohibition of discrimination, it is less certain that the positive entitlement to benefit from positive action enjoys a similar status.

23 United Nations Declaration on the Rights of Persons Belonging to National or Ethnic, Religious, and Linguistic Minorities, UNGA Res. 47/135 (1992), Art. 1, para. 1.

24 European Commission for Democracy through Law, Venice Commission Proposal for a European Convention for the Protection of Minorities, 5th meeting, 1991, Art. 3, para. 1.

25 Above, n. 24

26 Nevertheless, there is a hint in this direction in the Preamble, '[c]onsidering that the upheavals of European history have shown that the protection of national minorities is essential to stability, democratic security and peace in this continent'. See the Framework Convention for the Protection of National Minorities (FCNM), Preamble.

considered appropriate even to raise the possibility of active threats to existence as a prospect that needs addressing. Hence, it was deemed sufficient merely to express in the Preamble the resolve of the states parties 'to protect within their respective territories the existence of national minorities'.

Existence is nevertheless also protected through a number of substantive provisions of the Framework Convention. First, as was already noted above, Article 1 determines that 'the protection of national minorities' is an integral part of the international protection of human rights. This wording is an unusual departure from the careful language adopted throughout the other substantive parts of the Convention, which consistently refer to 'persons belonging to national minorities' in order to avoid the impression of the granting of collective rights.[27] Exceptionally, Article 1 nominates national minorities as an object of protection. The fact that the group as such, collectively, is the object of protection and must be preserved is emphasized in this way.

While the term 'ethnic cleansing' is not used, the Framework Convention does in fact protect the existence of minorities from destruction, displacement, or forced assimilation. Article 5(1) prohibits assimilation of persons belonging to national minorities, protecting in this way the existence of the group. Article 6(2) requires states to take appropriate measures to protect persons who may be subject to threats or acts of discrimination, hostility, or violence as a result of their ethnic, cultural, linguistic, or religious identity. Article 16 of the Convention prohibits measures which alter the proportions of the population in areas inhabited by persons belong to national minorities.

In order to exist, a minority must be able to live without constant threat and pressure of active discrimination. Otherwise exodus or forced assimilation will result. As was noted above, the prohibition of discrimination is therefore the second element of the protection of minorities. Discrimination is, of course, addressed at length in the Convention, and in a number of other provisions, all of which have been considered in some detail in this commentary. Article 3(2) ensures that no disadvantages shall flow for individuals on grounds of having opted (or not) to be treated as a member of a national minority. Article 4(1) guarantees equality before the law and equal protection of the law and rules out any discrimination in this respect on grounds of belonging to a minority. Article 6(2) obliges the state to take active steps to protect persons belonging to minorities from threats or acts of discrimination. This applies not only to the activities of the state's own organs, but also to society at large.

[27] FCNM, Art. 12, para. 1 is not really an exception, given that it does not address individuals as holders of a right, but it is instead directed at the parties.

The Convention expands upon the duty to refrain from and to prevent discrimination by also encouraging the adoption of special measures. The issue of special measures marks the point where the concept of protection from discrimination on the one hand, and that of promotion of identity on the other, meet. Both require the state to take active steps to improve the situation of minorities. Nevertheless, the two are conceptually distinct. Special measures are adopted to give expression to the principle of non-discrimination. It is necessary in order to permit members of minorities to be able to enjoy equally the human rights available to all, or to participate on equal terms in all aspects of society. Hence, special measures are remedial. It would not be sufficient to protect minorities from new acts of discrimination. Instead, it is also necessary to overcome the consequences of persistently entrenched discrimination that is part of the structure of the society in question. Special measures therefore seek to establish a level playing field by removing the consequences of discrimination that has already occurred.[28] They are temporary. In contrast, positive action as part of the promotion of minority identity does not aim at achieving full equality. Rather, positive action is based on a distinction and seeks to maintain this distinction. The state is obliged to provide additional resources to enable minorities to maintain and advance their identity.

C. From Toleration to Promotion: Identity

A further stage in the development of minority rights concerns identity. While the rights concerning existence are part of *jus cogens*, identity is less well entrenched at the universal level. As was noted in the introductory part to this volume, rules concerning identity initially regressed after the Second World War. During the League of Nations era, positive rights relating to language, education, religion, and culture were established.[29] There was provision for funding for some of these activities and an element of self-administration of minorities in relation to them. These rights were subject to international supervision complete with petitioning mechanisms.[30] However, these commitments were limited to a number of states and certain minorities only. After the catastrophe

[28] United Nations Declaration on the Rights of Persons Belonging to National or Ethnic, Religious, and Linguistic Minorities, UNGA Res. 47/135 (1992), Art. 4, paras. 1, 2. Para. 1 provides for special measures to ensure that persons belonging to minorities may exercise fully and effectively all their human rights and fundamental freedoms without any discrimination and in full equality before the law. Para. 2 requires the creation of conditions favourable to the exercise of minority culture, language, etc.

[29] See F. Capotorti, *Study on the Rights of Persons Belonging to Ethnic, Religious and Linguistic Minorities* (United Nation Publications, New York, 1991), 18 ff.

[30] J. Stone, *Regional Guarantees of Minority Rights* (Macmillan, New York, 1932).

of the Second World War, they appeared to be thoroughly discredited and provisions relating to minority identity were no longer pursued. Instead, individual human rights were extended to all persons. Provided these rights were extended equally to all persons, it was assumed, no need for additional measures in favour of minorities would be required.

Minority rights, on the other hand, are often described as human rights 'plus'. That is to say, minorities must not only be protected in their existence, and from discrimination in the exercise of general human rights. The minority *problématique* requires additional measures to ensure that the minority can preserve and develop its distinct identity.

This fact was recognized, albeit in rather a limited way, in the International Covenant on Civil and Political Rights. To this day, Article 27 of the Covenant remains the only universally applicable conventional norm concerning minority identity. Given that the ICCPR was drafted in the 1960s it is not surprising that it takes a cautious view of minority identity. This can be described as an attitude of toleration. Through a negative right, the state pledges to refrain from interfering with the exercise of minimum attributes of minority identity. Accordingly, the article precludes states from denying to ethnic, religious, or linguistic minorities the right, in community with the other members of the group, to enjoy their own culture, to profess and practise their own religion, or to use their own language.

This minimalist and negative approach of the toleration of minority identity has been modified in practice. Over the past decade, there has been a move from toleration to promotion. The UN Human Rights Committee, the implementation and monitoring body attached to the Convention, has considerably broadened our understanding of the obligation contained in Article 27:[31]

6.1. Although Article 27 is expressed in negative terms, that article, nevertheless, does recognize the existence of a 'right' and requires that it shall not be denied. Consequently, a State party is under an obligation to ensure that the existence and the exercise of this right are protected against their denial or violation. Positive measures of protection are, therefore, required not only against the acts of the State party itself, whether through its legislative, judicial or administrative authorities, but also against the acts of other persons within the State party.

6.2. Although the rights protected under Article 27 are individual rights, they depend in turn on the ability of the minority group to maintain its culture, language or religion. Accordingly, positive measures by States may also be necessary to protect the identity of a minority and the rights of its members to enjoy and develop their culture and language and to practise their religion, in community with other members of the group. . . .

[31] UN Human Rights Committee, ICCPR 'General Comment 23' in Art. 27: 'The Rights of Minorities', 50th session, 1214th meeting 1994, A/49/40, I (1994) 107, para. 1, 6.

Through this formulation, the Human Rights Committee has addressed three issues: the proactive obligation to ensure performance of the obligation, the translation of the originally negative right into a positive obligation, and the addition of an inter-subjective effect. That is to say, in the view of the Committee, Article 27 requires the state to desist from actively denying to minorities the right to engage in the cultural, linguistic, and religious practices that are necessary to maintain their identity. The duty of abstention is transformed into a duty of action to ensure compliance.

Moreover, the Committee argues that it is not only state agencies that must comply with the negative and positive aspect of identity. Other actors within society, too, must respect the right to identity of minority populations. In a negative sense, they must not interfere with this exercise.

Finally, the Committee recognizes that the state is under an obligation to facilitate the activities that are connected with the identity of minorities. Instead of the negative obligation of preventing interference with such practices, the state is required actively to promote these through positive action. As was already noted above, special measures as part of non-discrimination aim to achieve full and effective equality, while positive actions recognize an inequality. Positive action reflects the fact that minorities have requirements that may exceed those of the other, dominant parts of the population who are already well provided for by the general public services. For instance, it may be necessary to offer additional funding to ensure that a minority culture can manifest itself, to cover additional cost of language education, etc.

Of course, one may ask whether a General Comment can in itself advance the understanding of Article 27 to such a considerable extent without losing its legally binding, conventional character. The authority of the Human Rights Committee is significant. Moreover, it can claim to be in the position of offering what is known as 'authentic' interpretations. That is to say, a body or international organization attached to an international treaty may enjoy authority to record and advance in an authoritative way the interpretation of that treaty. Moreover, the views of the Committee are of course anticipated in the UN Declaration—a document adopted by consensus by the UN General Assembly specifically with a view to adding to the interpretation of Article 27.[32] Article 1 of the Declaration encourages states to create conditions for the promotion of minority identities in general terms. Article 4(2) requires states to take

[32] Alan Rosas, in a contribution published shortly after the adoption of the Declaration, portrayed this expectation; see A. Rosas, 'The Protection of Minorities in Europe, a General Overview', in J. Packer and K. Myntti (eds.), *The Protection of Ethnic and Linguistic Minorities in Europe* (Åbo Akademi University, Turku, 1993), 9.

measures to create favourable conditions to enable persons belonging to national minorities to express their characteristics and to develop their culture, language, religion, traditions, and customs. This general principle is then developed into specific obligations, such as language rights and educational entitlements.

Identity is therefore supported in several ways in general international law. First, Article 27, which can be taken to reflect general custom, obliges states not to interfere with the manifestation of minority identity. Secondly, through the Declaration and the authoritative interpretation of Article 27 by the Human Rights Committee, a positive obligation to promote minority identity in general terms is also now reflected in general custom. This is, thirdly, reinforced by the specific obligations introduced in the Declaration concerning positive action for the promotion of identity in relation to education, culture, language, etc.

The Framework Convention significantly advances this branch of minority rights in general international law. According to Article 5, the parties undertake to promote the conditions necessary for persons belonging to national minorities to maintain and develop their culture, and to preserve the essential elements of their identity, namely their religion, language, traditions, and cultural heritage. While this language sounds softer than Article 4(2) of the Declaration (the parties 'undertake to', instead of 'shall'), this difference may be explained with reference to the more open, framework character of the Convention. Nevertheless, the Convention does in fact frequently use the word 'shall' where the more specific rights addressing the individual manifestations of minority identity (language rights, media access, use of languages, education) are concerned. These rights to identity are certainly more expansive in scope than the provisions of the UN Declaration and generally more precisely defined.

Along with a detailed discussion of full and effective equality, the bulk of this commentary has been devoted to an interpretation of these very provisions on the basis of the extensive implementation practice that has accumulated. This practice itself provides for a unique focal point for debates and discussions about the actual content of the right to identity of minorities and the state's obligation of its promotion. Such a detailed and authoritative discussion can be found nowhere else. Without it, it would be very difficult to form a view of the content of obligations concerning identity as they relate to actual problems involving minorities on a day-to-day basis. Examples might relate to claims to multilingual street signs, the use of language by public bodies, support for educational institution, etc.

In addition to advancing our understanding of the Convention's obligations to promote minority identity quite considerably, this practice can also be used in a broader context. For instance, at the universal level, the interpretation of Article 27 of the ICCPR and of the UN Declaration can now be informed by it. Indeed, the present attempts to generate a legally binding universal instrument on minority rights may profit from this advancing understanding of minority rights.

D. Co-governance through Full and Effective Participation

The third principal phase in the development of minority rights concerns a rather more fundamental shift in our understanding of 'the minority problem'. Minority issues have often been seen by governments as security issues. The very impressive advances in soft law on minorities of the OSCE have to be seen against this background.[33] Even the Council of Europe Vienna Summit of Heads of State and Government instructed the Committee of Ministers to address minorities, so 'that they can contribute to stability and peace'.[34] To this end, the Framework Convention was drafted.

Of course, the preamble of the Framework Convention refers not only to security concerns that motivated its drafters. For instance, it also refers to cultural diversity as a source and a factor, not of division, but of enrichment for each society. The third aspect in the development of minority rights, in addition to protection, and tolerance promotion, concerns the management of diversity in a democratic, pluralistic society. This concept requires a move away from the security dimension—the perceived need to buy off the threat of secessionist minorities or irredentist kin states through provision of minority rights. Instead, harmonious and inclusive minority and majority relations are valued in themselves—they are seen to be an essential part of governance itself. Minority rights are an important element in the management of diversity through co-governance by diverse constituencies.

Co-governance applies to society at large, permitting it to organize public decision-making mechanisms in a complex, multi-layered arrangement. In that way the constituencies most closely concerned with the items at issue can take authoritative decisions in relation to them. At the same time, they are precluded from taking decisions that violate the rights of others or the basic core values of the state in question. Co-governance is co-operative, providing for structures of dialogue and mediation through public institutions. One of

[33] The mandate of the OSCE High Commission on National Minorities (OHCNM) whose office arranged for the creation of many of these instruments relates to conflict prevention, and not only to minority *issue per se*.

[34] Council of Europe Vienna Summit of Heads of State and Government, Final Declaration of the Vienna Summit, 1993, Appendix II.

the elements of co-governance is subsidiarity, now a well-established principle in Europe. Minorities, as well as other territorially based constituencies, profit from it.

In relation to minorities, co-governance concerns two issue areas. On the one hand, there is the positive entitlement of minority constituencies to fully participate in public decision making. Secondly, persons belonging to minorities must have equal chances in all aspects of public life in a more general sense, including social provision, access to economic opportunities, and contribution to the cultural environment.

1. Decision Making

Provision for participation of minorities in public decision making consists of four elements. These are (*a*) direct representation in decision-making bodies, (*b*) provisions for consultation, (*c*) representation in public service, and (*d*) autonomous decision-making by the minority itself.

(a) Democratic Representation

Direct representation is of course already covered in general human rights law. The principle of democratic governance grants to every citizen the right and opportunity to take part in the conduct of public affairs. This can be done directly, or through elected representatives. It includes the right to vote and be elected at genuine periodic elections. Already in Article 25 of the ICCPR it is made clear that this right must be applied without distinction, including distinction as to race, colour, language, religion, national origin, etc.

The right to equal representation in human rights is added to by the *lex specialis* of effective participation established by minority rights. This right extends from the national level (parliament) to regional and local governance. In addition to its vertical dimension, it also applies horizontally, in relation to individual sectors of public decision making. For instance, there would be a requirement for particular representation in relation to educational matters, through effective representation in school boards, etc.

Minorities not only have the right to participate equally. According to the UN Declaration, persons belonging to national minorities have the right 'to participate *effectively* in decisions on the national and, where appropriate, regional level concerning the minority to which they belong or the region in which they live'.[35] Effective participation is more than equal participation. Effective participation may require the state to make special provision to ensure that minorities are represented, for instance where their demographic

[35] Above, n. 23, Art. 2, para. 3, emphasis added.

distribution, coupled with the electoral system, would otherwise lead to their automatic exclusion. The requirement of effective representation may therefore necessitate special measures, such as exceptions from electoral registration rules, from minimum percentage thresholds that need to be passed before a party can gain parliamentary representation, etc.

Article 15 of the Framework Convention restates this right to effective participation, although it does not refer especially to 'the region in which [minorities] live'.[36] While some would see Article 15 as merely a programmatic provision, this commentary has demonstrated that it is being implemented in a substantive and serious way. Moreover, despite the wide margin of appreciation granted to states where the design of democratic systems is concerned, the Advisory Committee has become increasingly forthright in demanding representation that is effective in practice, even if positive measures are required towards this end.

(b) Consultation

Even if minority groups manage to gain representation in parliament or in other bodies, they will obviously, at least at the national level, remain a minority and lack the ability to control decisions.[37] Consultation ensures that the views and interests of minorities are taken into account in public decision making where minorities do not control the primary decision-making process. Practice under the Framework Convention is also particularly rich in relation to consultation. Consultation can range from a right to virtual co-decision by minority representative bodies, to conciliation processes between the primary decision-making body and the consultation mechanism, to an entitlement for minorities at least to be heard before a decision that is of special relevance to them is taken. The implementation practice under Article 15 is unique in exhibiting the different attempts to ensure that minority constituencies can have input in public decision making. The Advisory Committee has also not been shy in demanding that such mechanisms should not only exist on paper, but that they must function effectively in practice.

(c) Representation in Public Service

Article 25 of the ICCPR guarantees access, on general terms of equality, to public service. This requirement also applies specifically to minorities and is covered, albeit less expressly, both in the UN Declaration and the Framework

[36] See chapter on Article 15 in this commentary.

[37] At times, minority-based parties will join coalition governments and exercise considerable influence.

Convention.[38] Representation of minorities in public service is a particularly important element of ensuring that minorities actually do feel that the state is characterized by genuine co-governance.

The failure of both instruments to address this matter in a more direct way is compensated for in the implementation practice of the Convention. States clearly exhibit a consciousness of having to meet the obligation of achieving adequate (if not always strictly proportionate) representation in public service. Moreover, the Advisory Committee has quite expressly demanded improvements in this area, in particular in relation to representation of minorities in the security and justice sector. These areas of public service are of course particularly sensitive, both to the dominant and non-dominant communities. Appropriate representation in justice and security institutions is therefore seen as an important indicator of successful co-governance.

(d) Autonomous Decision-making

The mechanisms of co-governance addressed thus far have all aimed to ensure that minorities can participate effectively in the processes of public decision making at all levels of the state itself. This not only satisfies the basic democratic requirements of modern state theory. It also serves the quite pragmatic purpose of ensuring that minority groups feel that they have 'a stake' in the overall state. In contrast, autonomous decision-making processes aim to ensure that minorities have control over decisions that particularly affect them. Instead of participation in the overall state, the aim is to gain space apart from the state for internal decision-making.

Article 2 of the UN Declaration, and Article 15 of the FCNM both provide for this space. Generally, there are two modes of ensuring autonomous decision-making. These are territorial autonomy and functional or cultural autonomy. As was already noted, in contrast to the UN Declaration Article 15 does not refer to a territorial dimension of minority co-governance. The implementation practice (and the explanatory report adopted along with the convention) nevertheless emphasizes territorial autonomy as one possible approach. This accords with the more general trend of encouraging subsidiarity in governmental decision-making and of generating more powerful structures of devolved local self-government that were noted already above. Nevertheless, territorial autonomy goes somewhat beyond this, given its specific design as a means to enfranchise a minority in relation to a portion of territory and in relation to substantive areas of governance that may be somewhat different to those

[38] In relation to the FCNM, this consists of the right to full and effective equality. See FCNM, Art. 4, para. 2, Art. 15.

that arise generally in the context of local government. The Advisory Committee has advanced certain aspects that need to be borne in mind when autonomy solutions are adopted. These concern the constitutional entrenchment of autonomy, the need to provide autonomous units with the resources necessary to fulfil their functions of government, and the need to protect the human rights of those who do not belong to the local majority.

Functional autonomy places the exercise of public decision-making powers relating to issues such as minority culture, religion, education, etc, in the hands of a minority body organized at state or regional level. This body may be representative of all minorities, or there may be bodies combining the different representatives of just one minority. Often, these bodies will also have authority to disburse funding made available not only by their own membership, but by the government. Such practices are highlighted in the state reports submitted to the Advisory Committee, although it has to be admitted that there appear to be some difficulties in the functioning of such cultural autonomy. One may also note that the right to the exercise of autonomous functions by minority representative organizations also implies duties. In particular, there is a duty to ensure that the minority representative process is in itself genuinely representative and operates democratically and in a transparent way.

2. *Effective Participation in Social and Economic Life*

Article 3(2) of the UN Declaration confirms that persons belonging to minorities have the right to participate effectively in cultural, religious, social, economic, and public life. In addition to the issue of access to points of decision-making that was addressed above, this requirement goes to the heart of diversity management. On the one hand, this provision, also reflected in the Article 15 of the Framework Convention, requires that persons belonging to minorities must have access to participation in the public life of the state as a whole.[39] However, going beyond this requirement, the state needs to ensure that members of all groups have the same chances of success within the state. As cultural and religious affairs, and access to public representation, have already been addressed through other means, this additional dimension relates particularly to the economic and social sphere.

Once again, the Framework Convention is establishing itself as the focal point for the recognition of the economic and social dimension of minority rights. While a similar provision has been part and parcel of the UN Declaration, it is chiefly within the context of the Convention's monitoring

[39] FCNM, Art. 15 oddly does not refer to effective participation in religious affairs.

procedure that the general principle of economic and social participation is filled out with concrete substance.[40]

III. Reach and Scope

Having established that the FCNM does contribute significantly to the substance of human and minority rights, the question of the reach of its provisions arises. Does the Convention extend these rights to the minority communities throughout Europe that would benefit most from their application? In the Preface, it was noted that this study is not principally concerned with investigating the actual impact of individual provisions on the lives of individuals. This is left to Advisory Committee and NGO reporting and other assessment mechanisms. Instead, this commentary has focused on an analysis of the development of rights and their advancing interpretation. However, even from this perspective, it is necessary to revisit the question of the reach of the Convention. For, if significant minority constituencies are excluded from its application, then they will not profit from its provisions, however advanced their interpretation.

The question of the reach of the Framework Convention has sparked considerable debate. This debate focuses on four principal areas: the membership of the Convention, the question of the definition of minorities, its possible application to citizens only, and the process issue of the identification of minorities that benefit from it.

The issue of participation in the Convention was a source of concern from the beginning. Even at the end of the twentieth century, minority rights were still viewed with suspicion by governments in Europe. The initiative of the Council of Europe Parliamentary Assembly of generating an additional Protocol to the European Convention on Human Rights was rebuffed on this account. The governments of the Council of Europe even reneged on the compromise that had been envisaged: there would only be a framework convention on minority rights generally, operating outside the Strasbourg human rights system. However, this would be compensated for by an additional protocol on cultural rights. That protocol never materialized.

[40] At the universal level, the International Covenant on Economic, Social, and Cultural Rights provides something of a forum on these issues. See the International Covenant on Economic, Social, and Cultural Rights (adopted 16 December 1966, entered into force 3 January 1976) 993 UNTS 3 (ICESCR). Within the EU, exclusion is of course being addressed, although on a general level and not specifically as a minority issue.

Given this caution on the part of governments, the spread of membership in the Framework Convention is truly astonishing. The Convention was adopted on 8 November 1994 and was opened for signature on 1 February 1995. It entered into force on 1 February 1998, having reached the requisite twelve ratifications some three months earlier. In fact, the number of states parties has nearly tripled by now, standing at thirty-five at the time of writing. The Convention has been signed, but not yet ratified by a further seven states (Belgium, Georgia, Greece, Iceland, Latvia, Luxembourg, the Netherlands). Andorra, France, and Turkey have not signed.

The Convention membership has been criticized in two respects. First, not all EU members are parties. Given the strong pressure exercised by the EU on applicant and candidate states to subscribe to minority rights by virtue of the so-called Copenhagen criteria, this has given rise to a not entirely unjustified allegation of double standards. Moreover, the EU permitted Latvia to enter the Union without having ratified. In view of the serious concerns expressed in relation to minority issues within that state during the accession process, this is surprising. Secondly, within the Council of Europe universal membership has also remained elusive, with a number of non-parties featuring significant minority problems.

Of course, further members will join the Convention over time. With respect to the next wave of EU candidates or applicants, it is to be hoped that the Union will insist in a more consistent way not only on membership of the Convention (Turkey), but also on actual implementation steps. Within the EU, pressure will build, also and especially from among the new members, for coverage of minority issues within the Union itself. While some present non-members may yield and join the Convention, this may prove more difficult in relation to others. France will not easily move from its view that it is a state of equal citizens, where there is no need or space for the concept of minority protection. Greece's position has been that minority issues are regulated exclusively by the post-First World War arrangement, in particular the Treaty of Lausanne. This has inhibited a more open stance on minority issues affecting communities other than those denominated as minorities in that arrangement. Nevertheless, it is inevitable that minority issues will increasingly be discussed in the language of legal claims, also in the reluctant states. This result will be attributable in part to the Framework Convention.

The question of the definition of minorities is of course the second controversial aspect affecting the reach of the Convention. The absence of a generally accepted definition of minorities is widely bemoaned in scholarship. And yet, a good and widely accepted definition of minorities exists in principle, certainly since it was expressed and refined in the Caportorti study on the rights of persons belonging to ethnic, religious, and linguistic minorities. A definition was also provided for in Article 1 of the draft for an additional protocol on the rights of national minorities to the European Convention on Human Rights adopted by the Parliamentary Assembly of the Council of Europe.[41] The Central European Initiative Instrument of the Protection of Minority Rights defines national minorities as:

> A group that is smaller in number than the rest of the population of a state, whose members being nationals of that state, have ethnic, religious or linguistic features different from those of the rest of the population, and are guided by the will to safeguard their culture, traditions, religion and language.[42]

John Packer, the former Director of the office of the OSCE High Commissioner on National Minorities, on the other hand, simply defines minorities as 'a group of people who freely associate for an established purpose where their shared desire differs from that expressed by the majority rule'.[43]

This conclusion cannot hope to rehearse the entire debate on the issue of a definition. This issue has been investigated at some length in this commentary, in the light of the attitude of the states parties to the Convention and of the Advisory Committee.[44] A number of common principles can be deduced from this. First, it is clear that a minority is defined according to objective and principally known criteria. Practice confirms that it is not a concept quite as open as the one advocated by John Packer. Instead, there is a significant specificity to the concept of minorities, and to the application of minority rights. Hence, it is not appropriate to seek to apply the concept in its legal sense to other groups that can be considered non-dominant within the state and that seek to advocate common interests (for instance, gays and lesbians, the disabled, etc.). It is true, the special provision for minorities is part of the management of diversity in an even broader sense within the state. This was noted in section II.D. of this conclusion. But while minority rights are part of the wider machinery of diversity mechanisms, they are also a distinct form of addressing diversity in a specific context. They address a special issue area with its own particular problems and challenges. Hence, it is necessary and proper to seek a trigger

[41] Above n, 1.

[42] Central European Initiative Instrument of the Protection of Minority Rights, 1994, Art. 1.

[43] J. Packer, 'On the Definition of Minorities', in J. Packer and K. Myntti, *The Protection of Ethnic and Linguistic Minorities in Europe* (Åbo Akademi University, Turku, 1993), 23, 45.

[44] Chapters on Arts. 1, 3, above.

point for the application of this set of legal rules that relates to the specific features of that issue area.

Nevertheless, the definitional criteria for the application of minority rights are not as restrictive as is sometimes presumed. Even the practice under the Framework Convention clarifies that 'national' minorities are not only those minorities that can boast an external 'kin' state.[45] A minority also does not need to be numerically inferior. Portions of the majority population of the state as a whole may find themselves in the position of a regional or local minority. The Advisory Committee has addressed such situations. In some states, the population balance may be highly complex, featuring no clearly established 'titular' majority, but a number of population segments that can all be considered to benefit from minority rights. One may even envisage situations where a numerical majority is structurally non-dominant within the state, rendering it a minority.

Hence, we are left with an understanding of minorities as national or ethnic, religious, or linguistic groups in a non-dominant position within the state that are motivated by a desire to express and preserve their common identity. Some governments would add the requirement that such minorities must have a long-established bond with the state, or traditionally (over several generations) inhabit a specific part of the state. This criterion is meant to exclude recently arrived communities (migrants, so-called 'guest workers'). The Advisory Committee has avoided a doctrinaire approach to this question. Instead, it has sought to apply the provisions of the Convention in an extensive way, while recognizing that some parts of the Convention can only be applied in relation to territorially settled minorities. As Professor Hofmann, the former President of the Advisory Committee, has reported in the introduction:[46]

> As regards the issue of the potential applicability of the FCNM also to persons belonging to 'new' minorities, the Advisory Committee noted that some provisions of the FCNM—such as Art. 11 (3) with its explicit reference to areas traditionally inhabited by persons belonging to a national minority, could only be applicable to 'old' minorities. In contrast, it is clear that Art. 6 FCNM applies to 'all persons living on the territory of a given state party' including to persons belonging to 'new' minorities. Furthermore, it seems possible to argue that other provisions such as Articles 3, 5, 7, and 8 could also be applicable to persons belonging to 'new' minorities.

[45] See, for example, P. Thornberry, 'The Framework Convention on National Minorities', *Baltic Yearbook of International Law*, 2 (2002), 127–33.

[46] See the Introduction to this Commentary by R. Hoffmann; see also R. Hofmann, 'Protecting the Rights of National Minorities in Europe', *German Yearbook of International Law*, 44 (2001), 237–57.

One may also note that the OSCE is at present considering the drafting of a further set of standards especially applicable to migrant communities. Presumably such an instrument would very much reflect the obligations applicable to recently arrived communities that have been identified by the Advisory Committee.

The problem of the permanency of the link to the territory is related to, but distinct from, the question of citizenship. For instance, there may well be minority populations that have inhabited territory for a considerable period of time, but that are lacking in citizenship. In other instances, groups of newcomers may rapidly acquire citizenship, but the state may nevertheless exclude them from the definition of minorities, given that they are not autochthonous. On the issue of citizenship, the universal human rights approach is significantly more generous than the position of some European governments, and indeed the wording of the draft protocol proposed by the Council of Europe Parliamentary Assembly.[47] While Caportorti initially added the requirement of citizenship, he later moved away from this position.[48] General Comment 23 to Article 27 of the ICCPR clearly states that 'the individuals designed to be protected need not be citizens of the State party'.[49] Asbjørn Eide, in his authoritative commentary on the UN Declaration, finds that '[p]ersons who are not (yet) citizens of the country in which they reside can form a part of or belong to a minority in that country.'[50]

Is the proposed restriction of minority rights then a particularity of the European concept of 'national' minorities? As has been noted in the discussion on Article 3, the Advisory Committee has challenged this view, especially, but not exclusively, in relation to groups who were deprived of citizenship of their state of residence due to political upheaval. Further practice is likely to add pressure on the restrictive position that is still maintained by some governments in Europe.

Even if there is emerging an understanding of the scope of application of minority rights in general, a number of states have claimed the right of nomination. This claim to state nomination is to be distinguished from the right to individual choice. According to Article 3 of the Convention, every person belonging to a national minority shall have the right freely to choose to be treated or not to be treated as such. This is the right of individual choice. Some states

[47] Above, n. 1, Art. 1(a): 'reside on the territory of that state and are citizens thereof'.

[48] Noted by P. Hilpold, 'Neue Minderheiten im Völkerrecht und im Europearecht', *Archiv des Völkerrechts*, 43 (2004), 80–3.

[49] Above, n. 31, para 5.1.

[50] A. Eide, Commentary to the Declaration on the Rights of Persons Belonging to National or Ethnic, Religious, and Linguistic Minorities (2001), UN Doc. E/CN.4/Sub.2/AC.5/2001/2, para 9.

argue, however, that they have right to determine, in the first place, whether there exists a national minority on their territory. If they find that there is no such minority, then the individual right of choice would be rendered meaningless.[51]

As was discussed at length in the context of Article 3, states have adopted a number of different devices to try and secure this view in relation to the Framework Convention, mainly through differing types of declarations or through limitations expressed in the state reports. The Advisory Committee has been rather courageous in challenging the positions of some of these governments, for instance in relation to Denmark. It has taken the view that governments are required to investigate the personal scope of application of the Convention in relation to their countries. While governments have a margin of appreciation in making a determination as to application, this has to be exercised consistently with international legal requirements, including the requirements of Article 3. Again, over time this approach is likely to reduce the room for governments to exclude groups that fulfil the objective criteria for minorities. The interesting concept of challenging exclusions on the ground of appearing to be based on 'arbitrary or unjustified distinctions' advanced by the Advisory Committee provides a mechanism for approaching these issues in legal, rather than political terms.

IV. Legal Character and Implementation

From the outset, the designation of the FCNM as a Framework Convention has led to some confusion, leading to some doubts about its legal character. Of course, it is clear that the convention is a treaty—a legally binding instrument. However, the framework character manifests itself in two aspects. First, the provisions contained in the Convention tend to be phrased in more general terms. As the Explanatory Report accompanying the Convention explains, these are 'programme-type provisions'.[52] While states are under a binding legal obligation to achieve the result stipulated in the relevant articles, they are often left to determine themselves how they will achieve this. This approach was justified with reference to the fact that the situation of minorities differs from state to state and that solutions to problems will need to be tailor-made. Secondly, the Convention is not directly applicable. It is not meant to be incorporated or

[51] See, for example, P. E. Dimitras, Recognition of Minorities in Europe: Protecting Rights and Dignity, Minority Rights Group Briefing, 2004.

[52] Preparatory Work of the Ad Hoc Committee for the Protection of National Minorities (CAHMIN), Explanatory Report to the Framework Convention for the Protection of National Minorities, CAHMIN H(1995) 010, 1995, para 11.

transformed directly into national law. Again, it is up to states to determine how they will achieve compliance with the principles of the Convention in their domestic practice. This also means that the Convention will not be subject to judicial enforcement through municipal courts.

In view of this fact, would it not be better to describe the Convention as soft law—a loose guide that is meant to socialize states over time into patterns of behaviour that might, then, be enshrined in hard legal obligations? Of course, one has to admit that the development of minority rights is lagging behind other areas of human rights. The process that has been undergone with respect to other types of obligations, moving from soft law standards (UN Declaration on Human Rights), to fairly general hard law obligations (Covenants), and then to even more specific, specialized obligations (Racial Discrimination, Torture, Rights of the Child, etc.) is still ongoing in this area. At the universal level, we have noted a very strong entrenchment of existence in human and minority rights. Identity is only reflected in one single provision in hard law, in Article 27 ICCPR. The move from toleration of identity to promotion has been achieved through implementation practice under that article. This has not been backed up by a further binding legal instrument. Instead, the soft law vehicle of the UN Declaration was used to advance the concepts of promotion of identity further and to add to its meaning. Moreover, the Convention will increasingly be a focal point of the emerging discussion about co-governance and the provision of chances in relation to economic and social aspects. In this way, the Convention can increasingly mark the fact that minority issues are not primarily security issues. They are matters of human rights and good governance.

In view of this background, the Framework Convention does well in establishing the first more comprehensive catalogue of minority rights in hard law. This commentary has revealed that a number of the obligations of states contained in the Convention are phrased in a form that is sufficiently precise to facilitate implementation. Other provisions might sound general, but the Advisory Committee, in its dialogue with governments, has given concrete meaning to them. In fact, the depth and quality of the dialogue that has taken place between governments and the Advisory Committee is equivalent and in some instances superior to that found in relation to other human rights instruments. States quite clearly treat the Framework Convention as a serious legal undertaking and report on it in a serious way. The Advisory Committee has also taken the view that minority issues are developing dynamically. Its demands on governments appear to be increasing over time. Moreover, the Committee seems to have higher expectations in relation to states that have already advanced further in minority co-governance than others. One might ask whether this does not undermine the claim that the minority rights enshrined in the Convention have a defined legal substance. After all, the Advisory Committee appears to regard this substance to be a matter of negotiation on a case-by-case basis. Are minority rights therefore nothing other than a guideline in negotiations conducted with governments? Are we witnessing here the degeneration of the concept of human rights into a view of 'human rights as argument' as opposed to human rights as unchallengeable and clear obligations? After all, human rights activists and campaigners are rightly criticized when they somewhat recklessly proclaim the existence of a new right to this or that. In so doing, it is said, they are devaluing the legal character of 'real' human rights.

Two differences apply, however, in the context of minority rights. First, as already noted, this field is still in need of development. Hence, the Advisory Committee has had to find a balance between, on the one hand, insistence on compliance with obligations that are, in its view, clearly established, and, on the other hand, arguing about the substance of other obligations. Where protection and toleration of identity is concerned, there is a hard legal core in general international law that is of course not challenged and not subject to negotiation. With respect to promotion and co-governance, some firm requirements have also been clarified in the early practice under the Framework Convention. These, too, are not subject to negotiation, at least not downward. In other respects, it is still necessary to establish the level of entitlement in relation to a number of issues. For instance, should there be provision for bilingual street signage in areas with a minority population of 30, of 20, or of 10 per cent? Even if it were appropriate to have a fixed standard that can apply to this question in all circumstances, it would need to develop (and is in fact developing) through practice.

Secondly, it is a unique advantage that this dialogue is forced to occur through the Advisory Committee mechanism. Instead of having to rely exclusively on NGO advocacy in seeking to improve provision by states, this dialogue is elevated to the intergovernmental level. While the Advisory Committee is an expert body, it functions with the backing and the involvement of the Committee of Ministers of the Council of Europe. Hence, the very same governments that show little appetite at present formally to negotiate an even more advanced treaty on minority rights are actively contributing to lifting the expectations of performance in relation to the Framework Convention. This is the real achievement of the Convention and of the Advisory Committee process attached to it.

Initially, of course, the implementation system of the Framework Convention was heavily criticized. It is easy to understand the sense of disappointment at the time. After all, an Additional Protocol to the European Convention on Human Rights had been envisaged initially, rendering minority rights justiciable before the Court. Instead, there was established what seemed to be a rather weak monitoring mechanism in the shape of the Advisory Committee, and this Committee was to operate under the control of a political body, the Committee of Ministers.

Again, it is necessary to consider the development of human rights generally. Typically, early human rights instruments will merely provide for reporting and monitoring. Often, this monitoring was conducted through a confidential process. There then might follow provision for a state-to-state complaints procedure. Then, a right to petition might be introduced. Such a right would generally be optional. That is to say, states parties would have the right to micro-manage their consent. They might accept the Convention, but opt not to subject their conduct to review through petition (or also sometimes through state complaints). Even where petition is available, this would ordinarily not be conducted as a strictly legal process. Instead, several steps for conciliation and negotiation with the state concerned would be built into it. Political bodies of the relevant international organization would retain ultimate control over the process. Only at the regional level, and only in relation to quite advanced and refined human rights systems do we find a fully judicial mechanism of international implementation. In short, full international justiciability of human rights tends to develop only over time, and after the rights have been quite firmly established both in international law, and in the corresponding domestic law.

The Advisory Committee has, in fact, done rather well in escaping from the limited mandate that may have been foreseen for it. It has access to a wide range of information, going beyond state reports. In fact, it now regularly receives (and actively encourages the receipt of) shadow reports prepared by credible NGOs or minority representative groups. It conducts country visits, where it tends to have access to all relevant constituencies. And it has managed to turn the monitoring process that was meant to focus on periodic reports into an almost continuous process of engagement on minority rights, through follow-on activities and other measures.

The Advisory Committee has also had the support of powerful 'friends'. For instance some friendly states have ensured that the lack of transparency in the Advisory Committee process has been partially addressed. In consenting to the early publication of otherwise still confidential documents they have generated an expectation that other states will be similarly open. There now exists a more or less general standard of expectation in this respect from which only a small number of states have dared to remove themselves. Finally, the Committee of Ministers has not placed obstacles in the work of the Committee. Instead, it has generally reflected faithfully the views of the Advisory Committee and added to its authority in this way.

V. General Conclusion

Minority rights are firmly established in general international law as far as protection of existence and from discrimination is concerned. These rights enjoy the special international constitutional status of *jus cogens* and *erga omnes* obligations. The Framework Convention reflects these rights, although somewhat indirectly inasmuch as existence is concerned. With respect to non-discrimination, on the other hand, the Convention advances our understanding of special measures. In this respect it stands in close relationship with universal instruments, including CERD, and with other regional instruments, including Protocol 12 to the European Convention and the new EU anti-discrimination legislation.

The Convention's true strength lies in adding substance to the principle of promotion as it relates to minority identity. It transforms the soft law of the UN Declaration into hard law in relation to the Council of Europe area, while at the same time adding substantively to the obligations contained in the Declaration. Moreover, the advancing practice of the Advisory Committee very significantly clarifies and expands the substantive obligations established in relation to identity. Moreover, while Article 15 appears somewhat condensed, the implementation practice of the Convention also introduces advanced diversity management through the principle of full and effective participation. This applies not only to co-governance, but more generally to the availability of opportunities in the economic and social area.

The Framework Convention has not in itself overcome some of the problems that have bedevilled the field for some considerable time, such as the question of the definition of minorities. However, once again, the Advisory Committee has taken an unexpected and rather enlightened turn. Instead of participating in a debate of principle, it has started to expand the actual application of the Convention even where governments have at times shown some resistance. While this battle has by no means been won, it is becoming increasingly difficult for governments to defend arbitrary or unduly restrictive views.

Of course, the situation of minorities is not fully or adequately described by the state reports and official exchanges that have been considered in this commentary. The real situation of minorities remains in some instances quite precarious. However, even in this respect the Advisory Committee has gone beyond the claims of states and taken steps to receive authentic information from the affected communities. It remains for the political bodies within Europe to help ensure that the reach of this most useful work can in future extend throughout the entire Council of Europe area.

APPENDIX 1

The Framework Convention for the Protection of National Minorities

Adopted on 1 February 1995, entered into force on 1 February 1998. ETS No. 157

The member States of the Council of Europe and the other States, signatories to the present framework Convention,

Considering that the aim of the Council of Europe is to achieve greater unity between its members for the purpose of safeguarding and realising the ideals and principles which are their common heritage;

Considering that one of the methods by which that aim is to be pursued is the maintenance and further realisation of human rights and fundamental freedoms;

Wishing to follow-up the Declaration of the Heads of State and Government of the member States of the Council of Europe adopted in Vienna on 9 October 1993;

Being resolved to protect within their respective territories the existence of national minorities;

Considering that the upheavals of European history have shown that the protection of national minorities is essential to stability, democratic security and peace in this continent;

Considering that a pluralist and genuinely democratic society should not only respect the ethnic, cultural, linguistic and religious identity of each person belonging to a national minority, but also create appropriate conditions enabling them to express, preserve and develop this identity;

Considering that the creation of a climate of tolerance and dialogue is necessary to enable cultural diversity to be a source and a factor, not of division, but of enrichment for each society;

Considering that the realisation of a tolerant and prosperous Europe does not depend solely on co-operation between States but also requires transfrontier co-operation between local and regional authorities without prejudice to the constitution and territorial integrity of each State;

Having regard to the Convention for the Protection of Human Rights and Fundamental Freedoms and the Protocols thereto;

Having regard to the commitments concerning the protection of national minorities in United Nations conventions and declarations and in the documents of the Conference on Security and Co-operation in Europe, particularly the Copenhagen Document of 29 June 1990;

Being resolved to define the principles to be respected and the obligations which flow from them, in order to ensure, in the member States and such other States as may become Parties to the present instrument, the effective protection of national minorities and of the rights and freedoms of persons belonging to those minorities, within the rule of law, respecting the territorial integrity and national sovereignty of states;

Being determined to implement the principles set out in this framework Convention through national legislation and appropriate governmental policies,

Have agreed as follows:

SECTION I

Article 1

The protection of national minorities and of the rights and freedoms of persons belonging to those minorities forms an integral part of the international protection of human rights, and as such falls within the scope of international co-operation.

Article 2

The provisions of this framework Convention shall be applied in good faith, in a spirit of understanding and tolerance and in conformity with the principles of good neighbourliness, friendly relations and co-operation between States.

Article 3

1. Every person belonging to a national minority shall have the right freely to choose to be treated or not to be treated as such and no disadvantage shall result from this choice or from the exercise of the rights which are connected to that choice.

2. Persons belonging to national minorities may exercise the rights and enjoy the freedoms flowing from the principles enshrined in the present framework Convention individually as well as in community with others.

SECTION II

Article 4

1. The Parties undertake to guarantee to persons belonging to national minorities the right of equality before the law and of equal protection of the law. In this respect, any discrimination based on belonging to a national minority shall be prohibited.

2. The Parties undertake to adopt, where necessary, adequate measures in order to promote, in all areas of economic, social, political and cultural life, full and effective equality between persons belonging to a national minority and those belonging to the majority. In this respect, they shall take due account of the specific conditions of the persons belonging to national minorities.

3. The measures adopted in accordance with paragraph 2 shall not be considered to be an act of discrimination.

Article 5

1. The Parties undertake to promote the conditions necessary for persons belonging to national minorities to maintain and develop their culture, and to preserve the essential elements of their identity, namely their religion, language, traditions and cultural heritage.

2. Without prejudice to measures taken in pursuance of their general integration policy, the Parties shall refrain from policies or practices aimed at assimilation of persons belonging to national minorities against their will and shall protect these persons from any action aimed at such assimilation.

Article 6

1. The Parties shall encourage a spirit of tolerance and intercultural dialogue and take effective measures to promote mutual respect and understanding and co-operation among all persons living on their territory, irrespective of those persons' ethnic, cultural, linguistic or religious identity, in particular in the fields of education, culture and the media.

2. The Parties undertake to take appropriate measures to protect persons who may be subject to threats or acts of discrimination, hostility or violence as a result of their ethnic, cultural, linguistic or religious identity.

Article 7

The Parties shall ensure respect for the right of every person belonging to a national minority to freedom of peaceful assembly, freedom of association, freedom of expression, and freedom of thought, conscience and religion.

Article 8

The Parties undertake to recognise that every person belonging to a national minority has the right to manifest his or her religion or belief and to establish religious institutions, organisations and associations.

Article 9

1. The Parties undertake to recognise that the right to freedom of expression of every person belonging to a national minority includes freedom to hold opinions and to receive and impart information and ideas in the minority language, without interference by public authorities and regardless of frontiers. The Parties shall ensure, within the framework of their legal systems, that persons belonging to a national minority are not discriminated against in their access to the media.

2. Paragraph 1 shall not prevent Parties from requiring the licensing, without discrimination and based on objective criteria, of sound radio and television broadcasting, or cinema enterprises.

3. The Parties shall not hinder the creation and the use of printed media by persons belonging to national minorities. In the legal framework of sound radio and television broadcasting, they shall ensure, as far as possible, and taking into account the provisions of paragraph 1, that persons belonging to national minorities are granted the possibility of creating and using their own media.

4. In the framework of their legal systems, the Parties shall adopt adequate measures in order to facilitate access to the media for persons belonging to national minorities and in order to promote tolerance and permit cultural pluralism.

Article 10

1. The Parties undertake to recognise that every person belonging to a national minority has the right to use freely and without interference his or her minority language, in private and in public, orally and in writing.

2. In areas inhabited by persons belonging to national minorities traditionally or in substantial numbers, if those persons so request and where such a request corresponds to a real need, the Parties shall endeavour to ensure, as far as possible, the conditions which would make it possible to use the minority language in relations between those persons and the administrative authorities.

3. The Parties undertake to guarantee the right of every person belonging to a national minority to be informed promptly, in a language which he or she understands, of the reasons for his or her arrest, and of the nature and cause of any accusation against him or her, and to defend himself or herself in this language, if necessary with the free assistance of an interpreter.

Article 11

1. The Parties undertake to recognise that every person belonging to a national minority has the right to use his or her surname (patronym) and first names in the minority language and the right to official recognition of them, according to modalities provided for in their legal system.

2. The Parties undertake to recognise that every person belonging to a national minority has the right to display in his or her minority language signs, inscriptions and other information of a private nature visible to the public.

3. In areas traditionally inhabited by substantial numbers of persons belonging to a national minority, the Parties shall endeavour, in the framework of their legal system, including, where appropriate, agreements with other States, and taking into account their specific conditions, to display traditional local names, street names and other topographical indications intended for the public also in the minority language when there is a sufficient demand for such indications.

Article 12

1. The Parties shall, where appropriate, take measures in the fields of education and research to foster knowledge of the culture, history, language and religion of their national minorities and of the majority.

2. In this context the Parties shall *inter alia* provide adequate opportunities for teacher training and access to textbooks, and facilitate contacts among students and teachers of different communities.

3. The Parties undertake to promote equal opportunities for access to education at all levels for persons belonging to national minorities.

Article 13

1. Within the framework of their education systems, the Parties shall recognise that persons belonging to a national minority have the right to set up and to manage their own private educational and training establishments.

2. The exercise of this right shall not entail any financial obligation for the Parties.

Article 14

1. The Parties undertake to recognise that every person belonging to a national minority has the right to learn his or her minority language.

2. In areas inhabited by persons belonging to national minorities traditionally or in substantial numbers, if there is sufficient demand, the Parties shall endeavour to ensure, as far as possible and within the framework of their education systems, that persons belonging to those minorities have adequate opportunities for being taught the minority language or for receiving instruction in this language.

3. Paragraph 2 of this article shall be implemented without prejudice to the learning of the official language or the teaching in this language.

Article 15

The Parties shall create the conditions necessary for the effective participation of persons belonging to national minorities in cultural, social and economic life and in public affairs, in particular those affecting them.

Article 16

The Parties shall refrain from measures which alter the proportions of the population in areas inhabited by persons belonging to national minorities and are aimed at restricting the rights and freedoms flowing from the principles enshrined in the present framework Convention.

Article 17

1. The Parties undertake not to interfere with the right of persons belonging to national minorities to establish and maintain free and peaceful contacts across frontiers with persons lawfully staying in other States, in particular those with whom they share an ethnic, cultural, linguistic or religious identity, or a common cultural heritage.

2. The Parties undertake not to interfere with the right of persons belonging to national minorities to participate in the activities of non-governmental organisations, both at the national and international levels.

Article 18

1. The Parties shall endeavour to conclude, where necessary, bilateral and multilateral agreements with other States, in particular neighbouring States, in order to ensure the protection of persons belonging to the national minorities concerned.

2. Where relevant, the Parties shall take measures to encourage transfrontier co-operation.

Article 19

The Parties undertake to respect and implement the principles enshrined in the present framework Convention making, where necessary, only those limitations, restrictions or derogations which are provided for in international legal instruments, in particular the Convention for the Protection of Human Rights and Fundamental Freedoms, in so far as they are relevant to the rights and freedoms flowing from the said principles.

SECTION III

Article 20

In the exercise of the rights and freedoms flowing from the principles enshrined in the present framework Convention, any person belonging to a national minority shall respect the national legislation and the rights of others, in particular those of persons belonging to the majority or to other national minorities.

Article 21

Nothing in the present framework Convention shall be interpreted as implying any right to engage in any activity or perform any act contrary to the fundamental principles of international law and in particular of the sovereign equality, territorial integrity and political independence of States.

Article 22

Nothing in the present framework Convention shall be construed as limiting or derogating from any of the human rights and fundamental freedoms which may be ensured under the laws of any Contracting Party or under any other agreement to which it is a Party.

Article 23

The rights and freedoms flowing from the principles enshrined in the present framework Convention, in so far as they are the subject of a corresponding provision in the Convention for the Protection of Human Rights and Fundamental Freedoms or in the Protocols thereto, shall be understood so as to conform to the latter provisions.

SECTION IV

Article 24

1. The Committee of Ministers of the Council of Europe shall monitor the implementation of this framework Convention by the Contracting Parties.

2. The Parties which are not members of the Council of Europe shall participate in the implementation mechanism, according to modalities to be determined.

Article 25

1. Within a period of one year following the entry into force of this framework Convention in respect of a Contracting Party, the latter shall transmit to the Secretary

General of the Council of Europe full information on the legislative and other measures taken to give effect to the principles set out in this framework Convention.

2. Thereafter, each Party shall transmit to the Secretary General on a periodical basis and whenever the Committee of Ministers so requests any further information of relevance to the implementation of this framework Convention.

3. The Secretary General shall forward to the Committee of Ministers the information transmitted under the terms of this article.

Article 26

1. In evaluating the adequacy of the measures taken by the Parties to give effect to the principles set out in this framework Convention the Committee of Ministers shall be assisted by an advisory committee, the members of which shall have recognised expertise in the field of the protection of national minorities.

2. The composition of this advisory committee and its procedure shall be determined by the Committee of Ministers within a period of one year following the entry into force of this framework Convention.

SECTION V

Article 27

This framework Convention shall be open for signature by the member States of the Council of Europe. Up until the date when the Convention enters into force, it shall also be open for signature by any other State so invited by the Committee of Ministers. It is subject to ratification, acceptance or approval. Instruments of ratification, acceptance or approval shall be deposited with the Secretary General of the Council of Europe.

Article 28

1. This framework Convention shall enter into force on the first day of the month following the expiration of a period of three months after the date on which twelve member States of the Council of Europe have expressed their consent to be bound by the Convention in accordance with the provisions of Article 27.

2. In respect of any member State which subsequently expresses its consent to be bound by it, the framework Convention shall enter into force on the first day of the month following the expiration of a period of three months after the date of the deposit of the instrument of ratification, acceptance or approval.

Article 29

1. After the entry into force of this framework Convention and after consulting the Contracting States, the Committee of Ministers of the Council of Europe may invite to accede to the Convention, by a decision taken by the majority provided for in Article 20.d of the Statute of the Council of Europe, any non-member State of the Council of Europe which, invited to sign in accordance with the provisions of Article 27, has not yet done so, and any other non-member State.

2. In respect of any acceding State, the framework Convention shall enter into force on the first day of the month following the expiration of a period of three months after the date of the deposit of the instrument of accession with the Secretary General of the Council of Europe.

Article 30

1. Any State may at the time of signature or when depositing its instrument of ratification, acceptance, approval or accession, specify the territory or territories for whose international relations it is responsible to which this framework Convention shall apply.

2. Any State may at any later date, by a declaration addressed to the Secretary General of the Council of Europe, extend the application of this framework Convention to any other territory specified in the declaration. In respect of such territory the framework Convention shall enter into force on the first day of the month following the expiration of a period of three months after the date of receipt of such declaration by the Secretary General.

3. Any declaration made under the two preceding paragraphs may, in respect of any territory specified in such declaration, be withdrawn by a notification addressed to the Secretary General. The withdrawal shall become effective on the first day of the month following the expiration of a period of three months after the date of receipt of such notification by the Secretary General.

Article 31

1. Any Party may at any time denounce this framework Convention by means of a notification addressed to the Secretary General of the Council of Europe.

2. Such denunciation shall become effective on the first day of the month following the expiration of a period of six months after the date of receipt of the notification by the Secretary General.

Article 32

The Secretary General of the Council of Europe shall notify the member States of the Council, other signatory States and any State which has acceded to this framework

Convention, of:

a. any signature;

b. the deposit of any instrument of ratification, acceptance, approval or accession;

c. any date of entry into force of this framework Convention in accordance with Articles 28, 29 and 30;

d. any other act, notification or communication relating to this framework Convention.

In witness whereof the undersigned, being duly authorised thereto, have signed this framework Convention.

Done at Strasbourg, this 1st day of February 1995, in English and French, both texts being equally authentic, in a single copy which shall be deposited in the archives of the Council of Europe. The Secretary General of the Council of Europe shall transmit certified copies to each member State of the Council of Europe and to any State invited to sign or accede to this framework Convention.

APPENDIX 2

Explanatory Report to the Framework Convention for the Protection of National Minorities

BACKGROUND

1. The Council of Europe has examined the situation of national minorities on a number of occasions over a period of more than forty years. In its very first year of existence (1949), the Parliamentary Assembly recognised, in a report of its Committee on Legal and Administrative Questions, the importance of 'the problem of wider protection of the rights of national minorities'. In 1961, the Assembly recommended the inclusion of an article in a second additional protocol to guarantee to national minorities certain rights not covered by the European Convention on Human Rights (ECHR). The latter simply refers to 'association with a national minority' in the non-discrimination clause provided for in Article 14. Recommendation 285 (1961) proposed the following wording for the draft article on the protection of national minorities: 'Persons belonging to a national minority shall not be denied the right, in community with the other members of their group, and as far as compatible with public order, to enjoy their own culture, to use their own language, to establish their schools and receive teaching in the language of their choice or to profess and practise their own religion.'

2. The committee of experts, which had been instructed to consider whether it was possible and advisable to draw up such a protocol, adjourned its activities until a final decision had been reached on the Belgian linguistics cases concerning the language used in education (European Court of Human Rights. Judgment of 27 July 1968, Series A No. 6). In 1973 it concluded that, from a legal point of view, there was no special need to make the rights of minorities the subject of a further protocol to the ECHR. However, the experts considered that there was no major legal obstacle to the adoption of such a protocol if it were considered advisable for other reasons.

3. More recently, the Parliamentary Assembly recommended a number of political and legal measures to the Committee of Ministers, in particular the drawing up of a protocol or a convention on the rights of national minorities. Recommendation 1134 (1990) contains a list of principles which the Assembly considered necessary for the protection of national minorities. In October 1991, the Steering Committee for Human Rights (CDDH) was given the task of considering, from both a legal and a political point of view, the conditions in which the Council of Europe could undertake

Source: Council of Europe (1995). Framework Convention for the Protection of National Minorities and Explanatory Report. H(1995) 010. Strasbourg: Council of Europe, pp. 11–26.

an activity for the protection of national minorities, taking into account the work done by the Conference on Security and Co-operation in Europe (CSCE) and the United Nations, and the reflections within the Council of Europe.

4. In May 1992, the Committee of Ministers instructed the CDDH to examine the possibility of formulating specific legal standards relating to the protection of national minorities. To this end, the CDDH established a committee of experts (DH-MIN) which, under new terms of reference issued in March 1993, was required to propose specific legal standards in this area, bearing in mind the principle of complementarity of work between the Council of Europe and the CSCE. The CDDH and the DH-MIN took various texts into account, in particular the proposal for a European Convention for the Protection of National Minorities drawn up by the European Commission for Democracy through Law (the so-called Venice Commission), the Austrian proposal for an additional protocol to the ECHR, the draft additional protocol to the ECHR included in Assembly Recommendation 1201 (1993) and other proposals. This examination culminated in the report of the CDDH to the Committee of Ministers of 8 September 1993, which included various legal standards which might be adopted in this area and the legal instruments in which they could be laid down. In this connection, the CDDH noted that there was no consensus on the interpretation of the term 'national minorities'.

5. The decisive step was taken when the Heads of State and Government of the Council of Europe's member States met in Vienna at the summit of 8 and 9 October 1993. There, it was agreed that the national minorities which the upheavals of history have established in Europe had to be protected and respected as a contribution to peace and stability. In particular, the Heads of State and Government decided to enter into legal commitments regarding the protection of national minorities. Appendix II of the Vienna Declaration instructed the Committee of Ministers:—to draft with minimum delay a framework convention specifying the principles which contracting States commit themselves to respect, in order to assure the protection of national minorities. This instrument would also be open for signature by non-member States;—to begin work on drafting a protocol complementing the European Convention on Human Rights in the cultural field by provisions guaranteeing individual rights, in particular for persons belonging to national minorities.

6. On 4 November 1993, the Committee of Ministers established an ad hoc Committee for the Protection of National Minorities (CAHMIN). Its terms of reference reflected the decisions taken in Vienna. The committee, made up of experts from the Council of Europe's member States, started work in late January 1994, with the participation of representatives of the CDDH, the Council for Cultural Co-operation (CDCC), the Steering Committee on the Mass Media (CDMM) and the European Commission for Democracy through Law. The High Commissioner on National Minorities of the CSCE and the Commission of the European Communities also took part, as observers.

7. On 15 April 1994, CAHMIN submitted an interim report to the Committee of Ministers, which was then communicated to the Parliamentary Assembly (Doc. 7109). At its 94th session in May 1994, the Committee of Ministers expressed satisfaction with the progress achieved under the terms of reference flowing from the Vienna Declaration.

8. A certain number of provisions of the framework Convention requiring political arbitration as well as those concerning the monitoring of the implementation were drafted by the Committee of Ministers (517bis meeting of Ministers' Deputies, 7 October 1994).

9. At its meeting from 10 to 14 October 1994, CAHMIN decided to submit the draft framework Convention to the Committee of Ministers, which adopted the text at the 95th Ministerial Session on 10 November 1994. The framework Convention was opened for signature by the Council of Europe's member States on 1 February 1995.

GENERAL CONSIDERATIONS

Objectives of the Framework Convention

10. The framework Convention is the first legally binding multilateral instrument devoted to the protection of national minorities in general. Its aim is to specify the legal principles which States undertake to respect in order to ensure the protection of national minorities. The Council of Europe has thereby given effect to the Vienna Declaration's call (Appendix II) for the political commitments adopted by the Conference on Security and Co-operation in Europe (CSCE) to be transformed, to the greatest possible extent, into legal obligations.

Approaches and Fundamental Concepts

11. In view of the range of different situations and problems to be resolved, a choice was made for a framework Convention which contains mostly programme-type provisions setting out objectives which the Parties undertake to pursue. These provisions, which will not be directly applicable, leave the States concerned a measure of discretion in the implementation of the objectives which they have undertaken to achieve, thus enabling them to take particular circumstances into account.

12. It should also be pointed out that the framework Convention contains no definition of the notion of 'national minority'. It was decided to adopt a pragmatic approach, based on the recognition that at this stage, it is impossible to arrive at a definition capable of mustering general support of all Council of Europe member States.

13. The implementation of the principles set out in this framework Convention shall be done through national legislation and appropriate governmental policies. It does not imply the recognition of collective rights. The emphasis is placed on the protection of

persons belonging to national minorities, who may exercise their rights individually and in community with others (see Article 3, paragraph 2). In this respect, the framework Convention follows the approach of texts adopted by other international organisations.

Structure of the Framework Convention

14. Apart from its Preamble, the framework Convention contains an operative part which is divided into five sections.

15. Section I contains provisions which, in a general fashion, stipulate certain fundamental principles which may serve to elucidate the other substantive provisions of the framework Convention.

16. Section II contains a catalogue of specific principles.

17. Section III contains various provisions concerning the interpretation and application of the framework Convention.

18. Section IV contains provisions on the monitoring of the implementation of the framework Convention.

19. Section V contains the final clauses which are based on the model final clauses for conventions and agreements concluded within the Council of Europe.

COMMENTARY ON THE PROVISIONS OF THE FRAMEWORK CONVENTION

PREAMBLE

20. The Preamble sets out the reasons for drawing up this framework Convention and explains certain basic concerns of its drafters. The opening words already indicate that this instrument may be signed and ratified by States not members of the Council of Europe (see Articles 27 and 29).

21. The Preamble refers to the statutory aim of the Council of Europe and to one of the methods by which this aim is to be pursued: the maintenance and further realisation of human rights and fundamental freedoms.

22. Reference is also made to the Vienna Declaration of Heads of State and Government of the member States of the Council of Europe, a document which laid the foundation for the present framework Convention (see also paragraph 5 above). In fact, the text of the Preamble is largely inspired by that declaration, in particular its Appendix II. The same is true of the choice of undertakings included in Sections I and II of the framework Convention.

23. The Preamble mentions, in a non-exhaustive way, three further sources of inspiration for the content of the framework Convention: the Convention for the

Protection of Human Rights and Fundamental Freedoms (ECHR) and instruments which contain commitments regarding the protection of national minorities of the United Nations and the CSCE.

24. The Preamble reflects the concern of the Council of Europe and its member States about the risk to the existence of national minorities and is inspired by Article 1, paragraph 1, of the United Nations Declaration on the Rights of Persons belonging to National or Ethnic, Religious and Linguistic Minorities (Resolution 47/135 adopted by the General Assembly on 18 December 1992).

25. Given that the framework Convention is also open to States which are not members of the Council of Europe, and to ensure a more comprehensive approach, it was decided to include certain principles from which flow rights and freedoms which are already guaranteed in the ECHR or in the protocols thereto (see also in connection with this, Article 23 of the framework Convention).

26. The reference to United Nations conventions and declarations recalls the work done at the universal level, for example in the International Covenant on Civil and Political Rights (Article 27) and in the Declaration on the Rights of Persons belonging to National or Ethnic, Religious and Linguistic Minorities. However this reference does not extend to any definition of a national minority which may be contained in these texts.

27. The reference to the relevant CSCE commitments reflects the desire expressed in Appendix II of the Vienna Declaration that the Council of Europe should apply itself to transforming, to the greatest possible extent, these political commitments into legal obligations. The Copenhagen Document in particular provided guidance for drafting the framework Convention.

28. The penultimate paragraph in the Preamble sets out the main aim of the framework Convention: to ensure the effective protection of national minorities and of the rights of persons belonging to those minorities. It also stresses that this effective protection should be ensured within the rule of law, respecting the territorial integrity and national sovereignty of States.

29. The purpose of the last recital is to indicate that the provisions of this framework Convention are not directly applicable. It is not concerned with the law and practice of the Parties in regard to the reception of international treaties in the internal legal order.

SECTION I

Article 1

30. The main purpose of Article 1 is to specify that the protection of national minorities, which forms an integral part of the protection of human rights, does not fall within the reserved domain of States. The statement that this protection 'forms an

integral part of the international protection of human rights' does not confer any competence to interpret the present framework Convention on the organs established by the ECHR.

31. The article refers to the protection of national minorities as such and of the rights and freedoms of persons belonging to such minorities. This distinction and the difference in wording make it clear that no collective rights of national minorities are envisaged (see also the commentary to Article 3). The Parties do however recognise that protection of a national minority can be achieved through protection of the rights of individuals belonging to such a minority.

Article 2

32. This article provides a set of principles governing the application of the framework Convention. It is, inter alia, inspired by the United Nations Declaration on Principles of International Law concerning Friendly Relations and Co-operation among States in accordance with the Charter of the United Nations (General Assembly Resolution 2625 (XXV) of 24 October 1970). The principles mentioned in this provision are of a general nature but do have particular relevance to the field covered by the framework Convention.

Article 3

33. This article contains two distinct but related principles laid down in two different paragraphs.

Paragraph 1

34. Paragraph 1 firstly guarantees to every person belonging to a national minority the freedom to choose to be treated or not to be treated as such. This provision leaves it to every such person to decide whether or not he or she wishes to come under the protection flowing from the principles of the framework Convention.

35. This paragraph does not imply a right for an individual to choose arbitrarily to belong to any national minority. The individual's subjective choice is inseparably linked to objective criteria relevant to the person's identity.

36. Paragraph 1 further provides that no disadvantage shall arise from the free choice it guarantees, or from the exercise of the rights which are connected to that choice. This part of the provision aims to secure that the enjoyment of the freedom to choose shall also not be impaired indirectly.

Paragraph 2

37. Paragraph 2 provides that the rights and freedoms flowing from the principles of the framework Convention may be exercised individually or in community with others. It thus recognises the possibility of joint exercise of those rights and freedoms,

which is distinct from the notion of collective rights. The term 'others' shall be understood in the widest possible sense and shall include persons belonging to the same national minority, to another national minority, or to the majority.

SECTION II

Article 4

38. The purpose of this article is to ensure the applicability of the principles of equality and non-discrimination for persons belonging to national minorities. The provisions of this article are to be understood in the context of this framework Convention.

Paragraphs 1 and 2

39. Paragraph 1 takes the classic approach to these principles. Paragraph 2 stresses that the promotion of full and effective equality between persons belonging to a national minority and those belonging to the majority may require the Parties to adopt special measures that take into account the specific conditions of the persons concerned. Such measures need to be 'adequate', that is in conformity with the proportionality principle, in order to avoid violation of the rights of others as well as discrimination against others. This principle requires, among other things, that such measures do not extend, in time or in scope, beyond what is necessary in order to achieve the aim of full and effective equality.

40. No separate provision dealing specifically with the principle of equal opportunities has been included in the framework Convention. Such an inclusion was considered unnecessary as the principle is already implied in paragraph 2 of this article. Given the principle of non-discrimination set out in paragraph 1 the same was considered true for freedom of movement.

Paragraph 3

41. The purpose of paragraph 3 is to make clear that the measures referred to in paragraph 2 are not to be regarded as contravening the principles of equality and non-discrimination. Its aim is to ensure to persons belonging to national minorities effective equality along with persons belonging to the majority.

Article 5

42. This article essentially aims at ensuring that persons belonging to national minorities can maintain and develop their culture and preserve their identity.

Paragraph 1

43. Paragraph 1 contains an obligation to promote the necessary conditions in this respect. It lists four essential elements of the identity of a national minority. This

provision does not imply that all ethnic, cultural, linguistic or religious differences necessarily lead to the creation of national minorities (see in this regard the report of the CSCE meeting of experts, held in Geneva in 1991, section II, paragraph 4).

44. The reference to 'traditions' is not an endorsement or acceptance of practices which are contrary to national law or international standards. Traditional practices remain subject to limitations arising from the requirements of public order.

Paragraph 2

45. The purpose of paragraph 2 is to protect persons belonging to national minorities from assimilation against their will. It does not prohibit voluntary assimilation.

46. Paragraph 2 does not preclude the Parties from taking measures in pursuance of their general integration policy. It thus acknowledges the importance of social cohesion and reflects the desire expressed in the preamble that cultural diversity be a source and a factor, not of division, but of enrichment to each society.

Article 6

47. This article is an expression of the concerns stated in Appendix III to the Vienna Declaration (Declaration and Plan of Action on combating racism, xenophobia, anti-Semitism and intolerance).

Paragraph 1

48. Paragraph 1 stresses a spirit of tolerance and intercultural dialogue and points out the importance of the Parties' promoting mutual respect, understanding and co-operation among all who live on their territory. The fields of education, culture and the media are specifically mentioned because they are considered particularly relevant to the achievement of these aims.

49. In order to strengthen social cohesion, the aim of this paragraph is, inter alia, to promote tolerance and intercultural dialogue, by eliminating barriers between persons belonging to ethnic, cultural, linguistic and religious groups through the encouragement of intercultural organisations and movements which seek to promote mutual respect and understanding and to integrate these persons into society whilst preserving their identity.

Paragraph 2

50. This provision is inspired by paragraph 40.2 of the Copenhagen Document of the CSCE. This obligation aims at the protection of all persons who may be subject to threats or acts of discrimination, hostility or violence, irrespective of the source of such threats or acts.

Article 7

51. The purpose of this article is to guarantee respect for the right of every person belonging to a national minority to the fundamental freedoms mentioned therein.

These freedoms are of course of a universal nature, that is they apply to all persons, whether belonging to a national minority or not (see, for instance, the corresponding provisions in Articles 9, 10 and 11 of the ECHR), but they are particularly relevant for the protection of national minorities. For the reasons stated above in the commentary on the preamble, it was decided to include certain undertakings which already appear in the ECHR.

52. This provision may imply for the Parties certain positive obligations to protect the freedoms mentioned against violations which do not emanate from the State. Under the ECHR, the possibility of such positive obligations has been recognised by the European Court of Human Rights.

53. Some of the freedoms laid down in Article 7 are elaborated upon in Articles 8 and 9.

Article 8

54. This article lays down more detailed rules for the protection of freedom of religion than Article 7. It combines several elements from paragraphs 32.2, 32.3 and 32.6 of the CSCE Copenhagen Document into a single provision. This freedom of course applies to all persons and persons belonging to a national minority should, in accordance with Article 4, enjoy it as well. Given the importance of this freedom in the present context, it was felt particularly appropriate to give it special attention.

Article 9

55. This article contains more detailed rules for the protection of the freedom of expression than Article 7.

Paragraph 1

56. The first sentence of this paragraph is modelled on the second sentence of Article 10, paragraph 1, of the ECHR. Although the sentence refers specifically to the freedom to receive and impart information and ideas in the minority language, it also implies the freedom to receive and impart information and ideas in the majority or other languages.

57. The second sentence of this paragraph contains an undertaking to ensure that there is no discrimination in access to the media. The words 'in the framework of their legal systems' were inserted in order to respect constitutional provisions which may limit the extent to which a Party can regulate access to the media.

Paragraph 2

58. This paragraph is modelled on the third sentence of Article 10, paragraph 1, of the ECHR.

59. The licensing of sound radio and television broadcasting, and of cinema enterprises, should be non-discriminatory and be based on objective criteria. The inclusion of these requirements, which are not expressly mentioned in the third sentence of Article 10,

paragraph 1, of the ECHR, was considered important for an instrument designed to protect persons belonging to a national minority.

60. The words 'sound radio', which also appear in paragraph 3 of this article, do not appear in the corresponding sentence in Article 10 of the ECHR. They are used in order to reflect modern terminology and do not imply any material difference in meaning from Article 10 of the ECHR.

Paragraph 3

61. The first sentence of this paragraph, dealing with the creation and use of printed media, contains an essentially negative undertaking whereas the more flexibly worded second sentence emphasises a positive obligation in the field of sound radio and television broadcasting (for example the allocation of frequencies). This distinction reflects the relative scarcity of available frequencies and the need for regulation in the latter field. No express reference has been made to the right of persons belonging to a national minority to seek funds for the establishment of media, as this right was considered self-evident.

Paragraph 4

62. This paragraph emphasises the need for special measures with the dual aim of facilitating access to the media for persons belonging to national minorities and promoting tolerance and cultural pluralism. The expression 'adequate measures' was used for the reasons given in the commentary on Article 4, paragraph 2 (see paragraph 39), which uses the same words. The paragraph complements the undertaking laid down in the last sentence of Article 9, paragraph 1. The measures envisaged by this paragraph could, for example, consist of funding for minority broadcasting or for programme productions dealing with minority issues and/or offering a dialogue between groups, or of encouraging, subject to editorial independence, editors and broadcasters to allow national minorities access to their media.

Article 10

Paragraph 1

63. The recognition of the right of every person belonging to a national minority to use his or her minority language freely and without interference is particularly important. The use of the minority language represents one of the principal means by which such persons can assert and preserve their identity. It also enables them to exercise their freedom of expression. 'In public' means, for instance, in a public place, outside, or in the presence of other persons but is not concerned in any circumstances with relations with public authorities, the subject of paragraph 2 of this article.

Paragraph 2

64. This provision does not cover all relations between individuals belonging to national minorities and public authorities. It only extends to administrative

authorities. Nevertheless, the latter must be broadly interpreted to include, for example, ombudsmen. In recognition of the possible financial, administrative, in particular in the military field, and technical difficulties associated with the use of minority languages in relations between persons belonging to national minorities and the administrative authorities, this provision has been worded very flexibly, leaving Parties a wide measure of discretion.

65. Once the two conditions in paragraph 2 are met, Parties shall endeavour to ensure the use of a minority language in relations with the administrative authorities as far as possible. The existence of a 'real need' is to be assessed by the State on the basis of objective criteria. Although contracting States should make every effort to apply this principle, the wording 'as far as possible' indicates that various factors, in particular the financial resources of the Party concerned, may be taken into consideration.

66. The Parties' obligations regarding the use of minority languages do not in any way affect the status of the official language or languages of the country concerned. Moreover, the framework Convention deliberately refrains from defining 'areas inhabited by persons belonging to national minorities traditionally or in substantial numbers'. It was considered preferable to adopt a flexible form of wording which will allow each Party's particular circumstances to be taken into account. The term 'inhabited . . . traditionally' does not refer to historical minorities, but only to those still living in the same geographical area (see also Article 11, paragraph 3, and Article 14, paragraph 2).

Paragraph 3

67. This paragraph is based on certain provisions contained in Articles 5 and 6 of the European Convention on Human Rights. It does not go beyond the safeguards contained in those articles.

Article 11

Paragraph 1

68. In view of the practical implications of this obligation, the provision is worded in such a way as to enable Parties to apply it in the light of their own particular circumstances. For example, Parties may use the alphabet of their official language to write the name(s) of a person belonging to a national minority in its phonetic form. Persons who have been forced to give up their original name(s), or whose name(s) has (have) been changed by force, should be entitled to revert to it (them), subject of course to exceptions in the case of abuse of rights and changes of name(s) for fraudulent purposes. It is understood that the legal systems of the Parties will, in this respect, meet international principles concerning the protection of national minorities.

Paragraph 2

69. The obligation in this paragraph concerns an individual's right to display 'in his or her minority language signs, inscriptions and other information of a private nature visible to the public'. This does not, of course, exclude persons belonging to national minorities from being required to use, in addition, the official language and/or other minority languages. The expression 'of a private nature' refers to all that is not official.

Paragraph 3

70. This article aims to promote the possibility of having local names, street names and other topographical indications intended for the public also in the minority language. In implementing this principle the States are entitled to take due account of the specific circumstances and the framework of their legal systems, including, where appropriate, agreements with other States. In the field covered by this provision, it is understood that the Parties are under no obligation to conclude agreements with other States. Conversely, the possibility of concluding such agreements is not ruled out. It is also understood that the legally binding nature of existing agreements remains unaffected. This provision does not imply any official recognition of local names in the minority languages.

Article 12

71. This article seeks to promote knowledge of the culture, history, language and religion of both national minorities and the majority population in an intercultural perspective (see Article 6, paragraph 1). The aim is to create a climate of tolerance and dialogue, as referred to in the preamble to the framework convention and in Appendix II of the Vienna Declaration of the Heads of State and Government. The list in the second paragraph is not exhaustive whilst the words 'access to textbooks' are understood as including the publication of textbooks and their purchase in other countries. The obligation to promote equal opportunities for access to education at all levels for persons belonging to national minorities reflects a concern expressed in the Vienna Declaration.

Article 13

Paragraph 1

72. The Parties' obligation to recognise the right of persons belonging to national minorities to set up and manage their own private educational and training establishments is subject to the requirements of their educational system, particularly the regulations relating to compulsory schooling. The establishments covered by this paragraph may be subject to the same forms of supervision as other establishments, particularly with regard to teaching standards. Once the required standards are met, it is important that any qualifications awarded are officially recognised. The relevant national legislation must be based on objective criteria and conform to the principle of non-discrimination.

Paragraph 2

73. The exercise of the right referred to in paragraph 1 does not entail any financial obligation for the Party concerned, but neither does it exclude the possibility of such a contribution.

Article 14

Paragraph 1

74. The obligation to recognise the right of every person belonging to a national minority to learn his or her minority language concerns one of the principal means by which such individuals can assert and preserve their identity. There can be no exceptions to this. Without prejudice to the principles mentioned in paragraph 2, this paragraph does not imply positive action, notably of a financial nature, on the part of the State.

Paragraph 2

75. This provision concerns teaching of and instruction in a minority language. In recognition of the possible financial, administrative and technical difficulties associated with instruction of or in minority languages, this provision has been worded very flexibly, leaving Parties a wide measure of discretion. The obligation to endeavour to ensure instruction of or in minority languages is subject to several conditions; in particular, there must be 'sufficient demand' from persons belonging to the relevant national minorities. The wording 'as far as possible' indicates that such instruction is dependent on the available resources of the Party concerned.

76. The text deliberately refrains from defining 'sufficient demand', a flexible form of wording which allows Parties to take account of their countries' own particular circumstances. Parties have a choice of means and arrangements in ensuring such instruction, taking their particular educational system into account.

77. The alternatives referred to in this paragraph—'opportunities for being taught the minority language or for receiving instruction in this language'—are not mutually exclusive. Even though Article 14, paragraph 2, imposes no obligation upon States to do both, its wording does not prevent the States Parties from implementing the teaching of the minority language as well as the instruction in the minority language. Bilingual instruction may be one of the means of achieving the objective of this provision. The obligation arising from this paragraph could be extended to pre-school education.

Paragraph 3

78. The opportunities for being taught the minority language or for receiving instruction in this language are without prejudice to the learning of the official language or the teaching in this language. Indeed, knowledge of the official language is a factor of social cohesion and integration.

79. It is for States where there is more than one official language to settle the particular questions which the implementation of this provision shall entail.

Article 15

80. This article requires Parties to create the conditions necessary for the effective participation of persons belonging to national minorities in cultural, social and economic life and in public affairs, in particular those affecting them. It aims above all to encourage real equality between persons belonging to national minorities and those forming part of the majority. In order to create the necessary conditions for such participation by persons belonging to national minorities, Parties could promote—in the framework of their constitutional systems—inter alia the following measures:

—consultation with these persons, by means of appropriate procedures and, in particular, through their representative institutions, when Parties are contemplating legislation or administrative measures likely to affect them directly;

—involving these persons in the preparation, implementation and assessment of national and regional development plans and programmes likely to affect them directly;

—undertaking studies, in conjunction with these persons, to assess the possible impact on them of projected development activities;

—effective participation of persons belonging to national minorities in the decision-making processes and elected bodies both at national and local levels;

—decentralised or local forms of government.

Article 16

81. The purpose of this article is to protect against measures which change the proportion of the population in areas inhabited by persons belonging to national minorities and are aimed at restricting the rights and freedoms which flow from the present framework Convention. Examples of such measures might be expropriation, evictions and expulsions or redrawing administrative borders with a view to restricting the enjoyment of such rights and freedoms ('gerrymandering').

82. The article prohibits only measures which are aimed at restricting the rights and freedoms flowing from the framework Convention. It was considered impossible to extend the prohibition to measures having the effect of restricting such rights and freedoms, since such measures may sometimes be entirely justified and legitimate. One example might be resettlement of inhabitants of a village in order to build a dam.

Article 17

83. This article contains two undertakings important to the maintenance and development of the culture of persons belonging to a national minority and to the

preservation of their identity (see also Article 5, paragraph 1). The first paragraph deals with the right to establish and maintain free and peaceful contacts across frontiers, whereas the second paragraph protects the right to participate in the activities of non-governmental organisations (see also in this connection, the provisions on freedom of assembly and of association in Article 7).

84. The provisions of this article are largely based on paragraphs 32.4 and 32.6 of the Copenhagen Document of the CSCE. It was considered unnecessary to include an explicit provision on the right to establish and maintain contacts within the territory of a State, since this was felt to be adequately covered by other provisions of the framework Convention, notably Article 7 as regards freedom of assembly and of association.

Article 18

85. This article encourages the Parties to conclude, in addition to the existing international instruments, and where the specific circumstances justify it, bilateral and multilateral agreements for the protection of national minorities. It also stimulates transfrontier co-operation. As is emphasised in the Vienna Declaration and its Appendix II, such agreements and co-operation are important for the promotion of tolerance, prosperity, stability and peace.

Paragraph 1

86. Bilateral and multilateral agreements as envisaged by this paragraph might, for instance, be concluded in the fields of culture, education and information.

Paragraph 2

87. This paragraph points out the importance of transfrontier co-operation. Exchange of information and experience between States is an important tool for the promotion of mutual understanding and confidence. In particular, transfrontier co-operation has the advantage that it allows for arrangements specifically tailored to the wishes and needs of the persons concerned.

Article 19

88. This article provides for the possibility of limitations, restrictions or derogations. When the undertakings included in this framework Convention have an equivalent in other international legal instruments, in particular the ECHR, only the limitations, restrictions or derogations provided for in those instruments are allowed. When the undertakings set forth in this framework Convention have no equivalent in other international legal instruments, the only limitations, restrictions or derogations allowed are those which, included in other legal instruments (such as the ECHR) in respect of different undertakings, are relevant.

SECTION III

Article 20

89. Persons belonging to national minorities are required to respect the national constitution and other national legislation. However, this reference to national legislation clearly does not entitle Parties to ignore the provisions of the framework Convention. Persons belonging to national minorities must also respect the rights of others. In this regard, reference may be made to situations where persons belonging to national minorities are in a minority nationally but form a majority within one area of the State.

Article 21

90. This provision stresses the importance of the fundamental principles of international law and specifies that the protection of persons belonging to national minorities must be in accordance with these principles.

Article 22

91. This provision, which is based on Article 60 of the ECHR, sets out a well-known principle. The aim is to ensure that persons belonging to national minorities benefit from whichever of the relevant national or international human rights legislation is most favourable to them.

Article 23

92. This provision deals with the relationship between the framework Convention and the Convention for the Protection of Human Rights and Fundamental Freedoms, reference to which is included in the Preamble. Under no circumstances can the framework Convention modify the rights and freedoms safeguarded in the Convention for the Protection of Human Rights and Fundamental Freedoms. On the contrary, rights and freedoms enshrined in the framework Convention which are the subject of a corresponding provision in the Convention for the Protection of Human Rights and Fundamental Freedoms must be interpreted in accordance with the latter.

SECTION IV

Articles 24–26

93. To provide for overseeing the application of the framework Convention, the Committee of Ministers is entrusted with the task of monitoring the implementation by the Contracting Parties. The Committee of Ministers shall determine the

modalities for the participation in the implementation mechanism by the Parties which are not members of the Council of Europe.

94. Each Party shall transmit to the Secretary General on a periodical basis and whenever the Committee of Ministers so requests information of relevance to the implementation of this framework Convention. The Secretary General shall transmit this information to the Committee of Ministers. However, the first report, the aim of which is to provide full information on legislative and other measures which the Party has taken to give effect to the undertakings set out in the framework Convention, must be submitted within one year of the entry into force of the framework Convention in respect of the Party concerned. The purpose of the subsequent reports shall be to complement the information included in the first report.

95. In order to ensure the efficiency of the monitoring of the implementation of the framework Convention, it provides for the setting up of an advisory committee. The task of this advisory committee is to assist the Committee of Ministers when it evaluates the adequacy of the measures taken by a Party to give effect to the principles set out in the framework Convention.

96. It is up to the Committee of Ministers to determine, within one year of the entry into force of the framework Convention, the composition and the procedures of the advisory committee, the members of which shall have recognised expertise in the field of the protection of national minorities.

97. The monitoring of the implementation of this framework Convention shall, in so far as possible, be transparent. In this regard it would be advisable to envisage the publication of the reports and other texts resulting from such monitoring.

SECTION V

98. The final provisions contained in articles 27 to 32 are based on the model final clauses for conventions and agreements concluded within the Council of Europe. No article on reservations was included; reservations are allowed in as far as they are permitted by international law. Apart from Articles 27 and 29 the articles in this section require no particular comment.

Articles 27 and 29

99. The framework Convention is open for signature by the Council of Europe's member States and, at the invitation of the Committee of Ministers, by other States. It is understood that 'other States' are those States which participate in the Conference on Security and Co-operation in Europe. These provisions take account of the Vienna Declaration, according to which the framework Convention should also be open for signature by non-member States (see Appendix II to the Vienna Declaration of the Council of Europe Summit).

Select Bibliography

Akermark, A. S., *Justifications of Minority Protection in International Law* (London: Kluwer Law International, 1997).

Alfredsson, G., 'Identifying Possible Disadvantages of Bilateral Agreements and Advancing the "Most-Favoured-Minority-Clause" ', Bloed, A. and P. van Dijk (eds.), *Protection of Minority Rights Through Bilateral Treaties* (The Hague: Kluwer Law International, 1999).

—— 'A Frame with an Incomplete Painting: Comparison of the Framework Convention for the Protection of National Minorities with International Standards and Monitoring Procedures', *International Journal on Minority and Group Rights*, 7 (2000), 291–304.

—— and A. Eide (eds.), *The Universal Declaration of Human Right: A Common Standard of Achievement*, (The Hague, Boston, London: Nijhoff, 1999).

—— and G. Melander, *A Compilation of Minority Rights Standard: A Selection of Texts from International and Regional Human Rights Instruments and Other Documents*, Report No. 24 (Lund: Raoul Wallenberg Institute, 1997).

Allott, P., *Eunomia: A New Order for a New World* (Oxford: Oxford University Press, 1990).

Alston, P. (ed.), *People's Rights* (Oxford: Oxford University Press, 2001).

—— and G. Quinn, 'The Nature and Scope of States Parties' Obligations under the International Covenant on Economic, Social and Cultural Rights', *Human Rights Quarterly*, 9 (1987), 192–206.

Amato, A., 'Good Faith', in Bernhardt, R. (ed.), *EPIL*, II, (1995), 599–601.

Apel, K. O., 'Plurality of the Good? The Problem of Affirmative Tolerance in a Multicultural Society from an Ethical Point of View', *Ratio Juris*, 10 (1997), 199–212.

Bank, R. and J. A. Frowein, 'The Effect of Member States' Declarations Defining "National Minorities" upon Signature or Ratification of the Council of Europe Framework Convention for the Protection of National Minorities', *Zeitschrift für ausländisches öffentliches Recht und Völkerrecht* 59 (1999), 649–75.

Bell-Fialkoff, A., 'A Brief History of Ethnic Cleansing', *Foreign Affairs*, 72 (1).

Berlin, I., 'The Pursuit of the Ideal: The Proper Study of Mankind', (New York: Farrar, Straus and Giroux, 1997).

Besselink, L., 'Entrapped by the Maximum Standard: On Fundamental Rights, Pluralism and Subsidiarity in the European Union', *Common Market Law Review*, 35 (1998), 629–80.

Bloed, A., L. Leicht, M. Nowak, and A. Rosas, 'Monitoring the CSCE Human Dimension: in Search of its Effectiveness', *Monitoring Human Rights in Europe* (Dordrecht, Boston, London: Martinus Nijhoff, 1993).

Boerefijn, I., *The Reporting Procedure under the Covenant on Civil and Political Rights, Practice and Procedures of the Human Rights Committee* (Anterwerpen: Intersentia–Hart, 1999).

Borowski, J., 'Commentary to Art. 52 of the Charter of Fundamental Rights', in Meyer, J. (ed.) *Kommentar zur Charta der Grundrechte der Europäischen Union* (Note) (Baden-Baden: Nomos, 2003).

Borowski, M., 'Commentary to Art. 53 of the Charter of Fundamental Rights', in Meyer, J. (ed.), *Kommentar zur Charta der Grundrechte der Europäischen Union* (Baden-Baden: Nomos 2003).

Bruegel, J., 'A Neglected Field: The Protection of Minorities', *Harvard Human Rights Journal*, 4 (1971).

Bultrini, A., 'Developments in the Field of the European Charter for Regional or Minority Languages', *European Yearbook of Minority Issues*, 2 (2002/03), 435–43.

Capotorti, F., *Study on the Rights of Persons belonging to Ethnic, Religious and Linguistic Minorities* (New York: United Nations, 1991).

Cartabia, M., 'Commentary to Art. 53 of the Charter of Fundamental Rights', in Bifulco, R., M. Cartabia, and A. Celotto (eds.), *L'Europa dei diritti, Commento alla Carta dei diritti fondamentali dell'Unione Europe* (Bologna: Il Mulino, 2001).

Cassese, A., *Self-Determination of Peoples: A Legal Reappraisal* (Cambridge: Cambridge University Press, 1995).

Cheng, B., *General Principles of Law—As Applied by International Courts and Tribunals* (London: Stevens, 1953).

Conforti, B., *Diritto internazionale* (Naples: Editoriale Scientifica, 2002).

Connolly, W. E., 'Taylor, Foucault and Otherness', *Political Theory*, 13 (1985), 365–76.

—— *Identity/Difference. Democratic Negotiations of Political Paradox*, Expanded edition, (Minneapolis: University of Minnesota Press, 2002).

Cot, J. P., *La bonne foi en droit international public* (Paris: Cours de l'Institut de Hautes Etudes Internationales, 1968/1969).

Dahm, G., J. Delbrück, and R. Wolfrum, *Völkerrecht* (Berlin: DeGruyter Verlag 2002).

de Varennes, F., 'A Guide to the Rights of Minorities and Language', (Budapest: Constitutional and Legal Policy Initiative (COLPI), 2001), http://www.eumap.org/library/static/libr0/l/6/se56p2w.pdf, 2 August 2004.

Donnelly, J., 'Third Generation Rights', in Brölmann, Catherine, et al. (eds.), *Peoples and Minorities in International Law* (Dordrecht: Nijhoff, 1993).

Economist Magazine, 'Migration in the European Union: The Coming Hordes', 15 January 2004.

Eide, A., 'In Search of Constructive Alternatives to Secession', in Tomuschat, Ch. (ed.), *Modern Law of Self-Determination* (Dordrecht: Nijhoff, 1993).

Ermacora, F., 'The Protection of Minorities before the United Nations', *Recueil des Cours*, 182 (1985), 247–370.

European Commission for Democracy through Law (ECDL), *The Protection of National Minorities by their Kin-State* (Strasbourg: Council of Europe Publishing, 2002).

Fitzmaurice, G., 'The Law and Procedure of the International Court of Justice, 1951–4', *British Yearbook*, 33 (1957), 203–38.

Fox, G. H., 'Self-Determination on the Post-Cold War Era: A New Internal Focus?', *Michigan Journal of International Law*, 16 (1995), 733–81.

Franck, T., 'The Emerging Right to Democratic Governance', in *American Journal of International Law*, 86 (1992), 46–91.

Frowein, J. A. and R. Bank, 'The Effect of Member States' Declarations Defining "National Minorities" upon Signature or Ratification of the Council of Europe's Framework Convention', *ZaöRV Heidelberg Journal of International Law*, 59 (1999), 649–76.

Galston, W. A., *Liberal Pluralism: The Implication of Value Pluralism for Political Theory and Practice* (Cambridge: Cambridge University Press, 2002).

Gellner, E., *Conditions of Liberty: Civil Society and its Revivals* (London: Hamish Hamilton, 1994).

Gilbert, G., 'The Legal Protection Accorded to Minority Groups in Europe', *Netherlands Yearbook of International Law*, 23 (1992), 81–93.

—— 'The Council of Europe and Minority Rights', *Human Rights Quarterly*, 18 (1996), 160–89.

—— 'Minority Rights Under the Council of Europe', in Cumper, P. and S. Wheatley (eds.), *Minority Rights in a 'New' Europe* (The Hague: Nijhoff, 1999).

—— 'The Burgeoning Minority Rights Jurisprudence of the European Court of Human Rights', *Human Rights Quarterly*, 24 (2002), 736–80.

Grammatikas, V., 'The definition of minorities in International Law: A problem still looking for a solution', *RHDI*, 52 (1999), 321–64.

Green, A., 'Blunkett has failed to wake up to the immigration nightmare', *Daily Telegraph*, 24 February 2004.

Groppi, T., 'Commentary to Art. 52 of the Charter of Fundamental Rights', in Bifulco, R., M. Cartabia, and A. Celotto, *L'Europa dei Diritti, Commento a la Carta dei Diritti fondamentali del Unione Europea* (Bologna: Il Mulino, 2001).

Habermas, J., 'The Inclusion of the Other', in Cronin, C. and P. de Greiff (eds.), *Studies in Political Theory* (Cambridge, Mass.: MIT Press, 1998).

Hannum, H., *Documents on Autonomy and Minority Rights* (Dordrecht: Martinus Nijhoff Publishers, 1993).

Hanski, R. and M. Scheinin, *Leading Cases of the Human Rights Committee* (Turku/Abo: Åbo Akademi University, 2003).

Harris, D. J., *et al.*, *Law of the European Convention on Human Rights* (London, Carlsbad: Butterworths, 1993).

Heintze, H. J., *Selbstbestimmungsrecht und Minderheitenrechte im Völkerrecht* (Baden-Baden: Nomos, 1994).

—— 'Bilateral Agreements and their Role in Settling Ethnic Conflicts', in Schenckner, U. and S. Wolff (eds.), *Managing and Settling Ethnic Conflicts* (London: C. Hurst, 2004).

Henckaerts, J. M., *Mass Expulsion in Modern International Law and Practice* (The Hague: Martinus Nijhoff/Klewer, 1995).

Henrard, K., *Devising an Adequate System of Minority Protection* (The Hague: Martinus Nijhoff, 2000).

Hilpold, P., 'Minderheitenschutz im Rahmen der Vereinten Nationen—Die Deklaration vom 18. Dezember 1992', *Schweizerische Zeitschrift für internationales und europäisches Recht*, 1–2 (Vienna: Manz; Baden-Baden: Nomos; Zurich: Schulthess, 1994), 31–54.

—— *Der Osttimor-Fall, eine Standortbestimmung zum Selbstbestimmungsrecht der Völker* (Frankfurt: Peter Lang, 1996).

—— 'Das Vorbehaltsregime der Wiener Vertragskonvention', *Archiv des Völkerrechts*, 34 (1996), 376–425.

—— 'Sezession und humanitäre Intervention—völkerrechtliche Instrumente zur Bewältigung innerstaatlicher Konflikte?', *Zeitschrift für Öffentliches Recht*, 54 (1999), 529–602.

—— *Modernes Minderheitenrecht* (Vienna, 2001).

—— 'Neue Minderheiten im Völkerrecht und im Europarecht', *Archiv des Völkerrechts*, 42 (Nomos, Baden-Baden 2004), 80–110.

—— 'Sezession und humanitäre Intervention—völkerrechtliche Instrumente zur Bewältigung innerstaatlicher Konflikte?', *Zeitschrift für Öffentliches Recht*, 54 (1999), 529–602.

Hofmann, R., 'Preferential Treatment of Kin Minorities and Monitoring of the Implementation of the Framework Convention for National Minorities', European Commission for Democracy through Law (ed.), *The Protection of National Minorities by their Kin-state, Science and Technique of Democracy*, 32, (Strasbourg: Council of Europe (CoE), Collection Science and Technique for Democracy (ECDL), 2002).

—— *The Framework Convention at the end of the first cycle of monitoring: Filling the Frame, 5th anniversary of the entering into force of the Framework Convention for the Protection of National Minorities, Opening plenary* (Strasbourg: Council of Europe, 2003).

—— 'Review of the Monitoring Process of the Council of Europe Framework Convention for the Protection of National Minorities', *European Yearbook of Minority Issues*, 1 (2003), 435–60.

Hurst, H., 'Contemporary Developments in the International Protection of the Rights of Minorities', *Notre Dame Law Review*, 66 (1991), 1431–44.

Jackson-Preece, J., *National Minorities and the European Nation-States System* (Oxford: Clarendon Press, 1998).

—— 'Ethnic Cleansing as an Instrument of Nation-State Creation: Changing State Practices and Evolving Legal Norms', *Human Rights Quarterly*, 20 (1998), 817–42.

Jacobs and White, *The European Convention on Human Rights*, 3rd edn., Ovey, C. and R. White, (eds.) (Oxford: Oxford University Press, 2003).

Jennings, R. and A. Watts, *Oppenheim's International Law*, I, 9th edn., (London: Longman, 1992).

Kimminich, O., *Rechtsprobleme der polyethnischen Staatsorganisation* (Munich: Mainz, 1985).

Klebes, H., 'The Council of Europe's Framework Convention for the Protection of National Minorities', *Human Rights Journal*, 16 (1995), 92–116.

Kymlicka, W., *The Rights of Minority Culture* (Oxford: Oxford University Press, 1995).

—— *Multicultural Citizenship* (Oxford: Oxford University Press, 1995).

Kunz, J. L., 'The Present Status of International Law for the Protection of Minorities', *American Journal of International Law*, 48 (1954), 282–7.

Leader, S., 'Three Faces of Toleration in a Democracy', *Journal of Political Philosophy*, 4 (1996), 45–67.

—— 'Toleration without Liberal Foundations', *Ratio Juris*, 10 (1997), 139–64.

Lerner, N., 'The Evolution of Minority Rights in International Law', in Brölmann, C. *et al.* (eds.), *Peoples and Minorities in International Law* (Dordrecht: Nijhoff, 1993).

McGarry, J. and B. O'Leary, 'Introduction: the macro-political regulation of ethnic conflict', in McGarry, J. and B. O'Leary (eds.), *The Politics of Ethnic Conflict Regulation* (London: Routledge, 1993).

Macedo, S., *Liberal Virtues. Citizenship, Virtue, and Community in Liberal Constitutionalism* (Oxford: Clarendon, 1990).

Magliana, M., 'The Autonomous Province of South Tyrol—A Model of Self-Governance', *Quaderno/Arbeitsheft*, 20 (Bozen, Bolzano: European Academy, 2000).

Mandelstam, A., *La protection Internationale des Minorités* (Paris: Recueil Sirey, 1931).

Marquardt, S., 'International Law and Indigenous Peoples', *International Journal on Group Rights*, 3 (1995), 47–76.

Martin Estabanez, M. A. and K. Gal, *Implementing the Framework Convention for the Protection of National Minorities*, ECMI Report No. 3 (Flensburg: ECMI, 1999).

Medda-Windischer, R., 'The Jurisprudence of the European Court of Human Rights', *European Yearbook of Minority Issues* (2001/02), 487–534.

—— 'The Jurisprudence of the European Court of Human Rights', *European Yearbook of Minority Issues* (2002/03), 445–69.

Mendus, S., *Toleration and the Limits of Liberalism* (Basingstoke: Macmillan, 1989).

—— (ed.), *The Politics of Toleration* (Edinburgh: Edinburgh University Press, 1999).

Meron, T., *Principles of Public International Law* (Oxford: Oxford University Press, 2001).

Merrills, J. G. and A. H. Robertson, *Human Rights in Europe: A Study of the European Convention on Human Rights* (Manchester: Manchester University Press, 2001).

Mookherjee, M., 'Exclusion, internalization, harm', *Ethnicities*, 3 (2003), 345–68.

Morsink, J., *The Universal Declaration of Human Rights: Origins, Drafting and Intent* (Philadelphia: University of Pennsylvania Press, 1999).

Müller, J. P. and L. Wildhaber, *Praxis des Völkerrechts* (Bern: Stämpfli, 2001).

Myntti, K., *A Commentary to the Lund Recommendations on the Effective Participation of National Minorities in Public Life* (Turku/Abo: Institute for Human Rights, Åbo Akademi University, 2001).

Nowak, M., *CCPR Commentary* (Kehl: Engel, 1993).

Oraa, J., *Human Rights in States of Emergency in International Law* (Oxford: Clarendon Press, 1992).

Packer, J., 'On the Definition of Minorities', in Packer, J. and K. Myntti (eds.), *The Protection of Ethnic and Linguistic Minorities in Europe* (Abo Akademi University, 1993).

—— 'Problems in Defining Minorities', in Fottrell, D. and B. Bowring (eds.), *Minority and Group Rights in the New Millennium* (The Hague: Martinus Nijhoff, 1999).

Pentassuglia, G., *Minorities in International Law, An Introductory Study*, Handbook (Strasbourg: Council of Europe, 2002).

—— 'Minority Issues as a Challenge in the European Court of Human Rights: A Comparison with the Case Law of the United Nations Human Rights Committee', *German Yearbook of International Law*, 46 (2003), 401–51.

Pernthaler, P. and P. Hilpold, 'Sanktionen als Instrument der Politikkontrolle—der Fall Österreich', *Integration*, 23 (2000), 105–19.

Phillips, A., *The Framework Convention for the Protection of National Minorities: A Policy Analysis, Minority Rights Group International* (London: Minority Rights Group International, 2002).

—— and A. Rosas (eds.), *Universal Minority Rights* (London, Turku: Minority Rights Group and Abo Akademi, 1995).

Pizzorusso, A., *Minoranze e maggioranze* (Torino: Einaudi, 1993).

Polakiewicz, J., *Treaty-Making in the Council of Europe* (Strasbourg: Council of Europe, 1999).

Raihman, Leonid, 'Media Legislation, Minority Issues, and Implications for Latvia', http://www.policy.hu/raihman/PolicyPaper.htm, 27 August 2004.

Ramcharan, B. G., 'The Concept of Protection in the International Law of Human Rights', in Dinstein, Y. (ed.), *International Law at a Time of Perplexity* (Dordrecht: Nijhoff, 1989).

Raz, J., *The Morality of Freedom* (Oxford: Clarendon Press, 1988).

Roach, K., 'The Uses of Audiences of Preambles in Legislation', *McGill Law Journal*, 47 (2001), 129–59.

Rönquist, A., 'The Council of Europe and National Minorities', *Helsinki Monitor* 6 (1995), 38–44.

Roosevelt, T., 'Every immigrant who comes here should be required within five years to learn English or leave the country', 1918, cited in Bryson, B., *Made in America* (New York: Morrow, 1994).

Rosas, A., 'The Protection of Minorities in Europe, a General Overview', in Packer, J. and K. Myntti (eds.), *The Protection of Ethnic and Linguistic Minorities in Europe* (Turku: Abo Akademi University, 1993).

Said, E. W., *Culture and Imperialism* (London: Vintage, 1994).

Schorkopf, F., *Die Maßnahmen der XIV EU-Mitgliedstaaten gegen Österreich* (Berlin: Springer, 2001).

Segesvary, V., 'Group rights: The definition of group rights in contemporary legal debate based on socio-cultural analysis', *Int'l Journal of Group Rights*, 3 (1995), 89–107.

Sepúlveda, M. M., *The Nature of Obligations under the International Covenant on Economic, Social and Cultural Rights* (Antwerp: Intersentia-Hart, 2003).

Simma, B., *Das Reziprozitätselement im Zustandekommen völkerrechtlicher Verträge* (Berlin: Duncker & Humblot, 1972).

—— 'Self-contained Regimes', *Netherlands Yearbook of International Law* (1985), 111–36.

—— 'Reservations to Human Rights Treaties—Some Recent Developments', in Haffner, G. *et al.* (eds.), *Liber Amicorum Ignaz Seidl-Hohnveldern* (Koln: Carl Heymanns, 1998).

Skurbaty, Z., *As if Peoples Mattered* (The Hague: Nijhoff, 2000).

Sperduti, G., 'Responsibility of States for Activities of Private Persons', Encyclopedia of Public International Law, IV (2000), 216–19.

Spiliopoulou Åkermark, A., *Justifications of Minority Protection in International Law* (Uppsala: Justus Förlag, 1997).

—— 'The Limits of Pluralism—Recent Jurisprudence of the European Court of Human Rights with Regard to Minorities: Does the Prohibition of Discrimination Add Anything?', *Journal on Ethnopolitics and Minority Issues in Europe*, 3 (2002), http://www.ecmi.de/jemie/download/Focus3-2002_Akermark. pdf.

Steketee, F., 'The Framework Convention: A Piece of Art or a Tool for Action?', *International Journal on Minority and Group Rights*, 8 (2001), 1–15.

Stone, J., *Regional Guarantees of Minority Rights* (New York: Macmillan, 1932).

Svensson-McCarthy, A. L., *The International Law of Human Rights and States of Exception* (The Hague: Martinus Nijhoff Publishers, 1998).

Taylor, C., *Sources of the Self: The Making of the Modern Identity* (Cambridge, Mass.: Harvard University Press, 1989).

—— *The Ethics of Authenticity* (London, Cambridge, Mass.: Harvard University Press, 1991).

Telalian, M., 'Mechanisms for Monitoring Compliance with Human Rights within the United Nations and the Council of Europe: Effectiveness and Prospects', in Vassiliou, M. and H. Psomiades (eds.), *Human Rights in the 21st Century* (Athens: Human Rights Defence Centre, Ant. N. Sakkoulas Publishers, 2001).

Thio, L. A., 'Developing a "Peace and Security" Approach Towards Minorities' Problems', *International and Comparative Law Quarterly*, 52 (2003), 115–50.

Thornberry, P., *International Law and the Rights of Minorities* (Oxford: Clarendon Press, 1991).

—— 'The Democratic or Internal Aspect of Self-determination with some Remarks on Federalism', in Tomuschat, Ch. (ed.), *Modern Law of Self-Determination* (Dordrecht: Nijhoff, 1993).

Thornberry, P., 'The UN-Declaration on the Rights of Persons Belonging to National, Religious and Linguistic Minorities: Background, Analysis, Observations, and an Update', in Phipps, A. and A. Rosas (eds.), *Universal Minority Rights* (Turku/Abo, London: Åbo Akademi University Institute for Human Rights/Minority Rights Group, 1995).

—— 'Basic Documents on Minorities and Indigenous Peoples', *World Directory of Minorities* (London: Minority Rights Group, 1997).

—— 'The Framework Convention on National Minorities', *Baltic Yearbook of International Law*, 2 (2002), 127–33.

Tomei, M. and L. Swepston, *Indigenous and Tribal Peoples: A Guide to ILO Convention* 169 (Geneva: International Labour Office, 1996).

Tomuschat, C., 'Protection of Minorities under Article 27 of the International Covenant on Civil and Political Rights', in Bernhardt, R. (ed.), *Völkerrecht als Rechtsordnung, Internationale Gerichtsbarkeit, Menschenrechte* (Berlin: FS Mosler, 1983).

—— *Human Rights—Between Idealism and Realism* (Oxford: Oxford University Press, 2003).

Treviranus, H. D., 'Preamble', *Encyclopaedia of International Public Law* (1984), 1097–8.

Tully, J., *Strange Multiplicity: Constitutionalism in an Age of Diversity* (Cambridge: Cambridge University Press, 1995).

Uerpmann, R., 'La primarité des droits de la personne: licéité or illicéité de l'intervention humanitaire?' in Tomuschat, C. (ed.), *Kosovo and the International Community* (The Hague: Martinus Nijhoff, 2001).

van der Stoel, M., *Peace and Stability through Human and Minority Rights* (Baden-Baden: Nomos Verlagsgesellschaft, 1999).

van Dijk, P., 'The Final Act of Helsinki—Basis for a Pan-European System?' *Netherlands Yearbook of International Law* 110 (1980), 97–124.

—— and G. J. H. van Hoof, *Theory and Practice of the European Convention on Human Rights*, 3rd edn. (The Hague: Kluwer Law International, 1998).

Verdross, A., 'Die bona fides als Grundlage des Völkerrechts', in *Festschrift für R. Laun* (Hamburg: Girardet, 1953).

Viljanen, J., *The European Court of Human Rights as a Developer of the General Doctrines of Human Rights Law* (Tampere: Tampere University Press, 2003).

Walzer, M., *On Toleration* (New Haven: Yale University Press, 1997).

Weckerling, M., 'Der Durchführungsmechanismus des Rahmenübereinkommens des Europarates zum Schutz nationaler Minderheiten', *Europäische Grundrechte Zeitschrift*, 24 (1997).

Index

The manufacturer's authorised representative in the EU for product safety is Oxford University Press España S.A. of el Parque Empresarial San Fernando de Henares, Avenida de Castilla, 2 – 28830 Madrid (www.oup.es/en or product.safety@oup.com). OUP España S.A. also acts as importer into Spain of products made by the manufacturer.

www.ingramcontent.com/pod-product-compliance
Ingram Content Group UK Ltd.
Pitfield, Milton Keynes, MK11 3LW, UK
UKHW022025150926
475595UK00013B/297
9780199207626